THE SPAS OF ENGLAND
2: *the Midlands and South*

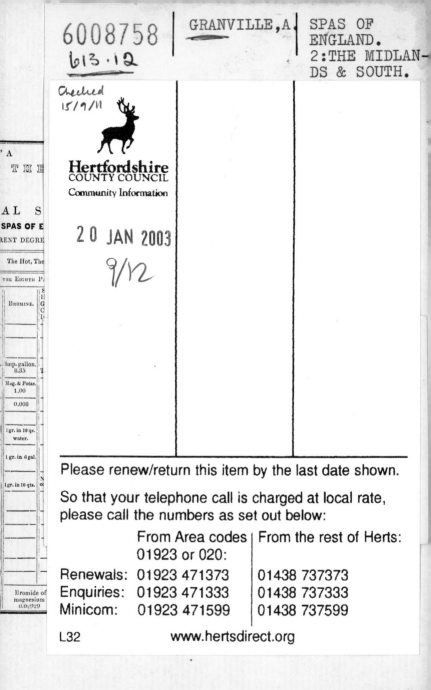

Spas of England
AND
PRINCIPAL SEA-BATHING PLACES

BY A. B. GRANVILLE, MD, FRS
WITH A NEW INTRODUCTION BY GEOFFREY MARTIN

2: *the Midlands and South*

ADAMS & DART

First published in 1841
This edition published in 1971 by Adams & Dart
40 Gay Street, Bath, Somerset
SBN 239 00086 2
Reproduced and Printed in Great Britain by
Redwood Press Limited, Trowbridge & London

Introduction

THE rise of the English spas and their intensive development in the eighteenth and early nineteenth centuries is a substantial but comparatively neglected part of modern social history. The history even of individual resorts has been unevenly investigated, and their collective contribution to our national patterns of behaviour has never been thoroughly assessed. The spas are ancient and hard-wearing institutions. From being places of pilgrimage and health resorts they became places of amusement, centres of social education, and then the models for resorts of a new kind, the sea-side watering places. The early sea-side resorts were at first crude and derivative, but they were adaptable, and were able to meet the demands which the new industrial society made for formal amusement and recreation. The older spas may seem anachronisms in the Victorian and twentieth-century world, but they did it a great service in their time. The interest of Granville's *Spas of England* derives as much from the date of its appearance as from its content: it is a landmark in the development of that vital and deeply interesting institution, the holiday.

The Spas of England is a survey of English resorts compiled in the early years of Victoria's reign, the work of a fashionable and widely-experienced London doctor. It was published in three parts in 1841, as a sequel to its author's influential book *The Spas of Germany* (1837), and it is a substantial and measured contribution to the topographical, medical, and social literature of its age. It did not, however, run to a second edition, and has remained ever since the only work of its kind. Granville believed firmly in the efficacy of natural mineral waters, and he found the spas in what seemed to be an assured state of prosperity. His commentaries upon them are often critical, for he was a shrewd observer, but he wrote always with a conviction that their fortunes and their general usefulness could be greatly increased. In fact it was the sea-side resorts that prospered and multiplied during the rest of the century, while the inland watering-places were able at best only to hold their ground. Granville's survey therefore showed them still in their prime, but on the eve of a slow and relative, but unmistakable decline. In consequence, despite its authoritative tone and evident good sense, his work took on an old-fashioned air, like its subject, as the century advanced. Even so, the book would have an historical interest, but its value is greatly increased by the far-sighted view that its author took of the sea-side resorts, which he also visited and carefully assessed. The relationship of the inland and the coastal resorts just at that time, and Granville's own personal history and interests, gave a distinctive quality to his observations. A proper appreciation of his work depends upon our knowledge both of the previous history of the spas and of Dr Granville.

The origins of the spas are lost in time. The springs at Bath and Buxton were used by the Romans, who may have found healing cults already established at both places. The high temperature of the waters at Bath, 120° Fahrenheit at the surface, must certainly have attracted attention at the earliest period of human settlement. Although resorts at thermal and saline springs took their generic name from Spa in Belgium in the sixteenth century, wells and rising streams have their own fascination, and religious and magical cults attach to them everywhere. In the Middle Ages it is not possible to distinguish medical centres from pilgrims' shrines; the springs at Bath were managed by the abbey, where medical skills were cultivated, but Buxton's reputation was maintained by the simple invocation of St Anne's well. There were shrines famous for healing, like those of St Thomas at Canterbury or St Alban's, where the presence of the saint's body or other relics was sufficient, but at

Walsingham, where pilgrims sought the Virgin Mary's house, two holy wells were associated with her cult. All these, and many other celebrated and obscure shrines in England and abroad, were places of resort, to which pilgrims travelled and where they sought accommodation. They were also, we may note, centres of a rudimentary trade in souvenirs, cap-badges and similar mementos, and occasionally the subject of literature which sought or served to publicise them. To the ordinary purposes of pilgrimage, religious devotion, and a divine aid to health, there was added at least on occasion a quest for diversion and for such gratification as travel affords.

At the Reformation the cult of the saints was proscribed and their shrines demolished. The monasteries were dissolved between 1536 and 1540, and images removed from all churches and chapels under an act of 1550. Pilgrimage was no longer a respectable and legitimate activity; those wells which survived as objects of devotion, and they were many, did so on the strength of local superstition. It was at this point, however, that science intervened to justify instinct. Physicians perceived that not all waters were alike, and began to ascribe curative powers to chemical solutions rather than to faith. It was a verdict from which present medical science would have to dissent, but it served. The first work in English on medical bathing, *A booke of the natures and properties of the bathes in England . . . Germany, and Italy* by Dr William Turner, was published in 1562. It praised Bath, but deplored its neglect by English physicians and their patients, saying that mineral springs on the Continent were better appointed and patronised. Granville in his day said much the same thing. Ten years later Bath and Buxton were both mentioned in the Poor Law Act of 1572 as places to which the sick resorted; the corporation of Bath had secured possession of the baths after the dissolution of the abbey, and at Buxton, where the wells had been closed by Thomas Cromwell's agent, the Earl of Shrewsbury had begun to build a bath-house and other amenities for visitors. In

1613 Anne of Denmark, James II's queen, visited Bath, and the citizens spent £1,000 on her entertainment; the town was already well established as a health resort, but there was no patronage like royal patronage.

Buxton was overshadowed by Bath in the early seventeenth century and developed more slowly, but the best indication of their joint success lay in the search for and discovery of mineral springs in other places. Of subsequently famous resorts, Harrogate was publicised in the late sixteenth century, the springs at Tunbridge Wells discovered in 1606, and the well under the cliff at Scarborough identified about 1625. Tunbridge Wells, which grew up at the junction of three ancient parishes and had no settled name until after the Civil War, was patronised in 1629 and 1630 by Charles I's queen, Henrietta Maria, but she also led her ladies to Wellingborough in Northamptonshire, which is not now celebrated for its waters. The most important of the new discoveries was that at Scarborough, where the accident of the spring flowing out of the cliff made an amenity of the beach and foreshore long before sea-bathing was in fashion. The promenade was not to everyone's taste: Celia Fiennes observed tartly in 1697 'all the diversion is ye walking on this sand twice a day at ye ebb of the tide and till its high tide and then they drink', but the habit survived. There were also horse races on the sands.

The rise of the spas testifies both to a demand for medical services and to a social need that they satisfied. Except in so far as the warm springs of Bath soothed the skin and relieved the pain of rheumatism, or other mineral waters served as aperients, the malady for which the spas catered best was hypochondria. Faith might work wonders at any resort, but the simple amenities which were offered to the convalescent and the ambulant patient were accepted gratefully by those whose real search was not so much for health as for diversion. The evolution of pleasure resorts was a long process, and one never fully accomplished at the spas themselves, but a substantial start was made in the seventeenth century. The reputation that several springs, and especially Bath's, enjoyed for curing sterility in women probably referred to the same facts. Cynics had their own explanation, but relaxation, a sense of well-being, and the stimulus of new scenes and company might well have benefited more marriages than they harmed.

That the spas survived the Civil War and the Interregnum shows clearly that their informal attractions still took a second place to their medical régimes. The republican governments regarded them morosely as centres of Royalist intrigue, which they were, but like gambling, idle conversation, and adultery, that could be considered a by-product, not the central purpose of their existence. The rule of the Saints and of Cromwell's major-generals would certainly have borne harder upon the watering-places if they could have been shown to be mere pleasure resorts. Even in the more self-indulgent society after the Restoration, when the country began to taste the benefits of colonial trade and there were dividends to be spent on pleasure, the spas were by no means transformed. Bath was visited by companies of actors from London, as it had been before the war, but it had no permanent theatre. The whole equipment of Epsom spa was a pair of small wooden huts. The chief diversion at Tunbridge Wells was to walk along the promenade from the springs that later became the Pantiles, but was only a path in the fields until 1676. There was a good deal of building and re-building in England in the later seventeenth century. Brick, stone and tiles replaced timber and thatch, and the elements of the agreeably self-assured style that we call Georgian were imposed upon a variety of local practices, but the spas were still modest places, the majority of them rustic rather than urban, and they did not attract more of that activity than was their due.

At the same time, some hundreds of new mineral springs were discovered and promoted in various parts of the country, some of them old holy wells refurbished, and others the reward of diligent tasting. They were particularly and naturally abundant round London, where places like Islington, within walking distance of the city, or Richmond or Epsom, a comfortable drive away, had a ready clientèle. Mr Sadler's wells at Islington survived as a resort in an age with other tastes; the springs at Streatham enjoyed a longer popularity for their own sake, but less enduring fame. What was plain in the late seventeenth century was that taking the waters, or affecting to do so, was as much a fashionable amusement as a medical fad, and that it could be gratified upon a very small outlay of capital was part of its general attractiveness.

A crucial change took place at Bath in the opening years of the eighteenth century. Mary of Modena, James II's queen, took the waters there in 1687, and then there were no royal visits until 1702, when Queen Anne came. The corporation appointed a master of ceremonies to supervise the arrangements made to entertain her, and no doubt feeling that the experiment had justified itself when she returned the following year, kept him as a permanent official. The post had an evident affinity with that of a twentieth-century festival manager, and some also with that of a nineteenth-century American sheriff. The first incumbent survived only until 1705, when he was killed in a duel. He was succeeded by Richard Nash, a professional gambler who had some experience of staging formal entertainments, and who now revealed an extraordinary talent for social organisation. Nash had some able associates, but his legendary fame does no more than justice to his career. He disciplined the visitors into a community, instilling an elementary but effective code of good behaviour, and inducting newcomers with irresistible ceremony. His autocratic rule served both to soften the manners of those who were sure of themselves, and to instruct those who were uncertain and who had come, whether they knew it or not, to learn. The lesson was of great general significance, one which worked with other accidents of English history to make a ruling class which was not as exclusively recruited as most of its contemporaries, and was less brutal in tone, more sensibly intelligent, than its predecessors. Nash was only one of its instructors, but a powerful one. His academy was the Assembly Rooms, which he helped to establish, and in which his gratified pupils first displayed what they had gathered of urbanity before they took it home with them.

It was now no longer enough for a successful spa to have a well, or even a pump-room, and a promenade: formal manners deserved a formal setting. While Nash refined Bath's society, the city's appearance was remodelled by a combination of two gifted architects and a far-sighted business-man. The elder and the younger John Wood, encouraged and supported by Ralph Allen, devised a brilliant series of architectural spectacles, through the Parades and Queen Square to the Circus and the Royal Crescent, that enlarged and transfigured the old walled town. The strong but disciplined originality of their work was a perfect setting for the transformed society of the spa, matching it with an unsurpassed display of architectural elegance. The whole device was the urban equivalent of the great country house and its park, laid out to flatter transient but demanding residents. It had little enough to do with medical draughts and therapeutic bathing, but much to do with assimilating wealth and other disruptive forces in society, and with establishing canons of taste.

The new Bath offered a pattern that other spas copied and developed according to their means and opportunity. Public buildings of more or less elaboration, a hall for assemblies as well as a pump-room, better accommodation than rustic cottages afforded, a circulating library, all became necessities, and their appearance a mark of success. A new resort could presume upon a little patience from its visitors, but not for long. The cult of the picturesque was only nascent, and still an intellectual rather than a practical taste: urban sophistication was not yet well enough established for many people to seek systematic relief from it. Tunbridge Wells, which had begun to take shape as a town at the end of the

seventeenth century, borrowed Nash in the summer, between
Bath's spring and autumn seasons, from 1735 onward.
At Buxton the Duke of Devonshire commissioned John Carr
to build the Crescent in 1781, providing an assembly room, a
news-room, and hotel accommodation as well as better-
appointed baths. John Carr's was the first crescent outside
Bath, and the precursor of many less ingenious adaptations
of the device. It gave Buxton the new lease of life that its
patron hoped for, closing the gap that had opened between
it and its upstart rivals. By that time, however, there was
more than the challenge of other inland spas for a resort to
meet.

As Bath and Buxton have thermal springs, they began as
bathing establishments, with the internal use of the waters
as a secondary, though subsequently important practice.
Elsewhere it was usual to drink the chalybeate waters, but
cold baths were offered in spartan tribute to the older resorts.
It had occurred to some physicians by the early years of the
eighteenth century that the sea was a natural saline bath of
unlimited potentiality, but we have no record of its regular
use for several decades longer. The earliest instances come
appropriately enough from Scarborough, where the first
marine promenade was a natural adjunct to the spa, and
where there was regular provision for sea-bathing by 1735.
At the same time, however, other hardy souls were visiting
Brighton, then a small fishing port, and with the encouragement of physicians who recommended bathing and the
drinking of sea-water as a supplement or alternative to
treatment at the spas, a score of similar places were patronised in the early years of George III's reign. By the end of the
century, the Prince Regent's liking for Brighton had made it
a resort as celebrated and as expensive as, though still less
well-appointed than Bath, and the king himself had raised
hopes of similar fame and riches in Weymouth by his visits
there. Together with Scarborough, the sea-bathing resorts
were in the same position as the inland spas a century earlier,
and that after only a few decades' growth.

There was one important difference, however, between the two groups at this stage of their development. The seventeenth-century spas in their own time had no rivals: the sea-side resorts, if they aspired to fashionable patronage, had to meet a formidable challenge. The contest looked an unequal one for some time; Brighton flourished during the French wars, but its rise was matched by that of Cheltenham, and the Regent's patronage, even after his accession as king, was not a universal commendation. The wars benefited all British resorts by inhibiting travel abroad, but even in the 1830s the advantages still seemed to lie with the spas. It is true that a wider taste for the picturesque and the cult of Romanticism lent a dramatic quality to the sea—it is interesting to compare Charlotte Brontë's reactions to Scarborough with Celia Fiennes's dry assessment—but in general the sea-side was a place for simple pleasures, including those of savouring makeshift accommodation. Brighton's amusements were raffish, and its lodgings extremely expensive; sober, even self-indulgent visitors were as likely to seek Bath or Cheltenham as Brighton or Sidmouth, and northern manufacturers, like the neighbouring gentry, looked to Scarborough before Blackpool. That was still the position when Dr Granville began to commend hydropathic cures to his patients.

Augustus Bozzi Granville was born in Milan in 1783, the third son of Carlo Bozzi, post-master general of the Austrian province of Lombardy. He was educated at the Collegio de Merati and at the University of Pavia, where he read medicine and received his doctoral diploma in 1802. His student days therefore coincided with Napoleon's invasion of Italy and the establishment of the republican régime, events which excited patriotic and radical sympathies in him, and led eventually to his renunciation of the Roman Catholic faith. Those sympathies, however, did not incline him to accept military service as a conscript in the French armies, and after some adventures reminiscent of those of Fabrice in *La Chartreuse de Parme* not long afterwards, he escaped by way of Genoa and Piacenza to Venice, where his brother, an Austrian civil official, helped him to take ship for Corfu. There he fell in with William Richard Hamilton, secretary to Lord Elgin, and later British minister at Naples. Hamilton offered the young man a post as physician to the British Embassy in Constantinople, and they travelled together through Albania and Greece.

Granville's subsequent career sustained the promise of these exciting but restless beginnings. Hamilton was recalled to England when they reached Athens, and although Granville took up his appointment in Constantinople, where he caught bubonic plague, he was induced by the accidents of friendship to apply for a commission as second surgeon to the Turkish fleet. After a brief tour of service in the eastern Mediterranean, he resigned and made his way to Spain. There he lived for three years, adding Spanish to his languages and learning to play the guitar, an accomplishment which, as he confesses, later proved a hindrance rather than an aid to his professional advancement in England. Having assumed the name of Granville upon his mother's death, at her wish, to commemorate his Cornish great-grandfather, he removed to Lisbon in 1806, and the next year was commissioned as an assistant surgeon on a British sloop in the Tagus. That his ship immediately took a prize in its way to Portsmouth, and that before settling in England in 1812 he should have been shipwrecked off Oporto and served in the West Indies, returning with Simon Bolivar's dispatches to the British government, was in no way out of character. He eventually retired from the Navy on half-pay in 1812, having married an English wife in 1809, and after a short stay in Manchester, where he was received into the Literary and Philosophical Society by John Dalton, he moved to London to establish himself in medical practice. In the process he lectured in chemistry at the Westminster Medical School, studied and practised for a year at *La Maternité* in Paris, and was eventually elected physician-accoucheur at the Westminster Dispensary. In the meantime he had acted as an interpreter at the Foreign Office, carried British dispatches to Italy in 1814, and fallen under the justifiable suspicion of the Austrian authorities during his travels in Lombardy, where he was arrested and detained as a spy. It was his belief, and that of some of his fellow physicians, that he might have saved the life of the Princess Charlotte in 1817, if he had returned sooner from his residence in Paris. It is a matter of which he wrote with some diffidence later, in Queen Victoria's reign, but one which he felt bound to mention.

For the rest of his long life Granville lived and practised in London, though he travelled extensively abroad, and paid a professional visit to the spa at Kissingen every year from 1840 to 1863. He retired after his last visit there, and began to write his autobiography, which was edited and published by his daughter in 1874. He died at Dover in March 1872. His self-confidence and vigorous spirit had roused some jealousies and made him enemies, but they were outweighed by the friends who admired his warm enthusiasms. He enjoyed a large practice, which he maintained with skill and vigour. In his early years in England he was befriended and encouraged by Sir Humphry Davy and Sir Joseph Banks, and his obliged patients included Palmerston, a man not readily blinded with science. Granville was elected Fellow of the Royal Society in 1817, and was among the first members chosen for the Athenaeum. His published works, which between 1812 and 1865 ranged over medicine, chemistry, public health, literature, travel, and politics, fill two-and-a-half columns of the British Museum catalogue; *The Spas of England*, therefore, falls near the middle of his professional and literary career.

Granville's particular interest in spas dated from the 1830s, although his taste for chemical analysis and what would now be called biochemistry went back to his student days. He was moved in 1836, following the success of a popular essay on the principal German spas by Sir Francis Head (*Bubbles from the Brunnens of Nassau*, 1835), to plan a

comprehensive work on the German watering-places.
The Spas of Germany appeared in 1837; its author showed
himself much impressed with the professional competence
of the German régimes, and the great popularity of the spas,
and although he had some rivals to contend with, he impressed
his readers. John Murray's first *Handbook for travellers on
the Continent* (1839) cites Granville on diet as a matter of
course, assuming that tourists who wish to take the waters
will recognise the English authority upon them. There may
therefore have been others than the handsome manageress
of the Grand Hotel at Buxton who reproached him for his
neglect of the English spas (*Midlands, p. 25*) and it was
natural that he should turn his attention next to them. He
travelled extensively in England in the summer and autumn
of 1839, and again in the autumn of 1840. He seems to have
made these tours much as he describes them in his book,
traversing northern England from Liverpool to the Tyne,
returning by Shap to the Fylde coast and the Mersey, and
then having worked from Buxton to Lincolnshire, passing
into the south-west via Cheltenham and Bath, to cover the
south coast from Torquay to Brighton. The resorts of the
Thames estuary, including the newly-discovered and short-
lived mineral spring at Hockley, are then treated before
Tunbridge Wells, but these were all places within easy reach
of London. Granville's work on the book was interrupted
by his treatment of Joseph Bonaparte, formerly King of
Naples and of Spain, and elder brother of Napoleon I,
whom he had attended regularly in 1838 and whom he
accompanied to Wildbad in the summer of 1840. That was
the urgent professional business to which he referred in his
preface, and which resulted in the sheets of the first volume,
printed in 1839–40, being held over until 1841, when the
whole work was issued.

The Spas of England is a single-minded but leisurely book,
abounding in discursive detail. As Granville says in his
preface, his object was to describe 'things as they are', and
he quite rightly supposed that his own experiences in

compiling the work were as consequential as the things
that he discovered. The result is not just a medical treatise,
which would now have a very limited interest, but also a work
of travel, topography, and social comment. Granville was a
busy, inquisitive man, used to making his way in strange
company, and sustained by the kind of self-confidence that
contrives to engage other people's interest in his affairs. His
belief in the medicinal value of the spa waters was ill-
founded, so far as we can answer for it, but it gives the
book a unifying theme and helps to direct his other observations. The modern reader may chafe at the stately
introductory dialogue and at some of the asides, and will
find the longer reported conversations incredible. Granville
himself had occasional misgivings, and at Shotley Bridge,
for which he mistakenly foresaw a glorious future as a
resort, he closed his notebook, 'lest I should be betrayed
into greater prolixity' (*Northern, p. 304*), but even his
undisciplined flourishes have an appeal of their own. There
are also many pungent reflections to set against them:
on the shortcomings of English hotels, for example, inspired
by the coffee room at the New Inn, Derby, or the realisation
that the popularity of Teignmouth as a resort for invalids
'does not seem to have much enriched its inhabitants'
(*Southern, p. 469*). Common sense and a wide experience were
valuable qualities in a physician; there are occasions when
Granville is able to compress the whole pattern of his life
into a single sentence. One such opportunity occurred in
Dorset: 'for a mere blow of sea air, such as one may get on a
quarter-deck, I know of no better place for an idler in these
parts than Weymouth' (*Southern, pp. 508–9*).

The most striking of Granville's general reflections are
those upon the railways. His journeys are in any case a real
and vivid part of the book, and he seized upon travel by rail,
not just as a dramatic and exciting novelty, but as a matter
of great social significance. His comments upon the management of the railways, on the difference in tone between
different companies or between stations ('as compared to

London, all the officers and servants at the Liverpool terminus are perfection' [*Northern, p. 15*]) are as illuminating as his descriptions of the night train's departure, or the bustle of the travelling post-office. His strictures upon the early companies were all justifiable, although some improvements had been made by the time the book was published. The legislative regulation of the railways, for which Granville called, proved to be a continuing and exacting charge upon nineteenth-century government, and a unified control, with all the advantages that a standardised policy promised, has been achieved only in recent times. The general tenor of Granville's discussion would be creditable if he had had a much longer time to sample travel by rail and to consider its significance: as a judgment upon the experiences of something less than a decade it was most shrewd and far-sighted.

The Spas of England is consistently and soundly informed by its author's own experience. Granville was a natural experimenter, always anxious to enlarge his knowledge, and his solemn records of his pulse and physiological sensations when he entered a bath were to him as much part of assessing a spa as was analysing its waters. It followed that he should also interest himself in the whole organisation of a resort, and in everything that its visitors were likely to do. Much of his detail is practical and eminently sensible: he comments as a matter of course upon the nature and cost of accommodation, not forgetting the cost of wax candles where charges were not inclusive (*Northern, p. 72*), and upon social life and provision of amenities as well as upon the ordering of baths and pump-rooms. He notices where people walk, and when and how they eat. The effect of the Blackpool air upon the appetite is well-observed, but Granville kept a sharp eye upon public dining-rooms at all times, and his strictures upon the ill manners displayed at the Half Moon Inn at Exeter conjure up the scene very convincingly (*Southern, pp. 458–9*).

Details of that kind are of more consequence now than the constituents of spa water, or the ill-advised use of metal pipes, but it is precisely the wide scope of Granville's interests that makes his observations valuable. One matter on which he would have been more precise if he had been able was the régime of the spas, but we can see from his testimony, as we might suspect on other grounds, that there was a laxness in the English that defied exact classification. German spas were undoubtedly better-ordered, but then their patrons were more amenable. Granville felt and said that the English started their day too late, and were apt to arrange it self-indulgently. He seems likely to have been right.

It is significant that Bath, which Granville praised highly and justly as a town, should have disappointed him in several details as a spa. There as elsewhere the patrons came too late to the pump-room, and they neither drank the waters nor used the baths as intensively as they might. The baths themselves were inferior to, at least in the sense that they were less ingeniously contrived than, those that a Continental resort of the same quality would have offered. The implication is that Bath, as agreeable and impressive by night, with 'the twinkling of all the gas-lights' (*Southern, p. 365*), as it was by day, was in the eyes of its visitors as much a place for idle diversion as it was a health resort.

Like the other inland spas, Bath was about to be sharply challenged by its upstart rivals on the coast. Granville himself could hardly be aware of the fact, but he sensed the potentiality of the sea-side resorts as he had already assessed that of the railways, and his comments upon them are particularly interesting. It was his impression that the English bathed less assiduously than other Europeans, yet the rise of the coastal resorts told its own story. The amenities that they offered were few and simple, and Granville was not deeply impressed by them as resorts for the sick and convalescent. His remarks upon the short-comings of Torquay, with its one level walk for invalids, varied according to the direction of the wind, and the hills that outfaced its 'asthmatic ... and pulmonic and ... phthisical' visitors (*Southern*, *p. 482*), are sharper in tone than most of his comments upon the inland spas. The contrast implied is a natural one, for if such places were judged as health resorts, then the superior amenities and experience of the older centres must have told in their favour. Only Bournemouth, in which Granville took a particular and markedly intelligent interest, really satisfied him in that respect. He deplored the thoughtless speculative building that he found elsewhere, and considered that if the new resort was properly planned it promised to be 'a perfect discovery', such a place as 'we vainly thought to have found elsewhere on the south coast of England' (*Southern*, *p. 512*). In the event, Bournemouth was developed much as Granville hoped, and the prescription proved a great success, but the real strength of the sea-side resorts lay in their freedom from the historic patterns of the spas. The only amenity that the new resorts needed to borrow from the old ones was the promenade, and even that was soon dominated by the beach. With the rapid extension of holiday-making through the middle classes and among the working classes in the nineteenth century, the most important qualities in a resort were accessibility and the capacity to grow: the railway provided the one, and the beach the other. Having no other models, the sea-side was likely to imitate the buildings and institutions of the spa, but its chief business was to range its visitors along the edge of the sea. By the end of the century the patrons had forgotten that it was a mineral water that they had come to seek, although the memory of ozone stayed long in their collective mind.

The chief interest of Granville's work therefore lies not in the matters that first engaged its author, such as the presence of iodine in the newly-discovered waters of Woodhall Spa, or the appointment of the baths at Buxton, but in its juxtaposition of two different styles of life. The tradition of the spas, for all their popularity, was aristocratic; the tradition of the sea-side, for all the distinction of its early patrons, was to be popular. The two institutions were closely connected,

both before and after Granville's day, but their inter-
dependence was particularly striking at that time, when
travel overseas was once again drawing off aristocratic
patronage from the English resorts, and when the great
popular holiday trade, which depended upon the steamboat
and the Thames wherries even before the railways were
built, had begun to transform the resorts of the south-east.

Granville brought some notable qualifications to his work.
His professional experience enabled him to speak authorita-
tively to his contemporaries on the central functions of the
spas, and also to look at their clientèle with an informed eye.
His upbringing and his cosmopolitanism saved him from
parochial judgements, although his attachment to England
was warm and complete. One personal preoccupation
emerges in the long discussion on the Roman Catholic and
Protestant churches that is attached to the passage on
St Mary's College at Oscott, in the section on the Midland
spas (*Midlands, pp. 192–217*). His Anglican faith was part of
Granville's Englishness, and to his original readers his
disconcertingly sudden excursion into Christian apologetics
would have been remarkable only for its studied mildness.
To Granville and his contemporaries it was an intelligent
man's business to concern himself with what was significant
in his world, a category of topics to which St Mary's College
belonged as naturally as the harbour works at Hartlepool,
the rocks on Brimham Moor, or the uses and shortcomings
of gas-lighting. In that, as in all other respects, the work is a
faithful portrait of its time, a reminder, like the history and
personality of its author, of the richness and variety that
characterised nineteenth-century England.

A. B. Granville, *The spas of Germany*, London, 1837, 2 vols. (illus.).

Paulina B. Granville, *ed.*, *Autobiography of A. B. Granville*, London, 1874, 2 vols. (illus.).

R. C. Hope, *The legendary lore of the holy wells of England*, London, 1893. (illus.).

R. V. Lennard, *ed.*, *Englishmen at rest and play: some phases of English leisure, 1558-1714*, Oxford, 1931. (illus.).

G. H. Martin, *The town*, London, 1961, bibl. (illus.).

J. A. R. Pimlott, *The Englishman's holiday: a social history*, London, 1947, bibl. (illus.).

MATLOCK.

THE

SPAS OF ENGLAND,

AND

PRINCIPAL SEA-BATHING PLACES.

BY

A. B. GRANVILLE, M.D., F.R.S.

AUTHOR OF "THE SPAS OF GERMANY," "ST. PETERSBURG," &c.

MIDLAND SPAS.

OLD WELL WALK, CHELTENHAM.

LONDON:

HENRY COLBURN, PUBLISHER,

GREAT MARLBOROUGH STREET.

1841.

PREFACE.

THE Author of " the Spas of England" cannot put forth the concluding portion of that work without apologizing for the delay which has unavoidably taken place in its publication. In glancing at its Contents, which in spite of every desire of curtailment, have extended over upwards of six hundred pages, the reader will at once perceive that observations, embracing nearly two-thirds of the island, and referring to between seventy and eighty places, whether Cities, Towns, Spas, or Sea-bathing Stations, personally visited by the Author, could hardly be embodied in the form of a continuous narrative within a narrower circle, or in less time than has elapsed since the appearance of the First Volume containing the Northern Spas.

The Author, moreover, had to consult various documents, obtain much useful statistical information, and correspond with several persons in the country, in order to secure to his performance that degree of fullness and accuracy as to facts and deductions, without which he felt that " the Spas of England" would never earn for themselves the character of faithfulness, as well as usefulness, which has been accorded to " The Spas of Germany."

Lastly, the Author had to contend against many interruptions incidental to a London medical practitioner at this peculiar season.

Notwithstanding all these causes of delay, however, it is hoped that these Volumes appear opportunely, and at the very period of the year when such a work is most likely to be wanted by those for whose service it is especially written, and who may purpose to pass the summer months either at a Spa or at some Sea-bathing place.

The Author next desires to call the attention of his readers to two particular features of the present Volumes. The first is the introduction of not fewer than three recently-discovered Spas of value, particularly the one in Lincoln-shire, of which no account exists in any previous work. The second is the greater extent given to the consideration of CLIMATE, the eligibility of certain marine residences for invalids, and the local peculiarities of places with reference to habitation and the recovery of health in England, than has ever been accorded to similar subjects in any other general work published in this country, even when those works have been announced as treating especially of such matters.

If this portion of his Work serve its intended object, that of supplying people in delicate health with a real HANDBOOK of CLIMATE, the Author will consider himself well repaid for his pains. Under this head he can with confidence point to his account of Torquay, Teignmouth, Dawlish, Southampton, Ventnor, Brighton, St. Leonards, Hastings, Dover, and, above all, Bournemouth, contained in the present Volumes,—which have been made to embrace at great length, and not, as in other works, to the extent of a single page or so, every particular concerning those places as residences, most likely to interest the class of individuals here referred to — unfortunately a very numerous one.

In concluding what the Author had to state preliminarily of the present portion of his work, he has to regret that the great length to which it has already extended, prevents him from making use of the notes he had taken of a few remaining, though minor, mineral springs, principally in the vicinity of London. These notes must for the present lie idle in his portfolio ; as it would be impossible, in justice to the Public or the publisher, to swell out farther with them the present Volumes.

If it may now be permitted to the Author to look back to his First Volume, he would avail himself of the present opportunity of so doing, principally with the view of performing a spontaneous act of justice to the managers and proprietors of that great railway which it had been his painful duty to comment upon in severe terms in the volume in question. Circumstances since the appearance of that publication having brought the Author frequently in contact with that establishment, he has been enabled to witness the many and important changes for the better, and the improvements as to order and regularity, that have taken place in its administration and the working of its details ; and he has great pleasure in adding, in his capacity of a medical man, that on the occasion of having to convey, a short time since, an invalid of great consequence, by a special train, from a distance of nearly an hundred miles, to London, the Author being placed in direct communication with two of the active directors, and the still more active secretary of the company, as well as with the principal officer who superintended the whole *trajet*, (which was effected in two hours and fifteen minutes,) he found them all, not only courteous and anxious to give satisfaction themselves, but strict and methodical in seeing that those who served under them should conduct themselves in the like manner, so as to ensure safety and convenience, as well as the best accommodation, for the illustrious patient.

While on the subject of the first volume, the Author ought also in fairness to make his acknowledgments to several private individuals, distinguished either in the literary or the medical world, not less than to the periodical press in general, (with a solitary exception that can neither hurt nor surprise the Author) for the encouraging manner in which they received his performance, and have urged him to its continuance. But fearing lest his words of gratitude should be misconstrued into expressions of solicitude for the like flattering reception of his present Volumes, he forbears from using them.

One single observation before concluding, he will take leave to make in this place, in regard to what has been said of a part of the first volume by a single private individual. He refers to the venturesome opinion attributed to a young physician settled at Harrogate, as candidate for public support in the absence of Mr. Richardson, (who has retired since the publication of the " Northern Spas") animadverting upon the account given of Harrogate in that volume. Without stopping to inquire how far it is consistent with candour and moral courage for any critical writer to impugn an avowed work under the safeguard of an anonymous attack, it might be justly retorted upon him, in pure kindness, that in endeavouring to defend Harrogate from what he has been pleased to call " the misrepresentations" of the Author of " the Spas of England," he ought himself to have carefully eschewed misrepresenting, through a pamphlet of fourteen pages of misquotations, misapprehensions, and misversions, what that Author had really said of Harrogate : bearing in mind all the time, that whatever was said by that Author was founded upon positive and undeniable facts observed by him, as well as upon information proceeding from resident parties far more capable than the young anonymous writer in question, to judge of the accuracy, the fullness, and on the whole the encouraging description of Harrogate, contained in " the Spas of England."

109, *Piccadilly, June* 20, 1841.

⁎ Some misspelling of names occurred in part of the First Volume, which the Author much regrets; such as " Wolsey" for *Worlsey*, " Cholmondeley" for *Cholmley*, "Travers" for *Travis*, " Woodwards" for *Woodalls*, " Hindewell" for *Hinderwell*, " Beavor" for *Belvoir*, " Valingate" for *Valimgate*, " Studely" for *Studley*, and " Castlegilling" for *Gillingcastle*.

CONTENTS

OF

THE MIDLAND SPAS.

CHAPTER IV.

DERBY—LINCOLN—MONKSWELL CHALYBEATE.

CHAPTER V.

THE WOODHALL OR IODINE SPA.

CHAPTER VI.

ASHBY-DE-LA-ZOUCH—WILLOUGHBY NEW BATHS—DERBY—RUGBY.

CHAPTER X.

LEAMINGTON.

CHAPTER XI.

LEAMINGTON CONCLUDED.

CHAPTER XII.

ENVIRONS OF LEAMINGTON—MALVERN.

CHAPTER XIII.

ROAD TO CHELTENHAM—VICTORIA SPA—STRATFORD-UPON-AVON.

CHAPTER XIV.

CHELTENHAM.

CHAPTER XV.

CHELTENHAM CONCLUDED.

ILLUSTRATIONS

TO

THE MIDLAND SPAS.

** *All communications respecting Errors or Omissions are requested to be addressed to the Publisher, Mr. Colburn, 13, Great Marlborough-street, London.*

SPAS OF ENGLAND.

SECOND GROUP; OR, MIDLAND SPAS,

AND

PRINCIPAL SEA-BATHING PLACES.

MIDLAND SPAS.

CHAPTER I.

DR. FORMBY, a respectable physician of Liverpool,
whom I accidentally met in the promenade-room at Harrogate, assured me that as many visiters now proceed to
Liverpool for the benefit of sea-bathing, as are known to

attend Harrogate for the purpose of drinking those mineral waters, or bathing in them.

That people should select a place which in reality does not enjoy the advantage of genuine sea-water, with an intention of taking sea-baths, somewhat puzzled me, until the learned Doctor explained to me that of late years a new sea-bathing place had been created, exclusively for the accommodation of the wealthier classes in and about Liverpool, who, having now nearly deserted the once fashionable Park Gate, on the Cheshire coast, gladly availed themselves of the new establishment to which the emphatic title of *New Brighton* had been given.

On a second visit, therefore, to Liverpool, the summer before last, my principal care was to make inquiries respecting this newly-risen Brighton of the north, and to proceed thither, if necessary, in order to ascertain its condition, and form an idea of an establishment which seemed to have commanded the attention of a medical practitioner by whom sea-bathing was evidently placed upon a par with mineral-water drinking.

Now, few persons are more ready than I am to admit the advantage to be derived from sea-bathing ; nay, I am prepared to contend that much more might be effected in the way of curing disease by means of the application of sea-water to the skin—and I will go further, and add, also, by means of a suitable internal use of sea-water—than has hitherto been accomplished. Long experience on this head,—my occasional residence on, and visits to the sea-coast in years gone by,—and my former services in the navy, when I had ample opportunities of watching the effect of sea-bathing on different classes of persons in this as well as in a tropical climate, have satisfied me of the immense benefit that may and might still more effectually be derived from the timely and judicious employment of sea-bathing. But I am not disposed, from any thing I have heard or seen, to go the length of admitting that sea-bathing is better than bathing in a mineral spring, or drinking of its waters.

This subject being quite akin to that which forms the principal topic of my present volumes, and being, moreover, one of great importance in a medical point of view, I may be permitted to dwell briefly upon its bearings and applications. After which, I will proceed to the description of New Brighton, and any other sea-bathing place which the Liverpoolians may have provided for their own particular use. It is not, however, a professed treatise on sea-bathing that the reader must expect in this place, but only a few practical hints derived from personal experience, to the exclusion of every species of theory or opinions peculiar to other people.

Two very important agents, endowed with peculiar virtues in reference to the human constitution, have of late years been much commended and employed in the practice of medicine. I allude to *iodine* and *bromine*, both of which have been detected by recent analyses in sea-water. The presence of the former, indeed, has been doubted by two high authorities,—SARPHATE, of Leyden, who found no such substance in the sea-water near the Dutch coast, and Professor DAUBENY, of Oxford, who could not detect iodine in the residuum of sea-water taken up near Cowes. But an analytical chemist of equal weight, Mr. Schweitzer, of the German Spa at Brighton, has shown, in a very recent analysis of sea-water taken near that place, that iodine is present in it, although in so minute a proportion that 174 pounds of the water contain hardly one grain of that substance.

With regard to the other active agent alluded to, *bromine*, its presence in sea-water is admitted on all hands, and, indeed, may be said to constitute an essential ingredient of every brine spring,—as I have shown both in my former work on the " Spas of Germany," and in the analytical table connected with the present volumes.

Independent of these, there are other very active ingredients in sea-water. The first is chloride of sodium, which exists in the proportion of one to thirty-five,—or, in other words, a pint of sea-water contains 216½ grains, that is to say, something less than half an ounce of common salt. The second is what medical men call muriate of magnesia, which is a combination of chlorine with magnesium—a salt endowed with well-marked properties on the human frame, and which constitutes one of the active ingredients of Pullna water, so generally used now in England, since I first made it known in this country, by my account and commendation of that water in " St. Petersburg" and the " Spas of Germany."

But, in addition to these active principles in sea-water, Mr. Schweitzer has found in that taken up in the Channel a considerable portion of a substance which we cannot consider otherwise than important, from its two constituent principles, although we have little direct experience as to its immediate influence on the human constitution as a medicine. This substance, which was first pointed out by Wollaston in sea-water, even before it was detected in mineral springs, is the muriate of potash or chloride of potassium, as it is called by the learned, six grains of which are found in a pint of sea-water.

To complete this analysis, it should be stated that the same pint of sea-water contains also eighteen grains and one-third of Epsom salts, eleven grains and a quarter of sulphate of lime, with a very trifling quantity of carbonate of lime.*

After this account it will be readily admitted, that sea-water is in fact a *mineral water* to all intents and purposes ; and that we may, therefore, look with as much confidence for beneficial effects from its employment, whether externally

---

* I have not mentioned another ingredient, muriate of lime, said by Lavoisier and others to 'be present in sea-water—because Schweitzer does not mention it as existing in that of the British Channel.

or internally, provided it be judiciously recommended, as from the employment of other mineral waters—proportionate to and in accordance with their respective chemical composition.

But this is not the whole question after all, if we adopt the views of one of the greatest luminaries of the medical profession, the late Dr. Hufeland, of Berlin, who, in speaking of sea-bathing, contends that its efficacy on the human frame is by no means to be ascribed to the chemical ingredients alone. " Since the sea," observes the Prussian professor, " is the habitation of innumerable organic beings who live and die there, it becomes impregnated with a quantity of subtile and volatile animal particles of which chemistry knows nothing, but which extraordinarily increase the stimulating power of sea-water. The smell of the sea already manifests their presence, and the whole of the neighbouring atmosphere receives from it a peculiar quality, which is exhibited in the characteristic appearance of organic nature in marine districts; in the strength and freshness of their inhabitants, in the peculiarities of the diseases of the latter, and finally, in the healing power of the sea breezes over certain complaints, especially of the lungs : nay, modern experiments, especially those of the excellent Hermbstädt, have shown that even the muriatic acid of sea-water is volatilized and mingles with the air; so that we may with justice affirm, that on the sea-coast not only the water but the air is salt, and acts as an especial stimulus on the frame. These volatile particles,—the life which the sea maintains outwardly as well as inwardly,—the perpetual agitation of the water and shock of the waves, with the electric and magnetic currents produced by that shock,—lastly, the modification of the atmosphere around a sea station—these form a whole in which we may well seek for the reason of those surprising advantages which are sometimes derived from sea-bathing."

If these views of Hufeland be correct, it is evident that sea-bathing, to be of the use he attributes to it, must be performed in the open sea, and in the most marine station possible ; and that the best sea-water baths prepared at home, or in a tub, though comprising all the fixed ingredients detected in such water, is yet not a sea-bath. Where the latter is genuine, according to Hufeland's experience, confirmed by the observation of many eminent practitioners besides, the effect is stimulating and reviving, by acting first on the skin, and secondly on the nervous, lymphatic, and glandulous systems, as well as on the organs of secretion.

" Although sea-bathing puts the whole frame into a state of agreeable and increased activity," continues Hufeland, " the nerves of the skin are, nevertheless, the organs most affected, and in which the power of sea-bathing as a remedy is most strikingly manifested."

But independent of excitation, which alone will not explain certain other effects produced by sea-bathing properly conducted, we must take into consideration the probability that the humours and structural substance of the human body are, in such as use sea-bathing or reside long in the immediate vicinity of the sea, modified by the chemical agency of its chlorine, muriatic acid, and muriate of soda, applied to the skin. Accordingly it has been found, that sea-bathing is most beneficial in lymphatic and glandular complaints, and in certain diseases of the skin : also, in gout and rheumatism, and lastly, in affections of the nerves,—respecting which, the power of sea-bathing is great and extraordinary, and often unique.

My experience coincides with the view taken by Hufeland, respecting the manner and *modus agendi* of sea-bathing on the human frame. That some of the active principles of sea-water penetrate into the body through the skin, and by combination with some of its juices, alter their existing condition, is a truth of which I have long been convinced. For some hours after bathing in the sea have I often noticed a continuous taste of salt in the mouth, accompanied with a slight bitterness, although

not a drop of the water had entered the lips during the operation of bathing. Mechanical absorption of the material water,
during the immersion of the body in the sea, is a fact admitted on all hands. Then, if absorbed, is it likely that a fluid
charged with so many distinct and powerful agents shall remain inactive in the midst of life, and within the vortex of
animal secretions, and excretions, and circulation? Certainly not.

I take it, that sea-water, particularly if used warm, and
recently procured from the sea, and employed in the immediate vicinity of the sea, produces two distinct actions
on our frame—the one of counter-irritation, or external,—
the other of modification, or internal. We have thus, then,
in our hands two of the most effective agencies to work with,
while endeavouring to remove disease or modify it; and it
must be the fault, indeed, of the medical adviser, if sea-
bathing proves either injurious or nugatory. Properly directed, its results must inevitably be good.

It were indeed to be wished that the English were more
inclined than they are to bathe,—especially in the sea,
for which they have such ample means. Their propensity is
not that way; or, at all events, it is, as compared to the *bal-
neomania* of the Parisians for domestic baths, and of the continental nations dwelling near the sea-shore for sea-bathing,
very greatly inferior. By a return recently made to the
Prefect of Police in Paris, it seems that the number of bathing-establishments of all sorts in that capital,—which, on the
termination of the war, was five hundred and fifty,—has since
increased to eight times that number.

One hails, therefore, with satisfaction any manifestation
on the part of a large community like that of Liverpool,
spread over a *quasi*-maritime region, to secure to themselves
the benefit of sea-bathing; and, in this respect, the people
of Liverpool and the country around—ill-favoured as they
are with regard to position in reference to genuine sea-water

—have shown their own conviction of the efficacy of sea-baths, by forming new sea-bathing establishments, and supporting them when formed, although placed at a somewhat inconvenient distance from the town.

Of these establishments, the principal one is New Brighton; the other has received the name of Crosby Waterloo—or simply Waterloo. Both establishments are much frequented during the bathing-season, and are well spoken of by those who have visited them. Thither, therefore, I repaired from Liverpool, to make myself master of every particular concerning them. Such of my readers as may be advised to use sea-baths, and who, living in counties nearer to Liverpool than to Margate or Brighton, desire to avoid the inconvenience, fatigue, and expense of proceeding to the latter places for that purpose, will not be sorry to peruse the account here contained of the sea-bathing places in question.

At twenty minutes after three, nominally at three P.M., I left the Prince's pier-head, in a good-sized steamer, nearly full of passengers, skirted the several docks, and admired particularly the new and splendid basins and masonry around them, honoured with the title of Waterloo; and dropping in this manner down the Mersey, along the coast, passed round the new sea-wall and nearly in front of Bootle, and Crosby Waterloo, when, taking to the middle of the stream, we steered towards the Cheshire shore, and made for the extreme end of a long peninsular prolongation, beyond and to the westward of the mouth of the river, where is seated

NEW BRIGHTON.

As we approached our destination, at the end of about half an hour's steaming, the green and lively coast of Cheshire, insignificant in other respects as it be, presents a pleasing contrast to the opposite shore we had just left, overwhelmed in brick and stone, without a single token of verdure. The water, too, looked more bluish and sea-like than it had appeared off Bootle and Waterloo, nearer to the *embouchure* of the river on the Liverpool side.

The steamer (and there is one every hour in the summer performing this crossing) comes in at the end and alongside of a skeleton pier, constructed of wood, which enables the passengers to land on the dry sand. Close on the right-hand side is the north-west fort, which guards the entrance into the Mersey, and near to it is the lighthouse.

New Brighton is a settlement of little more than five years' existence, planted among the numerous sandhills, of all sizes and shapes, barely covered with long and coarse grass, which crown in double and triple lines the northern termination of the peninsula or tongue of land previously alluded to.

It must have required some courage to have planted the first dwelling-house on such a waste, and still more to have expected to attract others to follow the example. Nothing can equal the air of desolation which prevails around. The few clusters of houses and villas that have since been erected in this perfect desert, tend only to make the scene of barrenness still more striking, and suggest the idea of a modern village overwhelmed in ashes after some dreadful catastrophe. But the temptation of the delightful and soft sands, and sloping shores, which offer to the wealthy Liverpoolians a genuine opportunity of dipping into pure sea-water, was too strong to be resisted, and all minor considerations were consequently dismissed.

An hotel, called Grave's New Brighton Hotel, is the first important building on the left, ascending from the pier, along a paved *chaussée* projected across the sandhills leading to some of the more elevated of those curious formations, on which a number of large houses, facing the north, have been erected, and were in the course of construction. The sandhills, in the direction of this line of communication between the landing-place and the upper buildings, look as if the sea had recently run riot among them, and had tossed them capriciously about. On these, houses are now being reared in regular succession, many of them on the more elevated brows of the hills inland, others below them, separated by an area of sand, which will be arranged as a carriage-road some day.

Smaller as well as larger marine villas are among the latter, which rest on some romantic and rugged rocks that project into the sea, at high-water, and are known as the Yellow and Red Noses. The style of architecture of the latter buildings is pleasing; the pointed Gothic, the cottage, and the Lombard styles prevail. Red-Nose villa, the residence of W. Rowson, Esq., is that which most attracts the attention of visiters. In the midst of the most unpromising waste have conservatories, greenhouses, and beautiful parterres been reared. Adjoining to it I noticed a pretty Elizabethan villa, on one of the Yellow Noses, beneath which I was led to explore a profound cavern, the work of centuries of sea-efforts, extending about a mile under the high ground.

In the same direction, overlooking the beach, are several other pretty villas, bearing the distinguishing appellations of Noughton, Stamford, and Portland, with a Tudor terrace.

The houses erected on the brow of the higher ridge of sand, inland, have more pretension to style, and are not unlike some of the best houses at Brighton. The Albion and Victoria, large boarding-houses, are among the first on the left, and the Montpellier crescent attracts particular notice. Houses, let to private families by the week or month, well furnished, and in every way as comfortable as can be expected in a place so recently started into existence, are among these ranges of showy buildings; all these have before, and about a hundred feet below them, the smooth and unruffled waves that wash the Cheshire coast, with the Irish ocean far visible on the left, and the Lancashire shore on the right.

The spectacle, to such as enjoy marine views, is pleasing

from the simplicity of its elements, and may serve to calm the nerves of the agitated invalid, or fatigued and exhausted merchant emerging from his perpetual counting-house prison.

Cliff Villa, a lovely spot, if such a thing can be made out of such a locality, terminates this colony at its farthest northwest corner. It stands on a rocky promontory, which the proprietor has, by means of artificial ground, converted into a species of garden. Near it is seen a row of Gothic villas, of two floors each, so arranged as to correct, by skilful contrivance, the inconvenience of the general and natural aspect of the whole settlement, which being directly northward, is of course much exposed, and renders the place unfit for a winter residence.

Yet every where the busy hand of man is rearing dwelling-houses still, making room for them on the brow of the rock, where none existed before, by clearing away the sand, or cutting down the crest of the cliff.

When once we have descended by a steep footpath upon the beach, we discover that the lowest range of houses, which from above looked as if it were level with the shore, stands rather at an elevation on a broad ledge of conglomerate sand, in horizontal strata; and that from the beach, the larger houses, already described as occupying the upper ridge of sandhills, such as the Victoria and Albion boarding-house, are not visible.

Bathing-machines are arranged in order on the delightful sands, which, by the bye, extend about five miles, as at Hartlepool, on the eastern coast of England, and are free from quicksands, besides being hard and dry soon after low water. A bath-house has also been erected, where both cold and hot sea-water baths may be had at a short notice.

The colony, new as it is, enjoys already all the luxuries of an old settlement. It has its pump-house, its billiard and its news room, with livery-stables, and other conveniences. Throughout the upper village I did not observe a single shop or storehouse of any sort, but provisions and water are carried about in panniers and small barrels, on asses, driven by little boys. Water of the purest sort is obtained from a remarkable spring, on the beach, covered by the tide at high water, yet perfectly free from any brackishness in half an hour after the tide has receded.

New Brighton, in fine, is a curious and extraordinary settlement of its kind, worthy of being visited, and I doubt not answering, in the summer, every purpose for which it was intended. It is the speculation of a man who I understood died about two years since, and has thus formed for his children a valuable property out of heaps of refuse sand, which he purchased for a trifling sum from a gentleman now living in the neighbourhood. The land so purchased has since been let on building leases, at 7s. 6d. per yard ; and for some in the rear of the Victoria Boarding-house, at the time of my visit, as much as 10s. per yard was given.

After having explored every part and corner of the colony, I again directed my steps towards the wooden pier. Taking the direction along the strand, and jumping into the five o'clock steamer, I was presently relanded, for sixpence, on the Liverpool wharfs.

The establishment just described is the sea-bathing rendezvous, *par excellence*, of the Lancashire people of note; but the middle classes, and the wealthy shopkeepers, have also their Brightons and Margates, in the sea villages of Bootle and Crosby Waterloo. The former is within a short distance north of Liverpool, along the shore of the Mersey ; and with Seaforth Church, and its own two obelisks near the beach, it forms a pretty marine group. The sands are favourable, but the water is hardly sea-water; it is seldom clear, and not very inviting. The road to it passes between a range of well-built marine villas ; but being roughly paved in the middle, like some of the worst French roads, it is very trying to the nerves.

At five and a quarter miles from Liverpool, beyond Bootle and Seaforth, on the same shore, lies the new marine settlement, called

CROSBY WATERLOO.

It is a village of considerable size, spread at a short distance from the low-water sands; and in front of it a long line of neat cottages, one story high, each having a shelving verandah over the ground-floor window, presents its face to the south-western horizon.

The Waterloo Hotel, a building with somewhat more of architectural style about it than the rest, being two stories high, forms the head of or entrance into the village from the Liverpool-road. Like the other and contiguous buildings, it has between it and the beach, a large expanse of sandy soil, barely covered with short grass. Below it the sands slope gently down to the margin of the sea, and on these are seen several bathing-machines arranged in a row.

The place, judging from appearances, seems much frequented. Its aspect is westerly, inclined a little to the south. New Brighton, on the opposite, or Cheshire coast, may be plainly seen from this spot, which being situated near the embouchure of the Mersey, has constantly before it a busy and lively scene of arrivals and departures of sailing-vessels and steamers.

Behind the village the country is one universal flat, except where the eye catches, on the right, the gentle elevation on which stand some of the streets, and the more recently-built houses of Liverpool. High winds blow often, and sweep along this coast, making, I should think, the marine houses somewhat uncomfortable upon the least approach of cold weather.

The principal division of the line of marine cottages be-

fore described, is called the Marine Crescent. Each cottage
has a small garden in front, and then the road of communication, beyond which is the flat green already mentioned,
which serves as a general promenade. An attempt was made
some time since to establish a rendezvous saloon, with gentlemen's baths and billiards ; but it failed, and the place in itself
is probably as dull as it looks wild and deserted all round—a
proper retreat, however, for quiet and sea-bathing on account of ill-health.

I examined the beds and sitting-rooms of the Waterloo,
and received a card of their terms, which are very reasonable.
For two pounds sixteen shillings a week, a single person may
board and lodge at this house, which in every way resembles
some of the best appointed hotels at other and more fashionable sea-bathing places. The coffee-room is airy and neatly
appointed ; the bedrooms are of moderate size, and all those
on the second floor look over the sands, and are consequently
preferred. Every thing in the house looks clean, including
the landlady, who seems moreover a quiet and pleasing person. The means of communication with Liverpool are frequent, omnibuses come and depart every hour in the day, at
the moderate fare of one shilling.

———

Once more I am plunged into the region of red-brick
mills, seven stories high, of factories and warehouses, with a
suffocating atmosphere, and grubby faces. In one word, I
found myself once again at the Royal Hotel, in Manchester,
whither the *senior* railroad but one in England bore me in
an hour and ten minutes from Liverpool.

Manchester, however, nowadays deserves a different character ; and on a more minute examination of the principal
and most central part of the town than I had been able to accomplish a few weeks before, when on my way through it to

Harrogate, I find it greatly changed for the better. An architectural mania seems to have taken hold of the wealthy factor, the warehouseman, and the cotton-printer; for instead of the huge unmeaning masses of red and dingy brick buildings, pierced with innumerable little square windows, we find now the houses of business externally decorated with columns, and porticoes, and frescoes, and pediments, and, in fact, ornamented like palaces. And these, in some of the principal streets, such as Mosley and Oxford streets, Spring-gardens and Fountain-street, have taken the place of what before were the dwelling-houses of the more influential citizens, who have removed to purer air and more favourabl situations, south of the little and foul river Medlock.

Anxious to witness the new improvements and superior arrangements introduced into a few of the most important mills and factories of Manchester, I lost no time in sallying forth in quest of a very old acquaintance, a well-known and able mechanician and scientific man, a member of the Society of Friends. Proceeding down Mosley-street for that purpose, the very man I wanted hailed me from the opposite side of the way, surprised to see me. He immediately acceded to my request of accompanying me to one of the principal cotton-mills.

Our first visit, however, was paid to the apartments of the Literary and Philosophical Society, of which we are both fellows, and where, twenty-seven years before, we had sat together at a full assembly of the members, listening to the learned discussions of Percival, Henry, Hull, and Dalton.

On the present occasion, I found the great philosopher last named in the little laboratory of the institution, staring at me as if struggling to recognise an old acquaintance, whom length of time, and his recent severe attack of illness had probably obliterated from his intellect. Yet there was still upon his countenance that peculiar smile of benignity which ever distinguished his otherwise striking physiognomy.

Dalton was in the act of endeavouring to loosen, with patient placidity, the stubborn glass-stopper of an empty bottle, and welcomed me with a single smile, after a moment's hesitation and a shake of the hand. Finding the effort difficult for him, "friend" Clare, by whom I was escorted, and who will, to the last day of his own useful life, cherish the gratifying thought of having been the favoured, as well as the constant, assiduous, and ever-affectionate friend and helpmate of the great philosopher, offered to assist him. But Dalton, gently withdrawing his hand, which held the bottle, from Peter Clare's friendly offer, proceeded to a little lighted furnace, heated the bottle, and presently loosened the stopper; after which, as if he had been exhausted by the effort, he sat himself down, and whispered with hesitation and difficulty some words, the meaning of which we could not catch. Peter, to rouse him, mentioned the last important papers on the Phosphates, which Dalton had forwarded to the Royal Society in the April preceding; hearing which, the philosopher instantly raised his eyes, and inquired if they had been read and published in the Royal Transactions. Having given him a satisfactory answer, and alluded at the same time to our former and frequent meetings in that very hall more than a quarter of a century before, I took my leave of this venerable man, who, besides the admiration he was wont to excite before his dreadful attack of illness, as one of the greatest, yet one of the most simple-hearted philosophers of his time, inspires, since that illness, and even commands, a still higher degree of respect, not unmingled with a feeling of commiseration at his present enfeebled condition.

From a sight of the great original, "friend" Peter conducted me to that very handsome and striking edifice, designed by Barry, the Royal Institution, (far outstripping in grandeur and beauty of form the building of the Royal Institution of London), in order to behold the effigy of the philosopher, executed larger than life, in the purest marble, by Sir Francis Chantry.

Although I had already seen this performance of Sir Francis at one of the exhibitions of the Royal Academy, surrounded by many other works of art,—and though I am no great admirer of that sculptor's classic taste and skill in delineating whole figures of an elevated character; nevertheless, the statue now before me, as it stood insulated in the square vestibule of the Institution, in its pure whiteness, and lighted from above,—pensive and meditating on some great mathematical truth, the limbs in a state of repose—struck me as being one of the happiest productions of the chisel of that artist.

It is related that, being asked the price he would charge for such a statue, the size of life, Sir Francis named two thousand guineas. Inspired, however, by his subject, and deeming it worthy of colossal dimensions, the liberal-minded sculptor executed his work considerably larger than life (the figure measuring eight feet), and thereby entitled himself to an additional sum of a thousand pounds; yet this he declined to charge to the subscribers.

It is not my present purpose to detain my readers with an account of my remaining peregrinations, escorted by my friend, over many highly interesting establishments in this great emporium of English manufactures; nor can I dwell on the architectural aspect of the various new or modernized buildings that have risen here in all directions. Still, one can hardly have been favoured with the permission to inspect the stupendous cotton-mills in Chorlton upon Medlock, near the Oxford road, belonging to Messrs. Birley and Co., in which sixteen hundred people are employed daily, whose weekly wages amount to 900*l.*, and among whom two-thirds of the number are females of young ages,—without desiring to record publicly, when an opportunity like the present offers, the sense of satisfaction and admiration which the sight of such a prodigious and complicated establishment cannot fail to excite.

This establishment I examined in detail for the space of two hours, from ten till twelve o'clock, when all the hands engaged in the cotton department, as well as the millwright, the mechanics, the joiners, the plumbers, the painters, the turners, the moulders, the smiths, and the masons—for all these are daily at work on these endless premises,—went to their dinner.

I took advantage of the latter circumstance to post myself favourably at the door, so as to survey every one of the adult and younger girls, as well as most of the boys, employed in these mills. I had already seen most of them at their posts in the course of the morning, standing before thousands of power-looms, (of which one room alone contains upwards of 600), or guiding, and placing, and arranging the 80,000 spindles which daily twirl in these mills, under a moving power equivalent to 397 horses, and which convert annually four millions of pounds of raw material into cotton thread ; and on both occasions I noticed few, very few individuals indeed, who appeared either weak or sickly, or in any way as if affected by the peculiar work they were engaged in, by the constant standing posture they are obliged to preserve, and the damp and hot atmosphere in which for eight hours a day some of them live. On the contrary, the majority of the grown girls had a smiling and good-looking countenance, neither emaciated nor bloated, and their figures appeared light, active, and free from any defect.

I can readily believe the story, often repeated in Manchester, which states, that when Sir Francis Chantry beheld this assemblage of young women in a cotton factory, he declared that were he in want of varied yet perfect forms and moulds of female structure, he should seek 'them in these very establishments. And yet how hardly have the master factors been dealt with by the philanthropist, for their supposed cruel and harsh treatment of these very creatures, whose frames were said to have been estropiated, and their health broken, by the severity of their employment!

As for the little urchins, many of them between eight and ten years of age only, whom I beheld in this place, engaged in several branches of light work—never has it been my lot to see a merrier set. They went through their allotted task, laughing and joking, with alacrity and unimpaired energy; and when I saw them issuing from the mills as the noon bell dismissed them to their dinner, so little tired seemed they, or so little pressed by hunger, that they would—like so many schoolboys just escaped from their gymnasium—stop by the road—wrestle—tumble about—throw stones—crack jokes together, and laugh immoderately; thus evincing at once what state of health they must have enjoyed at the time.

At the conclusion of my visit, one of the junior partners asked me, as a professional man, whether I thought the people in their factory looked as a certain great philanthropic lord had stated—miserable and slavish. Justice and truth demanded that my answer should be as decisive as it was immediate, in the negative : but how far the present state of things, which enabled me to give such an answer, be or be not the result of the act of factory discipline, which that lord, moved by the purest motives, has been instrumental in enacting, I was not prepared by any previous knowledge of the establishment to determine.

On quitting Messrs. Birley's great factory, and by their advice, we proceeded to a far different, yet equally surprising establishment,—the Locomotive Engine Manufactory, or, " the Atlas Works " of Messrs. Sharp, Roberts, and Co.

My friend Clare, who is himself an excellent engineering mechanic, explained every thing to me as we proceeded from one large compartment of these gigantic premises to another, and imparted information on many points, respecting which I was before in total ignorance, especially with regard to the locomotive engines for railway trains. Of the latter, many were in progress of construction which were destined for the railways in Belgium—as well as for that which leads from St. Petersburg to Tzarcoçelo.

The view of these two great establishments—in one of which a bulky mass of vegetable fibre is converted, as if by magic, into the finest cloth, through the ingenious contrivances of machinery; while in the other the rudest and most shapeless lump of iron is wrought and moulded into some of the most wonderful agents of power and motion—would induce one to think that if the ingenuity of man's mind cannot impart life to organic matter, it can, at all events, cause inorganic matter to live. For what else but life is that wonderful, complicated, and all-working movement, elementarily generated by heat, playing upon the particles of water, by which almost every artificial thing man wants in this world is created and formed?

And now farewell to an old friend, with hearty thanks for his kindness and cordiality, and away by one of the public vehicles, which in three hours and a half is to deposit me at my next station, Buxton.

Stockport, the most important town we passed through, like many others in Lancashire and Cheshire, I found nearly double in extent to what I had known it twenty-five years before.

One of the most splendid specimens in this country of via-ducts to carry a railway is now in course of rapid construc-tion; and will, when completed, be not only the longest and loftiest, but, from its situation, the finest object of that kind to be seen in an English landscape.

The country beyond it is beautiful, and assumed at every step a richer aspect as we kept ascending. At Whaley Bridge, the surrounding landscape, however, is more striking than upon the summit of a very elevated ground, where the first view is obtained of Buxton, with its gray buildings dotting the green vale, or scattered upon the surrounding hills. At Whaley Bridge, the Peak Forest canal comes in as a very pretty feature in the landscape.

This approach to Buxton from Manchester is not the finest. That from Matlock is the most imposing, as the whole road indeed is, from that place to Buxton.

I put up at the Great Hotel. It was full, and the last bed-room that remained unoccupied was assigned to my use.

CHAPTER II.

BUXTON.

THERE is a fragrance of aristocracy in the very air of this Spa, which at once bespeaks it the rendezvous of far different classes of visiters from those we have seen at Askerne or elsewhere, among the minor watering-places of the north. The very first *coup-d'œil* at the " Grand Hotel," as I surveyed the interior of that large building in my way up the principal staircase to the remote chamber assigned to me, showed me that I must take some pains with my toilet. Having done so, and again descended for the purpose of ascertaining from the landlord the address of Sir Charles Scudamore, whom I knew to be in Buxton, where he has for many years been in

the habit of taking up his abode in his professional capacity
during the summer months, I was encountered by a tall and
comely woman, wearing a cheerful smile on her fair countenance; who, accosting me with peculiar grace, inquired if she
had the honour of addressing the author of the " Spas of
Germany." I admitted myself guilty of the fact. " Then,
sir," exclaimed my fair hostess (for in that sort of character
I had soon to acknowledge her), " you have ruined us all,
by sending every one of our best English families and
countrymen abroad, with your book. Until you recommended the various baths in Germany by your description
and account of them, and enticed patients to go thither,
most of them were satisfied with what they could procure at
home. In the case of Buxton, and our own individual hotel,
the result has been most glaringly injurious. There was
Lord ——, for instance, a catholic nobleman, who came here
for the first time, three years ago, on crutches, and unable to
move even a finger. He got much better in six weeks, and
was induced to come a second time last year, when the benefits he experienced from these waters were even more manifest.
Yet, this year, nothing would satisfy him but he must go to
Wisbaden, where his lordship declares he is getting quite
well; and he adds, that the two previous years he spent at
Buxton had been productive of no earthly good to him:—
both ungrateful and unnatural. However, we are, thank
God, quite full just now, and we have no reason to complain.
But the season is short nowadays, and hardly of sufficient
importance to make it worth while for any landlord to con-
tinue the speculation of an expensive establishment like this;
Mr. Shaw's predecessor was ruined."

I hung my head like a culprit, caught in *flagrante
delicto*, and knew not what to say in extenuation of my
crime! I, however, urged the probability of some other reasons being the cause of the present apparent desertion of
Buxton, and my fair interlocutor was obliged to admit that

it wanted amusement and more society, and that in fact it was " a very dull place." She agreed with me also, that the sojourning of the Duke, the sovereign lord of the place, with three or four more leading people of *ton*, visiters to the Spa, determined to take the lead, and to get the people together, by giving them a ball or an assembly once a week, would soon bring about the restoration of the Spa.

" Here is, for example, the Marchioness of ———,* who is staying in this very hotel. She is inclined to favour a greater development of the social capabilities of the place, by dining herself at the *table d'hôte*, and mixing more with the rest of the visiters, though, as you know, she is a great lady at the Palace ; but as yet she hardly meets with any encourage. ment. In fact, all is yet to be done, and the beginning is but slight."

In all her remarks, Miss ———, my fair hostess, was per- fectly right; a truth of which I was not long in becoming personally convinced. For as what may really be called " the Spa" at Buxton lies in a nut-shell, it needed no greater industry or assiduity in the inquiries than I bestowed upon it, to ascertain, in two or three days, every particular merit and demerit appertaining to the place.

The hotel, in which I occupied a very comfortable room on the second story, looking north, forms the eastern termination or wing of that magnificent building (equalled in England only by one or two great edifices in Bath) called emphatically " The Crescent," with which the late Duke of Devonshire decorated Buxton, after the design of Carr, an architect of great merit in his days,—some of whose works in the city of York I have had occasion to mention.

At the opposite extremity of this semicircular range of Do- ric building, raised two stories high, above a rusticated arcade, which, though narrow, offers a convenient promenade in wet

.* Since a Duchess.

weather,—is another hotel forming the western termination
of the Crescent, and called St. Anne's.

The remaining oriental part of the building between
these two hotels, comprises various separate establishments; among which the post-office, and what here they
are pleased to style a promenade-room, are the most important. Immediately over the arcade, fluted Doric pilasters
twenty-six feet in height are placed between the windows of
the principal story all along the front, supporting a suitable
architrave and cornice, crowned by a balustrade which runs
continuously along the whole façade, and is returned at each
end of the building. The range of the compass in front of
the inner sweep of this Crescent, measuring in extent two
hundred feet, is W.S.W. and E.S.E.

While recording these notes in my tablets, at that hour of
the day when the gayest scene of social life mingles with the
natural beauties of Buxton, I was seated at an elevation
of about a hundred feet on the top of a green hillock, called
St. Anne's Clift, which extends east and west somewhat like
the sixth part of a mile, and is placed exactly in front of the
noble semicircular area of the Crescent, like a chord to an
arch. Over its surface, wide gravel walks have been cut in
various directions, the lowest of which, being laid out quite
straight, in the direction of the longest axis of the hill,
serves as a terrace, and is the most frequented of the walks
on the hill, because the most sheltered as well as the least
fatiguing.

The ample and semicircular area just mentioned, and
which now lies before and below me, as well as the arcade
beyond it, appeared thinly dotted with groups of men and
women, some standing, and others walking backwards and
forwards; while many more (single or in couples) I beheld
nearer to where I was seated, rambling about on the serpentine walks of St. Anne's Clift. They were listening to the
Duke's band, which plays (though not every day) between

eleven and twelve o'clock, and which seemed to be composed
of young lads dressed in a French gray uniform jacket and
caps.

At the west end of the lower walk on St. Anne's Clift is
the Drinking Well. I approached it to view the spring,
and did not remark that it was much resorted to by the per-
ambulatory invalids or visiters, among whom, I recognised
Marshal Viscount ———, the Marquis and Marchioness ———,
since raised to a higher rank by inheritance, the Honourable
Mr. E———, and a few, very few more of the *sommités*, who
had temporarily quitted the commodious apartments of the
Great Hotel, the head-quarters of those of " gentle blood."
St. Anne's, too, pours out at this same hour, from its equally
extensive range of rooms,—though not so choicely furnished,
or so choicely tended, — its inmates, the merchants and
their ladies from Liverpool or Manchester, the invalids from
Ireland, and a few of the squires with their spouses and
children, from neighbouring counties.

Beyond the Well, the surmounting urn of which only I
could perceive from the spot I occupied on St. Anne's
Clift, stretches the " Hall" with its ancient bath-buildings,
and another quadrangular arcaded edifice called the
" Square," behind which rises the new church * — its
portico partially seen in the landscape. This last mass or
group of buildings, clustered together, conceal the entrance
into the parterre promenade or " Serpentine Walks," which
wind along both sides of the Wye, and are situated at
a short distance from the said " Hall," being separated
from it only by the road. This latter, descending from the
western extremity (called Hallbank) of the very hill on

---

* This elegant structure is actually built on piles ; for though placed
upon a hill we have here quagmires and uncertain ground. Divine service is performed regularly in it, and in the old presbyterian chapel.
Not fewer than twelve reverends belonging to different rectories and
livings, have been known at times to volunteer their services during the
season.

which I took down this panoramic description, makes a circuit at the back of the Crescent to go and join another road leading into Low Buxton, on the right or eastern extremity of my picture.

Four or five substantial lodging-houses, with plain stone fronts and slated roofs, skirt this western road or Hallbank, descending *en echelons*, between the last of which and the shaded entrance into the promenade garden already alluded to, stands the public Billiard-room.

Such is the ensemble or grouping of this celebrated Spa, in its most important and prominent character, as seen from the elevated spot I selected—the best, in my opinion, for judging rightly of the place, and all it can offer of social resources and recreation out of doors, as well as of the movement and bustle of which Buxton is capable. The latter seems to be but slender; for in one hour after I had taken up my position on the hill, the show and hum of life in front of it had all disappeared.

This great centre of attraction at Buxton Spa is encircled at various rays of distance by loftier hills. That which backs the Crescent, and is seen to rise above it, is crested with a rich wood. Barren and moorlike are the western hills; whilst the one which shuts out the eastern breezes is crowned with a small village church and a few clumps of trees.

Many improvements suggest themselves to one accustomed to visit watering-places, which seem highly desirable at this aristocratic Spa. The two first and most prominent are a Kur-Saal and a more showy pump or well room. People should be enticed to go to the fountain-head to drink the water.

Early the following morning I proceeded to taste the water at the well, which is sheltered by a low Grecian canopy, where I saw many who attended to do the same; but they were all ordinary people, who deposited their penny contribution upon the stone-flag that covers the source. I saw none of the *crême de la société* drinking the tepid spring;—but perhaps it was too early, as few people were abroad :—in which practice of late rising, visiters at English Spas do err egregiously ; and those' medical men who suffer it to exist err still more.

A nearly decrepit old woman, seated before the scanty stream, with her shrivelled hands distributes it to the applicants as they approach her. Now it is one of the great attractions of the German Spas that smart female attendants are provided, and ever ready to supply the limpid and sparkling water in crystal or china beakers, which almost every visiter carries with him, without fee or reward ; not the slightest vestige of anything mercenary is suffered to appear in an operation which would cease to be natural were any pecuniary transaction mixed up with it.

Decorated well-houses, also spring-heads very neatly arranged with stone steps and balustrades, are conspicuous in Germany, and they have the effect of inducing people to congregate at the spot. Here the superior class of visiters seem ashamed of being seen to descend under the well-dome, and ask the old dame for a draught of the water ; they prefer having it sent to their lodgings or apartments—another most absurd practice which obtains only in this country. Could but these indolent persons behold the joyous, inspiriting crowds of [beaux and belles assembled, each with their beaker in hand, around the Therezenbrunnen, or the Sprudel at Carlsbad, or at the Ragozi spring at Kissingen, the example might convert them to early hours, and a more effectual mode of taking the mineral waters.

Arrangements of a similar kind as at those places might easily be accomplished at Buxton ; and, if necessary, the spring-head or well-house might be closed, after the morning hours, against intruders and mischief-makers ; suffering the surplus water which continuously flows from the source to pass into another stone basin, placed on the outside, for the more general and gratuitous use of the public.

As for a Kur-Saal, or Promenade-room, it is an absolute requisite for people who are drinking mineral, especially thermal waters. In a climate so uncertain as ours, a walk *sub divo* is precarious. That under the arcade of the Crescent is liable to the great objection of its being much exposed to draughts, and even to the sprays of rain beating in under it, in consequence of the considerable height of the arches, and the narrowness of the arcade—the latter being only seven feet wide. The stormy gales prevailing, as they must ever do, in this region of eleven hundred feet's elevation sweep at intervals through those arcades, and whistling with dismal violence, chill at the same time the poor invalid.

This and the preceding observation,—together with a third also, which I might make, namely, that the present promenade and news room at Buxton are really not worthy to hold the rank of an assembly-room in a market-town,—sufficiently show the necessity for a handsome Kur-Saal. Its site bespeaks itself.

There is, on the summit of the hill fronting the Crescent already described, an irregular area of some hundred feet. This should be levelled, and a Grecian temple erected upon it, with the principal or north front towards the Crescent, so as to receive all the reflected light from that amphitheatre, whereby the grave features of a Grecian portico would show boldly out. On the opposite side of the building another portico should jut out, upon a wide terrace facing the south; while the west and east sides of it might be shaded by an open colonnade, in communication with the south terrace. By these arrangements suitable exposure to the sun when desirable, and shelter from unpropitious winds when necessary, together with a general rendezvous in the centre protected altogether from the weather, would be completely secured.

A building one hundred feet by forty feet in the interior, and as many feet high, having a cassooned ceiling, and three quarter columns round the room to support a bold cornice;

with a gallery at one end for the orchestra; the whole lighted by full windows down to the bottom, and lateral doors leading out under the colonnade;—such a building I think would form a magnificent Kur-Saal—one worthy of the taste and munificence of the nobleman who takes so lively an interest in this Spa.

With such a patron it would be an insult to allude to considerations of expense, when speaking of such improvements as these; yet it may be observed, that an edifice of the class I have just suggested, in a place in which stone is so readily procured, could not cost any very large sum of money. But with such an example of tasteful magnificence before him as the Crescent exhibits to the admiring stranger, which an illustrious ancestor hesitated not in erecting for the embellishment of Buxton, at an expense of one hundred thousand pounds, and without which Buxton would have been nothing —it is not likely that his present descendant, no less illustrious, and equally munificent as a patron of the arts, will long delay in giving to Buxton two such essential and ornamental additions as a KUR-SAAL worthy of his taste and wealth, and a suitable WELL-HOUSE.

To the latter, such as it is, I proceeded, as before observed, early one morning, in order to test chemically the mineral water. The glass with which the old woman was about to supply me with the water is constantly kept by her at the bottom of the little bason, under the running stream, and feels warm to the hand when taken up full : hence I felt a moment of surprise upon putting it to my lips, to find the water cold to the palate.

The water has no taste whatever, and is rather insipid indeed, as compared with waters which have a lower temperature, — say forty-nine or fifty degrees. I measured the time it took to fill a half-pint tumbler, through the little silver spout, and thus ascertained that the supply is at the rate of six pints in a minute, or nine hundred and fifty-five gallons in the day exactly—a supply by no means abundant.

On reference to Sir Charles Scudamore's and Mr. Garden's analysis of this water, we find it to be so nearly allied to pure water, that the learned doctor is inclined to ascribe a large portion of its well-known power on the constitution to the presence of four cubic inches of azote in a gallon of it.

Unquestionably we cannot attribute much to chemical ingredients found in a mineral water of acknowledged efficacy, if, in the aggregate, those ingredients amount in quantity to hardly two grains in a pint. A fraction of a grain of muriate of soda, and a fraction of carbonate of lime—the two most prominent ingredients in a pint of the Buxton water—are not likely to impart to it much energy or power. But is half a cubic inch of azote in the same quantity of water likely to do it?

I have my doubts as to the presence of what is called azote in mineral waters. Mr. West finds it every where. There is not a water he has analyzed with which I am acquainted, and in which he has not set down azote as one of its constituents. Other English chemists have also mentioned it, as I stated in the Introduction. Strange that in none of the German waters I have studied, the same principle should have been detected by the very eminent analyzing chemists who performed the analysis. The water at Baden-Baden is the only one that has been mentioned as containing azote in very minute proportions; but that statement is not made by a *chemist* of note, and is not to be relied upon.

The question of azote in mineral waters is a doubtful one, at all events. I suspect it will be found to be atmospheric air somewhat vitiated by the processes of analysis; nor am I inclined to attribute much virtue or power of acting on the human frame to a fractional quantity of such a gas, did it really exist in a mineral water.

No: the efficacy of Buxton water, like that at Schlangenbad, which is of the same temperature, is to be ascribed entirely to that very temperature. There we saw, in a former work, a water producing particular effects, with very few chemical ingredients in its composition, but having a natural heat of 86 degrees. Here at Buxton, we have a water at nearly the same degree of heat, with fewer ingredients, still producing, not only similar, but even more energetic effects.

Those effects are seen even more strikingly produced by the application of a large quantity of the water to the whole body, than when only a small portion is taken internally. Hence, a plunge into the public bath, or into the more retired and elegant gentlemen's private bath, is always attended by phenomena which, whether during the immersion or after it, differ from those produced by ordinary water heated to 83 degrees of Fahrenheit.

In the public bath I saw many people bathing, three or four at a time, and several in succession. The operation with most of them was expeditious, the greater number of the bathers remaining but two or three minutes in the water, and being always in motion.

The water, from the dark colour of the rock at the bottom, and the darkness of the dome, (for it is in a vault under " the Old Hall,") looks, at first view, dingy and greenish; but it is as limpid, transparent, and colourless, as the one I drank at the spring. The form of the bath is an oblong square. The water surges about the middle, near the outer wall, to the height of four feet, and passes off at one of the extremities of the bath by waste pipes. Bubbles of air may be seen rising in succession from time to time. At other times a single one, much larger than the rest, will come up, to break at the surface.

The people bathing differed, it appeared to me, in opinion as to the impression made on them by the water. Some said it was very cold; others declared it was very comfortable. As the sun darted a slanting ray through the half circular window close to the vaulted ceiling over it, the surface of the water exhibited a gathering of scum, having an unusual appearance in any mineral water, which took away from me the temptation I had at first experienced of trying the effect of the Buxton water at this nearest point of its source.

The overflowing or escape of the surplus water through the waste pipes, is never so quick but that the said scum, or floating matter, remains too long spread over its surface,—as I witnessed during the half-hour I kept watching the proceedings of those who were in the bath. Indeed, one of the attendants comes now and then with a broom, and sweeps from off the surface the coarser particles, and thus restores to the water its natural appearance. But, at best, this is but mixing up with the water, or dissolving in it, the objectionable substance.

Altogether, the bathing in such a *piscina* was not such as to please my fancy; and when I beheld the class of persons, too, who kept coming in (for the access is free and the bath always open), and their dress and appearance—when I saw the pot-bellied farmer of sixty, half palsied, and the lame artisan with his black and callous hands, and the many who suffered from cutaneous disorders—all plunging together, or one after the other, in quick succession—some of whom would set about scrubbing from their hardened cuticles the congregated perspiration of ages, with a handbrush kept *pro bono publico* on the margin of the bath;—I say, when I beheld all these things, I confess my courage failed me, despite of my constant desire to try on myself, and ascertain by my own feelings, the effects of the various mineral waters I have examined.

Sometimes the most ludicrous scenes occur in these generalizing plunging-baths, where every body is admitted and at all hours of the day. A gallant officer of the life-guards, seized of a sudden with the "rheumatics," got leave for a fortnight from his regiment, and away he trotted to Buxton. There he found the place nearly deserted; but, as good luck would have it, among the few he met with an old friend. They agreed to bathe at the same time, and early, that they might avoid coming in contact with the "multitudinous." Accordingly, they both plunged into the dark stream early one fine morning, rejoicing in the privacy of the hour; as, by the doubtful light which reigns in the locality at all times, and still more so very early in the day, they could perceive no other bather. But what must have been the amazement of the gallant invalid when, upon raising his head above the water, whilst yet recovering from the shock of the plunge, he heard himself addressed with "How do you do, Sir Richard?" by a mouth spattering and spirting out water like a porpoise, and belonging to a head which had also just emerged out of the tepid stream, but at the furthest dark corner of the bath. Sir Richard stretched his neck towards the said head, puckered up his eyelids to sharpen his visual organs, approached the individual nearer and nearer, when, lo! he discovered that the "How do you do, man?" was no other than his tailor from Chester!

After all, I am assured that there is but three-quarters of a degree of difference between the temperature of this and of the gentlemen's private bath already alluded to, which lies to the north of the source, and is thus far cooler from being further removed from it. The latter bath I did not hesitate to try.

The water is here collected on the same level as in the general bath, but the reservoir or basin, which is an oval of considerable dimensions, is lined with white tiles. Upon these the water appears of a beautiful transparent light emerald-green colour. The reservoir is in a vaulted room, to which access is had by a glass-door, through a dressing-room, furnished with every convenience that one can desire in such an apartment. The attendance also is perfect.

There are two such private baths for gentlemen, and the same number for ladies : besides the public one for either sex. I should have expected a much larger number of both to have been necessary.

I entered the bath about twenty minutes before eight, A.M., my pulse at eighty-two. I had drunk half a pint of the mineral water some time before. The immersion was by the steps, and therefore gradual. The feeling of cold on the skin produced by the first approach of the water formed a striking contrast with the pleasing warmth of the atmosphere of the room. When I let myself down into the middle, and at the bottom of the basin, by holding the chain which hangs from the centre of the ceiling, the shock was precisely similar to what I have often felt when plunging into the open sea at the same time of the day and year. It took my breath away, and tightened the thorax, producing, however, not the slightest vestige of disturbance, either in the head or in the movements of the heart.

I partially got out and recovered my breath, and again plunged into the bath, all within two or three minutes. The water felt still cold, but not so as to affect the respiration this time. After the first four minutes, I being either standing upright on the tiles which felt cold to the feet, floating horizontally under the water, a degree of warmth began to pervade the body along its surface, and was evidently on the. increase at every half-minute. The skin felt soft—not puckered nor corrugated in any part, as is generally the case in warm water, and many mineral springs; when the hands were passed over the body, they glided readily over it.

Even after a few minutes longer, I experienced no inclination to sleepiness, and the head continued in the same state as when I went in. Before I left the bath, however, I ascertained that, contrary to the effect produced by an ordinary warm-bath, if I raised my limbs from the middle of the depth to nearer the surface, the difference of feeling, as to warmth, was what I should have estimated at about three or four degrees of increased temperature.

So much so was this the case, that quitting the position in

which the limb was previously stationary, and around which
the water felt as if it had grown cold, and raising it to the position before alluded to, I could have imagined that I had
placed my limb into a totally differently-heated water—into
one, in fact, of a regular tepid bath, so genial was the first
impression. But then it was only a *first* impression, which
soon vanished, to be again renewed by seeking with the limbs,
or any other part of the body, another and a new position.

At the expiration of about ten minutes, I might have
fancied myself, from my own feelings, in a bath of 94° or 95°,
or in a regular tepid bath; and this apparent feeling or impression was even stronger if I got on the steps of the
reservoir, and quite out of the water, and immediately plunged
into the water again.

Judging from this single experiment, which I have detailed
minutely for very obvious reasons, I should say that the
proper mode of using these baths would be, not to plunge,
but to walk gradually and quickly into the water up to the
chin, and out of it as quickly again. This operation should
be repeated at least three or four times, occupying perhaps
two minutes each time in doing it; and lastly, the bathers
should return into the water for the sake of a real bath, which
would then produce pleasurable sensations, and could be
borne very well and quietly for ten minutes longer, or even
a quarter of an hour,—during which time, the body would
receive the full benefit of these volcanic waters.

There is no disguising the fact : Buxton is a cold and not a
tepid bath, and only becomes tepid to the feelings by a little
time and management—the same as in the open sea—but not
in an ordinary water-bath at 83°. The difference here is, that
the warmth, when once felt, is a permanent sensation, were you
to remain even hours together in the bath ; whereas in ordinary water, tepid bathing, or the open sea, or in a river or
a spring in the sun, the water which at first might seem tepid,
would soon progressively feel colder and colder.

This difference, which it is of the most vital importance to bear in mind, in using mineral baths, is invariably to be observed in thermal springs, and is to be attributed (as I remarked elsewhere) to the peculiar nature of telluric or volcanic heat, as contradistinguished from the ordinary heat of our fires.

An hour after coming out of the bath, all the glow produced by it had gone, and the back felt chilly. This is owing to the low range of warmth possessed by the Buxton water (83°), and is not noticed in baths of a naturally higher temperature, such as those of Wildbad, Ems, Wisbaden, &c.

The aspiration of a recent professional writer on the Buxton waters, that they might be endowed with less energy, is something approaching to " fudge." I should rather wish that they were just 15 degrees hotter than they are; and I should then expect to find them useful in many cases of disease in which they are of no service now,—without becoming in the *least* hurtful to those which are at present benefited by them.

The most marked effect of the Buxton water is that of stimulation, whether the water be taken internally or used externally only. If artificial heat be added to them, and the temperature raised thereby to 96°, 97°, or 98° (and such a bath I tried twice, noting at the time every minute effect on myself), the result on the constitution is not a whit more stimulating than what is produced by the water at its natural temperature. The fact is, again, that the stimulation is due, not to thermometrical heat, but to the portion only of telluric heat inherent in the water.

The hot-bath at Buxton is administered in a particular way, which deserves a separate description. At the eastern extremity of the Crescent, close to the Great Hotel from which there is a covered way to it, is the new establishment for hot-baths, erected under the superintendence of Mr. Sylvester. When a bath at 98° is required, it is ordered the previous evening. The attendant, who knows how important it is to retain as much warmth as possible in the tiles, or marble lining of the bath, suffers the water which has been last used for hot-bathing in the day, to remain in the basin the whole night.

When I made my appearance to take a hot-bath at seven, A. M., one day, I found the basin so filled. By my ther-mometer I ascertained that the water in it was 86°. It had been used at 98° the evening before. It had consequently lost twelve degrees of heat in the course of the night. The appearance of the water, in which no soap or any other sub-stance had been used, was slightly milky ; and this is the aspect I found the Buxton water to assume when artificially heated, and suffered to cool down for several hours.

In letting this water out by the waste-pipe, I noticed that the attendant employed a species of scrubbing-brush to re-move a certain oily slime which adheres to the tiles, and then to clean out the basin. Water was then let in from two pipes ; the one conveying Buxton water, which by perpetual ex-posure to hot steam, is kept uniformly at the temperature of 86°, or there about ; the other letting in hot water, main-tained nearly boiling by steam also. In eight minutes I saw the basin filled, which is three feet deep, seven feet long, and three feet and a half wide.

The basin is sunk into the ground, so that the upper part is level with it. There is a step or seat at one end, about eight inches high, and four steps to go down into the bath, with brass railing on each side. This is rendered absolutely necessary to prevent accident from slipping down, on account of the particular nature of the deposit the water lets fall on the marble lining of the basin ; which deposit is peculiar to all thermal springs more or less, and is here to be seen in great abundance in the two public baths for ladies and gentle-men, when these baths are emptied for the purposes of being daily cleaned out, and the rock exposed.

The thermometer being suspended in the water all the time, and the temperature 98°, I felt my pulse at twenty-five minutes past six, A. M., rather below par, as to fulness, for me, and then descended into the bath, where I at once experienced those grateful sensations which warmth, applied to the body, invariably produces. I experienced quietude for the first five minutes, and found my pulse had got six beats lower, but was of double the fulness it had before; it felt like a soft but tense cord, and the beat was firm. In the next minute *my head*, which was particularly clear, and in a natural state before, became misty and heated. In the chest also, and throughout the body, I felt an inward increase of heat.

I was watching what would be the next effect, and expected an increase of these symptoms, which I never experience in an ordinary water hot-bath at 98°, but always more or less while bathing in thermal springs. They continued so for two or three minutes without increase, and then subsided, and merged into a general feeling of comfort, as experienced at first.

I continued in the water precisely fifteen minutes, during which no apparent difference of temperature had taken place in the thermometer. The water this time felt genial in every corner of the bath, and close to the very surface. It was beautifully transparent, and of a faint aquamarine colour. The minutest object could be perceived, but magnified considerably. The very lightest coloured hairs on the arms appeared dark from increased size, which seemed double their natural one at least.

Towards the last five minutes I repeatedly plunged my head into the water, but without any change of sensation resulting. As to the feeling of the skin, I missed completely, both when in, and immediately out of the water, that healthful *satinization* which people have so often experienced in some mineral waters abroad; Wildbad for instance, and above all others. The skin of the hands was not corrugated, as when they are dipped in hot water for some minutes, but it felt rough when passed over the body, as if it were a ground file. In other parts the hand could not be made to glide continuously, but would stick from the roughness of the surface.

When at the expiration of fifteen minutes I got out of the bath, the skin dried immediately upon the application of the warm linen brought by the attendant who was summoned for that purpose. There was not the slightest disposition to perspire afterwards, as is always the case on coming out of a more powerful thermal spring than Buxton; and although I returned home experiencing an agreeable sensation of genial warmth, which I certainly had not when I left the hotel in the morning (a morning both wet and stormy)— in an hour or two after, and through the remainder of the day, I was not sensible of any different feeling than I have in general.

There are only two hot-baths for the gentlemen, and an equal number for the ladies—with vapour and douche, or shower-bath, for each. This number of baths is not found to be small or insufficient, even when as many as one hundred and fifty baths in a week have been administered, according to the statement of the bath-woman. The price of the hot-bath is 3s., that of the gentleman's private bath of mineral water is only 2s.

There is room for improvement in this part of the Spa establishment of Buxton. The bath and antechamber should be kept more tidy. The brass work and stopcocks are suffered to be tarnished, and are never rubbed. The attendant on the bath, a young man, should wear a decent, neat, light-coloured dress and a clean shirt; instead of which he looked more like a grubby labourer just called from the plough.

The situation of the bathing-tanks themselves is ill-managed; for it is constantly exposed to the draught from the door between the bath and anteroom, the outer entrance into which is almost always kept open. A contrivance, too, of a wicker-basket with a pan of coals should be adjusted, with a view of supplying the bathers with the necessary linen —quite warm—in the room they are to dress in; instead of which, at present, they have to get out of the water, after ringing the bell for the attendant, and await his arrival with a single hot sheet, which he throws on your back, and disappears.

I asked Mr. Serjeant ——, a constant visiter at Buxton, why these little contrivances and improvements had not been already suggested and adopted. His reply was laconic and candid. " It's too much trouble."

In connexion with my account of the baths, I may as well state in this place, that I visited, with Sir Charles Scudamore, the Charity Baths, to which he is the senior physician, and saw him prescribe for some of the infirmary patients, whom he treated with great tenderness and humanity, taking down minutely their cases, in a room cold and stripped of furniture, and writing on a drum-head—the only sort of table he could find in the place. This charity has relieved, in the course of seventeen years, upwards of 21,000 patients, nearly 15,000 of whom had the gratuitous use of the baths and medical advice, &c. With regard to the latter cases, an account has been kept of the degree of benefit which they derived from the use of the waters, and from it we find that 12,608 have been dismissed, " cured, or much relieved."

According to my own theory of thermal springs, and the effects observed at Buxton, when the hot-baths, consisting partly of natural and partly of artificial heat, are regularly used, —I should say, that they would be much more and differently influential on the constitution and in disease than ordinary baths, in which the whole of the heat from the ordinary temperature of between fifty and sixty degrees up to ninety-eight, is artificial; and therefore it is, that I am not surprised at the wonderful effect said to have been produced by the hot-bath on rheumatism and faulty action of some of the internal organs, and should, on the contrary, have predicated precisely those results. In fact, we find that the joint testimony of patients and doctors of this and the preceding ages, is in favour of a particular action being the result of the Buxton hot-baths, and this agrees with my own experience.

But Dr. Robertson in his little work, entitled " Buxton and its Waters," goes further in his estimate of that particular action, and asserts that the energy is even dangerous. I have nothing to advance against such a doctrine ; as Dr. Robertson may claim to possess a larger practical knowledge of the Buxton waters than my own, for the ground of his theory. But *à priori*, I should not expect such effects as he has described ; nor did I experience them in my own person ; neither could I learn, from any of the several persons who assembled during my stay at the public rooms at the Great Hotel, that they had experienced such effects. The same I may observe of the many patients I have sent to Buxton.

My landlady, indeed, who is an exceedingly intelligent person, informed me that she had seen ladies who would plunge into the public bath without due advice, and be drawn out again in fits of hysteria. But these fits might have occurred if the said ladies had been suddenly plunged from a bathing-machine at Scarborough or Brighton into the sea, or had experienced any sudden shock of a similar kind. The first impression of the natural bath is that of cold and depression, as well as of a sudden constriction of the chest, suspending, or rendering difficult, the respiration. Such a series of feelings can never be said to be akin to " dangerous excitement ;" though a reaction, at some more distant period, may possibly take place. That, however, is what takes place also after cold affusion used in hot fevers, and, *cæteris paribus*, the two effects may so far be compared together.

The efficacy of the Buxton water used as baths at their natural temperature is more strikingly manifested in cases of general debility, partial paralysis, and that peculiar state of weakness which is the result of rheumatic affection, and repeated attacks of gout. In the latter cases, indeed, Buxton has acquired a well-known reputation; and to such as cannot have recourse to the more effectual waters of Wisbaden or Carlsbad, in that class of complaint, or with whose constitution the powerful and unjustly neglected springs of Bath do not agree, I know of no more desirable application for the occasion than this very water at Buxton. If care be taken to see that in all such cases every symptom of febrile irritability has disappeared from the system of the patient, the waters may be used internally or externally with safety. Sometimes the natural, at other times the artificially heated bath—and again, the pump or *douche*—will be found preferable during the treatment. These are points to be decided by the medical attendants on the spot, or by one well acquainted with the various effects producible by Buxton, though residing at a distance.

There is a result of arthritic affection which the practitioner often meets, consisting in an enlargement of the joints, which, if recent, I have known to be completely removed by the use of the Buxton water, applied as a *douche*. Indeed, either as a *douche*, or as a general bath, such patients as are plagued with stiff and enlarged fingers and hands from repeated attacks of gout, will find in the water at Buxton a means of relief.

Where I have seen the Buxton water perform wonders has been in persons who, having had annual, perhaps semi-annual attacks of genuine painful gout, have not courage enough to support pain, and fly at once to that curse of the human constitution, *colchicum*, to quell the "gnawing dogs," and purchase a lull from sufferings at the inevitable risk of multiplying the attacks of the disease. In such individuals the constitution is lowered below its standard, by the morbid condition left nearly always present, in consequence of the interference perpetrated against a salutary effort or crisis of nature; and it is also further depressed by the specific action of the drug generally taken in goodly doses to accomplish that interference. In many such cases that have fallen under my notice, much good has been obtained from two or three successive courses of the Buxton baths, used, of course, under proper precautions. I mention purposely that two or three courses are necessary, because I found that, in general, patients, doing infinite injustice to Buxton, think that if they have visited the place once for two or three weeks, they have done all that is requisite.

There is, also, another class of disordered constitutions to which I would refer, as having, in my experience, been greatly benefited by the warm Buxton bath at first, and the natural bath afterwards. These are the cases of exhaustion brought on from imprudence, either in very early or in adult life, and affecting the spine. They are generally accompanied by much languor, restlessness, without heat; and a sense of perfect debility in the back, without any specific pain. Such cases as these are wonderfully relieved by a course of the Buxton water, beginning with the warm bath, then using the tepid shower-bath; next the pump to the spine, and, lastly, a dip or two, every other day in the natural bath. In this manner I have lately almost resuscitated two cases, from a very distressing state of premature old age. The only thing to be attended to here is to discriminate accurately, at first, whether the debility of the spine be of the character I have just described, or an affection of the spinal marrow, or of the sheath covering it, or, in fine, of any of the branches of nerves that issue therefrom; for in such cases we have generally absolute or dissimulated inflammation, and the Buxton waters would do mischief.

In fine, I can conscientiously aver, from my extended experience of mineral waters throughout Germany, the Pyrenees, Italy, and England, that persons afflicted with any affection within the limited ranges of disease specified in this chapter, who require the aid of a suitable mineral water, will find that needful aid at Buxton, provided they abjure, on proceeding thither, the sad and interfering practice of constantly drugging their stomachs by way of *treatment*, and leave nature to nature alone,—namely, the mineral waters, and the pure, elastic, and bracing mountain-air of the Spa.

I might enumerate specific cases, to a great extent, of recovery from the Buxton water left to its own energy on the constitution, if I were so inclined. But in a work in which I must limit to a chapter or two all that I have to say respecting Buxton, I cannot find space for more than the following illustrations of the efficacy of its waters. They are all interesting, but the second is so in particular, as having occurred in the person of an illustrious member of the medical profession. I can vouch for the authenticity of the facts.

For twenty years has the Rev. ————, of Longhills, near Branston, rector of the latter place, and of Potter Hannoth, been in the habit of going to Buxton for the benefit of his health. He never carried thither any particular complaint, but was always poorly and felt weak after the exertion and labours of his profession through the year, and stood in need of recruiting his strength and the vigour of his body. These he never failed to obtain after remaining a month at Buxton ; but generally the benefit occurred two months or more after he had quitted that place. He both bathed and drank the water. The immersion was in the natural plunging bath, at an hour when none of the commoner people attended to bathe, which is à little before four o'clock. He used to remain only ten minutes in the water, which felt warm after the first sudden impression on the skin. He used to walk into the water— not plunge. He drank of the spring, but the water confined his bowels, and he was obliged to take simple aperient medicine, principally rhubarb. He attributes his present robust state of health to that practice, which he has followed annually, the present year excepted.

Not long since, the late Dr. Willis, who died at eighty-four, a very hale-looking old gentleman, used also to frequent Buxton at the same time, and found the utmost advantage from the bath. But he used to remain about half an hour in the water, and always began his course by taking two or three hot mineral-water baths. A curious effect of the Buxton water was noticed in Dr. Willis, after he had put his shoulder out, in consequence of a fall from his horse two or three years before he died. The joint was never afterwards supple, or, indeed, very moveable. His nephew escorted the worthy Doctor to Buxton the year of the accident, and saw him get into the bath. After a short time of immersion the articulation became more agile, though not to any considerable degree, except when in the water. This state of things continued for some days, the limb feeling comparatively easy, and its motion little, if at all, retarded while in the bath; at length the same benefit was experienced even out of the water; until at last there appeared to be a nearly complete recovery. Dr. Willis used first to take the warm baths of the Buxton water for two days, and] then the natural bath; his practice was to bathe four days and stop the fifth.

Mr. C—— knew the case of a Sheffield manufacturer whom he saw taken out of his carriage at Buxton a perfect cripple, and in a month beheld him again leave Buxton perfectly restored. His was a rheumatic complaint.

A General Ross, who had been wounded, was also a visiter at Buxton while my friend was there; the baths completely restored his health, which was impaired by an old wound in the right arm, producing constant pains, particularly in the night. The cure in that case was complete.

Having satisfied myself on the score of arrangement of

baths and the efficacy of the water at Buxton; the next object
of inquiry I had at heart was, to ascertain the origin of the
mineral waters themselves, and, if possible, the geological
structure of their locality. These are points of importance,
which I invariably make it my study to investigate at all the
Spas; but it is not always possible to succeed, as the investigation is at times difficult, and attended with obstacles.
Such has been the case with regard to Buxton.

The representation given me respecting the sources of tepid
water, both by the bath-man and the Duke's agent, Mr.
Haycock, whose urbane manners have made him a great
favourite in Buxton, is this : a principal source under the Old
Hall flows immediately into the public bath, through the
Sandstone Rock, of which latter rock the bottom of the bath
consists. This same source, before it enters the public bath,
by means of stone pipes, supplies a reservoir, from which the
gentlemen's private, or single, three-shilling bath is filled;—
the waste water flowing constantly from it into the large charity
bath. It also supplies the gentlemen's two-shilling bath, or
new bath, as it is called; and likewise the ladies' baths,
which consist in a similar manner of a public and two private
baths. But the men's public bath, which is over the principal
source, is said to receive from the bottom other smaller or
tributary streams.

In estimating, therefore, the total quantity of the water
from the principal source, we cannot assume any definite
datum or number from the quantity received in any given
time into the public bath, although its capacity is known;
for the auxiliary springs yield a part of the whole. But we
can estimate that quantity by approximation, and add to it
that which flows from the same main source in a given time
—(the capacity being known)—previous to any distribution
of its contents being made through pipes to the ladies' and
gentlemen's baths. This calculation I have not the means of
making; nor has it been satisfactorily made by others.

As to the distribution from the main spring, I only take it on report. No medical man on the spot has ever ascertained at the well-head, whether or not the arrangement is as it is represented above, on the joint testimony of the agent and bath-man. Every thing is under ground, and is not shown. Mr. Haycock tells me, that at the well-head the water surges to within two feet of the level ground, and that it is generally four feet deep in the shaft of the well. Now here, and at the bottom of this shaft, I think the temperature of the Buxton water ought to be ascertained, and the arrangement of the strata, if more than one, clearly made out. Why all this is kept as a mystery is to me surprising.

Against any interference with this well, or any attempt to augment the water by borings and experiments, the agent has always expressed objections, and probably with good reason. He fears that the very numerous land-springs in this place might come into play, and interfere with the thermal springs; and the nature of the ground being so uncertain, it would not be an easy task to explore it.

Whether it be desirable or not, or requisite, to have more water if it could be procured, I am not able to say; but judging from information obtained in looking over the bathman's register of the three-shilling bath, I find that as yet, in the present season, not more than four or five have bathed in a day in that bath—several more, but not a great many, in the new baths at two shillings—and the larger number in the public bath; and that, in fact, there has never yet been felt a lack of bathing-rooms, or of water.

I have already, though slightly, alluded to the climate of Buxton. I found it from experience (and I am confirmed in the observations by those of many patients who have repeatedly visited Buxton) such as is to be expected in all mountain regions in England: winter one day, summer the next. Winds hold their undisputed dominion, and sweep along the undulated surfaces with a violence at times terrific : but being free from permanent dampness, they do less mischief than elsewhere. I am myself, probably, one of the most susceptible persons in the world, in the way of " catching cold ;" and in town I never could walk in an evening dress, after dinner, the length of two streets, without getting one of those tiresome and unwelcome visiters, a sore throat. But at Buxton I walked out in that way in the evening, even when the wind was stormy, for an hour or two, and never experienced the slightest ill effect from it.

It rains a great deal in this place ; but the ground is soon dry, and one may walk immediately after with impunity. The architect of the Crescent had probably this peculiarity of the Buxton climate in his mind, when he judiciously surrounded the principal building with a covered walk, by means of an arcade. In addition to this convenience, at each end of the building he placed the two principal hotels ; so that each has immediate access, under cover, to a bathing establishment,—the St. Anne's Hotel to the natural Buxton water, the Great Hotel to the artificially heated Buxton baths.

Of the last-mentioned hotel I must speak in terms of praise, and to some extent; as it is in reality the rendezvous of all the *élite* of the visiters who frequent Buxton. I have had occasion, also, to spend part of one evening in the saloon of the " rival house," or the house "over the way"—of which I heard the inmates speak favourably. The same praise is due to the " Hall" Hotel adjoining it, which is placed immediately over the spring, and has a staircase leading directly down to the baths, as at Ems, Wiesbaden, &c.

Curiosity induced me to enter the precincts of two or three minor hotels in Buxton and Lower Buxton, all of which appeared comfortable ; but the palm must unquestionably be awarded to the Great Hotel, which for size, and the appearance of its principal apartments, may vie with the best Spa Hotels in Germany. There are not fewer than seventy-two best apartments in the hotel.

The Great Hotel occupies nearly half of the Crescent, beginning at the east end, and proceeding towards the centre. Its principal entrance is under the arcade; it leads to a great hall and the large principal staircase, both of which are common to the great ball or assembly room, as well as to the apartments of the hotel. On the ground-floor there is a small breakfast-room, and a large dining-room in which the table d'hôte is held, capable of accommodating one hundred persons comfortably seated. The principal floor is occupied by divers suites of apartments, more or less capacious, consisting either of two, three, or more pieces, suited for the accommodation of smaller or larger families who desire to live privately. Single sitting-rooms of different sizes, and of course different prices, may be had either on this or on the ground-floor; and many persons who do not like the constant ebbing and flowing of company, in a public or morning room at these places, engage such an apartment in addition to their own bedroom. A practice obtains here, such as I have described to be the prevailing practice in Germany, of inscribing the respective prices of every bedroom and sitting-room over the door; so that every body can please himself, and suit his choice to his purse—a circumstance which, coupled with the foreknowledge of the terms for board and servants, enables the traveller to ascertain beforehand the extent of the pecuniary outlay he is about to incur, during his *séjour* at Buxton.

When it is considered that the Great Hotel is intended to receive the higher classes of visiters, and that provision in every way suitable to their station has been made in the house, which (considering that the season lasts for a period of less than three months) must be onerously expensive to the proprietor,—the prices charged will hardly be deemed extravagant. I examined most of the apartments, and inquired with some minuteness into the economy and management of the establishment; and I am bound to say, that a person must be very fastidious indeed, who cannot find comfort and satisfaction in this establishment, especially in the private apartments. The proprietor, Mr. Shaw, seems to have spared nothing to render his hotel such as to deserve the support and commendation of its inmates; in which he has indeed consulted his real interest. He has, moreover, had the good fortune to secure the aid, and vigilant as well as indefatigable superintendence, of a lady who might do credit to a higher position in society, and who devotes her best energies towards giving satisfaction to all, but especially to the fairer portion of the company.

Were I to suggest further improvements in this establishment, it would be in the department of the men-servants who wait at table in the great banqueting-room; and in providing a larger and gayer morning or breakfast room. The proprietor would find it to his interest to establish such a room on the best floor, looking to the front of the house; and he should place next to it a billiard and chess room. Such accommodation would always secure to the Great Hotel the preference of a numerous, yet select class of men-visiters,—who, after all, whether bachelors or not, are the best supporters of a great hotel in a fashionable watering-place.

It will not do to compare lodging-houses with hotels at Buxton, either in the way of accommodation or expense. The latter is as much lower at a lodging, as the former is higher at an hotel. " I should say, that Buxton," writes to me an invalid lady who has been residing some time in the place, " does not contain more than eight or ten houses where the lodgings are comfortable, and of such an appearance as a lady would require. The lodgings I occupy are the best in the place, and are sometimes engaged by Viscount and Lady B——, who are constant frequenters at Buxton; indeed they are expected on the 10th of July (1840). This house, however, which is certainly the best in the place, is more expensive than one or two of the principal hotels for lodging; but a saving of nearly one-half may be made in the board for master and servant. A lady, her maid, and two men-servants, will be charged a guinea a day at the Great Hotel—whereas the same number of persons, it is supposed, could be boarded well for three pounds a week at a respectable lodging-house."

These domestic details I give on good authority, which is all that can be expected from an author in such matters.

The great ball-room, to which I have alluded in the preceding description, is a spacious and lofty apartment in this hotel, highly decorated in the Corinthian style, to which admission is gained by a large door in the centre of the principal landing-place, at the top of the great staircase. It is open every Wednesday evening during the season, which lasts from June till September, for a dress-promenade, to subscribers at a charge of ten shillings for the season, or at that of two shillings for a single admission. But these assemblies, I understand, are " dull work" to go through, as the two besetting sins of the English, shyness *cum* stiffness, are said to prevail on such occasions more than usual.

The English are incorrigible in that respect; and although they admit the sin, they make no attempt at reformation. It is either dull gaiety or gay dulness with them all, whether " at home," or at " quadrilles," or at a " *soirée musicale*," or at a " *déjeûner dinatoire ;*" in fact, at a funeral, *tout comme* at a wedding :—and " *voilà la société dans ce pays ci ; où le plaisir ressemble tant à l'ennui*," observed the Marquis de B——, as he was settling a long bill at Mivart's, after a heavy season of *gloomy pleasure*, and no sun, in London.

CHAPTER III.

ENVIRONS OF BUXTON—MATLOCK.

BEAUTIES of Buxton—Amusements within, and Enjoyments without—
The GREAT STABLES—The Windsor Stables and the National Gallery
—ROAD to Matlock—The Wye and its Marble Quarries—Approach to
Chatsworth—The Park—CHATSWORTH—The Palace and the Temple—
Splendid Improvements—THE QUEEN's Little Oak Tree—A SERRE
MONSTRE—The Largest Conservatory in Europe—Its Description—
A Mountain of Glass—A *Four-in-hand* Drive through Australia—
MATLOCK—Appearance, and Environs—THE SPRINGS—Old and New
Baths—Sir Walter Scott and Byron—THE HOTELS—Composition and
Efficacy of the Water—Author's Opinion—Temperature—Matlock
and Schlamgenbad—DRIVE TO BELPER—Willersley Gardens and the
Spinning Jenny—Difficulties of the Midland Railway—The ARK-
WRIGHTS and the STRUTTS—A large Fortune made by Chalk.

IN describing Baden-Baden among other " Spas of Germany," I felt it necessary to leave the task of giving an
account of its romantic environs to an author, who had performed it infinitely better than I could have hoped to do.
Even so must I act with regard to the beauties of the
country around Buxton;—its " wonders" and horrors; its
Peak and Tors; its Shivering Rock and Devil's Cavern; its
falls, its caves, and its mines.

So many able writers have tried their skill at portraying
this enchanting region, viewed during the summer months,
and among them more than one with so much success, that
I must refer my readers to those authors, if they feel any

inclination to know more of the " thereabouts" of Buxton than I am able or willing to give them. Even should they not wish to go further back than to my humorous predecessor, Sir George Head, who is the last of the topographic writers on the beauties of Buxton, they will be certain of finding in the " Home Tour" that which they will miss in the present pages.

There is hardly another Spa in England which can boast of so many resources to the invalid and the stranger fond of the beauties of nature, or the many productions, whether in geology or botany, with which the whole of the district around it abounds, than Buxton. This is no trifling boon to those who are compelled to pass a period of four or six weeks away from home, in the monotonous exercise of bathing and drinking mineral waters for the sake of health. It tends, indeed, to heighten the virtues of the Spa water, and helps greatly in restoring that elasticity and buoyancy of spirits, which is, at one and the same time, the cause and effect of renovated health.

The sources of enjoyment, too, within Buxton itself are neither few nor despicable; and what is, perhaps, more important to remark is, that contrary to the usual sordid practice of other English Spas, the high-minded and liberal nobleman, lord of the place, here willed it, that all such sources of amusements—the garden, the promenades, and the band—shall be without payment, and equally open to the poorer as well as to the richer classes of visiters. With all these advantages belonging to Buxton, it is a matter of surprise that medical men should not avail themselves more frequently of that Spa for their patients; for its reputation is not of the other day, but of two centuries.

My object, after so minute an exploration of the Spa itself, was, to push on to other and more important matters. But ere I quit the place, I must bestow a word or two on one of the most striking structures of its kind I have ever met with in my travels, and which, next to the Crescent, forms the most attractive, and probably the finest feature, in the general landscape of Buxton. I allude to the *stables*, a very extensive building, which cost about 20,000*l.*, and was erected by the same architect who designed the Crescent.

The form and arrangement of this structure are particularly felicitous and well studied; and it is only to be hoped, since the presiding architect over the hallowed region of Windsor is gone to his last bourne, that the artist to whom shall be intrusted the erection of the new stables at Windsor,—for which a sum of money was readily voted by the enlightened House of Commons of Great Britain of 1839, equal to that which another Parliament had scantily doled out to Wilkins for a National Gallery—it is to be hoped, I repeat, that he may not produce any thing worse than these very stables at Buxton.

An interior circle of one hundred and thirty-eight feet diameter, open above, is surrounded by forty-four columns of the Doric order, twenty-eight feet high, which support a handsome cornice and a roof over a circular ride, twenty-four feet wide, and well sanded—along which the horses are exercised in wet weather. Around this ride are a series of eight stables, containing eighty stalls, arranged in sections of a circle, they are lighted by windows in front, and there exists an uninterrupted communication between them, except at the four grand entrances into the building. It is within these four entrances under cover and on each side, that we find the doors of access to the stables.

Externally the building is of a square form, the angles of which have been cut off; and within these beveled angles there are other stables of eight stalls each, together with harness and saddle rooms. The elevation of the outside is simple and harmonious, consisting of a series of large semicircular windows on the basement, with a low story over, of dwelling-rooms having square windows. The centre of each of the four façades projects a little, and is surmounted by a pediment, under which is the great entrance into the inner circle of the building. The roof, which is slated, is high and sloping, and the building itself is constructed of stone.

Around the edifice, outside, is a spacious coach-house yard, enclosed by four lines of carriage-houses, some shut in, others open, or having only a wooden railing before them; each is capable of holding fifty carriages. In the angles there is an engine-house, and in the centre of one of the sides is a smith's shop. Altogether, it is the most complete establishment of its kind, and serves admirably the purpose for which it was intended—that of accommodating with stables and carriage-room the visiters living at the principal hotels during the season.

Having engaged one of the few public vehicles to be had in Buxton, I took the road to Matlock Baths, with the intention of visiting Chatsworth by the way. Mine was but a sorry conveyance—a *sociable*, as they are pleased to style these single horse four-wheel carriages, in which people turn their back to each other, as in a *sulky*. I had, however, the pleasure of being alone on this occasion, and had all the benefit of the prodigious shaking which an unballasted light spring-cart is wont to exhibit, as it proceeds along over a tolerably rough road.

Among the things wanted in Buxton, by the bye, are light and neat single-horse carriages, or donkey-carts and saddle-horses, to render excursions easy, and put them within the reach of all. It is incredible how much the knowledge that such an accommodation is to be found at a watering-place influences people in their determination to proceed thither.

Topley Pike was the first hill of importance we ascended, when about two miles from Buxton on the London road. The hills around are barren, save here and there, where plantations of fir-trees have been recently made. The Wye, not far from hence, leaps over two or three cataracts of small depth, and takes its course south-east.

In some parts, the lofty embankments by the roadside, exhibiting on their denuded surface the blue limestone, look more like gigantic ramparts, especially near Madder,— a name given to a few straggling houses placed on the brow of the Ridge, and overlooking the Chee Tor, the summit of which is plainly seen from the London road.

Where the road reaches the flat table-land, it divides into that which leads to Sheffield, through a district picturesque and romantic at every step, by Millendale and Monsaldale, and into the less interesting and tamer road through the village of Taddington, which leads to Chatsworth.

Taddington is a small mountain-village placed in a slight depression in the ground, with a smiling country around, from which a hilly road descends through alluvial banks partially tilled, leading into a narrow gorge that resembles, though on a smaller scale, the larger valley of the Wye. On the eastern side of this gorge shrubby thickets cover the surface, and the upper line is crested with gray rocks like crenated ruins; while on the opposite sloping wall, its green face is broken by projecting perpendicular masses of gritstone, whose horizontal layers and vertical fissures afford a footing to the various creeping plants that mantle their surface, and complete their perfect resemblance to old ruined castle-walls of gigantic size.

Emerging from this pass we once more enter the dale of the Wye, and admire its beautiful windings and clear sea-green wave, sweeping by the foot of a successive series of limestone rocks, smooth and rounded, covered with sheep pasture, or brushwood.

We had presently left Ashford and Ashford Hall, the latter the residence of G. H. Cavendish, Esq. M.P., the former worthy of being noted for its marble works—the first of the kind established in Derbyshire. This is the spot whence all our London marble and statuary shops derive their supply of marble slabs and ornaments, and whence almost all the grit-

stone balustrades, vases, and battlements in the new building at Chatsworth, as well as the massive marble doorways,
have been obtained.

The quarry where an exceedingly handsome kind of black
marble is obtained, lies close to the Wye, whose water serves
to turn the ponderous water-wheels which set in motion the
wooden machine destined to saw, grind, and polish the different marbles.

I halted for half an hour at the small town of Bakewell, to
examine the old chalybeate well—the water of which, having
a temperature of about 60°, is even now used for baths. But
its reputation is purely local; and the tourist stops a few
days in the summer at Bakewell, rather to enjoy the sport of
angling (which the liberal lord of the manor, the Duke of
Rutland, allows to all free liberty of doing, in the lovely
Wye), and the good cheer at the Rutland Arms, one of the
best inns in the county.

Hence to Chatsworth the road does not boast of any remarkable feature, save when arriving at the brow of a shelving part of it, the Vale, in which that magnificent seat of the
Duke of Devonshire, and its extensive park watered by the
Derwent, are situated, lies open to view. This prospect, seen
from a square tower, called the Duke's Stand, or hunting
Tower, peering out of a thick wood upon a hillock which I
beheld on my left, must be of the most enchanting character.

William Adam, of Matlock, published two years ago a
full and interesting Itinerary, much of which is in a poetical
style, but which visiters through this district will find of
great assistance. It is to be regretted, that instead of the
very indifferent sketch of a topographical map which accom-
panies the work, the author had not taken pains to draw up
a full map, in which the places he describes should, at all
events, be found. Such is not the case; and a map of the
Buxton and Matlock districts, marking the roads and principal objects of interest generally visited—the course of the

water, the gentlemen's seats, the villages, the elevation of the hills, as well as the geology of the surface—is yet a *desideratum*, and one which is well deserving the consideration of Mr. Adam, as it would prove a good speculation. A map, an inch to the mile, of the two localities with their respective environs, properly coloured, would be welcome by all those who are about to explore this favourite region.*

Leaving the carriage at a very neat inn just before the gates of the park, I proceeded through them on foot, passing by the side of a perfectly new Swiss-like lodge, of considerable size—fine and striking, because approaching to the real size of those picturesque buildings, and not a mere mimicking tiny imitation of them, such as one beholds on London roads, where citizens' villas rear their dusty heads.

The ground expands right and left, and keeps gently ascending. The green-sward neatly covers every spot, and the surface, chequered by extensive woods, either on the margin or ridges of the highest hills, or down their shelving sides, is dotted in the more level plane with clumps, planted in various directions, in a most artist-like manner.

I was directed to take the footpath to the left, along which I passed a drove of fine-looking deer, some with their towering antlers, three feet apart, sailing majestically along, or stopping at times as if to face the intruder; while others were gracefully butting against each other.

A summer's heavy shower presently overtook me, and I checked my steps under a wide-spreading lime-tree. The bell of Chatsworth church was knelling, and drew presently through the pelting storm many village belles in their holyday clothes, who, like myself, were compelled to shelter themselves under contiguous trees. Here, through a clump

* Some time after this chapter had been in print, my publisher sent me a second edition of Mr. Adam's " Gem of the Peak," which is enlarged, and in many respects improved. But the map, though somr .. uat embellished, is still deficient in the requisites I have pointed out.

and a long vista, I caught the first peep of the older part of the noble mansion I was in search of, and thither, without any further inquiry, in a few minutes afterwards I proceeded.

Although it was not a day on which admission is granted to the public, and to the Buxton visiters in particular,—a letter, of which I was the bearer, from the Duke's agent to the respected housekeeper, Mrs. Gregory, presently opened the gates to me, and ensured me the most urbane and kind reception from herself, as well as from her well-informed niece, Miss Browne, who is a model of a cicerone.

I must spare the reader an account of the state and other great apartments, or, indeed, of any division of the interior of this truly Italian and splendid palace, which, under the direction of his Grace himself, had just received, and was then still receiving, the richest and most gorgeous decorations,—the most prominent feature of which is, the profusion of gilding scattered in all directions, even over the entire of the window-frames and sashes—which are, moreover, glazed with plate-glass of large dimensions.

If there was a part of the interior of the building on which I should have loved to dwell in this place, it would have been the gallery of modern statues, which offered to my attention many specimens of art, both of this and other countries, but principally foreign, highly creditable to the authors; and also on the exquisite collection of original drawings, by almost all the best old masters of the various schools—which have recently been framed, arranged, and suspended in a long corridor over the principal story of the building.

But even here I dare not trust myself; for the theme might tempt me into too many digressions, although I might contend, as a valid excuse for introducing the present subject in a work like mine, that Chatsworth is one of " the lions of Buxton Spa", and as such within my province.

No; my chief object in coming to view Chatsworth Palace, was to enjoy the fine exterior view of that celebrated structure,—now rendered more remarkable by the extensive addi-

tions made to the north of the older building by the present
Duke, after the designs and under the direction of Sir
Jeffery Wyatville, the late able architect of the vast improve-
ments of Windsor Castle.

The finest effect produced by Chatsworth seen in perspective, is from the terrace in front of the great cascade. Two
sides of the old square building are seen—the south and east ;
at the end of which latter, towards the north, is the library; and
next to it the dining-room, with a little music-room adjoining ;
and further on the gallery of modern sculpture, the orangery,
and what is called the temple, within which is the great
ball-room and theatre. All these various and splendid apartments, from the library northwards, are the modern constructions alluded to, executed by Sir J. Wyatville, and have only
started into existence since 1820.

The south front has a still nobler effect, with its new plate-
glass, two in each window, and its massive frames richly
gilded and recently ; besides a grander flight of steps in the
centre, which has been substituted for the old one. Another
alteration, but not equally an improvement, is the having changed
a Dutch parterre in front of these steps into a common English
lawn. The former should be restored. A green lawn is insignificant in front of the best façade of so gorgeous a palace. It is
moreover, a monotonous feature, as the great slopes to the
eastward, towards the great artificial cascade, are also shelving
lawns; and the further ground, on each side of an oblong
sheet of water and lime-tree groves, where the fountain
throws up its jet of 92 feet elevation, is again a lawn-like
surface. It is furthermore totally out of character with
the Italian terrace and flower parterre, spread below the
balustraded terrace along the west front of the Palace—forming
altogether a magnificently-decorated area, along the margin of
which the Derwent is seen to glide, silent and dark.

Leaning against a singular sun-dial placed near the top of
the Duke's private walk, a striking view is obtained of the
grand square, or more ancient part of this palace, without

taking in a single portion of the new part of the building. It catches the grand front to the west, with its Ionic colonnade and pediment, overlooking the terrace and beautiful Italian parterre just alluded to, with a broad walk by its side. Along the edge of this, between each of the little acacia-trees, ought to have been placed those ancient marble busts and statues, supported on pillar-like pedestals, seven or eight feet in height, which now disfigure a small parterre of flowers, stretched almost in front of the group of stable buildings —a very striking architectural feature, by the bye, in the landscape. There, those works of art have not only been suffered to be covered by creepers, but some of them have even been, as it were, clustered together, by linking their respective neck with hanging bands of the creeping plants, under pretence of forming a species of *berceau!* Can this be good taste?

The little British oak planted eight years ago by her Majesty, as Princess Victoria, while on a visit to Chatsworth with her illustrious mother, who planted at the same time and in the same place (the Duke's private walk), a Spanish chesnut, is thriving beautifully, as the gardener assured me. In growing it has taken the lead of the foreign tree by at least eight feet in height, although both were in height alike when first set into the earth.

But not the least attractive of the many objects that claim the notice of the visiter in this fairy land, is one perfectly original and unique, just now starting into existence, which will command the attention of future visiters at Chatsworth, and to which the modern Parisians would unquestionably affix the title of " Serre Monstre." It is a truly gigantic conservatory, in course of erection, and probably by this time completed, at a short distance from the great water-works or cascades in the park. Here a spot of ground has been cleared of trees and shrubs, to the extent of two acres, one of which is being covered over with glass.

The merit of having first started the idea of such a conservatory belongs to Mr. Paxton, the Duke's head gardener, who may have borrowed a hint on the subject, either from the great *Serres* of the Botanical Society at Bruxelles, or from those erected in the Botanical Garden near Edinburgh, under the superintendence of my very able and excellent friend, Professor Graham, in whose company I had the satisfaction of examining that establishment in the autumn of 1838. I say this because the design of the outward form of those two conservatories, and of this intended one at Chatsworth, somewhat resemble each other.

Be that as it may, the mode of construction and the colossal dimensions of the Chatsworth Conservatory are without a rival in Europe, as far as my knowledge extends ; and of those Mr. Paxton is the sole contriver and architect.

The Duke, indeed, fearing that so gigantic an undertaking might prove above the strength of any single person—much as he has reason to value the talents and capabilities of his principal gardener—suggested to him the propriety of summoning an architect from London, with a view to consult him as to the best mode of carrying into effect the projected construction. This suggestion, however, was respectfully declined, and Mr. Paxton has very properly been allowed to proceed, and to carry into effect his own ideas and plans.

As that gentleman was absent at the time of my visit, I followed the escort of one of the under-gardeners, who seemed a very intelligent man, and who, to his other good qualities, added that of an unusual spirit of disinterestedness, which induced him to express to me a wish, that the house and grounds had been always thrown open to public inspection, without fee or reward to the servants. " Were I the master of this royal domain," said the enthusiastic floriculturist, " I would open the gates to every one that presented himself, as is the case indeed at present, but I would suffer nobody to give money to the attendants. It ill-becomes the servants of such a master to receive eleemosynary acknowledgments from strangers for performing their duty: their service is

their master's—it all belongs to him." In spite of this opinion
I deemed it expedient, on leaving the grounds, to act *vis-à-
vis* my patriotic conductor, as others had done before me ;
and my sentimentalist being probably loth to be the first to
establish a dangerous precedent, took what I gave him, and
thanked me for the same.

The form of this huge conservatory is that of a parallelogram, the longest side of which measures three hundred
feet in length, and the shortest one hundred and twenty-seven
feet. A wing eighty feet long will be added at the north
and south extremities, in immediate connexion with the
centre, so that the extreme length of the entire conservatory
will be four hundred and sixty feet, or about the tenth part
of a mile.

Around the principal area a solid stone plinth, or running sub-basement two feet and a half high, has been erected
upon arches, on which a glass wall, with a neat inward curve
of an elliptical form, has been raised to the height of forty feet,
where it rests upon a horizontal square frame of iron beams
supported by two parallel ranges of eighteen iron pillars, each
of a light and airy structure. From this frame springs the
lofty and bold glass dome, in the form of a square cone, with
a transverse span of seventy feet, up to an elevation of twenty-
seven feet; making the total height of this glass edifice at its
culminating point, sixty-seven feet.

The glazed surface will contain seventy thousand square
feet of glass, divided into slips each two feet long and six
inches wide, arranged in perpendicular rows, and so that
the slips of every two rows inclining to each other, form
acute angles upwards and downwards, giving to the whole
the appearance of a series of horizontal zig-zag lines of
panes of glass one above the other. By the peculiar
position of the narrow and light iron elliptical ribs which
serve to hold the slips together, constituting the frame-
work of the glass structure from the bottom to the top, both
the inner and external surface of the conservatory present a

succession of linear angular projections, an arrangement cunningly and appropriately devised to withstand the force and weight of hailstones during storms, as well as the violence of the sweeping whirlwind—which would then be broken in its career by the inequalities of the surface.

Of this huge mountain of glass the largest portion was already glazed, and seemed to me to promise the grandest effect when the whole shall be completed. Nor was the ingenious contrivance (equally the invention of Mr. Paxton's own mind) for glazing the flanks and loftiest slopes of this *Hill*, as well as for covering its ribs with paint, less entitled to admiration. Its merits are simplicity and complete success. I must leave my readers to guess how a dozen or two of painters and glaziers may be enabled to crawl spider-like, freely and nimbly, over a surface of such fragile materials, without either bending a single one of the slender ribs, or fracturing a pane of glass. The whole construction, in fact, reflects great credit on the ingenuity of its architect.

Here then, under this enormous dome, some of the best garden soil will be strewed on the levelled ground, to the extent of seventy thousand square feet, including both wings;—and in it will be planted, sown, or transplanted, every vegetable production that requires a permanent atmospheric heat, higher than what is peculiar to our own climate—a temperature for which a suitable provision has been made under the conservatory, by means of boilers and pipes, conveying hot water along corridors some hundreds of feet in length, and high enough for a man to walk upright in them from one end to the other.

The various plants, shrubs, and flowers of the two tropics, and Australia, will be reared in this artificial southern hemisphere, arranged in groves and parterres, as if they were growing naturally on the spot, without the appearance of pot or box of any kind; streamlets of running water, or standing pools, will give freshness to the sultry atmosphere ;

and meandering paths through these bowers, and a carriage-way across, and all round, will convey the enchanted visiter with ease to every part of this conservatory. Over the latter it is said that the noble proprietor intends to drive his visiters in a carriage and four—exhibiting a feat which has certainly never been performed *under* similar circumstances in England.

MATLOCK.

THE beauties of this region, coming from Chatsworth, first break upon the traveller as he crosses the Derwent over Matlock Bridge, at the bottom of the dale where the gigantic " High Tor" is seen to rise upwards of three hundred and ninety feet high, frowning with its broad mass of perpendicular rock, over the entrance into the hamlet of Matlock. The road is cut out of the stony bank on the right of the river, where the strata have a south-east dip, until we again emerge from the village, when the dale becomes once more, for a short distance, simply pastoral.

At this point, Matlock Bath, with the hotels and *museums* down to the river's edge, and the many private dwellings and villas, either scattered on wooded hillocks, or perched upon the naked heights of calcareous stone, relieved by the dark-green foliage of mountain trees, display all their varied beauties.

But this Spa demands a somewhat more minute description; although I cannot be expected to enter fully into the various details of the place in its character of a Spa—as I have done with Buxton—inasmuch as in the scale of watering places, Matlock holds an inferior grade. As a summer retreat, however, independently of its mineral water, it is superior to Buxton itself.

The village, or hamlet, consists of a row of neat houses, built at the bottom of a profound gorge or dale, on the right of the Derwent, following the crescent-like sweep of the river, which on its left margin laves the High Tor and other rocks of the same description. Ascending a gentle undulation of the road along this line of houses, among which appear conspicuous the Geological and Derbyshire Museums of Vallance and Adam, author of the Modern Tour through this region already alluded to; we arrive at a large hotel placed on an eminence which stretches north and south, with a western aspect, its face turned toward the rocky cliff of the opposite bank. It is the old Bath Hotel. The ground in front has been levelled and converted into a pretty parterre of some extent. This, which was once the natural bank of the river, exhibits yet, below the surface, and down to the water's edge, the stalactitious and stalagmitic concretions left by the tepid spring.

It is evident from this feature, that the mineral water must have poured down in broad sheets along the shelving rocks, and so over the bank into the Derwent, crossing that part of the ground which is now the carriage road.

Turning to the south, as we stand in front of the hotel, and looking towards the entrance into Matlock from Buxton, the scene appears much more varied and interesting. Below, and straight forward is the broad street we have just described, with its several hotels and lodging-houses, all neat, in good condition, and inviting. Among the former, I ought to mention, in particular, " The Hotel," at which I took refreshment, and found it an excellent country inn.

Higher and almost perched on what appears to be the perpendicular side of a lofty peak, among thick plantations of yew and maple, and the hazel, with picturesque clumps of dark mountain trees, several well-built and showy houses are seen; one of which, not the loftiest as to position, bears the title of " The Temple." The highest habitable points of this romantic crest are occupied by castellated buildings, called the " High and Low Towers." From the extreme edge of this hill on the right bank of the Derwent, to the edge of the equally lofty embankment on the left bank, (at an altitude of nearly 400 feet), the two opposite rocks seem almost to touch—a small space of blue heaven alone being seen between them.

At the extreme or furthest point of this line of perspective are the Fountain Baths and Gardens, a comparatively new establishment distinct from the " Old Bath" and the " New Bath." The mineral water here rises fountain-like out of a circular basin of durable limestone placed upon a pillar, and is allowed to overflow. The supply is rapid and abundant, and the temperature something lower than in the case of the other baths, which does not exceed 68° of F. A spring of this water has been covered over and suffered to expand in a reservoir, which serves as a most inviting and limpid swimming bath, adjoining to the new hotel, to which these springs belong.

A notion prevails here, that this water is much lowered in its temperature and diluted in its composition by land springs; in consequence of which, attempts have been made to separate them high up the hill, but hitherto without success. Fresh experiments were intended for the same purpose; and my own idea, formed from the examination of the locality, is that, if borings through the rock which supplies the spring at 60°, were made to a sufficient depth in the direction of the stream, water would be obtained at a higher temperature.

The good people of Matlock have never abandoned the hope of one day discovering a stream of mineral water warmer than that of Buxton ; in which case, they would certainly carry away the palm from that aristocratic Spa.

Nothing I could say,—had I even the vein of Darwin, who sung in his Cruscan verses these baths of Matlock, and the " Proud Masson," or Mountain of Abraham Heights, which overhangs " the Temple" and other buildings—or could I wield the descriptive pen of Gilpin,—would convey the vivid impression produced by the sight of this singular rocky and sylvan bowl, this deep and confined dale, within which Matlock lies—its dwellings lining the sides of the dale—the " dusky" Derwent shooting through it with its rapid stream— its outward boundaries formed by bastions of rocks covered with verdure. I stood in ecstasy, immersed in the contempla- tion of this enchanted scenery, on the margin of the parterre, in front of the Old Baths, and quitted it with regret. Could but a spring of water, fifteen or twenty degrees warmer than what now constitutes Matlock water be discovered, a very Wildbad would at once be formed in Matlock—the *ne plus ultra* of thermal Spas—leaving far behind Buxton, and the much over-rated Schlangenbach, or Serpent's Bath of Nassau.

The houses are built of stone, and are neat in appearance. They had been quite filled during the season—principally, however, by people of the class of farmers and small landed proprietors, who have taken the place of the high aristocracy which, in the palmy days of Matlock—when there were no " Spas of Germany,"—used to resort hither every summer for three months.

As a mere residence even during that period of the year, Matlock bath is desirable and tempting. The climate there is represented as being healthy. The air being constantly agitated by the currents of wind that sweep down the valley, we find an agreeable freshness prevailing in the summer ; while by the protecting influence of the " Heights of Abraham," great shelter is afforded from the cold winds of the north and east in the winter. Hence, that season of the year is said to be milder in Matlock, than in more southern climates ; and medical men are disposed to consider it as admirably adapted for invalids.

For either a permanent or temporary residence, the place offers excellent and sufficient accommodation, upon particu- larly easy terms—much below those of Buxton.

The *Old Bath* house stands at the head of the list, and with justice. It has, moreover, the merit of having been the

site of the first spring discovered in the place, to which circumstance Matlock Bath owes its existence.

A ball or dancing room, highly decorated and with a
carved ceiling, forms one of the ornaments of the hotel, and
used once to be the scene of much hilarity and harmony.
But music's sweet sounds are seldom heard now-a-days in
this handsome apartment.

As Gilsland Spa acquired additional interest from the
" love" of the great necromancer of the north, " sweetly met
and sweetly requited,"—so has this very assembly-room of
Matlock acquired celebrity from the " love" of a necromancer
of the south, whose romantic attachment for the heiress of
Annesley had not the same happy result as that of his great
poetical rival. In this room, Byron and Miss Chaworth
met and loved.

The *New Bath* house, second in seniority, but not inferior
in comforts and accommodation to the former house, sustains
a high character as an hotel. It is a building forming the
three sides of a quadrangle, the north wing of which, being
the most modern, contains many spacious rooms—erected
over the tepid bath, discovered second in succession. This
hotel has a beautiful garden for the use of the guests, who
admire greatly the order in which it is kept, and its wide
spreading lime-tree a century and a half old. The fountain
of the tepid stream is placed, with a glass tumbler ready at
hand, just at the spot where the dwellers have to pass—as
if to tempt them with a sight of the salutary spring.

" The Temple," more beautifully situated, as we have
seen, than any other hotel, " Walker's Hotel," and " Hodg-
kinson's," deserve equally to be mentioned as worthy of praise,
in their character of houses of entertainment.

Of the composition of the water, little can be said. No
regular quantitive analysis of its chemical contents has ever
been made ; and we only know from Sir Charles Scudamore's
account of it, that it contains a very small quantity of solid

ingredients, principally consisting of sulphates and muriates of magnesia, lime, and soda. Dr. Thomson holds Matlock water to be slightly calcareous, and almost pure. The tepid springs rise at an elevation, it is said, of 100 feet above the river, and are conveyed by pipes, covered over, into baths and basins. The most important of these, after passing through the premises of the Old Bath, forms a beautiful water-fall, and flows into the river, over the rough bank of Tufa.

Sir Charles Scudamore has a sweeping sentence respecting the efficacy of these waters, which would at once settle the pretensions of Matlock to the rank of a Spa. " I do not feel authorised," observes the learned physician, " to extol the water as a remedy in any particular class of disorders."

I have but a limited experience to set against this *dictum ;* but from the taste of the water—the presence of carbonates and muriates of the alkaline earths—and the effects it had on myself as well as on some two or three patients I sent thither, I should consider Matlock water, drank freely as a common beverage through the day, to be likely to prove highly beneficial in dyspeptic and nephritic affections.

There is probably not another ride of ten miles in the north of England, continuous and uninterrupted, that offers such an interminable succession of beautiful features, as that distance of ground from Matlock Bath towards Derby, pass-ing through Belper and Milford. Keeping the line of the Derwent dale, which it follows in most parts, nearly parallel, the road traverses some of the finest gorges and open country that are to be seen in mountain districts, or in this region of the Peak—the road itself being as fine and as good as any in England.

Matlock, in our days, is extending further south, particu-larly from and beyond the Old Bath ; and cotton-mills are intruding their columns of dense smoke at the lower extremity of the hamlet. Here, at no great distance, are the celebrated Willersley gardens and grounds, the residence of a descendant of him who, from the humblest state in society, raised himself and his generation to an unexampled pinnacle of fame and wealth, through a simple contrivance (the jenny) for spinning cotton, as a substitute for the more sluggish hand of man. His *château* is seen to advantage at the turn of the road facing a rocky portal, which leads to a chapel under the cliff. The pleasure-grounds are most liberally thrown open to the visiters of Matlock twice a-week, and are much frequented.

The road continues to skirt the elevated and rugged cliffs strewn with broken masses of gritstone, among which trees of every sort are seen to fasten their aged and knarled roots. The scenery is all the way eminently beautiful to within two miles of Belper. The Midland Railway was contending with no trifling difficulties, just about here, excavating a tunnel deep into the rocky bank of the Derwent, and crossing the latter over a rudely constructed bridge raised on single piles, and again cutting down the limestone rock beyond it to complete a profound excavation. These difficulties, however, have since been surmounted, and the public has just been admitted to the free use of so convenient a line of communication, which not only brings so many places and towns together at once, but also brings the south nearer to the north.

As we approach to Belper, the aspect of the country changes into a rich agricultural district, which was at the time covered with the heaviest and most promising crops.

From an insignificant village not many years since, Belper has risen to the important station of a manufacturing town, and is extending further every day in all directions, thanks to the activity and enterprise of the Brothers Strutts, the partners in industry and success with old Sir Richard Arkwright. The next market-town also, Milford, is swelling into great importance, under the same prosperous and fostering care.

It is curious that all the cotton-mills on the Derwent,

whether belonging to the Strutts or the Arkwrights, continue to be worked by water. This is a wonderfully fortunate circumstance for the industrious classes engaged in the works, and equally so for the inhabitants generally of the places where such cotton-mills are established. Their health and comforts are not bartered away by a heartless manufacturer, in a dense and smoky atmosphere or in moist and heated rooms, for a few hundred or thousand bales of goods annually produced at these mills.

The present Arkwright is the son of Sir Richard. He has an income derivable from estates worth perhaps 400,000*l.*, which he manages himself without any steward or agent. Mr. Strutt, the M.P., also is the son of Sir Richard's old partner, who is, I believe, still alive, and of very advanced age. The good fortune of this gentleman, who was originally brought up in Sir Richard's factory, is narrated thus :— The thread wound round the bobbing after its being spun, used to ride over the end of the bobbing or reel and break. It slipt or slided over, and Arkwright could not remedy the defect. Strutt was walking one day with him, when the latter said to Strutt, " If you could but find out the way to make this concern work better I would make a man of you. You shall have a share in the business." " How much ?" instantly enquired Strutt of his master. The amount was immediately mentioned, and Strutt being satisfied, at the same time relying most confidently on Arkwright's honour, took out of his pocket a piece of chalk, and proceeded to chalk over first one bobbing and then another, and so on to twenty bobbings, so that the thread could not pass or slide over the surface so treated, and kept therefore in its proper place.

Arkwright saw this, and admired its simplicity, and desired Strutt to do the whole; which being accomplished, Arkwright completed his bargain by giving Strutt a share in the concern, and treating him thenceforward as his partner.

On another occasion Strutt was asked to remedy another great defect in the machinery, connected with the ravelling of the thread or web. Strutt asked for a pair of scissors, cut off a bit of the flap of his own coat, made a small round washer with a hole in the centre, placed it under the wheel, and thus prevented its vibration, by which the ravelling of the thread was occasioned—a glaring and injurious defect in every species of cotton manufacture.

The old gentleman, who is in full possession of his faculties, is said to be anxious to dispose of the whole of his prodigious concern, which affords employment to nearly all the hands in Belper and Milford. He, I am told, will be satisfied with a moderate sum, and leave, as a bonus, 100,000*l.*, of the-purchase money, to lie for use in the concern for some years, at the smallest rate of interest for it, and without interference on his part.

Such are the men who rise from nothing by dint of genius of some sort or another, coupled with skill, assiduity, industry, mechanism, ability, and above all " honesty."

CHAPTER IV.

DERBY—LINCOLN—MONKSWELL CHALYBEATE.

English Grumblers abroad—Look at Home—AN ENGLISH COFFEE-ROOM —True to the letter—DERBY General Rail-station—Fresh Robbery from English Farmers—First View of the CITY OF LINCOLN— Splendid Cathedral and Panorama—The Lunatic Asylum—THE NON-COERCIVE SYSTEM—MR. HILL AND DR. CHARLESWORTH—The Bishop of London and the Quakers—*Palmam qui meruit*—Results and Calculations—The HANWELL ASYLUM—Statistical Facts—Curious Deductions—Females require more Restraint than Males— Dormitories and ingenious Contrivance—ALCOHOL AND RELIGIOUS EXALTATION the parents of Insanity—Dr. Charlesworth's Doctrine —Moral Discipline of private Lunatics at Lincoln—Objections of the Author—MONKSWELL Chalybeate—Monk's Abbey—THE SPRING —Chemical and physical Characters of the Water—Composition and medical Applications—Strongly recommended by the Author—SUG-GESTIONS for abating Establishment—Water preferable to Tunbridge Wells.

ENGLISH travellers, whilst in Germany, are incessant and loud in their complaints of the few comforts to be met with at an hotel, and of the rough, uncouth manner in which their meals are served.

But look we at home.   How stands the case here ?   See,
for example, what takes place at any hotel either at Liverpool,
Manchester, or any where else.   Take we, for instance, the
Royal Hotel in the last-mentioned place.   After having your
luggage tossed in the most cavalier manner on to the pavement from off the top of the omnibus which has just conveyed
you from the rail-terminus at the distance of two miles, your
leather-box torn, your portmanteau scratched, and the writing-
desk let fall on the floor by *mere accident* (whereby if it does
not break or fly open, its contents are, at all events, prettily
deranged) you are left shivering in a thorough draught of
wind, between the entrance and the back-door leading into the
yard, waiting for a sour-faced, sulky housemaid, who tells
you she has no room, or only one, at the very top of the
house.

After this encouraging introduction, if the waiter happens
to be tolerably civil, you may obtain an answer respecting the
locality of the commercial, or coffee-room, in which you are
desirous to take shelter.   Here, famished and tired, you
survey all round the pew-looking boxes, in which nothing
but their naked tables stare you in the face.   The room is
lighted by a hanging gas-burner, which has blackened the
ceiling, and threatens suffocation.   You take your seat
on a narrow, sloping, black hair bench, or form, two feet
away from the table (a fixture), and await the accomplishment
of your bidding for tea, and " something to eat."

This arrives at last. The caddy is handed to you with tea-
dust in it, and some drab-coloured sugar is laid before you
to sweeten it.   Toast, swimming in butter, and almost glazed
with it; a couple of eggs, through whose hundred fractures
the best of their contents has been oozing out; a tongue,
the coriaceous covering of which defies the serrated edge of a
white handled knife, whose blade has been cleaned into a
wafery thinness, and would be an object of curiosity, but for

the still more marvellously ridiculous accompaniment of a three-pronged fork, of bright steel, of a doll-like diminutive size ;—all this apparatus is thrown carelessly before you upon the naked Honduras, without the smallest white rag upon it to gladden your eye, or a napkin to comfort your fingers and lips; it being against etiquette, that a table-cloth, which is an admitted appendage of a noon repast, or breakfast in the morning, should deck the table when something of an identical repast is made in the evening.

At length the well-brewed tea, within the queen's-metal, arrives, and you begin your meal, eyed and ogled by every inmate of the opposite boxes; some lounging, " Times in hand," after a chop; others, sipping their diluted bohea, with Niagara-noise; and many laying the unction of gin-and-water to their stomachs.

This monotony is enlivened by the popping out of an impatient cork from a soda-water bottle, called for by a youngster who is just come in from half-price at the play; or by the fresh arrival of some shivering outsider, per mail, or per rail. Still, your own uninviting repast proceeds, and you are just beginning to find it palatable, and enjoying a little peace, when lo! " boots" pops in, and proceeds through the ceremony of *déchausséing* half a dozen people, exhibiting their soiled *chaussettes* to the submissive servant, who adorns the stripped extremities with slippers, that have received Heaven knows how many not over delicate feet before.

Such a manœuvre is rather more than your stomach can stand, and the desire to pursue your evening meal is so instantly checked by it, that in despair you pull at the summoner that hangs just over the table, and order the waiter to clear the cheerless board.

Now, surely, between such a picture, not a tittle exaggerated, and one at a *table d'hôte*, or even at a *souper à la carte*, in any of the hotels at Kissingen or Wisbaden, Carlsbad, or Marienbad, there is unquestionably some difference ; but on which side the favouring weight preponderates, all unprejudiced and candid readers will find no difficuly to determine.

The fact is, we never think of what we suffer at home, when by mere circumstances we happen to be in the midst of strangers abroad, where you are expected to conform yourself to their customs and habits.

I have been reminded of these notes, which were taken down from nature at Manchester, by what I again beheld around me in the coffee-room of the *New Inn* at Derby, whither I arrived after my excursion from Buxton and Matlock. This hotel boasts of being in the close vicinity of the residence of Mr. Strutt, M.P., and of the new and lofty Catholic chapel then just about to be completed after the design of Mr. Pugin. The same routine as at all other houses of entertainment was gone through here, with the same farce of waiter, boots, and chambermaid, and finally with the same bill—at which, however, I had no reason to grumble.

Derby is emerging all at once from an almost sepulchral lethargy, or indeed impending sepulture,—thanks to the intersecting lines of rail-road which will bring hither people from all the quarters of England. The bustle has already began, after years of increasing deathlike stillness, and the consequences of it are immediately visible in the constructions that are every where going on ; in the new houses that have started into existence as if by magic ; and in the public improvements that have taken and are taking place in many parts of the town.

Professional engagements, which had accumulated during my absence to visit the Northern Spas, now compelled me to return to London ; and as good fortune would have it, I found myself at Derby on the first day of the opening of its railway to town—that is, within little more than seven hours of my intended destination. I had ticket No. 1, no passenger having yet gone by the train, which the men appointed for that purpose did not seem to manage as if familiar with their work or duties. Fearfully and tremblingly therefore did I take my place in the well-stuffed carriage, and committed myself serenely to my fate.

That fate, however, was propitious, as will appear in another part of this volume; and in the afternoon of the same day on which I left the terminus at Derby, a little before noon, I reached London (at the distance of 130 miles) in safety.

The temporary station at Derby is near to that of the Midland Counties Railroad, which as yet performs only to Nottingham, and very regularly. It is also near the intended station now erecting for the North Midland, and will itself, judging from the designs exhibited to me by a director, be one of the most splendid buildings and establishments, if not the very finest, in this country. It is expected, however, that the three will combine, and be under one common roof in the " Old Meadows," an open place contiguous to the old London road, now possessed by the three several companies, where the buildings, and offices, and stations will occupy the area of twenty-five acres, which the Derby and London company have now for their own separate use.

In the mean time one of these railroads has since extended its usefulness as far as Leeds, and consequently to York ; and hence the same facility of conveyance which has enabled us all along to reach Liverpool in nine hours, will now transport us to the archiepiscopal See of Yorkshire in the same period of time.

Has it ever occurred to political economists and statistical calculators to consider and reflect on the quantity of bread, or food of some sort or other—the amount in fact of the earth's produce—which the extension of all these unnumbered rail-lines has swept and will sweep away from the agricultural surface of Great Britain ? For in most parts (so it happens) the rail-course has been through fair soil, round about farms, and across corn-fields, annihilating much productive land as it proceeds onwards to form the new line of communication. Every inch of this is robbed from the farmer.

This notion is any thing but ridiculous, as my readers will find if they will take the trouble to cast up the many miles of straight railways already established in England, and square that distance by the average width of any railroad, taken both at the bottom where the rails are placed, and at the top of the two sides of deep cuttings. The amount total will assuredly astound them.

We have heard of opposition made to every new railway started, because it is to pass too near a park, or to cut up a pleasure-ground, or annoy with its clacking noise and sooty emanations a nobleman's seat, or a wealthy citizen's villa. But has it ever been urged as an objection, that the bread, already scanty, will, by the establishment of every new rail-course through the plain, be further diminished?

My engagements once fulfilled in London, I lost no time in resuming my tour through the midland region, in search of mineral springs, that either had enjoyed or deserved to enjoy reputation. Within the last three years one such was discovered in the fens of Lincolnshire, respecting which I had heard various reports, all tending to make me wish to see it. In this desire I was confirmed by the letters I received from one or two physicians in the neighbourhood, who were acquainted with the mineral water in question; and to Lincolnshire therefore did I proceed.

The county-town is, *per se*, an attractive object to a traveller, were it only for that magnificent specimen of a highly wrought and richly ornamented protestant temple which it possesses, and which justly takes its place amongst the first and most imposing of the ancient cathedrals in this country.

The first burst of the city of Lincoln, towered over to an immense height by that glorious cathedral, which comes suddenly and unexpectedly upon the traveller, as at the end of a

long level drive of many miles he reaches the brow of
Cannick-hill, is grand in the extreme. It more resembles the
spectacle of some of those foreign cities we meet in Alpine
districts, than of an ordinary English town.

A wide hollow, or plain, along which courses the tiny
Wytham from west to east, lies at his feet, and separates the
cliff on which the traveller has been almost involuntarily
arrested, from a similar, yet loftier hill opposite, which, like
a screen to keep out the northern blasts, stretches in nearly a
straight line parallel to, and not far from the river. The
centre of this ridge is crested by the glorious edifice of
Gothic craft; and few like it are to be seen in Christen-
dom. Hundreds of red brick houses, with their red tiled
roofs, beginning at the margin of the river, spread gently upwards and sideways upon the hill, until they actually creep up
to the summit, to encircle the House of God. Here and there
a single dwelling, with more pretension to modern fashion,
exhibits its white or stone coloured front, contrasting with and
diversifying the monotony of the general red mass.

High above this mass, on the western side of the cathedral, the running wall of the ancient castle appears prominent, bearing aloft its keep and round-tower, but dwarf-like by the side of the gigantic structure of the church.

Beyond the castle wall, a smaller, yet elegant looking building intrudes its quiet Ionic portico and low pediment on our attention, and reminds us of the Lincoln Asylum for lunatics, which has already acquired so much renown, though but young in the career of usefulness. Immediately below it, and in many other parts of the general mass of buildings, patches of green, or some more extensive fields, are seen to spread and stretch right and left, varying the universal tone of the landscape.

The view of the cathedral on this, the south side, is not so picturesque as when the building is seen from an angle-point; it is, however, much more imposing, from the extent of its flank, which occupies nearly one fourth-part of the whole visible area of the great assemblage of dwellings of human beings thus brought at once and unexpectedly under our cognizance.

As the spectator advances, and prepares to descend the long and steep Cannick-hill, the landscape unrolls more and more before him; and whilst on the right the eye reposes still on the green valley of the Wytham, it wanders on the left to remote points over the fertile plains of Lincolnshire as far as the neighbouring county of Nottingham. In respect to position, no other cathedral in England, not even Durham, stands more proudly or advantageously than that of Lincoln. It is a sight worth a long journey to behold.

Enjoying, as I did, for the space of two years, in Paris, under the immediate eye of Esquirol,* and the unfortunate Hebreard,

* I learn, since this was written, that this highly gifted and philosophical physician has been added to the long list of those choice spirits whom death has snatched away in the course of twenty-five years, from the time of my enjoying the benefit of their instructions and friendship.

the one at La Salpêtrière, the other at Bicêtre, two of the most extensive public institutions for the treatment of mental disorders, the opportunity of witnessing their method of practice, it is not surprising that I should have sought immediate admission to the Lunatic Asylum in this city, which we have seen to form a prominent part in the general landscape of the place.

Although I had seen the establishment a few years before, it was but hurriedly, and without any professed object. Now, on the contrary, the recent introduction into the asylum of a new system of moral management of the patients, under the guidance of a young, indefatigable, and skilful resident medical superintendent, gave new interest to the place, and tempted me to deviate from my own immediate object in coming to Lincoln—the examination of a chalybeate spring of ancient fame in its neighbourhood.

The better to judge of the importance of the change effected in the internal government of the asylum, I visited it alone at first, unexpectedly, and without divulging my medical character. The Lincoln Asylum, I may say, courts such visits. I repeated mine a second time for more ample details, being again accompanied by Mr. Hill, the medical superintendent; and lastly, I had the satisfaction of examining it for the third time in company with a noble earl and ex-minister, whose hospitality I was at the time enjoying, and who, in his capacity of vice-president of the institution, deemed it his duty, without first acquainting the officers of his intended visit, to go and see for himself the truth or misrepresentation of the facts alleged in favour of the new, or non-coercion system.

That his lordship was satisfied with the result of his visit, I have authority to state; and that I became myself convinced, after repeated examinations, of the eligibility of the plan, under certain conditions, I am free to confess, and do so with pleasure, as I felt at first incredulous of its practicability.

A learned and eloquent prelate, who never lags behind when the cause of humanity needs advocates, has, at a recent meeting of philanthropists in London, alluded to the great and happy innovation in the treatment of those who have unhappily become insane, which is so fully exemplified in the asylum of Lincoln ; and he did not forget to refer, with perfect justice, to the Italians, the first originators of the improvement in question. His words well deserve being quoted in this place ; and although in his general view of the question the right reverend prelate seems to have entirely forgotten, or to have been ignorant of, the extent of the merit which belongs to the Lincoln Asylum, in furthering the humane and sound principles and practice of the non-coercion plan, but has simply alluded to the experiment now making of that plan in the Hanwell institution, the manifest and mere imitator of the Lincoln Asylum, it is not a little gratifying to the advocates of that system to have the metropolitan bishop in their favour.

" It has been proved by experience," observed the Bishop of London, " most satisfactorily, that if it was wished to proceed with any reasonable prospect of success in the attempt to mitigate, to ameliorate, and eventually to cure insanity, means must be adopted which were directly opposite to those which until lately had been deemed necessary, and which indeed had been considered as the only course to take. But the happy truth had at length been arrived at ; and at the present moment there was not a person in the country who would not admit that the treatment of the insane, in order to insure a prospect of an amelioration of, or recovery from, the malady, must be gentle and mild. The experiment had been tried first in one of the asylums in Italy, and had been related by one of the greatest ornaments who had ever adorned the surgical profession (the late John Bell, of Edinburgh). That individual had, in one of the journals of his day, published a detailed account of the arrangements of some of the lunatic asylums in Italy, and therein pointed out the advantages which had been derived by the adoption of a humane system of treatment, and contrasted them with the results of another plan observed on the continent and in this country. The harsher plan of treatment, however, continued in England until within a comparatively few years, when some members of the Society of Friends made attempts which were attended with such results as went to prove that the course of treatment, which upon their suggestion had been tried in the Retreat at York, was one most eminently calculated to produce the beneficial end. That treatment was one of mildness and gentleness."

To the efforts made by the Society of Friends in this cause, I trust I have done ample justice in another part of my present publication; but, in speaking of a true and full execution of the plan of not coercing patients, applied to a large lunatic asylum, in all cases of mental disturbance, no matter of what nature or degree, one is bound to defer the palm of originality and perseverance to Mr. Hill, whose work on the subject has probably led the way to a totally new era in the management of insane persons. It is Mr. Hill who has the merit of having proposed and undertaken the execution of a method which entails a prodigious increase of labour and responsibility on the medical attendants, and consequently (in the case of the Lincoln Asylum) on himself; a labour and responsibility, indeed, in which the whole intrinsic value of the system consists. For it is well to declare at once, that every patient suffering under insanity, no matter how violently he may be affected, may be managed without the usual and hitherto employed means of restraint, which occasionally extended to torture and corporal punishment, simply by increasing the number of keepers, and insisting on a never ceasing exercise of vigilance over their charge.

If the medical superintendent himself be not also for ever present and watchful over the keepers, the system will assuredly not work continuously and successfully. The causes for irritation from the conduct of patients, and the temptation to resent them by a stretch of authoritative interference and severity on the part of their keepers, are unfortunately too frequent ever to justify the hope that, without the watchful eye of a superior officer, or the fear of it, subordinate officers will strictly and invariably execute their trust in harmony with the views and intentions of the head of their department.

Accordingly I found that Mr. Hill hardly ever left the house, and was at all hours of the day mingling with the patients, watching them and their guardians at the same time. " In order to become personally assured," observes the last Report on the state of the Lincoln Lunatic Asylum, " of the effect produced upon disorderly patients by the substitution of a system of watchfulness instead of restraints, the house-surgeon spent three hours daily, for thirty-eight out of forty successive days, among those particular patients and their attendants; and had the satisfaction to witness good order preserved, without either violence or intimidation on the part of the latter, throughout the whole period."

This, in an institution containing but an hundred patients, may be practicable, and with so zealous an official as Mr. Hill, it has been found successful as well as practicable. But how will the system work in an establishment of eight times that number, with only one medical superintendent resident? There, much of the trust must necessarily devolve on the inferior officers; and when that is the case, one can easily foresee what will be the result. We must not be too ready to believe what may be reported by friendly committees and their chairmen, who, in their earnest desire that the plan of non-restraint should succeed in a particular asylum with which they may be connected, see and report success where time has not yet been afforded for the full play of the experiment. To judge of the true and final value of a plan like that of Mr. Hill, which enlists so soon the sympathies of the good and the humane, as applied to extensive lunatic asylums, we must await the slow operation of a much longer period of time than has yet been allowed at any other institution than that of Lincoln.

In the question of economy as connected with this subject, it is not my province to enter in this place. That the non-coercive plan of treatment will increase the expenditure of every lunatic asylum that shall fairly adopt it, I cannot for a moment entertain a doubt; for not only must the premises be enlarged in consequence, and much of the interior locali-ties altered; but the number of keepers must be augmented, and all of them must be better paid, in order that they may be obtained from among a far better class of people than that which has hitherto supplied this order of attendants in a lunatic asylum. The public economist, however, will not disregard this branch of the question; and perhaps it will be found in the end, that owing to the increased expenditure of public money consequent on its execution, Mr. Hill's plan will be considered inadmissible in such large establishments as Bethlem and St. Luke's, and the several county lunatic asylums.

These observations I took the liberty of making, in the course of one of my visits, to the senior physician of the asylum, under whose grey hairs, bushy eyebrows, and bril-liant quick-moving eye, one readily discerned the skilful and right-thinking practitioner. After a first introduction, he soon put me at my ease, by conversing freely und unreserv-edly upon the subject which engrossed my attention at the time, and by frankly avowing himself the staunchest advocate of the plan, as well as of the originator of it. In the course of one hour's conversation he displayed great shrewdness and ability, as well as fluency of discourse; and, to one like myself, who loves to study character, the frank and almost blunt manner of the speaker received, according to my think-

ing, additional effect from the association of a costume not unusual among provincial physicians, though very much so in
London.

The doctor, I found out, is rather dogmatical in his
opinion, yet original withal. For example, I had told him
in-doors—after we had seen together the whole establishment,
every part of which he threw open and described to me with
great animation—that I thought the medical officer to whom
the asylum owed so much was badly paid.

" Not at all," said he; " I have no notion of making a
man's situation so comfortable, that he shall never think it
necessary to look out for another much better.   No one
works half so well, and heartily, and zealously, as he who is
anxious to better his condition.   When our medical resident
thinks that he has been here long enough to deserve a better
salary, and he can get that elsewhere, let him go and get it—
it is his due; it is a regular promotion : we shall rejoice for
his sake; it is right he should get it, and I never look to
keeping him.   Whenever his character with the profession
and the public shall have been well established, and he may
choose to form and keep a private institution of his own for
the treatment of persons afflicted with insanity, he will be
sure to succeed in the speculation; and therefore why tempt him
to stay, by the offer of a higher salary than he has at present ?"

Mr. Hill was born in Lincoln, of parents engaged in trade.
He was apprenticed to an apothecary at Louth, and passed
his examination in London. He afterwards was appointed
surgeon to the Lincoln Dispensary with Dr. Charlesworth,
who, marking the young man's merit and worth, and being a
daily witness to his indefatigable exertions, as well as attention
to his duties, befriended him.   As his health was not of the
best, and the duties of the Dispensary became very laborious,
Mr. Hill, with Dr. Charlesworth's assistance, watched for a
vacancy in the office of house-surgeon to the lunatic asylum,
and when it occurred he was unanimously elected.

Being of a turn of mind given to statistics, Mr. Hill, soon after his appointment, looked into all the registers of the asylum, and began to tabulate the facts therein contained. In doing this it is probable that he had seen how progressivel the coercive system in the asylum had been reduced to a very low degree without any injurious effects, and hence he was induced to think that he might dispense with it altogether.

Mr. Hill has the merit of having succeeded in completely abolishing that system among the patients in the Lincoln Asylum. In justice, however, to the medical officers and boards, who have been very active and zealous in the discharge of their respective duties during a series of years previously to Mr. Hill's appointment, it is right to state that that gentleman found the plan of non-coercion more than two-thirds adopted already, measures of restraint and the use of restraining instruments having been reduced very considerably before his connexion with the asylum. This he himself very candidly puts forth in his book, by transcribing from the register of the asylum the various resolutions passed from time to time, and the measures adopted accordingly for the utmost possible diminution in the employment of coercion, and for substituting simpler and less aggravating modes of coercion when such was deemed absolutely necessary. Thus it appears from a comparison of the table of restraints for 1830, with the table for 1835, given in the appendix to Mr. Hill's book, that whereas, with a number of patients in the house, during the first of these years, amounting only to 92 (male and females included), the total number of instances of restraint had been 2364; in the latter of these years, with a number of patients greater, namely, 108, the total number of instances of restraint had only been 323; being a diminution of five-sixths of the number in the former year.

Mr. Hill, too, had the good fortune of finding the senior physician, an experienced and able practitioner, not only friendly disposed, but a warm advocate of the little or no re-

straint system ; and with him some benevolent and philanthropic clerical members of the weekly board, dignitaries of
the Lincoln Cathedral, who showed a praiseworthy readiness
in co-operating for the adoption of a system which had
humanity to recommend it.

How far the system is applicable or not to very large
establishments, such as the Hanwell Lunatic Asylum for example, in which from 700 to 900 patients are to be treated, it
is not for me to consider. Whether it would be desirable to
do so will depend, not only upon the safety with which, as it
appears, the system can be applied to patients, judging from
the example of the Lincoln Asylum, but upon the results that
will hereafter be observed to follow its adoption with regard
to recoveries.*

As yet, taking as a guide Mr. Hill's own tables and statements, it would seem that the recoveries under the coercive system have exceeded those under the non-coercive
system by nearly thirty-five per cent. If then, the usefulness
and advantage of a mode of treating lunatic patients is to be
determined by the number of recoveries effected, the three
years' experiment by Mr. Hill has proved that his system is
not so good as the one followed during the years antecedent
to his appointment.

The grounds for such an assertion are these :

During the years 1829—30-1-2-3-4-5, while the coercive system was pursued in the asylum, there were treated
264 patients, including those already in the asylum on
the first of January, 1829; of whom 117 were discharged
recovered, being one in two and not quite ½th. But during the
years 1836-7-8, while the non-coercive system prevailed,
195 patients, including those who remained in the asylum on

* This application to Hanwell has since been made, its superintending physician having previously paid a visit to Mr. Hill for that purpose. The good results are as yet ambiguous; and while they are
vaunted by some, they are disputed or denied by others.

the first of January, 1836, were treated, and of those 65 only were discharged recovered, being one in three. I have purposely omitted to add to the total number of patients treated under this system, the patients reported in the statistical tables as having been re-admitted in consequence of relapses, as I find such patients to average nearly the same number in each year, under both systems, so that their omission cannot vitiate the relative proportion of recoveries. This then, it appears, is nearly thirty-five per cent. in favour of the coercion system.

But if the non-coercion system does not exhibit yet a vantage ground when examined in reference to the number of recoveries it produces, the rate of mortality under it (which is, after all, a better conclusion) proclaims its superiority over the opposite system, inasmuch as we find it in the latter to have been nineteen and a half, while in the former it was only fifteen per cent.; the suicides being almost always checked by it.

It remains to be seen whether this superiority is obtained at a much higher rate of expense; and for this purpose it would be important to ascertain the average cost of each patient treated in the asylum, from the time of his admission to that of his discharge, under the former and present system. For this calculation I have not at present sufficient materials. It will be necessary to include in the expenditure entailed by the system, the interest of the money employed in enlarging the premises, and altering them to suit the views of the promoter of the system.

In the meantime, some curious facts and philosophical deductions may be obtained, by the consideration of the statistical reports, regularly made for the last fifteen years, of the state of this asylum. In looking over the data furnished by such reports, of which Mr. Hill availed himself in his lecture on the management of lunatic asylums, delivered at Lincoln in June, 1838, when the author was only twenty-six years of age, and which he subsequently published,—I was struck with that gentleman's statements and numbers respecting the coercive system, and have embodyed them in a summary table, shewing at one view the working of that system even under a conscientious and well-directed management. My readers, I trust, will not grudge me the space I devote to the recording of these condensed facts, and the reflections that follow; for the subject, apart from its intrinsic importance, is one that must soon command general attention.

Summary of the total number of Patients who have been subjected to Coercion in the Lincoln Lunatic Asylum, during a period of eight years, both by day and by night, and with regard to females as well as males. Compiled from the Statistical Tables published by Mr. Hill, resident-surgeon.

Number of Patients.		Times Restrained by Day and by Night.	Hours Duration of the Restraint.	Number of Patients.		Times Restrained by Day and by Night.	Hours Duration of the Restraint.
1829	M. 26	1129	13,312	1833	M. 22	461	5,012
	F. 13	598	7,112		F. 20	648	6,991¼
1830	M. 37	1690	19,763½	1834	M. 21	285	3,093½
	F. 17	674	7,350		F. 21	362	3,503½
1831	M. 96	426	4,433	1835	M. 14	135	1,194
	F. 13	578	6,397		F. 14	188	1,680
1832	M. 36	790	8,769½	1836	M. 2	2	14½
	F. 19	611	6,902		F. 10	37	319¼

The total number of patients subjected to restraint, male, and female, amounts to 311; being 184 males, who were confined 4918 times, or 55,592 hours; and 127 females, who were confined 3696 times, or 40,255 hours.

From which it appears that every female, relatively speaking, had required to be restrained fourteen hours and a half more than any of the male patients.

The proportion of the patients restrained during the eight years, compared to the total number of patients admitted or re-admitted in the course of that time, has been 311 of the former to 344 of the latter, which is the total of admissions during the eight years, in the relative proportions of 190 males to 154 females.

One of the improvements introduced by Mr. Hill in pursuance of his system is the dormitories, almost entirely established for the prevention of suicides, so frequent under a former regimen. On being asked whether it was the apprehension of such cases being likely to be numerous, that had led him to place so many beds in dormitories instead of cells, Mr. Hill answered—" Yes; and that the larger proportion of lunatics in the asylum were disposed to suicide."

The cells on one side of the dormitories, all of which have excellent beds and beddings, and clean sheets, are for such lunatics as are dangerous to others, and are locked up, but not restrained, at night. At the end of the dormitories is a square sleeping-room, containing seven or eight beds, for ordinary quiet or convalescent patients. In this the night-guardian has to register the time, at every quarter of an hour of his watch, by pulling the string of a clock, so constructed, that one of many steel pegs projecting from the circumference of the dial-plate is pressed in by a spring, put in action by the string, when pulled by him at the proper period, which is every quarter of an hour. That period past, without the string being pulled by the guardian, who may be asleep, the dial turns round the space between two pegs, the peg passed over being left out in consequence. This cannot be pushed in by the hand afterwards, and remains, therefore, an irrefragable proof of the want of watchfulness on the part of the attendant.

Mr. Hill attributes the greater number of bad cases to the frequent and inordinate use of ardent spirits, and the next largest number to religious enthusiasm, devotion, or perplexity of mind on religious doctrines.

Dr. Charlesworth, in the course of his conversation, broached a doctrine of his own, to which Mr. Hill assented, namely, that all mental diseases are diseases of atony, requiring strength, good food, air, and exercise. He abjures and abominates every species of depletion, and places no reliance on remedies of any sort for such maladies.

" Lunacy is a complaint that must have its course. If at

the commencement of the disease all sources of irritation, excitement, &c. &c., be removed, the course will be of short duration, and so in proportion to the length of time that has elapsed between the attack and the removal of the patient to a retreat away from friends and familiar objects."

I have reason to know that the late eminent Dr. Willis partook very much of this opinion, but could not be prevailed upon to believe that the total absence of coercion, even to the abolition of the *long-sleeved smock-frock* for patients who were inclined to do harm to themselves and to others (all of whom Mr. Hill allows to be at full liberty), would ultimately prove so beneficial as its advocates expected.

Setting aside this important question of the abolition of every species of restraint from a lunatic asylum, which in that of Lincoln has so far succeeded, though not without much struggle, and some schism in the councils of the institution ; and unwilling to enter the lists with Dr. Charlesworth upon the subject of a non-medical treatment of insanity, I cannot remain equally silent with regard to another branch of the moral management of patients in the Lincoln Asylum, and which consists in mingling together purposely, and upon principles, the private with the ordinary patients, when they are all out in the airing-grounds.

Within doors, the private patients have separate apartments,* which, though well arranged, and usefully furnished, are not equal, for the charge of a guinea, or even fifteen shillings a week, to those in the York Retreat. But when out of doors, no distinction is made among the patients ; and the reason given me by Mr. Hill is this, namely, that they would not be separated in the streets were they not confined, and

---

* All patients, except real paupers, pay certain charges per week for board and lodging, attendance, and medical treatment. These charges, generally speaking. are moderate. and suitable to the rank of the patient, of which the regimen of the asylum admits three. The first rank pays 1*l.* 1*s.* per week ; the second rank 15*s.* per week ; the third rank, males 9*s.*, females 8*s.* per week.

that, though made to live together with the pauper patients in the asylum, the better class are not bound to converse or hold intercourse with them.

With deference, I hold this to be an extremely bad reason for the practice, while, at the same time, I contend that there are many good reasons for its non-adoption. True, a wealthy lunatic, or even a sound man, as he walks through the streets, mingles with beggars, is passed by the filthy, and may at every step find himself among bad characters; and yet he neither feels insulted, nor derives injury from the admixture. But that admixture is transitory, and of short duration. Moreover, the man who is desirous of avoiding it, may choose another street, another walk, another part of the town; and may change his course as often as he pleases to eschew such company : nor can the man of low degree, even where the medley is inevitable, come up and elbow you, stand still when you stand still, follow you persecutingly when you walk away, stare you in the face, mock, and spit at you,—which I have seen, and every body has seen, to occur a hundred times in an assembly of men bereaved of their nobler faculties. The reason therefore is a bad one, because it is inapplicable, and the two conditions of circumstances are quite distinct.

But for not adopting the practice of mixing the private with the pauper patients, there are many excellent reasons.

First. The man of education, and who has been brought up as a gentleman, mad as he may be, may retain his feelings of delicacy and pride; he will be better dressed, and be shocked (how do we know he is not inwardly so?) at being associated with those whose coarse garments, coarse habits, rude manners, filthy tricks, and want of cleanliness, mark them out as of an inferior class. And if so, then the perpetual association, the inevitable company of such, their obtrusion on the same path, or along the same walk, must inwardly offend and irritate, and thus far impede the recovery of the man of a superior caste.

Secondly. The sight of persons bereaved of their wits by hard inebriation from potent liquors, inducing the worst species of insanity, can ill accord with any anticipation of cure in the case of a gentleman or gentlewoman afflicted probably only with melancholy, or an aberration of a refined sort, as most of the mental disorders of that class of people are. The latter, therefore, will probably be irritated at, and ultimately, perhaps, (through constant association,) be driven to imitate, the grosser ravings of the low-born.

Thirdly and lastly. As the progress of recovery in all insane persons greatly depends on their power and means of conversing upon the very topics respecting which their reasoning faculties have been damaged ; but so that they who are to converse with the patient as a means of cure, shall, by gentle and cunning gradation, turn his thoughts into a sounder channel ; it is manifest that such a progress towards recovery will be retarded, and the damaged faculties be damaged still farther, if other patients, themselves in the worst state of low and coarse ravings, are to have a daily opportunity of forcing their conversation on the less afflicted and more refined invalids.

On the whole, and under every aspect therefore, the admixture of the better with the worse, of the low-born with the educated class, of the gentleman and the pauper, which obtains in the open airing grounds at the Lincoln Lunatic Asylum, is injudicious, uncalled for, and calculated to retard, if not altogether to mar, the recovery of the superior and private classes of patients.*

* Just before going to press with this part of my MS., which has been ready for many months, I received a letter from Mr. Hill, wherein I regret to find it announced that he had vacated the office he held in the asylum, for reasons by no means creditable to the feelings of those who ought to have patronised so meritorious and indefatigable a medical

MONKSWELL.

Leaving Lincoln by the Broad Gate, and following a narrow, rural by-lane, which, at the distance of two or three fields on the right, runs a nearly parallel course with the Witham, we discover the remains of a small and rude Gothic chapel, inclosed within a paddock, known by the country people as the Monk's-house. These vestiges seem to mark the seat of a sort of hermitage planted here by some recluse, on the margin of a mineral spring (a holy well probably), away from the bustle of a city which at one time had the rank of a petty capital.

Though evidently not belonging to the best age of that style of building, the Monk's-house, or Abbey (as it has also been called with singular inconsistency), is nevertheless an object worthy the attention of the stranger.

My purpose, however, was with the mineral spring itself, which now, thanks to the liberality of the proprietor of almost

officer. He, at the same time, communicates his intention of establishing an asylum for the reception of patients of a superior rank, as soon as he shall meet with a suitable house; and thus the conjecture anticipated by his kind friend, Dr. Charlesworth, is about to be realized.

all the lands hereabout, is protected by a stone water-course, having steps leading down to the spring, and a narrow, straight channel by which the superfluous water, overflowing from the covered stone basin, makes its escape down and across some grazing-fields, thus reaching the Witham at the distance of about three hundred yards.

The temperature of the water, repeatedly tried, was 51° F., that of the external air at the time being 60°. Taken up in a glass tumbler, the water appears colourless, and beautifully limpid, dimming instantaneously the external surface of the glass. I tasted it very deliberately, and drank a full half-pint of it. I found it particularly pleasant, fresh, and without any decided taste, unless at first one may fancy it somewhat sweetish.

There is no excess of air of any sort disengaged from the water, even after agitation, which hardly produces any bubbles in the liquid. None of the latter adheres to the glass. The stone channel is actually covered with a reddish yellow ochre, from deposit, yet the water over it is perfectly limpid and free from colour.

I concluded from this superficial observation, that in this water oxyde of iron is slightly suspended by carbonic acid, and almost wholly thrown down on the water coming in contact with the atmosphere as it emerges from the earth at the spring. Else it is strange, that with such a quantity of the oxyde as the sediment in the water-course would denote, there should not be something approaching to the taste of iron in the water ;—for most assuredly in drinking it no one would suspect the presence of that mineral in it.

The stream is very abundant and incessant. It evidently proceeds out of a superior stratum in the same hill on which the cathedral stands, at about a mile and a half eastwards. Large pieces of iron-stone are found in that direction, and are even to this day to be observed in the old walls, where they have been very generally employed, alternately with blocks of lime-stone rock. These latter masses, obtained from quarries in the immediate vicinity, have often in them round or oval nodules of iron-stone, of considerable size.

Not many hundred feet westward of the " Monk's Well," apparently derived from the same ridge, is another very abundant stream, which pours down the side of this hill, crosses the road, and proceeds on to the river. At all times the water of this spring has 40° F., only of temperature, and has been used for many years for a cold-bath, in a house erected for the purpose on the upland. It is limpid, colourless, and wholly free from any vestige of steel.

If a bottle-full of the Monkswell water be kept carefully corked and sealed for four or five days, and then tested, not the slightest indication of iron in it can be traced, nor is there any notable precipitate at the bottom of the bottle.* Yet, tested at the spring-head, with either gall or prussiate of potash, it is found at every trial to indicate, immediately, as well as abundantly, the presence of that metal. There are also indications of carbonate of lime in the water, and magnesia, but none of the muriates or sulphates.

On evaporation, a pint of it was found to contain $8\frac{3}{8}$ grains of solid ingredients, $1\frac{3}{4}$ of which is an oxyde of iron ; the remainder is a combination of calcareous magnesia ; ingredients which render the water extremely useful in all cases of dyspepsia attended by acidity, in green sickness, female debility or obstruction, cachexy, and all those cases of glandular relaxation, torpor and flabbiness of muscles, which are likely to be benefited by preparations of iron.

The water, as may be inferred from the above experiment, will not keep, or if at all, certainly not beyond one day, however carefully bottled. It must therefore be drank at the spring-head ; and administered in that way, it will be found extremely useful. Having ascertained its composition and

* See Introduction, page xxxiii., vol. I., for the reason of this phenomenon.

nature, I was not long in prescribing it, during my short so-journ in Lincolnshire, to persons in the town, particularly to two or three cases of young females, in all which instances the effects were highly satisfactory. I afterwards conversed with a gentleman who had drank for some days of this spring, a patient of Mr. Hewson, the able surgeon of Lincoln, who was kind enough to lend me his aid and his laboratory for in-vestigating both this water and that of Woodhall Spa, to be presently noticed. In his case, one of general acidity of the stomach, the benefit had been very manifest.

I engaged Mr. Hewson to use more generally this natural and valuable preparation of iron, either as mineral water only, by sending the patient from Lincoln to drink it at the spring, or by using the dry sediment in doses of ten grains to a pint of common water, or what would be still better, of soda-water.

The people of Lincoln have here within their reach a useful water, if they will but know how to use it; and if Mr. Mainwaring will add to his previous liberality a little speculation, by erecting a small resting or pump room near to the spring, with a dry walk leading to it; and still better, if he should erect at the same time in one of the lower fields a swimming-bath, for which the supply of water is most amply sufficient, open to the air, and with an adjoining room for the convenience of dressing; a dip or two in it during the summer, rapidly executed, would prove a wonderful auxiliary in the re-storation of strength, with those who have been long labour-ing under general or partial debility, unattended with fullness of blood, palpitation at the heart, or frequent head-ache.

I most gladly avail myself of the present opportunity of awaking the attention of those who are within reach of this chalybeate spring, to its sensible and beneficial properties, which I can conscientiously recommend as being equally im-portant as those of Tunbridge Wells water, and in some respects preferable, being more generally applicable to various constitutions. But I again repeat, the water must be drank on the spot, for it will not bear carriage.

The reputation of the neighbourhood of Lincoln, however, as a mineral-watering place, will not rest hereafter on the fame of the "Monkswell" spring alone, now first divulged to the present generation ; but upon a much more important dis-covery, made within the last twenty years, though rendered available only, since 1837-8, of a mineral water, remarkable for the potent ingredient it has been found to hold in so-lution to a larger amount than has hitherto been found in any other mineral spring in this country.

CHAPTER V.

THE WOODHALL, OR IODINE SPA.

History of its Discovery—Look for Coals, and find Mineral Water—Establishment of the Spa—Its Locality—Buildings erected, and Buildings required—The Well—Pumping Objectionable—Iodine Suspected and Detected by the Author, and Mr. Hewson—Presence Proved by West's *Analysis*—Larger Quantity of it present than in other Waters in England—Physical and Chemical Character of the Woodhall Spa Water—Its Taste and Medical Virtues—Diseases cured by it—Influx of Visiters — Hotel — Bath-rooms — Accommodations and Charges—Improvements Necessary—Addition Suggested — Lincolnshire Salubrity — The Fenny District and its Drainage — New System effectual — Agricultural Advantage — Gidantic Project—Recovery of vast Tracts of Land—Prolific Influence of Lincoln Climate—Dame Honeywood.

From one of the resident physicians at Horncastle, in the immediate vicinity of the mineral spring alluded to at the conclusion of the preceding chapter, I obtained the following succinct particulars respecting the history of its discovery.

" In the year 1819, some speculators, under the idea of finding coal at Kirkstead, near Horncastle, caused a shaft to be sunk at that place, 100 yards deep; they then bored 100 yards deeper, when the works were discontinued, as it was stated, for want of money. Immediately on the discontinuance of this attempt, a gentleman, owning an estate in the parish of Woodhall, about a mile distant from Kirkstead, was induced, without previously boring, to sink a shaft thereon, of 280 yards in depth.

" Boring was then had recourse to, which was carried 120 yards deeper, when this scheme, like all the preceding ones, was abandoned as hopeless. In this trial no regular account was kept of the strata passed through, but from the information and specimens received, it appears that the sinking was commenced in the clunch clay, which was found to be 120 yards in thickness ; they then passed in succession through forest marble, cornbrash, oolite, Bath freestone, lias, clunch clay again; then a rock, composed of carbonate of lime, siliceous sand, alumine, a greenish substance resembling chlorite, and a portion of mica, in which many terebratulæ were embedded. In this rock the sinking was discontinued. Of the boring no other account has been obtained, than that they left off in a stone of a light colour. A brine spring was found at about 170 yards deep, which was the only water met with.

" Several years then elapsed, the shaft was covered over, and nothing more thought of it, until at length the property coming into the possession of T. Hotchkin, Esq., his attention was drawn to the water, in consequence of several persons collecting what escaped from the shaft into a neighbouring drain, and reporting favourably of its curative properties. He erected a small bath for private use; numbers flocked to it, and surprising cures were performed ; from which he was induced to provide accommodation for the public."

Thus far my medical informant. About a twelve-month after the completion of the accommodations here alluded to, of which I shall say all that is needful presently, a meeting of the medical gentlemen, and of many of the gentry in the neighbourhood, took place at the New Hotel at Woodhall, for the purpose of celebrating the anniversary of the opening of the Spa, which seems to have fully established its claims and identity as such on that occasion. At that time, however, no one was in possession of an accurate analysis of the water; and its virtues were only conjectured from analogy, or deduced empirically from the result of some practical experiments made with patients, who derived great benefit from the water. Being in the neighbourhood, and feeling an interest in the matter, I paid several visits to the Well, and suggested the propriety of procuring a perfect and correct knowledge of the chemical composition of the water —a suggestion which, with many others that I threw out on the spot when visiting it afterwards in the company of the proprietor, Mr. Hotchkin, that gentleman immediately adopted.

Nature presents hardly a single feature of interest around this mineral spring ; yet much has been effected, and more may be done, to render what was before desolate and unattractive, or is so still, less uninviting, and ultimately, I may say, even agreeable as a summer residence for two or three months.

Situated within a mile and a half only of the eastern bank of the Witham, and lower in its level than that stream, Woodhall, the small village which gives its name to the Spa so accidentally discovered, stands in the midst of a flat tract of land, which is often covered with water. Yet unfavourable as this situation may at first sight appear, there is nothing that judgment combined with taste, and a persevering spirit, aided by wealth, may not accomplish to render the spot one of gay and fashionable resort. Think of the origin of Leamington Priors, on the banks of a narrow and muddy stream ; or of Cheltenham, once a miserable gathering of paltry hamlets placed in the hollow of a valley, damp, cheerless, and clayish.

A belt of fir plantations of recent growth, yet sufficiently tall to exclude the north and north-east winds, stands fortunately at a very short distance from the Well, and affords one of the means to be employed for embellishing the place. The new grounds, to the extent of some acres, are now marked out around the spring, the land having been previously extensively drained, so as to exclude all moisture from the foundation of any buildings that may hereafter be erected upon it.

Not far from the Well a neat and unostentatious edifice has been erected, which serves as an hotel, honoured with the name of Victoria Hotel, the only rendezvous for the visiters to the Spa. Its two principal fronts are to the south and west; and in connexion with it are two ranges of stables, separated by a large courtyard.

The baths are in a distinct building, closely adjoining the Well, and consequently at a distance from the hotel,—an arrangement that has been found inconvenient by the bathers, particularly the ladies, although the distance be not considerable. In general, where the thing is admissible, mineral baths should be near or contiguous to the dwellings of the invalids in public places like the present, especially where the climate is so variable, and the ground liable to get wet.

Here, at the Woodhall Spa, such an arrangement is not only admissible, but called for, and likely to prove materially advantageous to the whole establishment.

The fact is, that the present building in which the baths are situated, and that which contains the ranges of stables before alluded to (with their noisy annex " a tap-room"), should change places. Had the proprietor been properly advised by persons conversant in such matters, he would have connected the very neat building he has erected for the baths with the hotel, so as to form its eastern extremity. A more imposing and uniform front would thus have been obtained; and an opportunity afforded of securing symmetry and effect to the building, by hereafter adding a similar wing to the other extremity.

Mr. Hotchkin being made sensible of the great advantages as well as necessity of some such an arrangement as this, from what I said to him, has decided upon forming a colonnade or covered way between the hotel and the bath-building, so as to make the latter quickly accessible when required. But a far greater improvement to the place would be to remove the tap-room and stables from where they now are,* for the purpose of rebuilding the former by the side of the present baths, for the use of that class of visiters (of whom I noticed a large number on the registers) who are likely to lodge in some of the cottages in the neighbourhood, and frequent the tavern for their refreshments ; and the latter in a still more remote part. A new wing should be added to the hotel, containing other and more commodious, as well as showy bath-rooms, for a very different class of patients.

If this Spa is to progress forward and flourish (and few establishments of this kind are better entitled to do so from their intrinsic worth), it is manifest that a set of bath-rooms very different from those at present in use will be required. It is not to be expected that my Lord-this, and Sir-that, will like to frequent the very narrow and insignificant bath-rooms as they now exist, and dip into the scanty space therein allotted for each bath-tank, from which the honest farmer in the neighbourhood, or the shopkeeper from Lincoln and Boston, have just emerged.

As there is an intention on the part of the proprietor to build, in connexion with the Victoria Hotel, a banqueting and an assembly room, the former of which might be used as a promenade room in the morning for the water-drinkers, the alterations I have suggested as indispensable will be the more readily effected, as, by enlarging the body of the hotel, through the addition of those two new apartments, the general line of buildings might be directed towards the well, so as to bring the new bath-rooms I suggest within a very manageable distance of the water-source.

At present, the water, which is pumped up from a depth of sixty yards by iron pipes, and conveyed by pipes of the same material to a reservoir for distribution, becomes charged

* The removal of the stables, I understand, has taken place agreeably to this suggestion, and various other alterations are about to be adopted at my recommendation.

with the oxyde of that metal, which it possesses not in its natural state. The marble slabs in the baths are stained with the brown marks of the same.

This accidental addition to the chemical ingredients of the water must naturally alter its character, and render it unfit to drink in the pump-room by many invalids, who ought not to take preparations of iron of any sort whatever. By it, also, the relative character and power of the water are changed altogether, and what was before natural is now partly natural and partly artificial.

As the great depth of the Well renders the employment of more than one pumping arrangement down the shaft necessary, the number of iron pipes employed in that operation, and of those which convey the water from the Well to the reservoir, and thence to the baths, is such, that a surface of not less than 210 feet of iron becomes exposed to the action of a large quantity of muriate of soda, or common salt, contained in the mineral water. An easy remedy to this would be to use baked earthenware pipes for all operations respecting the pumping and distribution of the water.*

There could be no objection to retaining a small reservoir of the water which shall have been in contact, by proper and judicious contrivance, with iron pipes, so as to keep for medical use the iodine water charged with a small proportion of soluble carbonate of iron. Such a combination, artificially prescribed, has been found in practice so truly excellent for the recovery of certain diseases, particularly affecting the

* While this sheet was going through the press, a most important invention called the *Hydraulic Belt* having been brought to my notice by a friend, of the simple yet most effective nature of which I satisfied myself experimentally ; I hesitated not in having it suggested to Mr. Hotchkin to substitute the same for the inconvenient, cumbersome, and expensive apparatus of pumps and pipes, and I rejoice to learn he has immediately ordered its adoption. This is an immense improvement, which I would recommend to all those who have to draw water from great depths. Its simplicity and effect are, even at first sight, most surprising.

weaker sex, that to have an almost natural mixture ready at hand, in any quantity, would be advantageous to both patient and physician.

My minute observations of the water, made on the spot, led me at once to suspect the presence of some more active ingredient in it than had hitherto been detected, and iodine was one of the principles which I conjectured might be found on a proper analysis, judging from the good results that had been obtained from its use in the treatment of certain diseases. The very large proportion, too, of common salt in it seemed also to warrant that conjecture.

Mr. Hewson, of whom I have already made honourable mention, undertook, during my temporary absence from the neighbourhood of the Spa, to make some preliminary experiments, and to prepare for others which we afterwards repeated together for the purpose of putting to the test his own and my conjecture above alluded to. The result was most satisfactory. Iodine was found present in all the specimens of the Woodhall Spa water, tried, after evaporating it to two-thirds, by applying the test of starch, sulphuric acid, and the still more delicate test of chlorine gas in its nascent state.

Having afterwards obtained a solid residuum of 329 grains of saline matter, deliquescent in its nature, from two pints of the water, I suggested that we should try a portion of this re-dissolved, for the purpose of ascertaining whether, during the evaporation of the water to dryness at 199° Fahrenheit, and the drying of the residuum at 212°, the iodine had escaped ; or whether, on the contrary, that important agent was still present with the saline matter, probably combined with some of the other ingredients. The result obtained after re-dissolving some of the said residuum in distilled water, and applying the chlorine test, was quite satisfactory, as to the presence of a considerable quantity of iodine.

Such being the case, I lost no time in urging on Mr. Hotchkin the necessity of immediately employing a practical chemist of well-established reputation, to undertake a complete scientific analysis of the water; and on this occasion, again, I ventured with confidence to name Mr. West, of Leeds, for that purpose.

That gentleman, accordingly, proceeded to the Spa, and remained on the spot until he completed his analysis, a full report of which he afterwards, at Mr. Hotchkin's desire, forwarded to me; and I must say, that in the course of my long experience in matters of this description, I have not met with a more able, a more elaborate, or a more philosophical examination of a mineral-water than this report of Mr. West.

From it it appears, first, that I was correct in my estimate of the importance likely to attach to the Woodhall Spa, in the treatment of scrofulous disorders in particular, on account of the presence of that powerful agent, iodine—besides bromine; and, secondly, that the quantity of iodine contained in this water is larger than has hitherto been detected in any mineral-water in Great Britain—being more than half a grain in the imperial gallon.

Mr. West's report ought to be published at full length, but its purely scientific character precludes its insertion in this place.

For my present purpose, however, it will suffice that I should quote a few of Mr. West's remarks on the inquiry he engaged in at my request, in order to give greater authenticity to my account of this new and important Spa. The ultimate analysis will be found in my general table.

" At Mr. Hotchkin's desire I forward thee the annexed statement of the experiments on the Woodhall Spa water, as well as of the report founded on them. In thy work the whole will probably shrink to a few lines, but as some of the results are remarkable, and the water is certainly uncommon, it is proper that thou shouldst be made acquainted with the processes resorted to. Thou wilt observe, that as usual with me, I confine myself to chemical statements almost entirely, and leave medical comments to medical men. * * * *

" The chief peculiarity of this water is the abundance, as

compared with others, of that active principle—iodine. It has been stated that the largest proportion before found in any British spring was one-tenth of a grain in a gallon.* In stating the present spring to yield about five times that quantity, I am guided by the most precise and delicate tests and experiments detailed in my report. * * * The iodine in this water, *without concentration*, may be shown, with proper precaution, by starch and chlorine,—a circumstance not recorded, as far as I am aware, of any other water in Britain.

"The total quantity of gases is very large; when fresh drawn up from a considerable depth it is remarkably ' brisk,' and may be compared to Champagne wine. The quantity of carbonic acid is unusually large."

To this I may add, that when the water was taken from the reservoir, and had passed through the iron pipes, a considerable quantity of iron was found in it on analysis by Mr. Hewson and myself. But Mr. West naturally was directed to procure the water at the bottom of the Well by means of bottles, and he then found no traces of iron in it; thereby confirming my original opinion, that to employ iron pipes to pump the water from the Well is highly objectionable, and is a practice which must be immediately put a stop to, with the only reservation already specified.

I may also state, in reference to one of the gases, pretended at first to be present in this water,—namely, sulphureted hydrogen—that the people at the Spa seemed to rely most upon the supposed large quantity of that gas contained in the water for its virtues,—hoping to rival Harrogate (the great object of envy in the north); but that I found by the usual tests on the spot hardly any trace of that gas, and I stated the fact at the time of my visit, much to the dismay of the parties interested. Mr. West's analysis bears me out in this point also; his remarks on that head are, " the sul-

* See Dr. Daubeny's Table of the iodine and bromine in certain mineral-waters of Great Britain.—*Phil. Trans.* 1830.

phureted hydrogen is in too small a quantity to be important—indeed *too small* to be measured."

But for the loss of this very ordinary and generally prevalent gas in the mineral waters of England, especially in Yorkshire,—the Woodhall Spa has been most abundantly requited by the detected presence of the two far more important ingredients already mentioned, iodine and bromine, particularly the former; and the public generally, as well as those who are more immediately interested in the Spa, may well rejoice at the substitution of two such ingredients for sulphureted hydrogen.

Lastly, I may state that the specimens of the water analyzed were taken at a depth of a hundred yards below the surface of the water, which is itself fifty yards below the mouth of the Well. The whole depth of the Well is about one hundred and seventy yards, seventeen or eighteen feet of which is through a soft freestone rock, from whose surface brine-water has been seen to percolate constantly, by the person employed to go down to examine and arrange the pipes belonging to the pump. These pipes plunge about twenty-five yards below the surface of the water.

Taken from the former depth in my presence, I found the water turbid or rather opalescent in its appearance; the taste was intensely briny, but neither bitter nor unpleasant. It is brisk and sparkling, and its temperature about 55°. Very faint indications of sulphureted hydrogen were obtained by acetate of lead when the water was tested immediately, but none shortly after it was drawn. Neither gall, nor prussiate of potash showed tokens of iron in it.

When taken from the pump out of the reservoir or cistern, in which it must have undergone some modification owing to the iron pipes, as I said before, the water is transparent but ochreous in colour. It froths a great deal when shaken, as if some mucilaginous or animal matter were present in solution, and the froth persists on the surface of the water a long time, adhering also to the side of the glass. When agitated to and fro in the tumbler, the water does not seem to wet the glass, but to slide over it quickly like an oily liquid, or rather as water would do over an oily surface. To the touch the water feels unctuous; so likewise does the deposit in the cisterns. The first impression on the tongue is unctuous, followed immediately by a strong briny taste, but not so much so as that of sea-water. It is not in the least bitter, and the saltish taste continues in the mouth for about ten minutes.

Here then we have an established fact, that at Woodhall, a few miles from Lincoln, there exists a most remarkable spring, supplying large quantities of mineral water, endowed with most important chemical properties, which, in the hand of a judicious and skilful practitioner, may be made instrumental in curing some of the diseases mostly prevalent in England, dependant on scrofula or glandular affections, and on disordered digestion, including symptomatic rheumatism, rheumatic gout, and gout itself.

This is indeed a wide and interesting field of practice, and one in which art may triumph while humanity shall rejoice. Like every other potent remedy, however, the Woodhall water must be prudently and sagaciously used.

A pint, and with some people half that quantity, acts as an aperient. It should be drank warm, — some of the mineral water being kept hot for that purpose, in a wooden cistern heated by steam conveyed through the body of the water by a worm of brass tinned inside and out.*

Though recently discovered, the Spa has not lacked visiters. On examining the register kept at the pump-room, I found from twenty to thirty inscribed in each day in the month of

* I am not satisfied that the process of tinning is a sufficient protection against the probability of a briny iodinated water being altered in some degree from exposure to the metal. Some other heating process must be devised.

August. In the space of seven weeks from the end of May, nine hundred and seventy had taken baths, paying three shillings; and altogether in the course of the twelvemonth, about two thousand had bathed. Those who drank of the water were only three hundred, and judging from the hand-writing of the signatures, as well as from the names, I should imagine that the majority of the visiters were farmers and people belonging to the industrious classes. Indeed neither the bath-room accommodations, nor the pump-room are calculated for very superior classes of persons. The pro-prietor must, to secure the latter, erect more suitable baths near the hotel, on the site of the present stables, as I before suggested, to which the conveyance of the mineral water from the Well through stone pipes, by a small steam-engine, would be an easy task.*

But if the accommodations for the baths be not of the first class, the hotel provided for the accommodation of the visiters is not liable to that objection. A very interesting young person, with an imposing figure and very intelligent counte-nance, active and apparently mistress of her business, has been placed at the head of the establishment. In her company I went over it in detail, and was much pleased with the arrangements and accommodations within it, particularly of the bed-rooms, of which there are several single as well as double. All the best of them have a favourable aspect, and some of them look over the fir plantation in the vicinity, or extend the range of their views as far as Horncastle one way, and the ruined remains of Tattershall, one of the best preserved castles of the pure Norman age in this country. Every part of the furniture and bedding is perfectly new and

* Before the expiration of the approaching season, much of this will have been accomplished; as the spirited proprietor, who has already laid out a large sum of money since my visit, is determined to spare no expense to render this important Spa deserving of the countenance of the better classes of society.

of the best kind, and no expense has been spared to secure perfect comfort.

The terms are not extravagant, and indeed much the same as those at all the spas in England. A single person may board for five shillings per day, and secure an excellent bed-room for one shilling more per night. If he has a servant, the latter will be boarded and lodged for three shillings per day. A private sitting-room is charged a guinea a week; but few need require that accommodation, as there is both a morning-room and a drawing-room for the use of the boarders.

Those who wish to live privately will find a private sitting-room and private boarding most convenient, and by no means extravagant, being charged six shillings a day for the latter, and three shillings for the former, or three guineas a week altogether. Surely the expense of twelve guineas for a month's course of the water cannot be said to be too large for the recovery of one's health. Perhaps the charge which might be reduced is that for the baths. Three shillings a bath is too much; invalids should be tempted, by some *bonus* in the way of a general subscription for the whole season, to use more baths than they do at present, when a person taking twenty-four baths in six weeks pays at the same rate for each bath as he who takes only half a dozen baths. This should not be so. The terms for drinking and the use of the pump-room are two shillings per week each person.

To some people the idea of sojourning in the midst of the fens of Lincolnshire while seeking health at the spring of Woodhall, may seem preposterous, as they probably attach to such a locality the old reputation of its being particularly unwholesome. But however just such an opinion may have been formerly, it has ceased to be generally applicable to the whole fenny district of the county, since the introduction of an extensive and most effectual method of draining. That method consists in drawing off from the lowlands the ordinary drain-water sufficiently early to allow room for the flood-water (whenever any such comes down) to pass away.

This is now effected by means of a twenty-horse steam-engine, in lieu of the windmills previously employed.

It is to be regretted that a plan which has worked quite well in the three or four fenny districts where it has been adopted for the last four or five years, should not have long ago been followed in all other parts of the county similarly situated. Had this been done, the farmers of some of the parishes near Lincoln, Boultham for instance, would not have had to deplore, as they did in 1839, the general submersion of their lowlands, whilst covered with crops of corn of a most beautiful and promising appearance.

The water collected in the sectional drains is pumped into the Delph, a large drain something like a canal, which runs nearly parallel to the Witham, and thence it either flows or is lifted into the river.

These successful operations have been the means of bringing much land, before useless, into cultivation; and the progressive improvement of those lands has been such, that very large crops of corn are gathered upon them now. Indeed, the quantity of wheat raised on every acre of well-drained fen, is larger than that produced by the same quantity of land elsewhere, in the middle part of Lincolnshire.

The corn is certainly not of so good a quality as that grown on ordinary lands; neither is it so heavy. This arises from the peculiar nature of the soil of a newly-drained fen, which consists of a loose black peat, generally eighteen inches, and in some places two feet, and even two feet and a half deep.

To obviate this difficulty in the arable soil, many of the farmers on the recovered lands have, within the last few years, adopted with great success the plan of "claying" the supersoil. Clay is found immediately below the upper loose peat stratum. Towards the end of the year men are set upon digging trenches a yard wide, and parallel to each other, the whole length of the field, with a depth of from four and sometimes five to six feet. They first throw up

and arrange on the one side of such trenches the supersoil,
and next fetch the clay from the bottom, and lay it along
the opposite side. The former is then thrown into the
trench, and the extracted clay deposited over it, while the
two soils are mixed near the surface, and their amalga-
mation completed further by the subsequent use of the
plough.

On such lands presenting a firm and consistent soil, I
have seen corn grown nearly as good in quality as that which
I had noticed on the higher lands in the vicinity of the
great Roman road, on the Sleaford road, and also on what
is called the " Clift Row."

After all, the true and effectual remedy for all the sub-
merged lands, and those still liable to such inundations,
among which I include those lands more immediately connected with the Spa which has formed the subject of the
present chapter, would be to enlarge the Witham, and make
the outfall at Boston more spacious than it is at present, in
order that it may carry away a larger quantity of water between tide and tide.

Connected with this important operation, comes naturally
before us that gigantic, yet plausible scheme, propounded
by the eminent engineer who superintends the wonderful
doings at Hartlepool, for the formation of a new general
outfall into the German Ocean of the waters of not fewer
than four rivers, the Witham included ; by means of which,
while their discharge into the great estuary called the WASH
would be greatly facilitated, and made more regular as well
as uniform (thereby improving not only the lands of Lincolnshire, but those of Norfolk), valuable land, to the extent
of 150 thousand acres, principally of alluvial deposit, would
be recovered, at the cost of twelve pounds per acre, the
average value of the fee-simple of which might be expected
to be at least forty pounds per acre.

This tempting speculation has been offered to the public
by a company, I understand, already formed and in earnest,

styled *The Company of Proprietors of the Great Level of the Wash.*

When I add that Earl Fitzwilliam, Lord George Bentinck, the Earl of Hardwicke, the Honourable Eliot Yorke, M. P., and others, are in the direction, my readers will readily conclude that this is not a mere wild scheme to catch the unwary.

Do I mention these facts, or enter into such matters for any purpose alien to the principal object of my present volumes? Far from it. The *assainissement*, as the French, with a word untranslatable, yet full of meaning, would say, of the lowlands throughout the extensive districts of Lincolnshire before mentioned, which must follow as the natural result of the success of such an operation as Sir John Rennie recommends, must render the climate near and about the Spas partially described in the preceding and present chapter perfectly safe; and do away with the old prejudices entertained against Lincolnshire fens. Hence my introduction of the matter just treated, and which I deemed it my duty to study, and submit to my readers.

After all, perhaps, the climate of Lincolnshire may not require my advocacy to prove not only its salubriousness, but its beneficial influence on longevity, as well as in promoting the multiplication of mankind, even before the draining of the fens had been dreamt of. For I find on the grave of Dean Honeywood, in Lincoln Cathedral, a registry of births and deaths (entered with a precision equal to that of her Majesty's registrar-general for births, deaths, marriages, &c.) which shows how prolifically the generations near the fens went on in the Reverend Gentleman's times. The said Dean of Lincoln, it appears, was grandchild of a dame Mary Honeywood, and one of three hundred and sixty-seven persons lawfully descended from her, all of whom she had seen before she died: viz.—16 children of her own body, 114 grandchildren, 228 great grandchildren, and 9 of the fourth generation—Total 367.

CHAPTER VI.

ASHBY-DE-LA-ZOUCH—WILLOUGHBY NEW BATHS—DERBY—RUGBY.

An Invitation — STAMFORD Springs — Stage-coach a Rarity—DERBY, Improvement, New Buildings—The New Catholic Church—Great Change in Derby occasioned by Railroads—Mr. Strutt's ARBORETUM — The Largest EMBARCADERO in England—First Opening of the Derby Line to London—Ticket No. 1.—Awkward Journey—RAILROAD SPEED—Gluttony and Philosophy—The Long Coach—ASHBY-DE-LA-ZOUCH—Source of the MOIRA Water—Its Physical, Chemical, and Remedial Properties—FOUR Analyses of the Water—all Different ! What ought to be done?—Bathing in the Moira Water—The IVANHOE Baths—THE HOTEL—Mode of Living at the Spa—STRIKING CASES of Cure—WILLOUGHBY New Baths—Rugby School—Road to Willoughby—The WELL—The Water—Properties Physical and Medical —Want of Accommodation—SUGGESTIONS—Excellency of the Water —Opinion of the Author thereon.

WHILE yet in the neighbourhood of Lincoln, busy in examining the geology of Woodhall Spa, and the agricultural capabilities of the country around it, I received from Dr. Hopkinson, a leading and much respected physician at Stamford, a letter inviting me over to that city, in reference to the principal object of my inquiries into mineral waters. " It would delight me," says he, " to see you as a visiter here. Stamford is very convenient on the north road, and if you would only let me know a few days previous to your coming, I will be ready to make your stay as interesting as I can. We have two or three mineral springs hereabouts : one rather out of the common way. These I should like to show you, and I will at the same time get together all the matter I can about Woodhall, respecting which you have written to me. I know your work on the Spas of Germany well enough to make me desirous of knowing the author and assisting him all I can in my humble way."

The invitation was a tempting one, and still more so from the very polite manner in which it was expressed. For some time I hoped to have been able to avail myself of it with a view to my intended publication ; but when the period arrived for proceeding thither, the calculated time of my absence from town, during which I had to perform a certain determined quantity of work, and the pressing engagements that awaited me in London, compelled me to abandon the idea of going to explore the springs alluded to by Dr. Hopkinson, for whose considerate kindness I beg to return him, in this place, suitable acknowledgments.

My object now was to direct my steps towards the mid-land counties, in search of certain mineral waters which seemed to me worthy of examination, judging from the information I had received and read about them ; although to the public at large one only of the whole number seemed sufficiently known—namely, that of Ashby-de-la-Zouch.

Accordingly, I made that place my next point of destina-tion ; and proceeded to Nottingham by the *old-fashioned* mode of conveyance — a stage-coach, which, by the bye, in the midland counties, is becoming more and more of a *rarity* every day, and will end by being " a wonder."

After a short delay in Nottingham, sufficient to inspect its staple manufactures, I reached at last the capital of Derbyshire by the neat and short railroad which connects the two cities.

DERBY, as I had occasion to state once before, exhibits strong marks of general improvement, by an extension as well as renovation of its principal buildings. The range of edifices, consisting of the royal hotel, a new post-office, and the bank in the corn-market, is a mass creditable to the town, The style of the front is an imitation of the late Mr. Wilkins's "peculiar," of which a tolerable specimen may be seen in the building of St. George's Hospital, at Hyde-park-corner, especially as regards the arrangement of the windows, which is by no means a commendable one. The principal feature of the whole range is the rounded angle, and here Grainger's-buildings at Newcastle were in the architect's mind when he designed the elevation.

Like Preston and Lancashire generally, and indeed a great many other places in England, Derby shows the daily increasing importance of the Catholics in this country, both as to numbers and wealth, as well as with regard to their staunch adhesion to the religious rites of their creed. I allude to the erection of a very large cathedral-looking chapel, which has been very recently completed. It is in what is commonly called the Gothic style ; but although the whole, especially the tower, looks imposing, when the several members of the building, either externally or internally, are examined separately, it is impossible not to be struck with the want of unity—a lack of a continuous spirit of invention, and a total failure in applying means to one end. No one, for example, who beholds the stately tower would expect to find side-windows of such paltry dimensions in the body of the church, nor such *mesquines* doors for lateral entrances ; still less (within the church) such petty side-aisles—a positive apology for those stately divisions of a large Gothic temple. As to the shafts which separate the nave from the aisles, and support a flat roof, though they are formed of clustered pillars, their general diameter is really so insignificant (bearing no proportion to the general size of the edifice) that they resemble more the single trunks of an old avenue of lime-trees than Gothic pillars, and are evidently disproportionate to their object.

The fact is that this building is two narrow for its length, and too lofty for its width ; defects that help materially to disfigure the façade of this New Catholic temple, which will be a striking, but not an admired nor a correct edifice.*

The junction of three railroads in this County-town, bringing travellers and goods from the north and the south, and also from the west, is already sensibly changing its character, its general appearance, and its importance. I remember the time when Derby, in spite of the silk manufactures, its lace, its hosiery, and its wrought iron and copper works, appeared to a traveller one of the dullest county-towns in the heart of England. It is now full of bustle, lively, and apparently in the enjoyment of greater wealth, comforts, and even luxury, than it has ever before possessed.

Simultaneously with these advantages, one is happy to see, —both from the spontaneous inclination of the citizens themselves, and the public and patriotic spirit of one or two of the wealthiest among them,—a corresponding advance made in the cultivation of the useful as well as the polite arts, and of many other branches of knowledge.

A relation of one of the representatives for the city, whose mansion I beheld not far removed from where the new Catholic church rises, is the spirited individual to whose exertion, and I may say munificent liberality, every citizen I spoke with seemed to attribute much of the improvements in and about the place. His picture gallery, which is probably destined for the ultimate use of his fellow-townsmen, is, in the mean time, open for their inspection, and serves to give them correct notions of taste in the fine arts.

This same individual is at present engaged in adding a feature to Derby, which will, of itself, form one of its best attractions. Under the well-known skill and taste of the author of many able and very useful works on agriculture and gardening—the only man whom government might have placed with confidence in the management of all the royal and public parks and gardens, if they were desirous of seeing

* The building was not quite finished when these remarks were written.

them always in their best attire and most favourable condition—Mr. Loudon, in fine,—an *arboretum*, or collection of trees and shrubs of every country, is just about being completed, by direction of Mr. Joseph Strutt, the spirited individual alluded to. The grounds extend to nearly eleven acres, including the gardens and buildings, for all which a sum of from ten to twelve thousand pounds has been appropriated, by the munificent donor of this beautiful as well as useful establishment to the town.

" Access to the arboretum," observes Mr. Adam, who has recently given a short account of it, " will be permitted on fixed days and at such times as will accommodate the artisan as well as the peer, and all parties whose time is more at their command. Here, therefore, the working classes of Derby will have a place of delightful resort, calculated alike to administer to their health and pleasure, as well as the refinement and cultivation of their taste, by affording them frequent opportunities of beholding the noblest combinations of artificial gardening."

The arrangement of the *arboretum* is equally ingenious and effectual. The scientific name of each plant, with its corresponding denomination in English; its native country or *habitat;* the family or natural order to which it belongs; its height; the year of its introduction, and many other particulars, are let into brick tallies, which, after being glazed, are stuck into the ground at a short distance from the plant.

But Derby promised fairly, at the time of my visit, to possess another equally striking and novel feature in the immense building which it was expected would be erected as a general station or *rendezvous* of the Midland, North Midland, and Derby and Birmingham lines of railway, if a coalition of the three companies could be accomplished, willing to work under one roof.

The head stations of the three railroads are near to each other on an open space of ground, called " the Old Meadows," contiguous to the old London road, and not far from the town, and it is calculated that the offices and buildings would occupy an area of twenty-five acres, with a continuous line of frontage to the principal edifice of upwards of a thousand feet. What a chance for an architect of genius and imagination !*

I happened to be on the spot, the day on which the line to London was first opened. As a matter of study and curiosity, I determined on taking my departure by it for the capital, whither a pressing summons obliged me to go for a few hours, although my destination was at the time to the Spas of Worcestershire and Shropshire. But the expected rapidity of my movements, in going and in being able to return by the same means in nearly the same time that under the old system of travelling I should have employed in proceeding direct to my latter destination, eschewing the journey to London, induced me to make the experiment.

All Derby was in a bustle on that eventful morning. The opening of the first railway from the town to the capital was the opening of a mine of wealth. I was the first on the spot, and had ticket No. 1. Every director was present. Preliminary experiments had been made daily for a week and upwards; yet every thing seemed in a state of confusion, every body spoke or commanded, and when the carriages were to be brought up to the temporary platform, it was found that something was to be done to the iron stop of one of those circular moving machines in the ground which serve to turn the vehicles. The operation was performed with bad and inefficient tools, and took some time to be completed. This was not very encouraging to me, who was silently watching every movement, and saw all the hesitation and whispering and going to and fro around me.

When all was ready, it was found that there were but few persons who would proceed, and the train ended by being

---

* This expectation has since been fulfilled, and the front elevation of this general embarcadero, I am told, is as magnificent as I had anticipated.

composed of three or four first-class carriages only, certainly very splendid and comfortable. With these we started for Stonebridge, on the London and Birmingham Railway, a few miles north-west of Coventry, where we expected to be taken in tow by a train from Birmingham. But we were not quite ready when the train came in sight, and it whisked along, giving us the go-by and leaving us in the lurch.

However, a locomotive with suitable fuel and water was soon procured and tacked to our three or four solitary vehicles, which started on their venture at the risk of finding every impediment and none of the ordinary aids on the road, inasmuch as we were interlopers on the line, appearing for the first time upon it, and not in our right and pre-concerted time.

The consciousness of this made my travelling companions in the same carriage and myself somewhat nervous: yet we could hardly help smiling, in the midst of our apprehensions, at the vacant and stupified stare of workmen we found on the road and our own line, who had just time to scamper off; and at the astonishment of some of the policemen who were seen running to take up their flags which they had not expected to be so soon called upon to wave again after the passing of the last Birmingham train; and above all at the gaze of wonder and curiosity of all the people employed at the different stations, upon beholding the arrival of a total stranger on their premises.

We made our journey good, nevertheless, though not without considerable anxiety, and I inwardly thanked my stars to find myself again upon my legs, passing under Hardwich's splendid arch at Euston grove, where we arrived in seven hours from Derby: no great performance truly, now-a-days, for a distance of one hundred and thirty-five miles !

Matters, however, have since been better managed in respect to this particular line of communication, which has been made both shorter and more convenient by bringing the intersecting line of the Derby upon the Birmingham Railway to London nearer Rugby. The whole distance is now performed in six hours.

Railroad speed, when most of the danger of that mode of travelling shall have been obviated by more prudence, better management, and a stricter *surveillance* on the part of the public authorities than has hitherto prevailed, will form a subject of interesting speculation. We hardly know what we have got by this extraordinary invention, for we are amazed, and have not yet set about calculating its results.

Let us take an example: Nothing marks time more effectually than the regular recurrence of our usual hours of repast. The lapse between breakfast and dinner is so brief that we may almost say that the first is hardly digested when we are summoned to the second. Now, to be able to say that in the short space of time which intervenes between these two repasts, you shall run over one hundred and thirty-five miles, (rattling, in that time, through not fewer than seven different counties on your way from London to Derby), will strike one with more amazement, and with the conviction that time has indeed been annihilated, than could any other computation of distance contrasted with speed. Yet such is the feat which a gourmand might easily accomplish any day in the week if he pleases, by means of the leviathan power that now regulates our movements.

We will suppose our traveller quietly at his breakfast at home in town at about nine o'clock, poring over the debates and quaffing his bohea, free and independent, and with all the world before him. A penny-post letter is brought him marked "Derby." It was written but a few hours before; the ink indeed may be said to be hardly dry. It might have been written over-night from Grosvenor-place, and yet not come to hand sooner. It brings an invitation from a frolic-some friend, to dine at Derby on that day, at a quarter before seven o'clock. "Good! I like the fun of the thing." It is half-past nine o'clock. "Get me a cab and put my things to dress in." Behold him at a quarter before ten o'clock starting from Euston-place, and lo! in three hours before the appointed time for dinner, our gourmand is at his friend's house at Derby, calling out for luncheon!

But that is not all. If the dinner be not protracted to what is now (thank Heaven!) no longer a fashionable hour, and the cellar of the Derby friend be not too attractive, his guest may leave him at half after eleven, reach home by six o'clock, go to bed, have a sound nap, and be again at breakfast at his own table at nine, where he was the preceding morning,—fancying that he had jaunted it down to Derby and back again in his dreams!

Now this may lead us to a little philosophy. The average rate of travelling on all the railroads in England by the first-class stations train, has hitherto not exceeded twenty miles per hour, including stoppages, and twenty-five exclusive of them. By the trains which call at all the stations, or what are called " mixed," the average rate has never exceeded *twelve miles*.* At the former rate, therefore, travellers, according to John Smeaton's well-known anemometrical tables in the " Philosophical Transactions," will have been scudding with the velocity of a " very brisk gale;" and it is only on extraordinary occasions that they will have been on the pinions of a "high wind," approaching to "a storm," when the engineer, pressed to make up for lost time, has pushed on his locomotive at the rate of between thirty and thirty-five miles per hour, or fifty feet per second.

Henceforth, therefore, the expression of " I flew like the wind," employed to signify the utmost speed, will no longer be considered as a poetical but as a *real* figure of speech; while, in order to express greater speed than that which hereafter will constitute our ordinary movements, it will become necessary to adopt the phrases of " we flew like a storm," or, " we went in a storm," which, according to the same

---

* This last rate of travelling may be the average, and as such I have found it reported in a public journal: but my own experience, even with all the delays perpetually occurring, gives me a somewhat greater rate of speed.

eminent engineer's experiments, before alluded to, mean, that we ran at the rate of fifty miles an hour, or seventy-four feet per second—the rate which we are promised to be conveyed at on the Great Western, when once completed, so as to arrive at Bath from town between shaving and breakfast, or, in other words, between half-past seven and ten o'clock in the morning!

As for the unfortunates who must travel by the "mixed," they will be exactly in the same predicament as those stage travellers who, upon the first introduction of the light four-inside post-coaches, rattling at the speed of ten miles and a half an hour on our astonished turnpikes, down to Dover or Portsmouth, were yet obliged, from motives of economy, to stick to the "long coaches," tracking along the whole of one night and the best part of the following day, at the truly Germanic pace of five miles per hour. The two classes of travellers will stand in something like the same relation as to expedition. But as to the chances of interruption in their progress, or the dangers of a smash, the *long coach* passengers of old would have had infinitely the advantage over the "mixed" passengers of the present day.

Mixed or unmixed, however, as the accommodation of the Derby line enabled me soon to leave town again, in order to complete what I had to do respecting the mineral waters of that neighbourhood, let us return thither, and discourse on a Spa which has acquired a certain celebrity within the last thirty years; I mean

ASHBY-DE-LA-ZOUCH.

There is an indistinct tradition in the place, that springs of mineral water abounded here in former times; and that the sick and the lame from far and near came to be healed by them. The real mineral water, however, which at present gives to Ashby its character as a bathing-place, cannot boast of having been so long known; for it was discovered at the bottom of a colliery, not longer than twenty-four years ago, during the progress of working a coal seam at the depth of about seven hundred feet from the surface. It is said to surge from various parts of the mine, at the rate of about two hundred gallons an hour, but in slender streams.

This mine, or colliery, called the MOIRA, being three miles from the town, the water could not be made available at or very near the spot; although, on its very first coming to light, it suggested by its marked and predominant taste, to those who first noticed it, the probability of its being endowed with medicinal virtues.

That taste is strongly saline; and the water indeed differs little from that of the ordinary brine-springs which, as we shall see presently, abound in that saliferous belt of land, connected in part with coal-fields, which crosses England in a diagonal direction, from N.E. to S.W., embracing, among other places, those about to be noticed in the succeeding chapter.

In this view of the case, I am inclined to place the mineral water at Ashby between the Woodhall Spa water and that of Tenbury Well, which will be hereafter described. The taste, however, is more intensely briny, and more decidedly bitter. I had some of the water sent to me on my return to London, and made good use of it, not only in experimenting its effects on my own constitution, but by requesting three or four courageous friends to give it a trial also.

When I look at the printed analyses of this powerful mineral water, I am sadly puzzled which to adopt as the correct one. By referring to the general table at the end of this volume, it will be seen that I have adopted Dr. Ure's analysis; but I have also stated that Dr. Thomson differs from him, in more respects than one, as to the constituents of the water. Professor Daubeny, too, who in 1829 discovered bromine in it, and published his researches in the " Philosophical Transactions of 1830," is at variance

· with Ure's experiments ; and lastly, in a " Guide of Ashby-de-la-Zouch," published in 1831, I find another analysis, which, in respect to one ingredient alone, the muriate of soda or common salt, differs from Dr. Ure in not less than 1796 grains and a half—a difference certainly not to be accounted for by the one analysis referring to a wine gallon, and the other analysis to an imperial gallon, of the water.

Equally do the two last-named analyses differ in the proportion of another ingredient ; one which, in my long experience of mineral water, I consider of so much importance, that on its being present in a larger or smaller proportion, depends, in my opinion, some of the most salient virtues of the water. I allude to the muriate of magnesia—a medicine with which I have obtained the most unlooked-for success in obstinate cases of dyspepsia, and other complaints of the digestive functions.

Well, then, in reference to this identical and important ingredient (and the reader of the " Spas of Germany" will bear in mind that it is principally on account of its presence in the Pullna, that I first recommended and made more general in England the use of that water now so much employed in London), Dr. Ure's and the analysis in the Ashby Guide are at variance by at least 190 grains in the gallon of water ! Who are we to trust to ?

Dr. Ure's analysis seems to be the one adopted on the spot ; for it is distributed at the baths, printed on a card ; while the one inserted in the Guide-book has not even a name attached to it as an authority ; unless, indeed, we are to surmise, from something stated in his preface by the editor, that Dr. Kennedy, the very estimable and respected physician at Ashby, vouches for its accuracy.

Be that as it may, every one interested in the question of mineral waters, and of the potent one at Ashby, which certainly, judging from its apparent physical and salient characters, deserves the attention of the profession, will re-

K 2

gret that such discrepancy should exist on the subject of the
intimate constitution of that water. In such a conjuncture
they cannot but form a wish that the plan I suggested in reference to several other mineral springs, the analysis of which
was doubtful before, may be adopted,—namely, of having a
fresh examination of the water instituted by a well-known
chemist *intimately acquainted with, and constantly employed
in*, the difficult art of analyzing mineral waters. And I
would suggest for that purpose, either M. Schweitzer, of
Brighton, whose elaborate analysis of sea-water I have already alluded to; or Mr. West, of Leeds, the gentleman
who so ably and scientifically analyzed an analogous water
to that of Ashby, and the water of Woodhall Spa.

As there are no gaseous ingredients mentioned in any
of the already published analyses, it is likely that none
exist, and in that case the Ashby water might with due care
be transmitted to either of those chemists for a fresh examination. At all events, I must repeat that, with such
glaring and very important variations as now exist in the
several accounts of the water under consideration, it is quite
impossible that a medical practitioner can recommend the
use of it with sufficient confidence.

The Ashby water is used principally for bathing. A few
drink it, in which case it is invariably mixed with warm
water. I have stated that the spring is at a distance from the
town. The water therefore is brought from the Moira mine
in carts or tanks, to the boats on the canal, and is thence
conveyed on a truck to a large reservoir at the baths.

These, which are called " IVANHOE BATHS," (probably because the Great Wizard of the North, in his interesting novel
of Ivanhoe, alludes to a castle in which Prince John held his
high festival, and which is supposed to have been the Castle
of Ashby-de-la-Zouch), were erected in 1826, after the design, and under the direction of an architect of the town,
Mr. Robert Chaplin, who erected likewise the   handsome

hotel which stands contiguous to the pleasure-grounds, and at a short distance south-west of the baths. Both buildings are of freestone, and of the Doric order.

I never descended into the mine to examine the locality from which the mineral-water springs, neither am I prepared from personal knowledge to make any observation upon the several appliances of this Spa; but as a lady, a patient of mine, who was directed to proceed to Ashby for her health last year, has supplied me in her letters with the best information that any person likely to go to the same Spa could desire, inasmuch as it can be depended upon as impartial and accurate, I prefer, with her kind permission, letting her speak, in justice to the parties interested in the establishment.

" I directed my course to this place, and I am very much obliged to you for having fixed on so beautiful and comfortable a resting-place. The hotel is surrounded by grounds, well laid out with walks in all directions, and the baths are adjoining. The former is a very handsome building, capable of accommodating a very large number of visiters, and admirably arranged. My apartments are in a corner of the house, quiet and cheerful, and so comfortable am I, that I shall certainly prolong my stay here. The baths, which consist of six bathing-rooms, and corresponding dressing-rooms for the ladies, with two waiting-rooms, on one side, and an equal number of bath-rooms for the gentlemen, besides a large cold swimming-bath and billiard-room on the other side, are kept in the best order. In the centre is a well furnished pump-room, used sometimes as a ball-room, fifty-two feet by twenty-seven, and is surmounted by a dome.

" The house is full all the summer and autumn ; but not in the winter. Residents in it may dine at the public table, and take all their repasts in that way, for five shillings per day, besides paying for servants; and half a guinea a week for a bed-room ; together with from ten to fifteen shillings more for a private sitting-room, if required. This hotel consists of a handsome hall, with parlours; a gallery above, round the house, with rooms; and an upper story of the same kind: excellent beds; and I was as comfortable as at my own home, without the trouble of *keeping order*. The house stands out of the town, has a varied prospect around it (the ruins of the castle, a beautiful object, included), and is altogether a desirable *séjour*. Indeed I have been much pleased, and met with great civility."

I may add that the charges for bathing are very moderate, and that almost every form of baths can of course be obtained at the establishment.

The Moira or Ashby water, taken internally, will act as an effectual aperient if drank early in the morning in the dose of a large glass mixed with warm water, the proportion of the Moira being about $\frac{1}{4}$ or $\frac{1}{3}$ of the whole. As an alterative, a wine-glassful of the same mixture of Moira and warm water, drank two or three times a day, will be of service. Some have it fetched, and drink it at home, others prefer going to the pump-room.

Many very striking cases of internal disease were mentioned as having been cured by the internal use of the water, as well as of rheumatic and paralytic affections, by immersion in the water tepid, sometimes by warm-bathing, and at others by warm spunging of the body with the water. A case which had made great sensation at the time, was that of Lady C——y, who recovered entirely under the use of this water; and I have been informed, that the Rev. Dr. Evans, head-master of the school at Market Bosworth, was in possession of the particulars of a case of recovery even more striking.

In bathing, the water occasions a sensation of itching, and often produces so much exhaustion at the time, that restoratives and rest are required before the patient can return home. But after that has subsided, much vigour returns.

The Moira water is never heated, as it would throw down its salt. When a hot or a warm bath is required, plain boiling water is added in adequate proportions. It is hardly necessary to explain that the water has received the name of *Moira* from the circumstance of the Earl of Moira, Marquess of Hastings, being the lord of the manor, and principal proprietor in the place.

Ashby has the further advantage of being well located, of enjoying very pure air, and of being surrounded by beautiful drives, and many noblemen's seats, houses, gardens, and parks, among which Calke Abbey and Melbourne Hall deserve particularly to be mentioned.

Whilst on a visit at Colonel W——'s, in one of the prettiest parts of Yorkshire, during my northern tour, I conversed with not fewer than three persons, two ladies and a gentleman, visiters like myself, who, upon learning my errand, of one accord strongly recommended my examining a mineral water in Warwickshire, the name of which even had never come to my knowledge. It was said to be of the same nature as the one at Harrogate, and the place to have, of late, become much frequented as an incipient Spa. The individuals here alluded to had, each in his or her separate case, derived great benefit from the water in question, and all agreed in stating, that although they had not been able to bear the sulphur water at Harrogate, to which they had been recommended, they had felt no inconvenience whatever from the water at Willoughby new baths, or

WILLOUGHBY SPA.

Learning, therefore, one day, as I drove into Rugby, that I was in the vicinity of the place, I engaged a light carriage at the Spread Eagle in that smart little town, to carry me thither.

Before I took my departure, however, I wished to indulge myself with a well-pondered survey of as much of the exterior of the new Gothic building of the famed grammar-school of Rugby as its position would allow. Internally, I knew I should have nothing of interest to see, judging from the interior of Eton and Winchester and Westminster colleges, with which I am acquainted, and in which one looks in vain for any of those decorations, appliances, and accessories which enrich so much most of the colleges at the two universities, and the two catholic establishments of Stonyhurst and St. Mary's Oscott.

As a seat of learning, indeed, under the auspices of its present highly-esteemed head-master, so well known among the admirers of classical knowledge and English literature, I am aware that I should have found the interior redolent with scholastic lore; but as I look for something else in collegiate life, connected with discipline, the formation of character, and the means adopted both to bring out the good and hidden qualities of some, and to repress the precocious and obtrusive evil propensities of others—which *something else* I knew is rarely to be met with in English colleges—I purposely avoided a visit within doors.

This new Gothic structure, I well remember, made some noise when it was completed a short time back. I neither recollect, nor did I inquire for, the name of its architect. From the street which faces the gateway, the building looks insignificant, and of no great extent. But it gains upon the observer as he walks along its exterior, keeping it on his left till the chapel comes in view, and, by continuing round the latter, bringing the open playground in sight, with its ancient and lofty trees, and garden-front. The latter, from the variety of its several parts, including the said chapel on the left, and the body of the building with its turreted portion on the right, forms altogether a picturesque group. There is much merit in the edifice; but for size, elevation, position, and importance, the new college of St. Mary, at Oscott, leaves this of Rugby far behind.

Judging from the little I saw (though I professed not to

form an opinion), I should imagine that the general discipline within these walls is not unlike what is met with in other similar institutions in this country, with some of which I am acquainted, namely, that much liberty is permitted to the pupils, who, provided they strictly attend to their studies, are left to learn by experience only the most eligible mode of acquiring the knowledge of how to live in this world with our fellow-men. In the very entrance or porch of the college, some of the scholars were " roughing it" or were playing at ball; while others, mere striplings, kept going in and out at full leisure and uncontrolled, bent on exhibiting themselves to advantage in the street of humble Rugby, by assuming the airs of dandies! On the play-ground, too, a great number of pupils of all ages were scattered and engaged in various ways, who seemed to be unwatched by any under-masters.

The road I took on my way to the new baths of Willoughby leads first to Dunchurch, and passes in front of Bilton Grange, once the residence of the purest writer of his time, Addison. Dunchurch itself lies on the eastern extremity of Dunsmore Heath, and the road thence to Willoughby Baths is through an open country, highly cultivated, looking at the time as green and fresh, though we were approaching November, as if it had been in the summer months. Scarcely a leaf had fallen, and none but the loftiest poplars were tipped with the golden hue of Autumn. Extensive pasture lands, dotted with cattle, stretched on the right and left of the road.

With all the appearance of wealth, which may be supposed to spring from a territory of such marked fertility, the soil being in general of the best description, the labourers' cottages in villages, and those which every now and then I noticed by the road-side, are the very emblems of poverty. Some are of clay, or of mud and brick-rubbish mixed, others of mud only, or of rough stone and timber. They are thatched, but the thatch is old, and in many parts decayed. Their walls are generally limed over, but the surface is broken and in patches. Such is precisely the appearance of Willoughby village, which is an assemblage of mud hovels and dilapidated cottages.

In the north, the proprietor of the gig one hires to travel in, or his son, or his hostler,—who usually drives you, and is not unfrequently a labourer besides, well acquainted with his own district,—helps you in your expedition with what he knows, if you will but properly question him : he is an index-post of great use if you will but peruse it fitly. But in these midland counties a gig conveyance is a sort of *half* posting, at a shilling a mile, with a *whole* postilion, who never knows any thing. Of all the classes of people travellers have to do with on the road, none is possessed of so little local information as your " boy," young or old, no matter which. " What is the name of that hill just there?"—" I don't know."—" Who lives in that fine building through that handsome gate, and at the end of that fine avenue?"—" Why it belongs to Squire ——, dear me, I forgets the name :"—and so on; no matter on what tack you put him, he will be sure not to answer the helm.

The way to the baths from the village is by a rough unmade road, or narrow lane, and across some fields towards the only part of the surrounding country, which presents the least appearance of a hill.

I stood now before the well, from which the water so much extolled by my Yorkshire friends is drawn. Honest Mr. Longstaff, who presented the appearance of a village schoolmaster, but who, as the proprietor of the premises, most cordially did the honours of his modest abode, in which he was as cordially aided by his respectable-looking helpmate, soon entered into an account of the manner in which the water was accidentally discovered about forty years ago—a manner so natural that it cannot interest my readers. He next proceeded to uncover the well to show me its depth, and the nature of the soil round the shaft.

The water stands at the depth of fifty feet from the surface, to which level it has been known to remain constantly, even on the days in which more than twenty baths had been served. The original borings, which were made in search of potable water, extended to 100 feet without detecting any, but two feet beyond that, the mineral water burst forth, and ascended to the pre-stated level.

Mr. Longstaff purchased the property, and let the well, but lost the rent, and now has taken it into his own hands.

I lowered my thermometer into the well, and found the temperature of the water to be 48° of Fahrenheit. On testing it with acetate of lead the presence of sulphureted hydrogen was immediately detected, but the quantity is small. Not wishing to judge of the water obtained by pumping, which is here also performed foolishly through leaden pipes, I had some of it drawn in my presence from the bottom of the well in a jug. Its taste is very pleasantly saltish, but has none of that bitterish *après goût* which indicates the presence of either the muriate of magnesia or of lime, or both. It is agreeable to the taste when drank cold, and feels soft to the palate. The most squeamish may drink it without disgust, in spite of the presence of sulphur.

My impression at the moment was, that the water is in *reality* what one of the springs of Leamington is *pretended* to be—a genuine sulphureted saline, suitable to the most delicate constitutions—well adapted, above all, for female constitutions, and also in certain maladies of children attended by the smallest suspicion of scrofula or worms, or accompanied by cutaneous eruptions.

Its being pleasant to drink is a very great recommendation; and in that respect it is superior to the strongest waters at Harrogate. It seems likewise to sit well on the stomach; and I feel disposed to think, from the little personal experience I have had, that, drank early in the morning with a small portion of plain boiling water—just enough to warm it —this sulphureted saline will prove sufficiently active as a purgative—one of the first, I may say the principal quality that a mineral water should possess, in order successfully to combat chronic or inveterate diseases.

In every respect I feel disposed to think that the Willoughby Spa water would prove superior as a remedial agent to some other springs in the neighbourhood, which have acquired a certain degree of renown, though not endowed with such *primâ facie* advantages as seem to belong to this place. I say *primâ facie* only, because the chemical analysis of the water itself has either never been made, or is so indifferent that it is never mentioned — at least to my knowledge. Mr. Longstaff had it not, and with some difficulty could I make the good lady of the well comprehend that a knowledge of the precise ingredients of the water was necessary before one could recommend it.

" Why so?" would the honest dame reply. " We know that it has done and is doing an immense deal of good to sick people—that it has cured Mr. *this* and Lady *that*, and the clegyman of our neighbouring parish, and that it has been recommended by the doctors at Northampton and Daventry, and even Warwick in spite of Leamington; and such being the case, where is the use of scrutinizing farther?"

Her lord, however, who had culled a bit of science in his intercourse with the world, soon understood the importance of my suggestion, and on my assuring him that an analysis by a reputed chemist would not be very expensive, he agreed to have it done.   Whether he has or not, and whether this last season has proved to him, by an encouraging increase in the number of bathers, that it is for his interest to attend to that suggestion, as well as to the many others which I took the liberty of giving him for the formation of a Spa, such as patients of any importance could visit and remain at,—I have not had the opportunity of ascertaining.

The place, as I saw it, wants every thing to make it fit to receive visiters. And as I contend that the water should be used as an internal remedy in preference to bathing in it—to which latter use it seems principally to have been confined—it is evident that many more people would attend, were there any accommodations besides the few neat little rooms in the dwelling-house of Mr. and Mrs. Long-staff.

The back of this house is to the south, and very pretty. In the horizon rises Staverton-hill due south. Shuckburgh (the name of which reminded me of that *naïve* correspondence between the lady of Sir Francis, who resides at this villa, and a fashionable daughter-in-law of a duke, which appeared in all the papers after its first publication in an able Sunday tory journal) lies to the left of Staverton. The grounds appeared in beautiful order, and the view is delightful. Opposite is the village of Flecknoe. All these places so seen are on the borders of Northamptonshire, like Willoughby itself, which is the first village within the line of Warwickshire. The highest ground about this district is seen from Mr. Longstaff's house, distant from the last-mentioned miserable village about a mile.

There is, not far from the house, an inn which had not yet been licensed, nor had it any accommodations at present; therefore visiters must secure board and lodging under Mr. Longstaff's hospitable roof.

The Lemm, a small insignificant brook, dignified as a river when it proceeds through Leamington, is close to the end of a large field to the south of the house, and in that direction we find a better approach to Willoughby Baths.

By it I took my departure towards Southam, on my way to Leamington, passing between Lower Shuckburgh and Napton, and crossing the Oxford canal not fewer than three times.

At the Craven Arms, in the market-place at Southam, an excellent inn, by the bye, I changed my vehicle, and, passing through a country tolerably green and full of trees for the distance of nine miles, but totally devoid of interest, I reached at length the king of the English Spas of the present day.

CHAPTER VII.

THE SALT-WELLS.—TENBURY.

The two Rival Spas—A Halt among Salt Springs—" Lady Wood's
Saline"—Taste, Appearance, and other Physical Characters of the
Water—Its Analysis—Advantages in Glandular Diseases—Absurd
Eulogiums—A Case of Cure—Accommodation—Approach to Dudley
—The Castle and the Cave—Commercial Inns—*Commis Voyageurs*—
French and English "travellers"—A Jolly Party—Sad Statistics—
A Blazing Atmosphere—Effects on Health—Mr. Murchison and the
Silurian System—His Opinion of the Origin of Mineral Waters—
Admanston and Salt-Moor Springs—Sir Humphry Davy's Analysis—
Dr. Lloyd of Ludlow—Tewkesbury and Droitwich—Tenbury Well
—Discovery and First Analysis—The Author's Visit and Opinion—
Road from Worcester—Lucky Farmers—The Ward Estates—Farmer
Chillingworth—Prince Lucien of Cannino.—Examination of Tenbury
Well by the Author—Its Geology—Experiments—Taste and other
Characters of the Water—Discrepant Analyses—A Fresh One Recom-
mended and Accomplished—Iodine Discovered—The Effect on the
Constitution—What is Iodine?—Disease cured by Tenbury Water—
The Spa quite in its Infancy—Every thing remains to be done.

As I am approaching the confines of the two most fashionable watering-places in England—the two rival spas of the
present day—Leamington and Cheltenham, my desire to
hasten thither becomes every moment stronger. The reader
who has kindly accompanied me so far through my excursion,
is probably even more impatient than myself to repair with
me to those renowned resorts of invalids and idlers, in order
to ascertain how far their rapidly-acquired reputation be a
just one, and upon what grounds it may be founded.

Yet, even with all these considerations, I must crave the
further delay of one chapter, and the indulgence of dedicating

it to the brief description of part of a group of mineral springs or wells which dot a curious, though by no means extensive district, from Dudley to Ludlow, and which embrace the Dudley Wells, Droitwich, Tewksbury, Admanston Spa, the Moor-Spring, and Tenbury.

It is necessary to clear the ground before us of two or three of these minor mineral springs, ere we proceed to treat of the more important ones in and about the same counties; inasmuch as the consideration of the latter, which it imports my readers to see fully discussed, may derive additional interest and light from the succinct information it is my intention to bring forward respecting the former.

When I say that the springs of which we are about to speak are minor ones, I do not refer to their chemical constitution, and the probable medical powers possessed through it; for in those respects they are probably far above in value those of Leamington and Cheltenham. But I call them minor, or of less importance, because they are either not employed at all, or very little, for the purposes of an ordinary spa, Tenbury excepted. The excursion is not a long one, and may be considered as episodical to our work. We shall afterwards return to Birmingham, and having taken a rapid survey of that neighbourhood, proceed on our road to the great Spa on the Lemm.

My steps were first directed to the

SALT WELLS,

near Dudley, which have since been distinguished by the euphonous title of " Lady Wood's Saline Spa."

The approach from Dudley, distant about two miles and a half south, is down a steep hill into a valley, and through a vast extent of coal-pits, all at work, presenting the same dreadful appearance as at Wolverhampton, Newcastle, Durham, and Bradford, with hundreds of heaps of coke burning, and a suffocating sulphurous atmosphere hovering above and around them.

The way is rough, tortuous, and difficult. It crosses the Dudley-canal, and at the distance of two miles and a half, as before stated, a gate for carriages and a turnstile for foot-passengers lead through a dell or gill down into a hollow, where the said Lady Wood's Saline Spa is found.

It is but a poor concern at present. The well, from which the mineral water is pumped by an ordinary pump, is covered over; and a small building had just been erected, like a cottage, by the side of it, with two indifferent looking bath-rooms. The supply of water is not plentiful, being about twenty hogsheads in a day only.

The water is clear, its taste is strongly salt, with a degree of bitterness so marked, though not unpleasant, that it will linger a long time on the palate. Its temperature, I ascertained to be 50° of Fahrenheit. Mr. Cooper, the London chemist, has found by an accurate analysis, which is printed and circulated at the Spa, 80 grains, and a little more than half a grain besides of saline ingredients, in the dry state—that is, without any water of crystalization. In a wine-pint of the mineral water, nearly fifty grains of that quantity are of common salt, nineteen are muriate of lime, and seven and a half muriate of magnesia. There is both a muriate and a carbonate of iron, making altogether a grain and a fraction; but neither iodine nor bromine has been found in the water.

From this it will be seen that as a chemical compound, the Lady Wood's Saline Spa presents a combination of ingredients, endowed with considerable discutient power, and might be employed with success in the treatment of glandular and scrofulous affections, provided they are not at their stage of inflammation. It cannot, however, be expected to act as an aperient, still less as a purgative, and so far it could hardly be employed without the aid of some other medicine which forms, in my opinion, a great drawback to the employment of mineral waters, and consequently to be avoided if possible.

In conceding thus far a decided and specific action on disease to the Salt-wells Water of Dudley, I do not mean to encourage the pompous and absurd eulogium inserted in the printed paper which gives its analysis, and where it is stated that the water had been recommended by the analyser himself, and all the eminent physicians in the neighbourhood, " as one of the best mineral waters in the kingdom, for almost *every disease* incident to the human body."

An honest and intelligent tradesman of Birmingham, whom I met in this expedition, and who was certainly not an interested party, assured me that the water had acquired more celebrity for the cure of weakness of limbs and palsy, than for any thing else. As a proof, he related the case of a friend of his who had suffered under a paralytic stroke, by which he was at once deprived of motion and vision on one side of the body, as well as of the power of speech, whereby he became totally unable to attend to business. He applied to this Spa, where he took several warm-baths, and drank some of the water for three weeks, at the end of which time he was completely restored. Yet the poor man had, in the first instance, tried every medical advice and means, including electricity, without any effect, and to the serious detriment of his scanty purse.

The spot or hollow in which the well-house stands, is surrounded by wood. The Salt-well Inn, at Netherton, perched on the top of a hill, and looking down upon the Spa, is the only house of accommodation for visiters I could perceive in the neighbourhood.

Ere I proceeded farther I deemed it necessary, on my return from the well, to halt at Dudley, in order to rest and refresh my horse for a couple of hours ; and this I did at the second best inn in the town, a sort of commercial house.

How interesting, by the bye, is the approach to Dudley from Birmingham, barring all the iniquities of burning coal-fields and iron furnaces! A series of hills appears in view before the traveller as he journeys onward, on the summit of one of the principal knolls of which peers Dudley Castle, in picturesque ruins; while upon another hill, much further on the left, the distant church of Netherton rises conspicuously. The sloping sides of the Castle Hill are covered with wood, into which the public is admitted, with Lord Ward's permission, for the purpose of walking, and examining a celebrated cave.

I have already had occasion to mention how convenient I had found it, in my travels through the country, where I was not personally known, to take up my abode at a commercial inn, and enjoy the advantages, privileges, and solid comforts of commercial travellers, in the room especially set apart for them. My modest equipage had indeed all that was required in its appearance to favour my scheme, which was still further promoted by the mode of conveyance I so often adopted " the single horse *chay* ;"—and the perpetual pulling out of my desk, to scribble away my notes, settle accounts, and arrange bills, on the commercial-room table, had also a knowing air of business.

Almost every country in Europe has that class of people whom in this country we call " commercial travellers." France had, at one time, not fewer than six or seven species of *commis voyageurs*, one or two of whom only, the *voyageur libre* and the *voyageur à commission*, resembled most the " commercial traveller" of England, emphatically so called. Since the *messageries* and *voitures accélérées*, however, have placed Paris and other great commercial cities within an easy reach of the provincial shopkeepers, all these commission travellers have disappeared, and none but the lowest in rank remain, which is little removed from that of a common pedlar.

Not so in England, for here commercial travellers are still

personages of importance, and far from dwindling in number; they have, on the contrary, rapidly increased, and like
rank grass, multiplied to such an extent, that it is no uncommon thing to hear, now-a-days, a modest shopkeeper in
a small county-town say, that " one sees nothing in the streets
but dogs and commercial travellers."

Nor is this all; for while multiplying in number, they
have also assumed, if not acquired, an air of increased importance in their own estimation, which is never so readily
acknowledged or assented to by any one, as by the
three classes of people following,—the smart, will-o'-the-
wisp-moving, coffee-room maid, who waits on them at table,
and has a wink for this one, and a pet word for that other,
so as to keep them all in good humour; the demure lass
who, brass-candlestick in hand, lights them to their chamber;
and lastly, the hostler, who washes their gig, and takes care
of their nags, after the "traveller" himself has peered into
the manger to ascertain that the corn is there.

When I entered the commercial room at Dudley, it was on
a Sunday, and at vesper time. Every one belonging to the
town was at evening service; but here I beheld around the
centre table, which, for the sake of greater snuggery, had been
pushed close to the fire, a merry party of four young men,
of the class just described, who, being at dessert, cracked as
many dry nuts as dry jokes, and drank bumpers of port to
" our noble selves." At the end of an hour the time of
reckoning came, and my jolly *fellow* commercial travellers,
who had, I must say, often tempted me with their invitation
to join in a glass, and who, from their attire in the tip-top
style of fashion, might have been mistaken for independent
gentlemen,—paid their eighteen shillings a-piece, like real
gentlemen, and took their departure, *cigare en bouche,* " for
a lark out of doors."

" Surely," said I to myself, " these people must be driving
a fine trade, to be able to afford themselves this sort of ex-

pensive mimicking of their betters. Do they or their masters suffer? Is not this another example of the miserable effect which the immense distance now existing between the industrious and the easy classes of society, (strongly marked by the excess of luxury displayed by the latter), cannot fail to produce;—namely, the creation among the former, (whose poverty appears only the more conspicuous by the contrast,) of either a strong feeling of envy, which ends in murmurs and discontent, or a desire to imitate the extravagances of their superiors, which must terminate in ruin and a prison?"

Judging from the sad statistics proclaimed by the chief magistrate of London in 1839, at a dinner given in support of the funds of the "Society of Commercial Travellers," the probability of the last-mentioned lamentable results in regard to that class of people, seems no longer problematical. His lordship upon that occasion stated, that the total amount of money paid by the Society to members who had declared on the funds for the year was 11,109*l.*, and to the families 8866*l.*; while the money received by the Society from members was only 3272*l.* As to the number of claimants that had been relieved by the sums in question, they were not fewer than 1118, and consisted of 362 members, 319 widows, 384 children, and 53 orphans!

Misfortune and ill-health may doubtless be admitted as two of the acting causes of such distressing results; but that extravagance in squandering present gains, and improvidence in not securing for themselves or families the needful succour on a rainy day, by subscribing to the Society's funds while the sunshine was abroad, must be failings of no ordinary frequency among commercial travellers, is proved by the numbers recited at the Mansion-house, and illustrated on a small scale by my little adventure in the commercial room at Dudley.

It behoves me to state, after having laid such stress on

the awful appearance and condition of the atmosphere throughout the whole region of blazing fires I had just been traversing, and which resembled a large town burning to the ground, that in no part of that district, without exception, did I notice the smallest vestige of any ill effect produced by such a dense and sulphureous atmosphere, either on the young or the middle-aged of both sexes; all of whom, on the contrary, appeared healthy and with a good complexion, while many were well-looking and had a pleasing countenance.

After this example, and that of Bradford described in the first volume, who shall venture to say aught against the heavy and smoky air of our great Babylon, in point of salubrity?

———————————

Being on my way to Tenbury, there to examine a recently-discovered well of briny water, the recent analyses of which, by Professors Brande and Daubeny, had been communicated to me by the proprietor, I felt desirous of making myself acquainted with the most recent facts and theories respecting this class of mineral springs, which in Worcestershire particularly (on the borders of which Tenbury is seated), and in Shropshire as well as Cheshire, have attracted considerable attention on the part of the physical geologist.

For this purpose I had recourse to that very elaborate and important work of R. I. Murchison, Esq., which treats of a series of rocks that had not been classified by geologists before him, occupying a definite place in the general stratification of this island, and first seen and studied by that author, in that part of England and Wales which Tacitus states to have been inhabited by the *Silures,* and hence called *Siluria.*

To this system or group of rocks, which previous writers, speaking of some of the oldest deposits of the earth's crust, (among which those rocks are to be found), had not separated into particular formations, Mr. Murchison has affixed the distinguishing appellation of *Silurian:* for how could he have described in an intelligible manner objects that had either been confounded with others by the geologists who preceded him, or had not been properly picked out from the rest, and classed,—unless he had previously and collectively defined them by a distinct generic denomination ?

Obliged, by a similar consideration, to find distinguishing appellations for the subdivisions of his new group of rocks, the same Author has followed the example of old Father Smith, the late eminent practical Scarborough geologist, in his mode of subdividing another group of rocks of distinct geological structure in England, called the *Oolitic.* For this purpose Mr. Murchison has borrowed from the names of the localities in which the particular subdivisions of his silurian group appeared more conspicuous, the distinguishing denominations he has assigned to them. These sub-divisions, of which he admits four, he has called *formations*, in obedience to the practice of geological writers ; and the way in which he has distinguished them has been by adopting a corresponding topographical prefix : thus—1, The Ludlow; 2, Wenlock; 3, Caradoc ; and 4, the Llandeilo formation.

But as these *formations* cannot always be very distinctly separated the one from the other (for No. 1 and 2 will occasionally appear as if forming a whole, and so will No. 3 and 4), our author has adopted the terms of " upper silurian rocks" to denote No. 1 and 2 together, and " lower silurian rocks," to denote the two other numbers combined.

It is farther to be observed that each of these sub-divisions is characterized by the presence of a corresponding series of organic remains.

I trust I have made myself understood to the generality of my readers, and to those of the fair sex in particular who may not be conversant with geology, by giving them, without any display of learning, or many technical terms, with which unfortunately modern geology is *hérissée*,—a succinct and plain description of a work, containing a series of geological researches which, in one point of view, bears on the subject of my present chapter, and on that of my volumes generally. Such a work, and so recent too, could not be passed over in silence in a publication on the mineral waters of England, particularly where they seem blended with the silurian system. That work has excited the most lively interest in the scientific world of this and other countries; nor is it too much to say, that from the industry which seems to have presided over its execution, not less than from the splendour of the unrivalled map, and other illustrations by which it is accompanied, Mr. Murchison's volume has stamped his fame as a philosophical as well as practical geologist of no ordinary character.

In regard to myself I only hope I have not done him injustice by my brief *résumé* of the intention of his work, or misapprehended his meaning.

Well then—Mr. Murchison has taken occasion, in the work in question, to discuss the subject of mineral springs whenever they occur in his silurian region; and in so doing he has set an example worthy of imitation to his contemporary geological writers, who seldom condescend to take that subject into consideration, as I have shewn in speaking of thermal springs and telluric heat in a former publication.

The springs principally noticed by Mr. Murchison are some of those to which allusion was made at the commencement of the present chapter, namely salt or briny springs; among which I had selected for a particular description those of Admaston, two miles from Wellington in a north-western direction, and of Saltmoor, two miles from Ludlow in a south-eastern direction.

Unfortunately, the death of a respected fellow-practitioner, Dr. Du Gard, of Shrewsbury, on whose accurate knowledge of Admaston Spa, and personal assistance in examining it myself, I had depended, occurred just at the time of my intended visit, and prevented the accomplishment of my

wishes. As a spa, however, Admaston is entirely neglected.

Tewkesbury New Spa and the briny sources at Droitwich
would equally claim a notice in this place, as being important
members of the group of " Salt-springs" referred to in the
introductory part of this chapter. But in neither case is
their rank as mineral watering-places such as to call for, in
a publication like the present, more than a passing record of
their existence.

With regard to the SALTMOOR spring, the facts alone of its
having been once a place of great resort for invalids (though
never in the style of our modern spas) and of its water having
been analyzed by the first chemical philosopher of this country, the late Sir Humphrey Davy, are sufficient reasons for
my more extended introduction of the subject.

Mr. Murchison, in noticing this spring, and after having
quoted an old and rough estimate of its component parts
made by Dr. Lloyd of Ludlow, proceeds to frame an ingenious theory as to the origin of the water. I know not how
far we may be warranted in classing it with the Salt-springs,
as its name implies. Its real composition,—notwithstanding
two analyses, the one said to have been made by Sir Humphrey Davy, but most unfortunately mislaid by its proprietor,
Mr. Charlton, and the other quoted by Mr. Murchison—is not
truly known; inasmuch as the latter has since been declared
by its author to have been inaccurate, as may be seen from
the following extract of a letter from Dr. Lloyd, of Ludlow,
with which I was favoured in January, 1840, in reply to
inquiries I took the liberty of making respecting the spring
in question.

" The analysis quoted in Mr. Murchison's work, was made
by me many years since ; but with too much haste and, I
fear, inaccuracy to be depended upon. Since I have been
favoured with your letter I have again examined the water.
The result of this examination varies considerably from the

statement quoted by Mr. Murchison; indeed I believe the water has undergone considerable change. It has not now a trace of sulphureted hydrogen, with which it once abounded. Its salts at present consist of *muriate of soda,* with sulphate of soda, and carbonate as well as sulphate of iron.

" I consider it a very safe and efficient chalybeate, possessing also mild aperient properties in the quantity of a pint. It was in high local repute a few years ago; but probably owing to its distance from the town (two miles), it is not now so much frequented, though in my opinion it possesses qualities of high value, and I have no doubt it would be much resorted to were proper accommodations to be met with on the spot.

"The spring rises in the midst of scenery of singular beauty and variety, and has certainly advantages in this respect over any Spa in the kingdom."

I have allowed Dr. Lloyd to speak for himself for the information of my readers, as I have not seen the spring; although my researches into another much more important source to be presently described, had called me to within five miles of the place. But at that time I had neither read Mr. Murchison's work, nor received Dr. Lloyd's letter, and consequently was perfectly ignorant of the existence of Saltmoor Spa.

Judging from Dr. Lloyd's more recent account, then, it would seem that the Spa must not be considered as of the same class of that near Dudley, or of those at Droitwich, and Tewkesbury—all briny springs, and as such very important. But as Dr. Lloyd has not made a quantitative analysis of the water, that point must remain for the present undecided.

Tenbury, on the contrary, which is the well I have just alluded to when speaking of my journey to the immediate neighbourhood of Ludlow, a twelvemonth since, is a decided briny-spring, closely allied to the salt-spring near Dudley, though much more potent, for reasons which will presently appear ; and I had hoped, therefore, to be able to trace, in a successive line from Dudley to Ludlow, a regular stratum of the briny element in a south-western direction; as unquestionably there exists a continuous one in Worcestershire in a line southwards from Dudley.

Mr. Murchison thinks, if I understand him correctly, that the great subterranean store-house of rock-salt and briny-springs in England, is the red marl, or the upper member of the new red sandstone, though he has shewn us that many other deposits are also saliferous.*

THE TENBURY WELL.

This is another of the many mineral waters which the occasion of my inquiry into the Spas of England is likely to bring into public notice, and which, if properly managed, may be converted into a Spa of considerable importance.

As the well is but of recent discovery, and must be wholly unknown to the generality of my readers, I shall enter a little more minutely into the particular character and circumstances of the place than 1 have done with the rest of the group of springs forming the principal subject of the present chapter. Every thing is as yet in its infancy at Tenbury Well, although the mineral-water itself is perfect. But if the suggestions I took the liberty of making to the proprietor, and his declared determination to see them carried into effect, should hereafter be accomplished, and the mineral-water properly and judiciously employed, there can be no doubt as to the

* Mr. Murchison has recently proved that the red ground of northern Russia, in which so much rock-salt and so many salt-springs abound, is the *old red sandstone,* similar to this around Tenbury.

very great benefits that will result from the discovery of this well.

At the close of the year 1839, after my return from visiting most of the mineral springs of England, a gentleman called upon me, and placed in my hands two distinct analyses of a mineral-water which had been discovered in the summer of that year on his premises at Tenbury. The analyses had been executed by Professor Brande and Professor Daubeny. At the same time, a list of cases of disease which had already been benefited by the use of the water was communicated to me, including the instance of the recovery of the gentleman's own child, who, after drinking the water for a few days, expelled a number of lumbrici, five or six inches long, which I saw.

On inquiry I found that neither of the analyses had been made on the spot. Indeed, I suspected as much upon looking at the papers : for there was no mention made of any gaseous contents in the water.

As an additional reason for me to take notice of the newly-discovered spring at Tenbury, a letter from a most respectable physician, Dr. A. W. Davis, of Presteign, practising within twenty miles of that place, reached me soon after, vouching for the statements and representations already made on the subject. In consequence I was induced to run down to examine the well and its locality, and make every necessary inquiry into the real state of the case.

A distance of 133 miles in our days is nothing, and accordingly in a very few hours, thanks to railroads and quick coaches, I reached my destination. Yet not so quick but that I could, *more meo*, pick up a few notes by the way, on the country through which I travelled, the best part of which was new to me; and could also gather some information from a civil fellow-traveller or two.

Our line of road, after quitting Worcester, took the direction of the Abberley Hills, and on the left of the road was seen spreading what was once Lord Foley's, and is now Lord Ward's park, between Great and Little Whitley. There is an exceedingly pretty Italian lodge connected with the park; and I was informed also that the fresco paintings in Whitley church are celebrated. The park is screened from the north-west by the range of hills just mentioned.

A very intelligent farmer and his wife, who were journeying part of the same way, and seemed well acquainted with the neighbourhood, supplied me, very good naturedly, with as much information on many points of interest to me as I had time to inquire about. They stated that, in proceeding to Tenbury (of the fame of whose mineral spring they had but a recent and not very clear impression) by the line I had taken, I should find the road traversing a very pretty country as far as the hills, but one dreary enough beyond them, until within five miles of Tenbury; and such proved to be the case in reality.

I could not help noticing to my friend, the farmer, the state of the land right and left of the road, which had the appearance of good arable land. "Yes," said he, "it is good for barley and turnips. Wheat-land, just here about, you see little or none; but not far from hence, and in some parts, wheat-land will often produce as much as forty bushels an acre, which is by no means common in this country. Such land as that will let for thirty shillings an acre, while this which you see near us does not fetch as much as twenty. The general average, however, in this part of Worcestershire is twenty-five shillings. The facility of transporting the produce by the road and the Severn is a great help to good prices, as is also the vicinity of some principal towns, such as Dudley, Kidderminster, and Worcester. My honest informant admitted that, although within the last twenty years the English farmers had made several improvements in the

way of raising produce at a less expense, they were nevertheless still in the infancy of that important branch of agriculture ; and he was right.

Be it as it may, of such species of lands as are here
described, the Foley estate consisted, in the purchase of
which the trustees of the minor Lord Ward invested 800,000*l.*!
All the tenants on this vast estate are old and most respectable, having been upon it for a succession of generations. No marvel neither, if they pay but an average
rent of 1*l.* 5*s.* per acre, while they can raise forty bushels of
wheat on it, which they will sell in the market, at the average
price of the last many years, for 16*l.*, or 8*s.* a bushel !

What wonder then that Farmer Chillingworth, of Holt
Castle, which I beheld a little way off on my right, should
have become a rich man by renting six hundred such acres,
farmed by him in a way superior to that of any other farmer
in the neighbourhood, and penned with as many sheep, the
mere wool of which (when wool was not a drug, as it now is)
sufficed to pay his rents !

Farmer Chillingworth is a great personage in these parts,
as having risen from nothing to great wealth, through sheer
industry and perseverance, accompanied by honesty. He
keeps up the Castle as it formerly stood, spends little or no
money, goes to market himself and attends the audits, one
hundred of which he had been present at, when his health
was drank the year before. He is a bachelor, but has
sundry nieces to inherit his wealth. *Avviso ai poveri preti
della parocchia.*

Noblemen's and gentlemen's country residences were seen
on various points of the vast extent before us as we proceeded along, and my informant related that of such there
were many, and at one time of great consequence. Hardly
any of these, however, are now tenanted; and little or no
style is kept up in those that are. He well recollected the
time when a lad (and his portly dame nodded assent), that

at all the principal seats there was kept up a great state, and a stud of horses for the visiters.

My fellow-traveller seemed to make a distinction from his sweeping assertion in favour of Thorngrove, an ancient family-seat, near to which we passed before coming to Holt Castle. It stands on a slope, dressed as a park, and looks with its front to the north-east, the broad Severn running just below it. " There," said he, " there it was that Lucien, the brother of Napoleon Bonaparte, first resided when he was brought to this country, and the reputation he has left behind him was that of an exceedingly good man, charitable to the poor, quiet, gentlemanly, and clever. The general orders given to his domestic physician were, that he should see all the poor when sick, and supply them gratis with all necessary medicines. His departure occasioned much grief in the neighbourhood."

Alas ! he too is gone to his last account since this eulogium was, passed upon him by an honest and unsophisticated English yeoman, who, while pronouncing it, could not divine that his simple and feeling language in praise of the Prince of Canino found a response in the bosom of the person he then addressed. For that person had been well acquainted with the excellent qualities of the head and heart which distinguished the illustrious individual in question, and which were only second to those of another still more illustrious brother, the eldest of the same highly-destined family, whose days it has been my good fortune, under Providence, on one particular occasion to preserve. After having worn two diadems in the space of eight years, he too is come to spend, on the same free soil which Lucien had so long inhabited, the evening of his life, with unaffected resignation, and in the exercise of all the best virtues that can adorn the heart of man !

———

THE TENBURY WELL was discovered at the back of the

house of S. Holmes Godson, Esq. (brother of the member for
Kidderminster), who owns, in and about the place, considerable property, and seemed to me to be just the person
to encourage and promote in every legitimate manner the
success of a mineral water.

As usual, it was in searching for better potable water,
that the one charged with very marked mineral qualities was
detected. The hint of nature once given, every means was
adopted to profit by it. A shaft thirty feet deep was sunk,
three feet in diameter; it was lined with bricks down to the
water's edge, and the water was ascertained to be six feet
deep.

On my getting to the well I found that the water had
reached nearly to the top of it in the course of the night.
This phenomenon, I was informed, had occurred often before,
and the taste or sapid properties of the water were always
on such occasions impaired.

The examination of the situation of the well, and of the
ground in which the latter had been sunk, as well as of
the many specimens of rock dug out of it and preserved, satisfied me that upper, or land-springs, must inevitably pour their contents into the shaft, considering the dip
of the stratum in which the well is situated, and the nature
of that stratum. We were here standing on a part of the
old red system ; and judging from the first impression made
upon me by the mineral water, as well as by my own superficial observations around me, guided by what I had learned
in Mr. Murchison's book, I thought that we should find the
stratification of the well, below the fresh-water spring-beds,
(which here consisted of strong gravel super-imposed to blue
marl, the latter measuring somewhat more than ten feet, and
of a hard blue limestone, three inches thick, dipping from
S.E. to N.W.), to be red marl conglomerate, over a close
or compact cornstone, and below this other beds of the

old red sandstone, through some fissure of one or both of which last-mentioned rocks the mineral-water probably sprang.

A more minute examination of the well than had hitherto been instituted having been made soon afterwards, in consequence of my requesting that the well should be cleared of all its water, and secured from the land-springs, it was found that its geological arrangement corresponded exactly with the preceding supposition, thrown out and committed to writing by myself, on the spot.

The Tenbury well, therefore, is a briny spring belonging to the old red sandstone, in which the western part of Worcestershire abounds; but in the combination of its ingredienst, and particularly with reference to the presence of two new ones, which a fresh analysis has elicited, Tenbury water must, for the present at least, be considered as quite different from those found in that part of the country.

Having ordered the entire shaft to be exhausted of its upper water, down to five feet of water only in the well, I lowered the thermometer, and found the temperature to be 48°, that of the air being, at the time, 38° of Fahrenheit. The water, then drawn up, appeared turbid, but after resting a short time it became limpid. I could not find the smallest trace of sulphureted hydrogen gas; neither was there any disengagement of free carbonic acid from it, but I have since been told that it always sparkles now.

The taste is strongly salt, and bitter at the same time;— the bitterness continuing for a long period, but not so long as the taste of salt, which is the last to vanish. But this bitter taste is by no means disagreeable, is totally unlike the taste of a solution of common Epsom salts, and rather resembles that of Pullna water.

Immediately upon swallowing half a tumbler of the Tenbury

water, a disturbance, or rather commotion, is set up in the abdomen, which, upon a repetition of the same quantity of the fluid, after a proper interval, will be found in most cases to end in a way desirable under such circumstances.

The supply of water in the Well, since it has been secured from land-springs, has proved very abundant, and of permanent strength, and is likely to continue so.

We now come to its analyses. Professor Brande, who examined a quantity of the water sent to him, which must have been diluted by land-springs, judging from the results of his analysis, as compared with those of two other chemists, found in the imperial pint fifty-nine grains of common salt (chloride of sodium), and as much as fifty-one grains of muriate of lime. But Professor Daubeny, who analysed the water, subsequently, I believe, found only thirty-nine and a half grains of muriate of lime, but he detected as much as $89\frac{1}{6}$ grains of common salt. The specimen of water he analysed, therefore, could not have been much diluted. Professor Brande also found sulphate of lime and sulphate of magnesia, neither of which salts Professor Daubeny detected in his specimen. And yet the whole quantity of *dry* matter which each of the Professors had obtained by evaporation was nearly the same—there being $3\frac{1}{3}$ grains difference only —the one indicating 120 grains, and the other $123\frac{1}{3}$.

Here then had I again, as in the case of Scarborough Wells, and many other Spas I visited, more than one authority, but each of the first respectability in chemical sciences, to deal with, while endeavouring to learn the real composition of the Tenbury water. Another difficulty of coming to a right conclusion arose from my own notion, acquired on the spot, and while in the act of tasting and duly considering the water, that perchance it contained iodine, and probably bromine also, in which case the recently discovered Well would become far more important as a medical agent, while the cure of some of the cases of disease stated to me to have been healed by the water, would be readily explained.

Accordingly I recommended to Mr. Godson that a fresh analysis of the water should be made by Professor Brande, to whom immediate application was made through me for that purpose; and upon that gentleman's declining the appointment, owing to his numerous engagements, I advised that Mr. West, of Leeds, should be sent for down to Tenbury to examine the water on the spot.

This is what has been done, and the result of that chemist's analysis is the one which my readers will find in the general Table of Analyses at the end of the present volume. Mr. West has found the total saline ingredients in a wine-pint of the water to be below one hundred grains; he, like Professor Daubeny, could not detect a single trace of sulphuric acid, which Professor Brande found combined with two bases in his analyses. Mr. West has ascertained the presence of a larger quantity of common salt than either of the Professors; and of more muriate of lime than Professor Daubeny, though less of that substance than Professor Brande. But what Mr. West has detected further in the Tenbury water, which the two Professors do not mention in their analyses, besides some free carbonic acid, and nitrogen (azote), is a portion of iodine ($\frac{1}{19}$th of a grain) in an imperial gallon of the water, with marked traces of bromine also and potash.*

---

* Nearly at the same time Professor Daubeny having been requested by Dr. Davis to examine afresh a sample of Tenbury water forwarded to him, discovered iodine also. This fact, which he communicated to the Ashmolean Society on the 1st of June, 1840, was published in the "Athenæum" the following week. Mr. West reported the result of his analysis to the proprietor and myself, on the 18th of May preceding, announcing the discovery of iodine, but did not publish any account of it. The Professor was not aware of Mr. West's analysis till I communicated it to him some time this year.

The water, in fact, as it now appears, varies very considerably from what was previously believed to be its composition. I am, on the whole, bound to admit Mr. West's analysis as the most correct representation of the constituent parts of the Tenbury water.

Iodine, a substance I first mentioned as an important constituent part of the Woodhall Spa water, in which it is present in a much larger proportion than in the Tenbury water, is a name which during the last few years has made some noise in medical as well as purely popular works, although it is probably unintelligible to the majority of those who have seen it in print, or heard it mentioned. A large number of the non-professional readers, who may favour me with the perusal of these volumes, may be in that predicament. It is therefore important they should be told that that peculiar solid substance or matter, which in burnt sponge (once so generally employed as a domestic remedy for the removal of wens of the neck) imparts to that marine production its particular sanative property, is what has been called *iodine,** by the practical chemist, Courtois, who discovered it more than twenty-five years ago in France, while boiling certain marine productions, somewhat similar to the sponge, such as kelp, and other sea-weeds, &c., in the manufacture of soap.

A Genevese physician, led by the analogy of the sponge, in which the same particular matter as in the sea-weed was soon afterwards detected, was the first to think of employing the newly discovered substance, instead of the sponge itself (just as one uses now quinine instead of bark, from which it is obtained,) for the cure of wens in the throat and other analogous tumours. The result having agreed with the analogical theory of the worthy Doctor, and all succeeding brethren having followed his example with equal success, iodine not only became a standard medicine for the removal of all those diseases, but its employment was soon extended, with more or

* Because when heated it rises in *violet*-coloured vapours.

less good effect, to the cure of many other complaints, especially such as affect the glandular system.

Hence such mineral waters as have been found to contain iodine in this or any foreign country, have been justly considered as additionally valuable, provided the quantity present be not smaller than in the case of the Tenbury water; for however potent the substance in question may be as a medicinal agent, it should certainly never be administered in infinitesimal or homœopathic doses.

Such waters, however, are by no means common. Indeed, only two or three of them exist abroad, and in this country not many more. The whole inquiry is but a recent one, and was never conducted, perhaps, with that degree of strict attention which it has received from chemists within the last five or six years, and never more so than ¡during Professor Daubeny's investigation, and that which I was instrumental in having undertaken of the waters of Tenbury and Woodhall, in Lincolnshire, the latter of which, at present, can boast of holding in solution the largest quantity of iodine hitherto known to belong to any mineral water in England.

I believe that iodine was first detected in this country by the late Professor Turner in the water of Bonnington, near Leith. Next came Mr. Murray, who announced it, as we shall see by and by, as being present in the Gloucester Spa. Mr. Ainsworth was third in the field, in regard to the Cheltenham water, in which he contends he found traces of iodine. But it is to Professor Daubeny that the credit belongs of having been the first to ascertain, by a careful chemical examination of several British mineral waters, as detailed by him in the Philosophical Transactions for 1830, their proportion of that substance, the presence of which alone had been hinted at by his predecessors.

It will have been seen, however, under the head of Woodhall Spa, that all the proportions found by Dr. Daubeny are as nothing compared to that which that Spa contains, and which amounts to more than half a grain of iodine in the gallon. I have seen somewhere, (but I forget the precise work), that a chemist of the name of Cuff, at Bath, announced the presence of iodine in the water of that Spa, which he professes to have discovered by evaporating thirty gallons of the water. *A priori*, looking at the high temperature of that mineral water, I should say that Mr. Cuff was mistaken.*

Now the presence of iodine, in due proportions, in mineral waters is not only valuable because it imparts to it those properties (peculiar to itself) which in the hand of the physician have proved so useful for the removal of particular classes of disease; but also because it accounts for the cure of those very diseases accomplished by the employment of certain mineral waters before the existence of that singular substance in them had been suspected; so that the practitioner having been furnished, as it were, with evidence of the efficacy of iodine before he could imagine that he was employing it —evidence, consequently, not liable to error from personal bias or pre-conception—proceeds afterwards to the employment of those mineral waters which are known to contain the substance in question with redoubled confidence in its power.

The medical practitioners who recommended the Tenbury water before my visit to that Well, like those who employed the water of the Woodhall Spa under precisely similar circumstances, were exactly in the condition expressed in the preceding paragraph; and they will now proceed with increased confidence in the application of their respective waters to a variety of diseases, in which iodine, disseminated

* In one of the chapters on Cheltenham, we shall presently see that a larger proportion of this principle had been announced, some years before the date of the discovery at Woodhall, in the waters of that place; but the statement has not been confirmed by any chemist in this country; and is contrary to one made by Dr. Daubeny, two years before, in the Philosophical Transactions for 1830.

by the superior manipulatory hand of nature, is likely to be of essential service.

The cases of diseases cured or benefited by the Tenbury water, taken internally, reported to me upon good authority, are tolerably numerous, and extend to all those classes of disorders which are accompanied by internal or external glandular swellings, by fullness, stagnation, or congestion in some of the largest secretory organs ; also to liver complaints, inactive state of the intestines, scrofula, and what is vulgarly called scurvy. Employed externally, it has relieved gout, rheumatic gout, and paralytic affections.

In one or two instances of the latter diseases, in three cases of hepatic or liver dyspepsia, and as an alterative in mild complaints of the mesenteric glands, I have used with effect the Tenbury water, drank in doses of from ten to twenty ounces in the day, in divided portions.

As the water seems to bear well being bottled and transported, it may and has been recommended in that way to patients who could not run down to the borders of Shropshire. But in regard to the mode of administering the water in this manner, much remains to be done at the Well in bottling it, to prevent its being spoiled by keeping—a result I have seen happen on two occasions.

The case, already alluded to, of one of the children of the proprietor of the Well, whom I saw, is an interesting proof of the great and speedy efficacy of this water in verminous diseases attended by enlargement of the abdomen, and no doubt of some of its glands. Dr. A. W. Davis, of Presteign, who has favoured me with his opinion on the subject of the water, assures me that in all the varieties of dyspepsia, nephritic disorders, and scrofula, as well as in cutaneous affections, even to the most inveterate forms of *impetigo*, he has found the Tenbury water decidedly beneficial.

And now that I have fairly and very fully laid before my readers the nature and value of this new mineral water, I wish I could add that all is to be found at Tenbury that is required to make the water available on the spot, in the way of baths, pump and promenade rooms, hotels, lodging-houses, walks, roads, and other accommodations requisite to constitute it a Spa of the first class, by which visiters of the easy and superior classes shall be attracted, and at which, when once there, they shall be pleased to remain the necessary time. The contrary is the case; the proprietor having been, by the opposition raised against turning a footpath now extending across his grounds, thwarted, at present, from converting them in the best way to the use of the public.

This gentleman, indeed, appeared very zealous in the cause of the mineral water; and upon the assurance given that he would exert his utmost to convert into a suitable Spa the present establishment, which to this day wants every thing to make it so, I explored the whole neighbouring land, found it to be excellently and admirably adapted for the required purposes, marked the spot where the baths should be, and that on which the pump-room and promenade-room ought to be erected, in accordance to the best experience I have acquired at foreign Spas. I finally sent down one of my sons, a young architect, who had accompanied me in my tour through the German Spas and principal capitals of Germany, to survey the grounds, and chalk out the desired improvements and buildings. But no step has, in consequence of the above-mentioned dispute, been taken as yet to render Tenbury habitable for people of consequence, except that temporary baths have been run up in the very place which I deemed objectionable; a band has been engaged to play to those who repair thither to drink the water without making any lengthened stay in the place; a master of the ceremonies has officiated; and a general meeting has taken place, at which the prices of the baths and for drinking the water were settled. All these arrangements are of very little consequence compared to those which should be made, and which there ought to be a steady determination to carry into effect. [1]

And yet no place is more calculated to be a second Leamington than this very Tenbury, with its beautiful neighbourhood, and various interesting objects of both nature and art within easy reach of the Well. Neither is there in that part of England a mineral water which, when properly managed, aided by all the auxiliaries alluded to in my introduction, is likely to acquire a greater reputation.

Beyond the recommendation of its mineral water, therefore, I cannot at present proceed in regard to Tenbury, consistent with my straightforward system of stating in the account of my tour nothing but facts, and " things as they are," and not as they are *likely* to be. For the former will never deceive any of my readers—the latter might end in the disappointment of many.

I shall, therefore, await a future opportunity of detailing all the improvements and the requisite creations of a real Spa at Tenbury, when they shall truly exist, and I will then enter more particularly into a description of the many beauties of its neighbourhood.

CHAPTER VIII.

BIRMINGHAM, the city of brass-factories, and of riots,—
which about the middle of the seventeenth century was all for
revolution and rioting, and at the close of the succeeding
century became a partisan of royalty, and an enemy to revolution ; again to change, in the very next, or our present
century, from royalism to sansculottism, under the name of
chartism ;* but always and upon each change immersed in

* 1641-2. They rebel against Charles I., and declare for republicanism.
1791. They proclaim their hostility against the French revolution,

riots and the wanton destruction of property ;—Birmingham, I say, by the fortuitous circumstance of having been converted into a centre of almost numberless radii of conveyance or railroad-tracks to every part of the kingdom, is become a city of more than double its former importance.

If any one, either from the north, or the north-east, or the north-west, desires to visit the capital or proceed to the south, how can he do it better, at a cheaper rate, or more expeditiously, than by going through Birmingham ? And if the Londoner or any other traveller from the south, the south-east, and the south-west, desire to reach the opposite points of the compass in England, how again can he carry his intention into effect more advantageously than by going through Birmingham ? This was the case with myself on more than one occasion during my excursion to and from the different Spas of England ; and hence my introduction in this place of the name of that city.,

Birmingham, in fact, sees daily traversing its dense population many thousand strangers, who must all leave more or less of their wealth behind them.

Yet with all this, Birmingham complains of being poor, and really wears all around the livery of poverty rather than of opulence. Take away its celebrated Town or Music Hall, and the very striking gothic edifice, erected after the design of Barry, for the Grammar-school, founded under a king, who was never a king ; besides two other lesser, yet still handsome buildings—that of the Society of Arts, and the Parthenon ;— take away these, and what remains to illustrate this vast city, which, as the emporium of hardware, and the cradle of certain productions of art and mechanism, is probably better known,

and sackage, and burn the property of those who doubted the rights of kings.

1838. They riot and set fire to houses and shops, contending as chartists for principles not far remote from those of the French Revolution.

and its name more familiar to foreign nations, than that of any other city in England, the capital excepted?

It is in the last character that Birmingham shines with unrivalled merit. In whichever part of England you may be residing, the metropolis itself even included, if you apply to a tradesman for any thing out of the common way in any branch of human ingenuity, in which metals form a prominent part, the answer is almost always, " I must send to Birmingham for it."

And truly they are wise in so doing, for when one has been indulged, through the liberality of the proprietors, with a visit to Collis and Co.'s establishment, in Church-street, there to contemplate and admire almost every kind of manufactures, useful as well as ornamental, whether of silver, iron, brass, or copper, which are produced upon those endless premises; or with the examination of the finest display in the world of cutlery and steel articles, exhibited in the show-rooms of Messrs. Maplebeck and Low; it is impossible not to admit the policy as well as the justice of employing none but a Birmingham manufacturer, when we desire to possess in perfection any of those articles of luxury or necessity.

Wherefore, then, if the Birmingham manufactories be always at work, are its artisans grumbling and dejected; betraying symptoms of inward discontent, as they either pace the streets or group themselves in different parts of the town, looking as if they envied your better coat and hat, and could not bear the sight of your superiorly-fed looks, and cleaner complexion?

The question has been answered by Baron Dupin, in his admirable opening discourse on the statistics of trade. " Because the demon of discord has infused into the minds of the working classes the idea that they ought to be discontented; that they ought to protest in masses against the cruelty of their lot, against the unequal portion which has fallen to their share of the productions of the soil and national in-

dustry; and finally that they are born not only to an equality
of rights in the eye of the laws (which, in fact, they enjoy),
but also to an equality of fortunes and salaries, which no
people has ever enjoyed, or ought ever to enjoy."

Has there ever been, or can there ever be, an equality of
talent, exertions, and bodily strength, the real producers of
capital, and consequently of the means of realizing a fortune,
or deserving a higher salary? If not, wherefore insist upon
an equality in the distribution of wealth?

If the earth had indeed yielded its treasures without labour
on the part of man, if indeed capital were not the production of individual exertion, but, like the air we breathe, or the
water we *may* drink, were found ready produced, and within
the lawful reach of every one who chooses to take it; then
truly the socialist, and the chartist, and the agrarian, and
the leveller, and the equaliser, might exclaim against the
iniquity of the existing differences noticed in society,
with regard to all those comforts of life, and superior means
of enjoyment, which at present can alone be ensured by capital,
and the possession of which constitutes the abhorred distinction between he who has it and he who has it not.

What would the artisan himself say, who, having by his
greater attention to work, or by his superior acquired ability,
or by his greater power of prolonging the hours of labour,
owing to better bodily health, succeeded in earning in one
of Messrs. Collis's numerous departments of manufactory,
double the amount of wages earned by a fellow-handicrafts-
man in an adjoining department,—should afterwards find the
surplus reward of his own superior merits and exertions claimed
and shared by the latter, on the plea of equalising the wages
of each, in virtue of some such levelling law as your present
philosophers are striving to establish? Would he not protest against the iniquity of such a law as applied to himself? Or what would be the feeling of any other of the
Birmingham artisans, who, having at the death of an in-

dustrious and economical parent become possessed of larger means of subsistence than those afforded him by his own labours merely, should hear his right to the enjoyment of the superior comforts of life so acquired, disputed, and a share of them demanded by a less fortunate fellow-workman, under the same plea of equalisation of wealth? Would he not exclaim against such a forced and manifestly unjust distribution?

And yet, the latter as well as the former class of artisans is to be found now-a-days in the ranks of the discontented, who, at times, are seen parading the streets and other public places in Birmingham, with minds poisoned by demagogues, murmuring at the superior comforts, better means of living, and *display* of wealth (which is, in fact, its *distribution* precisely where most needed), by which certain other classes of society, apart from themselves, are distinguished! Do they forget that those same classes, (since gold is not like air and water, which we may all have if we but desire them,) could not have reached their envied station, either now or at any time previous, except through the very means by which the superior workman, or the workman who has inherited from his father the result of better workmanship and a saving of wages, has reached his own preferable position, the enjoyment of which he would consider it a hard law to be compelled to share with others who have not deserved it?

It is curious that when you come to talk quietly and *tête-à-tête* with these murmurers and malcontents (unless it be your spouters, lecturers, or ringleaders), they are unable either to assign a cause for their dissatisfaction, or to point out the means of removing the latter. " They are out of work,"—that is all I was ever able to learn or gather from them, whenever, during some of my inquisitive rambles, I accosted any of the *désœuvrés* about the streets of Birmingham, Leeds, Manchester, Preston, and Halifax. But is that a reason why the entire frame and constitution of civil society, which is of many centuries duration, and has been the most powerful engine in bringing mankind to its present very far superior state of worldly happiness, should be shaken, broken down, and torn up by the root?

Immersed in these reflections, which, at the time of the visit to Birmingham I am now recording, were naturally suggested by the very recent occurrence of those disgraceful outbreaks of popular commotion that have since formed the subject of parliamentary consideration, I left the field of those commotions to direct my steps towards more congenial scenes in its immediate neighbourhood, where science and learning offered to an inquisitive traveller opportunities of mental enjoyment not to be neglected.

The supply of water for domestic purposes in such a densely populated city as Birmingham, deserved some consideration at the hand of a physician; and into this I inquired before I proceeded farther. A very intelligent tradesman and artificer with whom I conversed on this point, and who is himself an old inhabitant and housekeeper, assured me that the ordinary water of wells in the town is almost everywhere contaminated by the percolations of waste water from the factories, and, when drawn, appears generally greenish, and has a metallic taste. The poorer people, who cannot afford to pay water-rates, and must be satisfied with the well-water, are constantly subject to eruptions of the skin, particularly on the hands and legs.

A stranger, on his first arrival at Birmingham, if he chooses to live in lodgings, should take care that the house he is to inhabit does not derive its water from a well (the drinking of which will excite *internal commotion* of a painful sort), but is supplied from the reservoirs near the Sutton-road and the Canal, from which Birmingham receives some of the purest water, by means of a powerful engine, which forces the water even to the highest floor of the loftiest building.

Soho next claimed my attention; but, much as I was

struck at the view of that field of Watt's greatest achievements in perfecting that most wonderful combination of physical force and mechanical ingenuity—the steam-engine —which has now nearly changed all our previously received notions of the relation between time and distance, and between labour and production,—it would ill become me, an unskilled man in such matters, to attempt a description of that spot in this place

Rather let me turn to the contemplation of Aston Hall, not far removed from Soho. This stately fabric, seen at the termination of a long avenue of trees, after having rang with the carousals that usually attended the visits of Charles to his friends and adherents (it had done so during two days previous to the disastrous fight at Edgehill), and after having been battered by the parliamentary troops, became the seat of one of the greatest benefactors of mankind—of him, on whose account *Soho* has become better known throughout the civilized world, than, as a watchword, it had been to the troopers of Monmouth.

Following afterwards the Sutton-road until I had left the village of Erdington behind me, where that awful tragedy of Mary Ashford was perpetrated, in which her foul destroyer, Edward Thornton, was destined to renew in our days the singular spectacle of a " trial by battel," I drove across the country for two or three miles on my left, in order to reach St. Mary's College at Oscott.

That the Papists—some of the earliest and most determined of the dissenters from the pure and primitive Apostolic Church of Christ—are increasing in number in this country; that they are assuming, at this present time, an attitude of importance which none of the other classes of people who dissent from the religion of the state, the truly Catholic and Apostolic, arrogate to themselves; that they are actually enjoying privileges, honours, and immunities which, since the expulsion of the second James, who took Father Edward Petre the Jesuit into his privy council, and welcomed Ferdinando d'Adda, the Pope's nuncio, to Windsor, had never been accorded to them;—all these are facts so glaring that to deny them would be to deny the light of day.

In the course of my extensive tour through England, particularly in the northern counties, I declare that the tokens and appearances of Romanism met me in so many places that I could almost have fancied myself travelling through a Roman catholic state. I do not remember having seen more places of worship, or many much more magnificent ones among them, in the Roman catholic state of Baden and even Bavaria (except in the capital of the latter), than I have noticed in my peregrination north of Birmingham. I was admiring, one day, a recent and very imposing structure of Mr. Pugin, having the outward show of a cathedral, which had just been opened for the Roman worship, when a gentleman well acquainted with that skilful architect assured me that he was then engaged in superintending the construction of twenty-two other Roman catholic churches, principally in the Gothic or English style of architecture, in which Mr. Pugin is known to excel.

Indeed, their chapels and churches in England and Wales are said to be upwards of five hundred, many of which are larger and handsomer than the majority of the churches of the dominant religion; besides twenty convents, and not fewer than nine colleges in England alone for the education of the Roman catholic youths.

One of the latter institutions, conducted by the Jesuits at Stonyhurst, I have already mentioned and described in a previous volume.* A second, still more important, and one which deserves, on every account, the attention of my Protestant readers, is that the title of which I have placed at the head of the present chapter. As it laid in my way more than once going to and from the Spas of the midland counties, I

* In that account there are two typographical errors, as "Ascott" for "Oscott," and "Brownhill" instead of "Brownbill."

could not resist the temptation of visiting it ; the more so as I knew that among the students of the establishment there were three or four belonging to Roman catholic families of the highest respectability and exemplary character, with whom I had been in habits of professional intercourse.

Another motive for such a visit I found in that universal attention which the subject of education, with or without the aid of the church, commands, at the present moment, in this country, especially in reference to the Romanists. Such a motive is indeed paramount, and my readers can hardly blame me for introducing into my present work, as an episode, the account of the new college of St. Mary's Oscott. Thither, therefore, I drove from Birmingham on Sunday, the 27th of October, 1839.

Within the last three or four years an almost barren tract of land, part of an elevated plateau, distant about five miles north of Birmingham on the road to Sutton-Colefield, and a little to the left, has been invested, by the liberal support of the Roman catholic gentry, and the munificent donations of one of the higher clergy of that creed, with an importance which, though unperceived at this moment, may and will exert, at some future period, a commanding influence through a very extended sphere of society in England.

In the centre of that previously barren spot, over the surface of which parterres of flowers, green-plats, and serpentine walks have been traced by a skilful hand, and plantations raised as screens against the colder winds, and a noble extensive parapeted terrace erected, commanding a vast panorama before it—in that centre an imposing mass of building has been reared, which presents one of the most striking and solid examples of the Elizabethan style of architecture that has been executed in modern times. That building is St. Mary's College, which, with its adjoining Gothic chapel, is the combined production of Pugin and Potter of Lichfield.

The edifice, which is of red brick with sandstone ornaments and accessories, extends nearly three hundred feet in length, with its front to the south, and contains within every possible collegiate accommodation which the classical, moral, and physical education of one hundred and thirty, or more, children of the Roman catholic nobility and gentry of this and of one or two foreign countries can require, or the theological instruction of young men destined for the priesthood can demand.

The engraving here introduced will convey to the reader a better idea, than any description of mine can, of the general elevation and appearance of the college, with its central square tower, over the entrance door of which are inscribed the words " *Religioni et bonis moribus.*"

To the right of the College, and connected with it, is the church recently finished under the special direction of Mr. Pugin, which has cost at least 15,000*l.* The view exhibits a processional ceremony performed in the open air by the clergy of the college, proceeding to a temporary altar erected under a gorgeous tent outside the chapel.

The origin of this institution and imposing building is shortly this: prior to the French revolution the Roman catholic clergy of this country were educated in France, Germany, Italy, and Spain. That ever-memorable convulsion, and the perpetual state of warfare which it led to between this country and France, as well as the abolition which ensued of almost every institution for ecclesiastical purposes in many parts of the continent, threw the Roman catholic bishops in England on their own resources, with regard to the education and formation of the required number of clergymen for their flocks; and they endeavoured to meet the pressing wants of the times by establishing in this country separate colleges under the exclusive jurisdiction of each. Circumstances rendered it expedient to combine the education of the laity with that of the clergy, and the practice has continued to the present time.

It was for similar reasons that the "famed" Maynooth College was established in Ireland in 1795, with the sanction as well as the pecuniary aid of government, continued ever since, for the special object of educating and qualifying persons to be parish priests. But there a first and very important error was committed in its organization, which has extended to this day its baneful influence over the results of that system of education. That error consisted in confining the object of the institution to the rearing up of none but young aspirants for the priesthood; instead, as in the case of the Jesuit's college at Stonyhurst, and of this of St. Mary, of devoting it to the education of laymen as well as ecclesiastics; thus tending to infuse liberality of sentiment among the latter, by bringing men of all classes and professions together.

Old Oscott was founded two years before Maynooth College,

that is about 1793, and the building was gradually added to, as increasing wants rendered that step necessary. Further and more extensive additions becoming again urgent, it was deemed advisable to erect a new edifice, instead of increasing the already unsightly pile of the old buildings. The new college, accordingly, was commenced in March, 1835, and opened in August, 1838, a little more than a year before my visit.

It at once bespeaks the liberality of the Bishop of Camby-sopolis, Dr. Walsh, the papist prelate of the midland district, as well as the thriving condition of the old college institution, that the necessary funds for the purchase of the land, the construction of the building and for its furniture, amounting to about forty-five thousand pounds, have been supplied partly by the former and partly by the latter.

This fact, as far as it concerns the college itself, shews one of the advantages to be derived from combining with the ecclesiastical the secular education of many young people; inasmuch as by such a plan pecuniary resources are obtained, which render the establishment what it ought to be,—independent of all government subvention, and of course control, on the one hand, and of all eleemosynary support, which would be derogatory, on the other. And yet the pecuniary charges made at this establishment for the secular education of youth are exceedingly liberal.

Not satisfied with merely contributing towards the establishment of the new college a great part of his own wealth, which he so well knows how to distribute in works of charity and benevolence (as I learned from various quarters), the pious and reverend person just named has added another precious gift to his previous munificent donation of money, by presenting to the college a collection of 12,000 volumes, well known as *La Biblioteca del Marchese Marini*, at Rome, the publisher of a new edition of Vitruvius, from whose executors the books were purchased by Dr. Walsh. These 12,000 volumes, which, including duty and carriage, cost nearly 3000*l.*, were incorporated by desire of the donor with the library of the college, which amounts now to about 18,000 volumes.

This library is rich in the writings of the Fathers, and in ecclesiastical history, the classics, and classical archeology. It is also well supplied with literary and scientific journals, and with the transactions of literary and scientific bodies. It moreover contains a valuable collection of tracts in the various departments of literature and science, formed by Cancellieri and Visconti, being part of the Marini library; and grievous was the mortification experienced by the learned at Rome when this unique collection was transferred from thence to England.

A very handsome room, fifty feet long, has been assigned for the methodical arrangement of the Marini library, adjoining to which is the much larger, lofty, and covered apartment, containing the remainder of the college library—forming the west termination of the grand façade of the building.

To this and every other part of the establishment I was conducted by the professor of mathematics and mathematical physics—a secular priest, like the rest of the principal instructors of the establishment; who, with the utmost readiness and urbanity, shewed and explained to me whatever most attracted my attention. Mr. Logan, the gentleman in question, had been deputed for that purpose by the Rev. Dr. Weedall, the rector of the college, a person of most amiable, mild, and winning manners, by whom I had been kindly received after the celebration of their morning service.

From the library, my curiosity led me to the Museum before I proceeded to take a more general survey of this very extensive building, in which no expense appears to have been spared to render it most effectually applicable to the various purposes it is intended to accomplish.

The Museum is one principally of religious antiquities, and is situated in one of the upper rooms of the central tower.   Mr. Pugin, who, though a layman, fills in the college the office of professor of architecture, considered as a branch of art, is a principal contributor to the Museum. The Earl of Shrewsbury, also, has made many important additions to the collection by his numerous donations, among which I may mention a complete set of canonicals, three in number, with a stole and cape, most profusely and tastefully wrought in gold and embroidered in silk, to represent various figures of saints and bishops, so accurately finished, and the colours so vivid, that the whole would seem to be the work of the other day, and by the most skilful hands.   Yet they were discovered accidentally, not long since, in some recondite place in the Roman catholic cathedral of Waterford, supposed to have been concealed in it in order to save them from the rapacity of the protestants.

Whether this last expression was meant to apply to the triumphant soldiers of William of Nassau, who, having reduced the popish garrison of rebellious Waterford to extremities in 1690, compelled them to surrender nearly at discretion ; or whether it refers to a much earlier period (1617), when the exorbitance of the papists obliged the government to banish all their regulars, which at that time did in great numbers swarm almost everywhere in Ireland, and to issue a proclamation against the papist clergy,* I was not able to determine.   The exquisite workmanship of the canonicals certainly would incline one to consider them as the production of the more recent of those two periods ; and so do their freshness and high state of preservation.†

* October 13th, 1617.—*Cox's History of Ireland.*

† These objects are evidently of foreign handicraft.

Not far from where these splendid objects were displayed, the worthy Professor pointed out, with some degree of exultation, another object contained in a glass case, and by him considered as a proof of the loose and ready way in which Roman catholics are often accused of murderous crimes against protestants. That object was a short dagger of well-tempered steel, which bore inscribed on one side of the broad end of its richly-gilt blade, near the hilt, the words, " Memento Godfrey, Ætat. 12, 1678," with a death's-head; and on the other side, " Pro Religione Protestantium." " The murder of Godfrey," said Mr. Logan, " was ascribed to the Roman catholics at the time; but when the dagger which inflicted the fatal wound was examined, it exhibited the above tokens of a protestant murderer's knife:"—a very unsatisfactory proof this; for the papist who could encompass the death of an innocent youth, would not scruple at fixing the odium of that foul act upon the protestants themselves, by using the poniard of one of the defenders of the reformed religion, whom he had probably murdered before or robbed of his weapon.

There is a small painting in this collection, exceedingly well preserved, its colours most vivid, which appeared to me to be the work of Giotto, as it strongly resembles some of the paintings on the walls of the Campo Santo, at Pisa, known to be the production of that earliest of the Italian masters. It represents Christ, of mature age, placing a diadem on the Virgin Mary, while cherubims sound the organ at their feet, and angels stand on each side.

As a specimen of the handicraft of some of the converts to the Romanists' creed in China, another very curious picture, representing the Madonna and Child, was pointed out to me, supposed to be about one hundred and fifty years old, and to have been brought over from that empire by one of the missionaries. It seems executed by scratching the quicksilver at the back of a looking-glass into a design of the group, the heads and hands being afterwards painted of a dark ochre colour. The drapery of the Madonna and Child are of gold-tinsel pasted on the back of the glass, and so is the halo around the heads, which are decorated with diadems of sham jewellery.

The Archeological Museum is only one of the many appliances contained in this college for aiding the professors and assistant-masters in the work of instruction. There is also a costly apparatus both for mechanical philosophy and chemistry, as well as incipient collections of natural history. These are placed in various parts of the building, the internal arrangement of which seems deserving of all praise, whether for amplitude of room, cleanliness, order, and the suitable style of its solid yet tasteful furniture. It is a model for a college worthy the attention of those who, in these times of renovated zeal for education, are, or are likely to be, at the head of collegiate institutions.

The great staircase, of oak, in character with all the essential parts and ornaments of this Elizabethan edifice, leads to a very spacious and long corridor, parallel to the entire front of the building. The strangers' room, a very handsome apartment, is on this floor. It contains a central oak table, with chairs to correspond, covered with green velvet; and I noticed around the walls a series of alto-relievo carvings in wood, representing the several events of the Passion of our Saviour. They were purchased abroad for the college, are of an oval form, and about ten inches in diameter. Paintings presented by Lord Shrewsbury are to be seen in this room, as well as in the library and along the corridor.

Below the latter, on the ground-floor, a similar corridor, with a tesselated pavement, leads to the grand refectory for the general students, to that of the priests, and to the dining-room of the " philosophers." There is likewise the great room for general study, which is a gallery fifty feet long by fourteen feet wide, wherein the scholars are arranged on parallel forms in two series, with the prefect and sub-prefects of studies seated on elevated rostra, overlooking the whole room, and maintaining the strictest order and silence.

Small libraries of reference exist for each class, even down to the youngest children of eight years of age.

At the back of the principal building two wings project about sixty feet, forming a quadrangular court, with the playground beyond it, which is upwards of six acres in extent, and will be soon sheltered from the north and north-east winds by a very extensive and growing plantation.

In the upper floor of these wings are the dormitories, which are far superior to those of Stonyhurst, admirably as I, at the time of my visit, thought the latter calculated for their intended purpose. As at Stonyhurst, these handsome and well-aired apartments are arranged with a number of single beds and curtains, but of better, more showy, as well as uniform materials, so as to constitute a succession of separate sleeping-places, one for each student. When occupied by the students, they are watched by appropriate superintendants, who visit every apartment frequently during the night, to enforce order and perfect silence.

Into these apartments the boys retire at about nine o'clock, P.M., in regular procession, accompanied by sub-prefects, some of whom are also stationed on the different landing-places of the great staircases leading to the dormitories.

The personal surveillance practised over the actions of the students extends to the play-grounds, both to the one out of doors and to those in doors—of the latter of which there are several, for such of the boys as cannot or choose not to play in the open air. Among the amusements, gymnastic exercises and tennis-ball are much and properly encouraged.

This system of vigilance is a system of prevention; and works marvellous results. Hence, although the general discipline of the establishment is a firm one, and the inculcation of good manners as well as of moral principles is a leading principle of it, penal inflictions are never necessary, and the object of education is attained by moral checks only. For similar reasons, no " fagging," bullyism, or *supercherie* of any sort, is allowed among the boys, and any overbearing on the part of some towards others is instantly checked.

Nor is it to be supposed from this, that the mode of life led by the students must be that of a recluse; for in no establishment of the same intention have sources of gaiety and means of amusement been more liberally provided, in the shape of music, fencing, and dancing rooms, besides all other diversions of out-of-door exercises.

To carry this system into effect no mean Staff of officers is required. Accordingly I found, upon inquiry, that independent of the rector and vice-rector, the prefect of studies, and the prefect of bounds or discipline, there are twenty-four superintendants, exclusive of the professors and teachers, and thirteen priests.

As the establishment professes to prepare young men for matriculation at the Universities of London and Dublin, at which Papists are admitted for degrees, for which reason the form of studies has been altered so as to suit it to the London curriculum,—and as an application has been made (so I understand) to government, to permit the students of Oscott, when once they have matriculated, to return to their college to complete the higher studies previously to taking their degrees, it is manifest that the course of studies to be pursued at Oscott will be of the most comprehensive kind. It is, in fact, already so, although students are not admitted, at present, older than fourteen years of age.

But if the application just alluded to should be granted, young men will continue at this college until the usual period of life at which under-graduates generally quit their colleges at the English universities.

Ample provision exist in the present Staff of the college for such an extension of education; inasmuch as there are already two professors of Greek, and two of Latin, a professor of history and geography, one of philosophy, another for mathematics and mathematical physics, one for experimental philosophy and chemistry, one for natural history; lastly, a professor of theology, for those who intend to embrace the ecclesiastical state.

The professors of classics and mathematics are assisted by numerous masters, and there are also resident in the house native teachers of the French, German, and Italian languages, with all of whom I had the pleasure of conversing at the plain but abundant mid-day repast in the combination room, at which I was hospitably invited by Dr. Weedhall, after some hours spent in examining the establishment.

Looking at one of the half-yearly examination papers, which extends to every branch of knowledge taught in the college, from the highest class (philosophy) to the lowest, including the rudiments, it is impossible not to admit the superiority of the arrangement of the studies and selection of authors over those of some other national colleges in England. If, indeed, all that is there set down has been taught and learned, and has afterwards been displayed by pupils, under fifteen years of age, at a public examination of several days, the sooner some other collegiate establishments in this country look to themselves, and strive to come up to what is here done, that they may not lag behind in the great work of public education, the better will it be for those confided to their instructions.

This is said without any reference to the question of the religious creed which certainly imparts its peculiar colouring to some of the studies at Oscott, though it does not take away from the general character of the instruction given its comprehensiveness and perfect adaptation to many institutions of protestant foundation, guided by more enlightened principles of religion.

One great, and I would almost call it, national advantage to England, arising from such institutions as Stonyhurst and St. Mary's is, that they render unnecessary the temporary emigration to a foreign country of the children of its wealthier Roman catholic subjects, and of the young men who desire to enter into the priesthood. Very few, if any of them, are ever sent away now to France or to Italy for their education, as was incessantly the case half a century ago; a circumstance which tends to keep them steadfast in their allegiance as true Englishmen, despite of any feeling to the contrary which a diversity of opinion regarding the religion of the state might be supposed to engender. After a residence of many years at Rome or in a Roman catholic college on the continent, apparently for the purposes of education, how many were there not, in former times, who returned to England perfect foreigners in their hearts, imbued with the strongest prejudices against this country and its dominant religion?

CHAPTER IX.

OF the truth of the surmise contained in the concluding
period of the last chapter, I soon had a convincing proof in
the person of a most respectable-looking Roman catholic
gentleman, the father of a young priest, just returned from
Rome, who had, in company with his son (originally a pupil
in the Old College at Oscott) been to visit a younger son
now pursuing his education in the New College.

We recognized each other in the evening in the public

coffee-room of one of the principal hotels at Birmingham, as having met in the chapel of St. Mary in the morning; and upon my acquainting him with the apparent effect which the pompous ceremony there celebrated had had upon an honest citizen of Birmingham who had escorted me that day to Oscott, as well as to other places in the neighbourhood, he engaged readily and with a vivacity beyond his years, in a deliberate discussion with me,—first on the merits and value of the respective liturgies of the Romish and Protestant churches, and next upon a few of the leading points of difference between the two creeds.

On my reaching St. Mary's on the day already mentioned, accompanied by the honest escort just alluded to, we found every body at chapel, into which we were courteously invited to enter by a servant of the institution.

A priest in his white surplice and a golden stole was in the act of *reading* a sermon to the assembled congregation,—a practice unknown in Roman catholic churches on the continent, where the preacher either delivers his discourse extempore, or from memory; in which latter case he is occasionally prompted by a person who sits behind the pulpit, in such a way as not to be observed. The sermon, generally a short one, forms part of the ritual of high mass or great festivals, the ceremonies of which are suspended during its delivery, and then the officiating clergy and attendants present remain seated in their respective places.

To enter at this very moment of time into the body of a large and imposing edifice, having a single nave, but lofty and of great length, with a proportionate breadth, though without columns or any other striking architectural ornament, and to glance immediately as well as uninterruptedly at a multitude of apparently devout persons assembled within it, would alone, under any circumstances, be sufficient to excite attention in a stranger. But here that multitude was not, as in the churches and chapels of the protestant faith,

composed merely of the many who attend the service, separated into groups of various numbers shut up in pews, and
of the single minister who read it. The contrary was the
case; for besides the countless numbers of lay people of
both sexes, arranged, without the appearance of the smallest
confusion, in parallel lines on both sides of the nave, where
they occupied about two-thirds of the length of the chapel,—
we beheld also two hundred youths of gentle blood, students
of the college, neatly and uniformly dressed, similarly arranged
on cross benches, with their superintendants at their head;
while beyond them scores of priests, deacons, subdeacons,
and acolytes, the former in their splendid vestments of gold,
the latter in scarlet tunics, surmounted by a short white surplice, were seated in pompous hierarchy, on dignified stools,
which rose gradually from the floor to the wall on each side
of the inner or sacred space in front of the great altar—
itself gorgeously decked and brilliantly lighted by massive
candelabra, bearing lofty tapers around the tabernacle.

These were the things by which my honest burgher of
Birmingham, who had never entered a popish church before,
had been particularly struck. But when, at the termination
of the sermon, he beheld the high priest, followed by his two
deacons and the acolytes, moving towards the altar; and
there, after bowing before it, and going through many secret
prayers and open ceremonies, he saw him incense the symbols
of the Eucharist and the altar itself, to be himself, in his
turn, incensed by one of the deacons—when the volumes of
curling smoke from the censer rose and expanded through
the church with a fragrance which reached to where we
stood—when the full swell of the majestic organ, accompanying the human voice, was heard immediately above us,
its cadences directing the melodious harmony of the anthems,
the ejaculations of the chaunting priests, and the responses
of the congregation, — O then the protestant burgher of

Birmingham stood enthralled, and marvelled at every thing
around him !

Apprehensive lest he should in any way cause a disturbance of the service by his astonishment and admiration,
I whispered to him that, since we could not conform to the
many outward tokens of worship which were expected from
Roman catholics during mass, particularly as the high priest
was about to pronounce the words of consecration, and to
adore and elevate the host—we had better leave the chapel—
an object we easily accomplished, for upon entering it we
had kept respectfully out of the crowd and near to the
door.

Having reached the terrace, my simple friend, who seemed
lost in amazement, declared he had never suspected the
Romanists' church service to be so much more imposing
than our own, and added that he had never felt himself so
irresistibly drawn into real devotion as at that moment.

I had by this time resumed my note-book, and was proceeding to take down my observations of the general and particular character of the elevation of the building, when presently I missed my companion, and learned from a solitary
man in authority, who was guarding the grounds during the
hours of church service, that he had slipped into the chapel
again, out of which indeed I saw him issue with the crowd
at the conclusion of the mass.

" I am quite determined," said he, the moment he perceived me, " to come here again next Sabbath day ; and I
wonder that all the people of Birmingham do not flock to this
place of worship, to feast their eyes on the splendid dresses of
the priests, and their pompous ceremonies, to have their ears
delighted by most heavenly music, and their sense of smell
gratified by the outpourings of the swinging censers."

" Just so," exclaimed the venerable looking father of the
young priest, whom I mentioned before, addressing himself

to me as I concluded my anecdote; " the Birmingham burgher is right, and the example of his conversion (for I cannot doubt but your travelling friend will be a convert to our holy faith after next Sunday) will show that the liturgy of the Roman catholic church, in other words, the mass, is a more captivating form of religious worship for the followers of Christ than that which the disciples of Luther have adopted."

—" There I think you are in error," I replied ; " my protestant friend, as he himself stated, was struck with the richness of the vestments, the pompous ceremonies he saw performed in the course of an hour by many people in gaudy dresses, and by the intoxicating effect of the oriental perfume issuing from the censers, as well as by the music ; but he said not a syllable as to the nature, character, and words of the service, or as to the meaning and intention of the prayers uttered by the priests, in which, truly, the liturgy consists, and not in the outward forms only. How could he indeed have formed any opinion on either of those essential points, when the principal part of the service is purposely mystical, its language wholly unintelligible to him, and (even supposing it to be intelligible) when many of its prayers are expressly muttered so as not to be heard by the congregation ? What would be the effect produced in the way of exciting and keeping up devotion in any denomination of christians in England, if upon entering á protestant church to pray to God with his fellow creatures under the directing voice of a pastor, an individual were to hear the latter read from the desk the various prayers in an unknown tongue, and find that even some of those were designedly uttered in such a tone of voice as not to be heard ? Could such a christian be edified or benefited by a liturgy so read or pronounced ?

" And yet even in such a case, were the organ and the human voice, accompanied by many instruments, to swell out at the same time in melodious strains—were aroma to be scattered

about the altar,—and were multitudinous assistant clergymen
to be moving to and fro in the performance of their respective
functions; many, like the unlettered Birmingham burgher,
whom you claim as a convert, would be reconciled to the
gross absurdity of the whole, and consider that, provided the
senses were but gratified, the intellect and the heart need not
be consulted in matters of religious worship.

" This is precisely the history of my Birmingham friend at
the chapel of St. Mary. He was caught by the forms, and
never troubled himself about the substance. Had the service
been ' low mass,' instead of the pompous high or ' solemn
mass,' the effect would have been far different; and thus it is
that we ought to compare the respective merits of yours with
those of our own liturgy. If pomp is to be taken into the
account, as necessary to excite devotion, then we must quote
our own cathedral service on all great and solemn occasions,
when the bishop, and dean, and archdeacons, and canons,
and minor canons, and prebendaries, and many of the regular clergy, with choristers and chaunters innumerable, all
in their respective vestments, take a part in the celebration of
the liturgy, cheered, gladdened, and inspired by the organ,
and other instruments of sacred music.

" The true catholic and apostolic church of England has
preserved for all solemn occasions, and in suitable places, in
common with yourselves, many of those pomps and ceremonies which appertained to the primitive church, and which
are neither a mixture of the expiring pagan forms passing
into those of the christian faith at the period of its first pro-
mulgation, nor a direct misinterpretation (not to say
violation) of the written word of the Divine Founder of our
faith—like many of those you have retained from the time
when, as popish followers, you separated yourselves from the
church preached by the Apostles and the holy fathers, their
successors. But I again repeat, these forms do not constitute the liturgy, they are only its accessories.

" We must therefore compare your ordinary and daily mass with our usual church service on Sunday, setting aside the daily service in all parochial and metropolitan churches, at which what is called the communion service is not read. So viewed, the Romish equally with the English liturgy, is composed of two parts,—the common prayers and those of the Communion. The protestant allots generally an hour and a quarter for the two parts, which are kept distinct, and are invariably followed by a discourse. The Romanist mixes the prayers and the Communion throughout, and omits the discourse, and despatches the whole in fifteen or twenty minutes.

" The worshipper of the mass, on attending, generally takes a book of devotion with him, and prays with himself during the celebration of the mass, most of which is inaudible to him, and were it audible, must be unintelligible. For how many popish devotees can there be in a large and mixed congregation who comprehend the ancient Roman language, in which the mass is said? In most of the English popish chapels or churches, and throughout France, in the present day, a missal containing the Latin service, and its translation in the vernacular tongue by the side, is used by the educated Romanist; but even then the devotional exercise is ' individual,' is not in common with the surrounding brethren, and has no direct communion with the officiating priest; for the latter oftener than not is not heard through the service, except in some few parts. Surely, nothing of this is calculated to inspire and maintain devotion.

" Let us for one moment transport ourselves into a Roman catholic country, where the exercise of that religion is unrestrained by national customs or hostile laws, as being the religion of the majority; and let us enter one of their great parochial churches to see how the ordinary daily liturgy, ' the low mass' (without reference to any great festival or ceremony, plenary indulgences, *quarant'ore*, vespers, octaves, and other occasional prayers) exercises its influence in promoting and maintaining devotion, and a solemn impressive worshipping of God. Take we Saint Roque at Paris in our way, or Sainte Gudule at Brussels, or Santa Maria della Salute at Venice, or the Duomo at Milan, or Santa Maria Maggiore at Rome, or, lastly, St. Filippo Neri at Naples.

" In all these extensive and magnificent temples there are many chapels or altars, in or before each of which, and sometimes in three or four of them at the same time, low mass is said on Sundays and other days, from an early hour in the morning until noon or an hour later. A few devotees are seen before each of them, seated either upon benches, or upon chairs which they transfer from one place to another, kneeling or sitting, while a few are standing. Some read a book of devotion, others attend only to what the priest is doing, and seldom catch what he is saying, although, through frequent repetition of many of the Latin expressions, invariably alike in all masses and on each day, they can guess at a great deal. A few have a missal either in its original language or translated, by means of which they can follow in silence the officiating priest. A little boy, or at the most two such, (sometimes with surplice, but oftener without any) attend on the priest, pronounce the responses, and help him in some of the most solemn parts of the ceremonial forms of the mass, such as handing the wine to him for consecration.

" During the whole of the time that the mass endures, which, in good truth, is short enough, the frequent passing to and fro of listless and idle perambulators or strangers attracted by curiosity, or of devout people going from one chapel to another, disturbs those who are attending to the service. The aisles of those imposing temples seem like open streets, with as much and constant a thoroughfare, and nearly as much bustle and noise; so that collective devotion and inward meditation are perpetually intruded upon ; whereby individual as well as congregational worship is made less effective and imposing in your churches, by the ritual of your Divine service.

"That this is what may be called your liturgy—the one to be properly compared with the liturgy of the English church, and not your ' high mass'—is evident from the fact that the latter is seldom celebrated as compared to the former, which is, in good truth, the more frequent means the Romanist has of joining in public devotion and supplicating his Maker in common with his fellow creatures. Most of you are contented with one mass, others will daily attend two or more ; and when inflicted as a penance by the ghostly confessor after auricular confession of sins, some will attend a dozen masses in a day. All this has come within my own knowledge.

"To say that I have never seen tokens of sincere devotion in any such persons as in the midst of noise and bustle attend mass, and are evidently and wholly absorbed in the one sacred thing before them, would be a dereliction from truth. But the general impression of the impartial beholder who visits the principal churches alluded to on ordinary occasions is, that distraction, absence, and inattention prevail in them over devotion.

"It is, however, only just to make a distinction in favour of the Roman catholics of England, who, from the disposition and arrangement of their places of worship, as well as from the peculiarity of the manners of the country, being less exposed to all the causes of intrusion, interruption and distraction so common in the great churches of the continent, evince as much devotion as their countrymen of the dominant religion do in their own churches.* Yet even among them, when the ordinary

* I have had already the satisfaction of rendering this justice to the English Romanists in a previous publication. Indeed, the supreme

service only is celebrated, the remarks made before on the mass apply with equal force.

" Look now to the Divine service in an Anglican church, and to its form of worship and liturgy. Free from all mystical ceremony ; uniform throughout the kingdom ; borrowed from the primitive church of Christ in many of its parts, and consequently simple as well as beautiful, and the more beautiful and simple because drawn up in the vernacular language of the worshippers,—its import is perfectly intelligible to the meanest understanding, although in composition and choice of expression, or even of single words, it can vie with the finest efforts of philological science. Such a liturgy is not only calculated to inspire and keep up a feeling of devotion, but is capable of opening the heart of the most hardened or apathetic, and lending it words wherewith to supplicate its Maker for grace, peace, and forgiveness, in unison with all the brethren around, mutually inspiring each other, and cheerfully attending, following, or re-echoing the set words of prayer solemnly pronounced by the minister. Not the slightest disturbance or interruption, except by mere accident, can occur to this one great and congregated act of public worship offered to the true God. Every one's eye is upon every one, while the spirit is directed above; and the appearance of reverential awe and attention which uniformly prevails around the officiating clergyman (unlike what we have seen to take place around the altar at which the priest celebrates low mass) is both cause and effect of itself; whilst the two are to be found in the peculiar ordinances and arrangement of the service, as well as in the uniformity of time, place, and prayer adopted.

" What a cheering, pleasing, and encouraging idea to the

head of their church has scarcely another foreign community under his spiritual sway so respectable or sincere, as well as profusely liberal in support of their faith, as the Roman catholics of England.

protestant christian is that which must strike him when, on
the sabbath-day, and in the bosom of his parish church, surrounded in devout congregation by most of his fellow citizens
of the same faith, called together for the same purpose, he
raises his voice to the throne of God, and reflects that hundreds of thousands of fellow-worshippers are, like himself, engaged in praising the Creator of all things, and
in bending their knees in adoration of HIM with the same
solicitations, in the same words, and in the same language, and at the very same moment of time throughout
the realms he inhabits! Such an idea, I avow, has often
increased the fervour of my prayers, and imparted, in my
estimation, a greater solemnity to the religious ceremony
of the hour."

—" Yet," observed my patient and attentive interlocutor,
" how many of your protestant brethren, even including
some of the clergy, have at all times, and in these days
more loudly than ever, complained of the existing liturgy,
particularly of some parts, and above all, of its extraordinary length! The latter objection I have so often
heard made, that I should think it must prevail to a great
extent; and where the complaint has been conceived, there
devotion must have been damaged and listlessness prevailed.
Now, by the short duration of our ordinary mass, we eschew
the possible occurrence of such a feeling; and when solemn
mass, a service necessarily much longer, is celebrated on
stated days, listlessness is precluded by the very ceremonies and accessories which attracted the serious attention
of your travelling companion."

—" I doubt much," was my reply, " whether a natural
want of devotion had not preceded instead of followed the
complaint made by some individuals against the length of
the English liturgy. I will admit, however, that some truly
religious and conscientious christians have urged special
objections, which seem plausible, to certain parts of the

service; a circumstance by no means marvellous, considering that those objections are urged against what is of human devising, namely, the order and form of the service constituting the liturgy, and consequently, like all human things, fallible. Some object to the length of that service, as you have stated, not because there is *too much of it*, but because there are in it many repetitions which seem unnecessary. But such an objection is equally applicable to your own, though much shorter, service of the mass, in which the priest repeats many times the same *introits, prayers, offertories, secrets*, &c. Still, if repetition tend not only to prolong the general service unnecessarily, but likewise to diminish the effect it would otherwise produce on the congregation, we are entitled to consider it as objectionable.

" The repetition of the same prayer within a short space of time, some think, takes from its effect on the mind and heart of those who utter it. In an especial manner, say they, ought we to avoid repeating more than once, during the same period of daily worship, our great act or profession of faith—the Creed—which should not be pronounced but in the most solemn and emphatic manner, and never with any variation in the words of its context, as occurs when that solemn declaration of our belief is read aloud in the order of morning prayer, and again in that of the communion. The latter, which is the one originally settled at the Council of Nicæa, and which the Romish as well as the Anglican church adopts, declares, and pronounces in common, without the smallest variation,—being more impressive and comprehensive than the more ancient ' symbol,' or the so-called Apostles' Creed,—should be the one, and only one, assigned for our service, and ought to be most emphatically delivered at the very beginning of that service, immediately after the confession and absolution. It is then that the repentant and absolved christian, feeling within him the high and consoling character with which he is invested, exultingly proclaims his faith in those tenets which have served to secure him that character.

" In the litany (others of the objectors remark), which is intended to comprehend requisitions of every possible kind, we have (if it is to be read every Sunday), all that we can possibly ask. We ought not, therefore, to repeat under another form, and with many more words, prayers with the very same objects. What earthly ruler or potentate to whom we owe allegiance, and from whom we expect protection, should we venture to address with a petition for an especial favour twice or thrice at the same audience, varying only the words of the petition or prayer?

" We find another set of devout christians in the English church, whose objections are not to the length but to the manner of the service. Some of these think, for example, that the first prayer of the preacher on entering the pulpit, and before beginning the discourse, should be an extempore invocation, and always varied, like the result of inspiration. A set prayer, they contend, has no, or very little effect in preparing the souls and minds of the devout to take in the holy words that are to follow. We either see it read by the preacher, or know it to proceed from the faculty of memory, and we cannot imagine it to be the effect of an innate feeling of true devotion, when we hear the same clergyman repeat, Sunday after Sunday, the same prefatory aspiration or prayer for aid in enabling him to deliver properly the word of the Lord, and his congregation suitably to receive it. An extempore orison at such a conjuncture would be free from all such objections; nor can it be considered unsafe, as stated by some people, to leave to the preacher the liberty to compose such a prayer, lest he should introduce into it foolish, or ridiculous, or heretical expressions; when we know him to be entrusted with the very privilege, but much more extensive, for the next hour, during which he may, either extemporarily or from some written pages, deliver whatever his views or his imagination may dictate.

" The effect of a spontaneous prayer of invocation before the sermon, varied on every sabbath day, was the first means by which Irving, at the commencement of his pulpit career in London, acquired that celebrity which led the loftiest spirits and the greatest orators of the age, Sunday after Sunday, to the Scottish Chapel, in the vicinity of Hatton-garden, but which he so lamentably lost as soon as he began ranting, and went on every year raving more and more, in proportion as he lost himself in metaphysical abstractions and absurdities.

" Lastly, some object to the general duration of the sermon. To be effective, and command uninterrupted attention, a discourse need not extend beyond thirty-five minutes.

" It has struck me that by removing these various objections, the duration of the whole service might be so shortened as to admit of three full morning services instead of one, thereby gaining that which seems at this day to be so deficient— church accommodation for the increased population of each district, without spending money to erect new churches, but allotting some of it instead for the support of additional clergymen to each church. A full morning service of an hour and a half duration, at ten, twelve, and two o'clock, would leave scarcely an excuse to any one for not attending church on Sundays. It would also have the additional advantage of affording to the humbler classes (who now attend only the minor service of the evening, because they are occupied in taking quietly their midday frugal meal with their children, an indulgence they enjoy but once during the week,) the benefit of being present at one of the full services of the morning, followed by the solemn service of the Communion, which they so seldom, if ever now attend."

—" You have abstained from touching," said my papist friend, " upon another great objection which obtains in the case of almost every parochial protestant church and even chapel in

England that I have accidentally entered, where the unbecoming sight at once obtrudes itself on your attention, of a greedy pew-opener, pocketing shillings or sixpences from stray visiters as fast as he locates them in pews, until the very fobs of his waistcoat bulge out with the coins. I made my way into a fashionable chapel at the lower end of Regent-street, one day in November last year, and gave my shilling to secure a seat in one of the pews, as I was anxious to hear a favourite preacher. I saw afterwards six more persons in succession do the same thing. You cannot have failed to have observed this practice in the different churches you must have visited in the course of your excursions from one Spa to another. Now, if money is to be paid by a stranger on entering a protestant church or chapel, it ought surely to be either as an offering towards the support of the incumbent, or for the poor of the district. But that a servant should traffic in seats in the house of God with such as are desirous to hear his Holy Word, is scandalous; the more so as the traffickers generally dispose, for the time, of pews and seats appropriated or belonging to individuals who have already paid for the same. Are not these traffickers like the men whom our Saviour expelled from the temple?

" How different is the case in a Roman catholic church. There the seats are all free, and the whole space belongs to all who come to occupy it; the smallest coin is, in some few churches on the continent, demanded from the devotee by some poor woman for the accommodation of a chair when no other sitting accommodation remains; but in our Roman catholic chapels in England, even that trifling semblance of traffic is forbidden. The only appeal to the congregation is for charity during part of the service, generally while the sermon is proceeding, in the same manner that your deacons or churchwardens receive oblations for the poor during the Communion-service collection, or at the doors on particular occasions. A young acolyte in his proper vestment, and sometimes a common attendant, tenders a small leather bag as he walks through the groups of assembled devotees, receives their voluntary and very moderate contributions, which are afterwards carried to the sacristy, emptied out in the presence of the principal priest, taken an account of, and laid in store for the poor or the necessities of the church. Such subventions, being perfectly of an eleemosynary kind, and not for the private lucre of an individual, lose at once the character of mercenary hire, drink-gold, or simony in fact, which the slipping of shillings, one after another, into the hands of the pew-openers in church for their individual gain, most unquestionably resembles, and is therefore to be abominated."

Thus far did our dialogue proceed respecting the influence of the ordinary liturgy of the Anglican and Romish church, in promoting, fixing, and keeping alive true devotion among their worshippers, by their respective rituals; without any reference to those much more important differences existing between them, which in reality constitute the foundation of the two religious creeds. I felt that subjects of so awful a nature were scarcely within the province of two discussing laymen, and I am equally sensible that their discussion at full length into which we again engaged on the following morning, is not strictly admissible in this place.

After long argumentations, quotations, and references in attack and defence of the leading points, by which the Roman christian faith is prominently characterised, I left my friend to the consideration of many queries, naturally suggested by the singular positions for which he contended in support of the holiness of his own church; and to those queries he was not then prepared with satisfactory answers.

—" As the followers of that church," I observed to him, "while defending their particular tenets, contend for something which they hold to be ' positive' and ' infallible ;' whereas, upon that subject, we are satisfied with a system of denegation only ;

it behoves them to. adduce proofs of the correctness of their affirmatives out of the same written evidence, whether inspired or historical, from which we derive our reasons for protesting against the manner of their early separation from the true apostolic church, and their dissent, in practice as well as interpretation, from the words of Christ, as handed down to us in writing by his Apostles and their disciples, to be the foundation and pillar of our faith.

"To begin with what is most important. In which of those Apostles or disciples—nay, to come nearer as to time, in which of the first teachers of christianity immediately after them, for the space of more than two hundred years, can the Romish churchman point out a single passage to show that those holy followers of their Divine Master ever called together the devout christians in order to pray to God, and upon such an occasion took a portion of bread and wine, consecrated them by means of the sign of the cross and the whispered words of ' *Hoc est corpus meum,*' &c. employed by the priest of the present day at mass,—ate the one and drank the other,— firmly believing them to be the real and self-same body and blood of the Saviour, and taught their congregation to believe the same ; instead of simply considering those elements as the representatives of the spiritual presence of the body and blood of HIM in remembrance of whom, and of the foundation of HIS religion, they were instituted ?

"We deny that any such passage exists in written evidence ; or that, at any time after the death and resurrection of their Master, when the Apostles went about ' preaching and breaking of bread,' they proclaimed and believed in the corporeal presence of Christ's natural flesh and blood on all or any of those occasions. Consequently, the ordinary mass of the Romish church, which is, in reality, nothing else but the communion of the priest under both forms, and under the firm conviction just alluded to, preceded, accompanied, and followed by prayers in the presence of the people, is not of apostolic origin or authority.

" But should the Romish churchman retreat from written evidence, as insufficient for his purpose, to oral tradition, and pretend that by it an authority is obtained for believing that the miraculous transformation of the spiritual into the real body and blood of the Saviour was taught by the Apostles and the immediate disciples of Christ, then let him single out such an authoritative tradition in any part of the volumes of the oldest of the uninspired writers. Let him point it out in CLEMENS ROMANUS, for instance, who, besides having been Bishop of Rome, the third in succession after the Apostles, had seen and conversed with the Apostles whose preaching was still sounding in his ears, and was contemporary with many who, like himself, had been instructed by the Apostles, and had heard all their traditions. Or let him refer for the same purpose to the more learned books of CLEMENS ALEXANDRINUS, a zealous convert to christianity of the second century, who, abounding more than any other christian writer in knowledge of every description, including that of heresies and schisms in the primitive church, would certainly, if he had heard of such, not have omitted a tradition involving so portentous and miraculous an exhibition of God's power, repeated at all times and at all hours, at the bidding of every priest, no matter how many thousands of them may be engaged simultaneously through the Roman catholic world in celebrating the mass.

" I cannot call to my aid just now, with equal certainty, the authority of a third holy father of the christian church, IRENÆUS, whom the papists will certainly not reject, and who, having been a diligent collector of apostolical traditions, must, if such a one as they assume had existed in his time, about the closing of the second century, have recorded it. I have no means of referring to his writings; but if the tradition in question had been there recorded, the Romish churchman would most assuredly have brought it forward."

—"What!" exclaimed the startled papist, "do you not hold the words of the Saviour himself, at the Last Supper, sufficient to establish the dogma of transubstantiation? Surely you are not ignorant of the fact that even Luther himself declared, in perfect despair, that the interpretation given to those solemn expressions by the church of Rome, was the only part of its creed he could not demolish and overcome. And have not those very words of the Holy Founder been farther and fully commented upon and expounded in the way in which our church receives them, by the most inspired and enthusiastic of his Apostles—Paul?"

—"It would be useless for us, unlearned in these matters," I answered, "to attempt to go through the varied and endless arguments, comments, and subtile disquisitions to which those questions have given rise, from almost the very first moment of the introduction of the dogma under consideration into the religion of Christ by certain of the bishops of Rome, (long after the Apostles), down to the present day, including the very learned and recent opinions on that subject of one of the exemplary members of your communion, Dr. Wiseman, well known at the college we both visited this morning. He, and all those who contend for the material transmutation of the elements of the Eucharist after the consecration, assert that such a doctrine *has always been held* by the church of Christ from the time of the Apostles; and in support of their assertion they refer us to certain passages in the writings of the Apostles, which, they insist, prove that in partaking of the Eucharist, they firmly believed that the bread and wine they took were the real body and blood of Christ.

"On the other hand we, who reject such a doctrine, and deny that the passages so quoted convey the meaning attached to them by the Romanists, consider the words of the Saviour, as reported by three out of four Evangelists, and commented upon by St. Paul in more than one instance, to have been figurative; and we look upon the sacramental bread and wine as tokens that the body and blood of the Saviour are *spiritually* present at our partaking of his Holy Supper, as they were *materially* present in the person of Christ, when the Apostles were made first partakers of it, at its first institution.

" You admit (so I find it in a very able work, entitled, ' Dictionnaire des Hérésies,' &c., by PLUQUET, a staunch Romanist,) that although the words in which the followers of the church of Rome express their notion as to the nature of the Eucharist are quite plain, yet that they convey SOMETHING WHICH IS DIFFICULT TO COMPREHEND; and you confess also that the meaning we attach to the words of that sacrament expresses a THING EASY TO CONCEIVE, though you pretend that that meaning is contrary to the rules of ordinary language.*

" Upon your own shewing, therefore, the difficulty of the question would seem to be one of words and not of substance; since we must firmly believe that if there existed two ways of conveying his intended meaning to the Apostles, when Christ instituted the Lord's Supper, the one easily comprehensible, the other difficult to comprehend, the Saviour would naturally have preferred the former.

" But because that meaning is admitted by us to have been figurative, you, the Romanists, contend that such could not have been the Saviour's intention, as he had nowhere prepared the Apostles to receive, in a metaphorical sense, the words he pronounced at the institution of the Eucharist. The answer to that observation is short and conclusive. Through-

* " Le sens des catholiques est très-facile dans les termes; mais il exprime une chose difficile à concevoir. — Le sens des réformés est opposé aux règles de langage—mais il exprime une chose très-aisée à concevoir."—PLUQUET *Dictionnaire des Hérésies*, vol. i.

out the New Testament, Christ is represented as addressing the Apostles, and his disciples, in a metaphorical language. He has compared himself to a door, to a tree, to the true vine, &c., in order to convey more impressively his meaning on various occasions. That this has been his general practice we have no less an authority for believing than Christ himself, who near the close of his career, and subsequent to the institution of the Holy Supper, having declared it to be expedient for the disciples' sake, that HE should ' go away' (John xvi. 7 and 25), and again taught them various things in a mystical sense, exclaims, ' These things have I spoken to you in proverbs ; but the *time cometh* when I *shall no more speak* unto you in proverbs.'

" Does not this declaration go to shew that Christ had hitherto employed a figurative or metaphorical language to convey his meaning and precepts to his disciples, as one more suited to their till then untutored understanding, and likewise more akin to the habits and customs of oriental people ?

" Your churchmen rely much on their own assertion, that Christ had never led his disciples to expect, by any figurative expression used at any time previous to the Last Supper, that he would compare bread with his body, as a metaphorical mode of instituting the principal ceremony in the Eucharist. This is an error. Has not Christ pointedly alluded to such an intended metaphor, when he said, shortly before, ' I AM THE BREAD OF LIFE ?'

" What could have been the object of the Saviour in instituting the Sacrament by means such as he employed, following up the idea that he was ' the bread of life,' when being seated at the table with his disciples, to eat the Passover which he had ordered two of them to prepare, ' he took bread and gave thanks, and brake it, and gave unto them, saying, This is my body which is given for you.' And the same of the cup of wine, taking which he said, ' This cup is the new testament in my blood which is shed for you ?'

" The object was evidently a twofold one. First : To explain to the disciples farther than he had hitherto done, his forthcoming crucifixion, in which his body would be broken, and his blood spilt to secure eternal life to them and the rest of sinners, for whom it was given by the Father as a redeeming sacrifice. Secondly : To establish by a simple conversion of the ordinary Jewish rite of the Passover, which Christ had met his disciples to celebrate under the levitical law, into His own Holy Supper,—a perpetual commemoration of that redeeming sacrifice of body and blood which was to be productive of such mighty and everlasting effects on mankind. Hence the concluding words : ' This do in remembrance of me.'

" Are not these natural and very intelligible inductions from the process adopted at the Lord's Supper ; and such as even the church of Rome herself adopts? Then why invent also, as she does, any additional explanation of the two ceremonies, which renders the whole thing unnatural, and as her own advocates admit, *incomprehensible*, and places the Saviour in contradiction with himself? For I will not say what many pious and religious prelates and commentators have already said much more forcibly ;—how could Christ's real body and blood be ate and drank by the Apostles, when it was Christ's body, and the blood that animated it, which were the instruments whereby the bread and the cup were handed over to them. I will only ask in my turn—How could Christ expect to impress on the disciples' minds, as it was manifestly his will and intention to do, the fact that his body was about to be led to sacrifice and be broken for their sins, if he at the same time told them to eat that body and drink that blood, before the real sacrifice was accomplished ? And again, to what purpose could such a real, instead of a symbolical eating of Christ's body have served, which was not effected by the latter only ?

" The two ceremonies, therefore, of breaking the bread and

drinking the cup, and the words by which they were accompanied, could only have been emblematical; and I hold,
individually, upon this subject the further doctrine, that in
the like manner that God the Father had, in the olden
dispensation, instituted, under a covert meaning, the rite
of the Passover, (of which all the congregation of Israel
was to eat, but no stranger, unless by circumcision he had
first become like one of them,) in order that it might be a
link to bind the people together, as a sign that ' the strong
arm of the Lord had redeemed them from their captivity in
Egypt,' and also that it might serve as a ceremonial test,
or token, by which that favoured people of God might be distinguished ; so God the Son, acting in his Divine nature,
while yet in human flesh, instituted likewise under a covert
meaning, the rite of the Holy Supper (the Passover of the
new dispensation) to be a test or token by which his favoured
people would not only commemorate his death and their own
redemption from sin through it, but also shew that they ' are
followers of HIM who died on the cross, Christ the founder
of their faith.'

" In the same way, then, that baptism was made the
sacramental ceremony by which those who wished to enter
into the profession of the Gospel were to be introduced into
it,—so was the sacrament of the Lord's Supper made a ceremonial token of recognition among those who had adopted that
profession. In this respect the Founder of the Christian faith
did not differ from the founders of any other religion existing
in the East in his time, who all had established some particular
token and password by which their disciples and followers
were to know each other.

" That this must be the case, is made manifest by Christ
himself in that part of the Gospel which first led me to adopt
the present view of this debated point of difference between
your church and the church of England, and in which I
find that, soon after the establishment of this token of re-

cognition among the professors of Christianity, the Saviour used it himself in order to make himself known after his resurrection to Cleophas and his companion 'whose eyes were holden,' and could not recognise Jesus until he gave the sign and password.

"To awaken their knowledge of HIM, he began at Moses and all the prophets, expounding unto them in all the Scriptures the things concerning himself; and yet they knew him not; although, as christians, they must have been aware, through the instruction of the Apostles, of the applicability to none but Christ of all he was saying. But when, presently, Christ sat at meat with them, and *he took bread and blessed it, and brake and gave to them,* then 'their eyes were opened and they knew him.' Upon which Christ, having accomplished, by the application of his own established token and word among his followers, his desire of being seen by the disciples after his resurrection, 'vanished out of their sight.'

"You must admit that this gospel fact alone, better than any learned disquisition, proves the intention, the object, the use, and the real meaning of the Lord's Supper, and of the words that accompany it; and that its meaning is not the one which the Romish church has attached to it—TRANSUBSTANTIATION.

"There is, therefore, not the smallest vestige of Divine, apostolic, or primitive church authority for the most mysterious, incomprehensible and astounding dogma of the church of Rome, which forms the basis as well as motive of the mass so often brought before its worshippers, and the nonattendance of which, at least once on every Sunday, has been declared by that church to be a sin, to be expiated by a given number of years in purgatory, unless forgiven by the priest after auricular confession."

Such was the first of the queries I left for the meditation of my zealous popish interlocutor at Birmingham, and the same I would present for reflection and a reply to any of his fellow-believers.

Suitable queries, also, I ventured to put to my accidental friend, respecting the authority for another startling dogma of his church, whereby private confession of sins is commanded and made a sacrament, to precede necessarily, according to the tenets of that church, the true sacrament of the Eucharist, whenever the devout, during the mass, intends to partake of the latter.

—" Admitting," said I, " that the solemn declaratory words of the Saviour to his Apostles, ' Whosoever sins ye remit, &c.,' had conferred upon those holy men the high privilege and faculty of hearing the confession of sins made by the christians, and of absolving them, being penitent ;—in what part of the same Scriptures, or of any of the written records of the Acts of the Apostles, or of their successors for the first two centuries, is it stated, that either the former or the latter, in consequence of their own interpretation of the words of their Divine Master, had insisted, in any one instance, on a detailed enumeration of every sinful thought and deed being privately made to them by the penitent sinner, as a condition for receiving absolution ? Or, if no written evidence can be produced for such a dogma, but only some supposed tradition, shew me the holy father of the primitive church before the third century who has mentioned and specified such a tradition as having come down directly from the Apostles.

" ' Confess your faults one to another.' This expression of St. John distinctly points to the meaning we should apply to it, namely that we should publicly and in the presence of one another confess our sins ; and in this sense the injunction was interpreted by the primitive and early christians ; for they publicly, and in places of worship, declared their own transgressions and prayed for forgiveness.

" But how can such an expression be applied to the mode in which the Romish church has ordained the confession of sins to be conducted, namely, in private, and always to a priest, and to a priest only ? Had such been the intention of the Founder of our faith, would he not have coupled a distinct and specific injunction for a previous confession to the Apostles, at the same time that he imparted to them the power of absolving or retaining sins ?

" The confession of sins, inculcated in the New as well as the Old Testament, and in many places, was the purely fraternal confession of one to another, or of one to many, or of many, publicly, to an Apostle, as was the case with the thousands who came out of Jerusalem and Judæa to St John the Baptist, confessing their sins that they might be baptized. Would the Church of Rome contend that that transaction proves the establishment of auricular confession by the Scriptures, and that the Baptist had heard from each of the thousands of penitents who came to him, their individual and private confession ? Such a supposition is not only absurd but impossible.

" Not only there are no traces of auricular or sacramental confession in the Scriptures, but in the precepts even given by the holy fathers of the church, respecting confession of sins during the first three centuries, no vestige is to be found of sacramental confession as understood by the Romanists; not even in TERTULLIAN, who wrote a book on the very subject of penitence, and would have mentioned the practice of private confession to a priest, had it existed in his time."

In the like manner one might go on testing by queries and appeals to holy records the nearest to the time of the Founder of the christian faith, the many other dogmas or notions of the Romish church, which they hold distinct from the Anglican church, and for which they have neither a written nor a *real* traditionary authority.

But I have preferred limiting to the two important ones just disposed of, my introduction into a work like the present of a subject so alien to its real object; because the one being directly and the other indirectly referable to the form of Divine service of that church—the mass, which was the origin of my conversation and discussion with the stranger at Birmingham, who considered the mass as vastly superior in *words and deeds* to the liturgy of the Church of England,—it became necessary that I should venture upon such an introduction, for which, moreover, there is a somewhat parallel example in a recent and well-known work nearly analogous to my own.

My conversation ended at last by my pointing out to my popish friend that they, the Roman catholics, were, in fact, the real dissenters, or rather schismatics from the christian church, and not we, the so-called *protestants.* For as the Apostles, who had been sent abroad to instruct the uninitiated, had taught by their gospels and acts all converted christians to assemble together, and when so assembled to pray, and publicly to confess their sins, that being penitent they might receive absolution for the same;—to love the Lord their God with all their hearts, and to sing psalms to his glory, which the inspired writers had prepared : to search and read the Scriptures, both of the old and new dispensation: to obey the Commandments: to proclaim aloud their faith and belief in the Divine and triunal essence of Christ, his redemption of the world, his life, death, and resurrection; and finally, to eat of the bread and drink of the wine in thankful commemoration of the mediatorial sacrifice of Christ;—(and they had taught nothing else except the performance of good works by precepts and deeds) ;—the Anglican church had a right to consider herself as the true, the catholic and apostolic church, inasmuch as its liturgy or manner of worship embraces with the strictest precision all these apostolic injunctions, neither adding to, nor taking from, their meaning and intention.

" Now you of the Romish establishment," added I, " on the contrary, have not only taken from and added to the meaning and intention of the apostolic injunctions, but have entirely perverted the words as well as the objects of some of them ; and what is still worse, you have interpolated and mixed up with the worship of the Founder of our religion, the worship of many of his sainted followers, constituting them and addressing them as mediators or intercessors between God and his creatures; whereas the only mediator is, and can only be, the Divine Founder himself.

" You have been unmindful of the apostolic counsel to the Colossians, ' Beware lest any man spoil you through philosophy and vain deceit, after the TRADITIONS of men, after the rudiments of the world, and not after Christ.'

" You have, in fact, so altered the substance as well as the principles of the christian worship, that, compared with the best account we possess of the primitive church, it would be difficult to believe the religion of that church and yours to have sprung from the same source : and these vast differences you only began to introduce two, three, and even four hundred years after the foundation of the faith, and some of them even at a much later epoch.

" Had the christian religion, like all the human systems of knowledge, been one susceptible of gradual improvement, then the progressive changes you have introduced into it might have been accepted, if necessary, in order to forward its amelioration.   But the religion of Christ, like himself, was perfect at its birth ; and his injunctions to the Apostles were not to amend, improve, or add to the code of doctrines, principles, and precepts which during his lifetime he had revealed, preached, and enforced by his example ; but to go and ' preach the kingdom of God,' in the manner he had himself taught, as necessary to constitute a christian, and to ensure his salvation.

" That church, therefore, is less likely to be wrong which is the least removed from the rites, tenets, and doctrines of those primitive times ; and such is the case with the Anglican church : and may God vouchsafe that the church of Rome of the last sixteen hundred years may return to the state of faith and practice of the church of Rome of seventeen or eighteen hundred years ago, resuming her former purity and sanctitude."

CHAPTER X.

LEAMINGTON.

ORIGIN and rapid Progress of Leamington—What it was, and what it is
—The ROYAL HOTEL—Company—Table d'Hôte—Socialism—Accom-
modation—The MORE FASHIONABLE HOTELS—The Lansdowne and the
Clarendon—The Imperial—The Regent and its Table d'Hôte—Charges
extravagant — LODGINGS and Furnished Houses—New Buildings—
Eligible Situations—Streets and Shops—Reckless Speculations—Ruin
rather than Fortune—Who is the Cause ?—The ROYAL PUMPROOM—
Its Architecture and Defects—The SALOON—The Public Walks and
MALL—Aristocratic Patients—North-west Winds and Early Fogs—
The MINERAL WATER—Pumping again—Physical Character and Taste
of the Saline—First Impressions—Its Use in Medicine—The FIVE
WELLS—Analysis of Leamington Water—Pretended Sulphur Water
at the Pumproom—Its probable Source—MRS. LEE's Sulphur Well
—Lawyers not friendly to Mineral Waters—The OLD WELL—to be
Preferred — Mode of Drinking it—The ORIGINAL WELL—Goold's
Establishment the best at Leamington—BATHS—The Leamington Salts
—Mineral Water genuine and abundant at Leamington.

FEW of my readers who have reached "years of discretion" will fail to recollect that eighteen or twenty years
ago Leamington was almost a *terra incognita* to the *élite* of
society in this country. What is it then which has changed
so quickly the station of that Spa in the estimation of the
public, and, for the last ten years, but particularly within the
last seven years, has caused the said *élite* to congregate together

in that place in countless numbers, determined to go thither and nowhere else ? For that there are at that Spa, at this very moment of my writing, dukes and their duchesses, marquesses, earls, and barons, with their coroneted partners —not to mention the many Ladies Augustas and Louisas, baronets and their spouses, besides military knights and their ladies—no one can affect to be ignorant, who peruses those daily gossips of fashion, the newspapers.

This is a problem we must endeavour to solve.

Dr. Short, a learned Theban in his days, howbeit he dwelt and wrote in such a place as Sheffield, proclaimed in his two large quarto volumes on the mineral waters of England, exactly one hundred years ago, that people strove in vain to make something of the mineral springs of Leamington ; for that, instead of containing nitre, as it had been pretended by some cunning resident doctor, they were nothing but " a puddle of weak briny water."

There was, therefore, a Leamington, and something of a mineral water in it, even a century ago ; but nobody thought of the one nor cared for the other, until a rhyming cobbler, Satchwell, assisted by an honest friend, set about erecting baths for the invalids, and procure decent accommodation for their service. Success so far crowned his endeavours, that it was soon found necessary to look out for some more mineral water besides the one already known, in the discovery of which Satchwell and his friend were not disappointed.

Still the place continued in obscurity for many years, notwithstanding the preceding efforts of half-a-dozen physicians from Coventry, Birmingham, and Northampton, to bring it into notice ; and the visit of a solitary specimen of aristocracy to the Wells, " *an Honourable* Mistress Leigh," is recorded in the history of the times, as a proof of the wonderful progress the Spa had made towards notoriety.

It was Dr. Lambe who, in 1794, in a paper descriptive of the Leamington waters, published in one of the volumes of the " Memoirs of the Manchester Philosophical Society," first gave Leamington that lift to fame, which attracted thither not fewer than three duchesses in one season, who determined at once to bring Leamington to a par with Cheltenham, then in great vogue, and likely to cast Bath and every other Spa into the shade.

A search was instituted for more water, and again *it was found*. This made the fourth spring discovered in the place since the " briny puddle" of Dr. Short. A fifth, a sixth, and a seventh, however, came in sight in the course of time; so that, by the end of the year 1816, just twenty-five years ago, Leamington Priors boasted altogether of as many mineral springs as Cheltenham. Indeed, it seems to me that, as fast as the last-mentioned fashionable watering-place added to its discovered treasures of mineral waters, Leamington, to keep pace, as it were, with its rival, never failed to discover soon after an equal number of springs.

All these, nearly clustered together, were found in what is called the Old Town, or more properly speaking, in the original village south of the river Leam, with the exception of one which lies to the north, and close to the bank of that river. Beginning at that spot, over which what is called the Royal Pumproom has been raised, a new town, spreading wide to the eastward and to the westward, and creeping up a gentle acclivity northwards, has been forming within the last twelve years, and is still progressing.

Such is the brief history of this now highly fashionable Spa, which, a little more than thirty years ago, had only " The Dog" and the " Bowling Green" as houses of entertainment to tempt the visiters withal; besides a few rustic cottages for the convenience of the invalids; but which now boasts of a dozen of the most superb hotels in England.

My *pied à terre* on this, as upon a former occasion, was the Royal Hotel, for it lies handy in the way of one who

reaches Leamington by the eastern road—not the most interesting of those which conduct to this Spa.

For the purpose I had in view, the Royal is as comfortable a house of entertainment as any of the best hotels in
the place ; and probably more convenient. Bachelors, as
well as married people, have assured me of this. Its interior
arrangement is good. The principal part of the establishment is its large dining-room, in which nearly all the inmates assemble to a copious breakfast, with every morning
luxury; and again, at a table-d'hôte dinner, presided over
by one of the senior dwellers in the house. The company
then retires to the withdrawing-room for the evening, where
cards, music, and conversation are introduced, to enliven
and cheat the duller hours of a Spa-residence. I have met
with many select and agreeable persons at these convivial
meetings ; and were I to take up my abode for a time, as a
visiter, at Leamington, rather than be bored with expensive
lodgings and housekeeping, I should settle, by preference, in
this very house, and enjoy its public dinners.

The most amusing part of this species of socialism is the
mutual contribution of chat, small-talk, and scandal, which
every guest at the table brings, and pours out *pro bono* at the
hours of repast. So situated, a new comer at Leamington need
not remain longer than three days a stranger to the " low and
high doings" of the place, and will find himself in full possession of its red-book intelligence, and the *carte du pays* in
an equally short period.

The Royal, like most other hotels, has a spacious and
well-appointed coffee-room, but this is not much frequented,
for the reasons I have just mentioned.

The upper part of the house, which is very extensive, and
divided into many sleeping-rooms and apartments well furnished and with comfortable beds, is placed under the superintendence of an upper housemaid, who manages the service
of that department with the help of several under servant-

maids, with great regularity and civility. The rooms are
of good size and lofty ; but, with the exception of those to
the north and a few to the east, none have a pleasant look-
out. Altogether, the appearance of the building, its entrance-
hall and staircase, and the general aspect of the rooms, are of
sufficient importance to satisfy the greatest stickler for outward show in the hotel he is to dwell in.

I know I shall be considered a very Mohawk for detaining
my readers on such an hotel, instead of leading them at once
to the tip-top emporiums of fashion—the Imperial, the Clarendon, the Lansdowne hotels—superbly furnished and admirably conducted ; or even to the Regent, the only other hotel
where a table d'hôte on the footing of that at the Royal, and
even somewhat more magnificent, is kept. But to these I
leave their aristocratic or wealthy visiters to pay a just tribute
of praise. They pay in purse pretty smartly, and if that be
a recommendation for the rich and the noble, it is for them
to commend the establishments.

Of the charges at these places I need only say, that the
amount of a bill for drinking tea in the evening, and sleeping
one night at the Royal, and breakfasting next morning at
the public table (most bounteously supplied, to be sure,) was
thirteen shillings and sixpence, of which the servants took
one-third exactly. With dinner it would have been eighteen
shillings, which, multiplied by seven, gives us six guineas per
week, a sum of money for which a bachelor could be boarded
and lodged most comfortably at a German Spa for the space
of a fortnight at least.

At the Regent the charges are not inferior to those of the
Royal, and they are, in proportion, much higher at the other
great hotels, which are only family hotels, and have no table
d'hôte.

Copp's card makes it out that his board at the Royal, with
the use of the public rooms cost only three guineas a week ;
but when one adds another guinea for a sitting-room, with

an equal sum for a fire in that and the bed-room, and thirteen shillings and sixpence for wax and night candles, besides charges for servants, it will be found that the weekly sum I originally stated is the real amouut of the total charges.

Every thing in fact is extravagantly dear at Leamington. House-rent for the season is very high; lodgings are difficult to be had, and seldom under two or three guineas a week for two rooms. This is the case with those in Victoria-terrace, a very striking pile of buildings lately erected to the south and close to the bridge, resembling some of the best houses in our Regent-street, and having shops equally magnificent. But this, though a convenient, is not the choice part of the town. If the stranger desires to lodge himself more like a man *comme il faut*, he will secure a first floor in Union-parade, or Lansdowne-place, or in the Upper-parade, and pay from eight to ten guineas a week for the same. As to a whole furnished house in any very eligible situation, such a luxury, when to be had, is " pretty" and " dear."

With all the extravagance of charges, however, the hotel-keepers, as well as the proprietors of houses, make but a sorry business of their respective concerns, and the speculators in both, I trow, are burning their fingers. The old town has hardly had time to grow older, when a new one starts into existence. Who is to inhabit all these flimsy semi-palaces, it is not easy to conjecture.

Every road leading into Leamington has been seized upon and flanked with buildings. To the westward of High-street, on the border of the Warwick-road, a row of lofty houses rear their pretending heads, in imitation of those in Brunswick-square at Brighton, or in Kemp-town, but look in vain for dwellers. On the eastern side of the same street, round by " All Saints," the oldest church in the place, Priory-terrace terminates in another road, on the left of which rows of Gothic villas have started up in the last three years, called the Leam Villas generally, but marked distinctly by other names, such as Clifton Villa, Methuen Villa, &c. They face the south, and have opposite to them lines of other houses with greater pretensions, whose principal front being north, I should consider undesirable as residences. Here again, both among the villas, and these rows of larger houses, signs of more house-room than people can require stare you in the face.

All these buildings are south of the bridge. Northward, the fashionable Parade, over the broad and brilliant pavement of Union-street, the rendezvous of the beaux and belles temporarily dwelling in Leamington, pedestrians as well as equestrians, leads to many cross streets, at right angles with it,—Regent-street and Warwick-street in particular, in which houses without end, and shops, many of them as sumptuous as those in our Regent-street, have been erected.

I must likewise notice a range of tolerably fair-looking houses nearly adjoining to Newbold-gardens which latter are close to the bridge, and extend along the bank of the Leam eastward. This range has an inclosed green before it, and a terrace fronting the parade. Beyond it is Regent's-grove, Hamilton-terrace, and Lanark-villas, all of them with a north-west aspect. Opposite to the former of these places is the Victoria boarding-house, on the left of Bath-street, looking down the grove. Its rounded front, with six columns on the first story, resting upon rusticated piers, produces a good effect; which is more than can be said of the larger number of the new buildings in Leamington, where more out-rages have been committed against genuine taste and sound rules in architecture than could have been expected, at this time of day, even in this country.

This multitude of houses of every description—this launch-ing out of builders, and shop and hotel keepers, into thought-less speculations—has been attended by incessant changes in the ownership of property, followed by bankruptcy. Many begin with a magnificent shop one season, who are com-pelled to close it before the next. A bold and high-spirited hotel-keeper has struggled through several seasons, who has taken his place at last in the Gazette; while some other less unfortunate speculators in brick and mortar, having come to the wrong end of their purse, have been glad to make over their responsibilities for whatever they could get, to some successor, equally bold in the undertaking, and destined, probably, to be equally unsuccessful in the end.

Now all the mighty doings just described in the way of building, and which are of recent date, nor would ever have been dreamt of twelve years ago, are the work of one man—the cause and prime mover of the bustle, the start, the progress, and the increase of Leamington; and that man is a physician, of whom we shall say something anon. It does not require the foresight of Merlin, Murphy, or Madame Krudener to predict, that if the said great doctor does not let his mantle fall on some well qualified and equally lucky esculapius, Leamington without him will be what Brighton is already becoming, now it is without the King—an extended mass of modern dwellings, most of them mouldering and falling into decay: for as the reputation of the mineral waters was not the cause of the present crowds of people of fashion and rank who visit Leamington, so will it not be of sufficient weight to keep them faithful to that practice, when the waters only, and *no other* attraction, shall remain to distinguish Leamington from other Spas.

That I have entered into this the least interesting, though by no means the least important, of the details connected with Leamington, namely, house-room and accommodation for the visiters, ere I proceed to examine the mineral waters themselves, which these visiters are supposed to come to Leamington to drink, will not, I trust, be imputed to any bad taste on my part. Having so done, I may now fulfil the latter part of my duty, without interruption from the interference of more ordinary subjects, and give continuously the narrative of my proceedings and reflections on what may be considered as the medical part of the question and its auxiliaries.

Although the last discovered, the springs over which the Royal Pumproom is erected claim priority of attention. Every other spring in the place has something of a receiving-room attached to it, in which people meet to drink the water; but the *rendezvous* of the greater number of those who visit Leamington for the sake of the waters is the Royal Pumproom, which was erected twenty-seven years ago, after the designs of Mr. Smith, of Warwick, and at the cost of twenty-five thousand pounds.

Passing from the Royal Hotel up Bath-street, and crossing the bridge over the Leam, which was in my time undergoing considerable alterations and improvements, that have since been completed, the general mass of the building comprising the Pumproom, as well as the adjoining baths, appears immediately on the left, its longest front, one hundred and six feet in length, being laid parallel with the street, and nearly opposite Newbold-gardens. A wing projects at each end, thirty feet by twenty in extent, the sides of which, as well as the front of the building, are ornamented by a colonnade of duplicated pillars of the Doric order.

The general effect which such a building might have produced is perfectly *manqué*, from the glaring defect of its extreme lowness, being only thirty feet high; the columns of the arcade being of course lower—certainly not more than fourteen feet in height. Nor is the interior of the principal room much more striking, though its dimensions (seventy-five feet by twenty-eight) are more in accordance with taste. Still, to make good the claims which its *prôneurs* at Leamington set up for it, of being a building " excelling all the baths in England, and rivalling the thermæ of the ancients," one would have expected something better than merely four naked walls in the interior of the room, distempered over with a deep peach-blossom colour; having on one side high chimney-pieces of painted wood, and pilasters similarly painted, to imitate Sienna marble; with a plain white-washed ceiling, from which hangs pendant an ordinary chandelier, serving to light up at night four casts of statues in different parts of the room, besides the large counter at the upper end of it, at which the water is distributed in the morning.

The new Promenade-room at Harrowgate, and the recently-embellished Pumproom at Bath, and even the Montpellier Rotunda, at Cheltenham, I need hardly observe, cast this Royal Pumproom of Leamington into the shade.

However, at this room by early morn I attended more than once, in expectation of beholding the numerous company which I had been told was then in the place; for " Lea-

mington was quite full." But I looked in vain for more than
a few straggling parties, principally ladies, from eight till ten
in the morning. As they all, once or twice in the course of
that time, made their appearance on what is called the New
Mall and walks, in a species of pleasure-ground attached to the
Pumproom, I could not miss many of them, by following their
example, and examining each morning not only the quantity
but the quality of the visiters. The latter was everything that
had been represented to me. At Leamington, unquestionably,
no dross of society, or even ambiguous characters, will be found
among those who assemble at the Pumproom for their health
and the waters. The place is yet too choice and too costly
to admit of any but the very tip-top of society. Accordingly
one recognised the moment one entered the Mall, in the pale
faces of some fair damsels,—the hurried and puffing steps of
a portly Lady Gertrude,—the halting gait of a certain right
honourable,—and the saffronized looks of a haughty peram-
bulator, persons of importance in society, members of distinguished and well-known aristocratic families, or wealthy
commoners. But the number was never considerable upon
any such occasions, and formed a singular contrast, in the
estimation of one who has seen all the principal spas in Europe,
with what is witnessed at all the leading mineral watering-
places on the continent.

The conclusion to be derived from this fact is, that not one
tithe of the people who come to Leamington take, or are desired to take, the water; and such appears to be really the
case.

Of course, where nature has denied better means for a
public promenade around a pump-room, it would be unjust to
complain that the proprietors of this establishment (whose
exertions, as far as they have gone, merit commendation,
and might well be imitated in other places), had not provided
some gayer and more picturesque gardens and pleasure-
grounds than those I have just alluded to. The Leam,

which drags its sluggish course by the side of the Pump-
room, continues it along the margin of a large green field or
paddock, over which, and around which, is the only promenade for the drinkers of mineral water attending here in the
morning. The Great Mall, or that part of the walk which is
widest, and resembles a short avenue, is north-west by south-
east; and in the advanced state of the year, at which the
Leamington season begins, and with the ordinary climate of
the country, such an aspect is the very worst for people who
are made to walk between each glass of the mineral water
they drink, in order to promote a certain effect on the
internal secretions as well as on the skin. The latter is
checked by exposure to the winds which then prevail from
those two quarters.

I have seen, on a morning when the green paddock swam
with a floating *stratum*, two or three feet high, of white fog,
and the wind from the south-east forced dampness and chilliness into the very marrow of their bones, invalids of all
classes and ages tripping along with a rapidity that was
perfectly discordant with the notes then issuing from the
green kiosk where the band was located. These people
hoped by this means to ward off the almost inevitable consequences of exposure to cold, sore throats, and influenza.

In the Royal Pumproom, a respectable looking dame, by
no means a " *belle limonadière*," presides at the counter, and
distributes the water to every applicant who has entitled himself to that privilege, by inscribing his name in the book kept
open there for the purpose of a general subscription, either
for the season, or for a fixed number of days only. She
draws the water, *more anglico*, by that most objectionable
of all modes, a pump, whose pipes descend to the depth of
thirty-four feet in the well containing " the saline water ;"
but not so deep in that of the twin-well which supplies the
one charged with sulphureted hydrogen gas,—those being the
two sorts of mineral waters discovered on this spot.

The temperature of the saline water I found to be 52°.
Drank cold it tastes unpleasantly saltish; when warmed,
this taste is even more nauseous. As this water, according
to the analysis of the most approved chemists, contains a
larger quantity of the common salt (chloride of sodium) than
any of the other wells in the place, with not less than thirty-
three grains of muriate of lime and magnesia combined—both
bitter salts—it is not surprising that the taste of it should be
disagreeable. Of purgative ingredients it contains only
thirty-two grains and a fraction, and that is glauber-salts.
This proportion is not sufficient to render the water active;
the more so as its purgative action is somewhat restrained in
its operation by nineteen parts of a grain of peroxide of
iron in a pint of the water.

The first impression produced by the water a short time
after its reception, on persons easily affected by iron, is that
of headache, which continues sometimes till after breakfast,
or until after some decided effect on the *digestion* has been produced; but for the latter purpose a large quantity of it must
be drank, as I observed people to do, who scrupled not to use
for that purpose a huge tumbler I saw on the counter, that
positively frightened me. At whose recommendation they
do so, I know not; but I should be sorry to see any of *my*
patients imitating such an injurious practice.

In the hands of a skilful physician, this water, as an alterative, in diseases of glandular obstructions, attended by
visceral debility, without the least disposition to inflammation
or fulness, may prove highly beneficial; and as such I have
prescribed it with effect in several cases, after becoming
personally acquainted with its character and mode of
action.

In recent times additional ingredients have been detected
in the mineral waters of Leamington, by the aid of improved
analytical processes; but they are perhaps too minute in
quantity to add to the medical virtues of the waters. I allude

to iodine and bromine, both of which have been found by Professor Thomson, of Glasgow, in proportions of one grain of the former in eleven gallons of water, and one grain of the latter in ten quarts of water.

These proportions of the two principles in question, found in the saline water at the Pumproom, have also been detected at Robbins's Well, now the Victoria. It might indeed have been expected, that considering the geological bed out of which the mineralized waters are drawn at Leamington, all the wells that have been sunk or may yet be sunk into it, would supply a nearly analogous water. Throughout the district it is, as nearly as possible, the same as lias clay deposit, with saliferous marl, and subincumbent sand-stone rock, so uniformly disposed that the mineral water may with certainty be expected at depths varying only between twenty and sixty feet from the surface. Within that range are all the saline wells at present in use at Leamington; five in number, namely: 1. The Old Well (Lord Aylesford's). 2. Abbott's Original Well (Smith's and Goold's). 3. Curtis's. 4. Mrs. Lee's. 5. The Royal Pumproom.

Two other wells were formerly open, Robbins's, afterwards the Victoria, and the Bazaar Imperial Fount—in the latter of which there was the only chalybeate water known in Leamington. But these, at the time of my visit, were closed.

As usual with English mineral waters, the gaseous contents of these of Leamington are trifling in quantity. The proportions of carbonic acid are rarely more than three cubic inches and a half to the pint—too little to impart any taste whatever to the water. But here again mention is made by the analyzers of azote, to the extent of a half or three quarters of a cubic inch to the pint; with such proportions also of oxygen, given as distinct from azote, as confirm me in the suspicion that the azote so invariably detected by English chemists in the mineral waters of this country, and never by continental chemists in those of the rest of Europe, cannot be derived from any other than the common air usually suspended in all waters, and decomposed during the process of analysis.

As the composition of all the saline springs in Leamington, therefore, may be considered to be nearly identical, I have only inserted in my table the analysis of that of the Old Well, and of the Royal Pumproom, together with the analysis of the sulphurous water at Mrs. Lee's, which contains the largest proportion of sulphureted hydrogen gas of the three so called sulphurous wells existing in the place.

One of the latter, as I before observed, is that in the Royal Pumproom. I tested, as well as tasted, that water, which I found to differ most materially from the Harrogate water, and to resemble the one at Askerne, described in my first volume. It is a water having an exceedingly nauseous taste, and a most objectionable look besides, being of a dark yellowish green hue, with many floating particles in it. Doubtless the darkness of the colour may be ascribed to the folly of employing a leaden pipe to pump the water up with. Still its origin, which I feel convinced is in the bed of peat earth of that low piece of ground that lies between the south wing of the Pumproom, and the bank of the Leam (a very narrow space), would sufficiently explain the peculiar tint of the water; and such, I repeat, is the difference that will always be observed between the genuine sulphureted waters from rocks (which are the only pure and fit to use in medical practice), and those derived from bogs and quagmires. Add to it, that in the present instance of the sulphurous water of the Royal Pumproom, the source of which is on the very border of a small river, of a deep, dirty, and muddy appearance, thickish, and scummy on the surface, and receiving the drainage of the town,—the sulphureted hydrogen gas may, by the infiltration of such river-water through the bank, be derived, to some extent, from its decomposing ingredients. I merely throw out this hint, as of a possible case, not without the authority of experience derived from former and analogous cases.

I am inclined to look upon the sulphur water at Mrs. Lee's Wells as preferable, both from its taste and appearance, as well as from the copious change produced by the test I applied to it on the spot. Indeed the thing speaks for itself. The first water from the pump was slightly brown. It had lodged in the leaden pump and become decomposed; but it came up quite clear after repeated pumping, and then the test instantly detected the sulphur.

This establishment offers another instance of the ruinous effects of law-suits to defend property when invaded by one's neighbours, as we had occasion to notice at Harrogate. The original proprietor, finding the sulphur water of his well suddenly to deviate into what is now called the Imperial Fount, by the sinking of a shaft to form that new establishment, employed the men-at-law to protect his property and stay the invader. After a suitable length of quibbling, a proposal of arbitration was submitted to, but not until the unlucky man was ruined and compelled to shut up his establishment. The Imperial Fount people, on the other hand, did not fare much better, and their establishment also was closed, as indeed I found it at the time of my visit.

Mrs. Lee, however, having purchased the property of the former Well, caused it to be sunk fifteen feet deeper, and found the sulphureted water once more. The establishment, nevertheless, is but little frequented; and yet I should think the water deserves the attention of the medical men of the place, for many of the cases in which a saline water of considerable power, charged with sulphureted gas, is required. It approaches nearer to the milder Harrogate and Knaresborough water than any I have yet tasted, and is infinitely superior to the sulphur water at the Royal Pumproom.

The only genuine saline spring in Leamington, after all,

I imagine is the *Old Well*, in Bath-street. It is the spring originally noticed by Satchwell, which for a long time continued open to the heavens, when the water bubbled up freely; but which its noble proprietor, Lord Aylesford, ordered to be enclosed, allowing at the same time to the poor the free use of the water. A more modern and pleasing building was placed over it a few years ago, which, with some houses opposite, equally the property of Lord Aylesford, is rented and managed by Mrs. Squiers and her daughter, two very interesting persons, who contribute by their gentle manners and civility to render the well very popular and much frequented.

It is to be regretted that the objectionable system of covering mineral springs, and using pumps, should have been adopted in the present instance. The water of the Old Well is a genuine saline—has more glauber-salt in it than the water at the Royal Pumproom, and hardly a trace of iron. It is, therefore, the water *par excellence* in the place, and the one I should always recommend when I intend patients to drink the "Leamington water." The water is very clear, and when drank tepid, pleasantly saltish to the taste; its natural temperature is 48° Fahrenheit. Crystalized salts are prepared from it on the premises, which I have been assured by medical men are probably the best of those sold as Leamington salts.

My commendation of this water, however, must not be given to the exclusion of a similar approval of that of the "Original Well," discovered by Satchwell's friend, Abbott, and situate in the same street, where, after passing through many hands, and being called by many names, the establishment came at last under the management of Mr. John Goold, who holds it at present, and who improved the building by giving it a pleasing exterior. The water is as near as possible like that of the *Old Well*, and salts are prepared from it in the same manner, by certain chemists who have purchased that right from the proprietor.*

The part of Mr. Goold's establishment which demands especially my commendation, is his suite of bath-rooms, which are beautifully arranged, and fitted up in a style worthy of a private gentleman's residence, being well papered and carpeted, as well as lighted ; and the baths themselves tiled, deep, and wide. In these respects they are superior to those at the Royal Pumproom, which are nevertheless properly managed and deserving of patronage.

At Mr. Goold's there are eight baths, each having over it the necessary contrivance for the shower-bath. The walls are hung with *linen*, the border of the bath is of white marble, and there are four steps to descend into it. In the ladies' apartments, or dressing-rooms, besides every other convenience, I noticed that luxurious appendage to a lady's toilet, a *cheval* glass. Nor are the gentlemens' bath-rooms less luxuriously fitted up. In one of these I observed an invalid chair, by which a cripple may be easily lowered into the bath. For such as object to a very deep bath, there are two plain sarcophagus bathing-tanks, with only one step down to them.

A plunging-bath, fourteen feet by eight, and five feet deep, well lighted, is connected with the establishment. It is used cold in the summer, and is warmed towards the end of the season.

* With reference to the production of Leamington salts, I must not omit to mention a visit I paid to the manufactory of them at Mr. Herring's, an ingenious operative chemist in Bath-street, in whose laboratory, open to public inspection, the process is going on daily. Mr. Herring's process consists in simply pumping the mineral water from a well he sank four years ago on the premises, into a wooden trough ; it is afterwards condensed by boiling, and laid in zinc pans, placed on sand baths for gradual and slow evaporation ; the scum on the surface of the water being removed from time to time, until the dry salts remain behind in a state of granulation

In going over this extensive establishment, none of that appearance of mystery intruded itself on my attention, which is so often noticed when an inquisitive traveller of my own tribe begs for admission to similar or analogous institutions. The attendant shewed every part most readily, and explained the apparatus by which the mineral water is pumped up by a double-action pump—is warmed by steam-pipes—and by which the shower-bath is filled at the same time through a series of pipes, numbered according to the rooms, and discharged by the patient simply turning a cock, either for cold or hot water.   Every thing appeared genuine, and particularly neat and tidy; and I came away well pleased with the establishment, which, as well as that of the Old Well (where, however, there are no baths), deserves encouragement.

My readers must by this time begin to think that enough has been said of the Leamington mineral waters; although in the preceding account I have not included Mr. Curtis's baths and drinking-well, which ought not to be forgotten, as the former are quite as good as those at the Pumproom. The fumigating baths also of Mr. Fairweather, which differ not in the least from Mahomet's shampooing baths, may also be favourably mentioned.

I may now conclude what I have to state on the subject of Leamington mineral water with observing that two points are particularly to be noticed in its favour—first that it is to be had genuine, not the slightest suspicion of any mystification ever having attached to its production; and, secondly, that it is to be had in abundance.   As a drinking water, I readily admit the several moderate virtues which belong to such a class of saline waters; but, as a water to bathe in, I consider it as very little better than common sea-water. Used as a shower-bath, with or without the witch's silk cap on the head of the patient, so much employed in this place, and to be seen on sale even in the Pumproom,—it is not more efficient than ordinary water employed for the like purpose.   How

can it be otherwise ? After long immersion in the Leamington saline water, it is probable, and medical men believe, that some of its ingredients may benefit the body by
penetration through the surface, or by absorption ; but during
a sudden, rapid, and momentary ablution, what possible absorption of the component parts of the water can take place
through the skin ? If it be the shock that is relied upon, then
any water will cause that effect under similar circumstances.

CHAPTER XI.

LEAMINGTON CONCLUDED.

EFFICACY of Leamington Waters—Dr. Jephson's Negative Opinion—His Dislike of German Waters—Experience better than Vague Notions—AUTHOR's Ideas and Practice on this Subject—COMPOSITION of the Water—Ingredients—IODINE a farce—When and how to drink the Mineral Saline—Medical Consultation—PHYSICIANS and Surgeons at Leamington—THE ORACLE—Beach Lawn—DR. JEPHSON's History—His Character and Deserved Success—Monopoly of Public Confidence—STATE OF MEDICINE in England—Treatment of Symptoms and not the Disease—The " One Remedy" Plan of Cure—Celebrated Precedents—ABERNETHY, HAMILTON, and Others—Its Simplicity and Moral Influence—CERTAINTY *versus* Experiments—Force of Example—Medical Idolatry—CLIMATE—Whom it is good for, and for whom it is not—SALUBRITY, its degree—AMUSEMENTS—Leamington a dull place—ASSEMBLY ROOMS, and other Public Places—BALLS and CONCERTS—Circulating Libraries.

OF the efficacy of Leamington water, or Leamington salts, in the treatment of disease, there is no lack of medical authority ; but the one great authority regarding it—that of the practitioner who for many years might have successfully monopolized nearly the whole of the experience on this head—that great authority, I say, is wanting. Not only has that popular practitioner never expressed publicly his opinion on the subject, but even in private his testimony has never been of that decided character, to warrant my quoting it in support of the valuable medical properties of the water. Of mineral waters in general, indeed, I happen to know that the practitioner alluded to thinks very indifferently; and when I had the honour of an interview with him, after the publication of my work on the Spas of Germany, which had sent thither some thousands of patients who, of course, went not to Leamington that year, he ventured to speak unfavourably of the German waters, though he admitted he knew nothing of them from personal experience.

The prodigious number of happy results, however, that have taken place since, among those who have obstinately adhered to the practice of going to the German Spas, in spite of his *dictum*, may have worked some change in the opinion of that physician respecting them; and, if so, it is possible that he also may have formed a more favourable estimate of mineral waters in general, and of the Leamington water in particular. At present no one knows what he thinks of it, nor could I gather it from him at our interview. Very few of his patients, indeed, drink any of the water, and of those who do so, few drink long enough to affect their constitution in any sensible degree, or to modify their disease. Nor would it be possible to form any estimate of the medical value of Leamington waters from the results observed in the patients of the worthy practitioner here alluded to, even did they use those waters largely; since there is not one of them but undergoes a combined and well-followed-up treatment by medicines at the same time, on which, indeed, the successful practice of that physician is said to depend.

We must, therefore, turn to some other quarter for information, as to the particular virtues of the Leamington waters; and by so doing, as well as by reflecting on the composition of the water,—which, after all, is one of the best *criteria* of its medicinal properties,—and looking, also, at my own experience, I can with confidence state, that those waters will be found useful in many simple cases of disturbed or irregular digestion ; also, in incipient indications of the liver, or of the mesenteric glands ; in people who are undergoing a course of mercury ; and, lastly, in many glandular diseases accompanied by irritation or hectic fever.

These waters are not, *per se*, sufficiently active in urging the bowels, and frequently require the addition of Glauber-salts to render them so.

These observations respecting the intrinsic value of Leamington waters must be understood to apply strictly to the pure salines, without any iron, or at least with only a trace of it ; for where that mineral is present in a large quantity, —as in the saline at the Pumproom, in which it is stated by Dr. Loudon, the most recent writer on the subject, to amount to 0.956 of a grain, or nearly one grain in the imperial pint, —the use of the waters in any of the complaints I mentioned is incompatible.

The *Old Well*, and the *Original Spa*, or Goold's, are the waters mostly to be recommended as Leamington waters ; and so of the salts prepared from them ; for they contain barely a trace of iron.* As for the iodine of some of the Leamington waters, previously mentioned as having been detected by

* In a former note I described the mode of preparing the salts by Mr. Herring, at first from the Original Well, and now from a bore he made through a very red sandstone, at no great depth, where his public laboratory now is, when the water sprang up in a stream as thick as a man's arm. It was stated to me that four grains of oxide of iron were contained in a gallon of the water. But having tried in the presence of Mr. Herring himself the condensed liquor, as well as the natural water, with both tincture of galls and prussiate of potash, supplied most readily by himself, not the slightest trace of iron could be detected. The usual tests were also applied by me to the water in a very condensed form, under his inspection, for the detection of iodine, but none was found. I then declared to Mr. Herring, that, as both those ingredients were announced in his printed statement of the salts to be present in them, I should think it my duty to mention the negative results obtained by our experiments.

Professor Daubeny, who also ascertained its quantity, what importance can we attach to the presence of such a substance, which, in the proportion of one grain, is diluted over not fewer than eleven gallons of the water, or eighty-eight pints—a quantity that no patient, dwelling for a cure at Leamington, has time or inclination to swallow; for, supposing he drank one-and-a-half pints of the water a day (twenty-four ounces, or four doses each day) it would occupy him about fifty-nine days, or nearly two months, to receive within him *one* grain of iodine. This is homœopathy to the letter, and, like it, tolerably ridiculous.

With regard to the sulphur waters at Leamington, after the observations I have had occasion to make respecting them, it will not be expected that I can recommend the one in the Royal Pumproom. Speaking of this water, my excellent friend Sir Charles Scudamore seems to marvel that it will not retain its impregnation of sulphureted hydrogen gas, after it has been bottled for some months. " Whereas," says he, " the Harrogate water retains its gaseous impregnation seemingly undiminished for many months;" and then he proceeds to account for this marked difference, by means of some ingenious chemical theory. The thing is not so. The difference arises, as I before noticed, from the fact of the sulphureted water in question being simply the *découlement* from a peaty earth,—in fact, a *vegetable* sulphureted water, as I call all such to distinguish them from the real *mineral* sulphureted waters. If sulphur water is required for drinking or bathing at Leamington, that at Lee's must be employed.

All the saline Leamington waters should be drank in the morning, and almost always tepid. If the first glass were drank quite hot, the desired effect would be the more rapid and successful. They should be taken on an empty stomach; and, unless the atmosphere be foggy or very damp, the patients ought to drink them at the fountain-head, taking gentle and never violent exercise, at the same

time.   No saline mineral water is worth a jot to any body
who drinks it in the middle of the day, as I have heard
people say they had been recommended to do here, when
the stomach has already been at work to digest some beef-
steak-breakfast, much inculcated in this place.

In all these matters, however, the patient will probably
think it right, and for his own interest, to consult some one
of the respectable medical practitioners on the spot, particularly such as are not against mineral waters, and interfere least with their action on the system, by intruding and
disturbing medicaments.   To judge from the number of
chemists' shops, in appearance some of the finest in England
perhaps, and of which, in one short line only, from Bath-
street to the corner of Warwick-street, I counted not fewer
than seven—we might imagine that the prescribing system
at this Spa is in great vogue.   The mode in which medical
attendance is carried on explains this.   Instead of apothe-
caries visiting patients, and sending in medicines to remu-
nerate themselves for their trouble, agreeably to the very
absurd plan that has hitherto prevailed in England, and
England only, there are in Leamington three highly respectable prescribing surgeons, who attend patients, as physicians do, charging seven shillings for their attendance, and
sending no medicine.   My able and skilful friend, Mr. Mid-
dleton, senior surgeon to the hospital, and nearly related to
the physician of that name, to whom the mineral springs of
Leamington owe much, was the first, I believe, to introduce
this judicious practice, which has since been followed by
others.   Their prescriptions, of course, are sent to the chemists, and as there are upwards of thirty thousand permanent
inhabitants in Leamington who must require medical aid at
times, and as the occasional visiters to the Spa even will,
now and then, fall sick of accidental complaints, it is not
surprising that the display of brilliant flagons, darting at night
their prismatic colours against the opposite walls, or dazzling
the passengers with their violet rays, should be so considerable.

Of physicians there are also more than one; and hardly
a year passes but some new M.D. makes his appearance in
the field, which he however holds but for a short time; for
the one, and the only one, who seems to have monopolized
to himself the universal confidence of the patients, whether
visiting temporarily or residing permanently in Leamington,
is he to whom I have already alluded, and whose name, so
far and widely spread throughout the land, deserves that,
in a work like the present, it should have extended commemoration, even to the exhibiting of his residence, erected
by himself, and called Beech Lawn.

This simple and neat building, which has received within
it many thousand consulting patients, and which often re-
sounds with the cheering welcome of its hospitable master, is
placed in a most favourable situation in Warwick-street,
surrounded by a well-trimmed garden and lawns, and not far
from the fashionable promenade itself, one of the handsomest
streets in any provincial city of England, represented by the
vignette inserted in the last chapter.   It will be pointed out
in after years to future visiters as the habitation of one whose
success as a physician had no parallel in his own time.

The history of Dr. Jephson is encouraging to medical practitioners, and highly creditable to himself. Originally the partner of an apothecary, named Chambers, at a time when Leamington was but an indifferent Spa, he dissolved partnership, after some years of assiduous occupation, and sold his share of interest in the concern to a gentleman who is at present one of the three resident prescribing surgeons in the place. This accomplished, Mr. Jephson removed to an University, where he took his degrees, after which he returned to Leamington to practise as a physician. His old friends, and the reputation he had before acquired among them, soon procured him employment; and he succeeded so far in securing to himself a large number of the patients previously attended by the resident surgeons, as to excite murmurs of complaint that in returning to practise at Leamington, he had infringed the terms of his contract of sale. But not a shadow of just ground existed for such a complaint, since Dr. Jephson had now settled himself in his old quarters in a totally different character from that of a prescribing surgeon or apothecary.

The turmoil and opposition, however, set up on the occasion were very great, and the worthy physician was so much annoyed by them, that at one time he entertained serious thoughts of abandoning the field. He stood to his post, nevertheless, persuaded to do so by the many attached friends and patients who liked him too well to lose him. In process of time, he succeeded in silencing all opposition and detraction, by returning good for evil, and earning at last the affection, or, at all events, the good will, of all his brethren.

Dr. Jephson possesses great tact in the management of patients, and knows best when to assume the garb of severity, or even abruptness of manners, if their good requires it; for, at heart, there is not a kinder man; neither is there any other among the wealthy members of his profes-

sion raised to the summit of local fame who is more readily
or so extensively charitable.

In his attendance, when the case calls for such feelings, he
is all kindness, softness and zeal. He will not waste time in
repeating visits because desired to do so by some haughty aris-
tocrat, or some whimsical lady of fashion, if he thinks it unnecessary. On the contrary, he will absent himself for a week
from such patients. But where the case demands his vigilance
and attention, he has been known to repeat his visits more than
once daily, without the slightest reference to additional remuneration for his increased trouble. As often as six times in
one day have I known Dr. Jephson to attend a patient of
my acquaintance, while long danger prevailed during a severe
attack of inflammation, although otherwise overwhelmed by
engagements ; and yet no intreaty could induce him to accept
any other than the first honorary given to the physician.

This liberal turn of mind seems natural and a source of
gratification to him; as must be those splendid acts of benevolence and charity of his towards the lame and the poor of
Leamington, which are testified by the endowments he has
made of hospitals and other charitable institutions. Luckily
for humanity, an income, said to amount to twenty thousand
a year from professional exertion, enables this fortunate
member of our profession to indulge in these philanthropic
propensities ; and may he long live to enjoy the reward of
them in an approving conscience.

It is a study worth a few moments' attention to inquire
by what method an individual, so qualified and so disposed,
has been able to reach the station which Dr. Jephson at present occupies as a professional man; and a few general
remarks, perhaps, will assist us in this consideration.

In a country like England, where medicine, since the time
of Cullen and Brown, has been practised on no definite principle or theory whatever, but purely in accordance with the em-
pirical method—that is, by treating particular symptoms of a

disease either through the means of some *well-known* medicine or combination of medicines, or through the action of *new* remedies not yet sufficiently established—there will always be found some one popular medical man, be he a physician, surgeon, or apothecary, who runs too fast for the rest of his contemporaries, who outstrips all reputations, and defies every known calculation as to the success he is likely to have. Where an ordinary medical man would be just beginning, the fashionable favourite is already at the pinnacle.

Such characters profess no new philosophy—create no new system. Some of them adopt one, and only one, view of whatever human disorder falls under their notice, and always select the same prominent symptom as the one to be medicated ; while others, on the contrary, admitting the existence of variety in human disease, adopt yet the notion that one principal remedy only is necessary for their cure. I think I am not doing injustice to the highly-popular head of the profession at Leamington, in stating that he belongs to the class of practitioners who follow the last of the two above-mentioned plans. In this respect he but does that which many very popular members of his profession in this country, physicians as well as surgeons, have done before him, from time to time, and who, by following the plan in question, contrived to stand aloof and alone among the mass, like the oracles of olden days—their decisions being deemed final and indisputable.

Who has ever known Abernethy to prescribe any other but one medicine, or entertain any other but one view of every disease, although he admitted the vast variety of them that presents itself to the medical practitioner? and who was deemed, at one time, more oracular than he? Have we not seen a late physician rise into almost universal esteem and confidence in the Modern Athens of the north, who deemed the want of free purgation the only cause, and purgation the only remedy, of every disease incidental to man ? Has not a practitioner of surgery, not far removed from the metropolis, contrived at one time to absorb to himself all the reliance which great people have in the art of medicine, by following one only method of treatment, the bandaging or swathing of limbs or body under any circumstance of chronic disorder? In fact the examples of such men are innumerable.

The popular physician of Leamington, with equally great self-confidence, relies principally if not solely on the employment of preparations of iron, with or without sulphuric acid, as a sovereign remedy under one or two forms; to one of which he has given the name of " magnetic oxide of iron," —resembling in this respect an equally popular, and oracular, as well as wealthy M.D. at Bath, in the time of Charles I., of whom quaint Guidott says, that " he was very happy in (the glory of a physician) the cure of chronical distempers, which he effected chiefly by chalybeate medicines, which he was wont to say, were as true as steel."

The merit of the " one remedy" plan is its simplicity. It saves time and trouble to the practitioner, and it is not without a beneficial influence on the patients. To be treated as twenty, or twenty hundred other patients, including marquesses and marchionesses, have been treated before, is a circumstance calculated to inspire confidence, and one which leads every new patient to hope that he, like the rest of the many hundreds, will recover under the " one remedy" plan.

The advantages of this first moral result to the practitioner himself is that he sets about to cure the disease with equal confidence, and a sort of oracularism that produces great impressions. This combination of moral agencies stamps the medical practitioner as a worker of miracles. He becomes notorious, and people stimulate each other, as it were, to flock to him, in the firm belief that he has made some particular discovery in the art of treating disease which the rest of the physicians and surgeons, his contemporaries, have missed or cannot understand.

To endeavour to cure a disease by a succession of different remedies, according to the general method, is a course which bears in itself the character of experimental practice, and consequently of uncertainty in the expectation of cure. But the " one remedy" plan practitioner, who employs but one class of remedies in all cases, shews that he has no need of experiments ; for he is certain that in every case they will effect a cure. Hence patients, especially among the upper and wealthy classes, after having submitted to the trials of various remedies and means by their ordinary medical attendants or consulting physicians, all of whom have proposed some new medicine, and as often changed the treatment of their predecessors, without effecting any amelioration in the disease (and I allude to *chronic* diseases only, which form the four-fifths of a medical man's practice), run at last to the " one plan" practitioner, and blindly commit themselves to his infallible treatment.

One patient brings another. The force of example is contagious in such matters. What a hundred people will believe and swear by, will induce ten times a hundred more to do the same ; and thus a perfect oracle is set up in the end, by an increasing crowd of worshippers, who surround the idol, in the full expectation of being restored, through him, to the blessings of health.

England has seldom been without one of these medical wonders. It is not often that two such exist at the same time : they rather succeed one another. I am not here alluding to those irregular medical men who, in this country more than elsewhere, owing to the thorough ignorance that prevails among the public generally on the subject of medicine, contrive to achieve for themselves a high-sounding name ; for of these there is at all times a plentiful supply. I refer solely to regularly educated men, who either have the good luck to find themselves progressively (and generally in very quick time) carried to the pinnacle of popular celebrity ;

or who, endowed with peculiar talent, have studied the art of getting there. The celebrity of these men is a respectable celebrity, it seems to be deserved, it begets an enormous fortune, and fortune secures a name, even after the celebrity has disappeared.

Connected with the medical practitioners of Leamington, comes the consideration of its climate and salubrity. I met one morning a very old acquaintance of mine, remarkable for his height and corpulence, who had been domiciled at Leamington some months on account of his lady, then under the care of Dr. Jephson. He was grumbling through a wire muzzle, yclept a *respirator* (read *suffocator*), at the weather, and gave me a sweeping account of the climate of the place, in few but energetic words. " This place is damp and low," said he ; " there are too many trees about it, and it rains too often. In fact, it is a h— of a place for catching colds and sore throats."

A very sensible and clever lady, who has for many years been residing in the higher and gayest part of Leamington, where the New Episcopal Chapel, surrounded by rows of houses that rival those of Eaton-square, severally called Beauchamp-square, and Beauchamp-terrace (with Clarendon-square to the westward of them), forms the farthest vista of the principal street in the new town,—and who had very judiciously selected that situation as the most eligible perhaps in Leamington,—assured me that the air of the place is relaxing and damp, that people cannot get *braced*, as in many other places, and that it is too often wet.

Such are, in fact, the general observations made of this climate by those who are not personally interested in the success of Leamington ; and the meteorological reports, as well as the consideration of the geological structure in and about Leamington, would lead one to form the same opinion. Individually I should say, that for dyspeptic patients, and such as labour under derangements of the liver, accompanied by what people commonly consider as nervousness and nervous debility, the climate of Leamington is not the most desirable.

As to its salubrity, I need not offer any remarks after the able statistical report on Warwick and its district, inserted by Mr. Farr, in the second general report of the registrar-general for births, deaths, and marriages. There it will be seen, that the number of fatal diseases in that district, of the respirative organs and of the ogans of digestion, in 1838, was very considerable in proportion to the population.

There is another, and the last subject I ought to advert to in regard to this highly fashionable Spa before I conclude, —and that is, its sources of amusement; for they are as necessary to the completion of a perfect watering-place as the pump and bath rooms.

On this head my information is scanty, and that which I possess I would rather keep than publish, for it is not very encouraging. Leamington, in fact, is one of the most monotonous of watering-places. Families of the first *ton*, who have resided there for two and three successive seasons, have complained of its dullness. Of general society there is none. Private and exclusive circles in the evening are indeed formed among people who have been long acquainted with each other, but hardly ever is introduction into them allowed to a stranger.

Public and subscription balls during the season take place in a very showy and handsome apartment at the ASSEMBLY ROOMS; a building of considerable merit, by the same architect who erected the Royal Pumproom. Concerts and other musical festivals are held in the PARTHENON, a high sounding appellation for a modest edifice, which has nought to assimilate it to the superb structure of ancient days, whose name it bears, save the representation in basso relievo of the Panathenaic procession, after the originals in the British Museum.

The public or circulating libraries form, in reality, at stated hours of the day, as at most of the English Spas, the centres and rendezvous of whatever there is of bustling life, fashion, and idleness in Leamington ; and of these there are several well worthy of the patronage of the public. ' Hewett's, as being connected with the Assembly-rooms, and next to it the *Athenæum*, which has the advantage of a garden and archery-ground adjoining to the reading-room (a great acquisition in the summer season), are, I believe, considered to be the best establishments of this description. I visited both, and could not help observing to some friends that the visiters to the ROYAL LEAMINGTON SPA (as the place is now emphatically styled by its inhabitants), have no reason to complain of the want of mental, whatever may be the deficiency of bodily recreation.

CHAPTER XII.

ENVIRONS OF LEAMINGTON—MALVERN.

If there be one circumstance more calculated than another to work mischief against a Spa, or against any other place of public resort for strangers, it is the fulsome, hyperbolical, and improbable eulogiums upon every thing concerning it, to be found in guide-books and local descriptions. In this respect, I must candidly declare, that " the Old" as well as " the New Guide of Leamington Spa," particularly the former, is obnoxious to such a charge in a degree far be-

yond that of any guide-book that I am acquainted with, of
any other watering-place in England.

According to the "Old Guide," not only do "the Royal
Baths and Pumproom, excel all the baths in this country
and the *thermæ* of the ancients," but the hotels are "magnificent, unique, and unrivalled in England;" the Athenæum "is the *ne plus ultra* of fashionable and inviting
places of resort;" the "Upper Assembly Rooms vie in
grandeur and magnificence and convenience with those of
Bath and Cheltenham;" and even the streets and rows of
houses not yet built, but only in embryo, are to be the
finest things in the world, "splendid, palatial, stately, grand,
and calculated to call forth the most unqualified admiration."
The trees are all "venerable and majestic," more so "than
any in the kingdom;" the footpaths and carriage-drives,
"are all delightful," many of them are "romantic," or lead
to "deep and bowery strolls for the indulgence of the pen-
seroso and the contemplatist." In fine, exclaims this hyper-
bolic writer, "to what height of greatness Leamington may
hereafter soar, who shall venture to conjecture? *** It will
soon rival Bath and Cheltenham, to both of which places it is
superior in many particulars, as none of them has roads so
good or a supply of water so abundant, neither do they possess a neighbourhood so rich in rustic beauty!"

The "New Guide," is by a very different hand, and does
not dip into the vocabulary of friend Robins, of the Piazzas,
Covent Garden; though even he, in his description, out-
steps the limits of reality a little. He, too, is enamoured of
the new town, but not so outrageously nor so ravingly as his
contemporary, and unlike him, instead of giving his own
sweeping opinion of the *alentours*, or country around Leamington, as being the most attractive in the world, he is satisfied
with modestly quoting the result of a curious ballot, which is
related to have taken place at a meeting "of those useful
and well-informed members of society who travel periodically

throughout the kingdom to execute 'commissions in trade and commerce*," held in London.   This ballot, it appears, was taken for the purpose of deciding which was the county district, within an extent of twenty miles, most abundant in picturesque scenery, &c. ; and on that occasion the palm was awarded to that district of which Leamington is the centre !

Now, the readers of the two preceding chapters will have perceived what sort of an impression the view of a Spa like Leamington, in its interior and various arrangements, in its old and new buildings, its resources and its accommodations, has had upon one accustomed to travel and to visit places of the same description, both in this country and abroad ; and they must have noticed that that impression was a favourable one.   But between admitting all that is true and good, as I have done, and subscribing to statements which must mislead the readers, and which neither the temptation of making friends, nor the fear of making enemies, should induce a writer of travels to adopt, there is a wide distinction.

The better alternative of that distinction I covet in my present pages, and that distinction leads me at once to differ from the exaggerated accounts and descriptions of the environs of Leamington, given by its topographers.   The neighbourhood may be of the very first water for a " hunt;" and that it is so, the very progress of Leamington town testifies; for we must be of good faith, and confess that *hunting*, fully as much as *water-drinking*, has contributed towards that progress.   But for the very reason that the neighbourhood of Leamington is made the centre of various distances to at least 140 covers, all within twenty-five miles, for the North Warwickshire the Warwickshire, the Drake's, the Atherstone,

---

* The reader will recognize in this *circumlocutory* description, our friends the commercial travellers of the first volume.

and the Pytchly hounds, — that neighbourhood cannot be either " romantic or picturesque,"—for in such landscape-features huntsmen delight not.

The truth is, that nothing can be so tame as the country within ten miles of Leamington—a circumference generally considered sufficient at all Spas for pedestrian or even equestrian excursions by the visiters. What can be more uninteresting than the two miles and a half of road which lead from the Spa to Warwick and its castle, westward? or even than the longer and tortuous bye-road leading to the famed ruins of Kenilworth, in a north-westerly direction? Yet those are the two principal lions of Leamington's surrounding scenery; and to them all strangers are invited to proceed, as the *bonnes bouches* of enjoyment which Leamington affords in the way of excursions. Can the warmest advocate of this royal Spa point out any other attraction of this sort, that is not a mere gentleman's or nobleman's park, or some well-wooded and undulating spot, without romance or interest, and such as abound in every part of England? Unless, indeed, it be the tranquil and pleasant retreat of the redoubted Sir Guy, Earl of Warwick.

The most attractive and commanding view of Warwick Castle, with its Cæsar's and Guy's towers, is obtained by standing before the left-hand parapet of the stone bridge, which, with a single arch of a hundred feet, spans the classic river Avon. The river itself, in this part, is narrow, and by no means picturesque: but the embattled walls and grey sloping sides of the towers, descending with their mantling of ivy and lichens towards the margin of the water, offer a prolonged line of the best preserved and most striking castellated structure in England. Nor does the eye at first discover that the foundation of this ancient military fastness is upon a rock of its own colour and material, which here rises precipitous from the river side, and seems to form a natural continuation with the superstructure.

The privilege granted to every visiter, by the noble proprietors, of examining their baronial residence, connected with
these imposing vestiges of chivalrous and feudal ages, induces, very naturally, a vast number of strangers to flock to
the castle. Few of them, however, halt to contemplate the
exterior, but, crossing at once the dry moat (now changed
into a green and ornamented shrubbery) by means of a
stone bridge in front of the ancient gateway, pass through
this, and enter the inner court, to be wrapt in sudden amazement at the sight of fortifications, parapets, and turrets,
once rugged, but now covered over with the smooth clothing
of ivy.

The long embattled wall that runs by the north side of
the court, reminds the visiter that to one of its unfinished
towers the hands of the usurping and cruel Richard gave a
beginning. These vestiges, which surround three-fourths of
an otherwise narrow area, stand in front of the private
residence of the lords of Warwick, itself forming the front
or south boundary of the court.

Through the wainscoted interior gothic hall—which bears
upon its lofty walls the appropriate armour and weapons
of the age of those who, if they did not found, at least
enlarged and fortified, this almost impregnable and massive
structure,—the visiters are conducted to the different state-
rooms. Some of them will even push their curiosity to the
exploration of the private apartments when the family is
absent. The whole suite of the former, in a line extending
to about three hundred feet from east to west, is seen at
one view by any one standing in the Great Entrance Hall,
from which also may be perceived, through the casements,
the quiet landscapes and distant prospects of the country
lying to the south.

Why, among the other ancient weapons in the hall, those
curious remains were not placed which are believed to be
the various pieces of Guy's armour, and which are now ex-

hibited, with somewhat of a ridiculous association, in the
porter's lodge? Surely, if the corslet and gauntlets that
clad the limbs of a traitor-knight,—Monmouth, "King of
Taunton,"—have merited a place in this armoury, those which
protected the bosom of a gállant and gallànt warrior ought
the more conspicuously to be seen in it !

The reader will excuse me for not escorting him along
this *enfilade* of rooms, and pointing out to his attention the
several paintings and portraits that cover the walls of every
one of them.   Rather let us hurry through the gardens
and pleasure-grounds tastefully laid out by Brown, to reach
the celebrated Warwick Vase—deposited in that most inap-
propriate of all buildings, as a shelter for its invaluable contents, a greenhouse !

My readers, who have probably contemplated often, at the
British Museum, that most splendid collection of ancient
vases, formed by a British minister at Naples, cannot be
ignorant of the fact that the same learned antiquary brought
to England an antique vase of white marble, discovered near
Hadrian's villa, which he afterwards sold to the late Earl of
Warwick.   Ever since that transaction, the vase in question
has been known under the appellation of the Warwick Vase ;
and has been repeatedly described and commented upon.
Some parts of it are restored ; and one of the masks or
heads of satyrs is modern, and of an inferior workmanship.

The decrepit, back-bent gardener, who showed me this
exquisite relic of Roman taste and luxury, observed that,
" When they dug out of the earth this here *waise*, which
will hold some hundred gallons of beer (in reality 163), one
of them there old-fashioned faces was broken, and they
made a new one in its stead, as you may see; but, la' bless
us ! it a'nt at all like t'others."

This quaint and *naïve* remark of the old pruner and
trimmer, reminded me of another equally clever observation

of a Leamington man to an acquaintance of mine. The keeper of one of the circulating libraries was asked whether he had any of the modern books of travels just published. " Oh yes," was the reply. " Have you got Spencer's Circassia ?"—" No."—" Lane's Egypt ?" — " No." — " The Spas of Germany?"—" You mean Granville's ?"—" Yes.'' —" Oh no : all them there books are so much alike the one to t'other, it's no use to get them."

I cannot help observing, and in this I am not singular, that a small elegant *tempietto* of stone would have been a much more appropriate receptacle for this very handsome specimen of ancient art, than the greenhouse in which it now stands, and where, moreover, it is but insufficiently protected from the injurious effects of the external air, as one may easily perceive by inspecting its surface.

Different far, in style of design and workmanship, yet fine of its kind, and calculated to rivet the attention of the stranger, is the display of architectural and monumental antiquity, by which the stranger at Warwick finds himself surrounded on entering that beautiful specimen of ecclesiastical structure of the fifteenth century, which is to be found in St. Mary's church, and is called Beauchamp Chapel. Small, yet perfect, and highly wrought in all its parts, this funereal temple, glittering with richly-gilded metal, profusely laid about in ornaments as well as monuments, and recording the state of the arts in this country four hundred years ago, presents a series of attractive objects, worthy of some hours' meditation.

The monument of the founder, Richard Beauchamp, who had had for his godfather a king, and was made a knight of the Bath by another king, who assisted at the coronation of a third, and enjoyed the confidence and high esteem of a fourth, Henry VI., in whose service he died before he was fifty years of age, is one of those altar tombs which admirably suit the florid style of gothic structure, but the merits of which cannot be analyzed even when we are inclined to admit them. The historical interest, however, which this, as well as the monumental tomb of Dudley, Elizabeth's ill-fated favourite, placed in the north side of the same chapel, is calculated to inspire, will always lead those to visit them who prefer such practical chroniclers of the olden days of England to many of her written records.

It was with the latter view that I visited the Beauchamp chapel; and for the same reason did I next proceed to examine those vestiges of the baronial castle of the last-mentioned unfortunate leader of the maiden queen's troops in Holland, which are still to be seen at Kenilworth. These, invested as they have been with intense interest by the magic pen of " the Great Unknown," form another of the points of attraction for the visiters at Leamington Spa.

It is thus, and thus only, that a place " of such extraordinary strength and largeness," erected by a chamberlain and treasurer of the First Henry, and by the next Henry forcibly snatched from the hands of that officer's inheritors, to be granted by another Henry immediately succeeding to Montford, Earl of Leicester, has acquired in modern times a renown which the extant relics had hardly before commanded.

The most complete and picturesque view of Kenilworth Castle,—that, in fact, which embraces most of the ruins of that once-famed edifice, whose massive chamber-walls " could many a curious tale unfold,"—is the one taken from the south-east angle. But the more partial perspective of the interior of Cæsar's tower, massive and dismal, because dismantled and broken, though bearing the semblance of indestructible strength, which is obtained on approaching the ruins from Clinton Green at the north, is by far the most interesting and romantic.

The sight of Merwyn's Tower, as the Necromancer of Abbotsford denominated the " Strong Tower," in which that arch-politician, Leicester, less of a husband than an ambitious lover, is made by Scott to precipitate his devoted Amy into perpetual silence and death,—is the principal motive which, in our days, tempts most people to undertake a pilgrimage to Kenilworth, and continues to attract the curiosity of every idler congregated at Leamington. I have seen these people in numbers, attended by a miserable cicerone, standing before the ruins, and looking at the several stories of this part of the edifice, called Lancaster's-buildings, endeavouring to trace the downward course of the devoted victim, and measuring in their imaginations more than with their mind's eye, the height of the deadly fall, until they actually shuddered, as if the crime had positively been perpetrated in their presence!

But I must not loiter amidst such scenes as these, connected though they be with the object of my account of Leamington; for other and equally important Spas further south await our visit, and I am impatient to plant my standard for awhile in Cheltenham.

Previously, however, to our proceeding thither, the reader will permit me to introduce, as if by way of episode, a brief account of Malvern, though that place comes not here in regular succession. The fact is, that not having on the present occasion (1839) visited that much vaunted summer residence, and the memoranda I am about to use for my short description being those I took down two years before, on the occasion of my being summoned thither to visit a patient who had been recommended to spend the summer months at Malvern Wells—I can only introduce in a somewhat irregular part of this volume my general account of that Spa.

MALVERN.

" Whilst Malvern (King of Hills) fair Severn overlooks,
   Attended on in state, with tributarie brooks ;
   And how the fertill fields of Hereford do lie ;
   And from his many heads, with many an amorous eye,
   Behold his goodlie site,—how towards the pleasant rise,
   Abounding in excess, the Vale of Evesham lies."

When old Michael Drayton, the contemporary of Shakspeare, indited in his " Polyolbion," or English topography in verse, the preceding quaint lines, an eastern aspect could not have been so objectionable in this country, as in every respect it is considered to be in our days; else he never would have made " King Malvern" look with amorous eyes to his own goodly site which had before it " the pleasant rise," towards which the vale of Evesham lies.

The very fact that the " pleasant rise," in other words, the " deadly east" stares in the face of Great and Little Malvern, seated at nearly the same elevation, on the range of hills called the Malvern Hills, would and must, with our present notions, disqualify those otherwise picturesque and well located villages, as residences for real invalids. Assuredly no one who had his choice of situation, being ailing in health and sound of mind, would voluntarily place himself where all the gales from the eastern points between north and south, might blow directly upon him, that wind being by far more inimical than any other to the human frame.

Such, however, is the true position of Great Malvern, standing as it does at the bottom of a valley which separates the northernmost summit, called " the North Hill," from the next and more southern summit known by the name of the " Worcestershire Beacon." The valley is one of many which, ravine like, run down at right angles from the eastern face of that long chain of hills that extends for about nine

miles, nearly in a straight line, north to south, from the Pale
to the Rye, dividing the county of Worcester from Herefordshire. These valleys, which bear the marks of having been at
one time water-courses, gradually widen as they descend
and open upon the dead level of the Severn.

LITTLE MALVERN, like its greater namesake, occupies a
position in another valley of the same description, immediately
under the Herefordshire Beacon, the highest and southernmost of the loftiest summits, three in number, that overtop
the whole range. Its front is like that of Great Malvern
to the east, but it enjoys superior advantages of situation in
my opinion, in consequence of the favourable geological
circumstance of the lofty beacon which rises behind it to an
altitude of nearly 1500 feet; retiring in this part of the range
from the straight line, westwardly, and thus forming a wider
amphitheatre around the village, which is in many places
thickly wooded, and better sheltered from the northern and
northwestern gales.

But although placed at the bottom of valleys, it does not
follow that either the one or the other of the villages here
mentioned lies low: for the contrary is the case; since, according to observations made by Mr. Leonard Horner, GREAT
MALVERN stands at an elevation of 273 feet from a common in front of the position of the village, called the *Links*,
at the termination of which plain there is the further elevation of the right bank of the Severn, which is itself between
sixty and seventy feet in perpendicular height; so that the
total elevation of the village is 340 feet above the level of the
river.*

LITTLE MALVERN, judging by my walk to that retired
village, distant about three miles and a half, on the morrow

* The Malvern Hills are part of a chain of trappean hills which Mr.
Murchison is inclined to imagine may have undergone a movement of
elevation subsequent to the deposit of the new red sandstone—a rock that
occurs largely in this part of England, particularly in Worcestershire.

after my arrival at the Great Malvern, cannot be at a lesser elevation; although, when the whole range of hills is viewed from a little distance, there appears in it a gradual decrement from north to south.

The two villages, therefore, are not in the plain, though in valleys, but are seated upon the eastern declivity of the hills which on this side rise almost abruptly, or, at all events, at a very considerable angle, from the level land that stretches to the banks of the Severn, a distance of about four miles.

Nothing that the pen of one fond and accustomed to the contemplation of landscape beauties can indite would be held to be exaggeration, after having enjoyed, from any of the various points of view on the rounded summits of these hills, the vast panorama which stretches before them, not only as far as where,

" Abounding in excess, the vale of Evesham lies,"

but much further. The eye wanders at once over the extended plain of Worcestershire, stretching for many miles to the eastward, diversified in its map by small wooded eminences which start up in detached spots. Numberless country seats and parks enliven the scene, and the highly-cultivated land, swarming with farms and neat villages, bespeaks in its appearance abundance and prosperity.

In the midst of this rich scenery the Severn is seen to wind its tortuous course, nearly parallel to the range of hills, from Worcester on the left, to Upton Severn, conspicuously visible below and in front of Little Malvern, and down to Tewkesbury on the right.

While thus engaged in tracking its career, BREDON HILL, the northern screen to the vale of Cheltenham, is perceived to rise conspicuous in the south-east horizon, where it serves as a guide to those endowed with keener vision for detecting, just below it, the humbler yet prouder Avon, which slowly courses from Evesham, and from much higher, towards and around the hill just named, going thence to mingle its water with the Severn at Tewkesbury.

MALVERN WELLS, a picturesque and retired hamlet, placed between Great and Little Malvern, will by many be considered as a far preferable summer residence to that at Great Malvern. It enjoys equally very extensive views, and affords excellent accommodation to visiters at different points of elevation on the brow of the hill. The least cheerful houses are those on a level with the road; but they have the advantage of being in some degree sheltered from the easterly wind. Higher up the hill is the WELL HOUSE, a commodious boarding-house, the upper rooms of which, opening directly upon the face of the hill, offer a warm shelter to those who are delicate of lungs, even late in the autumn. Another house of entertainment, also high up on the hill, is ESSINGTON HOTEL. The situation is commanding, and nothing can be more cheerful or inspiring, on a decidedly fine day, than the view of this house with its front brightened by a south-eastern sun, its back rooms screened by the hills from the north, and all around enlivened by pleasure-grounds, thickly clothed in many parts with luxuriant plantations.

Far different, however, is the aspect of this very house when one of those violent gales incidental to this region, and not uncommon, as admitted by its staunchest advocate, blows upon it from the east; for then every thing looks cheerless and dismal, and the inmates would fain, if they could, retreat to the back of the house, where, indeed, the principal front and apartments ought to have been constructed.

It is incredible with what pertinacity and strangeness of argument those who have had an interest in bespeaking a favourable opinion in behalf of the two Malverns with the public, have endeavoured to get over the great and almost fatal disadvantage of the eastern aspect of their favourite place. Nay, in a dissertation on the Malvern waters, (of the nature of which we shall treat anon), written some years ago by a learned medical practitioner, once resident in the place,—and in a still more recent description of the locality and its peculiarities, by an interested party, an attempt is made to prove that the eastern aspect of the two Malverns is not only delightful, because " the inclined slope of the ground to the eastward receives in the most favourable manner the first rays of the morning sun at a period when the air has attained its minimum temperature;" but it is also fortunate, because an " easterly current of air, meeting the lofty hills behind the villages, receives considerable check in its progress, and striking against them, will rebound, lessening the force of the wind, and counteracting its influence before it reaches the hill itself; similar to what we observe to occur when the ripples or waves of a pond strike against a wall or high perpendicular embankment, where the resistance of the water breaks the force of the next coming wave."

Ingenious as this theory may, at first sight, appear, were it true, it would only lead to confirm and increase the inconvenience of the eastern aspect; inasmuch as the " forward and rebounding current of air," in the case of an eastern gale, would take effect precisely over the devoted villages, in consequence of the screen of hills, against which this species of tennis-ball game of the wind is supposed to take place, being just distant enough to allow the "resilient current" to back as far as the village, there to meet with and " break the force of the next coming current:" thus shrouding, as it were, in a double coating of easterly wind, every dwelling and every individual in the place.

But the objection to a direct eastern aspect in England is not so much on account of the gales which may prevail at times from that quarter; for, after all, gales are not the most frequent phenomena of that wind at the season most favourable for invalids at Malvern. No; it is rather because that wind over-spreading for many weeks together every object with its grey, ashy masses, in extended and unagitated sheets,—sits upon them like an awful *incubus,* penetrating the pores of man and animals to the very bones, in spite of macintoshes and flannels, relaxing the fibres, irritating the more exposed membranes into catarrhal defluxions, awakening up the most forgotten pains of rheumatism into troublesome re-existence, and finally prostrating by its continuance the best energies, both of body and mind, of the resident invalid, who turns his back piqued and disappointed from the very panorama that had before delighted him—for he now sees it bathed in a vaporous greyish fog, distilling dampness.

Barring this disadvantage, which in the course of the Malvern season, including July and two following months, I admit may occur but seldom,—Great Malvern and Malvern Wells are residences much to be commended for the pure and invigorating air that more generally prevails, as well as for the pure and invigorating water that is to be found at both places. To breathe pure air and to drink some of the purest water in England for the space of three months, at the most favourable time of the year, are two circumstances in themselves sufficient to promote the ultimate recovery of many disorders, especially those which originate in indigestion, and have been previously treated by appropriate remedies.

But people should rise betimes for that purpose, and breathe the morning air, and not keep London hours, as I perceived to be the practice on my arrival at half-past eight o'clock in the morning, when I visited Malvern early in September, 1837. At that hour of the day I reached the BELLEVUE HOTEL, on the terrace immediately in front of the church or ancient priory, and one servant only was up at that time of morning, and none of the rooms were ready for the reception of travellers.

Being, as it were, compelled to kill time until I could procure refreshments, I sauntered in all directions through the little village, and noticed that most of the best houses had yet all the windows of the principal rooms closed and curtained, without a vestige of stir even in the lower apartments. Such also I found to be the case at the CROWN HOTEL, and at the KENT and COBOURG,—the situation of which latter house, by the bye, seemed the most favourable, being more in advance, and on the brow of the hill, nearer to the splendid and extended view which constitutes the great charm of the Malverns.

On another morning, wandering between seven and eight o'clock over the hills, and returning from examining the WYTCH, an artificial cut in the rock, which offers sections of the geological structure of that part of the ridge, and in so far is an object worthy the attention of visiters,—I encountered a few groups of sauntering ladies and children, who had been at the Holy Well at that early time of the day, and were returning to Malvern along the hills, brushing with their feet the dew that glistened yet on the short grass with which those hills are everywhere covered.

Symptoms of general life and bustle appear more conspicuous, however, as the day advances ; and during the many hours of a long afternoon in August or September, the NORTH HILL, on the right of Great Malvern, from the beginning of the road opposite the Library down to the Serpentine Valley, and round by the Ivy Rock, and up to the summit; and the loftier peak of the Worcestershire Beacon on the left, (to reach which the more easily, the Victoria Drive, at the commencement of its ascent, was completed a few years since,) with the Harcourt Tower upon it, and the Camp Hill, not to mention the New Walk to the Sugarloaf Hill—all these various points, placed at different elevations of the extended and broad incline of the Malvern Ridge, swarm with pedestrians, single and in groups, with explorers, solitary walkers, pic-nicers, and donkey-drivers, imparting to the whole scene the semblance of a gay fair, or of an occasional village festival—howbeit it occurs here every day, if the weather is propitious.

This scope and facilities for exercise—these opportunities of scrambling up precipitous mountain-sides, so as to put every muscle of the body in action, and test the strength and elasticity of one's lungs at the same time—this frequent inhaling of the purest air in a lofty region—these things, altogether, are the charms and attractions of the two Malverns, on which a medical man must depend for any sensible change he may wish to produce in his patients through their agency. In these respects the two Malverns surpass many of the more-frequented and fashionable spas in this country.

As to the Malvern water itself, I tasted and drank it in suitable quantities throughout the day,—first, at St. Ann's Well, where it issues in a very slender stream from the rock, and is received and distributed in a room that forms part of St. Ann's Cottage, a short way up the hill from Great Malvern,—and next at the Holy Well, already alluded to near Malvern Wells; and all that can be said in its behalf is, that its purity and almost entire freedom from foreign matters are its principal qualities. Whatever I have advanced respecting Ilkley water may be applied to the water of the Malvern springs or streamlets; for, in good truth, they are nothing else but *découlements*, like that far more important stream in Yorkshire, from the summit of the hills. The water, indeed, here at Malvern, is so managed in its course, when it reaches the so-called Wells (a most inapplicable term, by the bye,) that at first view it would seem as if it sprang from the place at which it is drunk; but on retreating behind the scenes the coursing down of the mountain streamlet is easily perceived, and may be tracked like any other beck or bourne along a mountain gorge.

Of the learned disquisitions written and published on this water, I shall not take any special notice. Still less will I enter into the consideration of the merits of a dispute respecting the pretended presence of steel in the water, which was once rife between two highly respectable physicians. Malvern water must be drank as a pure water, and as nothing else ; and to those who know the immense advantage of cooling a heated stomach, and of diluting thick blood, and of softening the acrimony of superabundant bile, by quaffing nothing but water of the purest kind for the space of two months, during which many other necessary rules of diet and regimen are observed ; to such persons I hardly need say that at Malvern they will find a boon of that kind in perfection, with all appliances to boot.

Judging from experience of the effects of a residence at Malvern, upon the several patients whom in the course of the last twenty-three years I have had occasion to recommend to take up their temporary abode in that region for a definite period ; I am bound to agree with several of my brother practitioners, acquainted with the subject, that after a course of the Leamington or Cheltenham waters, the Malvern water, and a residence on the Malvern Hills, at the proper season, are likely to be of infinite advantage.

The perfect simplicity of the water will be judged of by casting a glance at the Table of Analyses at the end of the volume.

CHAPTER XIII.

ROAD TO CHELTENHAM—VICTORIA SPA—STRATFORD-UPON-AVON.

Leamington's Greatest Star—STRATFORD—A Strong Temptation resisted—The VICTORIA Springs—The Queen's Hotel—Range of Baths—The SPA-HOUSE—Management of the Mineral Water—Luxurious Baths—The ORIGINAL WELL—New Spring—Anne Hathaway—Dr. Charles Perry—ANALYSES of the Spa Water—Discrepancies—Appearance, Physical Character, and Taste of the Waters—MEDICINAL Virtues—Dr. Jephson's Opinion—Situation and Improvements—SHAKSPEARE'S Cradle — Washington IRVING and Walter SCOTT—Albums — NEW-PLACE—Sacrilege — Recollections — The CHURCH — Shameful Dilapidation—Recent Repairs—The GREAT POET'S MONUMENT—ENGLAND'S PRIDE.

ALLUDING in the last chapter but one to the environs of Leamington Spa, and to the principal objects in that neighbourhood, which offer any attraction to the resident invalids or occasional visiters, I purposely confined my remarks to those situated within a narrow circle around that place of fashionable resort. To such, however, as can extend their walks or drives from four miles to a little more than double that distance, a spot of paramount and intense interest presents itself to their notice, such as no other locality in England is invested with.

My readers will at once guess that I can but refer to that thrice fortunate little town, which, seated on the placid and reedy Avon, without any pretension to intrinsic significance, has acquired, since the close of the sixteenth century, a renown equal to that of the birth-place of the Cæsars. Yes; ancient Rome is hardly more known through literary Europe than is the town in which Providence cast the nativity of the greatest poet that ever lived—imperishable SHAKSPEARE.

Informed by letters of the existence of a mineral spring at Stratford-upon-Avon, which had been recently analyzed by Professor Daniell, of King's College, and also by Mr. Phillips, I should have directed my steps thither, even had I not been prompted, from its vicinity to Leamington, to indulge my warmest admiration for the incomparable bard, by proceeding in pilgrimage to the humble dwelling wherein he first drew his breath.

Yet, after my arrival, and after regaling myself with a whole night's repose, in the very town in which that memorable event had taken place, I had the courage to resist the temptation, as I walked down Henley-street at an early hour the next morning on my way to the Spa, of entering the antiquated little building I saw before me, from whence hung a board with this simple but thrilling notice: " In this house the immortal Shakspeare was born !" I had a duty to perform first, and to that I applied myself with all speed.

It was one of those mornings in autumn, when

> " Envious streaks
> Do lace the severing clouds in yonder east ;
> Night's candles are burnt out, and jocund day
> Stands tip-toe on the misty mountain tops."

I took to the country in a north-west direction out of Stratford, and proceeding along-side of the Birmingham and Stratford Canal, for the distance of nearly a mile, I reached a pretty little spot, where a group of newly-erected buildings presented itself to my view, surrounded by shrubberies, and constituting what has been denominated the " Victoria Spa."

The country appears one uniform flat, being principally pasture land, lower in level than the canal-course, except at the north, where the horizon towards Birley and Snitterfield waves gently with low undulations, which were scarcely discernible, owing to the grey clouds into whose neutral tints they merged. In the whole circle of this flat panorama the only two objects that offered themselves conspicuously to the eye on turning round, were the pointed spire of Stratford Church, emerging from out of a clump of dark-green trees, not yet tinged by autumn ; and the " Union" rearing its vast mass of red bricks, yet by no means unsightly.

The most conspicuous of the buildings at the Victoria Spa is GREEN's HOTEL, the architectural form of which partakes of the Elizabethan, with the peaked and projecting roof in the barge-board style. Within this building nothing has been forgotten which can render such an establishment desirable as well as comfortable ; and I surveyed every part of it with some surprise that so much luxury and convenience, such as would satisfy the most fastidious *richard*, should have been brought together under one roof in so retired a place. But when I reflected that many of the invalids desirous of flying for a time from the toilsome engagements of fashionable life, yet accustomed to its alluring enjoyments, might seek a retreat in this tranquil and soothing spot; I could understand why such studied preparations had been made for their reception. The aspect of the house, too, is favourable.

The cottage-orné style of the range of baths adjoining the spa-house, or pump-room, is particularly suited to the character of the scenery around. The interior accommodation deserves as much praise as its external prettiness. As an establishment of this class, of its size, there is not any one of the baths at Leamington to be compared to it.

The form of the Spa-house itself is in the rustic gothic style, with a projecting and pendant roof, and is peculiarly tasteful and summery. It has two fronts; the one south, with a principal entrance under a portico ; the other east, with another entrance also under a porch. There is a pump in a recess of the spa-room, where the company assemble to drink the water. The water is drawn through three pipes from a covered well, placed at some little distance in the flower-garden, which extends about an acre in front of the east side of the building, and is neatly laid out in green plots, with a piece of water in the centre.

There are three baths for ladies, and as many for the other sex. Two of them are ordinary sunken baths, of good size and proper depth, lined with white tiles. The third is a plunging-bath, laid round with a dark cement, and its bottom tiled. That for the ladies is nearly twice as large again as the other ; and adjoining to it is a neat contrivance for bathing children. Agreeably to the fashion of Leamington, over every bath the usual contrivance for taking a shower-bath has been placed.

A remarkable degree of taste and liberality, such as I have not seen displayed in any other bath-rooms, except at Scarborough, is observable throughout this suite of apartments. The furniture is not only plentiful, but of the best materials ; and there is every luxurious contrivance, particularly in the ladies' apartments, even down to the tinyest slippers, lined with soft fur. The rooms are lofty, and hung with draperies, and means have been adopted for allowing the steam to escape. The dressing-rooms are equally good.

The original well supplies the water to the reservoir, through a double action pump; but I regretted to find here again, that not only the pipes which are to convey sulphureted water, as this is, are of lead, but the reservoir also is lined with the same metal. This error must be rectified, and probably is so by this time; for on my remonstrating against it in the proper quarter, and suggesting the substitution of glazed earthenware tubes, a promise as readily given that the alteration would be made.

A second spring, but not so strong as the first, was discovered more recently, nearer, and to the west of the spa-house; but when the Original Well is worked, the water in the second is lowered to the level of the former, showing that both waters come from the same source, and consequently the reservoir is filled with both.

Besides these, there is a well, called " Perry's Well," situated farther out in the pleasure-grounds, which is not now used, but which was opened to satisfy my curiosity.

Although the " Sweet Swan of Avon" has not sung either the virtues of the Stratford mineral water, or the rural beauties of its environs, howbeit he took his wife, Anne Hathaway, from the very hamlet of Shottery, in which the springs are situated,—it is unquestionable that the water under our consideration was known in his days, and enjoyed reputation in the district and through the country; as we find in some of the oldest records of the place. Dr. Charles Perry, however, is the physician to whom we owe the first professional account (such as it is) of the water in question ; and his work is remarkable rather for the display of the oddest chemistry possible, even in those times, than for the conclusions to which even his imperfect science had led him — conclusions that have been confirmed since, in a great measure, by subsequent analyses, performed, as I before observed, by two modern and excellent chemists, to wit, Professor Daniell, who examined the water sent to him, and consequently missed the gaseous contents ; and Richard Phillips, who proceeded to the source to analyze the water. Their respective analyses, however, agree but indifferently ; for their quantities are not alike, nor is the total number of ingredients in the water the same in both; the first analysis mentioning five, and the second six of them.

The former chemist found an imperial pint to yield $74\frac{1}{3}$ grains of solid contents; while the second, in a common pint has detected $81\frac{1}{2}$ grains of solid ingredients, one of which is bi-carbonate of magnesia, not mentioned in Professor Daniell's analysis. In a similar manner, the Professor has omitted altogether the presence of sulphureted hydrogen gas, for the reason I assigned just before. By examining the water at the very source, Phillips collected five cubic inches and a fraction of that gas in a gallon of the water.

Pumped from the Original Well, I found the water to strike the violet or tawny colour in a very few seconds, upon throwing in the smallest particle of pulverized acetate of lead, and the sulphuret of the latter metal soon swam on the surface.

The water, naturally, is of a very light stone-colour, pervaded by very minute blackish particles, which I attribute to the leaden surface with which the water is in contact before it is poured into the glass. But even when the water was drawn up direct from the well in the garden where the water is only twenty-seven feet from the surface, and twenty feet deep, its tint is yellowish, as I have had occasion to notice of all the sulphureted springs derived from moor-land, or as in the present case, from below what was originally a peat soil.

Its temperature is $54°$ F. It barely tastes saltish, and the *après gout* is somewhat acrid in the throat, like all such sulphureted waters. On the whole, however, the drinking of such a mineral water would not require the efforts and resolution on the part of the patients which a stronger sulphureted or briny water seems to demand.

As it may be supposed, I have had no experience of the medicinal virtues of the Victoria Spa water; but looking at its composition, as laid down by Mr. Phillips, whose analysis will be found in the general table, it is not difficult for a medical man to predicate the sort of cases of disease in which it would prove beneficial. Accordingly, I find it stated in the printed accounts, and I have heard the statement repeated on the spot by unquestionable and highly respectable authorities, that a course of the Stratford water has been found useful in certain disorders of the stomach, in the slighter affections of the liver, in cases of gravel, and those pseudorheumatic and gouty pains which persons with long-deranged digestion are so apt to have superadded to their other sufferings.

I consider the fortunate circumstance of the water holding in solution a full drachm of glauber-salts to the pint, associated with a moderate and consequently not hurtful dose of that potent agent of which we have discoursed at full length at Harrogate—sulphureted hydrogen—as the most favorable feature of the Victoria Spa water. The presence of the latter gas, when the water is not raised to too high a temperature for a bath, renders it, of course, highly efficacious in the removal of cutaneous disease.

I have been assured that Dr. Jephson, who visited the Spa, expressed himself favourably of its water. Dr. Thompson, the only physician practising in Stratford, and Mr. Pritchard, the surgeon, having the largest practice there, hold, I understand, the Victoria Spa water in great estimation, for the cure of rheumatism and eruptive diseases.

On the whole, one may fairly conclude that a large number, and more than one class, of patients, residing within easy reach of the Victoria Spa, and even many of those whose habitual dwellings are at a greater distance, if afflicted with obstinate and rebellious disorders of the character just now specified, and who may have obtained no relief from ordinary medicine, would find in this consecrated neighbourhood of the neat little town of Stratford, a Spa likely to benefit them to the same extent as if they were to fly for that purpose to more distant shores. Certain am I, that in very few places will they meet with more striking evidence of what may be done for the comfort, convenience, and even luxury of invalids, when zealous and liberal-minded men are engaged, as in the case of the VICTORIA SPA, in bringing about those desirable results.

I never prepared myself at any period of my life for a feast, or a scene of promised enjoyment, with more glee or expectation, amounting almost to excitement, than I did on the day on which, after having examined the very creditable establishment I have just described, I retraced my steps back to Stratford, to view all that remains there to remind us of the first and last home of Shakspeare.

A gentleman, native of the place, and connected with its municipal government, whom I had met opportunely at the Spa, having offered to escort me in his carriage to my destination, kindly pointed out to me the several approaches made to the Spa, and the meditated improvements which the increasing importance and prosperity of the establishment seemed to demand. One of the most striking among these will be the erection of a grand terrace upon a rising ground close to the Spa, with a carriage-drive, which will bring Stratford nearer than it is at present by half a mile.

It is to this gentleman, Mr. W. O. Hunt, that these various improvements, and indeed the whole establishment in its actual flourishing state, are principally due—he having brought together for that purpose a small number of gentlemen to co-operate with him in the undertaking. Under his guidance I soon found myself on the threshold of the half-timbered and unassuming house in Henley-street, before alluded to, in which John Shakspeare, the glover, the butcher, the wool-stapler, the alderman, and the high bailiff of Stratford, became the father of the greatest intellectual wonder of any age, in 1564—a little more than ten years after which memorable event, fickle fortune, which had thus lavished on him the choicest of gifts, utterly abandoned him, and suffered him to sink into such abject poverty, that when a writ was issued against him for debt, and a seizure ordered of his goods, the man-at-law was compelled to declare that "*Joh'es Shackspere nihil habet unde distr. potest levari.*"

One room in particular in this house rivets the eager attention of the visiters : it was in it that the great poet was born.   At his second visit in 1821 to this hallowed chamber, Washington Irving inscribed upon it these lines, which I read on the spot.

> " Of mighty Shakspeare's birth the room I see,
> But where he died in vain to find we try ;
> Useless the search, for all immortal he,
> And those who are immortal never die."

Albums in general tend but to exhibit the feebleness and puny condition of the human mind when suddenly called upon to commit to writing extemporary feelings or opinions. Of all the compositions or inspirations gathered in such collections, the simple names of the visiters often speak more forcibly than your truisms, apothegms, or quatrains inscribed to the genius of the place.   Many of those names are in themselves whole volumes, and a whole history suggests itself immediately on their perusal.   The three or four albums, successively filled with the names of the visiters at Shakspeare's birth-place, and here preserved, are no exceptions to this general rule.

But the entire house—its half-timbered walls—its cracked ceilings—even part of the scanty and crazy furniture of every room—bear some name, some verse, or some inscription to record the different degrees of enthusiasm with which those who visited this sacred cradle were inspired.   Scott, who has approached nearest to the imagination of the bard, could hardly find space enough, among the thousand names on the walls, to pencil his own, as he however did at his first visit on one of the corner piers that support the ceiling opposite the fire-place.

Such is the birth-place of him whom we venerate before Homer:

"But where he died in vain to find we try."

So sang Irving; and that a churchman should have, by a wanton act, given occasion for such a remark, how lamentable! A dead wall only marks now the spot on which stood the residence Shakspeare loved so well, and wherein he breathed his last deep—deep sigh. NEW PLACE, in fine, and behind it the garden in which the celebrated mulberry-tree grew to maturity, hewn down like the house by the same sacrilegious hand, exist no more.

The grandfather of the gentleman who was now escorting me had the good fortune and good sense to rescue from the general ruin a bit of the foundation-stone which, with the key-stone from the doorway, bearing a blank shield in carved relief, are now in Mr. Hunt's garden. This gentleman possesses also the last genuine remains of the mulberry-tree, in the shape of a handsome table.

Anxious to peruse to the last page this topical biography of the incomparable poet of Stratford, I hastened to follow my kind guide to the church dedicated to the Holy Trinity, which holds within its precincts the precious deposit of all that was perishable in Shakspeare. The church was just then undergoing extensive repairs, and with difficulty did I wend my way from the entrance to the chancel.

Strange that a principal, and indeed the only church in a town of some importance, of so much intrinsic merit as this edifice, which dates its origin as far back as the Conquest—a church, too, which contains the ashes of the most intellectual mortal that ever lived—should have been suffered to fall into decay, and even to be nearly threatened with demolition—at a time, too, when church building, church extension, and church room are the theme of general conversation, for which the people have cheerfully contributed out of their pockets much

of the necessary funds, although they have had the mortification of witnessing the rearing of some of the greatest architectural abortions and monsters in the way of churches.

In the present case, the town of Stratford, finding its holy
temple tottering to its very foundation, has at last mulcted itself
to the extent of three thousand pounds, to stay the ravages of
time, and remedy the ill effects of neglect on the part of those
whose duty more immediately it is to see that the existing
churches do not fall into decay, and become an object to
sneer at by the more zealous Dissenters or Romanists, who
liberally subscribe to keep their own places of worship in
proper repair.

The dilapidation going on in Stratford church was particularly visible in its interior, where, from dampness, the walls
from the floor to a height of nearly four feet had assumed
such an appearance as to make it dangerous to attend Divine
service in it. This arose from the soil having been suffered
to accumulate against the wall, on the outside, until it covered
the latter as high as four feet. When this was removed, as it
was even then in progress of being done, the walls behind
and parts of the foundation were found to be rotten. It will
scarcely be credited that in this adventitious and accreted
soil, burials had taken place to a very considerable extent; so
that had the double process gone on much longer, of accu-
mulation of soil and burials of dead in it,—the House of God
must, at last, have itself been buried among the dead.

Monuments and inscriptions, of every date, and to the memory of people of various degrees, adorn the chancel of this
Saxo-Norman temple, which had been renovated a few years
before by the care and under the immediate inspection of the
Shakspearean Club. But the eye of the stranger, forsaking
all these, is at once irresistibly attracted by and fixed upon a
projecting architectural monument on the north wall, bearing
the carved resemblance of the Poet, which the written and tra-
ditional report of his contemporaries and relatives, under

whose direction the indifferent work was executed, tends to make us believe to be true to the original.

What a noble fabric is here displayed over the pupilless eye-balls, to hold its inmate brain, from which the corruscations of a genius that has no second to compare it to, scintillated for a period of twenty years in rapid succession, until quenched by the hand of death! The cunning of the artist who wrought the lineaments of the bard may have been but indifferent, as some contend, especially " one of the most distinguished sculptors of our days;" but in the admirable geometry of his forehead here represented, nature and truth alone could have been the guides of the stone-carver.

And what wisdom, wit, philosophy, morals, religion, and keen appreciation of the beautiful, did once animate that stupendous part of Shakspeare's perishable frame! And that brow, too—

" —————— a throne where honour may be crown'd
Sole monarch of the universal earth !"

England may indeed be proud of this highly-favoured child of hers, whose unaided efforts of the mind alone have sufficed to place her, at one single bound, on a par with the more enlightened and intellectual nations of the earth—a post no kindred spirit or genius of hers had tended to secure to her before. Truly may one of the many admiring critics of the ever-living productions of Shakspeare say, that to estimate the benefits this country has received from them is quite impossible. " Their influence has been gradual but prodigious, operating at first on loftier intellects, but becoming in time diffused over all, spreading wisdom and charity amongst us. There is, perhaps no person of any considerable rate of mind who does not owe something to this matchless poet. He is the teacher of all good—pity, generosity, true courage, love. His works alone (leaving mere science out of the question) contain probably more actual wisdom than the whole body of English learning. He is the text for the moralist and the philosopher" (and why not for the statesman, the poet, and the painter?). "His bright wit is cut into little stars; his solid masses of knowledge are meted out in morsels and proverbs; and, thus distributed, there is scarcely a corner which he does not illuminate, or a cottage which he does not enrich."*

It is thus that the spirit whose corporal effigy I stood contemplating with admiration, in the church of the Holy Trinity at Stratford, ought to be viewed, as connected with the history of the human mind, of which, take him for all in all, this mighty genius unquestionably forms the most remarkable, astonishing, and unparalleled epoch.

Of him as a painter of the human passions in his writings, it was probably the intention of the artist that we should be reminded by the posture he has given to the half-length figure of the poet in the monument, where he is placed between two pillars and under an arch, with a pen in one hand, and the other resting on a scroll. It is in that character that all the nations of the earth blessed with enlightenment and civilization acknowledge and reverence his unrivalled superiority over all poets, ancient and modern, admiring and extolling him in consequence. Pens, too, without number, have at all times been engaged in commending the same wonderful peculiarity of Shakspeare's writings. But how incomparably more forcible is the bard's own language, (of which I was reminded as I viewed his effigy, with my feet standing on the " envious grave" that encloses his dust,) when applied, and by no violent stretch of

---

* To the admirers of Shakspeare who would wish to have a manual of his " Wisdom and Genius" always at hand, a sort of rich casket of his gems in moral philosophy, delineations of characters, paintings of nature and the passions, to dip into at pleasure, and so adorn their minds with them,—I would strongly recommend a beautiful pocket volume, published a short time ago by the Rev. Thomas Price, from whose preface I borrowed the quotation just given in the text, ascribed to a writer in the *Retrospective Review.*

interpretation either, to the delineation of that same striking feature of his GENIUS!

> " So on the tip of his subduing tongue
>   All kinds of arguments and question deep,
>   All replication prompt, and reason strong,
>   For his advantage still did wake and sleep.
>   To make the weeper laugh, the laugher weep,
>   He had the dialect and different skill,
>   Catching all passions in his craft of will;
>   That he did in the general bosom reign
>   Of young, of old; and sexes both enchanted."

POEMS.

CHAPTER XIV.

CHELTENHAM.

THAT the reputation of Cheltenham as a Spa is on the wane—nay, escaping fast from it—is a fact, the announcement of which will not sound new to a great number of my readers. I entered the place on the occasion of my present visit under such an impression, and I found that impression con-firmed by the contrasting difference I observed between what Cheltenham then appeared to me as a mineral watering-place, and what I had known it as such, personally and from experience, fifteen years before.

So soon acquired, and so soon gone! Is the nation then whimsical and capricious, by which such reputations are thus vouchsafed and withheld in the short period of a few years?

or have there been good and substantial reasons for the change? At one time it was Cheltenham and Boisragon; now it is Leamington and Jephson! In the meanwhile, the former place, in ceasing to be a Spa, has become a town of great resort and importance, even to the obtaining of the high privilege of being represented in parliament: while the latter is as yet only striving to be what its more successful rival and predecessor in popular favour is become already, even at the same risk and penalty of ceasing to be a Spa.

Be that as it may, no doubt exists but that a particular mineral water, and its due application to the cure of disease, was the main cause of giving to Cheltenham a locality and a name; and as such, therefore, I visited it on the occasion of which I am about to record all such particulars as are likely to interest or be useful to my readers.

The approach to the region of this Spa from Warwickshire is far more interesting to an observing traveller than either of the southern roads leading to it. Traversing for a considerable distance the same flat and tame sort of country as was observed around Stratford, our way laid at length to the top of a considerable eminence, from which a very extensive and rich valley opens to view, Worcestershire on the right, and Gloucester on the left sharing its beauties. Rounded hillocks appeared in successive lines, like the halves of so many gigantic beads laid on the ground, many of them thickly wooded, others in a state of more profitable cultivation.

The nearest road from the Victoria Spa to Cheltenham, would be that which passes at the foot of that remarkable range of hills which traverses nearly the whole length of the vale of Gloucester, in a north-east and south-west direction. But the conductor of a public conveyance often prefers a more circuitous route, for many and very substantial reasons;— and such was the case on the present occasion, when a *détour* by Alcester and Evesham was made in consequence.

Passing the latter town, which is well placed and clean looking, and crossing the Avon, over a narrow, ancient bridge, the road insensibly deviates more westwardly, as if intending to reach Tewkesbury. But it has no sooner neared that imposing peak, Bredon-hill, noticed in our chapter on Malvern, when coursing between it and two other important hills, the great and little Washbourn, the latter of which, richly cultivated all over, it skirts nearly parallel—it suddenly deflects southwardly at Teddington Cross, and descends continuously in nearly a straight line down into Cheltenham.

The sun was lighting up the broad western face of the Cleave-hills, which rise nearly twelve hundred feet in height, and shelter the town from the north-eastern gales; and the undulating and ever changing character of the high ground on our left, variously coloured by its rays, as we rapidly passed in front, offered a striking as well as pleasing contrast with the table-land at the foot of it, cultivated to the very edge of the road, though the soil be far from favourable for that purpose.

The entrance into the precincts of Cheltenham, by the Evesham gate, as one might call it, is calculated to make a most favourable impression on the stranger. The temple-like Spa building, called PITTVILLE, which first presents itself with its many columned portico facing the road, and the Pittville gardens that follow, with their fine row of houses flanking them to the east for a quarter of a mile, are the objects that rivet the attention of the traveller. His eye tracing afterwards the line of the Pitville-parade, and Portland-street, which runs thence southwardly down into the town, sees the latter spread as it were below him, at the bottom of a broad cup, with the outlines of an imposing mass of human habitations, crossed by the oldest street, High-street, right and left, and by the insignificant Chelt, a stream hardly known to visiters.

For old acquaintance-sake I put up at the Plough, an establishment which, with all the bustle and appearance of a large country inn, combines the comforts and neatness of one of your best hotels of a more *townly* character. That it is liked by many of the easy and upper classes of society is proved by the fact that it is almost always full; and but for the migratory nature of its inmates, the chances of getting even a mere *pied à terre* in it would be poor indeed. But of this and other hotels something more anon. My present purpose must be with the spa-features of Cheltenham.

There are four establishments in this far-famed watering-place, which have contributed to give it the character it once enjoyed in London, and to which it still clings, of a first-rate Spa, or the Spa of spas in fact. These vie with each other, by all arts and schemes imaginable, to centre individually in themselves the attention and patronage of the visiters.

If importance, as determined by public opinion only, often capricious and not rarely fallacious, instead of mere chronology, were to decide to which of the four ought to be assigned the first place, the palm should unquestionably be yielded to "the Montpellier," and next to the "Original Spa," followed by the Pittville and the Cambray Chalybeate.

The first of these, in its present or more modern shape, is a giant of comparatively recent growth, (as compared to the second,) which has absorbed almost all other establishments, and annihilated almost every competitor. Through which means and upon what grounds will be seen hereafter. The second, besides the sort of venerability that attaches to the seniors in anything, has the charm of historical recollections connected with it—recollections which are intimately mixed up with the inherent loyalty of a most loyal nation. Its means of maintaining its ground with the public have not been of so dashing a description as those resorted to by its more successful rival; and yet its grounds for maintaining a high standing, a standing equal, and in one respect, as a mineral-water source, superior, to that of its rival, are indisputable. The Pittville, for grandeur and beauty of architecture (barring some provoking eyesores) for its situation, and, let me add, for the genuineness of its spring (for such is my conviction), commands admiration, and is, perhaps, the finest establishment of the sort in England.　As for " the Chalybeate," or Cambray Spa, the fourth and last of the Cheltenham Spas under consideration, no effort will ever make it rise to more than its present mediocre station.　In the light of an auxiliary, in the treatment of diseases through the agency of the Cheltenham saline waters, the Chalybeate may be considered as useful.　But to render it a paramount source of general patronage and important results, like the chalybeates in Germany, it should, like them, be sparkling with a profusion of carbonic-acid gas, instead of lying, as it does, flat and stale at its source, with its heavy mineral.

To the first of these four establishments the reader will now be pleased to accompany me, ascending for that purpose the bustling street in which the Plough is situated, as far as what is called the *Colonnade*, and thence, following a dashing line of promenades and drives, flanked on the right by handsome and first-rate houses, and terminated by the showy hotel, called " the Queen"—enter by a crooked and narrow " avenue," into the Montpellier Walk—and so on into the Great Rotunda.　Here it is, principally, that the mineral water, which during the last thirty years has enjoyed so extensive a renown under the name of Cheltenham water, is distributed ; and here it was, that in the palmy days of Cheltenham, the visiters thronged in almost countless numbers.　They still frequent the place during the summer season, which extends from May to the end of October ; but an idea may be formed of the diminution in their numbers, when I state that the Subscribers'-book in the room, which I inspected on my arrival, could boast of eighty-two names only, inscribed during the entire of that month.

Many thousand pounds (so public report says) were expended in the erection of this splendid room and adjoining premises, by the successor of a gentleman to whom it is yet doubtful whether Cheltenham will owe any very heavy debt of gratitude. Henry Thompson, Esq., a person endowed with a spirit of adventurous enterprise, which from early life had led him to various parts of the world, came at length to settle in Cheltenham, in 1809, attracted by the reputation of its mineral water, at that time derived only from what has since been called " the Royal Old Wells." With the eye of a skilful speculator, he saw at once how much there was to be done in the place by energy and some ready cash. Having brought with him a sum of ten thousand pounds, he instantly set about buying land in the immediate vicinity of the Old Well; sinking wells in his turn; discovering some new mineral water at every step, each differing from the other; and ending by raising, first, a modest-looking pump-room for the distribution of the water—then, one of more pretension, which was subsequently enlarged—to be at length removed altogether for the present magnificent Rotunda, erected, as I stated before, by his successor.

The sinking of so many shafts into a soil that covers a whole lake of briny water could not do otherwise than lead to the discovery of mineral water; and thus far Mr. Thompson need not have incurred the smallest obloquy of having pretended to discover it. But when he averred, on the faith of certain analyses, that each of the wells he sank brought to light a different species of mineral water, then the profession and the public were startled at the assertion, and that long, amusing, and somewhat curious contention between the credulous and the sceptical took place, which is as yet of too recent a date to have been forgotten by the majority of my readers. The manipulation of Cheltenham salts at Thompson's factory was looked upon with suspicion; and the weekly journey to Epsom of a certain black waggon, which returned as regularly to the manufactory at Cheltenham, was supposed to be connected with the supply of some powerful ingredient for the preparation of these salts.

These misgivings on the part of the public seemed, unfortunately, to have been justified by the subsequent occurrence of that extraordinary exposure in which two persons, well known in the place, Adam Neale and Matthew, appeared conspicuous, and which ended in the admission that many dozens of pounds of Epsom salts had been thrown daily into one of the wells, not connected however with the Montpellier property. The conviction of the adulterating party in this case did but make the suspicion already existing against Mr. Thompson, though not an offending party, the stronger; and Cheltenham water, say what you will, has never since recovered from the rude shock its reputation received on that memorable occasion.

Be this as it may, Mr. Thompson himself, who is looked upon as the regenerator of Cheltenham, gave proofs in his own person, that its mineral water was of a nature in which he could place trust as a medicine, without tampering with it; for I am well assured that, during a period of fourteen years, and down to the day of his death, which took place at the good old age of seventy-two (and then in consequence of a surgical complaint), he used no other aperient than Cheltenham water, which he moreover used to drink daily. And in this the old gentleman was perfectly right; for Cheltenham water, in its unsophisticated state, is a genuine mineral water, containing but one specific set of ingredients, no matter where the water is taken, and varying only in the proportion of two of those ingredients, namely, the common salt or muriate of soda, and the glauber-salt or sulphate of soda. The greater or lesser quantity of either will be found to depend ŏn the greater or smaller depth at which the boring for mineral water has been made through the blue lias clay, over which Cheltenham is seated. An illustration of this fact occurred in my own presence during my last visit, while I was watching some deep excavations at the back of the Old Well Walk, in the Bays-hill Road.

To one accustomed to see nature's bounty, in the way of mineral water, held in esteem throughout Europe, and dealt out to the invalid applicant without guise or mystery,—the sight which presents itself at the Montpellier Rotunda is not likely to inspire confidence. A pyramid is placed behind, and in the centre of, a semicircular counter, exhibiting a number of spouts, which, projecting from and on each side of it, conceal a set of pumps, the handles of which are put in motion by a sulky rough-looking servant-man. His office is to fill the tumblers of the applicants with any of the numbered waters they may desire, as fast as his strength and agility will allow; and from No. 1 to No. 6, including a No. 2 (a) and 4 (a), more recently added to the rest,—the invalid may riot in his choice of water, and quaff as many half pints of it as he pleases for the same subscription of a guinea for the season, or the paying of one shilling for each morning. If his tumbler be placed under spouts No. 1, or No. 2, or No. 3, and the handles in the aforesaid pyramid are put in motion, he will get either a chalybeate saline, or a strong sulphureted saline or a weak sulphureted saline, water. Should he, on the contrary, feel tempted to try taps 4, 5, and 6, placed a little way from the aforesaid pyramid, and wait but an instant that the pump-handles may again be put in motion, he will then procure either a pure saline, or a chalybeate magnesian saline, or a strong muriated saline water. But there are supernumerary spouts or numbers besides, as before stated, of which No. 4 (a) is just now the most renowned, and this will supply, by the same pumping process, an ioduretted saline water.

Now all this display calls largely upon the faith and credulity of the bibbers. It is not thus that matters are managed in Germany; for there the good, honest, and unsophisticated people of the country could not be persuaded to swallow a single drop of any water which should be presented to them in so mysterious a manner, or the source of which they could not plainly see. Here, on the contrary, I firmly believe, that were the enumeration of the taps or spouts to be carried out to three figures of numbers, there would be found people enough to drink, and feel convinced at the same time that they drank different waters.

" Would you let me behind the scene," I inquired of a kind acquaintance, by whom I was escorted on the occasion of my present visit, and who is well versed in the proceedings at the Montpellier, " and suffer me to look into the various wells from which these many waters are derived ?" There was not another stranger in the Rotunda at the time, and my request, after a brief consultation with some person, was acquiesced in. On passing behind the large counter, a trap-door in the floor beneath the pyramid was lifted up, and the back part of the latter opened at the same time, by

means of which I could observe a series of leaden pipes connected with a pumping-apparatus, and leading from the
several spouts down a deep shaft which was so narrow that
the collected cluster of all the pipes nearly filled it, and so
prevented my seeing any thing beyond a few feet below the
surface of the ground. Personal evidence, therefore, of the
direction which these pipes may take in their way to the
various wells, I have none to offer, as no other means was
pointed out to me for ascertaining that fact: but the same
assurance was given me, which had already been and is perpetually given to the public by the proprietors, that each pipe
proceeds to a different and more or less distant well, containing the specific mineral waters, and the main shaft of
each of which Mr. Thompson had caused to be covered over,
and to be protected by a small building.

I tasted No. 4 (a), which is stated, on the authority of Mr.
Cooper, to hold in solution a quarter of a grain of hydriodate
of soda in a pint of the water. It is now drank more than
the old No. 4., once so popular, and now nearly deserted, as
I hear, by all. The water, mixed with some of it heated, has
the usual taste that all muriated sodaic waters have—not
quite so intense as the water of the Leamington Pumproom,
but much the same as that of Abbott's and Satchwell's wells
in that place.

With regard to Nos. 2 and 3, or the so-called " sulphureted
and weak sulphureted salines," I lament to say that after
pumping as much as could be got out of the pipes, and testing the water in both cases by the most delicate test, no indication whatever of the presence of the sulphureted hydrogen,
gas quoted in the printed analysis, could be observed. Indeed, with reference to one of those quotations in Mr. Cooper's
analysis, its amount, seven-tenths of a cubic inch, is so small,
that, issuing as the water said to contain it (No. 3.) does
through a length of leaden pipe, measuring not less than
between sixty and seventy feet, the alleged quantity of the

gas in question would disappear by combining with the lead
before it could reach the spout.

Has Mr. Cooper obtained the several waters he has analyzed at the Montpellier from the bottom of the well itself? I
am not aware of having seen in any scientific publication
the full report and details of the analytical process by which
that chemist has come to the conclusions given in his quantitative analysis of the ioduretted saline. Its composition, according to that analysis, seems so much more complicated
than that of any of the other waters of Cheltenham previously
analysed by Sir Charles Scudamore, Mr. Garden, and Professor Daubeny, that a detail of the chemical and scientific
proceedings would have been highly satisfactory; and indeed is required, before Mr. Cooper's alleged proportion of
iodine and manner of its combination, announced with so
much confidence, can be generally admitted. This observation applies even more strongly to the No. 5, or chalybeate
magnesian saline, in which Mr. Cooper has, with wonderful
precision, announced even more hydriodate of soda, than in
No. 4 (a), with traces of hydrobromate of soda. To those practical as well as philosophical chemists who know, after reading
Professor Daubeny's researches on the iodine and bromine of
mineral waters, and Mr. West's accounts in the same strain,
how difficult it is to ascertain the precise quantity of each
substance when both are present, and still more difficult to
decide in what manner of combination each of them is present: the announcement of Mr. Cooper's discoveries will
seem to require the testimony of that gentleman's scientific
report of his proceedings on the occasion.

On the subject of the assumed sulphureted waters also, I
find, that Sir Charles Scudamore, who had been led to expect such a gas in Nos. 2 and 3, from an analysis of them
made in 1817 by Brande and Parke, could detect no trace
of it a few years afterwards; just as I could not discover any
in the same waters in 1839, although in 1832, Mr. Cooper

had repeated the assertion of that gas being present in them. We must, therefore, conclude that the Montpellier's mineral waters vary in their composition at different times, oftener and to a greater extent than has been observed of any other mineral water in the world.

Upon mature and deliberate reflection I hold that at the Montpellier Rotunda, the invalid who is sent to Cheltenham to drink its peculiar mineral water, will find it in perfection by using the old No. 4; or even 5, where a small quantity of iron added to the saline, is not incompatible with his complaint. It is the fashion here to offer to the invalid who requires greater activity in the water he drinks, a concentrated solution of the Cheltenham salts in the proportion of two pounds to a gallon of water, which solution is always kept ready for that purpose, and is added to the natural water.

But it is at the " Original Spa," or Royal Old Wells, that I should seek for the real and purest Cheltenham water of the saline class; for in a pint of No. 2 there, according to Sir Charles Scudamore, we find a happy combination of a moderate quantity of common salt, with nearly a drachm of an aperient salt (Glauber's), and a sufficient proportion of very active alteratives, the muriate of lime and magnesia; and there is not a combination exactly like it, either in power or simplicity, in the Montpellier Rotunda.

The passing from the latter establishment to that of the " Original Spa," is rendered very convenient by their juxtaposition. Most of the visiters to the one consequently go over to the other, dividing their time equally between the two. Indeed so moderate are the charges made for the privilege of frequenting the several walks and drives in both establishments, that little as one is accustomed to see money demanded abroad for the same privilege, we are not disposed to find fault with it in this case. By this means the extent of walking exercise which the invalid may take in the morning, during the hours of drinking the water, is considerable as well as varied.   And in this respect Cheltenham has a superiority over Leamington which the latter can never attain.

There is so imposing an air of formality and antiquity in that beautiful avenue of elm-trees, called " The Old Well Walk," which forms the principal feature of the " Original Spa," that one is tempted to select it, in preference to the more gay, varied, and improving gardens and pleasure-grounds of the Montpellier, for a morning " constitutional walk."*   A double line of lofty, and well-feathered trees, forming a vista of twelve hundred feet in a direct line, terminated by the oldest church in Cheltenham, which is seen through the iron gate that admits the stranger into the walk from the Crescent, presents a stately promenade, highly calculated for the display of the gay and fashionable company which should frequent this, the oldest and the most genuine Spa in the place. In this respect the short and insignificant walk before the Long Room or entrance into the Montpellier Rotunda, is decidedly inferior to it ; and as a well-wisher to Cheltenham, I venture to express a hope that the sacrilegious hand of the joint-stock company which has been committing havocks on the Bays Hill estate, once the favourite retreat of royalty, will not level to the ground this beautiful feature of the Old Spa.

On the other hand, we look in vain to the latter establishment for that magnificence and grandeur in its pump-room, which we had noticed in the Rotunda, or Central Saloon of the Montpellier.

Here, on the contrary, modest and unassuming, as every thing that smacks of old age is, the Pump or Promenade-room consists of an ordinary long and narrow apartment, placed about the middle of the avenue, in which, as at the Rotunda, are seen the many spouts supplying, through the pumping system, that variety of mineral waters which it seems

* It is represented by the vignette in the title-page of this volume.

to be the mania or fashion to require. There is, however, less of quackery in the present case; for, although No. 1 and No. 2, as well as No. 3 and No. 4, and even 5, all in a row, stare you in the face, at the good lady's counter who manages the concern, and you might feel disposed to look with doubt upon the source of all these waters,—yet, by walking a short distance away from the building, the several wells may be actually visited and examined. Among them is conspicuous the Original, or Old Well, situated in the very centre of the walk. This was opened on two occasions at my request, and water obtained immediately from it by means of buckets, on which my observations were made and conclusions drawn, as was the case with water No. 2, already alluded to, and also with No. 5, or the strong muriated saline from the Orchard Well, which, however, is not now drank.

To another well in the garden, my attention was directed, the water of which is not brought into the Pumproom. I found in it manifest, though extremely slight indications of sulphureted gas, which I could no more detect in the so-called sulphureted saline of the Pumproom, than I or Sir Charles Scudamore had in the so-called sulphureted waters at No. 1 and No. 2 of the Rotunda. The fact is, there is not a genuine sulphureted water in Cheltenham.

Sir George Baker, one of the most amiable and classical physicians of the last century, first stamped the character and celebrity of the Original Spa by recommending the water of what has since been called the Old Well before alluded to, to the most illustrious patient in the realm—his sovereign, George III.—who was supposed to have recovered from a severe indisposition by drinking that particular water. That may be looked upon as having been the era in which the obscure little town of Cheltenham took its *elan* or first spring towards notoriety, and which led to all its subsequent brilliant and almost unexampled success.

Holding the mineral water of Cheltenham to be one and

the same in reality, though differing in intensity in some of the wells, it is not likely that we shall find any material variation in the taste of this or that number out of the great many that are exhibited, whether at the Original Spa, the Montpellier Spa, or at the Pittville. The general physical character is that of a gently saltish and rather bitter water. This impression, as usual, is modified by the addition of heat, or by dilution with ordinary hot water. But in the latter case its sensible effects on the system are considerably quickened.

CHAPTER XV.

CHELTENHAM CONCLUDED.

GENUINE Water at Cheltenham—Geological Structure—SOURCES of the Mineral Water—Author's Inquiries—Medical Effect—My Own Experience—ERRORS and CASES—Liver and Dyspepsia—The PITTVILLE —Its Superb Structure and Gardens—Its Mineral Springs—The CAMBRAY SPA—Recapitulation of the Good Effects of Cheltenham Water—The MONTPELLIER BATHS—Medical Attendants—The FOUR LEADING Physicians—A Growing Town and a Declining Spa—Building Mania—Value of Houses, and Architectural Taste—Aspect of Houses—The PROMENADE—JEARRAD the Beautifier of Cheltenham— The IMPERIAL HOTEL—Widow Joseph—Old Bachelors and Crusty Port—" THE QUEEN "—Inside and Out—EXPENSES at Hotels—A Specimen—Character of Society at Cheltenham—The HIGHER CLASSES— Thirlestane House and LORD NORTHWICH'S Gallery—Arts, Letters, and Sciences—Periodicals and Reading-Rooms—AN ABOMINATION— Is Cheltenham a Dull Place ?—Subscription Balls—Musical Promenades—Out-of-door Amusements—CLIMATE.

IT is a growing error on the part of the public, especially in the metropolis, to think that genuine mineral water is not now, or was never to be found in Cheltenham, and to talk flippantly, as one hears people do occasionally, nowadays, of the supposed prevalent practice of manufacturing and *messing* (as I heard a medical person say) the mineral waters. Take it as it is, whether as issuing, according to Mr. Murchison's supposition, from below the lias bed which overlays the whole vale of Gloucester, in the centre of which stands Cheltenham ; or from between the lower strata only of the said lias bed, according to another geologist of the place, and my own personal observation,—a mineral water charged principally with from twenty to fifty grains of common salt, and from a half to a drachm of glauber-salts, also with three to eight grains of the muriates of both lime and magnesia in a pint, exists, and may any day be found in Cheltenham, by sinking a well less than one hundred feet deep.*

Such a water, in passing through the several beds of lias and sometimes of the detritus from the oolitic rocks of the neighbouring hills, here and there spread over the subincumbent stratum of lias clay, is probably modified in its composition, and may acquire other properties. Still, the great and fundamental principles will ever be the same as originally

---

* At the back of Lansdowne-place not fewer than five wells have been sunk, communicating with each other by pipes gathered up into a pump, placed under cover. The springs, which run north and south, were found at a depth of one hundred feet, where the two estates of Mr. Thompson and Bays-hill adjoin. The blue clay was here found as deep as the borings had proceeded, namely, one hundred and fifteen feet, and it might be deeper. Conversing, one day, with the well-digger who was engaged at the time in an operation of that sort on the confines of the Bays-hill estate, I learned that the water of the five wells just mentioned, and that which he was then in search of, and which, indeed, he had found, was the same that had been discovered and much used for preparing the famed Thompson's salts twenty years ago. It was then distinguished from the rest by the number *four*; but since the alleged discovery of iodine and bromine in it by Mr. Cooper, it had been qualified still farther by the affix (a). To find this 4 (a) the diggers had seldom to proceed deeper than seventy feet, when the first "weepage" would be seen running horizontally (and not ascending perpendicularly) along with the dip of the strata of the lias, which is here from east to west. In order to find a full reservoir, however, they had frequently to go down as deep as one hundred feet; and it had been constantly observed by this man that the water was more strongly impregnated with saline particles the lower in the west end of the strata of clay they searched for it. That the spring of No. 4 (a) in the present instance ran westwardly, was proved by the sinking of the very well my informant was then engaged in completing—which was done with the view to cut off the mineral water from the Bays-hill estate lying close and at the east.

predicated, and it is a folly to suppose they have changed since. Hence, when we speak professionally of "Cheltenham water," we must understand it to mean a naturally medicinal compound of the description just given.

And truly such a natural compound, judging *à priori*, or even from analogy only (supposing we had not already sufficient evidence of the fact), must exert a notable influence on the human constitution. A person in good health could not go on drinking with impunity a pint and a half (the quantity to which I should limit an invalid when using it) of such a water day after day for a month. Even were it not to act as an aperient, which is likely to be the case with many people, as the *genuine* Cheltenham water is not sufficiently endowed with that character,—the result of such a daily potation as is here supposed would still be found to have considerably *altered* the condition of our water-bibber. And it is precisely as an agent calculated to *alter* the animal fluids that the Cheltenham water will never disappoint the medical practitioner or the invalid who judiciously employs it as such.

I am here assuming, I trust, a becoming tone of authority, instead of one of doubt and diffidence, as I did when treating of mineral waters (like that of the Victoria Spa at Stratford for example) of the medical virtues of which I knew nothing individually; for in the application of Cheltenham waters to disease I have had sufficient scope for experience during twenty-three years' medical practice in the metropolis. The result of that experience has led me to a conclusion which at once explains the real virtues and former success of the Cheltenham water; while it points out the cause of its recent failures in the cure of disease, and consequent abatement of its popularity. That conclusion is —that to ensure the good effects of Cheltenham water, one must use it only at the close of visceral or functionary disorders, whether of long or short duration, which have been previously treated by appropriate remedies calculated to remove the principal features of the disease, but leaving yet much to be done for the completion of the recovery. That much which ordinary remedies, however skilfully prescribed, cannot effect, the Cheltenham water will be found to be just the agent for accomplishing. Where more has been attempted by means of this water, disappointment has followed; and as such attempts have been repeatedly made of late years, and are constantly being made, either through the advice of medical men, or the spontaneous determination of invalids themselves, — it follows that disappointments have been equally frequent, and a corresponding loss of reputation on the part of the water has ensued in consequence.

I would illustrate my position by a single example taken from what, in our days, may be considered as an almost every-day occurrence in medical practice. There was a time, say twenty years ago, when a patient labouring under extensive disease of the liver, commonly so called, and no matter how produced, whether by a residence in a tropical climate, [or from sedentary life and anxiety of mind, or through frequent imprudence committed at the table, would first undergo that suitable treatment under a skilful physician, which sooner or later, and *alone*, does successfully overcome this class of disorders. But inasmuch as even the skilful physician and the most appropriate treatment could not do all in such cases; and as after having cancelled the positive disease by remedies, the medical attendant often found it difficult, if not impossible, to restore by the ordinary means the constitution to its normal state—a thing only to be obtained through the agency of such chemical combinations as were found ready at hand in the Cheltenham waters; our patient was generally recommended to go thither, where he seldom failed to complete his recovery in the short space of four or six weeks. Vast numbers of cases of this description have come to my knowledge.

Of late years, however, as I before remarked, a patient under similar circumstances would not think it necessary to submit his case to any preliminary treatment, but would at once proceed to Cheltenham. Your sickly, jaundiced, and deeply-damaged orientals, on their return from their baneful presidencies to England, will frequently act in this way, and when once at Cheltenham, will instantly begin their own cure by means of the water, and the water principally,—in the expected good effects of which, however, they are disappointed. How could it be otherwise? Failure indeed might have been expected; for the Cheltenham water *per se* is incapable of curing any disorders (except indeed some slight cases of indigestion), though admirably calculated to assist in completing the cure of almost every disease and functional malady of the organs of digestion.

Viewed in this light, Cheltenham offers an immense resource to the medical practitioner; and thus recommended to invalids and convalescents, Cheltenham may be certain of a constant and vast concourse of visiters, who will there find what they require—health—and will be pleased and praise Cheltenham accordingly.

But we must not omit to pay our special visit to the third of the four enumerated establishments at Cheltenham—the one we descried while descending the Evesham road, as the first and most attractive feature in the landscape, and known by the name of PITTVILLE. It is scarcely possible to imagine a more favourable position in the immediate vicinity of *old* Cheltenham than the one which this new Spa, the creation of fifteen years, occupies, upon an eminence commanding an extensive view of the town and country around, facing the south, and sheltered from the more objectionable winds in a very effectual manner. Taste and judgment, such as are not often to be met with in our days among speculative builders,

have presided in the present case at the erection of the principal buildings, not less than in the distribution and arrangement of the many rides, promenades, and pleasure-grounds,
by which they are surrounded. A foreigner, accustomed to
view many of the most renowned places of public resort on the
Continent, must be forcibly struck, on approaching Pittville,
by the beauty and decorations of that establishment, even after
having admired the many other showy and striking buildings in
Cheltenham, as well as the Rotunda and gardens of the Montpellier. A more refreshing picture in summer-time can hardly
present itself to him in these parts of the country ; and when,
after meandering through luxuriant shrubberies, and crossing,
by either of the two elegant stone bridges, the spacious and
ornamental sheet of water which has been adroitly pressed
into the landscape, he ascends along the grand promenade
to the terrace, stretched before the entire front of the Pump-
room, or CURESAL, and enters the latter,—surprise at the
interior of the building, and admiration of its proportions and
elaborate finishing with marble and scagliola ornaments, will
be added to his admiration of the external picture.

Around three sides of this edifice ranges a handsome
colonnade, which supports an upper terrace, at each end of

which a colossal emblematic statue has been erected. These colonnades, and the central dome by which the building is surmounted, form a very striking and commanding feature in this vast estate of Mr. Pitt, the spirited proprietor, who has skilfully laid it out in terraces, lawns, squares, and streets, nearly the whole of which are occupied with handsome houses.

Pittville, lying to the east-north-east of High-street, half a mile distant perhaps, or not so much, from it, has the only inconvenience of being thus far away from the centre of buzzing life, the shops and the hotels; a circumstance which, instead of operating in its favour as it ought to do, considering it as a retreat to which real invalids visiting Cheltenham ought to repair, has operated in reducing the merited success of that establishment. A mineral water is found abundantly at the Pittville Pumproom, which has been analyzed by Professor Daniel, of King's College. It is somewhat similar, in the proportion of two of its principal ingredients, to the saline water No. 4 (for a long time the pet water of the Montpellier), but superior to it as a medicinal combination, inasmuch as it holds sulphate of magnesia, and bicarbonate of soda, which the other water has not. So that no excuse is left to such as require good air, a comfortable residence, delightful scenery, absolute quiet, and Cheltenham water, for not choosing his *séjour* on the Pittville estate. The Pittville colony was about to be (and is probably by this time) lighted with gas at night, like the Montpellier establishment, and a number of private watchmen in livery were to be in constant attendance.

The second spring at this Spa, called the weaker saline, is hardly deserving of the name of mineral water; yet when a very weak and simple solution of muriate of soda is required, it may be found useful.

What shall I say of the fourth and last of the enumerated establishments in Cheltenham, the CAMBRAY Spa, or chalybeate, except that it lies near at hand to the central street, and not far removed from the imperial walks ; that it has had a renovated Gothic hexagonal building raised over it of late, and that no less a person than Faraday was the chemist who analyzed its contents ? It tastes sufficiently astringent and saline to declare its own ingredients. As an auxiliary in the treatment of certain diseases by means of the real Cheltenham water, the pure chalybeate may sometimes be of service ; but people come down here to use the alterative and saline springs peculiar to the place, and not steel-water, and therefore the Cambray Spa is not likely to be much frequented.

Enough has already been said in the course of the present chapter to give my readers an idea of the medicinal purposes to which Cheltenham waters may be usefully applied. In a popular work of this description, a more extended and elaborate disquisition, on the various maladies in which they may be recommended with advantage is hardly necessary. But it may not be amiss to recapitulate, first, that as a gentle aperient, the daily use of which, in suitable quantities, does not, like the more common saline purgatives, weaken the tone of the digestive organs, and is therefore admissible in many cases when such purgative would prove injurious,—Cheltenham water is deserving of favour ; secondly, that as an alterative, properly speaking, after protracted mercurial treatment, and to cleanse the system generally by slow and imperceptible changes in the condition of the fluids, it is much to be commended.

There is hardly one of the more important diseases of the chronic kind, which affect the functions of the stomach or liver, that could not well be classed in one or other of the two categories just specified ; and therefore Cheltenham water is admissible in the multitudinous disorders which owe their origin to the derangement of those functions. But in the treatment of these complaints there is something more besides mineral water to be attended to, and that is climate, as we shall see in the sequel.

I have never found the Cheltenham waters useful in derangements of the female constitution.

Cheltenham is a drinking Spa, as must appear from all I have stated. But it deals in BATHS also, howbeit they are but little in favour, and the accommodation for them I believe to be limited to one solitary establishment. The Montpellier Baths are so far unique, for they have no rival of any sort in Cheltenham. They afford every convenience for the purpose intended, and I need not enter into any further description of them. Their approximation to the Great Laboratory of the " Real Cheltenham Salts," renders it easy for the people at the Baths to employ hot water or even the vapour, for the various processes of bathing. That laboratory is open to public inspection, but the process of manufacturing the salts can hardly be of sufficient interest to my readers to warrant my introduction in this place of a professed description.

It may be readily anticipated that where there is so much genuine mineral water to dispense, and so great an influx of invalids to drink it, the supply of medical attendance to direct its use cannot be inconsiderable. Accordingly we find that Cheltenham, with a population supposed to amount at this day to thirty-eight thousand inhabitants, boasted in 1839 of not fewer than twelve physicians, and of upwards of thirty practising surgeons, besides a very large number of minor medical practitioners. So that in point of medical aid Cheltenham is even more favoured than the metropolis, in proportion to its huge population.* The

* The shrewd editor of a very able little manual for the stranger in Cheltenham, called the *Annuaire*, speaking on this subject in his number

high name of the principal among the physicians is too well known to require any eulogium of mine in this place. Dr. Boisragon has enjoyed for a long period of years the leading practice of the place, and has endeared himself to the inhabitants by many acts of philanthropy, and the repeated efforts he has made to forward the interests of Cheltenham, and improve its character in the scale of scientific and literary instruction.

To the profession at large, Dr. Baron is perhaps, strictly speaking, better known, in consequence of his able pathological work, which first secured him that reputation under the favouring wing of which he ascended to the highest degree of favour at Gloucester,—until a fatal epidemic induced him to change the field of his exertions, by settling in this place, where he occupies a high station as a practitioner.

Of a third popular physician in Cheltenham, Dr. Gibney, I can also make honourable mention as the author of " A Medical Guide to the Cheltenham Waters," which has met with success ; and it is grievous for me not to be able to add to the list of the living eminent physicians the name of one dear to me from old friendship and fellowship in a public service, who, since my visit, has been gathered to his fathers—I mean Dr. Coley, of Cambray. Few medical practitioners enjoyed a larger share of the public confidence than did Dr. Coley at one time.

It is known that all these professional gentlemen place confidence in and prescribe to invalids the use of the mineral waters; which, however, as I had occasion to state already,

for 1838, contrasts the state of Cheltenham in 1800 and 1837, in this manner:—" In the year here referred to, the celebrated Dr. Jenner appears to have been the only resident physician practising in the town. There were five surgeons, one chemist and druggist, and five attorneys. The contrast of 1837 gives us seventeen physicians, twenty-seven surgeons, twenty chemists and druggists, and thirty attorneys !"

are unquestionably less resorted to in these days than they were formerly.

But after all, Cheltenham may now feel inclined to care little about, and rely less upon, its mineral water as a means of present or future attraction to strangers, either for the purpose of inducing them to reside permanently in the place, or for an occasional visit only. It has attained, in the short period of thirty years, that zenith or altitude of fame, which has proved sufficient to convert a small village with three thousand inhabitants, seven hundred and sixteen houses, and one solitary church, "St. Mary's," into a large town with thirty-eight thousand inhabitants, nearly eight thousand houses, and not fewer than seven churches, and from fifteen to twenty chapels. Among the former deserves especial commendation that very fine specimen of ecclesiastical gothic, Christ Church, a proprietary church, just completed at an expense of seventeen thousand pounds, (including seven hundred pounds for the organ) after the design and under the immediate superintendance of its indefatigable architect, Mr. Jearrad, in whose company I had the satisfaction of going over every part of it shortly before its consecration.* It stands on the north-western slope of Bays-hill, with a new, wide, and straight road in front of it, opening into the Lansdowne road, with one branch to the left, to Lansdowne-crescent, along Lansdowne-terrace. The new road is called the Christ-church road, and measures have been taken for covering all the extent of ground on its right with dwellings and streets.

The extent to which this building of new houses and entire new districts is carried on in Cheltenham has scarcely any parallel, except in the great enterprises of the regene-

* A very fine stone pulpit, with stairs, supported by stone pilasters on a pointed arch, a stone altar and altar-piece, introduced into this structure, deserve particular attention.

rator of Newcastle, of whom honourable mention was made
in the first volume. Not only are detached villas multiplying in all directions, but in the short, lapse of the two years
between my last and previous visit, the Lansdowne grounds,
the Christ-church estate, and that of Bays-hill, as well as
the Park estate, in the centre of which is placed the
Zoological and Botanical Garden projected in 1837, exhibit
so many little new towns, reared with a rapidity perfectly
astonishing. Of such many more are projected, and several
in course of erection. The process of clubbing together the
purses of half-a-dozen speculators in bricks and mortar, is
indeed a powerful means of quickly spreading over the map
of a country a number of dwellings, and such has been the
process principally resorted to in Cheltenham.

One would imagine that the town will be overbuilt at last,
and that more brickwork has been going on already than it
will be possible to find occupants for. Yet such is not the
case ; nay, the contrary is so ; for no sooner is a building
reported to be ready, than inmates are found equally ready
to enter it. The effect of such a multiplication of new buildings of every kind has been that of lowering the rent of the old
houses—so much so indeed, that for the same annual sum
which only procures you a decent-looking house in London,
you might lodge yourself in a palace at Cheltenham. Not
so, however, with regard to the more recent creations of Mr.
Jearrad.

I am bound to admit that, in many of these latter structures, much better taste and architectural skill have been
exhibited here than at Leamington. The very active, intelligent, and able architect, just named, to whom Cheltenham is indebted for most of its best and ornamental buildings, has secured his favourite town from the obloquy of
being a mass of unmeaning and often defective façades, as is
the case in many of the more modern towns, and Brighton
amongst them.

All the modern buildings, however, are not equally to be commended. The Lansdowne terrace, for instance, is heavy, from the lengthened repetition of the same heavy design from the first house to the last. A portico of four Ionic columns and a pediment, placed in front of the first story, the said portico resting on a projecting ground-floor, is a feature which, repeated as it has been, a great many times " all in a row," becomes ponderous, as might have been expected.

In the Crescent, on the contrary, the houses are too plain. Not so with regard to many of the detached villas in the vicinity, especially such as may be designated " The Italian Villas," for they are some of the finest specimens of Mr. Jearrad's inventive genius. Two of the latter were purchased, at the time of my visit, for five thousand pounds each, by parties who were in the occupation of them as permanent residents of Cheltenham. Indeed, the value attached to houses in these quarters is almost beyond comprehension. The very houses I have alluded to in Lansdowne Terrace will let, unfurnished, at 100*l.* per annum; and the two largest at each end of the terrace for 250*l.* !

Is it wonderful, after these examples, that property in Cheltenham should have so increased in value, that when the " Plough Hotel," which, in 1806, had been assessed at 65*l.* only, came to be rated in 1837, that amount was raised to 1500*l.* ! And whereas the total contribution from Mr. Thompson's property to all the local rates (including the poor-rate charge) was in that same year but 40*l.*, it is now upwards of 4000*l.** Such are a few of the wonderful effects arising from the reputation of mineral waters!

I wish I could speak in the language of commendation of

---

* These statistical data were furnished me by the editor of " The Cheltenham Looker-on."

the judgment displayed in the selection of the aspect for the new buildings, whether as detached or as connected edifices. No particular attention seems to have been paid to so important a point in questions of house building—a point so often neglected, and yet so essential! Houses here, on the contrary, seem to have been fixed at hap-hazard, or with reference only to some rigmarole and fanciful representation of certain geometrical figures—a parallelogram, for example, or a parabola, or a crescent, both concave and convex! Forgetting all the while that, by such a disposition, many of the houses entering into the arrangement must, of necessity, have an unfavourable aspect. This error, however, is not peculiar to Cheltenham. Here it was early illustrated by the houses right and left of what is called emphatically the Promenade. Those on the left, ascending towards the Montpellier, are all of small dimensions, most of them having but one story above the basements, and showing what Cheltenham was when it began to be something, after the Colonnade was built. The loftier and more pretending erections which have since started into existence on the right, mark the progress of the place, and the increased demand for grandeur and luxury, as Cheltenham became larger, more fashionable, as well as more wealthy. This promenade, with its one row of trees on one side, and two on the other, reminds one of the Alamedas in the southern cities of Spain, flanked by noble buildings, and affording a wide carriage-drive in the centre, with an ample pavement for pedestrians on either side. The foot-pavement, in this instance, is at least thirty feet wide. But striking as this line of walks must be admitted to be, its position is unfavourable in reference to the prevailing winds; while that of the houses themselves is equally so, in reference to solar aspect.

On the left is seen conspicuous the noble portico of the Literary and Philosophical Institution, also the work of Mr.

Jearrad; whilst among the more showy palace-looking houses on the right, stands out very prominently the Imperial Hotel.

The mention of this renowned house of entertainment in Cheltenham reminds me that I have promised at the commencement of the chapter to say a few words on the subject of hotels. Widow Susan Joseph keeps the Imperial, which is essentially the rendezvous of, and is supported by, Old Bachelors, many of whom dwell in it permanently, and rule the roast. These domineering seniors have laid it down as a law, that the good landlady shall not keep a table-d'hôte, at which that "most abominable of all abominations, woman," shall be admitted. They love to have their chops and mulligatawney all to themselves; and the presence of any thing so refreshing and animating as a member of the fairest portion of the creation would throw them into a state of listlessness, inimical to sound appetite. No lady, therefore, appeareth at the Imperial table. O the felicity of these great tubs, who having crammed until every single puckering of the inner coat of their ventricle has disappeared, and its whole amplitude is distended to advantage like the surface of Green's balloon when ready to start, sit after dinner to savour, by well-measured glasses, twenty-six to the bottle, a goodly magnum of the best port! *Crusty* like their darling liquor, any thing in the shape of civility or ceremony, until after a nap and a full digestion, is what they neither will afford, nor can bear. At night, and in their favourite coteries, *à la bonheur*,—" Richard's himself again," and one meets these old gentlemen with pleasure on such an occasion. But as to their haunt, the Imperial coffee-room, *procul esto profani!*

Widow Susan, however, in order not to disappoint the many friends who desire a quiet and civil boarding-house for both sexes, has established one or two of them on each side of the Imperial, unconnected with that showy hotel.

Not so showy is the Imperial, however,—at least in regard to architectural grandeur,—as that first of all the hotels of English Spas, "the Queen"—of the striking elevation of which I here represent in a vignette a faint resemblance.

This very extensive and lofty edifice, the largest of the kind in this country, is erected on the site of one of the mineral Spas, once in vogue at Cheltenham, under the two-fold appellative of Sherborne and Imperial; and was begun, completed, furnished, and opened for the reception of company, in the short space of one year. It is built by shares, I understand;—several resident gentlemen having come forward to assist Mr. Liddell in his undertaking. The establishment, after having been admirably conducted by him, ever since its opening, has just passed, I am told, into the hands of another person, who, as he has paid his predecessor for his interest in the concern and goodwill the large sum of five thousand pounds, will not find it an easy matter to make people believe that his charges are likely to be moderate.

To the interior of this splendid establishment I cannot do justice, except by saying that, as the people of Cheltenham considered it almost a disgrace, before the building of the Queen, that their town, with all its natural and artificial advantages, possessed no "hostelrie" fit for the accommodation of families of exalted rank visiting the place in great numbers,—they may now, with equal truth, boast that they have at last such a hostelrie for that purpose, as it would be impossible to name its competitor in any other part of England. Such a situation, too, and such magnificent and extensive views as are enjoyed from all its apartments, particularly those of the second and third story, would alone suffice to constitute " the Queen" the head-quarters of the leaders of ton and fashion in Cheltenham. The proximity, also, to all the principal walks and drives, as well as to the pump-room of the Montpellier and of the Original Spa, is not one of its minor recommendations.

And what might be the expense of taking up one's abode in such a palace, either to live privately in it—as there is plenty of scope for doing; or to use the general coffee-room, a spacious apartment, howbeit not sufficiently lofty; or to share in the table-d'hôte, for which ample and first-rate accommodations exist in the house? I cannot answer the question; but, judging of what I know of the Plough charges (though living, domestically speaking, is more reasonable at Cheltenham than in London) I should expect the expense to be just such as would suit the pockets of " the first in the land," for whom the hotel was specially intended.

A notion may be formed of the *easy* rate at which " a single gentleman" may live at the Plough, by glancing at one of the bills I saw in the hands of a person of that class. The board and lodging (the former in the coffee-room) were charged three guineas, and two more for a private sitting-room. It being winter-time, a fire was kept in that room, and another in the bed-chamber, for the latter of which three shillings and sixpence, and for the former seven shillings, were set down. As mutton candles are not the most pleasant things in the world to have under one's nose, our " single gentleman" indulged in real wax, for which a charge of seven shillings and sixpence was made; which, with the payment for a night-lamp (eighteenpence) and the usual allowance of seven shillings to the servants, constituted a general total of six pounds, eleven shillings, and six pence per week !

Now it is a fact, that " a single gentleman" could not, if he wished it, spend anything like that sum of money (amounting to about seventy-five florins) at the very first and most fashionable hotel in Germany—say Klinger's at Marienbad, or the Bellevue at Wildbad—with a much superior board, and equally abundant in every respect, besides lodging and other accommodation, to say the least, equally good. The charges at the German house for all those things together would not exceed five florins a day.

I overheard, one day, in the public room of one of these hotels at Cheltenham, an animated conversation, which might have induced me to form a hasty conclusion of the character of its permanent resident population, were I, like some travellers, disposed to take a mere general observation as the result of lengthened experience. The interlocutors seemed to be middle-aged men, and one of them had just greeted the other as a newly-landed visiter at the Spa, of which the former appeared to be an old *habitué*, or resident. " Yes, indeed," observed this knowing personage, " we have the reputation of possessing more spinsters and old maids, more widows and half-pay yellows from the Indus and the Ganges, together with lots of methodists and tee-totallers, than are necessary to render the place as dull as ditch-water ; and yet you will hardly find another watering-place in England that exhibits more of the worst symptoms of a fashionable Spa than Cheltenham. We have here male as well as female coquettes—modish fribblers—carriage-calling, shawl-adjusting, and poodle-petting creatures—whose whole life is spent in devising one day how they shall spend the next with as much enjoyment and at as little expense as possible. You will know them at once by their gait, looks, dress and address, whenever you choose to take a turn or two on the promenade, or peep into the Montpellier or Imperial at the *watering*-hour in the morning, or two hours before the close of day. As for the higher classes of people, you will find them to keep as much aloof from the rest as any of the proudest families in the higher classes of society in the metropolis, whose manners they ape, and whose habits they have adopted. They begin their day's operation for health at ten o'clock in the morning, instead of inhaling the fresh breeze of early morn while drinking the water ; and their operations for pleasure at ten o'clock at night—having, moreover, introduced the fashion of suppers !" (I shuddered at these words, and said to myself—" Is it thus that mineral water is expected to do good ?").

" Cheltenham in this respect has at length reached the olden renown of Bath, and is the only one of the gossiping, intriguing, and highly-fashionable watering-places that has had the felicity of becoming a true *pendant* to that once celebrated Spa. Leamington is striving to become one also, but it is as yet too young in the career of bathing-places. Brighton would have been so ere now, had it possessed, as we do, a permanent as well as a fleeting transitory population of consequence. I will show you, Charles, half-a-dozen well-marked characters of the description I have just alluded to, if you will take your breakfast with me to-morrow at the Queen, from whence we will sally forth on the adjoining walks and haunts ; after which I will regale you with a visit to Thirlestane-house, there to feast your eyes with, some exquisite pictures collected by my Lord Northwich."

From an angle in the Suffolk road an imposing building is perceived, with an Ionic portico of four columns, which presents itself surrounded by a garden within a high wall, at the confluence of the Thirlestane with the Great Bath road. It is Lord Northwich's mansion, which was originally erected, at an enormous expense, by a gentleman named Scott, who did not survive its completion. It was subsequently added to and greatly improved by the present noble proprietor, who became its purchaser, and has rendered it really a mansion fit for a nobleman. Its principal architectural elevation faces the Bath road, and is consequently west-north-west. The entrance has a more favourable aspect; and an exceedingly pretty Ionic pavilion, of great width, has been thrown over it, for carriages to drive under, and thus shelter them whilst the company is alighting.

On entering, a very neat oblong vestibule with a coved roof, supported by Ionic pillars, leads first to the library on the right,—in which there is a painting by Velasquez over the chimney, of the greatest beauty, representing Don Luis D'Hiero, minister of Philip IV. A Holy Family, ascribed to Raphael, attracts also attention; and not less worthy of admiration is the Birth of Jupiter, a large painting by Giulio Romano, preserved by a glass.

In the suite of drawing-rooms, consisting of three apartments, or divisions, lighted by two windows and glass doors, and occupying the front part of the house, but sadly overlooked by the neighbours—several rich paintings are displayed around the walls and on *chevalets,* many of which are of great value. The Marriage of Mary, by Rubens, a grand painting, in the execution of which that dashing master had evidently Paul Veronese in his eye, rivets first the attention of the stranger; but a rich and fresh performance of Raphael, representing a Holy Family—a St. John half-figure, by Leonardo—a pretty valuable Schedoni—the Schoolgirl, and the Alchymist by Teniers, formerly in the possession of Joseph, king of Spain; these soon call him away from the contemplation of the larger picture, to share among them his admiration.

The great dining-room has three corresponding divisions or compartments, containing also several valuable paintings by old masters, among which is, over the side-board, a Giorgione, the Woman taken in Adultery, and one of the many recumbent Venuses ascribed to Titian, over a grand Canaletti, which hangs above the fire-place, and on each side of which is a Claude, of undoubted origin, though not in the usual warm style of that charming master.

On the whole, the view of this choice collection is a great treat, to which, through the kindness of the noble proprietor, the public is admitted daily, Sunday excepted, from one to five o'clock.

Thus far the admirer of the fine arts residing temporarily at this Spa, can find means of indulging his taste in a manner hardly to be met with at any other watering place in England. Nor is the lover of natural studies less fortunate when temporarily abiding in Cheltenham on account of his health; for the Zoological and Botanical Gardens, though indifferently supported by the public, offer him sufficient resources for his pursuits.

To the literally and philosophically inclined, the institution whose fine building I previously noticed on the grand promenade, is calculated to afford a constant fund of information, not only through the collection of books, specimens of natural history, and fossils from the neighbourhood of Cheltenham, but also by the several courses of lectures which take place in the theatre of the Institution during the session, commencing in October, and terminating in May. It may well be imagined that in a place like Cheltenham, containing perhaps, permanently, a larger number of idlers than is to be found in the metropolis in proportion to its population,— reading-rooms to devour newspapers in, and circulating libraries for the propagation of whatever the fashionable publishers of the day may choose to stamp with the coin of their name in the way of fiction,—must abound; and such is in fact the case.

Of periodicals of native growth there are not fewer than five; four of which are strictly political, while the fifth professes to be only a pleasing gossiper of court news and fashion, and . *looks* neither to the right nor to the left for political controversies, which it leaves to the *Conservative Chronicle** the *Cheltenham Journal*, the *Whig Examiner*, and the *Radical Free Press*. In its peculiar department the *Looker-on*, the fifth paper alluded to, has sustained its character since its commencement in May, 1833, with ability and success. What votary of fashion frequenting Cheltenham can plead guilty of ignoring the existence of *The Cheltenham Looker-on?* Mr. Davies, its proprietor, conducts the circulating library and reading-rooms adjoining the Rotunda, which I must say seem to be everything that one can desire in the way of such establishments. Perhaps I am partial to it, as being the first place of this kind in Cheltenham I became acquainted with four years ago; but in its conductor (who is moreover the author of the *Annuaires* already mentioned, as well as of a very clever little guide-book to Cheltenham,) I met with so much intelligence and quaint dry humour, as well as every appearance of honesty of purpose, that in recommending principally his establishment I but follow a just and natural inclination. There is no corner in Cheltenham where a real " Looker-on," indeed, could ensconce himself with greater advantage than in this snuggery of books and prints, to catch in the very act of their " doings and misdoings" the great and little actors of either sex, in the semi-comico lugubrious daily drama of this watering place, and " mark their mould and fashion."

While yet in the immediate vicinity of the centre of attraction, the Montpellier rooms and walk, I cannot forbear hinting to those who have the management of the latter, that if they were to peruse in the " Spas of Germany" my justly expressed reprobation of a certain unbecoming arrangement which obtains at Carlsbad, in the covered promenade

---

* This was the favourite paper of George the Third, while he resided at Cheltenham for his health, and continued to be supplied to His Majesty after he left the place. It then advocated Whig principles.

of the Sprudel, they would not permit one of the same sort, equally objectionable, in the " Montpellier walk,"—respecting which the good honest Germans might justly retort upon me for my reproval of them with a " look at home." Indeed the indecency here is even more glaring, as the entrance to the objectionable retreats is close to the top of the public walk, and no bibber of mineral water detaching himself from the throng of promenaders of both sexes, to dart down the trellised footpath leading to those retreats, can fail to have the eyes of every one upon him. This demands instant reform.

Cheltenham has the reputation of having become of late a tolerably dull place. My information, obtained from patients and residents of every class, is of a most contradictory character ; some pretending that there is too much " sober seriousness" in the place, while others exclaim against its frivolities. To see the eagerness with which every occasion, either of the anniversary of a charitable society, or of an ordinary festival, or even of a political rejoicing, is made use of as a peg to hang a ball, a concert, or an assembly upon, one would not imagine Cheltenham to be either dull or ascetic. There are winter, and spring, and summer-season subscription balls every Monday, for which healthful and desirable exercise at a watering-place, Cheltenham possesses one of the most elegant and highly decorated assembly-rooms, erected sixteen years ago, at the enormous expense of fifty thousand pounds.

There is a *vacation* ball, which comes on at Christmas, and is distinguished by merry faces and Christmas cakes. Then in behalf of some " orphan asylum," the Cheltenhamites have a ball ; and a ball they will have again when the master of the ceremonies appeals to their kindly feelings for a suitable return for his polite attention to them and their visiters. This last-mentioned ball, by the bye, is said to be, generally, one of the most brilliant affairs of the season, as the gentleman who happens to fill at present the honourable post of master of the ceremonies (an officer in the army) is universally and deservedly esteemed. On such occasions, seldom less than eight hundred persons assemble to honour him with their presence, as the families of nearly all the most influential and fashionable of the residents, as well as of a great number of those who live even at some considerable distance from Cheltenham, make it a point to join in the festivity.

Nor is Cheltenham behind-hand in love for the sister art—music, both vocal and instrumental. There are chamber quartetts, philarmonic meetings, and concerts without number. But the musical promenades which take place in the evening, four times a week during the summer, either in the pump-room and promenade-walk of the Montpellier, which are brilliantly lighted up for the occasion, or in the adjoining gardens, are the greatest favourites.

The drama on the contrary has always been a so-so affair, except when the stars from the metropolitan firmament used to shoot down from their spheres into the vale of Gloucester; and now the edifice itself having been destroyed by a recent fire, little or no chance is offered in the place for histrionic display.

For out-of-door amusement, the Cheltenham stag-hounds, and the Cheltenham races, on one of the *loftiest* race-grounds in England, offer the most conspicuous opportunities. The pack is kept up by subscription, and hunting throughout the winter season is secured to the residents and visiters at an annual expense of something like six hundred pounds. But these subscriptions do sometimes lag behind, and the concern then gets to leeward. A meeting, however, is soon called together, a few speeches are made, the debts are presently liquidated, and then goes on as merily as ever this neck-breaking, life-jeopardizing, inspiriting and manly sport of the English.

But have the people at Cheltenham a climate suited to

all these out-of-door amusements ? What says Mr. Moss of High-street, who has for so many years taken notes of the weather and all its phases ? With regard to winds, yes; with regard to rain, no. Our meteorologist, who by the bye is deserving of every praise for his untiring observations in this respect, makes it out that they have at Cheltenham 243 days when the wind blows from the South-east, South, South-west and West; and only 122 days from the opposite or northern and eastern quarters. And such must in fact be the case; for the range of the Cotteswold hills, which rises at least eleven hundred feet above the bed of the Severn, cuts off those winds from Cheltenham, while its open situation to the south and west, courts as it were, the blowing in of the winds from these latter quarters.

The effect of this natural arrangement as to temperature has generally been that on an average the thermometer, for a period of seven years previous to 1837, had seldom been lower than $21\frac{3}{10}°$ of Fahrenheit; while the highest average in the summer has been 65°.

But then this advantage has been more than counter-balanced by the too frequent occurrence of rain, necessarily occasioned by exposure to the Atlantic gales of the south-west, coming heavily charged with moisture, which instead of passing over the town on its wingy clouds, scudding before the gale, is arrested in its progress by the said hilly barrier of the Cotteswold, and discharged in heavy and constant showers. Accordingly I find it admitted by Mr. Moss, that not less than two feet nine inches of rain has been the average quantity which has fallen every year. Now, this quantity of rain falling upon a soil which, below an insignificant deposit of alluvial detritus from the adjoining rocks previously described, presents many feet of blue or brown clay, must tend to keep the atmosphere over and about Cheltenham in an almost perpetual condition of humidity; and so it is that we find it when we reside any time in the place ; and so I found it more or less on every day of my three visits to that Spa.

A warm and at the same time humid atmosphere, however, is good for something; and accordingly we find asthmatic people, and such as have delicate lungs, comforted by simply breathing the Cheltenham air. Another class of patients who find the inhaling of such an atmosphere advantageous, are those who suffer from acute organic disease of the liver, occasioned by long residence in tropical climates. But I must declare it to be against my long experience in the observation of atmospherical influence on disease, that such a warm and moist, and consequently relaxing air, can be of service to he more ordinary disorders of the digestive organs, as stated by some of the advocates of the Cheltenham climate.

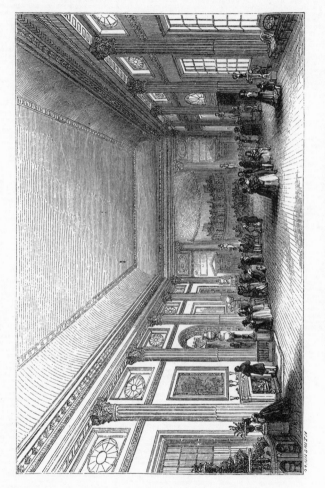

THE GREAT PUMP, OR CONVERSATION-ROOM, AT BATH.

THE

SPAS OF ENGLAND,

AND

PRINCIPAL SEA-BATHING PLACES.

BY

A. B. GRANVILLE, M.D., F.R.S.

AUTHOR OF "THE SPAS OF GERMANY," "ST. PETERSBURG," &c.

SOUTHERN SPAS.

WEYMOUTH.

LONDON:

HENRY COLBURN, PUBLISHER,

GREAT MARLBOROUGH STREET.

1841.

CONTENTS

OF

THE SOUTHERN SPAS.

SOUTHERN SPAS.   *a*

CHAPTER VII.

EXMOUTH—TEIGNMOUTH.

ROAD TO TORQUAY.

CHAPTER VIII.

TORQUAY.

CHAPTER IX.

DAWLISH—WEYMOUTH.

NOTTINGTON AND RADIPOLE SPAS.

CHAPTER X.

BOURNEMOUTH.

CHAPTER XI.

ISLE OF WIGHT—SOUTHAMPTON.

SANDROCK SPRING.

CONTENTS.

CHAPTER XII.

BRIGHTON.

THE ROYAL GERMAN SPA.

CHAPTER XIII.

HASTINGS.

ST. LEONARDS—DOVER.

CHAPTER XIV.

SOUTHEND.

HOCKLEY SPA.

CHAPTER XV.

TUNBRIDGE WELLS.

ILLUSTRATIONS

TO THE SOUTHERN SPAS.

SPAS OF ENGLAND.

THIRD GROUP; OR, SOUTHERN SPAS,

AND

PRINCIPAL SEA-BATHING PLACES.

SOUTHERN SPAS.

CHAPTER I.

GLOUCESTER SPA—GLOUCESTER.

The Avon—Way to the Gloucester Spa—The Pump-room—Discovery of the Mineral Water—Its Physical Character—Bath Rooms—Hotel and Boarding-houses—Dr. Baron and the Spa-woman—Exaggeration and Refutation—Professor Daubeny's Analysis—Presence of Iodine—Absence of Sulphureted Gas—Medical Virtues of the Water—Carr Glowe—Gloucester City not in the Movement—First View of the Cathedral—Its Interior—Roman Architecture—Statue of Jenner—Vaccination—Tardy Interference of Government—Plain Questions in regard to the Alleged Failures of Vaccination—Prejudice of the Lower Classes—Indifference—Author's Inquiries and Publication on this Subject—Splendid Monument—Fate of Eminent Physicians—Ingratitude of the Higher Classes—The late Dr. Baillie—Flaxman—The Noble Cloisters—Contrast in Architecture—Penury Wood and his Old Bank.

Many of my readers who can only associate the name of Gloucester with its superb cathedral, will wonder, on reading the title of the present chapter, at the mention of any Spa connected with it. Yet so it is: and having been myself informed of the fact while on my journey, I felt it my duty to proceed thither, and inquire into the truth of the statement.

As my way to the next important watering-place from Cheltenham laid to the banks of the Avon and the Severn, a halt was both natural and desirable, at a place where the last-mentioned and more important river, after travelling as an inland stream for one hundred and fifty miles, first becomes a marine estuary, and is spanned over by its last bridge.

To find a source of mineral water also in the place was an additional temptation for a short visit.

Leaving the Turk's Head, a superior sort of inn in one of the principal streets of Gloucester, and quitting the town by Southgate-street, I reached, at the end of a short walk, a handsome iron gate on the left of the road, opposite one of the streets which lead to the port, and, entering it, I proceeded along a private road, the left side of which is flanked by a line of houses, evidently of recent erection, and certainly of a superior class to those I had seen in old Gloucester. On the right, or opposite to them, a grass-field skirts the road, which insensibly expands into a green level ground of some extent. It is on this ground that the mineral springs were accidentally discovered in 1814, and it is here that a very neat Spa-house has been raised over them.

The surrounding plain being skilfully laid out in shrubberies and wide gravel walks, arranged in curves and serpentine lines; a promenade of some extent has been obtained around the two green paddocks, of which the ground consists. One of these, extending immediately behind the Spa, is surrounded by high and well-trimmed hedges of hawthorn. To the south, beyond these pleasure-grounds, a low range of hillocks, running from east to south, may be perceived, the highest of which, looking much as Hampstead does when viewed from the Regent's-park, is sufficiently close at hand to enter, with its green grassy clothing, into the features of the tiny landscape by which this well-arranged Spa-region is encompassed.

These walks, even at the very early hour of the morning at which I visited them, were enlivened by a few of the visiters, who were taking their prescribed exercise between their glasses of water. Their *tournure* bespoke them of the better classes of inhabitants.

Behind the building containing the mineral springs there is a billiard-room, and other conveniences, such as one would desire to have in a place of this kind, removed from the bustle of the city. The walks are shaded by belts of trees on one side, which impart to the whole the character of a private park.

The pump-room is a plain, oblong square building, about thirty feet in length and twenty feet wide, with a door at each end, and one in the centre, exactly opposite that never-failing incumbrance of almost all the English spa-rooms, the counter, at which the water is distributed by means of a pump. A low veranda runs along the front of the pump-room, and is returned partly at the sides, to shade promenaders from both sun and rain.

Here, as at Cheltenham, we have many spouts yielding mineral water. No. 1 draws the water from a well in an adjoining field ; another, not so strong, pumps it from a source immediately under the counter ; while a third draws the water from a source (the original one) near a private house at the entrance into the Spa.

While digging the foundations for the house just mentioned, a spring of water was tapped which, on the workmen tasting it, they found to be anything but agreeable. It was soon ascertained that it contained common salt and iron. In consequence of this, further search was made to the depth of eighty feet, when the strong saline well, which constitutes, properly speaking, the mineral water of the Gloucester Spa, was discovered.

The taste of this last-mentioned water is perfectly briny, without any bitterness, or *après goût* of any sort: it is a clean, soft, oily, and salt taste when the water is drank cold, which becomes more intensely salt, and not so pleasant, when it is drank mixed with some of the same water previously heated. By my tests I could not detect either sulphureted gas or iron in the water I tried.

The pump-room, I was assured, is well frequented; indeed, I could perceive from the subscription-book that such must be the case. The visiters generally drink a pint of the water at once, or half a pint twice. This quantity immediately or shortly afterwards acts as a purgative.

There are four very convenient bath-rooms, one of which is for ladies. From four to five invalids, perhaps, bathe here in a day. The committee of gentlemen (twenty in number) who have taken the whole concern into their hands, by shares, have spared no pains or expense to render the establishment worthy of patronage. From my slight description, even, it will be seen that they have contributed everything in their power, not only to the usefulness but to the decorations of the Spa.

In the private road by which we approached the Spa there is a good-sized hotel facing the south, with gardens and the open country before it, and ample accommodations within.

The good lady, whom I had rather puzzled and perplexed with my inquiries, as well as by my repeated tasting and testing of the different waters in her presence, was quite enthusiastic in her admiration of the salutary effects she had witnessed in many of the persons who had drank the water since she had been connected with the Spa-room. "Oh, had but Dr. Baron" (she exclaimed, turning round to other persons then in the room) "kept firm at his post—as he was in duty bound to do, for he had made all his fortune with the good people of Gloucester, whom he used to send in crowds, when sick, to this very pump-room—instead of leaving his patients in the lurch when they most needed his assistance, to go and take up his residence in a totally strange city to him—this Spa, which has been but indifferently attended to ever since, would have been in a very different state at this moment."

Being at the time entirely ignorant of this part of my skilful brother-practitioner's history, I could neither assent to nor dissent from the honest dame's remonstrance, so emphatically expressed. But I purposely report that remonstrance in this place, as I am thereby afforded an opportunity of declaring that by subsequent information, derived from sources less likely to be biassed in their opinion, I have learned enough of Dr. Baron's proceedings at the epoch alluded to— which was that of the prevalence of cholera in Gloucester, where the learned doctor was then the leading practitioner— to make me view this naked accusation of desertion of his patients, as one founded on pure exaggeration. Dr. Baron's character, as a man, stands not in need of defence either from me or any one else; but as the loose charge of the fair Gloucester Spa-woman has been occasionally bandied about, upon no better authority, even at Cheltenham, I should think myself guilty of a dereliction of that duty which ought to (does it?) bind together all the members of the same profession—namely, of upholding each other's character when unjustly assailed—did I not, from any foolish notion of delicacy, publicly vindicate that of an able practitioner and excellent man, though my acquaintance with him has been merely one of correspondence, and of a professional nature.

The Gloucester Spa water is, properly speaking, the first English mineral water in which iodine has been detected,* by the distinct experiments of Professor Daubeny; although Mr. Murray professes to have been the first to announce its presence in this Spa. As, however, the latter has not published

* The previous announcement of iodine, by Dr. Turner, in the waters of Bonnington, mentioned by me at page 164, refers to another part of the realm—Scotland; so that Professor Daubeny is in reality the first who discovered iodine in the mineral waters of England.

anywhere a regular scientific account of his alleged discovery, the statement of the presence of iodine in the mineral water under consideration is adopted on the authority of the Oxford Professor. His quantitative analysis will be found in the general Table. An old analysis of the water, said to have been made by Accum in 1814, is distributed at the Spa upon a card. But that analysis differs so materially from Professor Daubeny's that it is hardly possible to reconcile the one with the other. In Accum's analysis there are not fewer than seven solid ingredients mentioned, and the total amount of them in weight, in a pint, is 96¾ grains. In that of the Oxford Professor, the weight of the solid ingredients in the same quantity of water, is represented to be only 62 grains, and the number of the said ingredients no more than four. The first gives two grains of carbonate of iron, which the second does not mention; but in return the latter has one grain of iodine in fifty gallons of water, and one grain of bromine in ten quarts; which the other analyzer could not have noticed, as neither one nor the other of those substances was known at the time.

Professor Daubeny's silence respecting the alleged presence of sulphureted hydrogen gas and iron, shews that he was not more successful in 1836 than I had been in 1839 in detecting those substances in this water.

I have had not the slightest experience of the Gloucester Spa water, medically speaking. Its composition assimilates it to the pure saline water of Cheltenham; so that one may place confidence in the published statements of medical practitioners, of its efficacy in all those diseases for which the Cheltenham salines have been successfully employed.

A peep at the " CAER GLOWE," or the " Bright and Splendid Town" of the Old Britons, the place in which the great Norman Conqueror, many hundred years afterwards, loved to sing his Christmas carols in the midst of his barons, was the next natural thing for me to indulge in, after visiting the Spa; and after it a visit to the cathedral and its unequalled cloisters! What stranger can put his foot in Gloucester and not hurry thither to see both?

Gloucester is certainly not in the movement; except that it is brilliantly and profusely lighted with gas at night. The building-mania so visible everywhere in this country has not reached this place. There are indications of a new square, with rows of modern houses on three sides of it, in the immediate vicinity of the Spa; and red bricks have been lavishingly heaped together in two or three different parts of the city, and fashioned into two bastiles, the jail and the Union, as well as into a third building, the Infirmary. There is also a more recent edifice, with greater pretension to architectural style, of which I shall speak anon. But beyond these we look in vain for any other symptoms of progressive improvements.

Of the many old houses, several there are which look like deserted palaces, and must have been the old residences of the magnates of the land. In one of these—a very large and ancient pile, not unlike the courtly mansion once the residence of Henry VIII., which I described as being occupied by Dr. Simpson at York—resides the leading physician of Gloucester. He has facing him the high tower of the Cathedral, and the polygonal building of the Shire Hall close at hand.

There is a quaintness and singularity in the exterior walls of the cathedral, mixed with much richness of detail in some of the windows and the porch, which arrest the attention of the stranger at once, and make him almost overlook the signs of dilapidation so strongly marked on the sandstone buttresses and mullions. The square tower springing to an elevation of 225 feet, with its terminal parapet and four ornamented pinnacles, strikes the eye as being much loftier, on account of the great length and comparative lowness of the anterior part of the temple, out of the centre of which it rises, and also, owing to the precise symmetry of the parts of which the tower is composed, consisting of two equal stories correctly repeated. The richest and most imposing view of the whole body of the cathedral is at the north end from the gardens.

How impressive is the view of the nave? Those short Norman thick pillars, supporting the semicircular arches, are massive and imposing, and so is the simple roof or vault over them. Different indeed is the effect produced by the two pillars nearest to the great western end, raised anew from the ground two centuries later, and upholding a ceiling diversified by rosettes, ribs, and intricate tracery of the finest description. Take it all in all, this is the cleanest, whitest, and most neatly-arranged interior I have seen in the course of my extensive peregrinations through England. It is exactly a century this year since it received its present coat of a creamy tint, which is perfectly preserved. Here the dean has not had the bad taste, as in another cathedral, to which I have referred in the present volume, of removing all the monumental tablets and ancient records affixed to the shafts and walls, but has left them as they stood, in picturesque and ornamental effect.

I like much the simplicity of the early Norman character of architecture. It is a beautiful transition from the Byzantine and earliest Christian Greek style, so grave and chaste, to the richer, luxuriant, but in my mind, not so impressive Saxon, improved upon by the subsequent changes and additions of English architects.

Is there a medical man, or a mere philanthropist, who could enter this magnificent temple and not recollect that in it, among many other monuments of vanished greatness, there exists one raised to the immortal discoverer of vaccine inoculation! There stands the monumental statue of the great benefactor of mankind, in an imposing, erect attitude, seen on the right immediately upon entering through the western door. It is a praiseworthy effort of Sievier's chisel, obtained by subscription, at the head of which was Dr. Baron. The front panel of its pedestal originally bore Dr. Jenner's name, and the date of his death ; but these indications were four years ago obliterated, by order of Dr. Baron, and I could not learn from my informant, one of the vergers, the reason for such a proceeding.

Casual or not,—the mere effect of chance observation, or of a well-reasoned train of reflections, (for to both processes it has been ascribed by contemporaries),—the discovery of vaccine inoculation, as an effectual preventive of that great scourge, the smallpox, is an event, the gigantic result of which to the whole population of the world in future ages, we have hardly had yet sufficient means of justly appreciating. It is therefore in future ages that the name of its author will be held up to the veneration of every nation upon earth, from the surface of which an exterminating plague will have been swept away by the universal adoption of his discovery.

Strange, that in a question of such importance, the government and the legislators of the country in which that blessing to mankind took its origin, should have hesitated for a period of forty years, before it lent a helping hand to the medical profession, in endeavouring to extirpate smallpox from among us, by propagating the practice of a simple operation !

Have the public authorities hesitated in the performance of their duty until now, because a few solitary cases of failure had occurred in the attainment of the expected benefit from the Jennerian operation ? What are those cases, or double or tenfold their number, were even so many to occur, as compared to the millions of contrary and entirely favourable results ? Why do not sceptical people interrogate themselves, thus :—How many in our own families—how many in the families of our acquaintances—how many in the families of other people living in the same village, in the same district, in the same streets with us, have we known to have been afflicted with the smallpox during the last thirty or forty years, but especially among the present generation? How many thousands and hundreds of thousands of people have lived and died within these last thirty years, who never had the smallpox through life, owing to early vaccination?

Then let the contrary questions be asked : what family before 1800 used ever to escape decimation by death from smallpox ? How many of every family were there who, having survived the infliction of that disease, had had their lineaments and physiognomy permanently disfigured, or their senses and the most delicate organs of the body irreparably damaged ? Do we not, all of us, who are past the half century, remember that, of the remnants of the last generation, we had seen every second or third person bear indelible marks on their countenances of having gone through the severe phases of a loathsome disease ? And do we meet with such examples among the juniors of the present age ?

These are the homely and home questions I usually put to those parents who resist the salutary practice of vaccination on behalf of their offspring, because they doubt of its real efficacy, and listen rather to the hundred-times-told tale of such and such a case of smallpox having occurred in spite of vaccination ; as if examples of a second attack of smallpox, after the full course of that disease artificially inoculated, had not occurred in the same individual, much more frequently than in regard to vaccination.

Among the humbler classes, the principal cause which has retarded the progress of vaccination has been an unconquerable feeling prevalent in the breast of the parents, that nature had better be left to take its course. Where the mischievous practice of smallpox inoculation has been admitted among some sections of these classes of people, it has been forced upon them by low-minded practitioners, for the sake of mere lucre, and the pitiful amount of a bill for medicines, which were necessarily administered during the course of the artificial disease, but which are hardly ever necessary during the progress of the vaccine inoculation. That same motive is at work still, and will not be suppressed by the recent Act of Parliament, which is insufficient for the intended object of propagating vaccination.

During the ten years that I filled the responsible situation of senior physician to the Royal Metropolitan Hospital for sick children, founded by myself twenty-one years ago, I ascertained that though the feeling of the industrious classes in favour of the old practice of smallpox inoculation, as compared with that in favour of vaccination, was only as one to two,—that of perfect indifference in regard to both practices, and as to whether a child should be suffered to catch or not the natural disease, was, as compared to the love of vaccination, as ten to one.

On this interesting subject I published, eight or nine years ago, a curious coloured diagram, exhibiting to the eye at one view, without any aid from arithmetical computation, the march of these three different feelings among the humbler classes of the metropolitan population. It was represented by ascending and descending lines, differently coloured, which were calculated on a scale furnished by the total number of registered cases of sick children under twelve years of age, amounting to some thousands, that had come under the notice of myself and my professional colleagues at the institution here alluded to, during a period of ten years.

This digression on vaccination, while I am standing with my readers before the well-executed marble figure of its discoverer in Gloucester cathedral, will not be considered inopportune; especially at a moment like the present, when some decisive public effort seems likely to be made to forward the views of that patriotic and benevolent man.

How instructive in history, in biography, in statistics, in literature, in feeling, and in the appreciation of the fine arts, is the perusal of those congregated monuments which one beholds all around in these magnificent temples to God! What volume is more instructive to him who knows how to read it? Gloucester Cathedral, though not so rich in this respect as the Pantheon of Westminster Abbey, is yet a museum of many interesting mementos.

What can be more beautiful, and at the same time more affecting, to a lover of gothic art and the ancient history of these realms, than that exquisite canopied monument of the florid perpendicular, placed over the figure of Edward II., murdered in Berkeley Castle, and erected by the third Edward, and here called " The Shrine," to which pilgrims for ages after resorted, and paid homage and oblation? Not only is the carving of the canopy one of the finest specimens in this country, but the recumbent figure of the murdered monarch is one of the very few of that class in existence which possess real sculptural merit, particularly the face, whose expression of pain and resignation is admirable.

Another murdered prince is here represented in what may be considered as the finest specimen of wood-carving of those times. It is Robert, Duke of Normandy, a very noble and handsome person, who was starved to death in Cardiff Castle, ætat. 26 years.

If the biography of men somewhat nearer to our times interest us more, we may cast our eyes on the curious monument of Alderman Jones, of this city, who had been registrar to six successive bishops; mayor of Gloucester three times; friend and contemporary of Shakspeare, whom he survived but a few years, and whose monument in the chancel of Trinity church, at Stratford, was adopted as a model for this, by order of the alderman himself.

Medical men, after devoting their whole lives and energies, their honest endeavours, judgment and experience, to the service and for the benefit of the better classes of their fellow-men, so seldom meet with the sweet reward of grati-

tude in the continuous support and confidence of their
patients, that it must be refreshing to one of that profession
to find here recorded, in a monument from the design of Sir
Robert Smirke, an exception to that dismal fact, to which
the late Dr. Baillie (than whom no medical man was more
entitled to public confidence) bore testimony, by often observing, just before his death, to the author of these volumes,
that of all the great families he had attended during his
long and successful career, not more than four or five had
stuck to him as patients with constancy through life! And
yet no man had a greater number of friends than Dr. Baillie,
or a larger practice. What monument has the public raised
to that eminent physician? Or what monument is the
memory of an equally eminent surgeon, as devoted and as successful a servant of the public, and recently taken from us,
likely to receive at the hands of those many hundred families, or their survivors, whom both the physician and the
surgeon just named have been instrumental in saving from
death or the pangs of disease? None. A monumental
record of their imperishable names and merits has indeed
been raised, or ordered, since their departure; but not by
those from whom such a testimonial would have been an act
of justice. It has been raised by contemporary practitioners,
as an evidence of their admiration of departed excellence.
Strange that the art which tends to save our citizens' lives,
should never have met with the public guerdon of national
gratitude, which has been so profusely lavished on those who
most excel in the art of death!

Here, in the cathedral of Gloucester, Fry, a surgeon of
the infirmary, and an excellent man, who died in 1811, has
had his memory perpetuated, in a monument to which I have
just referred, and which forms the pleasing exception already
alluded to, of having been erected by public subscription of
all his friends and patients.

There is a beautiful specimen of Flaxman's art (one of the

few choice geniuses in sculpture this country can be proud of) not far from the last-named monument, which I cannot omit mentioning before I take leave of a scene where I could have lingered long. A lovely female figure (of Mrs. Morley) is rising out of the sea with her infant child. A winged angel, equipoised in the air, lifts her by the hand, while two other angels, equally on the wing, look on. The figures appear to be *appliquées* on a blue slab behind, like a very *alto relievo*. Mrs. Morley died after childbirth, on board ship, while on her way from India to England, and received the burial of those who plough the deep. Flaxman has wrought a pretty and affecting idea out of this incident. The motto inscribed over the figures is—" The sea shall give up the dead. 1784."

I must not trespass any longer on my readers' patience ; although the delight I experienced at the view of the finest Gothic cloisters in the Christian world, attached to this cathedral, would have warranted another short delay. But the pen refuses the task of describing, even in the short popular style I have adopted, that which has already been vividly and correctly delineated by architects and antiquaries of merit. The finest perspective view of these matchless corridors is obtained from the south-west angle, which takes in the two best sides.

To an admirer of contrast in architecture, particularly when connected with odd recollections, a short walk down Westgate will afford such a one as cannot fail to attract notice. It is the old dwelling of the rich notorious miser, whose ill-apportioned millions left at his death, have been melting yearly under the hot grasp of the law. I allude to the late Mr. Wood's house, who had dignified it by the name of the Old Gloucester Bank—contrasted with the new and splendid erection of the Gloucester Joint Stock Bank, at the corner of College-court leading to the Cathedral. These two banking-houses are sufficiently near to each other to enable one to compare them together at one view, and mark in the outward show of the one, and the beggarly, though picturesque look of the other, of which I here present a view,

the immense strides which ideas of pomp, luxury, and ostentation, without any real increase of wealth, have made since the owner of the humbler dwelling, with more treasure at his command than ten times the amount of the wealthiest county bank of the present day, used to stand at his shop-door to invite customers to step in and do business with him,—as represented in the sketch.

As to the more modern structure, which serves to form the contrast (and which I do not think it necessary to represent here), its palace-like front, though showy, exhibits, in the combination of the several members of which the front elevation is composed, a violation of the laws of architectural harmony not common even in this country. The first and second floor centre windows are placed in the space between two Corinthian columns, occupying the centre of the house, and resting on the basement-story, which projects from the wall as much as the whole diameter of the said columns, and no more. But by the side, and close to each of these, is a square pillar, wide as the diameter of the columns, and projecting from the wall with its base and capital as much as they do, and consequently flush with them. Then comes the side windows, placed between the square pillars and a pilaster of the same width, but only an ordinary *appliqué* pilaster of two or three inches projection, with which the outline of the elevation terminates. The effect of this strange combination in a width altogether of not more than fifty feet, is of the oddest kind imaginable. Still, as a contrast to Wood's old bank, it is, as I said before, a palace, and may by some be taken either as a proof of the progress which architectural spirit has been making in England in recent times; or only as an example of what people nowadays think of the necessity of outward show in business as compared with what they thought of it eighty years ago.

CHAPTER II.

I OUGHT perhaps to introduce in this part of my narrative a
short account of NEWENT Spa, another of the many mineral
springs to be met with in the vale of Gloucester, situated
about eight and a half miles from that city, near the Hereford and Gloucester Canal. But my personal data of information respecting it are too scanty. Mr. Murchison, in the
able work previously alluded to, considers it as a highly
sulphurous medicinal spring, formed by the surface-water
flowing upon the inclined bed of a coal-measure (anciently
worked in this place), which contains much iron pyrites, decomposing the latter so as to become impregnated with the
disengaged sulphureted hydrogen gas, and then rising to its
original level, through cracks in the stratum of new red sand-

stone, which here, as almost everywhere, overlays the coal-measure.

Newent is seated on the new red sand-stone ; and just about where the Spa is, Mr. Murchison discovered a fault in that rock, as well as in the coal-seam below it; and this break in the strata would certainly afford sufficient room for the up-coming of the sulphureted water which constitutes the Spa.

But then in such a case, according to the same able geologist's view previously mentioned, of the origin of saline springs, the Newent water, by passing through the various members of the new red sand-stone, which forms the crust of the soil here (including, I suppose, " the saliferous red marl"), would be charged in its passage with brine, in addition to the sulphur brought up from the carboniferous stratum.   That is to say, the Newent Spa water ought to be a strongly *saline* sulphureted water. Now is it so in reality ? I have no means of answering that question ; but I regret this the less, as Newent Spa is hardly of that character which requires it to be described fully among the principal watering-places that form the subject of my present volumes ; and I have only alluded to it in this place as an object of geological interest.

ROAD TO BRISTOL.—Until it reaches the little village of Newport, in the vicinity of Berkeley, the road from Gloucester to Bristol is tame and uninteresting.   Grazing-fields are traversed in succession, with herds of cows wandering over them whose milk is destined to produce the " single" as well as the " double Gloucester." The only redeeming features in this flat region are the Painswick Hills, on the left, whence that useful marble is quarried which is so much employed in buildings throughout this country. It was whilst seated on the summit of one of the loftiest of this range, watching the slow progress of the siege of Gloucester, that the ill-fated British monarch descended of a lovely and a still more ill-starred queen, gave that ominous answer to one of his children who was anxious to know when they should return home : " Alas, my son ! I have no home !"

From Newport forward, however, and up to the very threshold of the " metropolis of the west," as the Bristolians are pleased to call their city, the surrounding country opens and expands into the beautiful valley of the Severn, flanked on the west by the Welsh hills, and skirted near at hand on the east by the line of limestone-hills, which, beginning at Painswick aforesaid, to the south of the famed *Via Erminia* of the Romans, and in continuation of the Leckhampton Hills, near Cheltenham, follows a S.S.W. course by Stroud, Dursley, Wotton, and Chipping Sodbury, as far as Bitton and Marshfield, immediately to the north of Bath. From many parts of this road (which, by the bye, is kept in most excellent order, being upon a limestone bottom, hardened by the black-rock material from Bristol,) some exquisite points of view are discerned, both in the wide expanse of the subjacent valley of the Severn, whose very tortuous windings are now and then brought into the landscape,—and among the distant grounds bordering on Monmouthshire, clothed by the magnificent forest of Dean, and watered by the Wye.

In spite of the strong temptation held out to a stranger newly arrived in Bristol, after a lapse of twenty years since a previous visit, of loitering at that most showy hotel called the Great Western (a very fine and imposing Corinthian building just erected not far from College-green), I left it, soon after my arrival, in a fly for Clifton, the *ultima Thule* of my wanderings in this direction,—impatient to take cognizance of a place which has acquired so much celebrity in modern times as a station for invalids.

CLIFTON,

moreover, offered another object of attraction to one engaged, as I was, in the exploration of mineral waters in England—

namely, its *Hot-wells*, as they have been called. But the principal motive of my visit being that of studying the place under the twofold consideration of its climate and of its peculiar adaptation as a residence for people of delicate chest, I directed my inquiries, as I now devote my description, principally to those two highly-important points, without omitting, at the same time, what it was necessary to make myself acquainted with—its mineral springs.

My head-quarters were fixed at once at the Gloucester Hotel, and I sought for a room on one of the upper stories (No. 8) in the body of the hotel itself, which enjoyed a view of the cliff,—having declined a better and larger room in what is called the private house, adjoining, and in connexion with the hotel department.

In the coffee-room a young man sat by the fire, whose physiognomy and tone of voice, and whose whole appearance, bespoke the motive that had brought him to Clifton at this commencement of the inclement season (Nov. 1839). He was dressed in a fashionable style, and held occasional conversation with a healthy-looking young friend, whose demeanour denoted at once the superior class of society they both belonged to. The affectionate and sympathising looks which this youth cast now and then towards his friend, as the latter, after a long, deep, and cavernous cough, would exhibit signs of complete exhaustion, showed him to have come hither as the companion, and perhaps nurse, of one whose span of life was not likely to be long. The poor sufferer survived that dreary winter at Clifton, but succumbed at last under the fatal load of tubercular consumption on the approach of the succeeding cold season.

The coffee-room we were sitting in, though not to be compared to those at the principal hotels in Cheltenham or Leamington, is nevertheless a large and comfortable apartment, and I should say particularly warm, free from draught, and a proper sitting-room for invalids in winter. The house possesses also a very spacious assembly-room, ninety feet in length, thirty-five feet wide, and in height thirty feet.

I had scarcely left my bed, at early morning, on the day after my arrival at the hotel, while every soul seemed still at rest in that vast establishment, when such a discordant *charivari* of tin trumpets was set up in all directions in the streets, (reminding me of the " stirring times" of horn-blowing newspaper glory, ere Mr. Sturges Bourne put a *quietus* to that stunning practice,) that I wondered how any invalid, particularly the hopeless consumptive, bathed in his cold morning sweat around the neck and over his chest, could, under such a disturbance, prolong his slumbers into a more advanced period of the morning, so as to cheat a few more of his hours of suffering. These tin horns I found, on looking out of the window, announced to the still half-slumbering servant-maids, just roused from their chambers, the approach of a set of noisy striplings carrying morning rolls and muffins for breakfast, in wicker baskets. Surely, the last police-act might have extended its powerful and long arm, in behalf of sickness, even unto this nuisance, though at the distance of one hundred and seventeen miles from the capital.

There is no question as to which rooms I should recommend to an invalid living at the top of the house in this hotel. As a sleeping-room, the one I occupied, being completely sheltered from the north and eastern winds, would be the most preferable; while the room opposite and facing the south, enjoying, as it does, the prospect of a seaward view, and the glorious sight of a western sun, when such ever shines, cheering and delightful during the short-lived days of winter, would admirably answer for a sitting-room. There is a passage between the two, but the *trajet* is short. I doubt, however, how far your large bow-windows, cheerful though they be, whether facing the north or the south, can be kept warm in winter in this country, when placed opposite the entrance-door, which must be so constantly in use.

The position of the several dwelling-houses of the first and second class, in a colony of invalids like Clifton, is the principal and most essential point to be considered, by a medical man who desires to give useful and conscientious advice to the patients he may recommend to spend the winter there. That point has not been touched upon in other publications with the minuteness of details, without which the information could be of little service either to the patient or to the medical adviser, who may not himself have seen the locality. If, therefore, I have entered somewhat tediously and minutely into the description of the various positions which offer at Clifton the best resources in the way of habitation, and by so doing the reader finds that I have been even more than usually dull, my motive for such a course must be my apology.

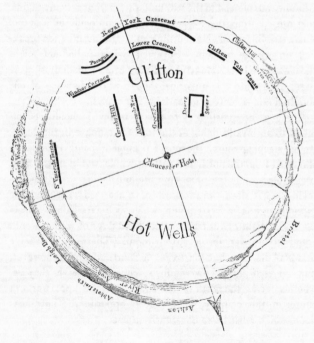

I have introduced into this place a circular diagram to illustrate my topical description. As they appear from the N.N.E. windows of my sleeping-room at the Gloucester, the several ranges of buildings in Clifton and around it have been set down in my *Circlorama*, and the bearings of their fronts marked by compass.

The highest placed, forming an arch of nearly two-thirds of the northern semicircle is the Upper Royal York-crescent, which looks S.S.E. and S.W. The Lower Crescent faces a little more the W. and W.S.W. The Clifton-vale houses, with verandas, on the slope of Clifton Hill, run north and south nearly, with their front to the west : further beyond these Clifton Church is perceived. Windsor-terrace, with its beautiful architectural façade, looks S.S.E. and Albemarle-row, at a right angle with the hotel, is dead east.

Turning now into the south room, its ample bow-window opens a curvilinear prospect of great beauty and extent. The village of Hotwells, close to the water margin, sweeps at some little distance below. The busy haunts of Bristol occupy the left of the picture, and the romantic, enchanting wooded scene of Leigh Wood and Leigh Down, with a peep at Abbot's-lodge, encircle the right-hand horizon, beyond which imagination carries the observer to the Bristol Channel.

This last-mentioned view to the south of the Gloucester Hotel, lies before its principal front on Gloucester Terrace, where its entrance, showy and inviting, is nevertheless not so highly placed as that of the back-front of the house, the level of which is higher, from the circumstance of the hotel being built against the side of a hill.

I have not seen a portion of landscape any where in England that reminds me so forcibly of Ems, as St. Vincent's-terrace, placed some hundred and fifty feet below the table-land which crowns Clifton-hill, and on which are clustered the several buildings just named, and many more. The river here is wider and deeper than at Ems, and, being a tidal river, exhibits its depth of muddy banks whenever the stream ebbs. The water is not so limpid; and there is also too great an approximation to the margin of the river, of the opposite well-wooded hill. At Ems, on the contrary, the hills on the farther bank of the river are placed at a greater distance from the water-side, owing to an intervening expanse of cheerful fields. Still the position of the houses, the terrace in front of them planted with trees, and above all the rugged and lofty rock behind, which both towers over and comes close home to the back windows of the said houses, are points of resemblance not to be overlooked by one accustomed to make comparisons of places.

The houses on St. Vincent's-terrace are in good style, and their aspect westerly. They are most effectually sheltered from the south-east, east, and north-east winds, as they bend inwardly within a niche of the rocks behind. Opposite, or on the left bank of the Avon, a screen of green-clothed hills tempers the gales from that quarter, without being too near to prevent ventilation, which is, on the contrary, promoted by every tidal change in the river, so beneficial in other respects, and in a medical point of view, salutary also. The side-glance down the river, as far as the celebrated rocks, which the inhabitants of these houses may enjoy, gives an additional interest to the locality.

The situation of St. Vincent's-terrace, therefore, cannot fail to be of the most genial and warmest kind for invalids, and must be preferred to any other in the place during the winter season. It is the *Lung' Arno* of Clifton, and if people had been wise in our days, instead of perching themselves upon all the peaks and obelisks of the great mighty rock, strewing palaces in all directions over its highest summits, for the sake of distant views and cheerful panoramas, without much consideration as to aspect and local influence for invalids,—they would have prolonged St. Vincent's-terrace close up to the new Hot-well house, and taken down also the shabby low huts in a line with the terrace, placed between

its south end and the village of Hotwells, in order to re-
place them by handsome boarding-houses. They would
also have enlarged, and beautified, and lengthened the
terrace in front, making it a most convenient promenade for
invalids, to bask in the western sun during the winter months,
between twelve and two, or between eleven and one o'clock,
on all such days as the tide is high at that hour.

As I am speaking in behalf of consumptive patients, or
such as are threatened with chest complaints, and of the
best mode of sheltering them during the colder months of the
year, I may state that the objection I hold against a lofty
wall of natural rocks coming close to the back of the houses,
as at Ems, and in this very place of St. Vincent also, does
not apply to the latter in the way it does to the former, to
which it was strongly directed in my work on the Spas of
Germany; because there, nervous, dyspeptic, or hepatic
patients, are made to reside during the warmer months of
the year, when they require no shelter, 'but, on the contrary,
a free circulation of air all round.

I have no doubt as to the fact that the Cliftonians have
been mistaken in their local arrangements, while expanding
their colony. The excuse urged in their defence, when I have
ventured to make the preceding remark, has been, that the
largest number of patients, or rather visiters, who frequent
Clifton, go thither during the summer, for pleasure as well
as to enjoy the beauties of the country. The invalids, on the
contrary, who arrive in winter, are few in number. Be it
so. Yet the latter should have the benefit of the best dwellings and in the most appropriate situations.

It will be expected of me, before I proceed farther with my
description, that I should, in this place, offer my opinion as
to the real advantages which Clifton offers to persons suffering from pulmonary complaints in their various stages. My
reply shall be brief.—The result of the last twenty years'
experience has not come up to the expectation formed of its
salutary and genial influence. Clifton has probably never

been more generally recommended by medical men, particularly by those of the metropolis, for patients in a certain delicate state of health, than during the last thirty years. The expansion of that formerly insignificant village, and the important changes in it that have taken place in consequence, in the course of that period, exceed almost all example. It is still flourishing; and building is still proceeding with vigour, although not quite so briskly as formerly. There must have been, therefore, some good reason for all these improvements and additions, which cannot be attributed to any other cause but to the strangers who come to the place, either for a prolonged or for a mere temporary residence. Still the sanative effects of such a situation in the case of visiters labouring under pulmonary affections, have not been confirmed by a sufficiently large number of happy results to warrant one in setting down the place as on a par with Nice,—to which Clifton has been abstractedly compared. Nevertheless, Clifton has its particular advantages of temperature, air, and locality, which in the hands of a judicious practitioner may be made available in many cases where probably no other situation or measure would avail; and therefore it is to be held in estimation and used accordingly.

THE HOT WELLS.

This is evidently a misnomer. Water from a spring, marking at the utmost but 76° of heat, may be called *subtepid*, but is certainly not *hot*. Its real temperature, however, is seldom found to exceed 73° of Fahrenheit, as was the case during the repeated experiments I made, after having had the water pumped for nearly three-quarters of an hour, before it could be obtained at that degree of heat.

This took place in the new Hot-well house, the style, solidity, and taste of which are worthy of praise. The whole building is of the Tuscan order, with the pump-room in the centre, projecting in the shape of three sides of a hexagon. It has a narrow portico on each side, with some deeper recesses, within one of which, access is had through a door to the interior of the pump-room. Behind these porticos are the baths. Each Tuscan column, without a base, has behind it a square pilaster to correspond. The whole building, however, is low.

I tasted the water at the highest temperature we could obtain, namely 73° Fahrenheit, as I mentioned. Though not insipid, it is not so pleasant as that of Malvern or Ilkley. Its chemical ingredients are few and simple; the whole amount of them in a pint of water being only six grains, and of those the most active, namely sulphate of soda, being present in the proportion of not more than two grains. The water, therefore, chemically considered, is not one endowed with sufficient power to produce any very sensible effects on the constitution, unless drank largely and for a long continuance. Still I can believe that if such a water be employed for general use, and upon all occasions, by the resident invalid labouring under irritative fever, and also in certain stages of phthisical complaints, it will be found highly serviceable. Doctor Carrick's commendation of the water in many of those cases of consumption which at one time were more frequently sent to Clifton than in the present day, and among whom that resident physician's experience was considerable, served to add to its celebrity, now somewhat abated. There was a time, not far removed from us, when Bristol water, as it used to be called, was forwarded to all parts of the kingdom well bottled; but that practice is almost entirely discontinued now. If this water possesses any particular merit above all other slightly saline waters, it is that which depends on its excess of heat over the ordinary temperature of mineral waters; and that excess is lost, of course, when the water is sent away from its source.

The late Dr. Saunders considered Clifton water to be the safest mineral water for use in England, and looked upon it as being endowed with both diuretic and diaphoretic virtues. In this statement he has been confirmed by the opinion of the practitioners on the spot, with one of whom, Dr. Fairbrother, I had the pleasure of becoming acquainted during my stay at Clifton.

From the bend in the parapet, opposite the Hot-well house, at the spot where the self-registering tidal gauge is inclosed in an iron box, what a stupendous view presents itself, looking northwards, at the descending windings of the Avon, hemmed in between its lofty and wooded banks! It is rocky on the Clifton side, and wooded on the side opposite. Here, on a point of the hill, topped by Leigh Wood, a square solid pier, like a large tower of stone, somewhat pyramidal, has been raised, which is to hold fast the suspending chain on the west bank : while on the summits of St. Vincent's Rock, on the east bank, perhaps one of the most striking objects in English landscape, stands the tower (not far from what is called the Swiss cottage), which is to be both the support of and the entrance to a bridge, balanced in the air across the Avon, spanning a space of 630 feet from cliff to cliff, and leaving the stream below at a depth of 230 feet.*

Those who walk from St. Vincent's-terrace, northwards, or who reside in the houses on that terrace, will enjoy daily and hourly one of the most magnificent sights which nature and the wonderful imaginings and works of man can contribute to produce. For the lover of the picturesque alone, this view, with the further embellishment of the " Zig-zag Walk," along which pedestrians ascend by gentle acclivities to the heights of Clifton Downs, will form a subject of the most striking character, worthy of the pencil of Salvator and Claude combined, as there are features in it suitable to both those great masters,—the lovely and the terrific.

The " Zig-zag Walk" just mentioned, leads up the cliff to

---

* This vast undertaking is slowly approaching to completion.

CLIFTON SUSPENSION BRIDGE, OVER THE AVON.

Sion House spring, the shaft of which bored through a mountain limestone rock, is upwards of 346 feet in depth. Though situated higher than the hot-well spring, the new spring seems to be identical with the water of the older one in temperature, as well as composition. This new spring now supplies all the inhabitants of Clifton with water for domestic purposes. The aspect of Sion Hill is westwards, and its summit nearly level with the bridge pier on Leigh Wood side. A circulating library, a boarding house, and the adjoining baths, with a spacious pump-room, together with Prince's-buildings, occupy the finest point of this elevated region, than which there is none higher on the Down, excepting the observatory erected on the site of an old Roman encampment.

The topographical details of this region, dry and uninteresting as they may seem to an ordinary reader, are yet due by me to those who may have to consult this volume for practical information respecting the localities to be preferred for a residence on Clifton Heights. It is thus that I dealt with respect to those in the village of Hotwells, and it is but just that the upper village, as Clifton may be properly called, should be treated in the same manner. Patients are often heard to say " Oh, Doctor such-a-one has ordered me to Clifton." " But *where* in Clifton?" "As to that he said nothing—I must see when I get there." Is that fair? Unquestionably, to people labouring under complaints of the chest, troubled with coughs or tracheal disease, or tormented by rheumatism, the loftier region of Clifton village and Clifton Down is not the most propitious. They must either confine their ambition to some of the sheltered houses midway in Hotwells, or descend lower still to St. Vincent's-terrace. But there are many invalids and convalescents who, even in winter, require a more refined and bracing atmosphere, and a well-exposed situation in an elevated region; and many more who, during the summer months, could bear with no other situation. All these people will find in the upper part of Clifton what they stand in need of.

Turning from Sion-hill houses or from Prince's-buildings, we find some parallel streets running at the back, in an east and west direction, in the centre of which is the Mall, fronted by the CLIFTON HOTEL, with its face to the west. This is a showy and goodly building, of considerable extent, well placed and well frequented by people of the highest class. In it are the Assembly-rooms, where balls and other entertainments are given in the season. The view in summer from either of the floors of this house is magnificent; few hotels in England can equal it. Looking down on the space below, arranged like one of those new oblong squares at Brighton, which run at right angles from the sea, we have on the left Caledonia-place, well named from its due northern aspect, but not eligible on that account; and on the right a far prefer-able row of houses in process of building, with a southern aspect, called the New Mall. Many excellent lodging-houses and a boarding-house are found on the one side as well as the other.

To such as like to soar in the air, the Royal York-crescent, before slightly alluded to, perhaps (though not so grand in appearance as the Royal-crescent at Bath) the largest range of dwellings perched so high in England, presents plenty of house-room, with its far-sweeping reach to the south, as if in its concave surface it aimed at concentrating all the slender rays of heat which the sun, in such a climate, sheds during the winter. But there is, a little way below, a competitor for the same advantage, and not an unpretending one, which strives to secure its own share of it. I mean the Lower-crescent; and certainly the report of those who dwell within its well-appointed chambers proves that it has competed most suc-cessfully.

At the end of these two crescents, those great *echélons* of the cliff swarming with human beings,—the " Paragon," as if in mockery of all nice discrimination of climate, sends its bow outwardly to the east, scarcely bordering on the southern verge; and the effect of such a position is strongly marked on its walls, which are black, smutty, and disfigured.

But the prettiest position, after all—the one which combines all the elements of a mixed view in such a place as Clifton—taking within it the city of Bristol and its floating harbour, and on the right the wooded bank of the opposite shore, with enough of the river to enliven the picture—is Windsor-terrace. Besides a most favourable and elevated position, its houses have the additional merit of being tastefully built and decorated, of being inclosed within iron gates, and of having a terrace walk in front, not so wide, indeed, as that which reigns all along the Royal York-crescent, yet superior to that as being sheltered by trees.

After all my lengthened peregrinations in this popular place, I am induced to conclude that as an hotel, quiet, comfortable and fit for an invalid, I would select the GLOUCESTER. I would take lodgings, if I could get them, for a permanent residence, in Windsor-terrace; I would bribe some one to let me have a house in the greater crescent, if I wished to live in the temple of the winds; but if, *par malheur*, I were coughing and wasting, I should shrink or ensconce myself down upon the terrace among the buildings of St. Vincent, with the tepid stream of the Hotwell close at hand, wherewith to quench hourly my fevered breath.

I requested the favour of half an hour's conversation with a lady long resident in Clifton, who had received me kindly on my arrival, and whom I soon ascertained from her answers and remarks to be quick and intelligent. My object was to obtain all necessary information respecting household matters in Clifton, and any other intelligence she could give me.

It appears that neither in the Gloucester, nor in any other hotel, is there a *table d'hôte*. An attempt was made to esta-

blish one in the former, some years since, but after struggling
in vain, the attempt was given up; as few, very few, of those
in the house would join the general party at the table, and
the bachelors or single persons lodging in different parts of
Clifton, who it was expected would take advantage of such an
accommodation, and come from their own solitary lodgings to
dine there, never, or very seldom, attended.

There is but one boarding-house for the convenience of
those who like to reside in such establishments, at which, of
course, there is a common table for all the inmates; but that
establishment is only struggling to keep afloat, and will probably not succeed in the end.

No: the plan here is either to secure distinct apartments
in a first-rate hotel, and agree to be boarded at a certain
fixed sum per week, or to engage private lodgings, of which
there are a great many good ones, and rather reasonable, and
so keep house. Housekeeping to a regular resident is not
quite so dear as in London; but to a stranger it is fully as
dear, and perhaps even more extravagant. All the *désagré-
mens* peculiar to lodging-houses in London or elsewhere—
such as musty and close rooms, old fashioned and scanty
furniture, indifferent attendance, and a desire on the part of
the landlady to be made partaker of the good things a lodger
has any longing for, and orders for himself through his own
servant—all these petty inconveniences accompany the living
in lodgings at Clifton. Still there are here, as elsewhere, exceptions much in favour of a residence in lodgings,
and at Clifton, perhaps, such exceptions are as numerous as
in any part of England. To them, therefore, the visiter to
Clifton, when the summer season has gladdened the heart
of the invalids who are sent thither for the benefit of their
health, repairs to secure both summer and winter quarters.

Of the better class of lodging-houses, and the same may
be said of the hotels, some stand upon a higher ground than
others. The Gloucester Hotel, as I before observed, is
placed low down the hill. The Clifton Hotel, on the con-

trary, and the Bath, are high on the hill; but the two latter are not so desirable as the former for real invalids, although, being far gayer from their situation, they are preferred even by the ailing in health, much to their detriment.

At these hotels there is almost one uniform rate of charge, which may be taken on an average at two guineas a head per week, besides the additional charge for a private sitting-room, when required, and fire. Two families, consisting of four and five persons, with one servant, can be well housed during the winter, and well boarded, in the private part of the Gloucester Hotel, each occupying a floor, and having all meals provided for them and served on plate, and managed by a separate housekeeper appointed solely for their service, at a charge of ten guineas a week. I feel convinced, from what I have seen of the establishment and the enormous cost they are at to keep it up, that such a charge is barely a remunerating one for the winter.

However, such, and no other, is the scale of public living at Clifton. The residents of course manage things differently, and, judging by the class of persons who select Clifton as their permanent residence, it is to be supposed that they find living cheap, else they would not sojourn all the year round in such a place.

Clifton is hardly a watering-place now. It is either a colony of half-pay notables, who have lineage and little cash, or it is a station of transition for Wales and Ireland, and also for the West Indies and (now) America. The *Hot-wells* have ceased to attract. Few people, if any, drink of their semi-tepid sparkling water—fewer still bathe in it. The rock of St. Vincent pours out its ancient stream in vain. As in the oldest times, the seafaring man alone seems to be the admirer of the fair Naiad—the steady and constant worshipper of its salutary wave.

Why these wells have been styled "Hot-wells" it is not easy to conjecture. 76° of Fahrenheit, a warmth 22° below that of the human body, is not such a comfortable thermal state in a mineral water as to make it worth while to run the risk of a long journey in order to enjoy its effects. Seven degrees lower than Buxton's, and 40 lower than Bath's, its temperature offers but little temptation for either bathing or drinking. Still there are at least 26 degrees of volcanic heat in it, in addition to the ordinary degree of heat which marks the temperature of ordinary water, in relation to the surrounding atmosphere; and according to my theory even 26 degrees of such heat is worth a whole steamer of artificial heat in the treatment and cure of disease.

Not only very few people now ever trouble the Wells as far as drinking the waters medicinally, but it would seem as if physicians had forgotten to recommend its use. They still send patients, though not so many as hitherto, to Clifton; but it is for the expected and supposed advantages of its climate, to which I fear they are disposed to attribute sanative virtues that in reality do not belong to it. We have here a high station exposed to the open and broad S.W. sweeping the surface of the great Atlantic, and wafting over the hill, to proceed to the interior of England, depositing, in the meantime, its enormous showers on this spot.

I asked my cheerful and very civil young hostess, a relative of Mr. Ivatt, the very attentive proprietor of the hotel, what sort of climate they had in such a region; and her candid answer, in one particular at least, settles the point better than any reference to meteorological tables, " It rains a great deal." Meteorological registers fully confirm Miss Ivatt's plain statement; for on looking at the Tables published by Mr. Jones, we find that, in the course of six years, from 1830 to 1835, there had been 1108 days of fair weather, and no less than 1032 of rain, without counting 51 days of snow. It had, therefore, rained almost every other day throughout that period. This is sufficiently dismal.

It rains at Clifton perhaps more than in most parts of western England—probably as much as in Devonshire (which is saying a great deal). True, the limestone rock quickly absorbs the rain through its strata, and the surface is, in three hours after the rain has ceased, as dry as possible; true, too, they have hardly any moisture or dampness in the air from that very reason; nevertheless, the season of rain is any thing but a gay season, and such a one is too often repeated in the district.

The air is light, and very little burdensome to the lungs, —which I believe to be one of the advantages of the situation of Clifton; it is also of the purest description—as much so as its beautiful crystaline water, and this, for reasons which must be obvious to the commonest observer, provided he *be* an observer.

In regard to temperature, Mr. Jones gives us a more cheering view of Clifton. The *absolute* lowest temperature had seldom been more than 11° below the freezing point, and that only for one day, and the highest was 85°. The *average* heat, however, in winter is much more favourable. The coldest days are in December and January, the warmest in July and August. The most prevalent winds, as might have been expected, have been from the south-west. Westerly winds have prevailed next in frequency, and after them the north-west and north-east; but there have been more south than easterly winds: all which facts tend to prove that the air, barring its moisture from rain, must be of a mild and genial character, and therefore suited to the patients generally sent to live in it—namely, those labouring under consumption.

But does the climate of Clifton favour either the recovery or the prolongation of life in such cases? Or are not, on the contrary, many unfortunate patients sent here who have no chance of a recovery? What a lamentable and distressing sight it is for a conscientious physician, who accidentally casts his eyes on such invalids, to behold the one I found in the coffee-room of the Gloucester on my arrival, fully knowing that he has come hither under hopes which must and will inevitably be disappointed!

" The medical men are more generous or more discriminating nowadays," observed my intelligent informant " in regard to sending patients from home to such places as Clifton. Formerly, when a physician, driven to the end of his wits in respect to any particular patient affected with chest complaint, recommended that patient to Clifton, in most instances it was a corpse that arrived here, either already as such, or very near being made one. Hence it was not an unusual occurrence to hear of such and such a patient being dead soon after we had heard of his arrival; and the churchyards at Clifton testify to this untoward and imprudent state of things; but such a thing seldom occurs now."

But what says that able, most valuable and well-digested register of deaths from disease, contained in the official report, published by the registrar-general, and collated and commented upon by Mr. Farr. Looking at the tables and computations of that work, we find that in what is called the Clifton district (exclusive of the city of Bristol) the mortality from consumption, in 1838, had been 98 males and 102 females; while at Bristol, in the same year, it amounted to 253, both sexes included. The relative population of these two localities, in January, 1839—assuming as a guide the progressive increase that is likely to have taken place since the census in 1831—would be as 61,609 for the Clifton District or Union, and 64,183 for Bristol. Now, I find, by a perusal of the documents preparing for next year's publication, kindly allowed me by the officer, who has taken great pains to supply me with positive data, that in 1839 there had died of consumption in Clifton district 112 males and 98 females, and in Bristol 141 males and 160 females. The result of these two years' observations, therefore, will give us an average annual mortality from consumption of 332 out of 100,000 living in Clifton district, and of 431 in Bristol—the mean of deaths of both localities being a rate of 381, which is but slightly below the mean annual mortality from the same complaint in all England and Wales, and is higher than in six other extensive country districts, tabulated by Mr. Farr at page 87 of the report before mentioned.

This then is not a very encouraging account of the beneficial influence of the climate of that particular portion of the English territory in which Clifton is situated, on consumptive patients; for with a total population of 125,792 living beings in 1839, it had lost 511 from consumption, of whom 253 were males, and 258 females. Of this number the village of Clifton proper had had twenty-three cases in an estimated population of about 15,000; but, in the preceding year, the mortality in the same village had been much larger and principally among strangers—people of condition—amounting to forty-six, or double the number of 1839. In this respect, however, Clifton had had the advantage of Bath during the two years in question; for out of an estimated population of about 70,400 inhabitants, 540—that is, 198 more than at the rate of the Clifton mortality in the same years—had died of that most fatal disease, which, according to Mr. Farr, attacks with most destructive partiality the female sex.

I cannot close this already overlengthened chapter more impressively, since we are upon this melancholy subject, than by quoting Mr. Farr's own very emphatic words respecting it. " Thirty-one thousand and ninety English women," he says, " died in one year (1838) of the incurable malady (consumption)! Will not this impressive fact induce persons of rank and influence to set their countrywomen right in one particular article of their dress, and lead them to abandon a practice which disfigures the body, strangles the chest, produces nervous or other disorders, and has an unquestionable tendency to implant an incurable hectic malady in the frame? Girls have no more need of artificial bones and bandages than boys."

Mr. Farr had before very justly stated, that compression by costume prevents the expansion of the chest, and with the indoor life which English women lead, deprives them of free draughts of vital air, whereby the altered blood deposits tuberculous matter with a fatally unnatural facility.

CHAPTER III.

BATH.

BATH — Rome and Edinburgh — Approach to the City at Night—
Scenic Effect—The WHITE HART—TOPOGRAPHY before Balneogra-
phy—The Old and the Modern Cicerone at Bath—Origin of its Mo-
dern Renown and Prosperity—Doctor GUIDOTT—Plan of Bath in his
days and our days—Situation of the City—Surrounding Hills—The
AVON—Position of the Hot-springs—CIRCULAR PROMENADE through
Bath—Successive Improvements—The two WOODS—Lansdowne—
Bathwick—English Florence—Great Pulteney-street—Sir W. Pulteney
—Countess of Bath and Duke of Cleveland—Back to where we
started—The KING's and QUEEN's Public Baths—BATH and BADEN-
BADEN—Old Fashion—What Harm ?—NEW ERA at Bath—Wisdom of
the Corporation—Mr. GREEN and Mr. SIMMS—A powerful rescue—
Bath likely to resume its rank in England as " King of the Spas"—
KING's Public Baths—Quantity of Water from its Source—PUBLIC
AND PRIVATE BATHING—Important Suggestions and Valuable Changes
—Numerous Contrivances for Invalids—Ample Resources.*

OF all the Christian cities,—Rome excepted, whose ancient
edifices and recollections have no parallel,—BATH presents
the most striking amphitheatrical spectacle which a traveller
can behold, as he approaches it for the first time. Edinburgh
might dispute with her the palm of grandeur, as it does that of
extent and of singularly beautiful scenery marked by contrast.
But it is in that contrast alone which her olden structures
offer to the more modern ones that her superiority consists,

* I have drawn the largest portion of the materials of this and two
succeeding chapters from another and recent publication of mine on
Bath, the correctness of the details of which has been approved by local
judges and experienced observers. I therefore offer my information
to the readers of the " Spas of England" with increased confidence.

and not in that uniform harmony of imposing edifices, reared in the lapse of scarcely two thirds of a century, and crowning many heights, arranged in concentric and ascending circles, by which "the city of the waters of Pallas" is distinguished.

Viewed in a dark and serene night, Bath awakens in the spectator feelings of surprise, such as even "the Eternal City," under the like circumstances, fails to excite. It was at such a time that I entered Bath on the occasion of my present visit, the third I paid to that city with the intention of studying more particularly its claims and resources as a Spa.

As we approached the city nearer and nearer, coming from the south, a sight burst suddenly upon me, the effect of which seemed as if produced by one of those magic representations of a night-scene introduced into French ballets, where, in the midst of darkness, hundreds of enchanted palaces appear, one placed higher than another, until the highest seems to touch the dark azure vault, and with their glimmering casement-lights mock the dazzling stars of heaven. The twinkling of all the gas-lights, profusely arranged in front of the many terraced edifices and crescents placed on different hills, and alone visible; while the buildings themselves were just distinguishable in the shadows of night; and the splendour thrown over the streets nearest to the steep road down which we rapidly descended into the town, passing at the same time under the high Gothic arch that supports the Great Western railway, to enter Southgate-street—all these things combined, presented to my mind a scene unequalled in any city, except perhaps that of the Scots, before mentioned, when approached from the north in the night time.

I halted for the moment at the White Swan, in Stall-street, a sort of Hatchett's hotel, handy for a traveller who wants only a *pied-à-terre* for a short time, sufficiently well attended, and convenient from its immediate proximity to the baths—the centre of attraction of the place.

As I hope to be useful not only to English readers but to foreigners also, while writing the present tour through England in search of a particular object which cannot fail to interest the latter, and which, indeed, has already interested them, as I have had means of knowing since the publication of the first volume,—it is important that I should introduce them, in the first instance, to a panoramic view of this magnificent city, ere I proceed to describe those wonderful sources of thermal water which form the origin of its celebrity.

To English readers, indeed, a particular description of Bath might appear superfluous; yet, even to them, or at least to such among them as are likely to have recourse to its mineral springs for the benefit of their health, a topographical account of the place they are to reside in for a temporary purpose, accompanied by opportune reflections on the various aspects and contingencies of the localities best suited for their residence, will probably not be considered as undesirable.

In the early days of the modern reputation of Bath, the task of a cicerone must have been a comparatively easy one. Having, in the first place, pointed out to the stranger in " Stawles-street," the King's and the other baths, and next the Grove, and the Abbey, with two or three sorry houses of entertainment, or the Town-hall, converted at that time into a ball-room as well as a gaming-room, his duty was at once accomplished. When the extraordinary man, who unquestionably was the means of imparting to Bath an European celebrity, first entered that town " he found it one of the poorest cities in England, its buildings being extremely mean and the inhabitants rude and unpolite." " In these days," says a spirited writer in a recent number of the most popular magazine in the North, " Bath was a pretty village : its grand place of association seems to have been a bowling-green ; its chief promenade was a double row of sycamores, and its principal employments yawning, and drinking those waters *which nothing but the most extraordinary fear of death, or the most singular insensibility to foulness in taste and smell, could ever have reconciled any human being to touching after the first drop."*

This writer who, but for his testifying to the indifferent condition of Bath in the early days of the last century, in confirmation of what I before advanced, I should not have pressed into my service on the present occasion, considering how *completely erroneous and the very reverse of reality* is his conception of the nature and character of the Bath water —answers my purpose well, and therefore do I quote him; since he too attributes to the same extraordinary individual I have alluded to the beginning and rapid progress of modern Bath. It is, therefore, from the commencement of the reign of upwards of half a century's duration, of the remarkable personage in question, that we must date the origin of that vastness and importance which the Spa about to be considered acquired in recent times, and which consequently call for greater exertions on the part of any modern cicerone.

What reader, on the perusal of the preceding paragraph, does not at once recal to his mind the days of Beau Nash, "the monarch of Bath," and its most renowned *arbiter elegantiarum?* To the third descendant of a Florentine citizen, Signor Antonio Guidotti, settled in England in the early part of the reign of Edward VI., by whom he was knighted, belongs the credit of having revived the fashion of the Bath water. In his quaint performance of 1676, called "A Discourse of Bathe and the Hot Waters there," Dr. Guidott, the descendant alluded to, a bachelor of medicine of Oxford, strove to bring those waters into repute again, in spite of the great opposition he met with from almost all the faculty. He laboured incessantly, and much against his own pecuniary benefit, in extending the knowledge of the health-giving qualities of those springs; and thus paved the way

for that brilliant era which began thirty years later, under the
roseate wand of Nash, and continued, as before stated, for
nearly half a century after him.

By casting a glance at the plan of Bath which accom-
panies Guidott's book (1676), and then at the fine map of the
same city and surrounding suburbs published a few years
since, we perceive at once what prodigious, and certainly
unprecedented an extension the exertions of a zealous
physician, followed by those of a master of the ceremonies
(both intent on rendering available certain valuable mineral
springs) have been the means of giving to a place which is
now five times larger than at the commencement of the last
century, and has a population of upwards of seventy thousand
inhabitants instead of the previous one of only one-sixth of
that number.

Like Baden-Baden, to which as a spa, but not as a city, it
may be compared, Bath lies at the bottom of a valley, encompassed by a triple circle of hills, rising higher the farther
they are removed from the city. But the valley here is
wider and more circular in form than that in which the
German Bath is seated; and the lesser or nearest hills are
more splendidly grand, from the greater number of striking
buildings with which they are studded, as well as for their
beautiful verdure, the gardens and plantations which decorate their surface.

From whatever point of the old or new city we cast our
glances around, a height, an eminence, or a hill presents
itself, with its own peculiar beauties, natural and acquired.
Being all of them parts of a great oolitic range, their shapes
are gracefully rounded or waving; and whether we trace the
steep ascent of Claverton on the east, up to the down or
table-land on its summit, raised 600 feet above the sea level
—or turn round to the loftier range of 813 feet elevation,
called Lansdowne Hill, to the north-west, passing for that
purpose over the lovely eminence of Bathwick in the north-

east; we find every part of the horizon occupied by some picturesque rising, once barren, and almost inaccessible, but now of easy access and teeming with busy population.

In the midst of these hills, all of them bearing distinct and familiar names, with various altitudes of from four to eight hundred feet above the level of the ocean,—the old city of Bath itself being only forty feet above that level,—the Avon, coming from Bath Hampton, in the farthest north-east, is seen winding and turning as it descends into the level valley, laving the foot of the western slope of Bathwick, and skirting with its right or northern bank the old as well as the new town; finally quitting the latter around the south-western base of Lansdowne-hill,—to enter the rich meads and pastures, among which it loves to loiter and meander, ere it reaches the small town of Keynsham on its way to the port of Bristol.

On the narrowest tongue of land which the sudden bend this river makes from its north and south to a north-west course, is seated the Old Bath, or the Bath of the Romans, with its hot springs occupying the centre; and near to them is the celebrated Abbey Church, and the no less famed Orange Grove, with the north and south parade and the pumproom. A wide and nearly straight line of streets from the southernmost or Bath bridge towards the north, cuts the old city into an eastern and western part,—in the former of which are found the localities and objects I have just mentioned, including the two principal springs; while in the latter, the remainder of the hot springs, the two principal hospitals, and the theatre are located.

Old though this part of Bath may be, in reference to chronology of buildings, yet it has been in almost all its parts modernized and embellished, either through the steady and judicious interference of a vigilant corporation, or by the hands of private speculators. Its former antique air therefore is gone; but with it have disappeared also the many low, obscure, and ruinous buildings which encumbered the most frequented thoroughfares, or blocked up the venerable Abbey Church, now wholly insulated; and several narrow and crooked streets have been widened and made straight, among which is the very street I have especially alluded to, being the principal entrance into Bath from the south and south-eastern counties.

The upper or north end of this line, Milsom-street, worthy of the proudest metropolis, and the rendezvous of all the gay world at one particular time of the day, leads us at once into the heart of what may be considered as the second or intermediate city of Bath. It is the creation of the last sixty or seventy years, the work of the two eminent and untiring architects, the Woods, father and son, and rose upon an extended and naked acclivity, which has positively and entirely been covered over with those very striking edifices whence the glory and peculiar beauty of Bath as a city are derived. This doubling of the original city was the result of that singular attraction imparted to Bath by the palmy and glorious days of its now-departed " monarch," which brought strangers to it not only from every part of England, but from foreign lands also.

Queen-square, and a little higher up, the Circus, a perfectly unique assemblage of handsome dwelling-houses, rich in architectural decoration, at the termination of Gay-street, itself one of the finest in England, occupy the centre of this newer section of Bath. To the right, and not far from it, the " Upper Rooms" (a very extensive building, of which more anon,) will naturally attract the attention of the stranger ; while if he should emerge from the Circus in a western direction along Brock-street, the grandest amphitheatre of palaces, the Royal Crescent, will suddenly appear before him, arranged upon the slope of a hill, and commanding the most extensive view of the city, with one of the finest public parks in England immediately at its feet. The handsome and straight line of Marlborough-buildings seems to flank on its left this noblest of crescents, as a foil perhaps to its curvilinear sweep.

But the extent of the beautiful and grandiose in buildings

as well as position,—the work principally of the last twenty years,—does not stop here; for ascending still higher, and spreading wider to the east and to the west, as it creeps upwards in a northern direction, the new city has taken possession of the high common and its descending slopes, and there established its Cavendish, Somerset, Lansdowne, and Camden crescents and places, its St. James's-square, besides many handsome and wide streets, gardens, and plantations, together with many other open places for public recreation.

In the midst of this new and aristocratic colony, thus scattered on the summit of Lansdowne, the hill in question, Mr. Beckford's multiform tower of stone and wood rises to an elevation of 154 feet, out of beds of flowers and shrubs, forming a conspicuous object, not only to Bath, but to every remote corner of the valleys of the Avon and the Severn, in very mockery of the tiny but more historical monument erected, not far from its more lofty rival, to Sir Bevil Granville, slain in the civil wars whilst fighting for the good cause against the army of a rebellious Parliament.

From any one point of this gay scene, rich in buildings of the highest order in the class of domestic architecture, a glance cast in the direction of the south-east embraces at once another magnificent sweep of succeeding hills, the nearest slopes and knolls of which are, as in the case of Lansdowne, covered with buildings, principally arranged, however, in this case, as detached villas with their surrounding gardens. This fourth region of modern Bath, known under the general name of Bathwick, is separated from those already noticed by the Avon, between the left bank of which, and the foot of the hill in question, a level tract of land, a quarter of a mile wide, and twice that length, presents as it were a new town, strongly contrasting by its exquisitely-finished buildings, its magnificent streets, and open squares, and the general air of grandeur that prevails over the whole district, with the oldest part of the city first of all alluded to, to which it lies exactly opposite.

It is this part of modern Bath that strongly reminds one of Florence and some other of the principal cities on the Continent; in none of which, however, will the traveller meet with such a double line of private residences, intercepted by squares and gardens, around which equally superb private buildings have been reared, as he will discover here, while standing on the furthest threshold of Pulteney-bridge, with his face turned to the north-eastward.

Here, looking down Argyle-street as far as where it expands into Laura-place, he sees the double line in question continued to the distance of nearly half a mile,—first contracting into one of the most striking streets in Europe— Great Pulteney-street—then expanding again into a wide and extensive hexagonal plantation, called Sydney-garden, around which many handsome houses are suitably arranged— to terminate at last in the new wide and straight road to War- minster—a work of recent years, and by far one of the finest drives of many miles out of any city in England.

Well did the original promoter of this immense addition and improvement, Sir M. Pulteney, and the Countess of Bath, his daughter, who followed up the spirited design of her sire, merit, at the hands of the inhabitants, the distinction of having their names perpetuated in the several and principal divisions of this splendid section of their city: and how fortunate for the citizens that the same intentions in favour of modern Bath should have been afterwards adopted and carried into effect by the nobleman at present in possession of this immense property!

And now, the visiter being brought back by a circular tour of Bath, made since he set off on his panoramic view of the place from the centre of the *old* city, to a point exactly opposite that on which the principal hot-springs surge; and having moreover made himself at once master of the general topo- graphy and distribution of the place, let him follow me across the Avon, from east to west, over the new and pretty bridge that spans that river, exactly opposite the east end of the North- parade, whence, after leaving Wilkins' elegant Doric portico of the Literary Institution on our right, we may pass down York-street, and presently reach the KING's and QUEEN's BATHS.

I had never paid so much attention as on the present occasion to the value and peculiar fitness of Bath as a Spa of the very first order if properly managed; and, unquestionably, the sight of that profuse supply of volcanic water uppoured from the bowels of the earth, by that impetuous spring which presently fills the two ample reservoirs designated by the names just mentioned, was calculated to impress my mind with the conviction that Bath equals in importance, and nearly so in power, Baden-baden—the Spa so much resorted to by Englishmen. This position I shall prove before I have done with the subject.

It is natural that a stranger who has read the stirring history of Bath in its palmy days, should feel impatient to behold the two public baths or springs of hot water into which ladies, full toiletted and *bien coiffées*, are said to have waded up to their chins, at an early hour of the morning, escorted by their cavaliers, thus to enjoy together the luxury of bathing in the open air in hot mineral water, varying from 99° to 104° of temperature, but much hotter in the centre or over the source.

The practice of associating the two sexes during the operation of public bathing, which prevailed in England as well as in foreign countries down to a very late period, has been a subject of never-ending animadversion, until, as in the case of Bath, and I may say almost everywhere else, at present, regulations have been wrung from the authorities to put a stop to it. At the time of my visit, the hours and days in the week for the bathing of the one sex were arranged so as not to interfere with that of the other, by allotting alternate days to each. Dame Wakefield, who boasts of upwards of twenty-two years' services as an attendant in the ladies' department, would fain have persuaded me, at our interview, that she had not given so many baths as before to ladies, since the separation of the sexes and the prohibition of promiscuous bathing. "What harm did it ever do, or could it do," she would say,

" to see the nice dear creatures go down the steps out of their private undressing-rooms, and enter the bath with their bathing-wrappers, made of rich stuff and fashionably cut, down to the feet and hands, and fastened to the waist,—their hair gathered up under a very elegant *coiffe*,—walk up through the water to shake hands and exchange morning salutations with the gentlemen of their acquaintance already in the bath, attired in the very pink of fashion? One might as well object to their walking together, or meeting and greeting each other in the GROVE, in dresses not very far different. There they are immersed in air—and here they are immersed in water. Of the two, the latter is the most decent element, as it is not quite so transparent.

> "Oh! 'twas a glorious sight to behold the fair sex
> All wading with gentlemen up to their necks."[*]

The old dame must have been put up to this species of wire-spun reasoning in favour of a practice now entirely abolished, for it is too fine for a person of her class. True it is, as she assured me, that since its discontinuance she had not seen the twentieth part of the number of ladies bathe whom she was wont to help in that operation at the commencement of her career. But for such defalcation there are more legitimate and substantial reasons—reasons, too, infinitely less onerous to the feelings of delicacy and propriety which have ever characterized our fair countrywomen.

In the print facing this page are represented several buildings, above which the Abbey Church tower is seen. On the left is the great pumproom, and next to it is the entrance to the KING's and QUEEN's public baths, as well as to the private baths connected with them. The whole group of buildings just mentioned forms a pleasing elevation, which, when " Stawles-street" was the gayest and most fashionable promenade, and not, as " Stall-street" is at present, the busiest and most plebeian thoroughfare of Bath, must have forcibly struck the attention of all visiters.

See Anstey's Bath Poetical Guide—King's Bath.

THE KING AND QUEEN'S BATHS, BATH.

Of the interior of these buildings I formed but an indifferent opinion from what I saw around me—beginning at the vestibule, in which I was received by honest Master Ridley, exercising for upwards of twenty-two years the functions of bathman,—and passing down and through dark corridors and stairs to the baths, which are several feet below the level of the surrounding streets.

But a new day has dawned on all the principal establishments of the place since my visit. The corporate body of the city, who are guardians of the springs, had been for many years using their best endeavours to maintain their importance, and the usefulness of these two baths in particular. Finding, however, that, in their own hands, the baths thrived not, but that, on the contrary, the receipts for many past years scarcely covered the expenditure, they determined on placing them and the rest of the springs, baths, and appliances, under a different system of management, by letting them all for a term of years to the most eligible bidder.

Some such measure, indeed, had become absolutely necessary to save the King's and Queen's Baths from thorough neglect, and the private baths adjoining from their threatened declension. Such, indeed, had been the diminution in the number of bathers that, at my visit, Master Ridley considered it a subject of exultation that the baths he had daily administered during the season just elapsed had risen to the wonderful cipher of 25 per week !

The lapse of little more than half a year has worked a wonderful change since; and the two individuals selected by the corporation as lessees by a large majority of votes, including all the more influential members of that body, have by their prompt and unremitting exertions shown what can be effected in such a place and with such immense resources, when, instead of a committee of many persons not individually interested in the result, a smaller number of individuals, having a pecuniary stake in the whole concern, is invested with the power and authority to wield those resources to the best advantage. In fact, the individuals at the head of an establishment of this kind should, in order to secure success in it, not only have a pecuniary interest, but be well qualified also for the purpose; and such, there is every reason to believe, is the case in the present instance.

Two persons, Messrs. Green and Simms, bear the ostensible responsibility of all the present arrangements; and in justice to them, as well as in accordance to that system which I have followed throughout this publication, I am bound, as I am happy, to say, that I have hardly met in this country, in the course of my long peregrinations, with any proprietor or other individual connected with a Spa, who has evinced greater zeal, or better abilities—a readier disposition [to receive and act upon proper suggestions, or a more spirited determination to do their duty—than the individuals alluded to have already displayed. It seems as if they were resolved to raise Bath once more to that station as a Spa, which it ought never to have relinquished, and to which alone it is entitled in England—that of " King of the Spas."

Their qualifications, fortunately, are coincident with the object for which they have been selected, and would seem, indeed, to have pointed them out for the purpose. The association of a practical and experimental chemist by profession, well known in Bath, with a person who for some years past has taken an active part, from choice as well as profession, in the concerts and other amusements of the city, offers the best security that the salutary, not less than the diverting departments of the revived Spa will be conducted in the most effective manner. The mature age of the first partner, and the more youthful bearing of the second, by imparting to the personal manners of each their peculiar characteristic, will tend to make the two associates popular, and by a natural consequence give popularity to their enterprise. This, I am assured, has already been fully demonstrated by the experience of the last season, the first of their administration; and it shall not be for want of fairness and justice on the part of the author of the "Spas of England," who is about to develop to his readers the resources of modern Bath, if the next and every other succeeding season do not prove still more successful.

Under such impressions and with these views have I drawn up the present account and description or this truly Royal Spa, in which I have mingled, as best suited my object, what I myself observed or experienced with what, I am assured, has been effected since; not omitting the several improvements I suggested, and those which I have been told have already been adopted.

Of the latter class are those connected with the public baths previously alluded to. The objectionable entrance to them has been obviated by constructing, at a large outlay of money, a staircase from the vestibule in the centre of the building, which affords now an easy access to the King's and Queen's public as well as to the private baths.

The kingly appellation of the first is probably derived from its original dedication to good old King Bladud, a Briton by birth, an Athenian by education, and the supposed discoverer of these hot springs 863 years before the Christian era. His statue, such as it is, decorates the centre of the bath, which is railed round by a brass rail on brass standards, to point out the part where the temperature of the water is highest— being there 116° of Fahrenheit; whereas, all round and especially nearest to the surrounding walls, the temperature is hardly ever more than 100°. In these very walls are recesses and seats for the accommodation of the bathers, who have also the advantage of a covered place on one side of the bath, supported by a handsome Doric colonnade, to shelter them during unpropitious weather.

Some curious relics are here seen, in the shape of massive brass rings fixed by means of staples into the walls, on many of which are inscribed the names of individuals, several of them redolent of aristocratic recollection. By some it is presumed that these rings have been left by grateful patients as votive expressions of the benefit they had derived from the baths; but they seem to me in reality nothing more than the rings which served the invalid, and the feeble, and crippled patient to hold fast by, while standing erect in this large body of water, and on which the names of the owner was inscribed, to secure undivided possession of the accommodation as long as he was in a state to require it. It may possibly tickle the curiosity of many in our days to know who the magnates of the seventeenth century were who committed their sweet persons to the hot wave, and grasped these massive rings; I can supply the names of a few. Barbara, Duchess of Cleveland, A.D. 1674. Sir William Whitmore, Baron Knight, A.D. 1679. Thomas Windham, Esquire, 1664.*

The immediate access to the water is by small doors in the wall, and down a few steps to reach the pavement, which, in the King's Bath as well as the Queen's, was laid down afresh this year, and is, in virtue of more recent regulations, cleansed every day after the hours of public bathing. Formerly, such an operation was but rarely performed, and on one occasion such was the collection of rubbish of every kind found in it, particularly in the shape of nut-shells, cherry and plum-stones, that to account for their presence one must imagine the beaux and belles who paraded daily in this water, at a given hour, during Nash's reign, to have been excellent customers to the fruiterers of the day, and to have amused themselves in consuming their *denrées* during the operation of bathing.

* Antiquaries may make much of this species of catalogue; but the learning of the old city folks of London will not appear very conspicuous in the following inscription on one of the rings.

"Lydia White, Dawter of William White, Citesen and Draper of London, 1612,"

Some of the rings would seem to indicate that their usefulness for the purpose mentioned in the text was deemed sufficient to induce patients to fix them at their own expense as tokens of gratitude or charity. Thus we have

"Thomas Deloes by God's marcy and Pomping, Here formerly ayded, Against an Imposthome in his head, caused this to be fixed, June 13, 1693." And another

"In memoriam Providentiæ devinæ Anno Domini 1693.

"JASIEL GROVAL of London."

I find from a Memoir by Sir George Smith Gibbes, M.D., that the King's Bath and spring just alluded to, pours forth daily 184,320 gallons of water, or 128 gallons every minute, at the highest temperature previously specified. The dimensions of the bath itself being sixty-five feet ten inches, by forty feet ten inches, it fills in about eleven hours, and contains, when filled to its usual heght, 364 tons, two hogsheads, and thirty-six gallons of water.

The Queen's Bath, which is much smaller, has no spring of its own, and is supplied from the main source of the King's; and being farther removed from that source, though separated only by a wall, contains water at a much lower temperature, and is therefore more generally applicable for bathing. It is in this bath that I should recommend the introduction of a thick layer of fine sand (such as is thrown up by the main source in the King's Bath) over the pavement, which would render the walking more pleasant, and the warmth more agreeable to the feet of such as admire this mode of bathing in the open air. The surface of the bed of sand might be raked every time the bath is emptied, and the sand renewed altogether at distant intervals, as is done at Wildbad; which natural warm-bath the Queen's Bath would more nearly resemble: first, because of its more moderate degree of heat, being that nearest to the temperature of the human body; and secondly, because of the persisting uniformity of that temperature, occasioned by the incessant supply and simultaneous passing away of the water after it has reached a certain level. This is no mean recommendation of the Queen's Bath, and an advantage of the utmost importance in my opinion, which private baths, holding a definite quantity of water supplied once for all at a given temperature, do not possess.

After all, I have strong doubts whether this mode of bathing in very deep water of a high temperature, *sub divo*, the patient standing or walking the while, is calculated to produce always a good effect, or does not rather defeat its own purpose very often. I admit that in a few instances a considerable benefit is derived from the use of such large masses of hot water surrounding, under the canopy of heaven, the bodies of the patients ; for they can then move and agitate their persons in every direction, while a refreshing air fans their heated countenance and head.   But in the majority of cases requiring such water as that of Bath, bathing in a reclining and quiescent posture is in my opinion essential. The patients may be directed to move their limbs and body in the water now and then ; but to maintain the body in an erect posture, to exert all the muscles, and to fatigue the body by exercise during the operation of bathing, are circumstances which greatly militate against its good results, and in such cases, therefore, neither the King's nor the Queen's Baths can be suitable.

As to the private baths connected with the King's source, I was not satisfied with a mere inspection of them, but tried their effects on myself, and studied their capabilities. My notes taken on that occasion, as they lie now before me, speak but indifferently of the order and condition of that establishment,—which may be said truly to have had the aspect of " a house that is falling." I the more gladly, therefore, spare myself the pains of transferring them to these pages, as I am informed and have reason to believe, that a most extensive change in this department also, as regards cleanliness, comfort, and every convenience, has taken place since my visit. Proper arrangements have likewise been adopted in reference to the public baths as will enable the most fastidious lady or gentleman to bathe in the latter *each day* in the week, and not on alternate days only as heretofore.

The apartment too, containing the different sorts of *douche* baths, especially the *ascendante*, which is managed as at Ems, and the shower-bath, with every contrivance for hot and dry pumping on particular parts of the body—to the condition of all of which I could not have borne favourable testimony at the time of my visit—have all been since put in the most complete state of repair.   The formation of a vast cistern or reservoir (in 1833) capable of containing 32,000 gallons of water from the King's Bath source, raised by means of a small steam-engine, through a fountain in the centre, and other lateral pipes for the purpose of cooling it,—has afforded ample means of accomplishing these various objects, and of regulating at the same time the temperature of the water to be employed in them. This quantity of cooling water is renewed daily.

A new vapour-bath has likewise been erected, in which the patient may either have the whole body enveloped in the steam, or the person only, and not the head, thereby avoiding the inhalation of the steam. This is an object of importance as far as regards the natural steam of volcanic waters charged with the volatile particles of very active ingredients.

Of the particular effects produced on myself by the hot water in the King's and Queen's public and private baths, which approached nearest to those I once experienced in the thermal spring of Töplitz, as described in the " Spas of Germany," I shall say nothing in this place. A much fitter opportunity will present itself of stating those effects of the Bath water when I come to speak of the " Hot Baths" in the next chapter.

With all these appliances and uses of the volcanic water issuing from the King's source, there still remains as may be supposed on reading Sir George S. Gibbes's statistical data, an excess of it, which is disposed of in various ways, such as filling the tepid swimming bath, to be hereafter described, and furnishing the necessary quantity of water for the baths in the general hospital, placed at the distance of the whole length of a street called Union-street, whither the stream is conveyed by means of a powerful steam-engine, with very little loss of temperature. Still nearly the half of the general supply from the King's Bath spring remains unemployed,— or rather is suffered to run waste. We shall see by-and-by how readily and advantageously a large portion of this excess of water might be made available, and how necessary it will be hereafter, should Bath resume its wonted rank among the Spas of Europe, to adopt the suggestion I shall venture to submit upon this subject.

CHAPTER IV.

BATH CONTINUED.

The Cross Baths—Ladies' Tepid Bath—Conversion into a Wildbad
Bath—The Kingston or Abbey Baths—The Hot Baths—The finest
private Baths in England—Want of Success, and future Prospects
—Their Description—Effects of Mineral Water at 114?—Author's
Experiment—Bath, Baden,' and Töplitz—Suggested Improvement—
The Sudatory, or Reclining Room—Charges for Bathing—Hours of
Attendance—The Great Swimming or Tepid Bath—Source of its
Water—The Great Pump-room — Principal Entrances—Interior—
The Pump and the Serpent—Distribution of the Water—Military
Band—Great and recent Improvements—Others suggested—Prome-
nade Concert—Taste and Appearance of the Water—Popular Error
—Bath Water has no Sulphur—Pumps again—How to do without one
—Fashionables and their Promenade of the present day—The
Orange Grove and its modish Company in 1750—Masked Ladies—
Loungers and Oglers—Few now drink the Bath Waters—Cause
of Decline—Bath unjustly neglected—The most powerful Mineral
Water in England.

A short but wide and handsome street, along each side
of which runs an open arcade, and called Bath-street, leads
from immediately opposite the establishment just described
to an insulated building, which forms, as it were, a terminating vista to the street, once the fashionable lounge of this
noted Spa. The space in which the building stands is ren-

dered more conspicuous by the crescent-like shape given to the two ends of the street—a shape which has been adopted also at its commencement opposite the King's Baths. A cross once erected on this spot marked the spring of hot mineral water in which the queen of James the Second had bathed in 1687; and to that spring, which upon the subsequent removal of that memorial of royalty was converted into a series of convenient slips for bathers, and private apartments, containing a reclining slipper or sarcophagus bath, the name of the " Cross Bath" has been given. The temperature of the water here is the lowest of any of those observed in Bath. At the time of my visit the building was hardly ever open for use; yet I considered the establishment susceptible of many important applications; and I should have rejoiced to have found that since it had been converted into a spacious tepid bath, kept exclusively, and furnished most appropriately, for the use of ladies, at the moderate charge of one shilling admission, the arrangement had been eagerly resorted to. Such, however, has not been the case ; and the accommodation has consequently been turned over since to other bathers, as a second class plunging bath.

An opportunity offers at this source, and in this very building, of adding to Bath a valuable continental feature, which could not be otherwise than highly beneficial to the place, and still more so to invalids repairing thither with paralytic and other nervous disorders that require a permanent and milder degree of volcanic heat for their treatment. In two words I mean that the " Cross Bath" of Bath should be converted into a "Fürstenbad" of Wildbad. In the first place strew upon the hard pavement of the present swimming-bath a bed of soft white siliceous sand; and secondly, let the water springing from its natural source, rise over the sand about two feet and a half, at which level it should be maintained by means of a waste issue kept constantly open. Around the walls, and at short distances from each other, place suitable back-boards for the patients to lean against when seated or half-reclining upon the sand. The water will then reach to their chins, and by its natural, permanent, and never-varying temperature (which at this source happens to be little more than the temperature of the human body), will affect the patient equally from the first minute of his entering the bath to the last at coming out, thereby producing uniform results, such as are known to be produced by the baths of Wildbad.

The immense advantage of such an establishment will be soon apparent to such as will reflect for a moment, that at present there are but two ways in which an invalid can bathe at Bath. He must either use the public bath, and stand erect in a large mass of water hotter than his complaint may require, and when perhaps that complaint unfits him for the erect and constrained posture he must take; or he must have recourse to the Royal Private Baths, or a reclining or slipper bath filled with the mineral water, the temperature of which, being previously reduced, either by cooling or by the immediate admixture of cold water to the suitable degree—say 99—will not continue the same throughout the time that the bath lasts, but lose on the contrary four or five degrees during the progress of that operation. Whereas in the Cross Bath, arranged as here proposed, the water of the bath being never the same, but on the contrary changing continuously and always from the real and natural source, such a loss of heat or change of temperature in the bath could not take place.

It is impossible to calculate the prodigious amount of favourable results which the adoption of this plan would infallibly bring about. It would at once detain at home hundreds of people who seek health abroad through the process of bathing in thermal waters. Of course, connected with this bath, there should be suitable private dressing-rooms, where the patient, coming out of the bath, may quietly rest for a little time.

This proposed arrangement would not interfere with the

plan of having a tepid plunging-bath on particular days of the week in the same locality; for in such a case, the lower waste issue or pipe being closed, the water from the source would be allowed to fill the baths to the higher level even now adopted for the swimming-bath; and the substitution of the siliceous sand at the bottom would suit remarkably well its intended purpose in both cases.

The slackness just alluded to, observed during my visit in the employment of the natural resources of Bath in the way of mineral water, I had occasion to notice also in regard to another establishment, called the " KINGSTON BATH," but more appropriately the ABBEY BATHS, from the circumstance of their immediate proximity to the Abbey. In this spot was the Roman Bath, discovered in 1758, with a pavement at the bottom, perfectly well preserved, although the steps leading down to it bore marks of having been worn out considerably by the naked feet of the bathers. The temperature of the water differs but little from that of the King's Bath, between which and the western bank of the Avon the source of the Kingston Bath is situated. These are the only baths in the place which are not the property of the corporation. They are let to an individual who endeavours to keep them in a state deserving of public patronage. I examined them with attention, and am bound in justice to make this declaration.

But the establishment for bathing, which bears away the palm of superiority in Bath, and leaves all competitors behind, are the " Hot Baths,"—under which denomination are comprehended a range of private baths, a tepid swimming-bath, and two large open baths. Perfectly new, or modernized and reconstructed buildings have, within the last twenty years, given to this establishment an importance which, while it shows how much the authorities of the place had at heart the welfare of Bath, and its restoration to the rank of a principal Spa, ought to have secured to it the countenance of the profession, and the support of the public generally. Large sums of money were lavished on the occasion with judgment and much discrimination; and whether we look to external decorative architecture, or to internal fittings and tasteful establishments, as well as conveniences, we must admit that few establishments in Europe are superior to the one under consideration.

It might have been expected that after such efforts and such successful results, the extension of the practice of bathing would have been so considerable as to render the seven beautiful private baths which form part of this establishment, too few in number for the demand; and that soon after their completion, double that number of baths would have become necessary. Whether under the present management, as already alluded to, such a necessity will be felt or not, it is impossible to predict from any recent experience. Certain it is, that the success expected by the corporation fell far short of every just expectation, notwithstanding the very reasonable charges made, and the many facilities afforded; and it remains to be seen how far renovated zeal, a fresh outlay of money, greater individual exertion, with better skill and experience such as are now embarked in the working out of this grand feature of the " king of English Spas" will succeed in rousing a most unaccountable apathy on the part of the profession, and overcome the blinding influence of fashion.

At Baden-baden, from twenty to thirty private baths in each of six or more hotels, constituting altogether a series of 208 *baignoires*, suffice hardly to the wants of the place during the season;* and here scarcely a dozen private baths are in request or full use in a day; and yet it would not be difficult to demonstrate, that for many bodily disorders the Bath water is superior to, while in some others it is equally as good as, that of Baden, notwithstanding its originally higher degree of temperature.

* See " Spas of Germany," vol. i., page 21, first edition, and page 11, second edition.

It was in one of these private baths that I put to the test the immediate influence of Bath water at its natural and highest temperature on myself, the effect of which experiment I shall take leave to record in this place, with a minuteness which some general readers may be inclined to consider as tedious and unnecessary, but which, I venture to say, people ignorant of such influence and effect, yet desirous of knowing everything concerning them, will be glad to ascertain.

The ROYAL PRIVATE BATHS, as I find them styled since my visit, connected with the source called the "Hot Baths," consist of a series of apartments to which you descend from the level of the street in Hotbath-street; and to the left of the insulated building previously named, the "Cross Bath." A running and well-sheltered corridor affords access to those apartments, seven in number, as before stated, and perfectly new. Each apartment consists of a dressing-room, lofty, and lighted from above, well carpeted, and with a fire-place, a sofa, a dressing-table, and mirrors, besides every other convenience that the toilet of an exquisite even could require. Adjoining to this is the bath-room, equally lofty, and lighted from above, with the bath sunken four feet six inches into the ground, in the shape of the letter T. There are side-steps at the single end, or that which is nearest to the door, to descend by into the bath, and a seat at each of the other two extremities. Around the room sufficient space has been managed between the wall and the margin of the bath, for the attendant to walk along in case of need. Hand-railings of brilliant metal serve to help the invalid in the descent of the steps; and three brass-handled stop-cocks are placed within his immediate reach, for admitting the natural volcanic water, either at its natural temperature, or tepid, or lastly cold—the latter of which is kept (as in the case of the King's Baths) in a reservoir open to the air. These baths are lined with white tiles, and kept in a state of cleanliness and order not to be sur-passed in any other establishment of the kind.

The one I was about to enter contains thirteen hogsheads of water. I saw it emptied and filled before me with water direct from the source—an operation which occupied about ten minutes; but when the bath is prepared for ordinary use at a temperature of 98°, and the cold is admitted at the same moment with the hot water, the time required to fill such a vast basin is considerably shorter. The effects of such a mixed water and lower temperature I had already tried the day before, as I have had already occasion to mention. My object at present was to test a much higher temperature, in other words, the natural volcanic water alone; and this, therefore, was let into the bath, from the real source whence it issues at 114°, although, after the bath is filled, one degree of heat is lost at its surface.

The highest temperature of Bath water, it ought to be stated, is 120°, which is found in the Lepers' or Patients' Bath, connected with this same establishment; but this degree of heat is found below the pavement only. The next highest temperature is that at the King's Bath, which is 116°, though the thermometer marks two degrees more when lowered into the opening of the source. And, lastly, comes the temperature of the Royal Hot-Baths, 114° Fahrenheit at its source; the effect of which temperature, on my person, I find thus noted on the spot:

" I feel perfectly tired, nay aching in every limb, in consequence of having been on my legs exactly twelve hours since breakfast, without sitting down at all the whole time, and engaged in perambulating Bath and its environs. Since that repast I have tasted no food, and feel greatly exhausted. My head is heavy and dull, but not aching, with a return of the hissing noise in the ears to which I am subject in London after protracted fatigue, but which I had lost since I had been travelling. The pulse beats 74.

" On plunging the thermometer into the centre of the bath I found it marked 113½°, and the steam which rose from the surface of the water obscured the lamps with which the room was lighted. The attendant tried to dissuade me from entering the bath at that degree of heat; he had never witnessed such an experiment, and felt sure it must do me great injury. To calm his apprehension, I promised to proceed cautiously, and requested him to be in immediate waiting in the adjoining apartment, that if he heard me call he might rush into the bath-room, and let the cold water flow into the bath.

" I immersed the feet and legs into the water by descending three steps, but the sensation of positive scalding made me quickly retreat. In a few seconds I repeated the trial, and brought the water to my knees, by getting to the third step again : it was then bearable. I descended farther so as to bring the water as high as the lower margin of the thorax, and found it again scalding and painful for a few seconds, during which time the whole part of the body exposed to the water had become of a fiery red, as I could distinctly perceive through the beautifully-transparent semi-greenish fluid. These were but first impressions, for, in a few seconds, the heat became more bearable and even comfortable.

" Encouraged, I proceeded lower down, and brought the water as high as the breast. My breath became suddenly short, and I felt seized as if I had plunged suddenly into very cold water. It was but for an instant ; and I again found the temperature comfortable. I now lowered the thermometer deep into the middle of the stream, and saw it marked 114° of heat. My pulse beat heavy, full, round, and one hundred times in the minute. There was a slight increase of noise in the ears ; the head felt intolerably hot within, but neither heavy nor throbbing.

" I at length took hold of the two rails, and let myself

down fairly into the body of the water, floating between the surface and the bottom of the bath, the head alone being unimmersed. By this time the colour of a red lobster pervaded the whole surface of the body to an extraordinary degree; but, strange to say, instead of the skin of either the limbs or the fingers feeling, as it does when one plunges the hands or feet into ordinary water at a high temperature, crisp and corrugated, the reverse was the case, for it felt quite smooth and soapy.

" After ten minutes' plunging, I tried the pulse once more, which had by this time risen to 115. My temples throbbed violently, and the singing in the ears had become louder and louder; yet I was not sensible of any disturbance in the region of the chest. The bath-man was now summoned to let in cold water, which by agitation was presently mixed with the rest so as to bring the temperature down to 105, at which it felt deliciously comfortable, the disturbing symptoms in the head gradually subsiding. In thirteen minutes more I left the bath altogether."

I cannot describe the satisfaction I experienced on reaching the dressing-room, and attempting, after a few minutes' rest, to wipe dry the surface of the body; finding the same difficulty in accomplishing that operation which I had experienced, and so minutely described, in the case of the Töplitz water, and other thermal baths. Big drops of perspiration started in a hundred places, wetting the whole surface as soon as dried, and continued to do so for half an hour; the skin, at last, when positively dry, feeling as smooth as satin-paper : such being the effect of volcanic water, and of it alone. No ordinary hot-bath will produce anything like it; and upon such a specific effect of thermal water on the human frame is based the cure of many of those complicated disorders of limbs and joints which the thermal baths alone, whether of water or of mud, have been known to produce.

But in order to secure the full benefit of this effect, an

additional means is wanting in almost all the thermal bathing-establishments of Europe, and in this of Bath especially; I mean a sudatory, or reclining apartment, into which the bathers should retire on coming out of the bath, after having been properly rubbed and wiped, and where, being wrapped up in a suitable long dressing-robe, which each invalid might bring with him, he might recline at full length on one of the couches placed along the sides of the apartment, for three quarters of an hour, before he retires to his own dressing-room to complete his toilet. Here, either a cup of tea or of coffee, or of broth, or of milk, or of rum and milk, or even of cold water, or lastly a glass of the mineral water (each of these appliances, according to the nature of the case, and the constitution of the patient, and the effect which the hot-bath may have had upon him), should be administered; and as it is important that no sleep should be indulged in at this conjuncture, the sudatory, or reclining apartment, should be calculated to receive several bathers at the same time, and be a species of reception-room, where the assemblage of many persons, all intent on the same object, and each with equal hopes and anxieties, by affording occasion for conversation, mutual encouragement and mutual diversion, would become instrumental in promoting the success of the bath. Lastly, another advantage of the new arrangement would be found in the gradual transition obtained through it, from the heat of the bath, to that of the air of the dressing-room.

I strongly urge the present enterprising managers of the mineral waters at Bath, to introduce this highly important improvement (for such it will unquestionably be) in their " Royal Private Baths," at all events, if not elsewhere; and I entertain not the least doubt of its popularity and success.

I must just add, to the credit of the managers of these baths, that their charges are unusually moderate for the accommodation they afford, being only thirty shillings for thirteen baths, attendants included. An invalid, and perfect cripple, who should require the contrivance of a crane and pulley to let him in and out of the bath, as it exists in one of these private baths, would be charged only sixpence more. Equally reasonable are the prices for the *douche*, or dry pumping out of the water, consisting of three hundred strokes; or for pumping in and under the water, as well as for the ascending *douche ;* for all which useful applications of the Bath water there is every suitable convenience and machinery, improved and perfected moreover since the change of management.

In all these baths, which are open daily from ten o'clock in the morning till ten at night, (except from ten A. M., to eight P. M., on Sundays,) any degree of temperature may be procured below or as high as 114° Fahrenheit.

I may now conclude the narrative of the immediate effect of the bath upon myself. The head, for at least twenty minutes after I left the bath, continued to pour forth torrents of perspiration as fast as it was wiped, and in proportion did the singing in the ears diminish, until at last it ceased altogether. The sensations of heat within the head also disappeared ; and the feeling of absolute lassitude and aching of limbs with which I had entered the bath, had vanished completely ere I had reached my hotel close at hand ; where I did justice to mine host's simple but abundant fare in the coffee-room, with the sharp sauce of an appetite I certainly had not before I entered the water, notwithstanding my long fasting.

Contiguous to the Royal Private Baths is that elegant oval *piscina*, or swimming-bath, sixty feet long, twenty-one wide, holding thirty-six thousand gallons of water, the heat of which is kept at what is called a tepid temperature, by admitting the thermal water from the source of the King's Bath (as was noticed before) at the same time with other water from the same spring, previously cooled in a reservoir. The entrance into the building is at the end, and under the arcade, on the left side of Bath-street. A series of windows and a dome-lantern light the interior, around which are openings leading to separate and convenient dressing-rooms, whence the bathers descend by steps into the baths.

I saw this bath emptied after the operation of the day, and examined the floor, which they were cleaning previously to the admission of fresh mineral water, that was seen soon after to issue with great rapidity through the copper grating in an angle of the bath, so as to fill the latter in a short time, and thus make it ready for the morrow. Decimus Burton is the architect of this structure, which is highly creditable to him.

There is another cleanly octagonal bath not far from this spot, which I believe is used for charity patients; but I have said enough, and indeed I have already embraced in my description all that there is to be told, on the subject of bathing at this important Spa.

Bathing, however, is not the only operation and resource afforded by the Bath water; which is, on the contrary, as is well known, employed largely, or at all events has been and ought to be employed largely, as an internal medicinal agent. For this purpose there is the Great Pumproom, which, as it has been newly arranged and decorated since my visit, I shall describe, both as it was, and as it is.

My readers will at once form a correct and favourable idea of the interior of this showy saloon, by glancing at the frontispiece plate of the present volume; bearing in mind at the same time, part of the elevation of its exterior, from having looked at the plate facing the present chapter. On the architrave, supported by four handsome Corinthian columns, which decorate the front entrance into the pumproom, as seen through the open colonnade in Stall-street, stand inscribed the three first Greek words of the first ode of Pindar —" Ariston men idor"—as if to proclaim that the water to be drank within the edifice is of elements the best.

The internal area of the saloon has a pleasing form, from the circumstance of its having a curvilinear recess at each end, whereby the length of the room in the centre is eighty-five feet, though only sixty feet at the side. The width is fifty-six feet. Three-quarter Corinthian columns are set round the room, supporting a bold entablature, above which rises a coved ceiling, standing thirty-four feet from the ground. Suitable large windows and lunettes throw a profusion of light within the building, which, architecturally speaking, is much to be commended. A light gallery in one of the recesses, raised considerably above the ground, affords suitable accommodation for a band; while in the opposite recess, or that at the east end of the saloon, a posthumous marble statue of the *great* Nash, executed by Prince Hoare, at the expense of the corporation, is handsomely ensconced.

Immediately opposite the principal entrance, and in a semi-lunar recess, below a large painted window, a space appears, inclosed by a neat dwarf balustrade, bronzed and gilt, and surmounted with a marble hand-rail. In the centre of this space rises a fine pillar of the same material, supporting a vase; and a sea-shell at the foot of it, resting on rocks, receives the water which the mouth of an encircling serpent pours into it, whenever a pump is worked from behind. On the wall by the window are two inscriptions, containing appeals to the benevolent in behalf of the poor afflicted of Bath.

Thus I found the great pumproom at my last visit, in 1839, as far as arrangement and the distribution of its several parts. In other respects it seemed to me unworthy of Bath; for its general appearance was that of a barren and unfurnished apartment. But since the new management every part of it has been renovated. Sculptured groups and casts of some of the classical figures by Canova have been distributed over the room, which, with the farther introduction of crimson draperies, mirrors, candelabra, elegant stands for minerals, shells and plants, has been converted into a gay and showy saloon fit for royalty.

Here the volcanic stream is distributed to the subscribing invalid, at the moderate charge of half a guinea for one month, three and sixpence for a week, or fourpence a glass to the non-subscribers; the former being allowed, in addition, the privilege of *entrée* to the grand pumproom at all hours. Nor is this an insignificant boon, considering the present character and attraction of the place, and the high enjoyment it affords from the recently introduced first-rate military band, which performs daily during the season, from two till four o'clock, the choicest productions of Rossini, Auber, Strauss, and other favourite composers, aided occasionally by some first-rate *artiste* from the metropolis.

Formerly, the Bath orchestra and its pumproom musical performances were the theme of general commendation in England. With the decline, however, of the renown of the Spa, its musical attractions declined likewise; until at length the mere semblance of an orchestra remained, such as I myself heard as late as 1839, to scrape upon a few sorry cremonas the same eternal bars of Corelli and Handel every day at two o'clock. As might have been expected, this meagre performance ceased to attract within the pumproom any other than a score or two of idlers, many of them of the lowest order, to whom the doors of this great room had been equally thrown open, free of expense, as to the less vulgar and more select. Now, however, that the establishment of a moderate rate of subscription has enabled the managers to introduce, for a six-months' season, Promenade Concerts *à la Musard* the influx of visitors has greatly increased in number, as well as respectability, and a promenade in the great pumproom, at the noontide hours of fashion, is become *une affaire de rigueur* for the *élite* and the elegant of this beautiful city.

While groups of the latter are wandering about and contemplating the many objects of curiosity and *vertu* in the room, and before they proceed to their accustomed walks out of doors, whither we shall follow them presently, let us, *en passant*, taste the renowned mineral water. After repeated pumping, the stream from the mouth of the serpent had poured forth water at the temperature of 112° only. The day was very cold, and some degrees of heat were lost during the operation of pumping up the stream, for it has to ascend from the source in the King's Bath, whence, by means of a pipe inserted deep in the shaft, all communication between the water used for drinking and that in the bath is prevented. The taste is that of boiled water cooled down to the above temperature, with a hardish *après goût*, as if a little ochrey powder had been deposited on the tongue and teeth. The writer in a popular periodical, to whom allusion was made in the early part of this description of Bath, could not have drank of the Bath water to have represented it as he has done. It is in no way unpleasant. It is perfectly transparent, and almost colourless; the light sea-green tint observed in the private and public baths, where a large body of water is collected, is scarcely perceptible in a small quantity of it in a glass. This taste and appearance I noticed, also, in the public as well as private baths of the "Hot Baths," as I did also in the pumproom of the latter establishment, called the HETTLING pumproom, a detached building, in which the water I drank had a temperature of 115°. The peculiar creamy deposit noticed on the surface of the water at Ems, and at the Kochbrunnen at Wiesbaden, is entirely missed in the Bath water, which resembles, more than any other, the hot water at Töplitz, the temperature of which is, moreover, as near as possible the same.

It is incredible how difficult it is to eradicate an erroneous impression from the minds of ordinary persons. Here, as at Wiesbaden, and Gastein, and Töplitz, I found the bath-men and oldest attendants impressed with the notion that the Bath water holds sulphur in solution; and this error is propagated by the writers of guide-books, who assert that the water has "a fine sulphureous, steely taste;", whereas not a vestige of sulphureted hydrogen exists; as I proved, like many observers who have preceded me, by suitable tests on the spot. The

fact is, that the peculiar odour perceivable on approaching
the King's Bath, especially at noon, is a faint animal smell,
due to the presence of some extractive matter dissolved in the
water, and playing, most probably, an active part in the
category of its medicinal virtues, as at the thermal springs of
Germany just mentioned. But this erroneous idea of the
presence of sulphur in the Bath water is not that of the vulgar
and ignorant only, for we find it recorded also in the works
of people who ought to know better.

Before I leave the pumproom (I detest this vulgar appellation—why not adopt the Saxon word Kur-saal, or Angli-
cise it a little, as thus " Cure-sal") I cannot forbear repeating
the objection I shall ever take, in behalf of the public, to the
system of administering mineral waters through pumps.
Where it can be done, at all events, the source whence the
water is taken should be seen, and the water itself drawn
direct from it by the patient himself, or the attendant in his
presence, as is the case at the Old Well at Harrogate, at
Buxton, Gilsland, and Scarborough. It is that which forms
the charm of the Sprudel, the Ursprung, the Kochbrunnen,
and the Kraenchenbrunnen—all equally thermal springs, where
the invalid dips his cup and is satisfied. The means of procuring such a satisfaction to the invalid at Bath are easily to
be attained in the great pumproom. Remove the pillar and
pump; convert the present space, now railed in by the balustrade, into a sunken ornamented basin with circular steps
down to the bottom of it, which should be level with the
great orifice of the source in the King's Bath, placed immediately outside the wall; let the pipe which now conveys
the hot stream from the said source to the well of the present
pump continue to carry the same (after the pump has been
removed) into the basin, where, after being suffered to reach
a certain level, the superfluous water would be wasted ; or,
let the conveying pipe be sunk below the level of the source
in question, and its discharging extremity, being turned ver-

tically upwards, let a *jet d'eau* be formed, through which water shall be perpetually flowing in the centre of the basin. In this manner the most sceptical would be made to believe, the most fastidious patient would be satisfied, and the most indifferent will be attracted by the sight of Nature's undisguised and unsophisticated bounty.

But the last thrill of the corneto has just sounded from the band in the gallery, and the fashionable throng is sallying out of the saloon to spend an hour or two in visiting or walking, in observing and being observed, ere they sit down to their principal repast. This promenading is their daily bread. When the witty Christopher Anstey, in one of the lightest and most amusing satires in the English language, undertook (1766) to mark and hold up to ridicule the manners and follies of Bath as a watering-place, the theatre on which they were publicly displayed was not so extensive as at present, though perhaps more conspicuous, because more concentrated. Even as late as 1783, another elegant writer, who regretted that a charter of incorporation had been granted to Bath, gave as the reason of his regret that " Bath was such *a small* place." The north and south *P'rades*, as they were then affectedly called, or parades—the one for the summer, the other for the winter months—the neighbouring coffee-house (now, alas, desecrated by its conversion into a wine-vault) in which the choicest wits of the age assembled—and the ever-famed Orange Grove—these were the resorts and promenades, for many years, of the gay visiters and steady citizens of Bath.

Of this last-mentioned rendezvous of fashion, such as it was thirty years before the satirical poet by his pungent verses fanned its intriguing and agitated atmosphere into a perpetual tempest, I could form an idea (and the contrast with our present modest habits is an amusing one), from an old print I saw at Mr. George's, an intelligent and honest bookseller, intended for a large fan then much in vogue. Instead of the present circle of sycamores, planted of late years around the

obelisk, seven parallel rows of lime-trees spread their
shade *en quinconce* over the open area, the principal end of
which was towards the Abbey ; while at the opposite extremity
three or four houses, still in existence, attracted notice, from
the circumstance of one of them (built in that style of architecture which Vanbrugh, the creator of Blenheim, had rendered popular,) being at that time the residence of the Earl of
Burlington. The obelisk, or memorial, erected to the Prince
of Orange, then in England, and whose name the Grove
assumed in consequence, occupied then, as now, the centre.

The costume of the age is clearly delineated, in the many
groups of people who are sauntering up and down the
avenues of the Grove ; ladies in their *sacs* and fan, wearing
a mask, *à la Vénetienne,* which they hold with one hand to
their face ; clergymen in their silk gowns and white bands,
like Roman *Abbés ;* gentlemen with bag and sword ; some of
them in court costume, but others buttoned up to the chin in
a hunting-frock and square-toed hunting-boots that reach
above their knees. Some of the fair ones are seen promenading with hoops, and their head full dressed, without
either cap or bonnet ; while many of the cavaliers, equally
uncovered, disport their hats as an appendage of the *hand,*
like the cane of our modern exquisites. The noted Bath-
chairs, with their lusty bearers and fair cargoes within,
are seen at various points crossing the Grove ; and all seem
to be basking in a far different atmosphere than would be
found convenient in our days for such *bizarre* costumes.

This famous Orange Grove was not so large as the half of
Golden-square ; and where Burlington reigned supreme, now
Mr. Packer sells music, exhibiting his Broadwoods in the
very saloon which had so often re-echoed with the smart
sallies of the wits of the age of Pope.

Out of doors, in our days, the idlers and the invalids, with
a more extended field of very handsome streets, and of some
of the finest landscape views in England, have abandoned the

parades and the Grove, for far different and more distant promenades. Some, strolling leisurely up Union-street, turn aside into the paved alley, decorated with magnificent shops, and the name of Bond-street, out of which such as have sounder lungs will be seen slowly panting up the steep pavement of Milsom-street. Here a few of the more languid or indolent loungers terminate their outward course; and walking back with lighter gait and loftier head, descend the declivity, towering for a moment over many of their betters, who are seen in their turn toiling up the same very handsome street from the bottom, in order to reach the very showy transverse street formed by the York, the Edgar, and the Prince's-buildings. Goodwin, the SAMS of Bath, has planted here at the upper angle of Milsom-street, his circulating and subscription library, at whose newspaper-room window your old codger and septuagenarian, kept green by Bath air, Bath water, and Bath whist, spend their days and hours at the " witching time" of four in ogling the fairest portion of the promenaders, and staring the most modest among them out of countenance.

Others of the loungers, after the pumproom hours, not satisfied with these brief and monotonous turns, keep ascending step by step, higher and higher, all the way to the Royal Crescent, but over the most beautifully and evenly paved streets, the broad foot-pavement of which, laid with flag-stone, it is a luxury to tread. Thence they will trace their steps back by Brock-street and the Circus into Gay-street, —than which few streets are handsomer—albeit on a steep ascent. The character of its houses bespeak it as a fit quarter for aristocracy.

How few, however, of all this goodly company, even though they may have been seen to issue from the great Cure-sal, have partaken of its health-giving water, or of the baths! How few, compared to the good old times, learn during their temporary residence in Bath, that such things as baths of mineral water, and splendid sources of it, exist in the place they have selected for their summer or winter *séjour !* It is a fact, that although the number of people who now visit Bath is ten times larger than what went thither even in the days of the " Monarch," those who use its mineral resources are infinitely fewer in number.

It would have formed a curious and interesting object of statistical inquiry, to have compared the actual number of persons who bathed or drank the mineral water in those palmy days of this famed Spa, and at present. But I was not able to collect sufficient data for that purpose, as no registers have been preserved by any of the authorities in the place, of the number of former visiters, which might be compared with those in recent times. An idea, however, may be formed in the aggregate, of the difference that must have existed between the two numerical figures, favourable to the number in former days, from the fact that the great pumproom alone, or Cure-sal, with another smaller pumproom at the Hot-Bath, was let by the Corporation for no less than one thousand pounds per annum, and both were eagerly sought after as a provision for the widow of some poor decayed citizen of repute. Of late years, on the contrary, the same establishments have not payed their own expenses; and it remains to be seen whether the present lessees will succeed in making them do that and a great deal more, as their public spirit deserves. The experience of the first season has been very encouraging.

And yet it was not for want of public spirit and liberality on the part of the old Corporation, that the mineral water of Bath has failed gradually but successively to attract invalids to that Spa; for in the erection of the greater and lesser pumprooms, the public and private baths, and in providing many other appurtenances and appliances, the same municipal body expended upwards of one hundred and twenty thousand pounds !

This decrease in the reputation of the Bath water, and in the number of people who drink it, as compared with what was the case fifty years ago, may be traced to various causes, one or two of which it will be well to state in this place, in order that they may be eschewed for the future or rectified. Others I have already alluded to in the Introduction to these volumes. Thus much I will venture to assert beforehand, that this falling off of Bath as a medical resource of great power in the treatment of disease, is unjust and unmerited ; for England possesses not a more powerful Spa, nor an agent of the class of mineral waters more calculated to do away with the necessity of removing to a foreign watering place for the successful treatment of some of the most obstinate cases of disease.

The *genius loci* of Bath, speaking through the organ of an anonymous writer, at the close of the last century, in a small work entitled, " Bath Anecdotes and Characters," seemed almost to have foreseen one of the causes of its future decline as a Spa, by what he asserts of the conduct of medical men in his time. " Formerly," says he, " the physician of the place attended here (the pumproom), to meet the company in the morning ; and then a fee at coming and a fee at going away generally satisfied him. But, *tempora*, &c., physicians now expect a fee at least every other visit they make, and don't attend at the room ; which makes physic expensive." And he might have added—and the Bath waters also—for from the moment that such a practice obtained (as in the case, for instance, of the famed Dr. Moysey, who introduced it into Bath), visits were multiplied ; the interference of the Doctor with the action of the Bath waters became incessant ; and the patients soon found that they might as well have staid at their own homes ; for, instead of mineral water and fair play, they had nothing but physic and *to pay !* The witty author of the " Poetical Bath Guide," has admirably portrayed this in his description of the consultation of three doctors, who having talked of every thing else except of the poor sick man's case during their deliberation, ended by ordering physic as usual; which induces the old nurse thus to exclaim :

> " ———— 'Twas a shame he should swallow such stuff,
> When his bowels were weak, and the physic so rough.
> Declared she was shocked that so many should come
> To be doctored to death such a distance from home ;
> At a place where they tell you that *water alone*
> Can cure all distempers that ever were known."

A second, and very influential cause of the decline of Bath as a Spa, is its vast increase and almost unparallelled success as a city. There are now upwards of 60,000 permanent residents, who of course never once think of the mineral springs ; and as these have all been covered over or inclosed, whereas they formerly stood in the open face of day, and every stranger and traveller could see them as he passed, and be attracted by them, the chance of the latter halting in the place for the purpose of using the water is lost ; they, on the contrary, pass through Bath without ever once suspecting to what powerful and natural sources of mineral waters the city owes its origin and renown ; while of the native inhabitants, and of the people who visit Bath for pleasure and other motives, an extremely small number indeed forms part of those who apply for Bath water and bathing during the season.

The sixty thousand inhabitants who have crowded the place have surrounded the springs with extended lines of houses and streets, and public buildings, and squares—the best of all of which they themselves occupy. Strangers, therefore, are unwilling to plunge, when looking after health and tranquillity, into the turmoil and confinement of a large city, in the most crowded and busy part of which the springs and the baths are hemmed in. There is a reluctance to come to Bath, evidently on that account; and the *City of the Sun* began to lose character as a Spa, the moment she began to swell out into a first-rate city; which she now unquestionably is—fit to be the capital of a small kingdom.

CHAPTER V.

BATH CONCLUDED.

CHEMICAL Composition of Bath Water—The Latest Analysis—WALCKER of the German Spa at Brighton—The Older Chemists—Odd Notions—MEDICAL EFFICACY of Bath Water—Opinion of the Oldest Practising Physician in London—Recent Writers—BATH EXTERNALLY on Health and Disease—Compared to the German Hot-baths—Precaution necessary — *Bad-Sturm* at Wildbad a Nonentity—Proofs—STRIKING CASE of Recovery—Supreme Comfort and Delight of Wildbad—INTERNAL Use of Bath Water—Quantity to be drank—How—Practical Suggestions—Early Hours Essential—CHANGE OF SEASON proposed—DISEASES benefited by Bath Water—Enumeration—Struve's Mineral Waters drank while bathing at Bath—ADJUVANTS—Promenades—The VICTORIA PARK—The GREAT CRESCENT—A Colossal Head—Ill-fated Genius—OSBORNE, the self-taught Sculptor—The UPPER ROOMS—Description of the Interior—Their Renovation—Effect at Night—A Gala Day—Public and Private Balls—Ladies' Card Assembly—Fashions Change and so do Manners—Beau Nash Laws—Comparison and Difference—MUSICAL Parties—Dinners and Routs—Public Concerts—THEATRICALS—Food and House Rooms——HOTELS—York House—BOARDING HOUSES—Hayward's—CLIMATE of Bath—Statistics of the Weather—LIVING at Bath—That of Baden and Bath contrasted—Fresh Water—Police of the City—Bath-chairs and Hackney-coaches—MENTAL RECREATIONS—What remains to be done—Sir Isambard BRUNEL and the GREAT WESTERN—TRIP to Bath.

FEW mineral waters in this country have engaged a larger share of attention on the part of the chemist than the Bath water. In more recent times, (not to speak of obsolete analyses) not fewer than four or five different statements have been given to the public, respecting the chemical composition of this water; and although for medical purposes their general conclusions may be considered as somewhat analogous, theoretically and chemically speaking they vary in more than one particular. The distinguished chemist of whom I have spoken elsewhere, Mr. R. Phillips, takes the lead among the modern writers on the subject. Sir Charles Scudamore, who followed him, and was aided by Mr. Garden, and afterwards corroborated by Mr. Children, both well known as practical chemists of great experience, detected the presence of an ingredient which had escaped the attention of Mr. Phillips, namely, magnesia. In other respects there was something like a concordance of results, with this exception, that Phillips's analysis contains two carbonates which Scudamore's has not, while the latter mentions two muriates respecting which the former is entirely silent.

An industrious, and perhaps one of the most painstaking analysers of mineral waters, Mr. A. Walcker, who was too soon snatched by death from his post of director of the German Spa at Brighton, undertook a fresh examination of the Bath water, the results of which vary materially from those obtained by his predecessors, in quality as well as quantity. The exposition of Mr. Walcker's experiments, the fulness of their details, and the philosophical inductions he has derived from them, and clearly stated in his elaborate paper on this subject (inserted in the Journal of Science for March, 1829) leave no doubt on my mind of the accuracy of his analysis; and I am bound to say at once, that I admit it in full confidence, and in preference to any other.

Four years afterwards, the scientific professor more than once named in these volumes, Dr. Daubeney, made numerous experiments respecting the amount of gaseous principles n the Bath water, which have since been admitted as the representation of the real state of the case upon that one point; and, individually, I am quite ready to bow also to the correctness of the learned Professor's inference, that the city of Bath is probably indebted for its hot springs to the action of a volcano beneath it.*

Mr. Walcker had been educated under the immediate eye of the late Professor Struve, to whose skill and accurate observation of nature in the formation of mineral water, the world is indebted for that beautiful and perfect imitation of those waters which have for years been distributed at Brighton. The process of these imitations requires the nicest discrimination and knowledge of analytical chemistry, and that process was confided to Mr. Walcker as long as he lived. This fact alone suffices to stamp the analysis of the Bath water by so consummate an experimental chemist, with that character which such inquiries and their result ought always to bear in order to inspire confidence. I have, therefore, inserted in my general table of analyses at the end of this volume Mr. Walcker's results ; and I have only to add in explanation here, that neither Mr. Phillips nor Sir Charles Scudamore admit in their analyses the chloride of sodium (common salt), nor make any mention of sulphate of potassa or alumina in their account of the Bath water, all of which substances Mr. Walcker has detected. †

It is curious to notice how differently the simple-minded chemist of the seventeenth century viewed the composition

---

* Respecting the origin of heat in Bath water, the reader will not be sorry to learn what was the theory of the wiseacres 180 years ago, gravely propounded before the Royal Society. Master Joseph Glanvill (almost a namesake) saith " that two streames having run through and imbibed certain sorts of different minerals, meet at last, after they have been deeply impregnated, and mingle their liquors, from which commixture ariseth a great fermentation that causes heat : like as we see it is in vitriol and tartar, which though separately they are not hot, yet when mingled beget an intense heat and ebullition between them.—See " Philosophical Transactions," No. 49 (1660).

† Dr. Wilkinson, about forty years since, announced the presence of common salt in Bath water, and to a greater amount than Mr. Walcker.

of these mineral waters whose " vestal or sacred fire," as John Mayow called it, they were almost disposed to worship; while the latter chemist stoutly denied that either nitre or sulphur were dissolved in the " Bathes of *Bathe*" (Baden-baden), for reasons which, if alleged in modern times, would prove nothing to the purpose. Dr. Guidott, who came soon after him, denies the accuracy of the conclusions. Guidott was wrong and Mayow right; but Guidott discovered or suspected the presence of common salt, which was never afterwards noticed (except by Dr. Wilkinson) until Mr. Walcker analysed afresh the water. Both Mayow and Guidott knew of the presence of iron in the Bath water, which modern chemists have also detected; but, whereas, some of the latter find it in the form of oxyde, and others in the form of proto-carbonate; the former, or older chemist, thought it was combined with vitriolic acid, and called it *vitriol*,—no trifling difference, in a medical point of view, with reference to the medical applications of the water.*

One thing appears to me to have escaped the vigilance of all modern chemists, which the older had paid more attention to; and that is the prodigious quantity of carbonate of lime found deposited wherever the Bath water has come in contact with iron; so that the pipes and waterducts which serve to convey the water have been known, even as late as within these two years, to be nearly choked with the deposit or incrustation, by which the bore of the said tubes has been reduced to the smallest dimensions.

---

* Differences of opinion have existed as to the real presence of iron in the water, arising from the fact, that by the usual tests, especially tincture of galls, many people have failed to detect it. This arises from the rapid manner in which the iron is precipitated when the water cools. If, however, a piece of linen be dipped in the tincture, and suspended over the spring, it will immediately become brown or tanned—proving the presence of iron in this water. This experiment also shews that the vapour of such a water carries particles of the metal along with it.

Of the medical effects of a water which, besides being endowed with a temperature averaging 117° of Fahrenheit, is charged with eighteen grains and one-third of various active chemical ingredients in a pint, my readers will expect to hear much. In days of yore, wondrous were the effects which the Bath water was supposed to be capable of producing, even upon inorganic substances. "The Cross Bath," says honest Joseph Glanvill, "eats out silver exceedingly, and I am told that a shilling, in a week's time, has been so eaten by it that it might be wound about one's finger." This same writer, by the bye, who has a place in the Philosophical Transactions, records also another still more curious observation of his, which, besides showing the odd physical notions entertained in those days (1660) in England, marks a singular practice in the toilet of the ladies of that epoch. "When women," observes Glanvill, "have washt their hair with the mixture of beaten eggs and oatmeal, this will poison the bath so as to beget a most noisome smell, casting a sea-green on the water, which otherwise is very pure and limpid. This will taint the very walls, and there is no cleaning of it but by drawing the bath."

No subject has been more largely canvassed by medical writers than the action of Bath water on diseases; and assuredly its importance deserves the attention of my professional brethren, who seem to have nearly forgotten that such a water is in existence. Conversing one day, very lately, with a venerable and veteran physician, whose experience of forty-six years in London, during the best part of which he has been at the head of the profession, enables him to institute a comparison between what Bath was and what it is now in the hands of medical men,—he expressed himself unable to account for the very great difference. "When I first came to London," said he, "hardly one of the leading physicians of the day would consider any of his better class of patients as completely recovered from their malady unless they ended their treatment with a course of the Bath water. Sir George Baker, Millman, Pitcairn, Warren, and Dr. Ash, my then contemporaries, invariably followed this practice. Accordingly, we find under that date a variety of medical publications testifying to the great virtues of that water. Now, on the contrary, one never hears of a patient being ordered to Bath, except as it were by chance ; or, at all events, the number of those especially sent thither is very small. How is this ? The water cannot have lost its virtue all at once, and that it possessed much of it my own early experience in town fully testifies. Pity, then, that so efficacious and sure a medical agent should be so neglected."

This learned and accomplished scholar as well as successful physician was right. The profession should be told of this, and be roused from their apathy or forgetfulness on this subject.

Dr. Sigmond, in an elegant Latin dissertation, published in 1814, in which he quoted the names of the medical practitioners best acquainted with the virtues of Bath water (such as Charlton, Heberden, Wilkinson, Falconer, Saunders, and Gibbes), in support of his own faith in those virtues, endeavoured to bring back the profession to the employment of that water in disease. Sir Charles Scudamore a few years later equally contributed his account of the Bath water towards that very just and praiseworthy object. The testimony of all these writers and practitioners is uniformly in favour of the valuable properties of the water in question ; so that its recommendation in the present volumes does not go forth on the single authority of their author, but on that of many medical men of high reputation ; to which must be added the very favourable opinion expressed in 1822 by Dr. Barlow, a physician, practising in Bath.

The immediate effect of the Bath water employed externally on a healthy person may be deduced with tolerable precision from the minute description I have given of the sensations produced on myself. Of the many individuals who had tried the baths under various circumstances of health and disease, and whom I had consulted, few disagree in that respect. It may be stated in general terms, that Bath water used as a bath, stimulates the skin and strengthens the muscles. Furthermore, that it will render supple stiff joints, animate paralytic limbs, and quicken the circulation to such a degree indeed as to require caution in its use, and render it necessary to discriminate well the nature of the patient's constitution ere the bath and its various degrees of temperature are recommended.

In this respect Bath does not differ from many of the German thermal baths. Baden-baden, Töplitz, and Gastein, for example, as we have seen in " the Spas of Germany," excite the circulation and quicken the nervous power, often to a dangerous degree; so much so indeed, that in the case of Töplitz in particular, the common people either apply leeches to or get themselves cupped in the back before they commence or soon after having commenced the bath, and always with singular benefit. At Bath I have known more than once the necessity of similar measures having occurred; but there are medical practitioners at that Spa who are rather too prone to interfere with the active process of the bath by introducing and employing the lancet somewhat too liberally. One fact is quite certain, namely, that with a tendency to fullness of blood in the head to a well marked degree, or in cases accompanied by sanguineous congestions (fullness) of any of the most important internal organs—still more in active inflammation—the use of all the stronger thermal springs, those of Bath included, is dangerous unless preceded by bleeding of some sort or other. When the latter operation has been had recourse to under proper advice, even the patients labouring under the peculiarities of constitution just mentioned, and afflicted with diseases known to be essentially benefited by Bath water, or any other thermal spring equally powerful, may use them with perfect safety, and will derive the expected result—perhaps with even greater celerity.

Now these precautions and observations hardly apply to the thermal springs of a minor degree of natural heat, such as Buxton, Schlangenbad, and Wildbad. In the latter the slight precaution of bathing the head the moment one enters the bath with the same water, which naturally cools immediately after, suffices to protect any patient, though he be disposed to fullness in the head, from any immediate risk.

Of the dire effects of the *bath-storm* or (bad-sturm) tempest, proclaimed by a recent writer on Spas as referable to the last-mentioned Spa, my readers may rest assured that none have ever been observed by those who have been somewhat more than two hours resident in the place. During five weeks that I spent at Wildbad last summer (being my second visit) in charge of an important case of paralytic affection consequent on a foregone attack of apoplexy— which case recovered most completely—I did not see even once the smallest symptom of bath-storm, though I watched the patient during the whole period of each daily bath for the twenty days; and yet the tendency of blood to the head in this patient was manifest enough; for when a sudden, unexpected, and most vexatious moral affection occurred in the midst of those high spirits which returning health from the effects of bathing in the Fürstenbad had produced, symptoms supervened that rendered the application of leeches necessary, and under which the temporary inconvenience in the head was removed in the course of a few hours.

I had also the medical charge of all the English invalids at Wildbad at the time, and in not one instance did I notice the semblance of the pretended disturbances of the circulation, except in the case of two gentlemen, the one labouring under active gout, the other with swimming in the head, who having arrived at Wildbad from mere curiosity, attracted by the account in my work, one morning plunged into the hottest bath without consulting any one, and came out the worse for it. In these two instances the one got a severe paroxysm of gout immediately, for which I attended him afterwards; and the other pain in the head with increased swimming, for which I bled him, and he was relieved.

It is a most glaring mistake on the part of those who have not had any possible means of observing accurately, to state that English invalids have gone to Wildbad, and left it in a day or two the worse for its baths. Travellers of that nation have occasionally made their appearance there, whom mere curiosity had attracted to see that beautiful succession of valleys, far different from the tiny nooks and hills of Schlangenbad, and then disappeared; and some few unlucky patients, being misdirected by medical men unacquainted with those baths, have found them unsuited to their cases, and so departed after a short trial; but surely this is not to be attributed to Wildbad, as has been unjustly done. On the other hand, the expressions uttered by all the rest of the patients present at the time alluded to, nearly two hundred in number, at the delight and comfort experienced in the baths—particularly the Fürstenbad, which I originally commended—testified to the propriety of my recommendation.

Now this is precisely the state of things I should wish to see brought about in Bath, where the Cross Baths might be converted into a Fürstenbad. I will venture to aver that there will be no *bad-sturm*, nor bad storms either, in such a case. Indeed good old Dr. Saunders, whom the medical hydrologists of this country hold so much in respect, would more than smile at this over anxiety of some new labourers in the field of mineral water treatment, and perhaps laugh outright at their timidity, as to bathing in thermal waters: for he himself thought that Bath water, applied externally, exercised no more specific or stimulating influence than ordinary water heated to the same temperature ;—thus running into the opposite extreme.

Used internally, the Bath water is more likely to produce disturbance by its heating properties unless it passes kindly off as an aperient. This, however, it seldom does. Its chemical constitution is not of a character to produce that effect; it is rather more of a diuretic, and decidedly also a diaphoretic, than a purgative agent. To render it the latter, one should increase the natural proportion of Glauber-salt in the water, just as people do at Carlsbad when the Sprudel is found to heat the patient and not to purge, and additional salts are dissolved in the quantity of water usually drank: or at Baden-baden, when Carlsbad purgative salts are added to the hot spring to render it active on the intestines. Dr. Falconer has testified to the heating effect of the water, by stating that he had known persons whose stomachs received it most kindly and gratefully, but who were constantly thrown into a fever after the use of the water, although no apparent tendency to fever existed in the habit of body of the individual. Sir George S. Gibbes has likewise noticed this property of the Bath waters, of exciting feverish heat when taken internally; and he very properly adds, that when they prove grateful and refreshing to the stomach, they may be said to agree perfectly.

The quantity generally recommended to be drank is a pint or a pint and a quarter. I find Sir Charles Scudamore, and others before him, have advocated the use of that quantity in two doses,—the first of which it is suggested should be drank an hour before breakfast, and the second at one or two o'clock in the day. My long experience in mineral waters does not allow me to coincide with the propriety of any such mode of exhibition. *Mineral waters should be drank early in the morning,* and before any repast, and seldom in the middle of the day, and never in such large quantities at one time. In a few cases only in Germany are mineral waters, particularly of the thermal class, allowed in the evening as well as in the morning; but with the exception of some very few instances marked by peculiarities of constitution, they are never prescribed in the middle of the day, and always in small doses. There are good reasons for this practice, which repeated observations and experience have fully established.

As there is a minute proportion of iron in the Bath water, which, being diffused and held up in it by volcanic heat as well as carbonic acid, is rendered even more than usually energetic,—such patients as cannot bear the action of steel should allow the water to rest in the glass for a short time, and then drink the upper half of the contents only. According to Walcker's statement, part of the iron is precipitated instantaneously, when the mineral water, by pumping and pouring into the tumblers, mixes with the atmospheric air; and this is the reason why the effect produced by the action of the tincture of galls on the water just drawn from the pump, is slighter than one could anticipate. Still a sufficient portion of iron remains to render the use of the water objectionable in some cases, without the precaution just mentioned. Or a better mode would be to fill a white glass bottle with the water over night, and after decanting its contents carefully into another bottle next morning (when an ochrey deposit will be observed at the bottom, which is the protoxide of iron), plunge the second bottle into the King's Bath for a sufficient time to impart to it the temperature of that source, and then drink the required quantity in two, three, or four small doses of four ounces each, and no more; with a promenade on the parades, or on the new bridge contiguous, or in any other situation more eligible, between the doses. Those who fear not the presence of iron need not take all this trouble; still less will those patients do so, whose cases are, on the contrary, likely to be benefited by and require preparations of that mineral.

Sir Charles Scudamore has recommended the cooling of the Bath water for a few hours, so as to deprive it of iron by precipitation ; but he suggests its being afterwards warmed in the ordinary way. That will not do ; the ordinary heat is not the heat of the Bath water: else the Bath water, which in

the palmy days of that Spa used to be bottled and sent all
over the country, would have produced its wonted effect when
drank after it had been warmed by the ordinary mode, instead of having served, as I stated in my Introduction, to
bring Bath water into discredit by the constant failures which
followed its use when so drank. What physician alive,
no matter how aged, recollects any number of patients
whose cases derived benefit from drinking Bath water at a
distance?

No; the water must be drank at the fountain's head, and
always early in the morning, and not in bed; nor at a late
hour in the day, as patients at Bath are constantly doing;
for here, the Cure-sal, instead of being thronged with water-
bibbers,

" When the golden sun salutes the morn,"

as in all the splendid saloons of that description in Germany,
is empty at that time, and full only at the late hour of two,
post meridiem.

Of the propriety and common sense of the former practice,
and of the absurdity of the latter, it is needless to offer a
single remark in illustration. I could almost go the length of
stating that by the latter practice the very peculiar effects of
Bath water are entirely frustrated. But in order to carry
into effect the desirable change of hours for drinking the
Bath water, it would be absolutely necessary also that a
change should take place in the period of the principal
season for drinking the Bath water and for bathing. The
autumn and winter have hitherto been considered, the one as
the minor, the other as the principal season at this Spa; and
although there are always a few invalids who go to Bath in
the summer for the benefit of the water, the greater bulk of
those who proceed thither for the same purpose, have with
one common consent done so at the period of the year just
mentioned. At such a period, the state of the weather and

atmosphere, the prevalence of extremely cold winds, the late-
ness of the hour at which every one rises, and the darkness
that prevails at the earliest hour of, and till late in the morning, are so many impediments against carrying into effect the
wholesome and excellent practice of the Germans. Why not,
like them, therefore, select the most appropriate season of
the year for going through a course of the Bath waters,
namely, the months of July, August, and September, when
every thing around combines in facilitating the proper mode
of using the water, when the human frame is better prepared
to receive the benefits of it, when the water itself seems as
it were endowed with greater virtue, and when lastly, little
or no chance exists of catching cold, or of being debarred of
a proper out-of-door exercise,—nature on the contrary inviting the invalid to it by the display of all its rifest beauties,
and an early sunshine chasing him from his bed-chamber ?

If the patients who wish to avail themselves of the great
and important advantages of Bath as a Spa will take the
word of one who wishes them well, and who has had no
mean experience in these matters, they will all agree to alter
their time of assembling at Bath for purposes of health, from
winter to summer ; reserving the former season for a pleasant
residence in Bath, as offering, out of the metropolis, at that
period of the year, more resources than any other city in
England for that object. It is the duty of all those who are
interested and concerned in the Spa-appliances of Bath to
assist in carrying into effect this important and essential
change and suggestion.

Having said thus much, I have only to state farther, respecting the medical question of the Bath waters, that used
externally they will be found beneficial in many cases of
paralytic affections, chronic rheumatism, and cold, atonic or
unformed gout. When the latter disease has existed for
some time in its more decided character, and has become
chronic, attended as it generally is with stiffness of joints,

coldness of extremities, and deficient energy in the muscular action of the body, I have known the "*Bathes of Bathe*" to produce admirable results. In this I have the corroboratory testimony of Sir Charles Scudamore; which is all that a patient labouring under such a disease can desire.

Master Joseph Glanvill told the Royal Society many scores of years ago, that " Bath is good in *cold gout*, as they call it. An alderman of that city told me that when troubled with the fits of it he used to go in as soon as the fit took him, which then went off presently, and returned not in a considerable time after. He used to put his feet on the hottest spring in the King's Bath. But it has a contrary effect in *hot* gout, and some who are troubled with that distemper tell me that the bath puts them into a fit, if they go into it without preparation; or if they have the fit before, it inflames it more, and sends it about the body, and disables the joint, so that there is no treading on it for the present."

As to certain paralytic affections, the statistical records of the Bath Hospital sufficiently testify to their being benefited by the waters. I find it recorded in Dr. Sigmond's essay before-mentioned, that Dr. Charlton of old had known eight-hundred and thirteen patients out of nine hundred and sixty-nine, afflicted with various modifications of palsy, to have been either cured or considerably relieved. And in confirmation of this statement, I read, in the official report of patients treated at the Bath Hospital and Infirmary, between April 1839, and April 1840, now before me, that of four hundred and fifty-seven of those patients labouring under different forms of palsy, of rheumatism, and of sciatica and lumbago, one hundred and twenty-two were cured, and two hundred and thirty discharged " much better," all of them having used the mineral water. It is remarkable that in the paralytic affection common among painters, and produced by white lead, the Bath water seems to act almost as a specific remedy.

There have been cases of obstinate dyspepsia, sluggish

liver, and retarded or checked secretions in both sexes, which I have known to have been completely restored by a combination of the Bath water, applied externally, and a moderate quantity of it drank at the same time. Connected with this subject, I may just hint to my readers that patients labouring with the " hyppo," or the wretched hypochondriacs who are found to linger around the Kochbrunnen of Wiesbaden, and the Sprudel, at Carlsbad, were in the same manner known to congregate in former times at the King's and Queen's Baths in this place ; and if we are to believe the old ballad, entitled, " An Easy Cure; or, a Prescription for an Invalid at Bath," they did so with chances of success :

> " If, brother hip, you want a cure,
> At Bath a lodging warm secure,
> There drink the wholesome stream by rule."

Injections, douche, and dry pumping upon ailing parts, swellings or indurations, have been successfully employed in a variety of cases. In some of the most obstinate of the last-mentioned affections it will be found highly advantageous to use the pump, directing each stroke to the complaining part, while the patient is in the bath, so that the part in question be not subjected to the simultaneous, and I must add, inconvenient exposure to the atmosphere, as is the case when what is called dry pumping is employed.

There are a great number of instances in which the patient will not bear both the bath and the internal use of the water ; and in all such cases I have recommended, and do strenuously recommend, the drinking of some one of the cold and effervescent aperient mineral waters of Germany (those imitated by Struve will suit quite as well), as is done at Wiesbaden, at Töplitz, and at Gastein, at Ems, and Baden-baden, at which places, besides bathing, the patient uses some of the mineral waters alluded to, derived from the nearest natural source. Thus at Wiesbaden the *Paulinen*, or Weinebrunnen of Schwalbach, at Töplitz, and at Gastein, the Kreuzbrunnen of Marienbad are drank.

One class of diseases not mentioned in the foregoing enumeration of those benefited by the Bath water, I am bound not to omit,—and that is the class referable to the female constitution. During nineteen years' incessant practice as an accoucheur in the metropolis, which I only surrendered from ill-health five years ago, I can safely aver that I have had reason to be highly satisfied on many occasions with the Bath waters employed in more than one way. Indeed Baden-baden does not, in my opinion, afford better results in such cases, although it has been so much vaunted on that score; and Tonbridge Wells is decidedly inferior to it.

But in order to derive a full benefit from the Bath water in disease, and to give it a full trial for that purpose, invalids should not do, as it is the fashion in this country, go thither for a fortnight or three weeks only, use the water perhaps a dozen times, and then run away. A full course should consist of at least five or six weeks.

A Spa is imperfect as an establishment, unless it offers to the invalids some one or many of those ADJUVANTS on which I have largely descanted, both in my " Spas of Germany," and in the introduction to the present volumes. In that respect Bath again claims for itself the rank of " King of the English Spas." No place offers better or more numerous resources in that way than Bath, whether for out-of-door amusements, motives for exercise, or attractive objects for distant excursions, on the one hand ; or, on the other hand, for in-door pleasing as well as useful occupation, such as libraries, subscription-rooms, balls, fêtes, and even society —

yes, I say, even society, which will no doubt become even more select and desirable, should the influx of strangers of the better classes increase, in consequence of Bath recovering its pristine honours and splendour as a Spa.

Accompanied by Dr. Fairbrother, who had kindly come from Clifton, his usual residence, to escort me about Bath, after having visited with him the principal institutions in Bristol (of which, however, I must not say a word, as my volume is already becoming too bulky), I proceeded to view in detail many of the most attractive parts of the city, listening with pleasure to his explanations and anecdotes. In this manner even a complete stranger becomes quickly acquainted with the town and its inhabitants. Perhaps, for the latter purpose, a walk through that delicious garden, formerly called the " Subscription-walk, or Bath-park," but now the VICTORIA-PARK, in which all the *élite* and the *élégantes*, the equestrians and the curriculars, exhibit at a particular hour of the afternoon, affords the best opportunity. Thither, therefore, we bent our steps, entering by the Royal-avenue and through the Victoria-gate,

opposite to which, but at a considerable distance and forming a pleasing vista, rises the triangular obelisk, placed on a pedestal and supported by crouching lions, erected to commemorate that royal visit in consequence of which the park was honoured with its present illustrious name. Wide gravel walks, and straight as well as tortuous or circular drives, have been cut and opened over the slope of a vast hill, dipping to the south, which, with its many plantations, avenues, and groups of trees, presents an animated scene when carriages and pedestrians dot its varied surface.

It was yet the season of living nature, and the meads were covered still with luxuriant herbage. Parterres enamelled by brilliant flowers, or hedge-rows flushed with crimson and lilac hues, diversified the scene, which acquired a grandeur from the stately edifices that rise around its upper boundary line.

The centre of the latter is occupied by a structure perfectly unique in Europe—the already-mentioned Royal Crescent. A sweep of 100 three-quarter Ionic columns, sixteen feet high, marking the first or principal story of a series of palaces, which present themselves in a concave or quadrant form to the S.S.W. is the first feature that rivets the eye, as we look up from the principal avenue in the park towards the north. The intercolumniations of this grand curvilinear building contain the first and second floor windows, crowned by a beautiful entablature, the running frieze of which is both rich and elegant. It is a glaring fault here that the basement and sub-basement, forming the line of elevation from the lower margin of the principal story to the bottom of a very wide and deep area and at least forty feet in height, should not have been rusticated; and many might object also to the insignificant dimensions of the principal windows, as contrasted with so vast an extent of columns. Yet, after all, we will look in vain for such another colonnade in Europe.

One of the sights I would recommend a visiter at Bath to

enjoy, at night, is the effect of light, reflected by the large
gas-lamps in front of this very Crescent, and playing with
various tints over that lofty structure,—here marking the
principal features of the building with deep and dark, and
there with brilliant and dazzling lines.

Turning then our faces to the south and east, the general
illumination of the opposite hill, divided into lighted streets,
squares, and terraces, as well as of the lower city at the
bottom of the valley, will present us with a picture for which
we may look in vain in any other part of the world. As to
London, nothing that it contains can be compared to it, or to
the park I was just now describing. The Regent's-park is
handsome, and its endless lines of varied architectural elevation, albeit of brick and plaster, instead of being of freestone, is striking at first view. But all these are light playthings in their proportions, and the garden-grounds before
them flat and unmeaning, compared to what the Bath people
have the happiness and delight to possess.

It was a sort of gala-day, the one on which we paid our
visit to the Victoria-park. A grand colossal head raised upon
a pedestal, the latter erected from a design by T. Barker, Esq.,
had just been placed in an appropriate site of the park,
and thousands were crowding to behold this extraordinary
production of an untutored, and, as usual, an ill-fated
genius. How grand is the effect of a single colossal object rising insulated in the midst of space! Those who
have beheld the stupendous work of Gian di Bologna, the
worthy pupil of Michael Angelo, representing *Jupiter pluvius*,
cut out of a mass of rock at Pratolino, in Tuscany, will
readily assent to this proposition. But how infinitely more
impressive the sight if that object, like the one here placed
for the contemplation and admiration of the Bathonians be a
single head exceeding in dimensions that of Memnon, in the
British Museum, with features strictly ideal, yet stamped
with a sublime expression!

Poor Osborne! Born in penury—a mere shepherd's boy—
he died in misery—an admired genius, and a statuary worthy
of a place among the ablest chisels of either ancient or modern times. As a youth, he taught himself to model in clay;
then became a pupil of Bacon, the London sculptor, through
the patronage of an honest yeoman; and finally, after many
vicissitudes, settled at Bath, where, having put by a small
sum of money from the savings of what he had earned in exe-
cuting monumental carvings, he purchased a block of Bath-
stone, weighing upwards of six tons, and set about fashioning
it into a colossal bust. In this he succeeded; but the exertions cost him his life. After his premature death the head
was purchased by subscription for one hundred pounds, for
the benefit of the destitute widow and fatherless son, being
their sole legacy!

Many think that the bust represents the head of Jupiter, a surmise which the poor artist to the day of his death denied. The severe grandeur, majesty, and placid character of the physiognomy may bring to the minds of those who are acquainted with the statues of Jupiter, those noble and purest productions of Grecian sculpture; but the artist in this case cannot be charged with plagiarism in his work, which, on the contrary, is stamped with the character of originality. This novel and grand feature of the Victoria-park is a just and proud boast of the Bathonians, who ought to have converted it into a monument to the unrivalled and unfortunate sculptor, by making his grave under it.

Retracing our steps through the beautiful Circus into Bennet-street, the sight of an immense square building, extending from the angle of that street to the corner of Alfred-street, and measuring two hundred feet each way, unattached to any other house, attracted my attention. " These are the Upper Rooms," observed my kind escort. " It is here that, after the destruction of the ' Lower Rooms,' where the ' monarch of Bath' had held his sovereign court, and the proudest of our nobility, be they lords or ladies, had bowed to the dictates of one who, without rank, had power, and whose power acknowledged no control; it was here that the bustle of congregated fashion assembled. You shall see a sorry full-length portrait of that singular personage, and a better-executed bust of him placed by the new managers in these apartments, the whole suite of which must be prepared for a ball on a magnificent scale to be given to-night; and as I cannot prevail upon you to prolong your stay in Bath another day, so as to assist at this grand sight, which would have afforded you the best living panorama of all the rank, beauty, wealth, and importance now resident in this city— take a view at least of the *locale*, and say whether, for its intended purpose, as a public building, it be not one of the finest in Europe, if not, indeed, quite *unique*."

I have seen this edifice in all its gorgeous trappings for the temporary occasion, and its more permanent decorations ; I have paced the octagon, forty-eight feet in diameter, and the tea-room, seventy feet in length and forty-three feet wide, and the great ball-room, *en suite*, one hundred and twenty feet long, with a breadth equal to that of the preceding apartment ; I have been struck with the loftiness of these three principal rooms, which measure forty-two feet in height, and marvelled at the boldness of the architect, who, not content with this spacious arrangement, added to it a card-room longer than the tea-room, though neither so wide nor so lofty, but still of grand proportions. Access to all these apartments is had through a Vestibule in the centre of the building, which is, perhaps, the most perfect architectural feature of the whole fabric.

From this piece passages branch off to distinct cloak-rooms for ladies and gentlemen, right and left, and to the outer hall, chair lobby, and carriage drive ; whilst into the passages themselves open a spacious club-room, and two large billiard-rooms, which complete the suite, placed all on a perfect level, without a single step in the floor throughout, the whole range. I say that I have seen all this, and I add that in the course of all my travels I have not beheld the like at any Spa on the continent. In asserting as much, however, I confine my expression to the great number, size, harmony, and fine proportions of the several apartments, truly palatial, just enumerated in this place; for, with regard to striking architectural decorated edifices for the specific purpose of a pump or promenade-room, in which balls and dinners are occasionally given, the Kur-saals of Bruckenau, Kissingen, and Wiesbaden, are in every respect superior. The celebrated Conversation Haus, however, at Baden-baden, of which I have given a full description in a former work, though more grandiose in its exterior, is decidedly not equal in its interior to the Assembly, or Upper Rooms at Bath.

These rooms, which of late years had been utterly neg-

lected, as dark, dirty, and comfortless, and were consequently deserted, have been recently placed in a state worthy
of the most renowned days of Bath, by their present spirited
lessee, who nothing dismayed at the high rent demanded, and
the difficulties to be encountered, has remodelled and renovated the whole establishment. I attach so much importance to the innocent and inspiriting amusement of dancing as an auxiliary in Spa life, that I cannot but consider this
revival of the rooms as beyond all doubt of vital consequence to Bath. It would indeed be a cause of reproach
to that city, should its inhabitants again permit these rooms
to sink for want of patronage. Policy, and a sense of justice
equally call upon them to give the necessary support to the
enterprising individual on whom alone lies the entire responsibility of this great concern.

The rooms are brilliantly lighted with wax, in large glass
chandeliers, pendant from the lofty ceiling, and by large
semicircular lamps projecting from the walls, on ornamental
cantalivers; and it was stated by persons frequenting them
that the regulation of the temperature and due ventilation of
the rooms is perfect. Servants in handsome liveries are seen
treading with nimble steps the beautifully carpeted octagon
and card-room, obedient to the slightest call; while female
attendants neatly attired, wait in the dressing-rooms for the
ladies. At the various entrances, porters also in state liveries
see that the ingress and egress of the company is free and
unobstructed. In fact the whole establishment displays a
comfort and convenience, such as one meets with in a nobleman's mansion, but hardly expects in a place of public resort.

There is no question that, much as Bath has fallen in the
estimation of the public as a Spa (and most undeservedly so),
no place in England can be compared to it for all the appliances
requisite to constitute a Spa, and for this very branch of its
amusement, the Assembly Rooms, in particular. Every thing
connected with it is on a grander scale, in better style, more

ceremonious, though not affected, and manifests stronger signs of high life than we meet with at any of the other Spas in the country, no matter how fashionable.   Much of this is due to the superior class of people who habitually reside in the place during the winter, as well as to many of the invalids who visit the Spa both in summer and winter, and who belong to the aristocracy of the county, and take a part in the amusements of the place.   Several of these, both noblemen and commoners, will form themselves into committees, and either superintend the regular balls which are given every Thursday, from the early part of December, to the first or second week in May; or set on foot private subscription balls, several of which take place on Mondays, including occasionally a grand fancy ball; and certainly no range of rooms in England is better suited to the display of upwards of one thousand persons in fancy costumes, who generally meet on such occasions.   It is reported that the last season (1840-1), had been more brilliant than any preceding one in every respect, and I trust it may be taken as an earnest of what is to be expected for the future under the present system.   The effect of a full and superior band, such as I was told performs at present in the rooms, must indeed contribute greatly to give to the diversion of the place the most inspiriting and inviting character.

Nor is the very economical and moderate rate at which subscribers are called upon to contribute to these entertainments less remarkable, when we consider the object to be attained.   Most assuredly the sum of one guinea for each person's admission for the entire season ; or a three guineas subscription, which admits all the members of a family who reside together for the like period ; or the sum of five shillings for a single admission to each ball, is a charge no one can object to, even when increased by the slender additional contribution of six-pence a night, paid on entering, for tea, which is served during the whole of the evening. This, and the wise regulation which limits the time for dancing to between nine and twelve o'clock, are probably some of the motives that induce from three to five hundred people to assemble in these rooms on all those occasions. At the private sub-scription ball, however, the dancing hours are extended at pleasure, and all sorts of refreshments are given on a liberal scale. The introduction to all these public or private as-semblies can only be obtained through a friend, a subscriber, or a member of the committee. No " unknown" is admitted, on which point the master of the ceremonies is both vigilant and peremptory.

A remnant of the " old glory" of Bath may be traced in the still existing practice, nowhere else adopted in England, though very fit to be introduced into the first class metro-politan clubs, of a ladies' card assembly, which takes place in the " Upper rooms" every Wednesday evening, from seven till twelve o'clock, when from fifty to one hundred ladies and gentlemen meet to play at cards. But instead of the faro and lansquenet of the days of yore, a quiet rubber at whist or casino, without the smallest attempt at introducing high gaming of any sort, occupies the time of the company. The subscription to these assemblies, which is exceedingly low, begins in October, and lasts as long as there are four tables, which of late years has often been throughout the year; the attendance being, of course, strictly confined to persons eligible to the balls.

Nothing marks more distinctly the successive changes that have taken place in the manners, costumes, amusements, and intercourse of the superior classes of society, than the curious codes of laws framed by succeeding dictators (yclept M.C. S.), from Nash to Dawson, and later still, for the governance of the assembled " ladies and gentlemen," frequenters of the Lower and Upper Rooms.* " Bath and the Company," said

* " The Lower Rooms," with an M. C. to boot, who made laws also, are no longer in existence. They were destroyed by fire, and from their ashes arose the Literary and Philosophical Institution.

Nash, in an advertisement, when he undertook the office of *arbiter*, " are in a state of confusion." In those days a great duchess was likely to be rebuked for wearing a splendid point lace apron, worth five hundred guineas, at a ball, which in these times every one would admire, and the ladies in particular view with envy; or a pretty royal princess would be refused the very modest request of a little longer dancing, rather than that the laws of the ball-room (unalterable, like those of Lycurgus) should be violated. ´ Then ladies who intended to dance were forced to appear in a full trimmed saque, or an Italian *night-gown*, similarly trimmed, a petticoat with lappets, and a dress hoop; but not a " pocket hoop," for that was too small. On the other hand, a gentleman durst not stand up to dance a minuet, if his hair or wig had not been dressed with a bag, and himself was not clad in a French frock. All other dresses " being insufficient to attend on ladies."

These minute regulations, this strict adherence to etiquette, this institution, in fact, of the *ton* and *tournure* of courtly and quasi-royal balls, have been smiled and sneered at by the *parvenus* of the present day, who with a stiff black cravat, a coat and waistcoat thrown off the shoulders, a pair of hessian boots, a cane, and the hair *chiffonné*, contrive to sneak among their betters, with the pretensions of men of fashion, and thus swell out the too compact crowds at a modern ball. Yet we may easily understand that when they prevailed, and the enforcement of such laws allured the celebrated beauties of those days, whose names have descended to us—the Lady Anne Coventry, and the Lady Bampfylde, or the Lady Augusta Campbell, with the lovely Mrs. Powis, or Miss Kitty Gore—to the public rooms in Bath, there to grace a dress-ball; a spectacle, finer than any which Europe could produce, must have been nightly exhibited in Bath in those days, not only on account of the personal charms of the ladies, but from the magnificence of their dresses and that of the rooms in which they were assembled, as well as from the order, decency, and decorum observed on all those occasions.

To the preservation of the last-named proprieties, the company who frequent the balls of modern Bath no doubt can lay equal claim. Nor have the gifts of nature been lavished with a less profuse hand on the fairer portion of the assembled dancers in our days; still less can the present be deemed inferior to the former rooms in splendour. Yet the *ensemble* —the *coup d'œil*—the movements and the composition of a gala-ball at Bath, must be far less imposing now than in the glorious days of 1748—the most triumphant year of the reign of Bath and Beau Nash.

As akin to this kind of amusement, one might mention the occasional performance of public concerts in Bath. These, however, which were once a distinguishing feature of the Bath season, have not of late been successful; first, because people have become more fastidious on the score of music, and have got a finer ear, so that they are not pleased unless called to listen to professional excellence; and, secondly, on account of the many *soi-disant* amateur musical " treats" to which people are invited gratis. " Les prétendus concerts d'amateurs," says a modern observer of Parisian fashion, which is indeed the fashion of London, and many provincial cities, " sont aujourd'hui | multipliés d'une manière si effrayante, qu'ils sont devenus un veritable fléau, une peste, que nous appelerons *musical morbus.*"

Private dinner-parties and balls are also not unfrequent causes of interruption to the successful progress of public concerts, and even theatrical performances, the latter of which, indeed, are, as everywhere else, *en décadence* in Bath. Again, the mania of routs and *grandes soirées* has extended to that fair city, and seems equally to interfere with the far preferable amusements of public balls. People possessing noble and spacious saloons—and none have better in England than the grandees of Bath—are not satisfied unless they convert them, three or four times a year, into what old Talleyrand used to call "*une Macedoine sociale.*"

Of the social condition of Bath I know nothing from personal experience, never having had the good fortune to be long enough in that city to become acquainted with the state of society there. But having discoursed with two old residents well versed in the humours and ways of that modern Florence, though each differing in opinion as to its real and intrinsic merits or defects as a social city, the conclusion has forced itself on me, that Bath must be a much more desirable place to live in in our days, than it could possibly have been even during the glorious days of Nash, or the subsequent and closing years of the last century, so lamentably described by the author of the "Bath Anecdotes and Characters." Surely, dullness itself is far preferable, or no intercourse at all, to that frivolous gaiety and dangerous medley of castes and classes of people which prevailed at Bath about the year 1783, when the laying of snares for young women, intriguing with such as had a husband, hunting after the fortune of widows, and entrapping the unwary youth with more money than wit into a lansquenet club, held on a Sunday night at the Three Tuns in Stawl-street, formed the principal occupations of the majority of those assembled at Bath. Public sinning, infamy, and plunder were then reduced to a system of precision, not more awful in itself than disgraceful to those who permitted it. Sharpers, under the auspices of great men, and footmen, living in an easy style, set down as decoys, were ready for their work, even at noontide, in the gaming-room. People were always at hand to negociate the notes and bills obtained from the unsuspecting victim. Drinking deep was the predecessor of all these iniquities; and when payment was demurred to, threats were employed—first of disclosure, then of duels, and, lastly, assassination! Thank

God ! we may exclaim, that Bath is now a dull place, if such was the state of society half a century ago.

By this time my readers will begin to think that enough has been said of the principal auxiliaries peculiar to the Bath Spa, and that something ought to be mentioned respecting other adjuvants of no less importance to the invalid—namely, house accommodation, means of living, and objects of mental recreation.

In all these adjuvants I can, upon good authority, aver that Bath is behind no Spa in England ; nay, that it stands prominently forward as almost unique, both with regard to facilities of procuring excellent house-room, and for the supply of good food. After what has already been stated in reference to the extent of magnificent streets, and handsome dwelling-houses, with which one is particularly struck in Bath, it is hardly necessary to add that the simple visiter, as well as the invalid who proceeds thither with the intention of remaining on account of his health, will find every convenience he can desire in the way of house-room. If any farther testimony of this truth were required, we should find it in the parliamentary returns, moved by Captain Pechell, R.N., of the names of twelve cities in England which paid the largest amount of window-duty in 1840. Those returns elicited the curious fact that Bath, with one exception, is by far the largest contributor, being considerably above ten of those places, and only second to one—Liverpool ; the latter having paid in that year 22,550*l.*, while Bath had contributed 18,856*l.*

But it is notorious that, whether as regards hotels, boarding, or simple lodging houses, or, again, as to single and first-rate houses, Bath offers every possible facility.

Prominent among the establishments first-named, stands " York-house," a conspicuous building, very handy to the great fashionable lounge, Milsom-street, and always well known, I believe, even from the earliest times, as a first-rate hotel in Bath. Since the death of its former master, Reilly, the present spirited proprietor, Mr. Emeney, has, at one fell swoop, cleared away dirt and drones from an establishment which had fallen into inanition and decrepitude—made extensive changes in the interior arrangements and accommodations—beautified and repaired the houses throughout (operations which he had just completed when I visited it), and thus restored to it once more its former attraction and celebrity. It is the most frequented hotel in Bath.

I have already spoken of the hotel I dwelt in—the White Hart; and of the rest I took no notice for want of time; but I was informed that the Lion among them was one which had recently been fitted up with much style and elegance. It is admitted on all hands that the charges at all these establishments are moderate.

While speaking of the profuse supply of thermal water thrown up by the source in the King's Bath, and of the very large proportion of it wasted, I hinted at a suggestion I should have to propose, at a subsequent period, respecting this unemployed excess of mineral water. That suggestion may be comprised in a short query. Why should not the principal hotels in the town (as at Baden, Töplitz, and Wiesbaden) have the use of that surplus, conveyed to them by glazed pipes and a forcing-pump, so as to accommodate invalids with baths of the natural water, in or near their own apartment, at those hotels, where, in that case, suitable provisions should be made, and a proper remuneration paid to the lessees of the mineral springs?

Of the boarding-houses, that which captivated me the most from its appearance, and above all its very desirable situation, is Hayward's, in South-parade. The house is much frequented by both sexes—the charges being 2*l.* 10*s.* a week in winter, and 2*l.* in summer, including everything saving a private sitting-room. A handsome flagged pavement, fifty-two feet wide, stretches in front of the house to the extent of 538 feet, serving as a lounge for the invalid who loves to bask in the occasional sunshine of the wintry solstice. Beyond the pavement is a handsome carriage-road, and next to it a well-cultivated garden, with a varied prospect over Widcombe, Prior Park, and Beachen Cliff's high-towering hanging wood. Exposed thus freely to the south, and sheltered from all the other objectionable points of the compass, the delicate would find in this house an almost meridional climate.

Longford's, another eligible boarding-house, but principally for gentlemen, is well situated also, in the immediate vicinity of Queen-square. There is another in Princess-street, and a fourth in Duke-street, equally commendable, though not enjoying equally the same favourable front aspect ; but they, as well as the two first-mentioned houses, have the advantage of being close at hand to the great Cure-sal and the Baths. In summer, however, their situation would not be considered as equally desirable with that of another boarding-house near Laura-place, Great Pulteney-street, or with the lodging-houses to be found still higher on the different hills ascending north and north-eastwards.

I have often heard it discussed in society whether the climate of Bath be dry or damp, cold or temperate, much exposed to winds, and variable, or the reverse. An inspection of some meteorological journals for the last quarter of 1838 and two succeeding years (1839 and 1840), which appear to have been kept with singular precision by Mr. Biggs, of Charles-street, Bath, supplies us so far with positive data for safe conclusions. Upon looking at these records, then, I find that in twenty-seven months consecutively there had fallen five feet seven inches four-fifths of rain—that the year 1839 had had the largest share of this quantity—and that in general November seems to be the wettest month ; next June and July ; whereas February, March, April, and May, are more than usually dry.

With regard to temperature, the average degree of any of two daily observations of the thermometer standing in the

open air, for every day during twenty-seven months, has
never descended so low as the freezing point—the lowest
average temperature having been thirty-five degrees; while
it has never reached during the summer months a higher
average degree of heat than seventy-two degrees. In several
of what are called the cold months elsewhere, November,
December, January, and February, the temperature of the
external air at Bath, at three o'clock in the afternoon, has
often been 44-5-6-7-8, and even 49; which bespeak the
mildness of its climate in winter.

As for the direction and strength of the wind during the
two last years and a quarter, the same journal records thirty-
eight days of easterly winds in the last quarter of 1838,
129 days in 1839, and 119 days in the succeeding or last
year; making a total of 286 days on which the wind blew
from the east quarter during the before-mentioned period—in
other words, nearly one day in every three. We have seen
that, owing to its peculiar position, Bath is not exposed to the
full force of an easterly wind, except that part of the modern
city which is built high up on Lansdowne-hill. Bath-Hampton
stands as a screen, though in the far distance, between the
north-east and Bath; while Combe Monkton, the furthest,
and Prior Park, the nearest hill, act in the same capacity as
regards the south-east. And yet when blowing hard and
long, the direct east wind will rush down the sheltering but
distant slope of Claverton, passing over Widcomb in its
way, to envelop and annoy with its deadly gushes Bathwick
first, and next the older city, placed in the hollow cup of
the valley. The frequency of such a wind, therefore, is an
unfortunate meteorological feature for Bath; though in that
respect Bath is not singular. The next most frequent wind
is from the south-west, which generally brings rain. To this
the valley lies broadly open. After it, come the north and
north-west gales, with a dry nipping atmosphere. But against
these the fair city has an almost triple rampart of defence in

the Salisbury and Charmy Downs, the farthest and highest; and in the North Beacon, Sion, and Primrose Hills, the nearest. The genial breezes from the south, and the cheering and inspiriting westerly winds, blow principally in May and June, accompanied often by a cloudless sky.

On the whole, Bath's climate is as fickle as that of many parts of England. It is marked by nearly as many wet days as that of other places in the west; but the rain falls at stated periods of the year instead of being diffused throughout the year, or being nearly constant; and moreover, as was before observed, from the nature of the soil, the moisture is promptly absorbed, and the streets become dry with amazing rapidity. It is in its mild temperature, arising from the very sheltered position of the city just described, that consists the principal merit of the climate of Bath, and in the purity of the air; whereby invalids, any way delicate in their lungs, may with safety be recommended to sojourn in this city during the winter months, though they ought not to be suffered to bathe in the thermal spring before the more genial season arrives.

Perhaps, after all these mere learned and comparative statements, the safer mode of judging of the climate of any place for practical purposes is to take the opinion of a sensible and accurate observer who has resided long in it, and whose means of judging have been frequent, as well as judiciously and impartially used. From such an individual I have obtained the following information, which I committed to writing immediately after I returned to my quarters from a visit I had paid him.

" Bath air is what is called relaxing. I had a sister who, while she lived in old Bath, was subject to fainting and losing her voice; so that, though an excellent singer, she never could sing after a day or two's exertion. She moreover used to lose flesh. The moment she left her abode and went up the hill all these ill-effects disappeared, and she got strong again. This was repeated several times, so that there is no mistake. At last she found a husband in Wiltshire, on the highlands, and she has continued well ever since.

" But then" proceeded my informant, " this very state of neutrality between laxity and tone is probably the main cause that people who have got beyond the fervour of youth or of very robust health, live longer here than anywhere else. The candle burns dimly; for the combustion is lower and fainter, owing to the atmosphere it burns in; and therefore it lasts longer."

People have come to Bath almost decrepid, having, either through long illness or advanced age, got into a state that threatened immediate dissolution, and they have gone on living for ten or a dozen years more. I met a gentleman the day after my arrival at Bath, who had lived abroad a great deal, sparing himself not a little, and who afterwards expected, but did so in vain, to rally in London under medical care; and I asked him, " How do you get on in Bath since you have transferred yourself to this place?" " *Je vivote*," was his reply, using a very expressive French phrase, though applied generally to the means of living rather than to the state of health. But he meant to express that here his physical life went on slowly—and consequently was likely to be prolonged.

This, however, is only in the basin of the valley—down by the baths and thereabouts; for up the hill to the west, perched on the pinnacle of the rock, the flame is fanned as elsewhere, and the combustion is in proportion more active as well as destructive.

It is singular that in such a region or lower part of the town fever and typhus and other epidemical disorders, which will rage at times in the upper region, are seldom if ever known. Such at least is the information I obtained from a most intelligent and talented person who has been fifteen years in Bath, and in one of the oldest streets of the primitive part of the city.

Yet the mania has all along been, and is so still, to erect mansions higher and higher, on the western and northern hills, away from the salutary influence of the spring atmosphere, which here, as at Carlsbad, Wiesbaden, and Baden-baden*, exerts a salutary influence on the animal system, though the air may not be elastic. Hence your Royal Crescent and your Circus, already overlooking the spring's basin, are over-topped by the Somerset Place and the Lansdowne Crescent, and these by Lansdowne Square, and the Square at last crowned by Mr. Beckford's tower!

Living in Bath is very reasonable, and there are excellent markets for all sorts of provisions. All the topographers of Bath, both old and young, agree that Lansdowne mutton is "the best and sweetest in all Europe." No wonder either, if it be, as the same authors assert, "the best in England," for where is there any mutton fit to eat out of England?

Mountain water, beautifully transparent and pure, though

---

* Baden-baden, to which I somewhat compare Bath, suffers even more than the latter city from dampness, even during the beginning of the summer, but especially in the spring and fall of the year. When I published my account of that Spa I was not aware of this unlucky peculiarity of its climate. The parties who supplied me, at my visit, with information, which I could hardly be expected to have gained by *long* personal experience, were interested in keeping that fact from my knowledge. But many English patients of both sexes, who have resided the year round in Baden, either on the recommendation found in the description alluded to, or by my advice, have since communicated to me the result of their personal observations, which is to the effect above specified. During the hot months, or principal part of the season, that inconvenience is not felt so much; yet even then the evenings are damp; and one lady in particular, who suffered much from dampness, and had passed a year at Baden, when she came over to Wildbad last year to consult me, complained bitterly of the sad influence of the Baden air upon her nerves, and was revived by the mere inhaling for one day of the more genial and balmy atmosphere of the Würtemburg valley.

somewhat hard, is abundantly supplied by a company; and the river water, into which sundry city drains pour their contents, is never by any chance used for domestic purposes. Such a practice is left entirely to the metropolitans, who love to revel in the filthy solution of Thames water handed to them for potation and ablution, as well as for the dressing of food, by sundry companies at a very heavy charge. The Bathonians would turn in disgust from such a chalice; but the Londoner swallows its contents and says nothing.

Fuel is cheap as well as abundant. Coal is obtained in prodigious quantities between Radstock and Bath, and sold at very moderate prices. It has its defects, however; for it is hard to burn, and leaves behind prodigious quantities of something like red brick-dust after combustion.

This varied information I have deduced from conversation had with one or two persons well able from long residence to form a correct opinion upon these matters. The one was a clergyman, connected with one of the churches; the other an old messmate and captain in the royal navy on half-pay, who, with his *modicum* of his country's gratitude for his " tossings and woundings," had contrived to sail for many years over the tranquil waters of Bath, with a flying pendant and a wife in tow.

The city of Bath is profusely lighted with gas at night. The streets are very well paved, and kept clean; indeed the materials with which they are paved and flagged, as well as their dip or inclination, will not admit of dirt or wet after rain to remain, and make it a matter of no difficulty to maintain that peculiar cleanliness in Bath which has always proved particularly striking to strangers.

With vehicles and other means of conveyance, Bath is proverbially well supplied. Who has forgotten the *Bath chairs?* These and the hackney carriages are under wholesome regulations by the magistrates, and their fares are rather below than above what is fair. To be carried by two lusty fellows the distance of one thousand one hundred and seventy-three yards, or nearly two-thirds of a mile, for one shilling, must be admitted to be a cheap luxury.

It is needless to say anything respecting public conveyances of any sort for a journey to or from Bath, as these, with the exception of the railroad, will have probably vanished ere this volume can be generally read. Fifty years ago there was advertised as a wonderful performance, " a flying machine to London from Bath, at eleven o'clock every night, which arrives at seven in the evening of next day in London;" performing the journey in *twenty hours*. Other machines (which were not flying), were advertised to go in two days, or forty-eight hours. What say the dons at the Paddington Embarcadero upon this point? Why that they will send invalids from London to Bath in one sixteenth part of that time.

For mental recreation, I have stated that Bath possesses resources equal to those of a small capital. How far the Literary and Philosophical Institution which that city numbers among its public establishments, is made available, and the public libraries are frequented, I have no means of ascertaining, except from hearsay. The object, however, of my present chapters is not to give a full description of Bath, which I must leave to guide-books, but simply to enumerate the several resources afforded by that city as adjuvants to the Spa. It is thus that the invalid will be instructed how to occupy profitably his time in aid of the beneficial effects from the mineral water, by avoiding idleness and indolence, either of body or mind. It will therefore be sufficient to state generally, that there is no lack at Bath of the usual means for intellectual occupation.

There remain still two or three subjects of interest which I would fain have introduced into this account of the " King of the English Spas." I should have liked to have entered the portals of its cathedral-like Abbey Church, admired its many and exquisite specimens of Gothic tracery and carving there found, and its new stone Gothic altar-piece, and dwelt on its numerous and important monuments and tablets, ancient as well as modern, albeit arranged in a formal and stiff manner, so as literally to cover all the walls around. I should have wished, also, on emerging from thence, to have escorted my invalid visiter up to Prior's Park,

once the mansion of " humble" Ralph Allen, a sort of " fortunate youth" of his day, at whose hospitable board the brightest wits of the age, Sterne and Fielding and Smollett, with Warburton, Garrick, and Quin, had often assembled, but which is now converted into a palace for a Popish prelate of pious character, and into a college for the education of Popish youths. I should have desired, lastly, to salute the hallowed spot on which stands Bath Easton Villa, the Parnassus of Bath during the years 1750—60, presided over by a single muse, who invited the votaries of fashion and fortune to a refined social intercourse by rhyme and verses. All this it would have been a satisfaction to have accomplished; but I am warned of how much yet remains of my unfinished task in other parts of England, and how rapidly my volume is thickening; I must therefore close my description of the fair " city of Pallas," and of the " waters of the sun," by simply inviting all those who may have visited the foreign baths, Baden especially, and who have not yet seen the English " Spa of Spas" (as I trust it will soon again become), to proceed thither in numbers as soon as Sir Isambard, the magician, shall, with his *Great Western* wand, have brought Bath within three hours of the metropolis, and so judge for themselves of its superiority and importance.

444

CHAPTER VI.

ENVIRONS OF BATH—MELKSHAM SPA.

SOMERSET SEA-BATHING PLACES.

ROAD TO THE SOUTH-WEST COAST.

WELLS—GLASTONBURY—EXETER.

Corsham House—Bow-Wood and Longleat—The MENDIP Hills and
CHEDDAR—MELKSHAM Spa—Its Mineral Waters—Three Wells and a
Spa-house—Bristol Coast—Sea-bathing Places—WESTON-*Super-Mare*
—Pelagus of Sands—MINEHEAD—Mildness of its Climate—Journey to-
wards Torquay—Objects of Inquiry through Somerset—The TURBARY
—The POLDEN Hills—Hawkins and the *Psauri* Fossils—Approach to
GLASTONBURY—A Lias Village—WALTON Drive and HOOD's Monu-
ment—Magnificent View—Glastonbury Torr—The OLDEST CHURCH
in England—The George Inn and the Pilgrims—The RUINED ABBEY—
Harry the Destroyer—WELLS and St. Andrews—The CATHEDRAL and
the Bishop's Palace—The Allotment Colony—Its Success—The Worthy
Bishop—FRONT of Wells Cathedral—Its Interior—MONUMENTS—The
Philanthropist of Montacute—The CRYPT—Skull of INA—Favour-
able Position of the Cathedral—Progress into Devonshire—The
WELLINGTON PILLAR—TAUNTON—Descent into EXETER—A Coffee-
room Scene—Foreign and English Manners—Look at Home.

THE same reasons which restrained my pen, when treating
of one of its most interesting suburbs, Clifton, from dilating
at the same time on the many important establishments of
Bristol, where wealth, industry, and knowledge have made
rapid strides since my first visit in 1812, compel me to pass
over in silence many subjects of interest at Bath which

would have been justly entitled to consideration. But, as I approach nearer the conclusion of my Grand Spa Tour through England, space is failing me for more than a mere glance at many of the several topics,—such as those, for instance, which are enumerated at the head of the present chapter. Though, as a traveller, I have derived both pleasure and information from their contemplation, as a writer, I have no reason to conclude that a minute description of them would equally interest my readers. Of the environs of Bath most likely to awaken the curiosity of the stranger, those in the direction of the old London-road, but now upon or near the Great Western Railway, present a higher degree of attraction, as being the residence of titled rank, wealth, and taste.

It is impossible to visit that immense Gothic pile, CORSHAM HOUSE, and its splendid gallery of paintings ; or BOW-WOOD, the seat of the Marquis of Lansdowne, which lies a little to the right of the former, near the old Roman-road, without admitting the truth of my remark. How beautifully the latter mansion, by its noble station and architectural elevation, contrasts with the former building. Of the same character, but more seignorially imposing and extensive, is LONGLEAT, in another direction, though still within an easy reach of Bath, from whence the approach to the quadrangular structure of the Thynnes, over that fine Warminster road of which notice has been already taken, is beyond description enchanting.

But if the Bath visiter or invalid be more in favour of Nature than Art in the choice of objects for his excursions, then let him direct his chariot's course to the south-west ; let him mount, and again descend, the Mendip Hills, there to be lost in astonishment and awe among the Cheddar Cliffs, while looking straight up to catch a glimpse at the vault of heaven, between two nearly perpendicular rocks that rise eight hundred feet above the level of the valley where that well-flavoured cheese is manufactured which *gourmets* love to taste before a bumper of tawny port.

There is one of the environs, however, of which, in a book on mineral waters, I am bound to speak more especially; and that is MELKSHAM SPA. Two wells of, mineral water, respecting which I regret to say I have no modern and well-authenticated quantitative analysis, are to be found at the small town of Melksham, about eleven miles distant from Bath by the London or Great Western railroad. The one is said to be a saline aperient, the other a chalybeate. But a new spring, somewhat stronger, as a saline aperient, was discovered afterwards; so that Melksham is abundantly supplied with mineral water. A company was formed to extend, improve, and work out these several wells; and some lodging-houses, as well as a spa-house, were built in consequence. But I am not aware that the fortunes of this new health-giving source, so near the great leviathan Spa, have been prosperous; and here I must leave Melksham Spa.

The mania for sea-bathing is certainly not the one most conspicuous among the people of this country; and yet fewer nations love better than they to dwell on sea-shores at certain seasons of the year, be it only to look upon the glorious ocean, and listen to its roaring. Accordingly here, on a line of sixty miles of coast in the eastern and western divisions of the county, forming the English boundary of the Bristol Channel, Somersetshire reckons nearly as many bathing-places (so considered) as there are towns or hamlets possessed of a beach or a sand-strand before it.

Of these, WESTON-*Super-Mare* and MINEHEAD are the most frequented, and consequently the most fashionable places of summer resort. The former is situated at the foot of Ashcombe Cliff, looking south-westwardly, and forming the north horn; while the latter lies under the slope of a rocky eminence, called Greenleigh, constituting the south horn of Bridgewater Bay.

At Weston, the view of the ocean, and its use, are dependant on the incoming tide; for to such a length does the water recede at ebbing, that the sea, which at one time of the day does nearly lave the foundation of the newly-erected buildings rendered necessary by the increased influx of visiters, becomes in the next two or three hours a distant view only, or indeed almost a peep—leaving behind a Pelagus of sand such as is hardly to be seen in other parts of the coast. Upon these the beaux and belles of *Zomerzetshire* saunter away their duller hours.

At Minehead *c'est une autre chose*—albeit it has been stripped, by the ruthless hand of reform, of the mighty honour of sending a representative to Parliament. Here we have a regular bustling, fishing, trading sea-port, with a good deal of uninviting sea-water in one part, and a cleaner portion of sea-shore on the other, where strangers come to bathe from many parts of the country. But in regard to inns, lodging-houses, and baths,—as well as in reference to one or two public buildings recently erected at the expense of a patriotic individual—Minehead must yield the palm to Weston. The mildness of the climate, however, much more than sea-bathing, seems to be the real attraction to invalids at this place. I am not aware on what authority or authentic data the assertion is made, but Minehead is said to be the climate in which delicate flowers appear sooner and die later in the open air than in any other local climate in England. In the course of my excursions through the country, I had occasion to meet and converse with persons of delicate health, who had passed several winters in this dismal town, which has only its fine surrounding landscapes at the back, and the pleasing though distant prospect of the Welsh coast in front, to redeem its natural *tristesse*: they thought themselves much benefited by their sojourning in the place.

I am now wending my way to the south-western coast of England, with the view to examine the more important sea-bathing stations there, and more especially Torquay, which, as a medical man, claimed my most serious attention. No sea nook has been more talked of in this country, for the last fifteen or twenty years, than Torquay; and as a great deal of loose, flippant, and unsupported assertions for and against its climate have been advanced in books which are propounded as guides to the public, I deemed it an additional duty on my part to proceed to the place, and see with my own eyes, and judge for myself, ere I attempted to instruct others.

In my journey thither many were the objects that arrested my attention, and detained me from my ultimate destination. The desire of looking at the few small sea-bathing places I wished to examine along the coast of the Bristol Channel led me, in the first instance, to take the road from Bristol to Bridgewater, which, after crossing the two parallel and lofty ranges of the Mendip Hills already mentioned, enters a vast extent of marshy ground, called in some parts of Somersetshire the *Marsh* and in others the *Moor*, which spread from the coast to as far east as Wells and Glastonbury. The most curious objects on this road are the green knolls or hillocks that rise suddenly in the midst of this vast plain or morass; and of these Brent Knoll, 470 feet high, is the most conspicuous. These knolls are truncated cones of the newer red sandstone, supporting lias; but in the case of the Brent, the cone is capped by the inferior oolite.

The *Turbary* into which a large portion of this swamp or morass has been converted, is of the first class in England. Land for cutting turf in it lets at fifty shillings an acre, a higher rent than it will fetch afterwards when cultivated with corn. But to a naturalist that part of the district now under consideration is more interesting which lies nearer to Glastonbury, and the Polden Hills, those important lias ridges which supplied Mr. Hawkins (now living at Sharpham, not far from them) with the splendid collection of *Psauri* at present decorating the galleries of the British Museum. In the lias quarries at

Street, the finding of these fossil reptiles is by no means an unfrequent occurrence.

The sight of the Polden Hills, on the back-bone of which ridge runs the mail-road from Bath to Exeter, tempted me to halt for a day or two, at a picturesque little village, situated upon them, where one of my sons officiated as curate. Under his escort, and in his vehicle, I explored the ruins of Glastonbury, and retraced my steps as far as Wells, to admire its splendid cathedral. Both objects are worth a much longer deviation from the right road, and are equally deserving of a digression. Indeed, what better service can a medical guide to the English Spas render to the invalid who proposes to follow his steps than to afford him excuses for prolonging the diversion of travelling and seeing " strange things," whereby he may cast from his mind, through the contemplation of interesting subjects, the reflection of his own suffering condition ?

As we were descending the Poldens, our faces turned to the north-west to reach Glastonbury, the village of Walton offered, in its construction, a curious feature to our attention, besides another interesting object, the new residence of the Rector, Lord John Thynne, built I believe after his own design, in the Elizabethan pointed style. The village is considerable, and the peculiarity of its structure consists in the material used in the building of the houses, as well as in the latter having all their principal fronts turned to the southern sun. Near Walton and the adjoining village, Street, the richest and finest quarries of that curious clay formation called the blue lias, exist ; and the facilities of obtaining that indurated and easily worked material so near at hand, has induced people to introduce it in every form and shape in the buildings of the village. Blocks and slabs of it are used for that purpose, some of the latter of which I have seen standing up as fence walls, which measured ten feet square, and many more of them eight feet. Not only the houses and cottages are built

of this useful material, but some of the shops and cottages
have their very doors formed of one single slab of it. In
places where greater protection or resistance is required, substantial blocks of this lias, eighteen inches long, by four
inches in thickness, are employed in constructing a wall,
the top of which they render difficult of access, by placing
every alternate block on end, so as to form a sharp em-
battlement.

From Walton a very delightful carriage-drive leads over
a very extensive line of the Walton Hills, to a view of Hood's
naval monument, a meagre design of an ordinary pillar, having for its capital a combination of flags and the sterns of
ships. The prospect from thence is magnificent, principally
extending over the plain country, displayed like a green map
at the foot of the hills, and encompassed by the Poldens
and the Mendips. This last great parapet or mountain
wall, presents, even from this elevated spot on a fine day, one
of its most striking features, the celebrated Cheddar cliff, to
which allusion has already been made. This vast chasm,
which breaks the continuous and lofty ridge of the Mendips running from east to west, looks at this distance as if
man had striven to force its passage through the barrier. Far
mightier power, however, has caused this portentous fracture,
in days unnumbered and unrecorded; and its rocky and
gloomy side-caverns remain to tell the internal structure
which that fracture first revealed.

We had no sooner done admiring this astounding feature
in the horizon, than, carrying the eye five or six miles in advance of the Mendips, and nearer to us to the eastward, over
the *Turbary*, it rested at last on the pinnacle of one of those
green knolls which have been noticed before, and from the
top of which a tower of an unknown age overlooks the
country, and forms an insulated beacon to the surrounding
plain. The scene is hardly characteristic of this country; it
reminds one rather of the baronial castles on the Rhenish

Hills. It is the Glastonbury Torr, near to which Glastonbury itself, with its neat streets, and the abbatial ruins, is
seen to occupy the declivity of a slender eminence in the
plain. The first part of this, the oldest christian town in
England, that presents itself on a near approach, with its short
quadrangular tower, backed by the dark-green and wooded bank
of Glastonbury-hill, is the old church, reminding us of the very
first introduction of Christianity into Great Britain. By the
side of it rises even more conspicuously the newer church;—
yet old enough, having been erected by Andrew Bere, the
abbot. Few ecclesiastical structures, in the later style of
English architecture, present towers of so graceful a character, with highly wrought turrets and decorated battlements.

The landlady of the George Inn in Glastonbury, the
very house of entertainment kept by the olden monks for
the pilgrims who visited the celebrated abbey and monas-
tery, holds in her custody the keys of the precincts,
within which the important remaining vestiges of that grand
structure are now secured and carefully preserved. The
aspect and form, and recent renovation of the George, however, are in character with the recollection of the destroyer,
and not the preserver, of those glorious edifices; for they be-
tray, by their style, the Harry and Elizabethan times.

I will not allow myself the gratification of dwelling on the
exquisite impressions I received on entering these grandiose,
imposing, and magnificent remains; would that they were
placed, like Fountains and Bolton Abbey, in a landscape
more suited to the melancholy tone of grandeur they retain!
How happy the present proprietor of the abbey-land must
be, to have before him at all hours of the day such noble
vestiges, as seen from the principal apartments of his own
modern dwelling-house, built in a style of architecture to
harmonize with the venerable remains to which it is almost
contiguous! Many a time and oft, while in the act of contemplating the yet upstanding relics that are daily before him,

2 G 2

of one of the finest temples reared by christian worshippers, and while marking on their sandstone, ivy-clad surfaces, the different effect produced on them by the Vandalic hand that has destroyed, and the corroding tooth of time that has spared, must this modern "lord of the sacred glebe," blush for the scandalous and sacrilegious deeds of the debauched king of this country, who stained the page of English history at every step of his life; and who, in this instance, not content with the firm grasp he had got of their wealth, threw a destructive noose also around the throats of the wretched monks of the abbey, and strangled them on Torr Hill!

But I must hasten on to WELLS,—the cathedral of which even now, as I descended the hill on leaving Glastonbury, appeared conspicuous at the distance of about seven miles. Neither the pleasing tradition which carries us back to the years immediately succeeding that great event which secured our redemption; nor the sight of "Weary-all" Hill, and its yearly flowering thorn, by which that tradition is suggested,—shall detain us on our way to the capital of the Kings of the West Saxons.

To St. Andrew's well, which abundantly flows through part of the city, is the honour ascribed of having given its own name to it. But that honour might be successfully disputed by the locality or position of the city itself. Never was an assemblage of houses and streets so deeply sunk into a well as these appear to be, to the traveller who approaches the place from Glastonbury.

Two objects merit the attention of strangers in Wells; its Cathedral and the Bishop's Palace. But the philanthropist and the Englishman who love their race, must also feel an interest in a third object, peculiar to modern Wells—I mean the colony of allotment-labourers, formed by the venerable prelate, whose presence I had the regret of missing at the time of my visit, he being absent for the benefit of sea-bathing at Weymouth. A long acquaintance of twenty-four years had enabled me to appreciate the many acts of benevolence which have marked the career of this most venerable dignitary of the church, equally exemplary in his public as in his private life ; and I felt, therefore, not at all surprised to hear the head domestic at the palace describe with feeling and admiration this new work of judicious philanthropy of his revered master—the formation of the colony in question.

The allotments are just below, and to the south of the hills. There are about 500 tenants with a quarter of an acre of land each, for which they pay the yearly rent of ten shillings, and they succeed remarkably well. The bishop visits them every morning early on horseback. They attend morning and evening to their land : and employ profitably the rest of the day. A shilling is returned to them on rent day instead of giving them a dinner. Their conduct, I understood, is exemplary. In how many hundred parts of England that I have visited, might such a scheme be adopted, to the great benefit of the landlord, the improvement of waste lands, —and what is more important,—the amelioration of the condition of a wretched peasantry ! Will not the example of the good Bishop of Bath and Wells find many followers in England !

But the venerable prelate, whose life has been one of great activity, directs his eye to every thing that needs it. Thus his liberality and taste restored the famed hall, contiguous to the palace, which had been in ruins since the days of Edward IV., and in that way has he rescued from ignominious uses a noble building, in which the mock trial of Abbot Whytyng had taken place. That abbot's chair is in the bishop's private chapel, which has been beautifully restored. The moat, filled with quick water from the abundant well of St. Andrew before mentioned, surrounds the modern garden and inner court, round the embattlements of which runs a raised terrace within, and a gravel walk without at the foot of the wall; both of which, like all the rest of the premises, are kept in a state of peculiar neatness. Besides these arrangements and restorations, which are all the work of the good prelate, he has enlarged the great library of the palace, and at the end of the vast drawing-room has thrown out a very beautiful oriel window.

The front of the cathedral is the most complete in all its parts of any edifice of this class I have seen, except that the two side-angle towers so richly decorated and finished at their bases, particularly at the corners, are truncated and left unfinished. But the design of the front, as originally drawn, was here actually completed and finished in its minutest parts, and so are the sides and porches; though here the decorations are more sparingly distributed, and so far differ from the beautiful work of Lincoln Cathedral. The two front-angle towers, and the central one rising from the cross, are, like the Ripon towers, of two different heights; the upper part of the central and loftiest tower, with its three windows and double mullions, being of the finest construction.

The interior has a warm, bright, creamy colour spread over it, now of many years duration, though still perfect. There is nothing very interesting in the way of monuments here collected, except those of the older abbots and bishops. Among the modern memorials, one by Chantrey is pointed out in a very conspicuous place, destined to commemorate the worthy philanthropist of Montacute. It is an alto-relievo. The head is entirely detached and insulated, as well as the left side of the body, with the arm hanging over the back of a chair. A large gown supplies an excuse for a drapery, the folds of which, as they fall from the knee and thigh, are marked by the usual hardness and stiffness of this artist's draperies. The head is the part which claims praise for its execution and expression. It is indeed in that particular branch of statuary that this modern sculptor excels. The representation of any ordinary man, clad in modern clothing, and sitting in a chair (no matter what attitude you may give him), is not a very difficult object to represent: a model will supply all that is necessary for the purpose. But to finish and give the figure movement and life in spite of all the pictorial as well as classical defects of modern clothes, appertains only to the very superior class of sculptors: and those qualifications in the present figure are wanting. The monument cost 800 guineas. No lack of encouragement to the arts here!

The crypt under the church is remarkable, first for the very curious massive lock observable upon its outer gate, and secondly, for the arabesque iron ornaments on the panels of the second or inner door, over which the wings of the hinges so much admired expand. I, however, descended into it, not on this account, but simply to examine a human skull, flat, square, wide, and ample below the posterior part of the parietal bones, which was found some years since in a stone coffin under the centre of the nave. The bones of the skeleton were left where discovered, and the head alone was removed, and with it a copper vessel in the form of half an egg-shell (of dimensions sufficient to contain two pints of liquid), in which the heart of Ina, king of the West Saxons, was found swimming yet in some of the original preserving fluid, a portion of which, tinged greenish by the presence of the salt of copper, is still shown in a phial.

Wells Cathedral, placed as it is on a green, surrounded by the houses of the different dignitaries, and enclosed within Gothic gates, much better preserved than those at Lincoln, has the advantage of being seen unobstructed, and in a tranquil simple scenery wholly suited to its character. It is built of a strong freestone, which has, however, suffered in many parts; and even the clusters of small Purbeck marble pillars of the west front exhibit symptoms of decay.

As I quitted the Poldens, I left the fine and varied country behind me, and beyond Bridgewater I entered upon a far different-looking district, extending partly into Devonshire. The land appeared rich in meadows and pasture, and orchards filled with apple-trees, but is dotted with mean-looking villages, the houses of which are mostly of mud, thatched and white-washed. There is no imposing or attractive feature within sight of the road, throughout the whole extent of the district I traversed, either in the remaining part of Somersetshire or that portion of Devonshire which follows, and in which are principally found the properties of Lady Cox Hippesley, Lord Waldegrave, Lord Politmore, Sir T. Ackland, and Lord Cream, and the Earl of Egremont, who was a Captain Wyndham, R.N., of whom every one seemed to speak with respect and affection. Indeed the first small town we entered, after travelling about ten miles into the latter county, I mean Collumpton, more reminded me of the miserable-looking Jewish towns of Russia and Poland than of the usual neatness and show of comfort one expects to meet in England. Sir Thomas Dyke Ackland's, Killerton Park, is not far from this spot.

The first view of the great and dark range of the Black-down Hills, which come in sight before you reach Taunton, is the only redeeming feature. As we came close to it, while just about to enter Devonshire, the direction of the hills being west-south-west, and a little to the left of the road, there appeared upon the one nearest to the town of Wellington, towering alone, and pregnant with yet recent recollections of the hero whose deeds it is intended to commemorate,—the WELLINGTON PILLAR.

In this day's excursion TAUNTON was the head-quarters, and a visit to various parts of this comfortable-looking town, in which antique and modern structures are blended together, well repaid me for the sameness of my previous drive. The top of the very handsome tower of St. Mary's, a beautiful object which I descried many miles before we reached the town, has the same ornamented and curiously-wrought battlements and pinnacles which I noticed in Abbot Bere's New Church at Glastonbury. Many, indeed, of the churches in Somersetshire have the same character, as if they had been erected at the same time, or were imitations of each other. As in Lincolnshire and about the fens, so in this country, where the flats or marshes were rescued, not many years since, from almost perpetual inundation, the churches are large and handsome, with showy exteriors, and lofty quadrangular towers.

The general appearance of the population I this day beheld in my progress, and of their dwellings, was not calculated to make a favourable impression on a traveller. The inferior classes may be above poverty, but that seems as much as can be said of their lot. In partly agricultural districts in England, whether in Yorkshire or Somersetshire, no matter how far apart the counties may be, where the produce is dearly got and scantily obtained, no appearance of wealth or much comfort can be expected : such districts barely produce enough to support life and prevent positive starvation. The cultivation of apples, which yields only a precarious and uncertain result ; and even the more lucrative rearing of that useful weed the teazle, without which the Leeds clothiers cannot work, but which so frequently proves a failure,—may serve to put money into the coffers of a few farmers, but will give no surplus bread to the labourer. The consequent effect of all this is, an inferior development of physical beauty, and a corresponding deficiency in the unfolding of the intellectual faculties.

I apprehend that the statistics of the agricultural parts of Somersetshire, as applied to the inferior classes of people, confirm the foregoing notions. It is idle for a critic to smile with conceit, and treat with contempt the passing remarks of an observing traveller, merely because they *are passing* remarks. It does not require a residence of months or years among country towns, villages, and hamlets to judge whether they wear the aspect of comfort, and whether the people who live in them seem happy, well fed, and well constituted. Depend upon it, that the contrary state to all these things is soon seen, not in England only, but wherever else it occurs, for *il saute aux yeux*, and you cannot mistake it.

A steep descent into Sidwell and High-street brought my vehicle at a rapid rate, and somewhat at the risk of my neck, before the gate of the Half-moon in Exeter, where I found a most civil landlord, very attentive to his business, in the conducting of which he is ably seconded by his good help-mate and some very pretty daughters, in their appearance and manners altogether superior to their station. One must, how-ever, secure a private sitting-room at this house in order to be comfortable, inasmuch as the coffee-room, small and con-fined as it is, is nevertheless frequented by many and all sorts of people, most of whom are not of the most choice description. My own company was dismal enough. A coal merchant sat opposite me, calling for a third rummer " as before," extending, at the same time, his one-pint empty tumbler to the waiter, who nodded assent while he repeated the laconic words " Scotch whisky," whose powerful influence, by the bye, was even then visible in the gestures and squint of the dealer in black diamonds. On my left a " young gentleman" with his hat on was finishing his tea, sucking now and then the tips of his finger and thumb, which an instant before had held a square piece of buttered toast, and whistling in the intervals a tune he had heard at a masquerade ball, whence he had just returned. In the box behind me a portly elderly person had been for the last hour munching and swallowing oysters, lobster sallad, and North Wiltshire, with the loudest *gnam, gnam, gnam* of tongue and palate col-lapsing as it has ever fallen to my lot to listen to. Hot brandy and water succeeded large draughts of London stout; and while the mouth incessantly full, was thus sonorously masticating its contents, the nose, acting the part of a breathing proboscis, was whistling through a labyrinth of " Irish black-guard," which the pot-bellied gent was snuffing up, with great gusto and action, between every four or five morsels.

We talk of the German and of the Italians of the middle classes picking their teeth with the prongs of their forks, sweeping up the last drop of gravy from their plates with a bit of bread, and licking the point of their knife clean before they immerse it into the saltcellar to help themselves to some of its contents : but when we publish to English readers these nationalities, do we ever reflect on such little scenes at home as I have just described, in a coffee-room of one of the crack inns of an episcopal city of such notoriety? Which of these habits are the most revolting, or most inconsistent with the general notions of good breeding ?

CHAPTER VII.

EXMOUTH—TEIGNMOUTH.

ROAD TO TORQUAY.

WE may now bid adieu, at least for some days, to the Spas of England, and turn our attention to the principal Seabathing Stations on the south and south-western coasts, which public opinion, sanctioned by experience or the sentiments of professional men, has assigned as the most favourable retreat for certain classes of invalids during the inclement season. Among these, Torquay has almost monopolised, in our day, that reputation of superiority which, in years not long passed, had been shared by three or four other sea towns not far removed from it. To Torquay, therefore, I directed my willing and anxious steps—the more eager to reach it as I expected to derive much valuable information and assistance from a talented and skilful practitioner, Dr. De Barry, whom my occasional and indeed recent professional correspondence respecting certain patients I had committed to his care, had led me to expect I should find at his post. Alas! on my arrival, I encountered only the mourners who had just returned from consigning this young physician to an untimely grave! He had, with intense assiduity, attended, by night and by day, an interesting case of fever, which had proved fatal; and the same disease, developing itself immediately after in the physician, snatched him from among the living, even before the new-made grave of his patient had been covered with the greensward.

Ere we enter the precincts of the south-western asylum of condemned lungs, let us cast a retrospective and a superficial glance at the episcopal city we have just left. Exeter is not only a *transit* city for the south-west of England, but is itself in a state of transition. Ancient as York or Coventry, it is nevertheless losing, one after another, its characteristic signs of primordial life, and assuming a new character. Whether it be also, and at the same time, emerging from monkish superstition and its attendant darkness, it is not for a mere chance passenger to determine.

In its exterior, the city of Exeter, from being in a *transitive* state, offers some peculiar and startling contrasts as well as features. No one, for instance, can walk along its main street, the ancient way of the place from north-east to south-west, without having his attention attracted, first, by the buildings of a Gothic age, and then by those imitated from the Greeks and the Romans, either opposed to each other, or rising side by side—the one marking the days of

yore, the others those that are even now passing. High-street
and Fore-street in Exeter, to which I am thus alluding, are
perhaps in those respects as interesting as High-street, and
Cannongate, and Princes-street in Edinburgh would be, if
the respective elements of architecture of those separate
localities were mingled perchance together to form but one
successive line of buildings as in Exeter. Here we have, for
instance, the imposing elevation of the Free Grammar-school,
with its few yet grand Gothic windows and a fine gateway
on the one side of High-street, contrasting with the Corinthian and pretending front of the West of England Insurance
Office on the other side.

This last modern edifice and others that are seen in the
same street with many equally modern-built or modernized
dwellings, would lead one to expect a speedy and total
extinction of the venerable aspect of Exeter, by which all
travellers must have been, as I was, greatly struck, in passing
through that city twenty-nine years ago. That protracted
period of peace had not then arrived which followed later,
and which has permitted the people of this country to set
their minds on works of art and comfort, and, in this instance,
almost to obliterate the works of their fathers. But the
sight of the Guildhall portico, projecting with its dark
gloomy mass into High-street, recalls the ancient days of
fifteen hundred.

The prevailing tendency, however, is to cancel every mark
of teutonic time. All the old city gates have been demolished, or are in progress of being so. The castle of Rouge-
mont (a name fit for a romance) is desecrated by the presence
of an ordinary-built English session-house, and every inhabitant whose house happens to have an ancient front, a
projecting oriel, a carved gable, or a bay window, with mullions, and grotesque or arabesque figures, if he cannot rebuild
or reface his ancient and picturesque abode, will, at all
events, lay white paint thickly upon its surface, hang

Venetian screens before the windows, put up Italian balco-
nies, and superadd a Grecian portico to his door—thus
striving to conceal the olden date of his dwelling. The very
inn in which I resided is in this condition of transit. Still
the more ancient part within remains in *statu quo*, though
cleansed or enlivened by paint; and I rejoiced at the short
séjour I made in it, and loved the little low bedchamber I
then occupied, with steps to go down into, and steps to go
out of it, and its oak panels, and tall chimneypiece, and
mullioned windows,—for all these things carried my recollection back into the century when, probably, this identical bed-
chamber gave shelter and repose to a weary pilgrim, come to
visit the shrine in the Lady Chapel of the Cathedral Church
of St. Peter.

The exterior of this cathedral is inferior in design, state
of repair, and neatness, to many cathedrals I have seen in
the course of my general tour through England. The great
quadrangular north tower (the first seen on approaching the
ample churchyard through Broadgate) from its unusual width
and the peculiar arrangement of three or four rows of blind arches
on its walls, with a few narrow open windows only at the top story,
more resembles a specimen of the castellated than of the ecclesiastical style of architecture. On the eastern side, the face of
the building is quite black, and in a worse condition than
are some parts of the outside of Westminster Abbey. Of the
principal front one can only say that it is curious, but certainly
not striking. The many-figured advancing porch before the
great western door, secured by two flying buttresses, is but
a poor compensation for the barrenness of ornaments on the
north and south sides of the walls.

One of the few attractive features that arrested my attention in its interior is another and very different porch, placed
in front of the great screen below the singularly-shaped
organ, with three exquisitely-ornamented arches. It is a
feature quite unique among the cathedrals I have visited.

Eleven old paintings on stone, which were discovered about seventy years ago, under a coat of plaster of Paris, have been arranged over these arches, in an equal number of compartments, constituting a peculiarity sufficient to distinguish Exeter Cathedral from all others. This imposing structure has the great advantage of being encircled at the west and north side by a very wide and open area, around which are several ranges of houses, and among them two quiet hotels— the *Globe* and the *Clarence.*

Never did I behold, except in St. Martin's-le-Grand, in London, at the hours when mail-coaches arrive or depart, so great, so incessant a bustle of arrivals and departures of public and private vehicles of every description as I was a witness to for an hour or so at the New London Inn in High-street, near to the Public Rooms, between which and the inn a short street ascends to the castle and to the public walk of Northernhay. My .turn at length arrived, and I took my departure by the two-horse mail-coach on my way to Torquay. It was on the 6th of November I started—a favourable date for one who wished to judge of the proclaimed mildness of the climate in these parts during the autumnal and colder months of the year.

Foregate, a continuation of the principal line of streets I have described, ends in an almost precipitous descent on the bridge over the Exe, which is wide here, and takes a semi-circular sweep round the west part of the city. The view of the latter, from the centre of the bridge, spread over the acclivities to the south and south-east, with the castle very prominent, and Mr. Granger's seat and pleasure grounds next to it, forms by far the prettiest picture of Exeter, as seen from the south-west.

As far as Alphington the road winds through low flat ground. Here quitting the direct branch to Plymouth, it enters an undulating [district leading to the Earl of Devon's seat, Powderham, with the view of many detached villas, favourably situated in a very extensive country on the left, in which lies Topsham, at the head of Exmouth's harbour.

Before reaching the Earl of Devon's, the road winds round a hill of red sandstone, richly clothed with verdure, even at the advanced season of my visit, and of great extent, though not very lofty. It has been worked in some parts as quarries.

Losing now for a moment the view of Topsham and the river Exe, the carriage entered a hilly ground both east and west, on an elevated part of the former of which the Belvedere of Powderham Castle betokened the immediate approach to that mansion. A new lodge in the Gothic style, of red sandstone, was then erecting by the road side, as an entrance to the grounds, which comprise large pasture fields, green hills and wooded cliffs. At one part of the road, sunk within the deep cutting in the rock, a bridge of one arch brings the woods right and left of the road in communication. On emerging from this spot the great and little Haldon-hills come in sight, and the road then skirts the well-wooded bank of Powderham.

To reach Kinton, a small village, the red argillaceous sandstone has been deeply cut through in every direction, so that the village itself lies perfectly buried. Quitting this, the road quickly gains the shore of the wide estuary of the Exe, and reaches Star-cross, a place fit only for summer residence, and the houses of which are exposed to the east and south-east.

Exmouth is here fully seen on its promontory-like cliff on the opposite shore, and at the mouth of the Exe. Its church tower marks its locality to the mariner, and shows at once that the situation it occupies is in no direction sufficiently sheltered, either on the land or on the sea side; for it has behind it all the flat country as far as Rawleigh-on-the-hill, which is too distant to protect it from the north east, while all the east and south east winds meet and blow upon it from the sea. In any other country south of the Channel, such a situation

would perhaps be too hot in the summer months. Not so
here. At that season its local peculiarities would render
Exmouth a desirable residence; but decidedly neither it
nor its climate can be recommended to very delicate invalids
in winter; and although Exmouth has been considered the
oldest sea watering-place in Devonshire, and the genial
nature of its atmosphere has formerly been much descanted
upon, subsequent and longer experience has not confirmed
those high commendations. The influx of strangers is much
smaller than it was wont to be in former times, and invalids
have gone in search of a more sheltered and more genial
situation.

And yet this falling off in the attractions of Exmouth is
not for want of well-located and well-protected dwelling-
houses, since it possesses excellent accommodation of that
kind. Neither is it owing to any deficiency of walks, for the
Rock-walk, and the Terrace on the Beacon are cheerful and
convenient. No; it is, on the one hand, the somewhat exposed
situation of the town just alluded to, that has worked the
change of public opinion; and the defects of the sea-bathing,
which is in reality a bathing in the river, for it takes place
within the bar, and not on the strand.

Like many other sea-towns in Devonshire, Exmouth has,
in its immediate neighbourhood, a valley sheltered on all sides
from the winds, and capable of affording a genial retreat to
the afflicted with complaints in the lungs; such a locality,
indeed, is worthy of their attention. An easy and direct
communication obtains to it from either Exeter or Topsham;
but the access to Exmouth itself from the west shore, along
which winds the road to Torquay, can only be accomplished by
means of boats from Cockwood or East-town.

Quitting the latter place, our road, on leaving the coast,
took a sudden turn inland, and for a time fronted the two
ranges of the Haldon-hills, over the former of which are
thickly scattered the fine woods by which Mamhead, the

seat of Sir Robert Newman, is surrounded. This domain is extensive, and I was informed by a gentleman who knew the mansion well, that the view from thence towards Exmouth, and up-channel, passing over a very rich country, most of which belongs to the proprietor of Mamhead, is truly magnificent. With reference to a winter residence, however, the aspect of the hill is not altogether felicitous.

The stage through this district, as far as Dawlish, is very hilly, and quite away from the sea, which bursts again into view at half a mile on this side of the last-mentioned place, when the eye first catches the " Clerk Rock," out in the sea, and beyond it " Hope's Nose," forming the eastern point of the entrance into Torbay.

Into the village of Dawlish we descended immediately after, through another much more stupendous cutting in the sandstone, the strata of which dip to the east, and exhibit on their denuded surface a remarkable " fault." I did not halt to examine Dawlish this time, but reserved that pleasing task for my return. At present, continuing my journey over an incessantly hilly country, along which occur many cuttings, twenty and thirty feet deep at least, through a coarse-grained red sandstone, almost entirely disintegrated, we reached Teignmouth, after having enjoyed from the top of Teignmouth Hill a striking land-view of the town lying at our feet.

Teignmouth, to say the truth, appeared to me at first sight but a poor place, with its narrow hilly streets, and scanty accommodation, except down by the seaside on the eastern shore at the mouth of the Teign. Here are some houses very favourably placed as to aspect—modern built, and I am assured very comfortable. A little private business, and a desire to examine the more recent part of the town, detained me in this place. I relied upon regaining the lost time by crossing over to the opposite bank of the Teign by the new bridge. But that striking feature

2 H 2

of West Teignmouth, built partly of stone and partly of wood, and the longest bridge in England, being 1671 feet in length, was unfortunately broken at the time and under repair.

The engineer, Mr. R. Hopkins, who designed and executed this remarkable structure, at the cost of 19,000*l.* and opened it in 1827, calculated on a much greater power of resistance to the alternate action of the land floods rushing down the Teign, and of the tumultuous eddies of the sea driven in by the easterly gales, than the materials of which the bridge is composed have proved to possess. Those materials consist of stone for the abutment-walls, which are of great strength, and serve to support the ends of the bridge, itself constructed of iron and wood, and composed of thirty-four arches, independently of a drawbridge, which opens in two parts to admit the passing of large vessels into the inner harbour.

The *contretemps* of an interrupted communication by this bridge from West Teignmouth to Shaldon on the opposite side of the river, compelled me to make an immense *détour* in order to reach Torquay. We were, in fact, constrained to ascend the left embankment of the Teign as high up as Newton, in order to get into the higher road that crosses Milber-Down. The magnificent lengthened vista of the up-river, in many parts a quarter of a mile wide, and of the country adjacent to both banks, which a ride of this sort affords, is beyond conception gratifying. Though advanced in the month of November, and riding outside of a public carriage, with the wind blowing down the river, and consequently facing us, I felt as if we were passing through an atmosphere of a more genial nature than the one I had been in a day or two before. This impression on my mind became much stronger the further we proceeded inland.

To the right of the road, about two miles from Teignmouth, the slopes of the hills, arranged as it were in the form of an arch, and either well clothed with wood or cultivated, present several neat insulated houses, and a small village, called Bishopteignton, which have the benefit of a full view of the mouth of the river, as well as down channel on the one hand; and up the river and far inland on the other, with, besides, a rich prospect on the opposite side. This situation, which I purposely and thus minutely signalize, I should consider very desirable, provided the houses be well built and free from draughts, and so placed that the principal rooms shall open to the western sun. To invalids having delicate chests and requiring a *séjour* in this milder atmosphere for the winter, and whose nerves cannot bear the relaxing air, such as I hold the entire range of coast-air in Devonshire to be, this situation is one much to be preferred to that of the lower or east town of Teignmouth.

The influx of invalids who select Teignmouth for their residence does not seem to have much enriched its inhabitants; for, with the exception of the better houses by the sea-side in East Teignmouth, built expressly for visiters and already alluded to, besides a few of the streets, in which I saw some tolerably neat lodging-houses, rough-surfaced, and worked over with a greyish tint,—the town, particularly the upper part, is, as I before observed, poor and mean in appearance. Yet I noticed several vehicles with gay company, and many ladies riding on horseback in groups, while some were wandering solitarily, either mounted or on foot, in all directions. The laurestine was in full blossom, and some wall-flowers and geraniums were living out of doors near the sea-shore. Here the sea-bathing is not of the best sort, on account of the peculiarity of the beach, which is such that horses cannot be used to draw up the bathing-machines.

At Newton Abbot the work of construction was proceeding merrily. Long ranges of houses of considerable size were rapidly rising, and the place exhibited a sprinkling of fine people. The physiognomy of the Devonshire women is peculiar. It is marked by a very piercing eye and a sharpness of features which impart to the countenance a determined yet pleasing character. They have almost all fine and well-designed eyebrows, and the eye is generally black, or of a deep hazel colour, while their complexion is fair. A striking resemblance runs through them all, and a few of them have that *embonpoint* which is so frequently observed among women in other parts of England.

But the most satisfactory portion of this day's journey, to one looking after climate, was yet to come. Throughout the six miles which immediately precede the small town of Torquay, our way lay through a beautiful and rich vale,—winding sometimes at the bottom of it, with high grounds on our right, and at other times, cutting through a wood, or emerging now and then into the open country, which is densely wooded. At King's Kerswell a new road was making to pass over a hill, one of a series which form a most perfectly-shaded valley, completely encompassed by green hillocks, with some nice-looking houses turned southwards. From this smaller valley we entered one much more expanded, but still properly sheltered, and presenting, like the former, a warmer region, in looks as well as feelings, than I had yet met with in Devonshire. The perceptible difference indeed in the climate was very striking; and I should be inclined to recommend both these valleys to the consideration of those who have to select a winter residence for persons with damaged lungs and feeble nerves, in preference to the sea-coast.

Altogether, the drive of six miles from Newton Abbot, which I have endeavoured cursorily to describe, is calculated to please and inspire the invalid traveller with general feelings of hope for himself, preparing him for the fulfilment of those expectations which his medical adviser had led him to form when he despatched him on this journey to Torquay. There is much in these preparatory impressions, received on approaching a place to which an invalid is directed as the only asylum where he can hope for health. When they happen to be like those which this drive into Torquay cannot fail to inspire him with, the invalid considers himself half cured already, and his confidence and faith increase as he proceeds, until he firmly believes in the reality of the promised boon.

CHAPTER VIII.

TORQUAY.

Near APPROACH to Torquay—Encouraging Impressions—SAD SIGHT and first Experiment—Fair Evening and Rainy Morning—Sick Chamber Sounds—ASSES' MILK—Donkeys drawn by Horses—GEORGE III. and the Sea Coast—TOPOGRAPHY of Torquay—The Channel Fleet, Torbay, and the Officers' Wives—Localities of Torquay—SEMICIRCLORAMA—The BRADDON HILLS Villas—The HIGHER TERRACE—Rock House and the Castle—PARK PLACE—The STRAND—Victoria Terrace and Vaughan Terrace—Access to the Higher Levels—Pleasing Picture of Torquay—The ROYAL HOTEL—Its Favourable Situation—Stormy Day and a Calm Tropical Evening in November—The Torquay Band—HEARDER'S HOTEL—Inconvenience of Lofty Levels for Invalids—The "Frying Pan" Walk—The BASON and its Objection—Side Views of Torquay—HOUSE RENT and Price of Lodging—EXPENSES of Living—List of Visiters—Its Analysis—AMUSEMENTS—The Subscription Library and the BALL ROOM—Gas Light in Dwellings poisonous to Lungs—The CLIMATE of Torquay—The late Doctor De Barry—Heat and Rain—SALUBRIOUSNESS—Can the Climate of Torquay either cure Disease or prolong Life?—NUMBER of Deaths from Consumption in 1838 and 1839—Frequent tolling of the Death Bell.

THROUGH the opening of a wooded valley, along one mile of which the road proceeds, ere it reaches Tor-Moham's neat village, a sudden peep of Torbay is caught. The western sun was gilding a few lowering clouds just above the opening, and below them a distant line of the ocean appeared blue—blue as sapphire—a tint which all the hills on our right, as far as the southernmost head of the cove, " *Berry Head*," seemed to have caught. Descending thence by Torre Abbey, along a steep declivity, some of the more prominent features of Torquay, the haven of invalids I was in search of, successively presented themselves, principally towards the west and south, in which direction the well-wooded round hill, called the Rock Walk, with Rock House upon it, and the so-called Castle, were pointed out to me by the intelligent driver, who was formerly a medical practitioner, and still quite a gentleman in manners as well as appearance.

If the last few miles of road had been of a character to inspire feelings of hope in the bosom of those stricken with disease, who are wending their way to a winter retreat,—the *coup-d'œil* which that retreat presented, as the vehicle was yet hovering on the high ground above it, and gradually unfolded a goodly assemblage of white or stone-coloured gay-looking houses, around a still harbour, unruffled by any wind, was even more calculated to produce cheering and salutary impressions. These, by some readers, may be deemed trite and too trivial circumstances; but my experience as a physician has long taught me to attach great importance to them.

Having once gained the level ground of the little town, we were not long in reaching the ROYAL HOTEL, at the termination of the Strand. The room I took possession of faced the entrance into the little bay, and was directly south-west. I threw up the window to lose nothing of the most glorious and splendid sunset I had ever seen from an English coast. It was the 7th of November, and half-past four o'clock P.M.; yet the thermometer out of the window marked 56½°, one degree and a half above " temperate!"

Surveying my neat chamber to see what sort of quarters I

was to occupy,—the sight of "a spitting-pot," as a regular article of furniture by the side of those which generally adorn a washing-stand, spoke volumes to my imagination. I warrant me that no such sight ever presented itself at any other town in England. There was no such provision made in the chambers of the hotel at Clifton; but here every bed-room was furnished with it.

The morning which succeeded this lovely and almost tropical evening was as much the reverse of the latter as possible, and quite unfavourable. At a little after six it was raining very hard; and on inquiry in the coffee-room afterwards from persons, visiters like myself, who had been in the place since the middle of October, this morning-rain appeared to have been a daily occurrence for some time. All that was fair and balmy in the air through the night, (in the course of which I rose twice to test the outer temperature, and look to the sky from my casement,) I found, on waking in the morning, had disappeared. The ground was deluged with the rain, which was pouring down incessantly; while the distant shores and sea-marks were enveloped in mist. The temperature of my room was nevertheless 63°, that of the water 58°, and out of doors 54° of Fahrenheit; but in two hours it rose to and remained steadily at 60°. The wind was blowing from the south-east.

At morning dawn the sound of a cavernous cough, short, large, and followed by quick and ready expectoration, resounded from the bed-chamber to my left, the partition of which was very thin. It seemed to be the cough of a female. On the right, the adjoining bed-room had been the place whence a long, thin, sibilating cough,—dry, exasperating, and nervous, had been heard every five minutes through the short night I had allowed myself, namely, from two to six o'clock. At the latter hour the exhausted sufferer had probably sunk into a momentary slumber, beginning then his night's repose when all else were stirring and quitting their beds. "And each of these patients," said I to myself,—"each of these distinct states of bronchial or pulmonic disease and irritation, is to be healed by sojourning in the mild atmosphere of Torquay!"

This is but a miniature picture, after all, of what obtains more extensively in the fine and handsome buildings that surrounded me, and many of which sheltered under their showy architectural exterior more than one victim of that most destructive malady, consumption. My two next-room neighbours were only momentary inmates of the hotel, and would soon, in all probability, get billeted in some more private and comfortable lodgings, there to struggle with various luck through the approaching winter.

The events of this first night, and the sight that had greeted me on entering my chamber, sufficiently indicated the sort of place I had come to; but to remove all doubts, some dozen asses passed before my window, even at that early hour, driven from one great house to another for the purpose, no doubt, of administering their healing milk to invalids. I wonder that the judicious, though somewhat ludicrous practice, common in Paris, of conveying these useful animals in covered carriages drawn by horses, with a view of preventing the *échauffement du lait*, has not yet been adopted in this country, where we often behold three or four wretched-looking quadrupeds of the assinine race standing yoked together by a rope, at the door of some noble lord or lady, for a few minutes, and next driven by an unmerciful urchin as fast as sixteen asses' legs can galop to another remote grand dwelling, to deliver at each the heated draught.

Since George III. introduced the fashion of regularly going to the southern coast for health, London and other doctors have been in the habit of recommending to those who cannot or choose not to go abroad, the same description of residence in all cases of individuals of consumptive habit. The particular spot designated for this purpose has varied from time to time, having extended west and south, farther and farther every eight or ten years; from Weymouth to Sydmouth, from Sydmouth to Exmouth, and so on to Dawlish, and Teignmouth, and lastly and now to TORQUAY.

Now let us inquire how far this last change has been warranted by what might have been anticipated in making it, or has been sanctioned by the result obtained from it.

The peculiar position of Torquay is the first point that demands our attention in this investigation. Every one knows that between two remarkable promontories, the one (north) terminating in a limestone point, called " Hope's Nose," and the other (south), wholly of limestone, called " Berry Head," which projects considerably out of the straight line of coast between Teignmouth and Dartmouth, there lies a bay, about three miles and a half deep, inland, and entirely open to the east, called TORBAY. Its greatest width is about four miles from north to south, and the centre of its semicircular shore is marked by a small head of land, composed of the Exeter red conglomerate sandstone, standing out into the sea, called *Roundham Head;* near to which and to the south, a naval hospital was established during the war. Into this bay many a time and often have I sailed during that eventful period, while cruizing in a king's ship on what was called the channel-station.

About that time Torquay consisted of a small row of houses, with green blinds, principally inhabited by naval officers' wives, who lived there in the chance of the channel-fleet or some of its detachments anchoring in the bay, and their husbands being permitted to come ashore.

The northern promontory, or great headland of this bay, the axis of which has a north-east and south-west direction, consists of a compact and almost indistinguishable group of high sum-

mits or hills, two of which are called the Beacon, and War-
berry-hills, composed of a nucleus of red sandstone, cased
in almost by limestone all round, except at a small part of its
coast, facing the south-west, where what are called the Mead-
foot-sands are, and where the rock is an argillaceous shale-
grit; and at another portion of its coast, facing the north-
east, near a place called Ilsam, at which the rock is *trap*.
The entire surrounding coast of the promontory is bold and
rocky, playfully or picturesquely indented, and measuring in
its circular extent about five miles. Well then, at a place
where the south line of this great headland starts from the
curvilinear coast of Torbay towards the sea, with a direction
somewhat like a bow, the concave part of which faces the
west-south-west, is TORQUAY situated, the asylum of all such
as labour under the disease from which the two poor creatures
suffered, between whom I was hemmed in in my resting
chamber the previous night.

Torquay, therefore, is a very small bay, within the much
larger one, of Torbay ; and is moreover inclosed seawards by
two piers and quays, for one of which the inhabitants of a
previously insignificant fishing hamlet, but now the most attractive watering-place on the south-western coast, are indebted to Sir Lawrence Palk, who caused it to be erected
between the years 1804 and 1807. The second was not built
till sometime after, and thus a snug and secure basin was completed, exceedingly convenient, not only for small, but also
for other and more important craft.

Like its larger prototype, the bay of Torquay has its two
terminating headlands, and they consist of two of the most
picturesque hills imaginable, to the one of which I have
already alluded—namely, Rockwalk-hill; while the other,
or the opposite one, is known by the name of Park-hill,
terminating in the sea in a smaller hillock, called the
Beacon. If the reader will now fancy himself standing upon
the pier-head, in the centre of the little basin, his face

turned from the sea, and Rockwalk-hill rising on his left, while Park-hill is on his right, his eye will first be caught by a crescent-like screen of hills, forming a single gentle undulation down to the right and to the left, where it seems to approach as if it would join (but does not) with the two hills before mentioned. Thus then a crest of high land, almost continuous, and forming something like a figure between three sides of a square and a semicircle, appears to the beholder richly clothed with verdure, wooded, and well planted, and exhibiting on various points, and on many and different levels, whole lines of handsome houses, detached villas, cottages, pavilions, and terraces, all of them destined to shelter the occasional visiter, the stranger, and the invalid who seek for warm winter quarters. Of late years, however, several permanent residents of consequence have established themselves in some of the superior sort of these dwellings.

But as I consider position and aspect to be the first and most important points to be attended to in the choice of housesfor the winter residence of people with delicate chest—a consideration, by the bye, which in all works having a reference to climate, seems to have been regarded as of less consequence than the registering of their thermometer and barometer, to which most of those works have confined their inquiries—let us see how stand respectively these truly inviting, and many of them beautiful residences.

On the Braddon-hills, straight before us, a number of handsome detached villas, with plantations behind them, occupy the loftiest line, and serve as residences to the wealthiest of the permanent inhabitants. A little below them, on the slope of the hills, is the " Higher-terrace," to the left of which, in different parts of the acclivity, stand three or four detached, good houses, the Chapel, and Montpellier-terrace. Rock-house, a very showy pavilion, with verandas; and the so called Castle, appear on the Rockwalk-hill; while Park-place, with its lofty dwellings, stretches midway upon the acclivity of Park-hill, on many points of which, besides, peep from among the dense plantation single houses or groups of them to allure the visiter.

Descending now to the level of and around the basin or inner harbour, we trace at its head, running the entire length of the strand, which it goes to meet at one end, and at right angles, the Victoria-terrace on the right, and at the other end Vaughan and Carey-parade, behind the former of which, and a little higher up, is another row of houses called the " Lower-terrace."

This is the topical punctuation or dotting of the houses in Torquay, open to the sea, and behind which extend streets and houses, and other distributions of spaces and buildings, constituting the bulk of the increasing little town of Torquay, the busy part of which, in fact, is creeping up the hill, and ramifying in all directions. Access to all these various elevated regions of dwellings is obtained in two ways,—by flights of steps, and by inclined or ascending roads and streets. The communication from one side to the other is principally along the strand, but roadsteads exist much higher, which conduct those who dwell among the higher regions from one part to the other, without descending to that lower level.

Let the reader now cast a glance on the following diagram of the localities just enumerated, and in the semi-circlorama it exhibits, they will at once perceive the different aspects those localities enjoy. I traced this on the spot, taking as my point of departure the centre of the basin, with our faces turned to the land. With such a guide, either my medical brethren who may direct the invalid to spend the winter at this place, or the invalid himself, will be able to select the situation most suited to his case, or his habits, or the susceptibility of his constitution.

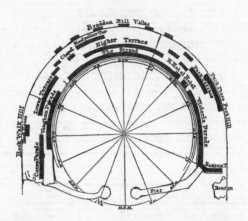

SEMI-CIRCLORAMA OF THE PRINCIPAL BUILDINGS AT
TORQUAY, WITH THEIR RESPECTIVE BEARINGS.

In adopting the present mode of conveying to the readers
of the Spas of England all the necessary information respecting the topography of Torquay, I render the best service in
my power to its inhabitants, whose principal dependance is
upon the arrival and permanent residence of strangers.

The view from the spot on which we have been all along
contemplating and analyzing the position of Torquay, is
exceedingly curious, and in England I should say unique.
It is in every respect a striking and pleasing sight, which
strongly reminded me of visits paid in days far gone to
some of the Greek islands in the Archipelago, in which it
is not rare to find a conical and well-wooded hill at the head
of a small and completely sheltered harbour, covered with
houses from the margin of the water up to the summit, like
a great pyramid of human dwellings.

An illustration of the advantage and disadvantage of certain aspects, taken from my own experience will probably not be
considered as superfluous.   The Royal Hotel, a house much
to be commended on every account, and in which there are

some excellent rooms, particularly No. 2, a three-windowed
room, with a terrace in front, over the portico, of good size
and well furnished as a sitting-room, occupies, as will be
seen in the semi-circlorama, one of the most desirable positions. By receding a little in a slanting direction at its
eastern extremity, this house is completely sheltered from the
E. and N.E. winds, and its front faces the S.S.W. The
N.N.W. gales, which sweep sometimes down the strand with
great violence from over the northern edge of the Rock-hill,
pass before the Royal Hotel, and affect it not ; whilst, on the
contrary, they go to impinge on Hearder's Hotel, which faces
that quarter, at the head of Victoria-terrace or parade, the
row of small buildings already mentioned, which are equally
amenable to this objection.

Of these two facts I had an early opportunity of ascertaining the correctness. Towards the afternoon of the day
the morning of which I described as having been particularly gloomy and wet,—a north-wester, which for a time
blew with some violence, cleared away presently the clouds,
and all was sunshine again. My room being at 62° of Fahrenheit, I placed the thermometer outside, close to the window,
when the mercury fell to 56° where it stopped, and no breath
of wind came in at the time. In half an hour I sallied forth,
crossed the strand in front of Hearder's Hotel to walk along
Victoria-terrace, and was blown upon by the strong north-
wester so as to be chilled immediately, the mercury of my
pocket thermometer, placed on a post for some minutes,
sinking at the same time to 52°. But I soon espied in what
part of the semi-circlorama I might take shelter from the gale,
and went over to the opposite side of the basin, to Vaughan-
parade, where, entering Mr. Elliott's Subscription Library,
I found his differential and self-registering thermometer
marking 57½°.

At eve again the breeze subsided completely, and the
town, as well as the basin and outward bay, were perfectly

still. The stars shone in their vault of azure, and the dark water, glassy and unruffled, had filled with the returning tide the little harbour, reflecting from its surface the few gas lamps placed at equal distances near its margin. The atmosphere felt as genial and pleasant as in a clear, calm, and summer evening in the south of Spain. Every body was abroad. Many houses, and our own among the rest, had their windows open (8th of November), and the Torquay band, at ten o'clock, came on the Strand to enliven the inhabitants and cheer the invalid to his early couch. During its performance I walked up to the " Higher Terrace," by ascending some steps at the back of the strand, and by following a winding path, which led me in front of that handsome row of lodging houses,—as I wished to judge of the effect of the music at that elevation, in the still atmosphere that surrounded it. Wind instruments, played in the open air, in the stillness of night produce a wonderful effect when heard at a distance; and my present experiment confirmed that notion by the additional delight it procured me.

On the succeeding morning, while on my peregrination through every street and winding path, mounting also each of the three principal hills that form the semi-circlorama, I repeated my visit to the same terrace, and was well repaid for the fatigue of the ascent, and greatly enchanted at the view of the bay from it and the inclosing shores. But it is well for one who has stout lungs, as, thank God, I am blessed with, to scamper, *à la chevreuil*, from one steep hill to another, and ascend from a lower to a higher terrace. The question is, how can the asthmatic and the pulmonic, and the phthisical, having no breath to spare, master the peculiarities and difficulties of these situations ?

This is in reality the great and prominent inconvenience of the place : that there is only one level walk for invalids, who may select, according to the quarter from which the wind blows, either the eastern or the western parade, or

BEACON TERRACE, TORQUAY.

again the "Fryingpan-walk" along the strand, filled in general with respirator-bearing people, who look like muzzled ghosts, and are ugly enough to frighten the younger people to death. A lady, with four daughters, whom I had recommended to spend the winter in the place on account of her own delicate chest, had left it in despair after a few days, on account of the want of a level walk a little more varied, and not quite so exposed to the gaze of every idler, as the strand. If Messrs. Carey and Shedden would permit a level road to be made under the rock by the Abbey Torr, Torquay would be delightfully improved.

The peculiar smell of the back water in the little basin, when the tide has been out some hours during sunshine and hot weather, is found particularly offensive to some temporary residents who live down on the level ground. At Teignmouth, I understood, typhoid fevers, from a similar circumstance, were by no means an unfrequent disorder among the poor and the cottagers dwelling close to the water.

The houses on the higher terrace, on the other hand, are exposed to another disadvantage, in having at their back, and in immediate proximity, the rock, with just enough of space between to form a gully or funnel for the north-western or south-eastern winds to sweep down it with concentrated violence. With all these drawbacks, however, the position and the character of some of the houses, whether of those clustered together, or of the detached ones, are very inviting, and must be pleasant to live in. The *Castle*, on Rock Hill, for example, is said to be a delightful residence. The view from it across the basin, extending from the east end of the "higher terrace" over all the scattered villas on Park Hill as far as its seaward termination, where the Beacon Terrace houses ascend *en échellons* the steep road which divides them from the Beacon,—is perhaps one of the prettiest side-glances at Torquay. Nor are the detached houses, or those in Park Place, on the acclivity of Park Hill, less desirable, but on the contrary more so than those just alluded to ; for not only is the side-view of Torquay from thence nearly as gay and pleasing, but the aspect is infinitely more favourable.

As for the Braddon Hills villas, their being chiefly mono-polized by permanent residents, proves in what estimation they are held ; yet money, money will, even here, dislodge a proprietor, and procure to a rich invalid, who is ordered to inhale pure air away from the immediate emanation of the sea, magnificent lodgings. Detached villas, however, seem to be the *furore*, and the Bishop of the diocese, who usually took up his abode at the Royal, has since, I believe, com-pleted a detached villa for himself.

It is to be expected that house-rent during the season, which begins in September, and extends generally a great way into the month of May, will be any thing but reasonable. We find, accordingly, that a house in the Higher Terrace, with two best bed-rooms, will not be let for less than five guineas a week. *The Castle*, of which I spoke, lets for thirteen guineas a week, but is well furnished ; a remark not equally applicable to the generality of lodging-houses in Torquay. Another detached villa on the Braddon Hills, at the time of my visit, occupied by the family of a noble Earl, was let at ten guineas a week ; and they will not let such houses for a shorter term than six months.

These high prices were beginning to frighten people away to other parts on the coast. At Teignmouth, an invalid would get, for two guineas a week, what is charged five at Torquay. Late as it was already in the season at the time of my visit, a great number of houses, which had in former years let well, could not get tenants—people having changed their opinions now-a-days in regard to high rents and high prices.

But to be away from the direct effluvia of back sea-water and sea-sprays, as well as from the relaxing, warm dampness of Torquay, which is balsam to the lungs, and poison to the nerves, I should ensconce myself for the winter, had I a damaged chest, into a plain, substantial house, on the high land before reaching Torquay, to which allusion has already been made. There,—after passing that tract of a few miles extent, which lies between the high ground of Milber-down, to the east, and Longford to the west, until it reaches King's Kerswell, (where a new road was making at the time of my journey to the Coast, by cutting through the western side of a high sandstone hill, which stands between the last-mentioned place and Coffin's-well,) we meet with a succession of pleasing valleys, from the gap made in the hill as far as Tor-Moham, which overlooks Torquay, but particularly on approaching Shiphay and Chapel-hill—on any part of which I would plant my standard during the inclement season.

The expenses of housekeeping and living in general at this place are moderate, and were I to judge from the charges made at my hotel, I should say cheaper than at Clifton, considerably more so than at Bath, and somewhat cheaper even than at Exeter. A family of a patient of mine, with four daughters, and suitable attendants, resided here for upwards of a year, or two winter seasons, and found their bills to amount to something like a quarter less than they would have been in London. A dinner for 3s. 6d., tea for 1s. 9d., and a bed-room for 2s., are charges not to be grumbled at in a fashionable watering-place ; and such were those at the Royal Hotel in my case.

The knowledge of something like this fact has probably induced persons of all classes, provided they are in good circumstances, to come to Torquay in the winter for the benefit of their health ; for certainly, although Torquay is at that season full of strangers, it is by no means full of people of condition. This was proved by the attempt made, in November 1838, by one of the booksellers, to publish a list of visiters, which attempt, however, did not and could not succeed, for there are not the elements for such a fashionable luxury. The place is too limited in its number of new visiters; and there is scarcely ever any fluctuation among them, as is the case at summer watering-places or spas. Nay, it is the very nature of the place to have, as it were, a permanent residentiary set of invalids, who hurry thither on the coming on of winter, distribute themselves in all the houses and lodgings that can possibly be had, and there remain stationary and ensconced until the warm sun of June again permits them to run up to the metropolis, or return to their country-houses.

The analysis of the attempted list (No. 1.) given me by a good-humoured gentleman from Wales, who recognised me on the " Fryingpan-walk," as having consulted me in town, and gave me an account of the company that generally congregate in Torquay, was rather amusing. He reckoned by his fingers the number of visiters, whom he had divided by classes; but I preserve no other recollection of his enumeration, than that there were eighty-two spinsters, nineteen medicals, twelve divines, and only two attorneys.

Now, all these, and many others besides, must desire to find some occupation or amusement to kill time with, in which I apprehend Torquay does not shine conspicuously. Still there are the subscription libraries, one on each of the three sides around the basin; there are fine shops to visit, particularly those on the strand; and finally there are your assemblies and balls at stated periods during the season, for which purpose the Royal Hotel possesses a ball-room of sufficient size, having an orchestra at its upper end, and its walls painted Etruscan fashion, with a lofty coved ceiling, from which hang three handsome chandeliers. I did not inquire whether the rival house or Header's Hotel, so immediately close to the Royal, could also boast of such a thing as a ball-room. Most likely it does; but the political mania being carried so far here as to impart even to the hotels a distinct political character, I did not choose to hazard a collision by an inquiry.

Before, however, I have done speaking of the Royal Hotel, I must express, as I did to its master at the time, my surprise that in the coffee-room (and one of small dimensions too) of a house of entertainment at which patients with loaded, congested, or irritable lungs, are likely to alight as a first *pied-à-terre*, the injudicious absurdity of introducing large argand burners of gaslight should have been committed, and having been committed, should not have been remonstrated against by the professional people in the place. Patients, such as I have alluded to, who are likely to enter this apartment on their arrival, are not, of course, benefited by the inhalation of so vitiated an atmosphere. I saw two of those who had arrived at the same time with myself, sorely afflicted in health, the one fainting after a sudden excess of cough on entering the room in question, and the other so affected in the head by the emanations of the unburned portion of the gas, that he must have fallen from sudden dizziness, had he not left the room immediately. The atmosphere was indeed so oppressive at the time in the coffee-room, that it was agreed on the part of the three or four persons who remained, and on my motion, to have the gaslights extinguished, and candles introduced instead.

The admission of gaslight into dwelling-rooms is one of the banes of modern improvement, or I would rather say, innovation, for improvement it is none; and I lament to say, it is one which has become very general in all the coffee-rooms of the South and West of England, where the gas is none of the purest, for the coarser sort of coals is employed to obtain it. Such a practice is a positive source of annoyance; and with some delicate chests, or ticklish heads, it inflicts downright injury.

We have now inquired into every particular concerning

the *matériel* of these celebrated head-quarters for consumptive people. Let us now turn our researches into the more essential requisite they are presumed to possess—an atmosphere whose genial and beneficial influence is to cure consumption, or at all events to prolong the existence of its victims.

The late Doctor de Barry contended most strenuously that the average temperature of Torquay was more favourable than that of Exeter, Bristol, London, Edmonton, Sheffield, Farnham, and Cheltenham. It exceeded that of London—for example—in January, 1838, by a mean of 9 degrees, the observations being taken respectively at Somerset House and Hyde Park ; and he moreover supplies us, along with his published tables giving the temperature of the severe months of January and February 1838, from which the preceding results are deduced,—a list of the averages of temperature in Torquay during the months of January, February, and March for the years 1828 to 1838 inclusive, which certainly appears gratifying, such averages being 40.3 in the first of those months, 43.4 in the second, and 45.6 in the third. But we have already seen that the mean temperature at Clifton and Bath was higher during those months and years, having extended from 44 even to 49, and therefore the contrast between Torquay and those places with which, in truth, it ought to be compared, is not in favour of the latter.

I think I have now said enough in point of temperature, as deduced from the most recent observations ; and it would be useless to reproduce, in this place, for the hundredth time, the evidence to be found in many other works upon the same subject. Those who wish to have more extended data, may refer to those works, particularly to " Blewitt's Panorama of Torquay," and to a very able paper of Doctor Coldstream, in the " Edinburgh Medical and Surgical Journal," No. 117.

There is one point, however, concerning this subject to which I must not omit to allude, ere I dismiss it altogether. A great stress has been laid by all writers on climate, on what has been called the *mean* temperature of a place, as a criterion of its mildness. All that has been said regarding Torquay, for instance, in that respect, is founded on no other evidence; and in giving or reasoning upon the temperature of Clifton and Bath, I have myself followed the common example of all writers. But such a mode is a fallacious one, and must mislead the invalid, who looking to it, determines on placing himself, in case of need, within the influence of such an average. Let us take an example. By looking over Doctor de Barry's short table of the mean temperature in January, February, and March, for a period of six years, the invalid finds that in 1833, the mean heat of January had been 41.8 degrees. "Well," says the invalid, "that is just the thing for me." And in 1838 he proceeds to Torquay from the very beginning of the year, in expectation of finding something like the same heat. When he has remained there the whole of January, he ascertains that the mean temperature through that month has fallen short by six degrees of the desirable one. But that is not all, for he will have gone through many cold days which he ought never to have been exposed to ; for in that same month and year there had been not fewer than twelve days when the thermometer in the morning was below *freezing*, and two other days when it was at the freezing point. What becomes then of the advantage of a favourable *average* calculated upon the whole number of days of the month, as far as the lungs of an invalid are concerned, if on those dreadful twelve days (nearly the half of the month), the thermometer, below 32 degrees, tells him that he is, in reality, in a cold and not a temperate climate ? Will the hotter temperature of from 40 to 45 degrees, which occurred on eleven other days of the same month, make amends for the very cold ones? *Pas du tout*, but much the contrary ; for this alternation of hot and cold days, with a difference of ten or twelve degrees from one to the other, is the very bane of an English climate, and the bane which, more or less, appertains also to local climates in England, much to the detriment of the poor invalids.

But there is the rain besides, and the moisture after it; and the incessant occurrence of the former, and the nearly permanent existence of the latter, which influence and modify the degree of temperature and its effect on the patients, and give a character to a place ; and on this all-important subject Doctor de Barry's tables are perfectly silent. My readers know, almost proverbially, that it rains *a very great deal* in Devonshire, and I must refer them to the published Meteorological Tables, if they desire to know precisely how many inches of rain fall in Torquay. Certainly not less than in other parts of the coast of that country.

The important part after all, in a work like the present, which does not affect to be a purely medical treatise, is to ascertain practically, what benefit consumptive patients, who are the principal people sent thither, derive from a sojourn in Torquay. For this purpose I shall avail myself of the information I culled, by permission, from those invaluable registers of mortality, which are now so ably kept, and collated, and worked upon, at the Registrar General's Office in Somerset House, and from which it is impossible to calculate how many beneficial results to mankind may henceforth arise. I shall simply, in the present instance, lay the facts before my readers, and limit myself for that purpose to the year in which I visited Torquay, and to the year preceding, leaving them to draw their own conclusions.

In the course of the first quarter of the year, 1839, there had occurred thirteen deaths from consumption in the parish of Tor-Moham, and the chapelry of Torquay, having together at the time an estimated population of 5000 inhabitants, calculated upon the known one of 1831, which amounted to 3582.

In the second quarter, there were again thirteen deaths

from consumption, six in the third, and lastly, ten in the
fourth quarter; makng a total of FORTY-TWO cases of consumption.   Among these are not reckoned either those deaths
which are reported by the registrar as resulting from " diseases of the lungs," or those which follow many other affections of those organs, independently of " consumption."

The number of deaths from the same malady, in the
corresponding first, second, and third quarters of 1838, had
been ten, nine, six,—total twenty-five; and as the volume of
register of the fourth quarter of that year was not easily accessible, I substituted the number of deaths that had occurred in
the fourth quarter of the preceding year (1837), amounting to
nine, which makes a second general total for four quarters,
THIRTY-FOUR, and a grand total for the eight quarters, of
seventy-six deaths from consumption, in so small a community, a mere village, in fact, as Torquay.   Of these, twenty-
five had been females, and fifty-one male patients. The oldest
was sixty-seven years of age, a female, and the youngest ten
years of age, a male.   There had been besides, among the
general total, three infants of the respective ages of eight,
thirteen, and thirty-three months old, two of them males and
one a female.   In general, the patients were of young age;
and if the six among them, aged sixty years and above, and
the three infants just mentioned, be left out of the account,
the average age of the rest who died of consumption will be
found to have been only twenty-nine and a half years; showing, at all events, that the climate of Torquay had not much
served the purpose of *prolonging* life in cases of that disease.

Neither will it seem to have ostensibly *cured* many cases of
consumption, if we consider of what elements the total number
of seventy-six deaths consisted, as I ascertained very readily by
inspecting the proper column in the register; It appeared
therein, that during the eight quarters in question, forty-four
strangers, all persons of condition, who had come to Torquay
from all parts of England, and even from Calcutta, with the

expectation of being cured, had all died instead; while in thirty-one permanent dwellers, or natives of the place, all belonging to the industrious classes, in whom consumption had first developed itself there, that fatal disease had run its wonted, awful, and unrestrained course in spite of the genial climate of Torquay.

This frequent tolling of the funeral bell—as every one of the forty-four patients of condition arrived at Torquay had died principally during the two first quarters of the year—this witnessing of obsequies once in nine days for a period of seven hundred and thirty days—must have been awful and thrilling to the rest, who were trembling on the verge of their grave with symptoms of the same devouring malady, consumption; and this is another of the serious disadvantages belonging to medical sanctuaries, as these " Montpelliers" have been called, in which people, stricken with a fatal disorder, are incited to take shelter and congregate, with, alas! too often delusive expectations.

I made the same remark to a gentleman, who seemed a shrewd and clear-headed man, in spite of his uncouth and farmer-like appearance, and who had been exceedingly civil in assisting me in my inquiries; but he parried this observation levelled at the salubriousness of his favourite and long-adopted place of residence, by declaring that, in that year, there had not been seen more than two or three funerals besides that of poor De Barry. The registrar-general, however, tells a different story; for in the very preceding winter of that same year, as will have been seen, twenty-six burials from consumption had been witnessed in Torquay, the half of which were of people of condition; and in the very quarter we were in at the time of the conversation, not fewer than ten more such funerals had taken place. One never can get an inhabitant of an unhealthy place to acknowledge the damning fact. Torquay, however, is not such a place; but neither is it all that has been said of it in an opposite character.

CHAPTER V.

DAWLISH—WEYMOUTH.

NOTTINGTON AND RADIPOLE SPAS.

Torquay not a sea-bathing place—The Tor-Abbey Sands and others in Torbay—Babicombe Bay—Pleasant Excursions—Darlington House —Ugbrooke, the Seat of the Cliffords—The Ness—View of Teignmouth from it—Inconvenience of Lodging-houses near the Shore— Advantages of those placed on the Hill—Their Favourable Aspect— Cliffden House—Rowdens—Desirable Residence for a Rich Invalid —The Grounds—Perpetual Spring—Charming Views—The Conservatory—Choice Plants and Grapes—A Bijou for a Rich Consumptive—Other Villas—Dawlish—Former and Present State—Accommodation—Sea-bathing — Rides, Walks, and Prospects—Climate— —Temperature highly Favourable compared with that of Torquay —Important Observations—Cheering Conclusions—The Sea Coast to Weymouth—The Upper or Down Track to Dorchester—Description—Axminster and Bridport—Descent into and First View of Weymouth — Magnificent Prospect—The Nottington Spa — The Radipole Spa—Their Chemical Nature—Reflections—Weymouth the most Cheerful Sea-bathing Place for Summer Pleasure—The Esplanade—The Sands—Sea-bathing and Warm Baths—Lodgings and Boarding Houses—The Pier—Pleasure Boats—Interesting Neighbourhood — Commins's Library and Reading-rooms—Preferable Quarters.

I must now entreat those readers who have hitherto accompanied me through my inland tour, to follow me in the somewhat rapid excursion I propose making along the southern coast eastwards, on our way home, for the purpose of casting a glance—for it must be but a glance—at such of the sea-bathing places as are most in vogue, or ought to be so. In doing this, we shall bear in mind that the only useful object of such an excursion must be, the ascertaining, first, where the best sea-bathing is to be obtained on the south coast; and secondly, which of the sea-bathing places worthy of special mention, offer the best resources of climate and situation for invalids or people in delicate health.

It will not be expected that in going through this concluding part of my task, I shall enter every nook, harbour, or inlet, or even visit all the principal towns on the coast. Neither is it necessary that I should assign reasons for selecting certain places, and omitting the rest. No doubt sea-bathing is to be found of some sort or other at all of them; and many of the places which I have not mentioned, may, in the estimation of other people, be considered as equally deserving of commemoration. My object, however, was not to publish a general survey of the coast, but to throw together, in the most convenient and useful garb I could give to it, such information as my personal visits and inquiry at the leading marine resorts for either summer or winter, enabled me to collect.

Torquay, as will have been seen, offers no resources in the way of sea-bathing. Near it the coast is rugged, and broken masses of red sandstone gird the shore. Below Cholston, a little place a short distance out of the harbour to the westward, there are the *Tor-Abbey sands;* and for such of the visiters at Torquay as can extend their excursions as far as Paington, two miles south, the *Preston* and *Polsham* sands may afford some chance of sea-bathing. But on the whole, Torquay, as I before stated, is not a place for the latter object; the less so, indeed, as it happens to be a winter rather than a summer residence.

During the hot months, those who wish to enjoy real sea residence away from the nasty effluvia of back water and receding tides, cross the great Headland, on which stand the Warberry and Beacon Hills before mentioned, and either by the ascending road towards Tor-Moham, leaving Ellicombe House at the foot of Warberry Hill on the right, and so on to St. Mary's Church; or by the more scabrous, yet more enlivening and gay route round the sea margin of the said Headland, reach Babicombe, or Babbacombe Bay. A more enchanting or beautiful, and I might call it romantic sea-inlet, is not to be found on the coast. There are some neat little houses, two or three of them near the sands, and others dotting the wooded slopes around; and the sea-bathing is tolerable.

This is not the only agreeable excursion in which an invalid may indulge in the neighbourhood of Torquay; for if he will proceed inland, he will find no lack of objects of curiosity, or a deficiency of pleasant drives. The roads in Devonshire were not long since proverbially dismal and difficult; but of late years much has been done in the way of improving them, especially in the vicinity of important places; and of that number are those leading in and out of Torquay. This improvement in the lines of communication has brought many tempting objects within the reach of the Torquay visiter, who will now hardly hesitate to extend his drive as far as *Darlington House*, for example, a short way on this side of Totness, there to inspect some of the largest and most antique apartments in the county; or to *Ugbrooke*, in an opposite direction, a little distance from Chudleigh, the charming seat of the Cliffords, in whose varied and delightful grounds the vestiges of a Roman encampment are easily discernable.

On bidding adieu to Torquay, I took the lower or sea-road, which towers over and along the rugged red sandstone coast, on my return to Teignmouth,—the view of which, by the bye, from Shaldon on this side of the river, is exceedingly striking, and displays to advantage many of the pretty villas and cottages *ornées* that are scattered on its acclivities.

To one standing under the lofty aspiring Ness, itself a sublime object, placed like a giant warder at the mouth of the
Teign,—East Teignmouth appears to expand northwards on
the opposite bank as far as the cliffs, under the shelter of which
sauntering groups seem to be enjoying the roaring of the incoming waves.   Behind the town and above it rises a hill,
dotted with many excellent-looking houses, some of which appeared to me to be well calculated for the residence of persons
of delicate chests, being protected by the higher chain of the
little Haldon Hills from the N. and N.W. cold winds;
and, at the same time, exposed to the full rays of the southern sun.

I next crossed over the Teign, along the celebrated bridge,
which, though then under repair, admitted yet of the transit
of an inquisitive foot passenger *par faveur ;* and I halted at
the hotel facing the sea.

To the capabilities of Teignmouth as a residence for
invalids during the inclement season (setting aside its indifferent qualifications as a sea-bathing place, of which we have

already spoken), I paid, at this my second visit, a little more attention. Much as one may approve of some of the lodging-houses and other dwellings in this place, particularly the superior and more modern ones to be found nearest the sea at East Teignmouth, there are objections against them, as far as patients of delicate lungs are concerned, which would induce me to recommend in preference houses on a higher situation. It is not pleasant, in the first place, to have the effluvia of the mud after a receded tide, constantly under your nostrils; nor is it always suitable to delicate nerves to be too close to the loud roaring of the lashing waves,—still less to be too near to their spray. Lastly, a direct exposure to the east wind is more disadvantageous when the patient lives near the margin of a river, than when on a hill and a dry soil. All these objections are obviated by selecting a residence either to the right or to the left of the very steep road which leads from Teignmouth to Dawlish, and which crosses the general hill before alluded to, forming the background to the former town, when viewed from the opposite bank of the river. Some of these houses I sallied forth to inspect, by walking leisurely up the hill; but, unfortunately, few are ever to be got when most wanted for invalids. First on the right, on going out of Teignmouth, is Cliffden House, a very pretty place, and one which seems to be kept in the highest order. This house is permanently occupied by its proprietor. Next is Rowdens, which, happening to be vacant at the time (though it was very soon afterwards occupied by a retired physician of my acquaintance, who has to lament the occasion of his seeking sheltered places of this kind for a part of his family), I proceeded to examine, looking at both the house and grounds in detail.

The first great feature that struck me upon entering the ground, at that period of the year at which we then were (the 11th of November), was their general gay appearance, and the aspect of spring around me, due to the profusion of ever-

greens, many of them choice, and the growth of warmer climates, planted and grouped in all directions. Indeed, these
had been suffered to luxuriate in an almost untrimmed and
unrestrained progression, so as nearly to block up parts of
the grounds that ought to be open—a strong evidence this
of the mildness of the climate, as well as of the richness of
the soil. This evidence was also strongly marked in the many
beautiful plants displayed in the long conservatory adjoining
the front of the house, most of the glazed windows of which
were thrown open to admit the genial air that even then was
breathing, and exhibited to view, pendant from their trellised
fastenings, such abundant crops of delicious grapes, as
might entice a delicate invalid to undergo the " *cure des
raisins.*"

The house itself is in the form of a one-story cottage
orné, with seven windows in front on the first, and four only,
but larger ones, on the ground floor, one of which serves as
the entrance into a hall that divides the dining from the
drawing room, over which are the sleeping apartments and
their accessories,—all fronting the south and south-western
quarters. The view from the boudoir windows is a perfect
picture. Stretching above the tops of the dense plantations
that spread from the dwelling down the declivity of the hill,
as far as the top of the cliff that looks over the sea, and among
which peeps out the steeple of East Teignmouth Church,—
the eye instantly catches the most distant sea-point, (the one
which marks the entrance into Torbay), and between it and
Teignmouth, lying immediately below, traces the rocky shore,
fringed with the indentures of Braddy's Cove and Babicombe
Bay, and, coming nearer, of Watcombe and Minicombe,
until it rests upon the great NESS, and the neat hamlet of
Shaldon adjoining. If from the latter point a slight turn of
the head to the right be made, then the up-river reach of the
Teign appears open to view to a considerable distance;
while, by reversing the direction of the head, the eye of the

beholder will hover over the Channel sea, studded with the fishermen's slender barks near at hand; and farther on the horizon, with the whitened top-gallant sails of more pretending vessels.

Much taste has been displayed in the original distribution and arrangement of the pleasure grounds at Rowdens, particularly in carrying through the continuous belt of plantations (which are evergreen) winding paths and extended walks, many of them between edges of flowers. The perfectly round walled garden, as part of the grounds, is itself a curiosity, on account of the two sloping banks of which it is composed converging at the bottom, and forming a most sheltered kitchen-garden, plentifully supplied with water by small pipes, which make the entire circuit of the walls. Indeed, of water, and that of a very excellent quality, there appears to be great abundance; for not only is this ground supplied with springs, but there are also not fewer than three wells in it. The little domain is of an extent of from thirty-five to forty acres; and with the presence and superintending eye of a master having taste, judgment, and a little money, might be made a most enviable residence for some of your wealthy invalids, anxious to prolong a life threatened by a destructive disease, and ever in jeopardy, unless spent in a spot like this, where sea and land, pure air, absence of effluvia, a warm aspect in front, and the back and flank protected by dense plantations, all unite in resisting the inroads of the enemy, consumption.

Many other prettily situated and some very showy residences I espied in my peregrinations, and took down the bearings of a few of them; Cambrian cottage, for instance, Grove house, West and East Cliff's cottages, and the residence of Lord Exmouth,—located in various directions. But although I cannot say, *ex uno disce*, after having described Rowdens; neither need I take up more space in giving a more particular account of other dwellings, when the latter residence can be referred to as a specimen of what can be procured in the way of superior house accommodation in the immediate vicinity of Teignmouth.

In former days Teignmouth had a powerful rival in

DAWLISH,

which lies but two and a half miles distant, northwards, from the last-mentioned house. Originally a mere village of fishermen's huts, in a narrow valley, with a small but never-failing stream, that runs nearly west and east, Dawlish has for the last forty years grown into a sea-bathing place *à prétension*, and extended itself from the sea inland. A row of neat-looking houses, many of them with a good aspect, and facing the south, run up the creek, near the little bridge over the narrow stream. On its left bank, which is at some feet elevation, another row of houses,—and among them a few that are let as lodgings, sheltered from the N.E. and E.—displays its modest front; while across the little stream where, the road ascends on its way to Teignmouth, I observed a third and very inviting range of buildings on the right. These have a fine sea view, with a precipitous cliff of red sandstone at their feet, from which an enormous detached mass stands upright, mocking the easterly gales.

The various residences just alluded to, all more or less desirable for invalids requiring a milder atmosphere in winter, have the advantage over those at West Teignmouth, and others on the Newton-road there, of not being like them exposed to the effluvia of a tidal river ; and the temporary dwellers in these well-situated buildings have, moreover, the gratification of a superior sea-beach, extending from north to south about a mile and a half, which is always firm and safe for riding and walking, with fine smooth sand, when a southerly wind prevails—the only one during which an invalid has any business with the sea-beach. The natural inclination of the latter is at an angle of only five degrees, so that the bathing is perfectly safe.

The rides and walks near to and about Dawlish are much varied. Shady lanes in sheltered valleys, during boisterous weather ; and fine open roads and tracts over the extensive heathy commons of Haldon and Holcombe Down, when the air is still and genial,—afford at all times recreation and motives for wholesome exercise. From these heights, magnificent and extensive views of the districts watered by the Teign and the Exe, and of the far distant Dartmouth hills, are enjoyed at every step in clear weather. The roads, too, have been greatly improved, and every convenience of frequent communication established between Dartmouth and Exeter, taking in all intermediate places of importance.

Yet with all these advantages, Dawlish, since the peace, has made no progress. While Torquay, before nearly unknown, has since that period kept advancing, and taken at length the lead, becoming a sort of winter Brighton, and eclipsing all other Devonshire watering-places,—Dawlish has nearly stood still, having few new lodging-houses, and being now distinguished only by its tranquillity, its fine air, and

fine coast, and its perfect exemption from the effluvia insepa-
rable from harbours and estuaries.

Thermometrical observations, as accurately made as those
of Dr. De Barry at Torquay, which have been kindly communicated to me by a very intelligent patient of mine, long
resident near the sea-shore, and at an arrow-shot from Dawlish, give a more favourable view of the prevailing warmth of
the air during the same months and years at the latter than
at the former place. The observations are made only with
reference to the range of winter temperature, with a six's index
thermometer placed in a north-eastern aspect, about thirty
feet above the level of the sea, and thirty yards from the high-
water mark ; and they show the greatest warmth by day, and
the greatest cold by night. For the former, the thermometer
was invariably observed at 2 P.M., assumed to be the warmest
hour of the day, and for the latter the index was consulted.
The observations extend over a period of five years, from
1835 to 1839, both inclusive, and for the five cold months of
the year, January, February, March, November and December ; the mean temperature of each of which months (taking all
the years together) has been at 43°, 45°, 45°, 49°, and
45° by day ; and 35°, 36°, 37°, 41°, and 38° by night. Now
the mean temperature of three similar months, January, February, and March, taken for five years (namely 1830-1-2-3,
and 8) at Torquay, according to Dr. De Barry's tables, have
been at 39°, 43°, 45°, showing an inferiority of temperature
as compared to Dawlish, in two out of the three worst months
of the year. If, therefore, we assume the comparative table
of relative geographical mean temperature for the same three
months quoted by Dr. De Barry from another work on climate, to be accurate, Dawlish will find its proper place between Pisa and Torquay. But the genial state of the atmosphere at Dawlish during the five years before alluded to,
appears even more conspicuous when we look at the highest

degree which the temperature reached in the day time and the lowest marked at night, in every one of those years, and in the course of January, February, March, November, and December ; for we find that in such circumstances the thermometer stood respectively as follows :

	January. deg. deg.	February. deg. deg.	March. deg. deg.	November. deg. deg.	December. deg. deg.
1835.—	H. 55 L. 39	H. 56 L. 39	H. 58 L. 39	H. 56 L. 42	H. 52 L. 35
1836.—	H. 50 L. 38	H. 50 L. 34	H. 54 L. 38	H. 58 L. 42	H. 58 L. 38
1837.—	H. 50 L. 35	H. 54 L. 39	H. 50 L. 32	H. 57 L. 46	H. 56 L. 41
1838.—	H. 52 L. 29	H. 46 L. 31	H. 58 L. 38	H. 56 L. 39	H. 58 L. 38
1839.—	H. 56 L. 35	H. 54 L. 38	H. 52 L. 38	H. 56 L. 41	H. 59 L. 39

This table speaks eloquently for itself, and there I shall leave the once fashionable and pretty hamlet of Dawlish.

Having already seen Exmouth, and the remainder of the coast from thence to Bridport offering no excuse but what a geologist alone could plead, not a writer on Spas, for loitering on his way to the next most noted sea-bathing places —I preferred returning to Exeter, and thence proceeding over the hilly tract that unites Devonshire to Dorsetshire, as far as Weymouth, my next place of destination. I feared lest by taking the lower road, or that nearest to the sea, I should be tempted by the captivating geological descriptions of the coast from Sidmouth to Lyme Regis, given by M. De La Beche and Professor Buckland, to extend my visit to that striking portion of the southern coast of England, which had just then become even more interesting than ever in consequence of a great recent slip or landfall.

Devonshire, to judge by the extensive nursery-grounds one sees near its capital, may be said to be the garden of the south. I had already seen, on my way to Dawlish from Exeter, one of the most extensive establishments of that sort in England, and now in quitting the same city, in the direction of Honiton, another nursery-gound, nearly as vast, caught my attention. The climate of Devon is favourable to floriculture, and the taste of the people lies much in that way. They have here many plants worth forty or fifty pounds each, raised from seeds.

As far as Honiton, our course lay through a fertile but tame country, with a few hillocks and extensive pasture-lands. But to a lover of the wild and amphitheatric—the rich by the side of the barren — the well-cultivated vale surrounded by ranges of hills capped with wood—to those who love to wander over vast and desolate heaths covered with furze, with here and there some parts of the denuded surface, to show portions of the constituent elements of the great oolitic formation;—to all these the drive from Honiton to within a mile of Axminster, on the verge of Dorsetshire, will afford in the summer a fine scope for admiration. At one particular spot of this tract, four miles short of Axminster, a peep of the sea is caught on the right, through the deep gap which forms the valley of the Axe, with its noted quarries of blue and white lias, and the little bay of Axmouth. Axminster itself stands on an eminence, in the centre of this great oolitic waste.

Neither the exit out of Devon, nor the entrance into Dorsetshire, is very inviting. A hundred hills, rising and dipping in all ways, and with every fantastic shape, over the level of the barren downs, (for many of the latter are so still), form the base of the country for miles around and as far as the eye can stretch. At the wretched cottage, thatched and decaying, called *Penn Inn*, where the two counties divide, the landscape is one of desolation ; and the chalk hills, now capping the great oolitic beds, appear tossed about in every direction. Through the summit of one of these a tunnel has been pierced, to break the steep ascent which crosses the last range of cretaceous hills towards Charmouth, and on the top of one of which, that comfortable-looking hamlet appears, with its bay before and below it.

Here we were assailed with hawkers of fossilized *ammonites* and *echinites* and *pentacrinites*, and many other stony-*ites*, all imbedded in marl or lias-slate, which are offered to the inners and the outers of every public or private vehicle that halts to change horses at Charmouth, as oranges are tendered to the stagers who start from Hatchett's or the Gloucester. The trade is a thriving one, and as organic remains are abundant in the lias formation at Lyme and its vicinity, particularly of the *Saurian* animals, it will never fail.

At Bridport, six miles further, we entered the south-east range of chalk hills, called the " South Downs," having their highest summit on our right, where they throw up a sort of escarpment that screen the sea-view from us, and form the bold coast so remarkable in these seas for its height and abruptness. Upon the very crest of all these lofty cretaceous deposits, as far nearly as Black Down, rising 817 feet above the sea, has the road, with provoking pertinacity, been made to pass, instead of taking the level valleys on either side of it. A considerable extent of these Downs, as far as my eye could survey, appeared to have been brought into a state of pasture, or partial cultivation ; but the soil, which is a thin loam over a rubbly chalk mixed with stones, is little calculated for the latter purpose, and consequently the agriculturist has not yet imparted the appearance of wealth to the miserable-looking thatched cottages, many of them tumbling to pieces, which one meets with huddled together, at great intervening distances, as villages or hamlets. Not a vestige of a tree is to be seen, except in two or three places, where within the last six or seven years an attempt has been made, with slow success, at raising a fir plantation. I doubt whether there be anywhere else in England so forlorn a stage as the one from Bridport to Dorchester ; and *en resumé*, I may say that for a pastoral and agricultural district, the whole of the line of country we passed through in Dorsetshire is but meagre and inferior; though in many parts it may be deemed picturesque during fine weather. The two sixteen-mile stages from Axminster to Bridport, and from thence through the chalk hills to Dorchester, are heavy, fatiguing, and desolate, and by no means a good specimen of England.

The descent from the last-mentioned neat and clean country town to the coast, and down to Weymouth, repays for all the fatigue and monotony of the preceding journey. As you turn your face directly south, and having passed that remarkable mound on which stands the Roman encampment, called *Maiden Castle*, gain the verge of the South Downs,—following the mail-road, and running down the southern declivity, with the pretty village of Upway on your right,—a most striking view of Weymouth, with Portland, the West Bay, and Wyke Tower, suddenly bursts upon you. But a public vehicle is inexorable, and you may not halt to enjoy it; on the contrary, the universal desire of the travellers is to *arrive*, and the team is urged on its downward course, regardless of any wish I might have entertained of halting to examine two Spas we actually passed through—

NOTTINGTON AND RADIPOLE,

until we stopped at the Golden Lion in the market-place, from whence I immediately transferred myself to the Royal Hotel in Gloucester-row, facing the sea.

The existence neither of Radipole nor of Nottington Spas had ever come to my notice, before or during my short exploring *séjour* at Weymouth. Having seen no one while there, nor sought even for a guide-book which would have instructed me on the subject, I left Weymouth without seeing either of those mineral springs. It was only after my return to London from my long and fatiguing tour of upwards of three thousand miles, which had lasted nearly three months, and had pretty well tired me of all Spas, that I received from persons directly interested in those springs, a printed account of them, and of the analyses of their water. Had i

been a reader of the " Philosophical Magazine," I might have
become acquainted with the nature of those mineral waters
from the accounts given of them in that periodical for 1833,
by the respected author, Richard Phillips. Such was not,
however, the case; and I am only now aware that both
Nottington Spa, which has been the longest known, and
Radipole Spa, which is of recent discovery, and is not very
remote from the former spring, are both slightly saline mineral waters, with sulphureted hydrogen gas.

Why the Nottington water should bear the emphatic title
of " the only pure sulphureted water discovered in England,"
and on whose authority such a title has been conferred upon
it, I know not. But I strongly suspect that the publication
to the world of so many never-before-heard-of sulphur
springs among the Northern Spas of my first volume, and
their analyses, will have shown that neither *per se*, nor on
comparison with others, can the Nottington water maintain its claim to such an exclusive appellation. What,
indeed, is there in that water according to Phillips's analysis? Why, in a wine-pint of it we find a total of four
grains and a little more than half a grain of solid materials,
besides one and a quarter cubic inch of sulphureted hydrogen
gas. If it be intended to state that, because the mineral ingredients are in so small a quantity, the water is the purest
of any in England, having sulphureted hydrogen at the same
time,—I answer, Nay. Look at Guisborough: the solid ingredients in that Spa amount to not quite three and a half
grains, besides its sulphureted gas, and it is therefore purer
than the Nottington Spa. If, on the other hand, the title
assumed by the Nottington Spa water is revindicated, on
account of the happy mixture of the particular ingredients
with sulphureted hydrogen, then an inspection of the analytical tables which accompany these volumes will be sufficient
to prove the unsoundness of such a pretension.

With respect to the more recently discovered sulphureted

water at Radipole, likewise analyzed by Mr. Phillips, there, the sulphureted hydrogen gas is less, but the solid minera_lizing ingredients are more than double in quantity. *Du reste*, the two waters are much alike, containing the same class of ingredients, except that the Radipole water has one grain of Epsom salts in each pint of water, which the other spring has not; and four times as much common salt as the other spring, and no iron,—which the Nottington Spa has, to the extent of the eight-thousandth part of a grain!

The wonderful cures performed by these waters, either drank or used as baths (always recollecting that at 98° of heat, three-quarters of a cubic inch of sulphureted hydrogen gas will have vanished out of the boiler before the patient gets into the water), are recorded upon the authority of so many respectable names amongst the profession, a list of which is printed, that it does not become me, who have had no experience whatever of the water, to doubt their assertion.

And now that I have reached

and in safety, and have adverted, *en passant*, to two more Spas than I had reckoned upon, what shall I say of Weymouth itself as a bathing-place? Why, that had I friends in perfect health, desirous of spending a couple of months during the summer by the sea-side on the south coast, and at the same time indifferent as to the particular spot they inhabited for that object, I would, on their asking my advice, tell them by all means to spend them at Weymouth. But I should not say so to any patient, labouring no matter under what disease; for the situation of Weymouth is not fit for *patients*. The mere fact of the town turning its back to the west, and of its right flank being screened from the south by the lofty headlands of Portland Isle, is quite sufficient with me to settle that question. For a mere blow of pure sea-air, such as one may

get on a quarter-deck, I know of no better place for an idler
in these parts than Weymouth; for he has only to lounge
backwards and forwards along the Esplanade, one of
the finest marine promenades I have seen in England, and
his object will be accomplished. If, indeed, the blowing
gales should be from the eastern quarter, he may get more of
sea-air than he may like, and probably be overwhelmed. I
happened to be travelling upon the Southampton Railway, as
far as Andover, one day, in company with a gentleman who
had been two years resident in Weymouth, and who praised
much its pure and invigorating air, and the cheerful ensemble
of the place; " but," said he, " my rheumatism won't stand
any longer the dreadful east winds, and my poor daughters
cough worse than ever since we settled there, and so we are
about to leave it at the suggestion of Sir ——, whom I had
just been to town to consult." Seriously speaking, this facing
of the east is a sad drawback to the place; but in the summer
that signifies less.

The sea-bathing is perfect at Weymouth, and the accommodation of about twenty or thirty machines always
ready near the centre of the Esplanade, kept in perfect
order, serve much to facilitate that operation. The sands
over which the bathers have to walk are well known, as

being of the finest description, equal to those of Scarborough in the east, and Blackpool in the west, and superior to any other in the south. The declivity of the shore is almost imperceptible, and totally free from those obstructions which are noticed on many parts of the southern coast; so that the most timid lady may indulge in the great luxury of open sea-bathing, with the additional comfort of perfect security, and of sea-water pure, clean, and transparent; in fact, genuine, unpolluted sea-water; which is more than can be said of some other pretending watering-places by the sea in this country. Neat and commodious warm salt-water baths also will be found on the South Parade, opposite the Harbour.

Beside the magnificent promenade just mentioned, nearly a mile long and about thirty feet in width, on one side of which ranges an uninterrupted series of houses of various sizes and styles of architecture, while below it the sands extend in the form of a semicircle of more than two miles,—Weymouth offers an advantage to the summer bather, which is not common at the most celebrated sea-bathing-places on the south coast, and that is, the facility of entering a yacht or pleasure-boat from the quay, without any danger, owing to the sheltered position of the pier and harbour. Hence the enjoyment of this species of sea-side amusement is much the order of the day at Weymouth.

A more interesting district to reside in than that which immediately surrounds the place, is hardly to be met with in the south-west of England, whether in point of its geology, rural scenery, fine prospects, extensive view, antiquities, or grand and often palatial residences of the noble and the wealthy. A visiter spending his summer at Weymouth need not complain that time hangs heavy on his hand, for he may find full and instructive occupation for every day of the period, without going over the same ground twice, if he has but energy, taste, and inclination, and should happen to enjoy that vigour and elasticity which the *séjour* in any of the many comfortable lodging-houses fronting the bay will not be long in imparting to him.

Of the latter accommodations few watering-places possess more, for the size of the town, than Weymouth, or better ones. It is scarcely possible to point out some as being preferable to others, without doing injustice to the rest. Mrs. Clarke's Boarding-house is in great vogue : not merely because it is delightfully and conveniently situated, as well as roomy and commodious within, but because many people will always be found who prefer a gregarious to a solitary life. But, as with many people the double enjoyment of having in the house a source of intellectual amusement, and out of the house the finest prospect of the beauties peculiar to the place, would be always a temptation, I should advise them to choose most unquestionably, and *par préférence*, Commins' furnished apartments, delightfully situated on the Esplanade, having a reading-room and library connected with them, to which admission is obtained by a moderate subscription, and where one finds everything one desires in the way of periodicals and modern works ;—no mean recommendation to a lodging at Weymouth.

CHAPTER X.

BOURNEMOUTH.

I LOOK upon Bournemouth, and its yet unformed colony, as a perfect discovery among the sea-nooks one longs to have for a real invalid, and as the realization of a *desideratum* we vainly thought to have found elsewhere on the south coast of England. This might seem, at first view, an exaggerated and sweeping opinion, had it been uttered by one less accustomed to judge of localities, climate, and topical peculiarities, than the author of these pages can be, after having visited *all the resorts* of invalids, abroad and in England. But in the present case, its truth and reality can be made manifest by any common observer, who can see with his own eyes, and can tell to other ⌈people what he has seen. This is precisely what I have endeavoured to do on the present occasion; and my readers must know by this time, that I have ever studied not to mislead them in my account of either foreign or English places suited for the reception of invalids. Bournemouth is one of the latter description, and eminently entitled to a separate chapter in a work of this kind.

Sometime in the month of February of the present year, a medical engagement having suddenly called me away from London for a day, to the neighbourhood of Bournemouth, I was requested by several gentlemen connected with that almost unknown sea-watering-place, to visit and give my professional opinion respecting it.

Having completed the object for which I had left home, I deemed this invitation the more fortunate, as it had brought within my knowledge a place I had passed over, when I explored the whole coast from west to east, in the preceding year, as has been seen in the last few chapters, and especially that portion which extends from Weymouth to Southampton including the Isle of Wight. On that occasion, though my way lay to the immediate vicinity of Bournemouth, I did not learn from any one I met or conversed with at Weymouth, Wakeham, or Blandford, aught of the existence of the incipient living colony at that place. But this singular want of information respecting it I ceased to marvel at, after I had seen and judged of its great peculiarity; nor did I subsequently find it extraordinary, that even in places much nearer to Bournemouth than the towns just mentioned, I should have found the people silent upon that subject, and

affectedly ignorant of its existence as a new and formidable
rival on the coast.

The impression left on my mind by my careful and attentive inspection of that rival will be best gathered, perhaps,
from the spontaneous opinion I expressed of its capabilities
as a residence fit for the most delicate valetudinarians, at a
public dinner given at the Great Hotel at Bournemouth, in
a style of excellence seldom surpassed even in the metropolis, with which a number of gentlemen from Poole, Blandford, and Christ Church had been pleased to welcome the
Author of " The Spas of England," whose first volume had
just been published. As that opinion was taken down at the
time, and found its way into the public papers, which gave
an account of the day's entertainment as well as of the various
speeches delivered on the occasion, and as I see nothing in
what I then stated which subsequent reflection and the
acquisition of additional and valuable information on many
topics connected with the subject, would induce me to change
or retract,—I cannot act more fairly by such of my readers as
are likely to require hereafter the resource now for the first time
about to be brought to their notice, than by quoting in this
place the very words in which I expressed my sentiments,
setting aside all preliminary and exordial matter and phrases.

" Having been requested to extend my professional excursion to this place, for the purpose of inspecting and reporting
upon what has been done, and remains yet to be done, by
the proprietors and well-wishers of Bourne, in order to make
it a place suitable for the resort of the better classes of
society requiring a southern climate in our island, I have
acceeded to your request. I have examined Bourne in all
its parts, under sunshine as well as during the prevalence of
wet and high wind. I have seen what has been done, and
have heard of what it is intended to do, in order to profit of
the many advantages which the situation of Bourne offers as
a watering-place; and I have no hesitation in stating, as the

conclusion of 'all my observations, which have extended through two whole days, and around as well as within the place,—that no situation that I have had occasion to examine along the whole southern coast, possesses so many capabilities of being made the very first invalid sea-watering place in England; and not only a watering-place, but what is still more important, a winter residence for the most delicate constitutions requiring a warm and sheltered locality at this season of the year. As such I hold it superior to either Bonchurch, St. Lawrence, or Ventnor, in the Isle of Wight. Though situated ten miles less to the south than the extreme point of that island, Bourne has the superior advantage of being rather more than as many miles to the westward, a circumstance that makes quite sufficient amends for the trifling difference in regard to its southern position. But Bourne has other claims to superiority over Ventnor, being in the centre of a beautiful curvilinear sweep of coast or bay, which, instead of being called Poole Bay, ought henceforth to be called Bourne Bay, the two extreme points or horns of which, equidistant from Bourne, serve to protect the latter from the direct influence of many of the most objectionable winds. But above all is Bourne superior to the back of the Isle of Wight, from its entire exposure to the south, with a full protection from the easterly winds, to which Ventnor on the contrary is indirectly exposed. I hardly need touch upon its superiority as a bathing-place to any in the neighbourhood, or along these coasts. It is as an inland sheltered haven for the most tender invalids, however, that I would call your attention to the great capabilities of Bourne; for we look in vain elsewhere for that singular advantage which Bourne possesses, of presenting two banks of cliffs, clothed with verdure even at this inclement season, running from the sea inland, with a smiling vale watered by a rapid brook or bourne, dividing them just enough to allow of a most complete ventilation, with coolness in the summer months, and yet affording a most protected succession of ridges upon which to erect residences not only for convalescents, free from positive disease, but also for patients in the most delicate state of health as to lungs.

" For the latter the many glens which run up the western cliff, and which I pointed out this morning to the gentlemen who accompanied me in my excursions, offer very beautiful retreats, surrounded by balsamic and almost medicinal emanations from fir plantations, which are found to be so beneficial in these cases. In fact, gentlemen, you have a spot here which you may convert into a perfect blessing to those among the wealthy who are sorely afflicted with disease, and who do not like to tear themselves from home to go in search of foreign and salubrious climates. I have pointed out to you in the course of my many rambles all that is requisite to be done, to make the place perfect, and it will be your own fault if Bourne is not soon an object of general admiration and attraction.

"But you must not commit the many blunders that have been perpetrated in other watering-places, especially on these coasts and farther eastwards. You must not let in strangers and brick-and-mortar contractors, to build up whole streets of lodging houses, or parades, and terraces interminable, in straight lines facing the sea, the roaring sea, and the severe gales, that make the frames of an invalid's bedroom casement rattle five days in the week at least, and shake his own frame in bed also. The laws of climate, of locality, of aspect for houses about to be erected, of position and arrangement, have hitherto been overlooked, neglected, or misunderstood. My experience, abroad as well as at home, has enabled me to lay down certain principles on all those important points which can alone lead to success. These I have communicated to you in the course of my inquiries, and shown you how they are to be made to apply to Bournemouth ; and if you attend to those suggestions, you cannot fail to see your ultimate object, the securing the growth and prosperity of Bourne, most triumphantly accomplished. This consummation I most heartily desire, for your sake, for the sake of future invalids, and for that of the members of my profession throughout England, who will then know where to send with full confidence all such patients as require the combined benefit of sea and land influence such as is possessed by Bournemouth."

This is the unbiassed and candid opinion I felt bound to express of Bournemouth when on the spot, and it seems to be too much in the interest of those who are connected with that young establishment to act up to it, to doubt of their adopting and carrying into effect the view and plans I then suggested. They must be sensible of the fact, that by not properly using their resources, their very first beginning a few years back proved a failure, until two or three other spirited and judicious proprietors stepped in to the rescue.

In order the better to comprehend the plans I sketched out on the occasion, and so form a correct idea of what Bournemouth is, as well as of what it is likely to become, I shall enter into a few brief particulars as to its situation and resources, and thus aid in giving " a local habitation and a name" to an incipient settlement on the most favourable point of the Hampshire coast, placed nearly in the centre of the southern coast of England, midway between the South Foreland and the Land's End, which has as yet no definite or permanent population, and which, so insignificant has it hitherto been considered by the topographer that we find in the adjoining county's map, an indication set down that a particular road from Dorsetshire leads " to Christchurch," without mentioning to Bournemouth, albeit the identical road passes through it. But the day is at hand when the latter indication will be substituted for the former.

Few people are unacquainted with Poole Bay, a gentle curvilinear sweep of coast, measuring about twelve miles along the shore, and nearly nine from the western point or head of the crescent to that of the opposite end. The former called *Handfast* Point, divides the little bay of Studland, a species of sea *cul-de-sac*, from Swanage Bay; while the other, named Hengistbury Head, marks the precise spot where the estuary of Christchurch ends.

The exposure of this fine bay (which is remarkable, by the bye, for a singular tidal phenomenon, to be alluded to presently, highly favourable to the inhabitants on the coast), is from due south to south-east. But from all easterly winds it is defended by the Isle of Wight, which sustains on its eastern and south-eastern coast the first brunt of the gales from that quarter, sweeping down channel. The prevailing character of the coast, geologically speaking, is a fine white sand; but yellowish and pinkish beds of sand occur, with some of the lower strata of an ashy colour, arising from the admixture of vegetable matter. With the latter species of sand there is associated sometimes, but at the depth of seldom less than fifteen or twenty feet below it, a thick bed of black bituminous clay, in such a way that as the ashy coloured sand is never found except under thick strata of other sands, either yellow or white, the said bituminous clay, properly speaking, is never met with nearer than from forty to fifty feet from the surface. Here and there, among the topping white sands, white pipeclay has been found, but neither continuously nor in thick masses, except near the cliff to the east of Boscomb, and at Big Durly-chine, where it is worked out and sent to the potteries in Staffordshire, as the purest and best material for the celebrated porcelains of that district. The writer of the "Bournemouth Guide," who has stated that the country around or near it, consists of hills of sand and *clay*, has not very accurately described the character of the locality.

The cliffs formed by these various strata, superimposed one over the other, vary occasionally in height, but except where a chine or valley occurs to interrupt the continuous line, their elevation is seldom less than 60, and often exceeds 150

feet. Of these chines in the sweep of coast now under consideration, there are several. Some are mere indentures in the
sand beds, more or less profound, due to the percolation of
water digging into the sand; others are real valleys, due to
the course of some important stream having, in olden times,
formed to itself a vale of level land, even with the sea, and
so kept apart the deposits of sand on each side of it.

Bournemouth is just one of these valley chines. It occupies precisely the centre of the sweep of coast I have been
describing, and appears from the sea like an opening through
the cliff, made by a stream of water, on each side of which a
sloping surface of white and yellow sand inclines from the
top of the cliff downwards, at an angle of 40° on the east,
and of about fifty on the west side. At the foot of the cliff
is the shore, covered with the usual shingle, being part of the
coarse, moderately-sized and multishaped gravel noticed in
strata of from two to three feet in thickness at the lower part
of the cliff, the largest proportion of which consists of fragments, some rounded and some angular, of indurated iron
clay. But between the foot of the cliff and the bed of sea-
shingle, there are in many parts of the strand wide and extended belts of sand, which at high tide offer an excellent
footing to the bather.

Near, and to the westward of Bournemouth, there are
other interruptions or chines in the cliffs, such as Little
Durly, Big Durly, Broad and Middle Chines, Alum Chine,
&c. But to the eastward, as far as Boscombe Chine, a
distance of nearly two miles, a single gentle and continuous
undulation beginning at Bournemouth, is observed in the cliff,
which at about its middle is upwards of eighty feet high.
The western declivity of this high land forms the eastern
cliff at the entrance of Bournemouth, which, like the one on
the opposite side (not quite so high), runs inland with undulating and waving surfaces, and in somewhat tortuous lines
—ascending on either side of a narrow but rapid stream,
until they are merged into three elevated heaths—Holdenhurst

Heath to the right, Poole Heath to the left, and straightforward, with a north-west direction, Canford Heath, in the
centre of which rises the Bourne, or river that gives the name
to our infant colony.

This peculiarity of its formation constitutes one of the
great merits of the locality as a retreat for invalids ; while the
chance circumstance of a gentleman retreating to this spot
some thirty or forty years ago, and planting all the sandhills
to the westward of the Bourne, or brook, with trees of the
Pine tribe, whereby the district has been converted, in the
course of time, into a sort of tiny Black Forest, is the cause
of another and most important advantage of the place.

The reader will now experience no difficulty in forming a
correct notion of the singularly favourable position of
Bournemouth ; but a walk or two of exploration for the purpose of noticing what has since been done to profit of such a
situation by other proprietors, particularly on the eastern
cliffs and banks of the Bourne, and of pointing out the absolute improvements that are called for, as well as the threatened errors that ought to be eschewed, will complete the
chapter more satisfactorily to my readers than any abstract
or general description of a place as yet undeveloped.

Two principal roads converge into the vale of the Bourne,
the one from Christchurch in the east, the other from Poole
in the west   Northwards and inclined to the eastward, is another, but minor road, which soon after quitting the vale,
bifurcates upon Holdenhurst Heath, leading to a cross-road on
the verge, and parallel to, the lovely and fertile valley of the
Stour, near to which are the towns of Wimborne Munster
with Canford Magna, Kingston, and Hecklenhurst.   The
road from Christchurch having reached the back of the lofty
cliff previously noticed, between Boscombe Chine and
Bournemouth, begins to descend gradually when it has
arrived before a lofty and imposing edifice, with a pretty
front, on which is inscribed the title of " Bath Hotel."

This building commands a view of the whole valley, and

particularly of the range of detached villas, which follow at a short distance lower down, and on the right of the same road. Few buildings in the way of sea-hotels at watering-places can boast either of a handsomer exterior, or of a better interior than this establishment; and as to its position, peering over the cliff and the whole bay on the one hand, and as far as the extended heaths on the other, it must be deemed unrivalled. Much judgment and taste have been displayed in the arrangements of the principal floor, on which there are many beautiful sitting-rooms, three of which, being capable of being thrown into one, will form a spacious and showy ball-room. But the second story bed-rooms, destined for servants, is a *manqué* floor, with windows like holes, and rooms small and low—too good for servants as to situation, for they enjoy the finest view imaginable—too bad for masters as to accommodation. This story should be rebuilt, and applied to a series of lofty and well-furnished bed-chambers, each of which would be a little Belvidere. Besides, to have rattling servants running up and down side-staircases at each end of the principal corridor which divides the best sitting from the best bed-rooms, and afterwards stamping with their heavy tread immediately over the heads of their masters and mistresses, is a most objectionable arrangement. Men-servants should never be in the same *corps de logis* with their masters, but made to occupy separate out-buildings at all great hotels.

The Bath Hotel has a parterre-garden on one side, with a lengthened shrubbery or plantation, through which the inmates, after a moderate walk of gentle descent, may reach the strand, and the baths built near it, or the bathing-machine not far off, or lastly, the marine library. This latter has recently been enlarged, and greatly improved with many upper and lower rooms, fit for a superior class of visiters who desire to occupy a place in a good boarding-house, and a most delightful marine residence.

The high road before alluded to, having left the hotel, skirts the range of detached villas just now alluded to, of various structures, including the old English, the Lombard, and campaniled forms, as well as the Swiss cottage. They are of moderate sizes, well built, and in all of them the inmates enjoy, from the first-floor room, a side view of the bay, which, however, they càn enjoy much better by ascending to the several kiosks and terraces at the top of the house, or upper balcony, as every house is possessed of such a convenience. Behind them extends, up the hill, a useful garden, by the side of which are the stables.

I had been hospitably received on my arrival, in an excellent house, the last but one in this series of detached villas, which is always let during the season by its worthy proprietor, and I could thus practically form an idea of the convenience and the desirableness of this situation. From my bed-room window, I caught on my left hand an extended view of the bay; below me, the same road, already twice mentioned, prolonged its downward course towards the right, until by a gentle sweep inclined to the left, it reached the level of the vale, crossed over the brook by a small wooden bridge, and was seen ascending on the other side towards the heath on its way to Poole. Just beyond the margin of the road, a young plantation and garden, reared on a flat level to a certain distance forward, descended a gently sloping declivity, to reach the vale of the Bourne.

Behind these villas, the continuation of the ascending hills, topped with wood, midway on which the houses are erected, screens them from the north-east winds; while in front of them, across the valley, rises that loftier range of sand-hills, once barren and naked, and now, as I before stated, covered with luxuriant and dense forests of fir-trees, the work of the late Mr. Tregonwell of Edmondesham, Dorsetshire, whose relict even now occupies the mansion he originally built for his permanent residence, at present surrounded with lawns and shrubberies, and embosomed amidst dense plantations. This ridge, running nearly due north and south, and most completely screened from all easterly winds by the opposite bank, is pleasingly varied with undulations. It is ever clothed in green from the nature of its vegetation, and serves to break the violence of the westerly gales, that would otherwise impinge against the detached villas of Bourne.

It is by exploring this ridge, on a few points of which only an insulated private dwelling-house has as yet been erected, that I discovered three or four retired glens, so lovely from their verdure, so tranquil from their position, and so warm from their sheltered aspect, that I did not hesitate a moment in declaring such spots to be the very thing that was wanted in this country, to render the south coast really and truly available in behalf of those who are afflicted with consumption.

" Here," I said to the gentlemen who were escorting me, "must be erected commodious and well-arranged dwellings for invalids of that class who happen to be wealthy, and who will not, as indeed in such cases they need not, expatriate themselves, and tear asunder, even before death, every tie that links them to a life, for the sake of prolonging that life. Here you will find a temperature, during cold weather, of from eight to ten degrees higher than on the table-land, or the sea-shore, the distant roaring of which will reach the patient's ears, muffled by the intervening wooded cliffs ; but the sight of which, and the inhaling of whose invigorating breeze, he may in one moment obtain, by issuing from his glen, and slowly pacing down the footpath which winds at the foot of the cliffs parallel to the course of the rivulet, until he has reached the shore. And when he has quaffed enough of the sea-air, warmed by the noon sun even in the coldest month of the year, he may return to his retreat, there to enjoy immunity from severe or brisk atmosphere, and the comforts which a dwelling suitably prepared and so sheltered will procure him.

Look around, and interrogate vegetation at this period of the winter (16th Feb.) The snow has left the ground, though it is lying heavy still on the high lands a few miles hence. We have had everywhere nipping frosts : see how every thing here on the contrary is green—how those geraniums out of doors have survived in freshness—how strong, vigorous, and untouched are those exuberant rhododendrons. Hark to the distant gale : it is a mere hissing that is heard in this sheltered spot—though you may see by the course of the clouds overhead, which scud before the wind, how boisterously it blows at sea. Is not this then the very haven that is required in England for those who tremble on the verge of consumption, or are already plunged into that destructive malady?"

Here, turning to a physician (Dr. Aitkin) who was of the company, a resident at Poole, and a very able and talented man, author of a work on physiology, and formerly a lecturer in Edinburgh, " I would urge you," I said to him, " to make inquiries into the comparative difference of temperature of these and other situations in Bournemouth, and see whether my surmise be not correct."

The time is come when that gentleman has been able to supply me with the information I required ; and what is the result of his inquiry ?—Why, this, as I collect it from a letter received only a few days since (May, 1841).

" I was certainly not prepared," he states, " to expect so complete a confirmation of what you asserted would be found, in respect to the difference of temperature on the tableland, and the valleys or glens you pointed out. I found on my first observation, on the 8th of March, at 1 P.M. with a fresh breeze from the S.W., at Mr. Polhill's favourite seat (high on the west cliff), that the thermometer, sheltered from the wind and in the shade, stood at 49°, and where the church is going to be erected, at 50° ; while in the different glens it ranged from 58° to 60°. By repeated subsequent observations I noted similar differences."

Here then the great desideratum for consumptive invalids is found; and if the proprietress of this blessed region is properly advised, instead of parting to speculating purchasers with her lord's estate (who, in planting it, and throwing the shelter and balsamic effluvia of a forest of firs around so many natural glens, probably looked forward to the destination for which I am the first to declare it to be fitter than any other place in England), she will apply herself to build insulated villas of different sizes, and properly located with gardens, and a general walk through the intended woods, inclosing the whole territory by fences, and making a handsome entrance into it near the wooden bridge or head of the valley, denominating henceforth the establishment, BOURNE-MOUTH PARK, and the dwelling-houses of the valetudinarians in it, the PARK VILLAS; with a perfect assurance that they will become celebrated all over the country as the best, the most promising, and the only real asylums for consumptive people of the higher order.

Nor are the detached villas already in existence, and alluded to on the slope of the east cliff, or the still more pretending, larger, and first-rate mansions built by Mr. Gordon, on the verge of a cross-road, fronting the south, and over-looking the beginning of the heath from their back rooms,—or, again, the Swiss cottages adjoining to these,—unsuited to people of delicate health. On the contrary, a great many of those dwellings are so placed as to be just the thing wanted for patients who are not far advanced in the disorder, and who yet require genial, pure and mild air, which they are certain of getting at Bourne—now from the sea, and now from the heath, or lastly from the fir-woods right opposite.

Such are the present resources in Bournemouth, and such the proposals I have to suggest as a medical man in behalf of suffering humanity, for creating others. But there is besides, a great deal to be done in the place to render it complete. At present the accommodations are not numerous enough:

many more houses must be built; a regular community or village must be encouraged to come and settle here, bringing along with them all the necessary useful arts and trades ; and lastly, a church must be erected. But in all these undertakings great judgment, discrimination, knowledge of the laws of climate, and, finally, taste, are required. An opportunity is now offered of establishing a real Montpellier on the south coast of England, and a something better than a Montpellier in point of beauty, for the upper and the wealthier classes of society, who ought to be encouraged and enticed to remain at home and spend their income in husbanding their health in England. They have been driven away from every point of the coast by the facilities afforded to the " *everybody*," and the " *anybody*," of congregating in shoals at the same watering-place, creating bustle, noise, confusion, and vulgarity. These and other inconveniences act as so many impediments to the recovery of health, in persons of refined habits; and your interminable terraces, parades, paragons, and parabolas of houses of every sort and size and description, which mere brick-and-mortar speculators have run up, wherever they thought the current of fashion was likely to direct invalids, have acted on the influx of the better sort of people, exactly in the inverse ratio of their own increasing numbers. What the result of such proceeding, has been to the place itself, I need not specify ; every one of my readers will bring to his mind, probably, some one example within his own knowledge, in illustration of my position.

Is it then the intention of the three or four proprietors of the land at Bourne to act in the same manner? If the engraving put into my hands as a view of Bournemouth as it is to be, is likely to be realised, then the place will be in the category of those I have just painted ; it will become one of twenty sea watering-places, just as tolerable and common, and will only be frequented as such, with slow progress and doubtful success. It is well to study effect, and to try to cover in concentric circles the whole face of the hill, which towers over the east sea-cliff, and at the back of the present villas, with lines of lodging and other dwelling houses, and crowning the whole with a Gothic church, placed in the centre of the summit, like a diadem—to serve as a beacon to mariners ; but it will not do for invalids with delicate chests and damaged lungs to climb up the Capitol, either to return home after a walk on the sea-shore, or to attend at church on a Sunday, to be blown away in endeavouring to reach the House of God, or blown upon on coming out of it by the boisterous south-wester,—and so, chilled into a pleurisy or an additional vomica, thereby destroying the benefit which Bournemouth is calculated to yield to the sick.

Has the architect, has the landowner ever reflected upon such a consideration as this ? In a colony of invalids, the Temple of God should be in a quiet, secluded, and rural spot. It should be easily accessible to all—to the villagers in health, who are occupied to the last minute with household affairs— to the valetudinarian who cannot walk far—to the feeble and the cripple who can only creep or must be carried ; and all of whom ought, above all things, to eschew exposure of every description. Such a spot I pointed out for that purpose, on the estate of Mistress Tregonwell on the eastern bank. There a plain, unassuming, but capacious and well-built rural church, without any pretensions to Gothic *niaiseries*, (for who can bear a church in a Gothic dress that is not as big as Lincoln, Wells, or York Minster ?) should be erected near the entrance to the park, whereby the invalid inhabitant of the Park Villas would have it near to them ; close to a spot where the villager's community would be principally settled, on the margin of the brook at the foot of Gordon Villas, that attendance may be made easy to the dwellers therein as well as to the villagers ; and lastly, not far removed from the present and any other detached villa, along the lower and upper roads ;—thus leaving no excuse to any class of inhabitants and visiters (as they will have, if the church is built on the top

of the hill) for not attending divine service. From the
high character for charity and liberality which the lady nobly
connected who owns the Bournemouth Park, as I have
called it, bears in the place, and among all who have the honour of knowing her, no doubt can be entertained that a
site, such as I have pointed out, would be granted by her.
Let the rest of the landowners who take a true interest in the
success of Bournemouth, and the spiritual welfare of its future inhabitants, contribute materials and money as part of
their tribute for the erection of a suitable temple, and their
charity will be blessed. Any other worldly or selfish view in
this affair ought to be set aside, and not allowed to have any
sway.

But are no other houses than such as are suited to far-gone
patients, with damaged lungs, to be erected in Bournemouth?
Are there not many other classes of people in easy circumstances who require, and may be benefited by, the pure and
invigorating, yet mild and temperate air of the place? Yes,
there are, and for such as these, provision should be made in
gay and airy regions, calculated to serve as much for the
summer as the houses before alluded to are essentially destined
for the winter season; for it is as a winter residence to a
select community of invalids and visiters, that Bournemouth
must become chiefly celebrated.

I ascended, on the second morning after my arrival, the
cliff behind the Bath Hotel, until I reached a spot from
which I overlooked the roof of that building, and placed
myself, at the distance of four hundred yards from it, in the
midst of the green and vivacious underwood which has grown
luxuriantly, though not very high, all over the surface of that
cliff, and on many parts of the land adjoining it, where,
moreover, many large clumps and patches of forest-trees
have grown.

The sea was on my left at a depth of sixty feet or more; I
looked towards Poole Harbour, and stretching my eye as far as
Swanage Bay and the Purbeck Hills, I saw below and before

me the mouth of the little river Bourne, discharging its meandering stream over the sand. The wind was E.S.E., and blew at my back; but as I had not reached the whole elevation of the cliff, that portion which still remained above me, screened me from the wind. Here, then, I stood on the most eligible, and at the same time, a most delightful spot, for building summer residences, either in the form of detached villas on several parts of the cliff, without destroying its heathy character, by removing too many of the shrubs with which it is clothed or (after clearing away enough of the latter near the verge of the cliff), in the form of a terrace or crescent facing the west-south-west, and enjoying the magnificent sea-view I have just described.

Upon another occasion, while exploring the opposite and western cliff, on which stands the station-house of the coast-guard, and while examining amongst others the little villa of Mr. Drax, a bijou, and its adjoining grounds, with a gentle-man who manages this property, I sallied forth on a terrace erected as a walk facing the roaring sea — a carriage-road lying below it. Here again a parade or line of summer residences might advantageously be erected. The view from thence along the coast, tracing Christchurch and Muddiford, encompassing the Needles and the western shore of the Isle of Wight, with an almost constantly passing and repassing of crafts and larger vessels in opposite directions, would be fully as delightful as that from the other side. In this way ample provision would be made for all summer visiters—for those, in fact, who, being otherwise well in health, like a retired rather than a bustling and noisy sea watering-place.

The character of Bournemouth, as an unique Montpellier, would be thus preserved intact; while, on the contrary, it would be damaged if you line your coast with a whole mile of monotonously uniform houses, or spread whole streets and squares in the plain, and convert a present garden into a future huddled town.

Bournemouth combines, to an eminent degree, the character of beautiful and sheltered rusticity with that of an open sea-side residence. To the first it lays claim by its perpetual clothing of green in winter, which, seen for ever out of every casement, cheats you into the belief that spring is come again; while, when the sun shines around, summer seems present out of doors, even in the dreary months of December and January. To the latter it lays claim, not only by the favourable character of the beach, and the easy access to the water, but also by the peculiar tidal phenomenon previously hinted at, which occurs between Spithead and Ballard's-head, (embracing the sea off Bourne) of course, whereby four tides take place every twenty-four hours, thus doubling the effect over any other situation on the sea coast, and affording to the bathers at Bournemouth a command of the tide every day.

Both these characters suit well the purpose and objects of the winter residents and invalids. Of the latter, two classes must be provided with accommodation;—first, those who labour under severe chest complaints; secondly, your dyspeptic, or such convalescents from other disorders as require pure sea-air and sea-water in perfection, as well as cheerful and inspiriting inland landscape, means for exercise on horseback, or in carriages, and other diversions. To be near the sea, and to be able to have recourse to its water or its breezes when necessary, yet not to be always and for ever saturated with either; to have it in one's power to turn to spots where its shingle-rustling, or the more loud roaring of its waves, cannot disturb you—to be, in fine, on the threshold between sea and land life, so as to take to each alternately as required, as a means of recovery from disease, or for the restoration of lost strength (and those means of the very best description)—these are the advantages which, in my estimation, nature affords at Bournemouth to an extent and of a character unequalled in any other place I am acquainted with on the south coast of England.

To render its superiority to the generality of sea watering-places still more conspicuous, the vale of the Bourne,—beginning at the present insignificant wooden bridge, which ought to be replaced by a handsome stone one, down to the beach, a species of narrow flat prairie, which divides the two banks before described,—should be converted into a regular promenade-garden all the way, with parterres and beds of flowers by the sides of the brook. That imaginative and skilful agronomist, Mr. Loudon, would soon make the prettiest thing in England of such a place, and he ought by all means to be consulted. At present, the vale consists of a narrow belt of peat earth lying over sand, on which a few miserable sheep are allowed to feed, or a scanty coarse grass is cut. It divides the west from the east banks, which are the inland prolongations, before adverted to, of the corresponding cliffs on the shore, and which slope down to the margin of the brook, both of them clothed by evergreen plantations and shrubberies, and crested with the rows of detached villas or single houses previously mentioned. The ittle brook itself, perfectly wild, shallow, and tortuous, and of no great width, meanders down the middle; but a little judicious management, by swelling out the banks in parts, contracting them in others, and deepening the bed here, or raising it there, so as to create a rustling fall or cascade, would readily convert an insignificant streamlet into a pleasing ornamental water-feature in the landscape. The garden, with suitable gravel walks, would afford to the weakest and the most delicate among the real invalids at Bournemouth the means of taking exercise on foot whenever any other wind but the north prevails; for to that and that alone would the garden promenade be exposed. At the mouth of the river a small estuary or cove, to admit a few pleasure-boats, might be established readily, and a short pier, *sans prétension*, yet convenient for landing on the beach in favourable weather, ought to be added. The only diversions of which the Bournemouth people would be wholly deprived, unless such measures as I here hint at be adopted, are precisely those of pleasure-boating and sailing, owing to the present total want of means for that purpose, unless the visiter extends his rambles either as far as Poole or Christchurch, there to procure what is necessary for those objects.

It is manifest, therefore, that nature has done every thing for Bournemouth, and that the hand of man has nothing to create, but only to fashion, and *suitably* and judiciously to convert to its own purpose. Of house accommodation there is perhaps a sufficiency for present want, and that at no great outlay. For the house I inhabited, for example, and which contains every sort of desirable and well-furnished apartments and convenience, beside coach-house and stable, garden, &c., six guineas per week are charged for the season; single floors or apartments are to be had considerably cheaper, and one may live, *en garçon*, for very little money. Provisions are obtained readily from Poole or Chriscthurch, whose well-supplied markets are equidistant from Bourne, and only five miles apart. Tradesmen are in the habit of calling for orders and with supplies every day; and soon a regular series of shops of every description will be established in the place itself, along with the progressive formation of a village. Milk, butter, and farm-house supplies of the very best description, the valley of the Stour abundantly yields. Water is plentiful and excellent. That which I washed in felt soft, and readily lathered with the soap, leaving the skin perfectly supple and smooth. It was drawn from a well in the house twenty-five feet deep; and other wells of water equally good are found a few feet deeper in other houses.

The water of the brook being of itself a never-failing and abundant supply, and likely too to be the principal one to be depended upon for the new community, when a regular village shall have been established on its bank,—I was particularly anxious to have it properly tested ; the more so, as at a consultation on the case of a patient residing at Bourne, with a surgeon from a neighbouring town, I had been told that a relaxation of the bowels generally followed the first use of that water, said to proceed from the drainage of the heath. Extraordinary as that opinion must have seemed to me at that time, inasmuch as it was at variance with the observations my long experience in such questions had enabled me to make, I nevertheless took not upon myself to gainsay it ; on the contrary, I requested Dr. Aitkin, the scientific and pains-taking physician of Poole before mentioned, to examine the water chemically, as well as the nature of the heathy soil through which it courses down to Bournemouth, and to compare the result with that yielded by the examination of what might be considered as the best water in his own place of residence. The nature of the experiments, and the conclusions arrived at in consequence, Dr. Aitkin has been kind enough to send to me, and I can only say that his opinion is most favourable with regard to the water of the brook, as well as to its source. " The latter is from among the gravel and sandy beds or undulations below the peat-earth on the adjoining heath, on which not a particle of manure is ever spread, and it consequently affords water free from infiltration of dung, from which very few streams of Britain are exempt."

Dr. Aitkin had also, at my suggestion, tested six of the wells of Bourne, to see if any iron was present in their water ; but after every possible trial, he had not detected the slightest trace of that metal.

To the same gentleman, whose professional services, by the bye, will be available to the invalids of Bournemouth, owing to the nearness of his residence, and his frequent visits to that place, I am indebted for a perusal of a very valuable

essay on the medical topography of the district of which
Bournemouth is the centre, read by him last year at the
general meéting of the Provisional Medical Association.
That paper, which I trust will be given to the public entire
at no distant period, enables me, after closely examining the
localities, to speak as I fully expected, very favourably of
the · climate of Bourne for warmth, equability of temperature and dryness. Indeed, considering its western
direction on the south coast, the climate of Bourne is
remarkably free from rain ; and what is better, when
the rain falls, it is quickly absorbed by an extremely
porous soil, consisting principally of sand. Dampness in
the atmosphere, therefore, is a rare occurrence at Bournemouth.*

* " It not unfrequently happens that the elevated downs of the Isle of
Purbeck to the west of Bourne, have their tops loaded with clouds when
the wind is (as it is termed) up channel, when, at the same time everywhere else, here the sky is clear. These clouds, caused by the colder air
on the tops of the downs, contribute much to the beauty and variety of
the scenery, and often combine in the most pleasing manner with the
august ruins of Corfe Castle, that rise from the midst of them, in
furnishing landscapes well worthy of the study of the painter. At other
times, heavy showers are seen falling in Purbeck, when not a drop is
felt at a short distance rom its borders.

" In the neighbourhood of Dorchester, the chalk downs divide into
two branches, the one proceeding along the shore of the channel
by Weymouth and Lulworth, and terminate at Peveril Point close
by Swanage. The other takes an inland direction towards Blandford, and approaches this district at Badburyrings near Wimborne.
Clouds and rain are frequently seen following the course of these
higher grounds, while in this immediate locality, if there are any
clouds overhead, they are at a considerable elevation. Again, while in
Purbeck on the one hand, and at Blandford, Wimborne, and along the
Stour to Christchurch on the other, rain frequently falls abundantly, this neighbourhood altogether escapes. Moreover, it is by no
means of unfrequent occurrence, to see the clouds overhanging Purbeck clearing away at Ballard Head, the air becoming clear as it
passes over the sea, till it reaches the Needles and high cliffs of the

As it is always gratifying to a medical man to be supported by the authority of his brethren in what he advances, I cannot deny myself the satisfaction of adding to the testimony already advanced in favour of the climate of Bournemouth, the opinion of an old and experienced general practitioner, also resident at Poole, Dr. Slater, from whose correspondence I select the following passage:

" I have had ample opportunities, in the course of thirty years' practice in the immediate neighbourhood, of becoming acquainted with the healthfulness of that interesting place (Bournemouth). From the undulating nature of the surface, conjoined to its southern aspect, and dry and permeable soil, it is in my opinion peculiarly fitted for the residence of invalids, and adapted equally to every season of the year. I have had patients at Bournemouth for the past two or three winters, and I have scarcely ever gone there in cold weather, without being struck with the extreme mildness of the locality, even contrasted with the places in its vicinity. The whole neighbourhood has as high a temperature in the winter season as any situation on the south-west coast of England,—with this advantage, that it possesses a drier atmosphere than places farther west. Having kept a meteorological journal for more than twenty years, I speak with confidence on this point. Unless the winter be very severe, it is an unusual thing to see snow on the ground for many hours together."

I have now said enough, I trust, to prove by the details of positive facts, and by descriptions taken down on the spot, the correctness of the assertions with which I set out in the present chapter, and which are to be found in my address to

Isle of Wight towards the east, where they again make their appearance. It also not unfrequently happens, that rain may be seen falling in every point of the compass, excepting in this district, of about ten miles in length, and not four in breadth."—*Extract from Dr. Aitkin's Unpublished Paper.*

the principal people interested in the progress and welfare of the place, that Bournemouth is the realization of a *desideratum* we had hitherto vainly sought elsewhere on the south coast of England.

CHAPTER XI.

ISLE OF WIGHT—SOUTHAMPTON.

SANDROCK SPRING.

Winter Retreats—Nature in Miniature —Shanklin Chine and Mock
Waterfall—Poesy is not Reality—West Cowes — Indifferent Sea-
bathing—Summer Residence—Speculation and East Cowes—Auc-
tioneering Flummeries—Improvements possible and desirable—Posi-
tion of East Cowes preferable—The Under Cliff—Popular Opinion—
Facts are' stubborn things—Letter from an Invalid's Mother—Vent-
nor—Its Temperature—Vegetation in Winter—The Doctor's Bou-
quet—Deaths from Consumption—Miserable Accommodation—Better
Prospects in store—New and Finer Buildings—Roads, Hotels, and
Boarding —Expenses of Lodgings—Bonchurch—Preferred by many—
Church Accommodation—South Easterly Winds fatal to the Undercliff
—The Sandrock Chalybeate—Its extreme Power—Medical Opinions—
Access to and beautiful Situation of the Spring—Taste of the Water—
A Ride across to Ryde—Southampton—Temperature—Soil—Advan-
tages of Gravel—New Way to keep the Feet warm—Southampton Air
unfit for Dyspeptic Patients—Excellent for Pulmonic Invalids—No
Sea-bathing at the place—Three great Rules for Patients at South-
ampton, and three great Districts—The way to improve and spoil
Southampton—The Back Water and its Effluvia—Useful at one time
to diseased Lungs—Supply of Water—Out-of-door Diversions.

It is not as a sea-bathing place that either the Isle of Wight
or the adjoining town of Southampton can lay claim to a niche
in the present collection of marine watering-places : for the
latter has ceased to have any sea-bathing, which, by the bye,
it never enjoyed in perfection ; while at the former, sea-
bathing forms the last of its recommendations.   No: it is as

retreats during the inclement season, principally for persons afflicted with various kinds of diseases of the chest, more or less of a serious nature, that I am about to consider them, in continuation of that series of analogous places farther west- ward on the south coast, which I have severally described in the preceding chapters. Having resided for three months in the island, for the benefit of my own health, and that of my children, many years ago, and minutely examined it in all its parts, especially around its marine boundaries, of which that to the south enjoys the greatest reputation for the mildness of its climate,—I should consider myself sufficiently entitled to speak on the subject, even had I not since paid other visits to it, or had I not had the advantage of other peo- ple's experience, who either upon other medical men's recom- mendation, or my own, had tried the effect of that climate in their own cases.

To such as love Nature's beauty in miniature, the Isle of Wight will afford pleasure and contentment. Its lozenge- formed surface exhibits almost every variety of landscape feature, from a valley to the summit of a hill, from a brook to a river, from a mere sea-inlet to a harbour or seaport. But all these objects, which so much resemble those to be seen in other parts of England, present themselves on so reduced a scale on the island, that one might fancy himself looking at grand and enlarged landscapes through an opera- glass turned the wrong way; so petty as well as pretty are they.

I well recollect the effect which the first view of Shanklin Chine had upon me, after having read the inflated account of the coast written by an enthusiastic and deceased divine, who declared that "no such country had ever occurred to his observation;" when I found myself on the shore looking up to a moderately lofty rugged rock, torn in twain at its summit by a fissure, and was told I ought to admire so ro- mantic and magnificent a sight. To heighten my surprise, some unseen hand, lifting up a small wooden sluice-gate, gave vent to some pent-up water, which forthwith formed a cascade of a single leap, narrow like a silver ribbon, and was presently again stopped for the entertainment of future travellers.

" Playthings these, my dear captain," said I, turning to a gentleman who escorted us, and whose office in the sea-fencibles had never taken him to other quarters of the globe, to see mightier and better objects.

" Playthings, my dear sir; what think you—not to go out of your own country—what think you of Flamborough Head peering over the eastern sea nearly five hundred feet, and its mighty caverns and subterranean lakes? What of the romantic Robin Hood's bay, with that most imposing feature, Stowbrow, reaching to an altitude of eight hundred feet? What of St. Vincent's rocks? and the stupendous chasm of the Cheddar cliffs? Your chines and your rocks are mere babies to these. But so it is: poesy has got possession of the minds of those who have written on the island, and they have set down as magnificently grand that which is only moderately pretty."

The most picturesque approach to the island is without comparison round by the Needles, sailing between Hurst Castle and Yarmouth road, up the Solent, and so on to the northernmost point of the isle, on which stand West and East Cowes, divided by the mouth of the Medina. Coming from the westward, this is the course. The shorter sea-trip to the island of those who can steam it from Southampton at stated periods of the day, to reach West Cowes, or from Portsmouth to reach Ryde, offers not a fraction of the interesting views which the former course affords, and which presents the island in perspective on the right, Lymington and the range of the New Forest on the left, and Porsdown Hills in front, backing the lands in the vicinity of Portsmouth. There is nothing striking or attractive on any point of the north shore of the isle, which is the only object that is kept constantly in sight during the *trajet* from either Southampton or Portsmouth.

WEST COWES is a delightful summer residence down by the sea-side, or westward of the castle, or up the hill peering over the shore; but the sea-bathing to be got there is fraught with difficulties, and not of the safest description. The charm of the place is in the maritime bustle that seems constantly to be going on, of vessels of all nations passing up or down channel, of aristocratic and wealthy commoners' yachts, aping the discipline and manœuvring of a king's fleet, and of steamers bringing cargoes of idlers and loungers three or four times a day, or taking them away again. West Cowes has one great disadvantage—it turns its face to the N.E.; but such an aspect in summer is not so inconvenient.

It is impossible to say what the spirit of speculation may not attempt hereafter as regards EAST COWES, if, as we may anticipate, the having brought Southampton withing three hours of the metropolis, should greatly increase the influx of visiters to the island. A project has been long on the *tapis* for converting the superb baronial structure of Norris Castle, and its surrounding well-wooded park, into a new marine settlement for persons of the highest rank and fashion. Without entering into the flummeries and exaggerations of an auctioneer's prospectus, it will be admitted by all, that the site of Norris Castle offers capabilities for establishing a far better sea watering-place than that on the opposite bank of the Medina, and of a very superior description. But never can either the east or the west bank of that river be a fit residence for persons of delicate health to reside in during the winter months, for both are exposed to the north.

Custom, medical opinion, and popular prejudice in some measure,—but only from the period of time when English invalids were prevented by the circumstances attendant on war from seeking a more temperate climate in foreign lands,—seem to have established as a fact, that for invalids, such as we have particularly alluded to in this and the preceding chapter, the UNDERCLIFF, or back part of the island, offers, as a situation, the best chance for recovery. This region, which, taken on a larger scale, may be said to extend from Shanklin Chine on the east coast, to Black Gang Chine on the west, is girded round with lofty and nearly perpendicular cliffs, which serve to condense and reflect the genial rays of an eastern sun from the very earliest hours of the morning, showering them down upon the villages of Bonchurch, Ventnor, and St. Lawrence, and the villas and detached abodes of the invalids there.   Till very lately, however, the accommodations for such invalids as are sent thither have been few, and of the most *mesquine* description ; but at present there is a fair prospect that such will not be the case in future.   A number of new houses are in the course of building at Ventnor, the one of the three places just mentioned, mostly preferred, for the intended object.

As it is always better to procure practical information where one can do so, than to profess or adhere to mere general abstract statements and declarations, I shall select the fullest and most recent account of this far-famed settlement for patients labouring under consumption, which has been supplied to me by a very intelligent lady, the mother of a cherished daughter threatened with that disease, over whom she hangs, and whom she watches with that devotion which none but a fond mother knows how to evince.   It was at my request that the account was drawn up, and at my request also it was made to embrace information upon every topic which it might be important for invalids or their friends to possess.   It was written at the conclusion of March of the present year.

"I can have no objections to giving you my impressions with regard to this place, Ventnor, as the task of describing its perfections will not occupy much time, for as yet it has not many except its climate.   Having been here since the beginning of November last, I can in that respect assure you it was *exquisite*, compared with any other place at which I have spent a winter. But as my experience only extends to a few of the counties in England,—and those not on the most favourable coasts,—and to one winter passed in the island of Jersey, and again on the northern shores of France,—I fear it may not be worth much. With regard to Jersey however, I must say decidedly, that I found this climate milder, and infinitely more salubrious, as well as more comfortable, to myself and my invalid daughter, from the dryness and cheering bright atmosphere.

" Although the winter we have just gone through was such a one as had not been known here before, the thermometer was never below 20 degrees out of doors, and that only during two or three nights. The state of vegetation is the strongest test of its mildness, for even after the severe frosts of January, our doctor brought us a little bouquet of chrysanthemum, roses, heartsease, and some annuals that had sprung up out of doors and were then in bloom. I have been delighted with its effect in keeping off the inflammatory attacks to which my dear child had been subject previously to our coming here ; and though she has fallen off during the last month of very fine but treacherous weather (easterly winds), it might have been prevented by more prudence and greater self-controul.

" The place is entirely occupied by invalids suffering from chest complaints, and every lodging was taken in the course of February. *More deaths than usual* have occurred here this winter, but only among those patients who had been sent here in a hopeless state.

" I am sorry to be obliged to admit the correctness of your observations with respect to the houses. This invaluable spot has been built upon in the very worst style imaginable, both as to use and ornament. The land has been let in small portions to needy people, who have run up cheap small houses for the sake of immediate gain; and consequently there are few houses that afford comfortable accommodation for invalids. It is necessary to seek long, and select well. But there are now some better buildings erecting, and the place is likely to be much improved before next winter. The roads of which you complained on behalf of the invalid travellers, are at present under substantial repairs; the shops have become numerous, and the principal hotel, well known to you, is being enlarged, and will have good baths attached to it. There are two other hotels; the Montpellier is by far the most sheltered as to situation. They all supply board as well as lodging, or the latter separately if preferred. The terms for the two united are two guineas per week for each person, with one guinea for a servant, and for this the fare is very indifferent; but you have it *en particulier*. The price of lodgings in general is two guineas a week for one sitting-room and three bedrooms, including the use of the kitchen, &c. But this price is raised to two guineas and a half in June, and to three guineas in July.

" We have just got into a choice spot, and a well-built house close to Bonchurch, which is the prettiest place in the island, and more sheltered than Ventnor. It is also beautifully embowered with trees, of which there are but few to be seen in Ventnor. The cliff is more lofty and verdant there, but not wooded and rocky as at Bonchurch. I am so sure that I must spend another winter here *at least* (trusting it will please God to spare my dear child), that I have secured this house for that time. In the common lodging-houses every one that comes here must put up with small rooms; there is nothing else to be got. Our own apartments are so, but they have the advantage of being loftier than usual. I understand that one or two leading London physicians have made inquiries through the doctor here, for accommodations for their patients, and would have sent many had the accommodation been fit for them. At present the best recommendation is the equability of its climate ; but the place is in its infancy, and consequently very deficient in many respects. I must not, however, omit to mention its beautiful church, built and endowed at the sole charge of Mr. Hamborougn, of Steephill Castle, at an expense of 8000*l.*, including the parsonage ; nor the kindness of Mr. Colman, the clergyman, to all the invalids who cannot attend divine service, as he visits them weekly to read and to pray with them. It would have been a wretched place but for the above offering, so gratefully made to the Bestower of wealth and all other good gifts."

For the correctness of the general and useful information contained in the preceding extract, I can in a great measure vouch from my own personal observations, particularly with regard to the inferiority of the lodging-houses, the want of judgment, and the haste with which they have been erected. The deficiency of good accommodation, indeed, is a great drawback, of which other patients of mine have also complained.

But a greater drawback still is the circumstance connected with nearly the entire of the most favourite district of the Undercliff, to which the writer of the letter slightly but feelingly adverts, where she alludes to the " falling off of her sick daughter during the prevalence of very fine but treacherous weather." In spring, and the earlier parts of summer, the wind from the east quarter generally prevails in Britain, giving rise to the keen and cutting blasts along the east coast, and to these the south-eastern shore of the isle is particularly exposed.

In this, as well as in many other respects, it will be seen that Bournemouth is superior to Ventnor, as I have stated in the previous chapter. With an equally warm climate, a dryer atmosphere, less of rain, and the most thorough protection against all easterly winds, as far as its present dwellings are concerned, Bournemouth may be said to be a paradise to consumptive people, as compared to the most favoured spot of the Undercliff. It is, in fact, the " Villa Franca"* of England, as Ventnor and Bonchurch combined may be said to be its Nice; and surely no one would hesitate as to which place to prefer for a residence in winter, in cases of consumption. I therefore trust that the people in whose hands are the resources and great capabilities of that fortunate sea-inlet on the Hampshire coast will strive, with judgment and skill, to render them valuable to society, and take a warning from the sensible remarks of my fair correspondent.

* Many of my readers will gladly learn the particulars of the climate of this highly favoured sea-side residence for invalids of delicate chests, which were drawn up and communicated to me by an English physician who accompanied Lady O—— S——, in 1817, and remained there with the most successful result during the latter half of the month of November, and three following months.

" Villa Franca is situated in a remarkably sheltered spot on the coast near Genoa, and most of the country residences possess the same advantage. The bay, lying north and south, is a remarkably deep one, and the surrounding hills rise from the very shore with great boldness; on the west and north, in particular, they reach to the height of four, five, and, I should think, six hundred feet, very abruptly, at an angle of inclination of 45°. On the east, the amphitheatre is less complete; the elevation attained is not great, and consequently the recess is here a little exposed.

" The extreme heat is felt a little before noon, and the extreme cold just at sunrise. A thermometer exposed to the north in the coldest days of February marked 50° as the minimum of temperature; the difference between that exposure and the south one being only one degree; showing how much the town is sheltered from those cold blasts so noxious in most other situations.

" The receding position of the town, at the bottom of a deep bay, scarcely allows of anemometrical observations; but inspections of the vessels lying off during the above period, showed a determined prevalence of easterly winds, with a dry air and serene sky, and of southerly winds. The surface of the bay is always calm and smooth during the four winter months: nothing beyond a gentle ripple has been observed on its surface.

" The prevailing weather is what is generally called in England very fine, but it is very frequently more than that, and what the English invalids here have styled *very, very* fine; by which is meant that kind of weather which

The Isle of Wight possesses another claim besides that of climate, and of a suitable residence for invalids, to the attention of an author engaged as I am in the consideration of British mineral springs; for it boasts of a chalybeate water of so singular a character as to have almost identified the celebrity of the isle in England with that of its

SANDROCK SPRING.

I never revert to the Isle of Wight but I think of its invalids' retreat on the Undercliff, and of its source of water strongly impregnated with alum and green vitriol, to be found not far from it, in the midst of that romantic and wild

is seldom or never seen in England—which must be seen and felt to be understood—and which is generally expressed by the words "Italian sky."

"November, 1817 (11 days).

Average maximum ther. 63° at 2 P. M.

Average minimum ther. 55° at sunrise.

One day cloudy; none of rain; one day thunder and lightning.

December, 1817.

Average maximum ther. $56\frac{1}{4}°$ at 2 P. M.

Average minimum ther. $48\frac{1}{2}°$, at sunrise.

12 days cloudy; nine days rain; one day thunder and lightning.

January, 1818.

Average maximum ther. $55\frac{3}{4}°$ at 2 P.M.

Average minimum ther. 49° at sunrise.

10 days cloudy; five days rain, one incessantly.

February, 1818.

Average maximum ther. $57\frac{1}{18}°$ at 2 P. M.

Average minimum ther. $50\frac{1}{4}°$ at sunrise.

10 days cloudy; three days rain; four days very windy, S.E. and N.W., the town sheltered from both; the lowest temperature in this month 41°, the highest 71°."

By way of a useful contrast, let us see how matters stand at the Undercliff with regard to rain and variation of thermometrical heat; assuming, for that purpose, as correct certain tables in a work containing some very brief notes on the climate of the southern coast of England, of which a new edition has lately been published, and from which my quotations are taken.

scenery, which the huge detached fragments from the cliffs above, and the elevation of the site of the spring, about one hundred and thirty feet from the sea-shore, on a bold and rugged wall of rock, have combined to form.

Either by tracing the Undercliff from east to west until we arrive to nearly the extreme southern point of the isle, on which rises St. Catherine Hill, and then ascending as far as the small village of Niton; or by mounting Steep-hill as you leave Ventnor, and proceeding through St. Lawrence to Whitwell, and so on again to Niton; we may reach, first, the Royal Sandrock Hotel, placed at the end of that village, and

The yearly mean temperature of the Undercliff is stated at 51.11, which includes the temperature of the summer months.

In this respect London is very little inferior to the Undercliff, for its yearly temperature is set down at 50.39.

Now *exclusive* of the summer months, we find the mean temperature at Villa Franca to be 56° : and such I am convinced will be found also to be the yearly and mean temperature of the glens in Bournemouth Park, when a sufficient number of observations shall have been made.

As to the mean variation of temperature at the Undercliff, contrasted with that of London, it is stated to be as 3.75 is to 4.01 (it should have been more correctly as 3.81 is to 4.19), a difference so trifling that it is scarcely worthy of notice, amounting really to .28 only, or not quite a third of a degree against the climate of London. It is in the mean variation of temperature during the coldest months alone that the superiority of the Undercliff to London appears manifest; for in November, December, and January, the difference is more than one whole degree in each month.

As to rain, the London differs from the Undercliff in a trifling degree; for there falls in the capital 26.686 inches of rain in the year, and 26.236 at the Undercliff. On reckoning the yearly number of rainy days at the latter place, we are informed that they amount to 144, whereas in London there are as many as 178 days of rain in the year.

But as compared to Villa Franca, the Undercliff is wet indeed; for in November, there are at the latter place 19 days ; in December, 10 days ; in January, 16 days ; and in February, 16 days of rain,—making a total of 61 days in four months; whereas in nearly the same period, or rather in three months and eleven days, seventeen days only of rain had occurred at Villa Franca.

next the aluminous chalybeate spring at Sandrocks, issuing half-way between Niton and the village of Chale.

The situation of the spring is extremely beautiful, commanding a view of the whole range of the Undercliff to the east, and of that part of the south-western coast of England we have so recently visited, to the west; while in front the wide expanse of the British Channel offers a never-ceasing source of attraction, in the numerous vessels and steamers that are tracking their silent way to and from distant climes.

Every provision and arrangement have been made by the zealous proprietor of the spring, to render it available to such invalids as resort thither for the sake of the water. No sooner had its composition been made known, more than twenty-five years ago, by an eminent scientific chemist, the late Dr. Marcet, than opportunities occurred to medical men in different parts of the country to test its virtues in several diseases. The presence of not less than forty-one grains of crystalized sulphate of iron in a pint of the water, at first deterred the practitioner from its free employment; nor was the addition of thirty-one grains of crystalized alum in the same quantity of the water likely to give him greater courage in employing it; the more so as in the same measure of the water there are only nineteen grains of saline matter, properly speaking, of a purgative nature. To what disease, indeed, *à priori*, could such a compound be applied?

The taste of the water is in itself so intensely styptic, that to drink even a wineglassful at first without being previously diluted, would require great resolution. To one liable to fulness of blood in the head, and of a warm and sanguine temperament, such an experiment would be positive death; and yet, even undiluted, the Sandrock water has been drunk, not only with impunity, but with excellent results. The fact is attested by the best authorities, those of Dr. Saunders, Dr. Latham, senior, Dr. Young, Dr. Calvert, Sir Charles Scudamore, and, above all, by Dr. Lempriere, formerly physician at the depot hospital on the island, on whose extended and successful application of the Sandrock water principally it was that others afterwards relied, for the propriety of using it in a variety of cases of disease, especially such as are accompanied by debility, prostration of the nervous energy after long miasmatic fevers, and in many disorders of the female constitution.

Viewing it, therefore, as a well-established British mineral spring, unique in this country as a chalybeate for its strength, though not in composition, since it resembles in that respect Horley-green and Calerley in Yorkshire, as well as the Hartfell waters in Scotland, I have deemed it my duty to insert its analysis in my general table, and to give this slight account of it, after a personal inspection, without however laying claim to any personal experience of its utility.

An excellent carriage-road, made over what had hitherto been but a trackless waste, would enable the visiter to regain the northern shore of the island by a far more romantic road without retracing his steps from Sandrock to the Undercliff, and so on to the seignorial residence of Appuldercombe and Newport, all which points of attraction I presume him to have visited before. Once safe in the villagé of Chale, after having escaped the horrors of *Black Gang Chine*, the traveller could easily wend his way along the sea-coast to Freshwater-gate, and so reach Yarmouth, having of course previously visited and expressed the usual degree of admiration at the view of the Needles and Alum Bay. The line of road hence across the country, from west to east, so as to reach the next attractive spot in the isle, RYDE, is easy enough; whence, after a passing glance at the principal hotels, the hot and cold baths, the range of bathing-machines drawn up on the extended sands, and the ricketty pier, the visiter might embark in the returning steamer for Southampton.

SOUTHAMPTON.

I have always been impressed with the conviction that, viewed under every possible aspect, Southampton offers to people having delicate lungs or irritable trachea, a retreat preferable almost to those found on the south-western coast, including Torquay itself. Having been well acquainted with the place for more than twenty-five years, and knowing the effect of the climate on invalids of all classes and constitutions, I can aver as much with perfect confidence. It is undeniable that Torquay, as we have seen, is more sheltered, is a greater snuggery, and a warmer place ;* but then there is too much moisture, owing to more frequent rain, as well as from the nature of the soil. For this reason it is a much more relaxing climate, inimical to nervous people of every description—more so than any other place on the coast from Sidmouth to Dartmouth.

In point of soil Southampton is greatly superior. Indeed one of its principal advantages is to rest on a high gravelly bank that separates the river Itchen from the bay, the fall of level of which in every direction is such that the streets are constantly kept dry. No sooner has the rain fallen than it is gone through the soil as through a filtering stone. An invalid, catching a glimpse of the noon sun in front of his dwelling during the winter, the moment after a heavy morning rain, can also safely face the air, and walk on the bare earth, as the one will not be found charged with the im-

* This last expression had scarcely dropped from my pen when I began to doubt whether such is really the case. On looking over a table of thermometric observations made during the last three months of 1838, and the first six months of 1839, and again during the month of January 1840, at one of the villas situated in the second region or district of Southampton, described in the present chapter, the average of each of those months seems to have been equal in most, and superior in a few instances to the mean temperature of Torquay quoted by Dr. De Barry.

mense dampness that hangs above ground for some time after rain in clay, sandstone, or even limestone soils; and the other will barely mark his shoes with moisture, for the moisture which the surface of clean quartz gravel retains after rain, is but a fraction of that which is maintained on the surface of any other species of soil except sand.

This of itself is an immense advantage. But there is another appertaining to a gravelly soil, which for health, and especially for such people as are obliged minutely to study every part of their own proceedings in order to preserve delicate health, is, in my opinion, of almost incalculable importance, though it has not been set forth by other observers or writers on climate. If attention be paid to the fact, it will be found that in walking over loose shingle, or angular flint-gravel, the feet become almost immediately warm, even when such gravel is yet wet from recently-fallen rain. Indeed, some people have suffered inconvenience after a long walk on loose shingle from that very circumstance; and the reason of that effect seems obvious : at each step the sole of the foot, pressing upon a plane of loose polyangular or round bits of flint, a general movement and rolling of the fragments takes place, producing friction on the sole of the foot, and, consequently, heat. This repeated every half-second, as each step is taken during a long walk, ends by exciting considerable warmth in the foot, and the promenader returns to his home with a quickened circulation in the lower extremities. But the gravel in such cases must be rather loose, as is the case in many of the streets, the roads, and walks about Southampton. Where it has been rolled and pressed down so as to form a dense, compact, smooth surface, like a mosaic pavement, especially if the gravel be of the smoothest sort, the effect is not so perceptible. Hence, I should always recommend to persons residing in large mansions in the country near the town during the winter, and having extensive pleasure-grounds,—or who are charged with the superintendence of paths and promenades near and about Southampton, to reserve a gravel walk exposed to the south-west sun near at hand, which shall be suffered to remain in a loose state, being merely smoothed from time to time with a garden-rake, and never rolled or pressed down. Such a walk will be dry sooner than any other after rain, and afford the pleasing and agreeable opportunity of warming and maintaining a comfortable warmth of the feet—an object of the first importance at all times and in all cases, but especially in those of invalids with delicate chests and tracheas, having recourse to Southampton air for refuge and protection from winter mischief.

It is a curious fact that, much as the climate of this neat and cheerful town is friendly to pectoral diseases, its influence on diseases of the digestive organs is of the very opposite character. Had I not had repeated occasions to ascertain the truth of this fact—had it not forced itself repeatedly on my attention—I could hardly have believed it. But so it is; and in the course of twenty-five years I have known whole families of dyspeptic people compelled to expatriate themselves from the land of their birth, and change quarters for good, after having repeatedly, but in vain, tried the effect of mere temporary absence from the hostile region, whither they would return when recovered from a severe attack of dyspepsia, principally of the nervous kind, but only to relapse again. On reflection, the reason of this result will appear evident; but as the present volumes are not intended for medical disquisitions, I must rest satisfied with simply having mentioned the subject.

Southampton never was or could be considered in the light of a sea-bathing place. It is certainly not so now that the all-devouring railway company, and its still more grasping twin-sister the dock company, have swept clean away the bath-buildings and the bathing-shores. Baths, indeed, of such sea-water as can reach so high from the Solent, are to be found at West Quay, and in Cuckoo-lane, near the pier, or even in one of the streets—Poland-street; but these would never form a temptation for any one to travel to Southampton, even though the swift-rolling train convey ye thither in three hours from the metropolis. No : Southampton, in a medical point of view, is only a desirable collection of comfortable lodging-houses, situated on a favourable soil, and within a peculiar friendly atmosphere, to which people betraying any excess of susceptibility in the organs of respiration may be sent for a temporary change. Fortunately, the many and extensive improvements which speculators of every sort have brought about, and which have served to substitute well-formed roads and convenient thoroughfares for the narrow and muddy lanes and alleys of a few years back, and to raise terraces and crescents of handsome dwellings, where the deep-cut trench, the hedge row and the barren heath only prevailed, have increased the accommodations of every class and value for such invalids as are here contemplated.

Three general rules, however, must be borne in mind in disposing of your visiting invalids at Southampton, according to the several kinds and degrees of indisposition under which they may labour. In the first place, your decided consumptive patient, whose case is purely and strictly of that character yet not bad enough to require the more sanative atmosphere of Bournemouth, may be sent to Southampton; but he must reside in the lower town and below bar, in some of the best streets to the left, or even in the principal thoroughfare of the town, which is now not only a beautiful, but an interesting feature of Southampton—its bustling activity and the gay company that generally parade it in the afternoon being, at the same time, highly favourable adjuvants to the locality. In the second place, if what is usually termed nervousness be a concomitant of the pulmonic tendency to disease, the dwellings to be selected must be such as are found above bar, going towards the London-road as far as where the turnpike used to stand, and thence inclining to the left in a slanting position, taking in a large tract of ground that has been covered with buildings of every description, arranged in streets, squares, and polygons, within the last twenty years. Rockstone-terrace, Carlton-crescent, and Carlton-house may be cited as some of these. Some detached villas there are on the outside boundary of this particular district, which mark as it were its termination, and the commencement of a third district or region for invalids. Their situation is most favourable; Bannisters is one of them, Clayfield, and Archers' Lodge two others, and a fourth is Bellevue, a large mansion facing the avenue to London, which enjoys the expansive and smiling prospect of the Itchen; though I should not consider the latter house so appropriate for a winter residence as the first-mentioned, or any other detached villa which may be built hereafter with the like aspect.

Thirdly, and lastly, those patients who, being visited with any sort of pulmonic disease in its incipient or merely threatening stage, are, also, unfortunately subject to dyspepsia, and require a more elastic medium to breath and digest in than is to be found in either of the two previous regions, must seek a higher district; and such an one, with excellent air and well-built houses, they will find on Shirley Common, recently enclosed by act of Parliament, and to which immediate access is had by Hill-lane, branching off the Romsey-road.

An invalid residing for the winter at Southampton should live on the first floor, and put a double sash to all windows that face either the east or the north, never ventilating the house but by a south or west window, which should be open some time at noon, whenever there is any sunshine. The best position to be selected for the two last months of the year, and until the end of the spring, would be a house which should receive the south-east sun, and have it until noon in one part, while in another part the setting sun impinges on the western casement to cheer the close of day. Such houses are to be found at Southampton in each of the three regions I have alluded to.

In point of residence for people of delicate health, Southampton, if public report is to be credited, will soon exhibit a novel feature, by the execution of a projected plan whereby the whole, or at least the largest portion of that well-wooded and cheerful bank of the Southampton estuary, or water extending between the Itchen and the Hamble, including the venerable remains of Nettley Abbey, will be converted into an assemblage of villas, and rows of dwellings with gardens. The situation is admirable, and the general aspect one of the most favourable description. A proper and judicious choice of spots for the erection of particular houses, or the formation of crescents and terraces (for in that everything consists) will render this locality the most to be preferred by invalids of the class first mentioned, who are anxious to benefit by the Southampton air.

I cannot believe another report made to me respecting the future destiny of the well-wooded ridge on the left bank of the Itchen just alluded to. The Dock Company may perchance require, in the immediate vicinity of their basons, close to the margin of the water, room for the erection of warehouses, and for that purpose a large portion of the ridge is said to have already been levelled and cleared. But they surely can never have seriously contemplated the notion of letting or selling the remainder of the ground to the south of the mouth of the river, and all along as far as Nettley Abbey, to a publican, for the purpose of building ordinary houses to accommodate the people employed in the docks, for whose Sunday amusement and edification the venerable ruins of the abbey too are to be desecrated, and its site converted into a tea-garden! Every chance of securing the best and a safe retreat at Southampton to people of delicate lungs in the first degree of that disease mentioned in this chapter, will have been thrown away quite, should such a barbarian scheme be carried into execution.

But there is no end of the pertinacity of error in building in this country as to situations. From the shore of the Itchen, just by the Ferry, a rising hill ascends gently towards the N.E. up to a village bearing the name of the river, and inhabited by people engaged in fishing. At the top of it is Pear Tree Green, which is exposed to the east. The village itself is in a dell, with miserable huts on each side. These demolished, and good houses erected instead, the place would offer a very sheltered, warm, and comfortable situation, having an excellent aspect for invalids with chest complaints, while the present industrious inhabitants would gladly exchange it for another lower down and nearer to their calling. But no : gentlemen prefer having their dwellings on the Green, exposed fully to the east winds, like those belonging to two gentlemen, who I believe once represented Southampton in Parliament, and that of a noble lord, who, however, has taken care to embosom his within a sort of plantation.

Those who object to the smell arising from the mud at low water, or dread its supposed effluvia, entertain in the case of the Southampton water, an estuary ten miles in length, and more than two miles broad, unfounded apprehensions. Indeed, as far as the class of invalids is concerned, for whose sake I should rejoice to see a judicious conversion of the Chamberlayne lands into mansions and villas, the circumstance of emanations from sea deposits being in their immediate neighbourhood is favourable rather than not. It is for this reason that I did not lay so much stress as others have done when writing about Torquay, on the inconvenience of having a small inner harbour, which at low water sends forth its mud effluvia ; although I admit that it is anything but agreeable. Nor can I be accused of inconsistency in maintaining, in the case of Southampton, a different notion from that expressed respecting Teignmouth. The whole difference in the latter case consists in the sheet of water at that port being a large river, bringing down and depositing before the town its own peculiar vegetable and animal impurities along with the mud left by the receding tide; whereas the sheet of water at Southampton is an open arm of the sea, in a direct line with Spithead, and the east part of the English Channel, as well as with the Solent in communication with the west channel. And as for the three river streams which pour their fresh-water tribute into the bay, their contributions are too insignificant to cause any impression different from that which I am disposed to attribute to the emanations of the Southampton water at low tides.

The atmosphere of such a neighbourhood, indeed, in the winter season must prove beneficial to invalids having incipient tubercular disease of the lungs, from being slightly charged (and it can only be slightly during cold weather) with bromine, and probably iodine also, both of which impart that particular marine smell to the uncovered bottoms of deep tidal bays. Whatever *debris* of vegetable or animal substance the retreating wave may leave behind, neither the length of time during which they can possibly remain exposed before they are again covered by the returning tide, nor the solar or atmospheric heat of an English climate during the winter (the only season I counsel invalids to sojourn here), can induce decomposition, still less putrefaction, so as to render them sources of mischief. I should be sorry to recommend to any patient or friend of mine to place himself close to the backwater at Southampton, between the pier and Milbrook for example, where, nevertheless, a terrace of small houses, called Bletchenden I believe, has just been erected; and still less on the opposite shore, with the face turned to the east, during the dog-days (if such days are ever given to make their appearance amongst us) or in any hot months generally. The effluvia from the uncovered mud at these times may really prove injurious, for reasons obvious to every understanding; but during nine months of the year I hold the Southampton water to be not merely harmless, but likely to be of good service.

I may close this summary medico-topographical account of Southampton with a general statement, that in point of auxiliaries to a retreat for invalids, so essential to the promotion of their health, the town abounds, and is every day acquiring new ones. In one only important article is Southampton deficient, namely, good potable water. What is now drank is derived principally from reservoirs on the common, receiving the drainage water of that extensive region; and Southampton has often been much distressed for want of a good supply of water. An attempt has been made at forming an Artesian well, but hitherto without success. The water of the several springs in the place is hard and unfit for culinary or other domestic purposes.

In point of any other auxiliaries, particularly out-of-door exercise, the place is abundantly rich. A quiet walk down High-street at two o'clock, when the air is dry and still, and when equipages and pedestrians saunter or course up and down the same line, as if the whole of the best company in the place had given themselves rendezvous for the purpose of one daily universal recognition; an extension of the same, as far as the Royal Pier, itself perhaps one of the greatest improvements of Southampton, and an object of curiosity, but to the invalid in particular one of diversion, from the variety of scenes he may witness upon it; at other times a drive over the commons and to the neighbouring mansions of the wealthy; or, crossing the Itchen over the bridge, or by the steam ferry, a ride in the direction of the Gosport road;—all these resources are offered to the resident invalid at Southampton, with many others to prevent *ennui*, kill time, and promote health-giving exercise in the open air.

CHAPTER XII.

BRIGHTON.

THE ROYAL GERMAN SPA.

BRIGHTON and the REGENT's Park—The Refuge of Convalescents—Two Miles and a Half of Lodging-houses and Hotels—SEA-BATHING Indifferent—Impediments and Objections—Ladies and Gentlemen's Bathing-machines—Where is Decorum?—The ROYAL BATHS—The Great Swimming-bath—MAHOMED's Baths—MAHOMED Himself—Life and Progress of an Hindoo Nonagenarian—An Arsenal of Trophies—Other BATHS—The CLIFFS—East and West Brighton—The Old Centre and the Old Ship—MARINE Brighton—INLAND Brighton—Private Palaces and Royal Hotels by the Sea-side—Residence too near the Sea injurious to many Patients—The GREAT CLIFF and the finest Sea-Promenade in England—Early Rising not in Vogue at Brighton—Fashionable Hours for Walking and Riding—GRAND DISPLAY—Air of Brighton, to whom Useful and to whom Injurious—The ROYAL GERMAN SPA—Its Origin and Progress—Description and Apparatus—The Pump-room—Distribution of the Waters—The Hot and Cold—Prodigious Sale of the Latter—Errors and Delusions—Argument in Support of Errors Confuted—The late DR. TODD—DR. HALL—The Artificial Waters—The NATURAL CHALYBEATE at Brighton—HOUSE ACCOMMODATION—Expenses of LODGING and HOUSE RENT—Objections of the Brighton Houses—COST of Living—Will be Cheapened by the Railway—WATER and other Necessaries—Dinner Parties—Gaslight and the Police—Dismal Environs of Brighton—The DOWNS—Its Barren Declivities converted into Forests—VIEW of Brighton from Land—St. Peter's Church—THE ROYAL PAVILION.

ON Brighton I need not dwell long. As well might I undertake a description of the new terraces on the east side of the Regent's Park, which, with the sea before them instead of the lawns, now the subject of a scramble between the patrician and the plebeian, might not inaptly represent your Portland or your Brunswick-terraces on the East Cliff and the King's-road at Brighton.

Yet to that celebrated place my attention is due, from its being the resort of a great number of real or fanciful patients tired of London, or anxious to give the slip to their doctors ; as well as from its receiving annually thousands of convalescents despatched thither by the doctors themselves. It commands attention also as being the place selected by the late skilful and lamented Professor of Dresden, Struve, for establishing one of those manufactories of artificial German mineral waters, for which he has acquired unfading celebrity, and which, in the present instance, has been denominated the Royal German Spa.

As respects the claims of Brighton for anything else—sea-bathing for instance—I may as well say at once, and that in a very few words—it is, in this particular, not bad, but it is indifferent. The shore will not admit of any better. From the east end of Arundel-terrace, Kemp-town, to the west end of Brunswick-terrace in the King's-road—a line of shore measuring more than two miles and a half in length, exposed to the south, south-south east, south, and south-south west (no better aspects than these)—there is not as much as a palm of good clean sands to bathe upon at high water. The bather, for this purpose, must wait until low water has uncovered such sands as lie at the distance of nearly a quarter of a mile from the shore, where the bathing-machines are ready to receive him. The shore itself, strewed with shingles, sinking and heavy, is in parts abruptly shelving and deep ; a circumstance which deters hundreds of people from bathing where the sea covers the beach ; added to which, the water is always foul-looking, from the number of sea-weeds that are constantly being thrown on the coast.

It is not long since there existed a still greater objection against bathing in the open sea at Brighton, which has since been removed by the establishment of the great parallel sewer, executed with praiseworthy spirit and judgment by the town authorities : first, along the East Cliff, completed in 1839 ; and next, along the West Cliff and the King's-road, which was in the act of completion at the time of my visit. By this arrangement the drainage and sewerage of Brighton are no longer suffered to mingle with the tidal water from a great many drain-pipes opening a little way on the beach, where I had often observed with disgust, before the recent improvements, the meandering streams of pollution issuing from those pipes, not far from where bathing took place, and in hot weather not only smelling abominably, but penetrating into the cellars of some of the houses.

Lastly, we may reckon as among the impediments to good sea-bathing at Brighton, those singular-looking divisions of the beach into sections or parts called *groynes*, on each side of which the shingle will accumulate, and form as many ridges or backbones at right angles with the cliff, and against which it is by no means pleasant to knock one's head or one's feet while diving or swimming.

All these untoward circumstances render the aid of bathing-machines absolutely necessary, in order to transport the bathers far enough into clean water, four or five feet deep. Accordingly we find these useful auxiliaries during the bathing season, ready on different points of the shore, and placed at such a distance as will secure the necessary quantity of water for a dip or a plunge.

At my last visit I found three stands of them destined for the use of the ladies, between Kemptown and the Old Steine ; and four for gentlemen westward of the Steine, as far as Regency-square. The attendants are principally old women ; but the ladies who used the machines on the beach at Kemptown, seemed to prefer being carried to their distant, and almost floating *cabinet-des-bains,* in the brawny arms of stout, broad-shouldered fellows employed for that purpose. It would be ludicrous if it were not somewhat indecent, to behold how fast these modern naïads cling to their lusty neptunes while the latter hurry through the waves with their fair cargoes, until they deposit them in the floating bath-room, where a female attendant is at hand to help and guide them in and out of the water. Such a practice, however, (much as it may be deemed objectionable) the dangerous appearance of the shore in this place would seem almost to sanction.

The gentlemen on their own side are not less objects of curiosity at times ; for many lacking courage after they have stripped to the skin, will stand on the outer steps of the machine, shivering and hesitating, their persons in the meanwhile wholly exposed, owing to the want of hood that ought to project over the steps, as is the case at all decent sea-bathing places. No attempt has as yet been made by the authorities to set this right, and the practice remains as a stain on the *gentility* of the Brighthelmstonians.

But though the open sea-bathing be not of the best—that in sea-water collected in the several bath-houses at Brighton is deemed unobjectionable. The most attractive of these establishments is the gentlemen's circular swimming-bath of Charles Brill, late Lamprell's, distinguished by its hemispherical dome from among the rest of the buildings on the Grand Junction Parade, in which a complete course of lectures on swimming is given for five guineas. Connected with these are the Royal Baths at the end of Great East-street, which had lately been refurnished and fitted up afresh, and seemed clean and well appointed, but without any of that luxury or style which I remarked at Scarborough. There is an air of freshness and of sweet atmosphere throughout Brill's house, which I missed in Mahomed's establishment, —the next one at hand.

One of the greatest curiosities at Brighton, by the bye, in

the way of bathing, is, not Mahomed's house—for that indeed recommends itself but indifferently, either for smartness, size, and sweetness of the apartments, or for any of those qualifications for which bathing establishments elsewhere are generally commended—it is Mahomed himself—SAKE DEEN MAHOMED, who is nearly as old as his more holy name-sake and prophet, who stands before you to tell his own story and panegyric, and narrates it erect, hale, firm, and without tremulousness of any sort, at the age of ninety-two! Out of pure respect for this quasi-century on two legs, one listens attentively to all he has to say. How he first entered the Indian army, and fought in all the battles on the banks of the Ganges and the Brahmapootra, and was at the siege of Chunarghur and Mirzapoor, and Heaven knows what other sieges, and got a commission, and found himself penniless by the breaking of his banker in Calcutta (no uncommon thing, by the bye, in that region), and how he came to Europe to work out the skill he had acquired by a few years' service in the *medical department*, to do good to suffering humanity, and become " a very celebrated character." Nor is this all; for if the nonagenarian notices that you look in the least incredulous at his narrated miracles, he insists upon drawing you towards the top of the stairs which lead into his kitchen, and there exhibits to you, hanging on every part of the wall, a museum of what he calls his " testimonials"—his trophies, in fact, in the shape of crutches, spine-stretchers, leg-irons, head-strainers, bump-dressers, and club-foot reformers, all regularly ticketed with as much skill as the ornithological specimens at the British Museum used to be a year or two ago as thus; " this is a duck, and there is a goose," so as not to mistake the nature of the objects. " And these," exclaims the Hindoo, " these are the tributes paid to my skill by the gentlemen whom my method of schampooing, and a particular oil I employ, have enabled to leave their cumbersome tools and utensils behind them." This extraordinary man settled at Brighton forty years ago, when there were only eight instead of the present sixty thousand inhabitants in the place.

I was well satisfied with Bannister's Baths, the next in order; they are equally as creditable as the Royal Baths or Lamprell's. He has six baths for each sex, with a separate dressing-room to each, and the back of the house is towards the sea.

Harrison's, Creak's, and the Battery Baths I also visited, and found them to be well calculated for their intended object.

In all these establishments, water is drawn from the sea on the coming in of the tide, by aspirating pumps moved by horse or steam power. By them it is thrown up into lofty reservoirs, in one of which the water is heated by means of steam-pipes, and whence the one and the other are ready to be let down into the baths as required. As the average charge for the hot-baths at almost all the houses, I may quote a guinea subscription for eight of them, except at Brill's, where the charges are lower.

But the cliffs, and not the baths are, after all, the great and striking features which distinguish Brighton from all other English sea-bathing places. Brighton—fashionable Brighton I mean—is wholly developed and spread in a long continuous line on the crest of a high shore to the east, which gently and insensibly slopes down to the west until it reaches the STEINE, where it assumes and continues on a flat and level ground for nearly a mile further westwards. The Steine on which the principal and central square has been formed, marks the bed of the ancient valley of Brighton, which creeping inland and upwards with greater and lesser width in a continuous line, passing by the Royal Pavilion, and subdivided into North Steine, the lawn of St. Peter's Church, and an open space higher up called "the Level," a little to the right of the London road, serves to separate most completely the town into two nearly equal parts, which might be styled East and West Brighton.

Old Original Brighton forms but a very small portion of this whole, and lies immediately contiguous and to the left, or westward of the Steine; and I remember well when the Old Ship (the very hotel I now selected, from cherished recollection) was, thirty-three years ago, the principal *rendezvous* of the sea-officers cruizing against privateers, between Beachy-head and Dunnose, and landing occasionally in calm weather on this shingly shore. A sort of watering-place reputation was even then beginning to dawn on Brighton, though a mere village at that time, with a population of about 8000 inhabitants.

The largest and best decorated *concert-rooms* are in this very hotel, the Old Ship, the coffee-room of which is greatly frequented. From this centre has Brighton spread right and left, keeping principally to the shore, for every one will have a peep at the sea.

In most of the provincial towns and places in England, and it is so of those by the sea-side, we find some peculiar feature or physiognomy that distinguishes them from the capital. But at Brighton none such exists. Walk from Kemptown to Regency-square, look not to the sea, and close your ears to its murmurs, and you will be inclined to believe that you are walking in one of the leading streets of the metropolis. Brighton is a portion of the " west end" of London *maritimized*.

Of late years, however, Brighton has been struggling to escape from the sea. It is creeping up inland, principally by the side of the valley before-mentioned; but the style of houses is hardly suited to the condition of persons whom a judicious physician would recommend to reside at Brighton for a change of air, in places like those I am now referring to, within the immediate influence of a vast range of chalk hills, so salutary in many cases,—not so much exposed to frequent draughts and gales,—and above all, protected from the immediate saline emanations inland of the sea, often injurious. In these respects, perhaps the locality I allude to is the best in Brighton; but it has not been properly worked out; for the present habitations in the vicinity of St. Peter's, for instance, or in Brunswick-place, or Hanover-crescent, &c., are fit only for people of humble fortune, and the buildings are in accordance with that object. The aspect too of these second and third rate houses is in most instances injudicious, and might have been easily made better.

The Richmond Hotel is one of the buildings in this direction, and at the head of the North Steine, which first attracted my attention. Its west-north-west aspect might suit many invalids requiring the bracing air of Brighton, without the positive influence of sea air. The Gloucester Hotel, on the other hand, which is also a very good-looking house, and well arranged, on the opposite side of the North Steine, is not so eligible, owing to its principal front and rooms being dead east.

Mr. Barry, disregarding all canon laws, and the ecclesiastical rules usually followed in such cases, has seated St. Peter's (the first public edifice of any magnitude, I believe, which he undertook on settling in this country, after his return from Italy, and which led to his rapidly fortunate career) nearly north and south, placing the principal entrance at the south, and thus subverting the universal rule which requires that the lateral entrances only of great Gothic temples, those of the transept, should be north and south.

There is another public building which, both on account of the lofty station it occupies in the heart of Old Brighton, and the singularity of its architectural arrangement, might be considered worthy of notice. It is the Town Hall, erected at an expense of 30,000l., and serving all sorts of purposes. But it is fortunately screened by many other houses, and the occasional visiter at Brighton often quits the place without ever suspecting that such an unsightly object exists in it.

Of the thousand people who are sent to the sea-side for a change of air, or the peculiar benefits of sea breezes, not one in five derives the expected advantage from their residence at Brighton, owing to the very circumstance of their choosing to dwell in the best and most tempting houses, which are all either immediately or indirectly contiguous to the shore. In this position they are too long and too much exposed to the direct inhalation of saline particles, which are notoriously hostile, in a majority of cases, to a vast number of diseases that might otherwise be benefited by a judicious selection of situations in the *vicinity* of the coast. The invalids themselves are not long in discovering this fact; and although almost all, at first, try to be splendidly lodged on the King's-road, and enjoy the luxuries of the Bedford, the St. Albans, the Royal Cliff, or the Royal Sea-house hotels, not to mention those of the Marine Hotel, and the boarding-houses on the Marine-parade,—a very small number of such invalids can prolong their sojourn there with impunity. They therefore change the lower plain, where they are in fact nearly on a level with the margin of the sea, and where the saline atmosphere will penetrate the chinks of their splendid drawing and bed-room windows, for a higher one, and take up their abode on the East Clift, in the magnificent saloons of the Bristol, or the private houses of Portland-terrace, or the semi-palaces of Lewes-crescent, and of Sussex-place. If mere elevation above the surface of the sea be not sufficient to protect from saline influence, then the many lateral squares and streets to be found branching off the Cliff, especially the east front of all such places, as Portland-place, the Marine-square, New Steine, will supply eligible residences.

The Cliff at Kemptown soars far above the sea-margin, to which a series of three descending terraces leads down in a symmetrical form, and with a very showy appearance. But once down to the shore, little or no temptation is to be found for plunging into the water, as the whole of this section of the beach in front of Kemp-town at low water is frightful to look at; an aspect which extends a great way into the sea. Add to which, the shingly shore itself is steep in parts, and very abrupt, and the bathing altogether would seem to be an operation of some danger.

It is from this identical spot, where the coast is highest at Brighton, that begins what I should call the great cliff. The corporate body of Brighton may indeed claim the merit of having in a most spirited manner caused to be executed, at an expense which would have appalled even the government, one of the finest, indeed the finest marine promenade in the world. One hundred and fifty thousand pounds applied to the erection of a lofty and solid sea-wall, in many parts sixty feet in height, and that wall supporting a terraced walk, with a wooden railing, and a wide, firm, and well-made *trottoir*, on which Bath-chairs for invalids are permitted to be drawn, and contiguous to which is a straight and ample carriage-way, flanked by a long and parallel line of houses, many of them of considerable architectural merit—such results, I say, and at such an expenditure of money, may well be considered as a Roman work.

" But we shall pay for it," exclaim the inhabitants, even while admitting the magnificence of the work. And so it is. Rates and imposts have accordingly been laid on the citizens and housekeepers, to defray the expenses of the mighty undertaking. Yet better to pay than be deprived of so imposing, so useful, so unique a promenade, which is indeed without a rival in any sea-town. It has made a difference of fifty per cent. to Brighton since this marine promenade has been completed, as compared to what it will be recollected to have been a very few years back, when the East Cliff was in a perilous, irregular, and unsafe condition, with many petty meandering sewers beneath, spreading around their stench at low water, and when the face of the cliff, uneven in its surface, served as the depository of all the ordure housemaids nad others might please to throw down, until swept away perchance by some friendly spring-tide.

In the simplicity of my heart, I bethought me that as people are sent hither to enjoy the sea-air for their health, they would be found at early morn pacing this grand parade; but early rising is not among the customs of the place. At seven o'clock I never observed a decent-looking person out of doors, and between that hour and nine, those only would be seen abroad who drove, walked, or crept along to the German Spa. But the mere visiter to the sea-side for the recovery of his health never appears, as he ought to do on all fine mornings, on the Great Cliff, there to inhale the purer and subdued breezes of the ocean at sunrise, when the salt exhalations are hardly begun.

"But it is now between three and four P. M., with a fine brilliant sunshine,"—so I read in my note-book;—"the sea is clear and still, and the horizon visible to an immense distance. The water is quietly creeping in, and covers the ill-looking beach. It had rained the best part of the morning, and the streets had been deserted ; but now the people, one and all, have sallied out of their shelters, and boldly face the dry and inspiriting air. What a wretched place Brighton is, if we take away the sun! True, there is not as yet the dense emanation of burning coals along the two shores, to contaminate their atmosphere; and the only annoyance peculiar to the place by which the front of the principal edifices facing the sea is visited, is the damp sea-fog, instead of the thick yellow and throat-tickling atmosphere of London, in which Monsieur Darcet detected the presence of sulphurous and sulphuric acid. Still without the sun, Brighton must be detestable, particularly if, at the same time, pouring and never-ending rain should confine the invalids to their bow-windowed chambers and parlours ; *Il y a de quoi se tuer d'ennui.*"

But when the glorious planet lights up the two cliffs, and sheds its genial warmth on places of public resort, the terraces, the piers, and the walks—when the pedestrians and their fair mates—when the equestrian groups, and the " flies," and the numerous and handsome equipages come forth to parade along, and fill those haunts of fashion from the Junction Parade to Brunswick-square westwards, and again from the Albion Grand Hotel to Kemp Town eastwards,—oh, then Brighton is enchanting ! and so it is indeed during the autumnal months, and for many days in winter also ; for which reason it is that the place has acquired great renown at that season, among invalids and wealthy idlers, and will continue to retain it, as long as British clime remains unchanged.

Yet Brighton air is not suited to all cases ; and in many, indeed, it is of a positive injury to the patients. Persons labouring under almost permanent febrile symptoms ; those who are frequently attacked with bile, or are in any way afflicted with bilious complaints attended with an irritable state of the intestines ; people who are subject to inflammatory complaints, who have a quick pulse, who labour under any suspicion of organic derangement of the head, or of any of its annexed blood-vessels : all such people will be unable to remain long at Brighton, without feeling, to their cost, that the air of the place is not the thing for them : it is too dry, it is too irritating, it accelerates very inconveniently the circulation.

On the other hand, the many hundreds of thousands of convalescents from any disease already successfully removed, who require merely the help of dry, pure, invigorating air for a month or so, to be themselves again ; or on whom a living panorama of artificial life, rather than the aspect of nature, makes a favourable impression, and aids to brace the nerves ; these indeed will derive prompt and lasting benefit. In fact and in two words, Brighton is a place for convalescents, not for patients ; and the rapidity with which in future people will be able to be despatched thither, will induce medical men to say, when dealing with such convalescents as want nothing better than air different from that of London to be made sound, " Go to Brighton,"—just as they used to say, " Go to Hampstead."

There is only one reason for sending real patients to Brighton, and that is the establishment of the German Spa already alluded to,—at which almost all the most efficient mineral waters of Germany are successfully imitated and administered to invalids, agreeably to a plan devised and fully laid down by Professor Struve. The opinion I entertained of this establishment from its very first introduction at Brighton, I fully expressed in the second volume of my work of travels to St. Petersburgh, while describing Dresden and its institutions, where the professor had established the original manufactory of mineral waters. The German Spa was then in its infancy ; it had existed but two years, and great difficulty was experienced in defending its interest against prejudice and incredulity. A patent for the beautiful process and machinery for manufacturing the mineral waters, which had been obtained for fourteen years, was about to expire, when at the close of 1837, after protracted discussion before the lords of the council, and a close examination of the author of these volumes, among other witnesses who testified to the novelty as well as the value of the discovery, a renewal of the same was granted for seven years more ; and it is a source of gratification to one who was among the first to encourage Struve in his undertaking at Brighton, to see it prosper in every way. As I have already alluded to the principles which led Struve to adopt his peculiar mode of imitating mineral waters, and partly described the process by which that imitation was successfully carried into effect, it will be unnecessary for me to repeat my former observations in this place. I would invite every one who feels an interest in mineral waters and is not so blinded by prejudice as to suppose it impossible to produce anything like a close resemblance of the natural waters by means of machinery, to go and visit that which is to be seen at work every day in the week, Sundays excepted, from the 1st of May till the month of November, at the German Spa—a smart-looking building in the south-east angle of the only decent plantation to be seen near or about Brighton, called "the Park."*

* A succinct summary description from Mr. Schweitzer himself of the practical working of the German Spa, as contained in a letter from that gentleman to me, under date of the 15th of February, 1837, will be read with interest by all who are likely to use the artificial mineral waters.

"The establishment is divided into two parts—the chemical and the mechanical part. The object of the first is to analyse the natural mineral waters, and to produce ingredients *chemically pure* for the manufacture of the same. The ingredients are united to each other according to equivalents, and the quantity of the same is established by a minute analysis. The medium by which they are dissolved is distilled water, for the production of which is constructed a particular apparatus, which when in action is never heated above 212° Fahr., and the level of the water is constantly kept up. This water is without any gaseous or solid contents except a little atmospheric air, of which it is freed in a proper apparatus by means of carbonic acid gas; in this state the water is ready for the reception of the ingredients. The production of pure carbonic acid gas is another principal point, and for that purpose several apparatus are constructed. On the purity of the carbonic acid gas depends greatly the perfection of the mineral waters. It is a known fact that chalybeates cannot be exported from their natural source without undergoing a material change. This difficulty we prevent by an able apparatus,—every bottle is filled with pure carbonic acid gas before the mineral water is introduced. Dr. Struve has entirely succeeded in producing a perfect imitation of nature, as he has paid the greatest attention to the most minute ingredients, and by his process dissolves those which have hitherto been considered insoluble; namely, phosphate of lime, fluate of lime, flint, barytes, &c. The mechanical part occupies itself with the machinery and apparatus. All the vessels are composed of many parts, which close hermetically. The vessels for the production of the mineral waters are connected by pipes with the gas pumps, which are again connected by pipes with the gasometers. The quantity of gas introduced into the mineral waters is controlled by mercury guages. The vessels for

Thither some hundreds of people, the average of whom will continue their attendance from four to five weeks, proceed every day between the hours of eight and ten o'clock, A.M., to drink such of the mineral waters as their medical attendant, or their own choice and fancy, or the recommendation of people who think themselves entitled to give an opinion, may have pointed out. The subscription is a guinea per week, which of late years 'has sufficed to defray the expenses, and yields a profit to the proprietors.

One of the defects of this place is the want of more ample space for walking; which can only be procured by a farther permission from the proprietors of the park, to whom application was about to be made for that purpose. The pump or promenade room in rainy weather is soon filled; for it is small, and has none of those gay and showy appliances which are so attractive at the German Kursaals. Unlike, too, what takes place at the German springs, the water-bibber here drinks in faith; for the water does not bubble up from the earth, but flows from a silver or glass spout, on the turning of the stop by the fair hand of the smart lass whom Mr. Schweitzer, the manager, director, and part pro-

the dispensation of the mineral waters connected with the pump-room are so constructed, that during the dispensation, the temperature and the proportion of gas are constantly kept to correspond with that of its prototype: for that purpose are the vessels furnished with thermometers and mercury guages.

" I hope this rough sketch will meet your wish, if not, I stand at your service for any further request.

" Permit me to draw your attention to two great advantages which our establishment affords to the public.

" 1. The dispensation of thermal mineral springs, which do not bear carrying any distance without a great chemical change—therefore unfit for export.

" 2. The exportation of chalybeates in a perfect state. The carbonate of iron, which you are aware is a most obstinate preparation, and exists only perfect in mineral waters, has never been kept in solution in artificial mineral waters, until Dr. Struve, by his persevering researches, succeeded in dissolving this problem."

prietor of the concern, has appointed for the purpose, and who is always ready with a civil answer to everybody, and a beaker of the respective water required.

The thermal waters, such as those of Carlsbad and Ems, are the first of the series, arranged in a line successively from left to right behind an elliptical counter in the pump-room. Next follow the cold mineral waters, including most of those I described in my volumes on the Spas of Germany, and one or two others of that country, besides the water of Saratoga in the United States. These cold waters are sent to every part of England, and I have authority for stating that owing to my strong and decided commendation of them, their sale has more than quadrupled from 1837, at which time the first edition of the Spas of Germany made its appearance, to the end of 1839, when an official report of the quantities sold was sent for my inspection. To facilitate the sale of those waters, agents have been appointed in London and other principal cities, and I have for many years been in the habit of referring my patients to one of them, Mr. Waugh, a most respectable chemist in Regent-street, who is charged with that sale at the west-end of the town.

Of course it is only the cold waters, as already stated, that are sold, and the entire aggregate quantity of those disposed of in the course of the four years before alluded to, converted into pints, has amounted to 217,956. This quantity of mineral water, large as it may appear, I have reason to believe, has considerably increased during the past and present year. Indeed, the number of those who attend at the Spa itself during the season, appeared also to have been considerably augmented in 1839, having then reached the cypher of 527, as I ascertained by inspection of the register in the pump-room, while in the year of my last visit (1840) the number was already 465 to the middle of September, with six weeks more of the season to run.

The only objection I can name to this multifarious mineral-water establishment of Struve, is one which subsequent experience only has forced on my attention; for, *à priori*, I could not imagine it possible that I should ever have cause for urging it. The facility which this bringing together of many mineral waters from all parts of Germany far asunder, under one roof, and within a single reach, has afforded to patients for mingling two, three, and sometimes four of them together, and swallowing them with an expectation of benefit, which is and must be disappointed, is the objection I must urge against the German Spa at Brighton, where alone that practice obtains, under some extraordinary delusion.

The very first person I beheld on entering the pump-room one day, was a lady who had some years before been under my care in London, and who now was in the act of drinking the Theresienbrunnen of Carlsbad and the Pyrmont together; while a relative of hers applied her glass successively to the spouts of Kissingen, Ems, and Pullna. And yet such things, which in the end must prove the ruin of the artificial mineral waters if persevered in, and which the first lamented and skilful director of the establishment, Mr. Walcker —to whose memory I was happy to find a modest monument erected in the Spa-garden—would never countenance by his own advice—such things, I say, have been defended; and certain medical men make it a practice to encourage them! On one occasion, I was referred by a person, who ought to know better, to what takes place at the Spas themselves in Germany, as a triumphant answer to my objection against so absurd a practice. But I challenged the individual to cite a single place in Germany where two or three waters of different parts of the world are mixed and drank at the same time. He will find at the several thermal baths where bathing is the order of the day, as at Wiesbaden for example, Baden, and Töplitz, that the patients are occasionally directed to drink of *some one* of the cold mineral waters imported in bottles from their respective sources, or the imitation of the same. Thus it is not unusual to order a regular course of the

Paulinen from Schwalbach to a patient who is bathing in the Kochbrunnen or Alderquelle at Wiesbaden; but in which of the Spas of Germany, in the name of good sense, has it ever happened, except at the German Spa at Brighton, that the Pyrmont, and the Ems, and the Pullna, have been ordered to be drank at one and the same time, as a regular and daily practice?

I would fain also make a remark or two with respect to the imitation of the thermal waters as contrasted with that of the cold mineral waters; but my sentiments on that all-important point are so well known from all I have said in my former writings, that I deem it needless to repeat them in this place. Every year's ulterior experience has confirmed and further elucidated those views—from which I did not abate one iota during the life of the eminent discoverer of the process for imitative waters himself,—nor have I reason to shrink from them now he is no more, and no better advocate of the contrary opinion left behind. I would ask a simple question on this subject: If the artificial Carlsbad water with artificial heat be as valid as the natural, how comes it that not a single pint-bottle of it is to be found among the quarter of a million of pints of artificial mineral waters manufactured and sold at the German Spa as before stated? Surely it would not be difficult to impart a coal-heat of 134° to a bottle of the Theresienbrunnen, without detriment to the in-significant proportion of carbonic acid gas it contains; for that quantity of the gas might be preserved, and in that case, a bottle of Theresienbrunnen ought to be as effi-cacious in its own sphere as any of the artificially imi-tated cold mineral waters. Why, then, is it I ask once more, that not one bottle of the Carlsbad or Ems waters has been sold?

The physician to whom the fortune of the German Spa at Brighton is mostly indebted, was the late Dr. Todd, a highly respectable and amiable man, who had formed to himself an extensive practice, the principal part of which, I am happy to learn, has fallen into the no less able hands of Dr. Hall, —who is well versed in the use of the artificial mineral waters, but not like his predecessor, fond of ordering two or three different waters at the same time.

Most people know that besides the German Spa, there is at Brighton a natural mineral spring—a chalybeate—with the particular virtues of which I am not myself sufficiently acquainted to say much about it. That it has been recently analyzed by Professor Daniel, and commented upon by Dr. Paris in terms of approbation, are sufficient reasons why I should mention in these volumes the Wick chalybeate of Brighton.*

* In both my first and second edition of " The Spas of Germany," I had occasion to point out the gross error committed by the author of a small work on the watering-places of the continent, in having compared the *Wick* chalybeate of Brighton with the *Bruckenauer* in Bavaria, than which, I declared at the time, no two springs could be more dissimilar. I felt convinced that the author had never seen the source he pretended to describe. The same writer, in a more recent pamphlet on " English Mineral Springs," published subsequently to the first volume of my present work, has made the following acknowledgment of the correctness of my charge against him, though without referring to the individual who pointed out his blunder. " In my former work (says Mr. Lee) I compared it (the Wick chalybeate) with the water of Bruckenau, which *I had not at that time visited* (a circumstance he suppressed before); but, in fact, no two springs belonging to the same class present a greater difference." This is not the first time that the same author has been forced to admit that in his prolific, but slender duodecimos on German waters, containing just as much information as can be found compiled in a gazetteer, he had ventured on descriptions of places he had never seen. In regard to Wildbad, I also convicted him, and made him acknowledge in his " Baths of Germany" (first part), that when he first described that Spa he had never seen the place. And now I venture to assert with equal assurance, that in his second and slenderer, and more meagre account of the " Baths of Germany" (second part), he has described Gastein without ever having seen it or examined it in person ; else he could not have committed the blunders of mistaking the *Schloss* for the Archduke's house and baths at that Spa ; nor described inaccurately the

But enough of drinking; let us now turn to eating and
living, with a few words as to house-accommodation, at
Brighton.

An acquaintance of mine, a man of the world, and a
medical practitioner, is in the habit of coming down here
regularly every year, for four months. He was occupying at
the time of my visit, on the best side of the Steyne, two parlours and two bedrooms, with his two sisters ; he himself being
obliged to live in the back parlour, in which, as in the other
apartments, there was just room enough to move in, and no
more. For this accommodation he paid three guineas a week.
Ex uno disce, &c. The town was quite full, that is, all

division of baths in Straubinger's establishment, besides other similar
peccadilloes. But Mr. Lee, who, in bringing forward, last March, his
little *bijou* cabinet volume, entitled " The Mineral Springs of England,"
aforesaid, is pleased to observe, that though he was told of the previous
existence of such a work as the " Spas of England," he did not think,
judging from the Spas of Germany, that the necessity of his own performance was in the least superseded,—Mr. Lee, I say, has been equally
guilty of palpable errors in respect to the home or national sources. For
example: he considers Malvern and Matlock as analogous springs, the
former of which, moreover, he had previously described as *scarcely tepid.*
(" Baths of Germany," page 45, Part II.) ; whereas every one knows
that Malvern is a delightfully *cold* water, and that no analogy exists between it and Matlock. He also gives a pretended analysis of the Scarborough mineral waters by Dr. Thomson, who never analyzed them ;
and though aware of the existence of the " Spas of England," he will not
quote from it the elaborate and very recent and only correct analysis
of these waters by Phillips, by which the ingredients and quantities
are shown to be as different as possible from his own statement.
And again, in treating of the Harrogate's Springs, preferring for his guide
(he himself not having visited the place) any other work than the hate-
ful " Spas of England," though the latter is the most recent of all,—Mr.
Lee repeats the mistakes of his predecessors, and talks of the *Crescent
Old Well,* which no longer exists, and of the *Crescent Hot Saline* Spring,
which has changed name, owner, and position. In fact, there is no end
to the inaccuracies and omissions,—setting aside the very superficial
manner of the little whole—contained in both the English and the German Baths of the author in question, who nevertheless imagines that his
productions will supply " *a desideratum* in English literature" (!)

that is decent and lodgeable was occupied. The lodging-keepers, therefore, make the most of their time, and know not how to ask enough during the season. A whole house on the east and west cliff cannot be had for less than from eight to fifteen guineas a week; and the sorriest lodging for a " single gentleman " in any of the cross streets on the east cliff is charged two guineas;—yet Brighton is over-built, and houses are constantly on sale. It is a curious sight, by the bye, to behold some of these, with their showy exterior, but stripped of their internal fineries, and as naked inside as the auctioneer's hammer can make them; and to see how flimsily they are built.

In many of the principal parts of Brighton, towards the sea, and even in Kemp Town, when a S. or a S.W. gale is blowing, one can hardly keep in the front rooms, for the wind will penetrate and force its way in spite of bolts and *serrures*. Light things are seen pleasantly dancing about the room, on the tables, or on the floor; the carpet of which, like a light sail spread on a lawn, is seen to rise and fall with each intro-sufflation.

The cost of living, in every article, is about 33 per cent. more than in London. Meat and fish are never sold during the season at less than a penny or three-halfpence per pound above London price. The tea and wine were represented to me as being of a very inferior quality, and yet sold at high prices. On inquiring of many of the strangers who have chosen to keep house, I found it universally asserted that it costs them one-third more than in London. Now this state of things cannot endure long after the railroad shall have come into operation. The tradesmen of Brighton must either lower the rents, and the price of their comestibles, or speculators will be found who will run down in two hours from London every morning, to place before breakfast-time on the kitchen dresser of their own town customers, all they now stand in need of; just as the butcher, and the poulterer, and the fishmonger, from Bond-street, run down to Belgrave-square and Cadogan-place to supply their customers.

One important article of diet—water—is indifferent at Brighton. It is supplied principally by a company, and it deposits a reddish sand, and is in colour dingy. It lathers tolerably well with soap, but leaves the skin rough. It should be used filtered for tea, and a small quantity of carbonate of soda added to it. In some of the streets there are pumps for public use, but their water is hard, and in a few places chalky, while in others it is evidently chalybeate. Excellent bread is to be had at times ; but the dairy supplies are not of the first quality.

With all these drawbacks, however, a *gourmand* need not despair at Brighton ; for were I to judge by the manner in which the table of certain *Richards* was decked at some *diners priés*, every luxury that imagination or appetite can desire, and money command, is of ready acquisition ; nor can the well-pampered guest, filled with the fumes of Gallia's effervescing liquor, fear any interruption on his way back to his quarters, for he will find the streets admirably guarded by a zealous police, and lighted with the blaze of gas-lamps.

The visiter at this wonderful resort of fashion should make up his mind to being satisfied, by way of general enjoyment, during his *séjour*, with the view of houses and the sea—the latter seldom enlivened by those objects which gives animation to its surface. The promenade on the pier, and a blow on its terminal platform, equal to that one gets on a quarter-deck in sailing down channel, are the only episodes to this eternally monotonous existence at Brighton. Nature offers no other resources.

Nothing can be more dismal-looking, barren, or discouraging than the general aspect of the immediately surrounding country on either side, or at the back of Brighton. Hillocks, more or less elevated above the town, with the peculiar round and smooth forms that chalk-hills assume, present their almost naked surface in all directions, and hardly a vestige of vegetation appears beyond the short hard grass that covers them. These serve as sheep-walks, or as downs to course and drive upon by way of exercise, for want of a better place. Here and there a reluctant crop of wheat has been drawn from the arid chalk and gravelly soil; and some more assiduous and cunning gardener has succeeded in forming enough of real soil to grow the ordinary herbage for the market. But even in such places as these neither the field crops, nor the aspect of the orchards and kitchen-gardens present to the rambler that *riant* aspect which adds a zest to the invigorating out-of-door exercise an invalid at a watering-place is desired and willing to take. In no direction, turn whichever way you list, can such an invalid discover a bit of lively landscape, or a refreshing patch of green, or a picturesque group of lofty trees, to feast his eyes with. This is a great drawback, and much felt.

It marvels me that no attempt has hitherto been made to convert these barren and exposed uplands and hills into forests of larches and other trees of the *Abies* kind, in imitation of the Duke of Athol's successful experiments in the mountainous and barren districts of Scotland. Twenty-five years of persevering experiments in that way, with the assistance also of the sewerage (now wasted) judiciously employed when the proper time arrived, would have produced a sheltered evergreen region around the town, affording to Brighton a new, attractive, and important feature for purposes of health. For, assuredly, nothing would contribute more to the promotion of recovery from disease, or prove a better corrective to the too drying and heating property of the air of the place, than the surrounding it with forest vegetation, and changing the upper surface of the chalk into a milder form of soil—a species of mould consisting of the altered chalk and the decomposed leaves of the forest trees.

A ride to the barracks, placed in the very centre of desolate hillocks to the east and north-east of the town, on going out of Brighton by the Lewes-road, as happened to myself on my way to Hastings, suffices to impress the mind of the visiter with the aspect of nature's destitution in the immediate environs of Brighton. Turning your face towards the latter as soon as you shall have reached the South Downs, and ere you attain the first spot of smiling vegetation nearest to the town, *Stanmore Park*, three miles distant,—you behold Brighton, thrown, as it were, into three great masses at the foot of converging chalk-hills, directing their course south and down to the margin of the sea, along which the principal succession of dwellings seem spread in an undeviating line. From this point the new church of St. Peter, standing at the back of the town, offers its Gothic slender pinnacles and elegant steeple to more advantage than when the church is seen quite near.

Viewed from this same or any other analogous position, the Brighton houses which constitute the inland part of the town, and which seem to have been purposely built for letting as lodging-houses, present two defects; they are too low, and the lower floor is seldom raised a single foot from the ground. From these defects even the Royal Pavilion is not exempt.

This latter singular-looking building would, nevertheless, possess infinite merit, were it not buried within a wall, without the view of either sea or country, such as it is. It should have been placed on one of the nearest downs in the north-east quarter, above Kemp Town, with a south-south-west aspect, and raised four feet on a sub-basement, at the same time screening it from the north and east winds by suitable plantations. The Pavilion would then have formed a marine palace fit for an English sovereign; whereas now, though head of the first maritime nation in the world, that sovereign cannot boast of a royal residence from whence she may contemplate the field of her country's glories.

CHAPTER XIII.

HASTINGS—ST. LEONARDS—DOVER.

By the Lewes-road I took my departure, at length, from Brighton. Lewes is singularly situated. Within a vast circular hollow, formed by rounded chalk hills sloping down towards it from a distance, a small elevation rises, on which the ancient capital of the county is seated, spreading itself down the declivities. A hill or two, bolder and more upright than the rest, and more crumbling with chalk and flints, stand close upon some of the houses. The road takes a most circuitous turn to double the town, and gives it the go-by to proceed Hastings-wards, offering not a single attractive feature until it reaches the seat of Sir Charles Lamb, three miles in the rear of St. Leonards, between which and Hastings a newly-made road now leads the traveller from London to both these adjoining places.

The invalid condemned by his medical adviser to seek a milder climate on the Sussex coast, who with his lungs threatened, flesh wasting, sleep unrefreshing, and night perspirations incessant, proceeds either to Hastings or St. Leonards, in hopes of recovering the lost health, or the better to husband the little of health and life he has left—such an invalid, I say, must not approach the place of his destination by the new road just alluded to, which, passing through Battel, rapidly descends the hill in a south-east direction till it turns to the right, and proceeds straightway facing the sea by Silver-hill and Tivoli, coming at last immediately upon the back of the east-end of the new town of St. Leonards, and terminating before the door of the Conqueror Hotel, between St. Leonards and Hastings. Such an approach, destitute of all beauty, or of any characteristic feature in the surrounding country, is in itself so dismal, that any invalid's courage may perchance fail him, and his hope sink within him, ere he is fairly housed in his new quarters. Magnificent as it may appear on the sea-side, with its showy and length-ened frontage, and cheering and beautiful as it looks when entered by its own direct northern road, St. Leonards, viewed from behind, and at the extremity of the road first mentioned presents nothing but a monotonous ladder of unfinished, ill-placed, and ill-sheltered houses, of dingy material, and but imperfectly inhabited, enough to damp every cheerful expectation.

The approach to Hastings by the old London-road, at the
foot of Fairlight Down, and at the upper end of High-
street, is far different from the one described, and truly
picturesque. An almost precipitous hill descends towards
a grove of ancient and lofty lime-trees, under which
the carriage courses in its downward way, having a lofty
range of sloping hills on the left or east side, screening the road from that wind, and an elevated ground on the
right, but more open, and admitting, therefore, the driven
gale from the south-west to visit an otherwise secluded and
sheltered spot. Such an approach is cheering as well as
soothing, and the invalid at the sight of it may well hug
to his bosom the sweet hope that he is about to halt in a
protecting and genial haven.

But, once arrived at his goal, he has yet to encounter the
formidable trial of an English hotel. The tendency to impose upon travellers at almost all these establishments,
whether at Hastings or any other popular sea-bathing place
on this coast, is evinced at the very first onset, when,—after
a little more or less *empressement* on the part of the landlord and waiters according as you alight from a carriage or
a stage-coach,—the chambermaid is rung for, and is seen
descending with leisure steps, in her fine starched cap and
chemisette, and clean apron, to obey the summons.

" A bedroom for the gentleman."—" This way, sir." And
up and up many interminable steps and stairs she leads you,
having previously scanned you from top to toe, until she
reaches the top garrets, throws open No. 47, beckons you in,
and you find yourself close under one roof and overlooking
twenty others, at the summit and at the back of the house.
" Is this all you have?" " We are all full—quite full."
" Then the porter need not trouble himself to carry up my
luggage—I'll walk on to another hotel." " Let me think

if you don't object to the back of the house, I can give you
an excellent room on the second floor. It is promised, but
I will make shift to oblige you." "What—no room at all
in front, eh?" "No, indeed; we have been full these three
weeks." And away we trot once more down winding stairs
and along tortuous corridors and dark passages, uniting a
new with an older house (the two made into one), when, at
last, a larger and somewhat better furnished chamber, with a
single window, is thrown open. The opposite wall is almost
within touch of the hand, and the back yard beneath, with
its scullery, and refuse water from garbage and cabbage, sends
up its effluvia in harmony with those from cabinet No. 0 next
door to the room. "No, no! my good lass, this won't do;
I shall be off to better quarters, and so adieu, my fair. I had
been strongly recommended to alight at your house, but if
this be the specimen of your reception of a stranger, I shall
not follow the example of recommending you in my turn."
"Dear me, sir, I am sure this is a most comfortable room.
You are very difficult to please. But, let me see; I shall
be obliged to disappoint an old customer in order to give you
satisfaction. Here is another room on the first floor in front.
It has every convenience, and a most beautiful prospect,
&c., &c." "So it has; and why not show it me at once?"
"Why, if we did so with everybody and always, when are
the *higher* and *inferior* bedrooms to be occupied? I only do
my duty."

And the girl is right; but inasmuch as an invalid seeking
Hastings for his chest has generally irritable nerves, which it
is important should not be excited, and as houseroom-seek-
ing is the first and indeed principal part of his business on
arrival, I have given my dialogue at the hotel I alighted at
as a specimen, that it may serve as a warning to all invalids
to write beforehand and secure a specific room in a specific
part of the house, and at a fixed and specific charge.

Indeed, beyond treating of residences and climate, I have

no other object connected with Hastings which could induce me to occupy many pages in these volumes,—for as to sea-bathing, one would hardly prefer Hastings to many other places; and since we have touched on the subject of hotels, we may as well dispatch it at once, condensing into a narrow compass whatever information I was able practically to cull during my recent visit to that winter-quarters of invalids.

It was at the MARINE Hotel that I alighted; a handsome-looking house, immediately facing the sea, at the west end of the Parade, not far from the principal library, the Pelham Baths and the Crescent. The road and a small terrace separate it from the shingly shore, which lies a few feet below the latter at low water. There are three apartments on each floor—the rooms in front having (as seems to be the mania of the place) bow windows and balcony, and the bed-rooms at the back being airy and spacious. They are all well furnished, and each apartment is charged 7s. 6d. per diem. There is a fine view of the coast and Beachey Head from its front windows. Hutchins, the landlord, seems most anxious to please his customers. The house is always full during the season, and might be made an exceedingly convenient as well as desirable residence for an invalid; for it has behind the shelter of the cliff, which rises to an elevation of nearly 300 feet.

Not many yards from this hotel, to the eastward, and nearer to the shore, is a still more showy hotel, called the ALBION. From the north and north-east winds, the streets of Old Hastings sufficiently protect this house; but its exposure to winds from other quarters is greater than that of the first-mentioned hotel. I should select the *Albion* in summer, and during winter the *Marine Hotel* for a residence. Of the oldest hotel in the town, perched up in High-street, the ROYAL SWAN, I shall say nothing, for assuredly no invalid would think of sojourning in so dull a neighbourhood; and

of the locality of two other similar establishments, the Royal
Oak and the Castle, I shall say a word or two when we
come to them in our perambulations.

I recollect when Old Hastings, seated in a very compact
manner, with its two parallel long and narrow streets, High-
street and All Saints-street, on the rising vale between West
and East Cliff, stopt by the sea-shore at the west end of
George and West-street, near the Battery and the Parade.
Westwards, the foot of the naked cliff was not then obstructed by any new buildings, which, however, have since
extended half a mile farther in a west-north-west direction,
following the line of the beach, over which, as well as upon
the acclivities inland, whole ranges of superior and good-
looking houses have been erected. The first and principal
part of these facing the sea is Pelham-place, consisting of
about ten houses to the right and to the left, united by a
range of shops, called the Arcade, above which peers Pel-
ham-crescent and its central church, with an imposing Grecian portico, on whose pediment are inscribed the words _Ædes
Sanctæ Mariæ in Castello._

It is at the back of these several buildings that rise to a
perpendicular height of some hundred feet the Castle Hill.
To the lover of the picturesque, the sight of this rock and its
ruins will prove a disappointment. The denuded face of the
cliff, which, to avoid the previously frequent avalanches of
broken fragments, has been cut down, is of an uniformly
dingy colour, consisting as it does of a hard gray tinted
calciferous sandstone at top, of a yellow soft friable sandstone in the middle, and beds of clay, slate, and ferruginous
sandstone in the lower part. The remaining vestiges of the
ancient fortress, which have been recently made stronger by
masonry paid for by some patriotic hand, instead of appearing picturesquely grouped, look like heaps of stones
recently piled up at random. A short rank grass covers the
upper surface of the hills, as it does indeed throughout the

range of the cliffs at the back of the town, and further on to
St. Leonards.

All the houses in Pelham-place and the Crescent—to the
latter of which one ascends by a series of steps at the east,
and an inclined plane at the west—face the south, and
have two floors, with large well-shaded bow windows, and
attics over them. Those to the west are open in front to the
sea, where bathing-machines are collected on the strand,
strewed with shingle. At the east end on the contrary the
view of the sea, except from the upper stories, is obstructed
by what are called the *Beach Cottages*, a few mean-looking
buildings, some of wood, and others of black-glazed bricks,
which totally disfigure the view of the Crescent and Pelham-
place from the sea. In winter the houses in these two localities offer the advantage to the invalid of a warm shelter in
the back rooms, which face the rock, and receive the reflected heat from its surface; thus escaping from the south-
east and south-west gales, to which the front apartments are
exposed.

Following the line of the cliff still westward of Pelham
Crescent, ranges of neat lodging-houses extend in continuation as far as Castle-street, formed by a triangular cluster
of well-located dwellings, near the Beach, called the *Caroline
Cottages ;* beyond which, doubling the Castle Hill by turning to the right, we find Wellington-square creeping up
with its long parallelogram towards Castle Terrace, in a
north-east direction. The Castle Inn is at the entrance of
this new part of the town, now deemed the most favourable
quarter of Hastings. The square is built upon three sides,
with good-looking houses, which stand, however, upon an
inconvenient sloping ground, inclined south-west. The
houses on the north-western side enjoy the sun the best part
of the day. In the morning the front of the houses opposite
look dark and chilly. A few of the latter may at the back
receive the cheering rays of the morning sun, but it can only

be in the upper apartments, as the western end of Castle Hill rises immediately between them and the eastern sun. They, however, enjoy a full view of the western sea from the upper rooms towards St. Leonard's and Bopeep, looking over the Baptist chapel, which, with the Castle Hotel, forms part of the square. The houses are small, having a very modest front parlour and two drawing-rooms, with as many bed-chambers. Those at the top of the square are of a superior class ; though not so much so as the houses on the west side.

Judging by the letting, I should conclude that the houses of the west and north end are preferred, as there was not a bill on either side, whereas on the east side there were several. At the north-west corner, two houses (30, 31), newly done up, with a full view of the sea, S.E., must be warm in winter : they are well looking externally, [with large parlour-window and drawing-room. Nos. 41, 2, and 3, south-west end of the square, have also been lately done up, and seemed to me well suited for delicate invalids, having the sun upon them the best part of the day. The back looks upon the Downs. All these houses have the advantage of being sheltered by the Kentish and York cottages, and the back of a handsome range of buildings, called York-buildings, forming a con-tinuation of Castle-street, from the direct violence of the sea gales ; and of being away from the saline effluvia so inimical to chest complaints, to both of which the lower buildings on the Strand, or below the West Cliff, are so much exposed. They have besides the farther benefit of country air at their back, which none of the buildings nearer the shore possess, on account of the lofty rock behind them.

Having now brought the visiter to the extreme or western limit of modern Hastings, close to the Priory-bridge, and enumerated all that is most important for an invalid looking out for a residence to know, I shall only offer one or two remarks on the general exposure of the place, and on the sort of open sea, or in-door sea-water bathing, to be obtained in it.

These straight lines of coast, such as the one on which both Hastings and St. Leonards are seated, which hardly ever assume the curve form, and never change into a shape like a cove, are much exposed as a residence, and for sea-bathing not to be put in comparison with the sands on the east or even the western coast of England, and are also inferior to Weymouth on the south-western coast. The shore itself is not propitiously formed. Its surface is broken by jutting rocks and reefs, and when from any elevation the eye rapidly runs along the whole line of it, from Hastings east cliff even to the farthest or westernmost point of St. Leonards, naught presents itself at low water but a space more or less wide, but hardly ever exceeding 100 or 200 yards, of coarse sand, from the sea wall to a well-defined reef of black rocks. It is only beyond that reef, and as far as the receded tide at the lowest ebb, that a smoother sandy surface may be observed. The shore itself is not abrupt in any place, and so far is better than at Brighton. It is also much cleaner, and the water almost always limpid, and of that beautiful hue, which has been called sea-green by common consent, so inviting to bathers. This appearance of the strand and beach is pratically manifest before my hotel, where about ten or twelve white painted bathing-machines, like those at Brighton without a hood, are placed on a small area of gravelly sand, left uncovered by the receding tide between the line of shingle immediately below the terrace, and the many reefs of dark rock about 200 feet beyond.

To the frequent gales from the south-west, the coast, and necessarily the houses built upon it, are awfully exposed. On such occasions one can scarcely venture to walk out in front of the buildings, the proximity of which to the beach is much greater than at Brighton. As it generally rains too on such occasions, the warm temperature of the day falls

considerably at sunset, and the evenings and nights are generally very cold.   In this respect again the difference between
Brighton and Hastings is very great.   At the latter place
they are often obliged to have fires in the house when
at the former nobody would dream of asking for such a comfort.   This actually was the case on the evening of my arrival
at Hastings from Brighton.

At the close of the year, or beginning of winter, a rainy
and a blowing day, with a south-wester, such as I once encountered at Hastings, must be most disastrous to invalid residents.   A soft air, with warmth and moderate dampness,
corrected by the presence of absorbing sandstone rocks
roundabout, may be useful to people of delicate chests ; but
to be shaken by an unmitigated storm of south-west wind
even within the confines of your own bedrooms, in the upper
stories of the several houses I have mentioned—where the
frail window-frames themselves are threatened at every moment with demolition—is more than any tender invalid can
well resist without injury.

That it rains frequently at Hastings is made manifest by the
published average quantity of rain which falls yearly in that
place, as contrasted with that which falls in London, being as
28.340 inches for the former, to 26.686 in the latter place ;
but on the other hand the mean yearly temperature at Hastings is greater than that of London, being as 51.11 to
50.39.

I also question whether the perpetually recurring thunders
of the swelling waves, first breaking against the reefs, and next
dashing over the sloping shingle during the morning tide,
which prevail on every occasion of a stiff gale from the
south-west, may not be considered as an unfavourable circumstance connected with the residence of a real suffering
invalid by the sea-side, where, as at Hastings, his dwelling
is in close approximation to the water,—as when he lodges in
Pelham-place or the Crescent, for example.   The incessant

roaring of the morning waters must, for some weeks at least, be an annoyance to a delicate person whose nights are probably disturbed by suffering, or that sleeplessness which frequently attends chronic and formidable maladies. It is not the gentle murmurs of rippling water over a pebbly bed, but like the discharge of distant cannon, or like the application of some mighty engine to a gigantic rampart for the purpose of overthrowing it. The noise is terrific, it is disturbing, and a patient with a night hectic upon him cannot soon reconcile his nerves to the thunder.

There is something soothing, nay, healing, in the perfect stillness of night, and the out-of-doors silence, so remarkably enjoyed at all inland watering-places, and more especially at the German and all foreign spas, after the first hours of the evening. Of such a blessing we deprive the feverish invalid for some time, or at least until he becomes accustomed to the incessant roaring, by placing him on the margin of a too frequently agitated ocean.

ST. LEONARDS.

To all the various objections just enumerated, St. Leonards, or in other words that long line of showy palaces called the MARINA, erected at the distance of three quarters of a mile from the Priory-bridge, close upon the shore, from which it is only separated by a promenade terrace, is particularly obnoxious.   And so will be all the intended new buildings for which the ground was preparing, and with which all the vacant space is to be covered which lies between the foot of Cuckoo Hill, (where the new London road over the cliff begins, near the west end of Hastings) and the east entrance-gate of St. Leonards, including what is called the Grand Parade. Some of these buildings exist already—the Verulam for example, and those of White Rock-place, all direct south, with the cliff close behind them, and more favourably placed as to exposure to winds than Pelham-place.

A square also is meditated in this part, to be called War-rior-square. This will prove an excellent locality in summer as well as winter, because the houses will have varied aspects—they will be farther removed from the water—not hemmed in between the latter, and a lofty cliff behind, neither be half so much exposed to the gales. The houses already in existence have an advantage, under the difficulty of their exposed situation, which those of Brighton have not—that of being built with greater regard to solidity and style, and being very like some of the most modern town houses.

Mr. Burton is an architect of acknowledged taste—the first perhaps to whom the Londoner owes the introduction of the more *riant*, gay, and cheering style of building that has since prevailed in the metropolis, over the gloomy sameness of long brick walls, pierced with a number of unadorned windows on each side of an interminable street. At St. Leonards he has again given proof of his power of invention and love of the beautiful. We should look in vain on any other coast in England for such a range of buildings as those he has raised below St. Leonards Cliff; of a superior order, though not so ornamented as some of his previous structures. None but the unrivalled crescents of Bath and Bristol is superior to the Marina of St. Leonards.

All this with pleasure I admit; but the architect will permit me to question the judgment he has exercised in raising so many dwelling houses, all equally exposed to one and the same aspect, however favourable with regard to warmth, which is of necessity subject to the visitation of both the south-west and south-east winds—the most frequent as well as the most objectionable winds on this coast. It is just such an error that I hope to see avoided at Bournemouth, where an equally inviting and superiorly clothed cliff would tempt another Burton perhaps to erect long lines of marine villas, but where also I trust more judicious Burtons will use the South Cliff sparingly, and cling to the East and West Cliffs inland, as the Burton of St. Leonards might have done, and as indeed he has done, in part only, around the vale and the basin on the higher ground, behind the Marina, as well as near about the handsome Doric structure of the Assembly Rooms, and still higher up the hill, as far as the north gate entrance into St. Leonards.

The whole of this last-mentioned and varied region must be a little paradise to invalids; and the houses, whether those detached as Italian or Lombard villas with gardens, or those placed in rows like a series of Gothic cottages, all equally desirable, are much sought after by the wealthy invalids, and always occupied. It is in this direction that we find the higher or north entrance into St. Leonards; and certainly nothing can be so cheering or more beautiful than this single approach, impressing at once with gay and happy ideas the visiting stranger, and giving him hopes of restored health.

The fault in its position, however, shall not prevent my doing further justice to the distinguishing feature of the Marina at St. Leonards. Two separate ranges of dwelling-houses of the first class, having a low arcade in front, which shelters the parlour-floor, extend along the shore nearly two hundred and fifty feet each in length, and by the side of a grand and loftier edifice of a whiter colour, and more pretensions to architectural ornaments, called the VICTORIA or St. Leonard's HOTEL. Before them is a wide and handsome carriage-way, by the side of which ranges a terrace or parade, partly gravelled and partly in lawns, nearly a mile [long, with seats, and supported by a stout sea-wall twelve or fifteen feet high. Opposite the centre building or hotel on the parade, stand the bath-rooms, with the library, the Bank and Post-office on one side, and a refreshment-room on the other. Below these are kept bathing-machines and pleasure-boats, which are hauled up off the strand by a windlass through a slip or cut in the sea-wall.

The Victoria Hotel has the appearance of a nobleman's mansion. A wide street runs up on each side of it, leading to other and less regular series of buildings constituting the town of St. Leonards, and also to that paradise of detached villas to which I have already alluded.

The entire mass of this sea line of buildings was occupied at the time of my visit. When the sun of January and February visits St. Leonards, and shuns the inland towns—when the sea at half-tide has covered the uglier part of the shore and reached the shingle—and still better when high-water comes up to the level of the sea-wall and looks truly beautiful— then the Marina, as a retired tranquil sea-bathing or sea residence, is far preferable to the cliffs of Brighton.

If another proof were required to convince the skilful architect of the Marina, that in placing a whole terrace of first-rate houses direct south and north, he has not followed the dictates of a climate physician, I should find it in the present state of the back-front of those houses, which faces the north, and in which is the principal entrance. The external wall of the parlour stories of this front, and still more so of the sub-basement and area, owing to their direful exposure to a sunless, damp, and cold aspect, were dripping with wet, looked stained and mossy, and the very stones seemed in a state of decomposition. For the sake of their health, I should be sorry to see my servants lodged in offices so situated. The contrast between the joyous, warm, and inviting front apartments, and the dismal and gloomy rooms behind, must be seen to be understood.

If my informants at Hastings are not mistaken in the details they supplied me with respecting the subject of house-rent and living, I may set both these important items down at one-fourth less than they amount to at Brighton. I was sorry to find the water equally as objectionable as that at the latter place; but with respect to every other article of food, they are neither deficient in quantity nor inferior in quality.

An old friend, whom I was sorry to miss at my visit, Dr. Harwood, a physician practising at both St. Leonards and

Hastings with deserved success, has written so fully on the temperature and meteorological occurrences on that coast, that I consider myself exempt from the necessity of touching upon the subject, but beg to refer my readers to his work. We differ somewhat in certain general points, but on the whole, and notwithstanding the remarks I have deemed it my duty to make, I am disposed to attach nearly as much importance as he does to the influence on certain pulmonic complaints, of a residence in Hastings or St. Leonards.

I have mentioned the bath-building on the Marina at St. Leonards, in which there are excellent accommodations for its intended purposes. In Hastings, proper, the best and principal private baths are the Pelham, close to the Marine Hotel. The horizontal iron pipe through which the sea-water is drawn in by a pump while the tide is in, may be seen projecting at low water on the beach, quite dry; so that sea-water is only obtained direct for a bath at certain times of the day. But there are reservoirs in the house for both cold and hot sea-water; and this arrangement for single baths, vapour and douche baths, is very creditable. There is also a plunging-bath, about ten feet square and five feet deep, which, however, has for the last two years been nearly useless, in consequence of some leak that has not yet been discovered. The charges for these various baths are much the same as at all other sea-bathing places on the coast.

The romance and beauty of the *alentours* of Hastings, of which one reads in the guide-books, must not be sought for immediately behind or upon the downs that overlook the town within three miles. True the general surface of the latter is somewhat less desolate-looking than that of the Brighton Downs; but with the exception of the Vale of St. Leonards to the extreme west, the slope of Fairlight Downs, the much talked-of Glen, and Dripping Well, and Lover's Seat near it; or, lastly, the entrance into Hastings before mentioned, by the old London road, to the extreme east, in all of which verdure and smiling features may be seen in the land-scape—the whole district within the before-mentioned dis-tance, presents but a poor-looking land, with scarcely a tree above a shrub, or underwood, some patches of which oc-cur here and there in the vicinity of a detached house or cottage.

Of the few more distant excursions recommended to in-valids, who find at Hastings every facility of carriage and saddle-horses for indulging in them, the one to BATTEL seems to excite most curiosity. The spot is in itself insignificant, and has no great recommendation, notwithstanding the still-remaining vestiges of its ancient abbey. But every one within reach of it thinks it of importance to visit and behold the place where a bold usurper of the Saxon throne of Eng-land fell by the hand of a still bolder usurper, the offspring of an illicit amour and a foreigner, yet the head of all the royal lines (with only a few interruptions) that have swayed ever after the realms of Great Britain ; and not only the head of royal houses, but the source and fountain of those honours and ancestorial distinctions (besides largesses and domains), by which the blood of four-fifths of the present distinguished families in this land have been ennobled,—the sovereign giver himself having none of that noble blood in his veins, but, on the contrary, bastard blood !

DOVER.

ON the 20th of September, 1827, I indited the following memoranda of my opinion of this place as a residence for invalids, which were soon after published in my work on St. Petersburgh.* A lapse of eleven years, instead of weaken-

* St. Petersburgh: A Journal of Travels to and from that Capital, through Flanders, the Rhenish Provinces, Prussia, Russia, Poland Silesia, Saxony, the Federated States of Germany and France. 2 vols. 1828, First Edition; 1829, Second Edition ; 1832, Third Edition, London: Colburn.

ing, has but confirmed the accuracy of my observations, which at the time had the merit of novelty on their side, to say the least of them, inasmuch as not one word had ever been written by any medical man before on the salubriousness of Dover, or its peculiar suitableness to certain complaints. Whatever results, therefore, advantageous to Dover may have followed the publication of those observations, I may claim the merit of having given them impulse—a merit which the late comptroller of the customs at Dover, a gentleman with whom I had formed a lasting acquaintance at the Isle of Wight, was never backward in acknowledging.

That results tending to the increase and prosperity of the place must have followed the public expression of my professional opinion respecting Dover as a watering-place, is manifest by its increased growth, and the constant influx of visiters during both winter and autumn. Look at what Dover was in 1827, and what it is now. Some of the houses on the Marine Parade had but recently been erected on speculation, and Liverpool-terrace was also begun, and here and there a house under the Castle Cliff was seen. In the open and flat ground which now divides the new buildings to the east from those to the west, and by the sea-side, stood, as now, the range of low buildings containing the baths, which were of recent date. But they were at that time away from nearly all important buildings; whereas they have now close at hand, right and left, ranges of lofty houses, and many of them of the first class, fit for patrician inmates. Who had ever heard, before 1827, of whole families, or even single individuals, selecting Dover, above all places in the world, for a winter residence ? Where were the suitable accommodations for any such, except at the four or five hotels, themselves so greatly improved and enlarged since, although as a transit port (on which those species of establishments formerly depended for customers) Dover has lost one-half of its importance? Now the same hotels are constantly full, as I have ascertained, with strangers who come to spend a fortnight or three weeks, and not with merely passing travellers. The lodging-houses, even in the heart of the old town, and all the newer buildings by the sea-side, are now in great request; and about Christmas, house-room is hardly to be had. It has been computed that from five to six thousand strangers congregate every season at Dover to enjoy those peculiar benefits which the place is particularly calculated to afford, and which I had first the good fortune to point out. For the sake of the patients themselves, as well as of the good people of Dover, I pray that these good results of my recommendation may be lasting. The following are the observations contained in the publication I have alluded to, concerning this place :

" As a professional man, acquainted with those diseases and constitutions which are benefitted by a residence at the sea-side, I may be permitted, in this place, to offer a few remarks on the situation of this sea-port town. Dover is much improved within the last few years in its appearance. It has been enlarged, particularly at the south-east end," (the Marine Parade and Liverpool-terrace), " and in many parts embellished. There is fair sea-bathing, with the most convenient establishments I have seen on this coast for warm and cold sea-baths, and for all other applications of sea-water to the purposes of health or cleanliness.

" The new as well as the old lodging-houses, are clean and on moderate terms. The situation of those nearer to the sea side, facing the south and south-west, is highly desirable, gay and warm. These are sheltered from the easterly wind, as is also the rest of the town from the winds of all the northern quarters, by the two celebrated ridges of rocks which flank the town, and wall it all round behind to a gigantic height. The air is pure, and by the recent improvements in the harbour, the retreating tide does not produce that penetrating smell, which to some delicate constitutions is so unpleasant and injurious. The vicinity of flint chalk, hanging in large masses about the outskirts of Dover, prevents all moisture from long loitering in the atmosphere that hovers over the town. I have often had occasion to remark, while cruizing in a man-of-war, a great many years ago, in this part of the channel, that during damp and very foggy days, when the whole line of coast was concealed from our view by a dense atmosphere, the white cliffs of Dover and the town were the first to emerge out of this concealment; not, as in ordinary cases by the gradual rising of the fleecy veil which hung before them, but by the almost sudden absorption of the vapoury atmosphere, which promptly disappeared, while the other part of the coast, as Deal for instance, continued in obscurity.

" To these local advantages, which are almost peculiar to this place, others are to be added, which are decidedly unique, and of the greatest value to the resident invalid; I allude to facility of transporting oneself to a totally different country and *climate* in a few hours, and to the daily *agrément* of witnessing as much of the bustle as is agreeable attending the arrival and departure of sovereigns, princes, and subjects of every colour, character, and degree, both males and females, with their bags and baggages, their smuggled articles, and articles which one should be paid for to smuggle. Then the pleasure of being the first to hear the news from foreign parts, and of listening to fifty *bamboches*, telling stories in every language on the surface of the globe, which by living at Dover one is sure to enjoy, is with many persons an invaluable recommendation to a country residence. To hypochondriac patients, too, this very circumstance renders Dovor a far preferable *séjour* to any other.

" Persons suffering from what have been styled stomach and liver complaints, labouring under dyspepsia, or indigestion, after having gone through a regular course of blue-pill or carbonate of soda, breakfasted on brown bread, and swallowed loads of mustard seed (I might now add, after having been homœopathyzed, and well drenched with brandy and salt), with little success, will find a residence of two or three months at this place more productive of good, by simply attending to diet, and using sea-bathing.

" To the bilious, instead of taking constant medicines, I recommend embarking, when the day is fine, on board a sailing-packet (or a steamer); and cross over to Calais or Boulogne in hopes of being made sea-sick. This operation empties the stomach more effectually than can be done by means of emetics, so justly esteemed in cases of obstructed or re-gurgitating bile. This plan may be adopted twice or three times in the course of a two or three months' residence, if oc-casion requires; and it should invariably be followed by equitation or airings in a carriage, extended some distance into the country.

" With these recommendations I have sent to Dover a considerable number of patients within the last eight years (1820-8), all of whom have got well, and have liked the system and place exceedingly ; and as the people there are civil, and all the necessaries as well as luxuries of life are to be procured at a reasonable rate, there appears no reason why Dover should not be included in the list of those sea-port towns which enjoy the patronage and good opinion of the London physician."

And Dover has since been included in that list, and London physicians have for the last ten years been in the habit of re-commending it to their patients labouring under stomach affections, or to the merely convalescents, as a most desirable autumnal and winter residence.

I have only to add, that whereas one or two masses of buildings formerly constituted the Marine-parade, five ranges of houses are now erected in it; each range separated by a street at right angles with the beach, and by two square open places, here called Lawns; namely, Guildford-lawn, and Clarence-lawn, built on two sides, east and west; and farther, that between the locality of the Baths, and the York Hotel, on an area which in my time was barren or encumbered with rope-walks, &c., the splendid Waterloo-crescent, and the Esplanade have been constructed for aristocratic families.

But on these points and collateral questions, so interesting to an invalid, practical and positive information being the only desirable one, and that which I am always anxious to tender to my readers, I have obtained permission from an old and valued friend and patient of mine, to insert in this place a brief statement, the result of personal experience and observation, obtained only two years since.

" The houses in Waterloo-crescent are very large, and are often let to several families in floors. In all the other buildings the houses are of more moderate sizes, and let from six to ten guineas per week in the season, and for about half that price in winter. The Lawns are much approved, being removed from the great noise of the sea. They consist of five houses on each side; I paid for mine, in Clarence-lawn, six guineas: two rooms on a floor, moderate size, but large enough for a small party, very clean and perfect, with a beautiful view of the Castle.

" There is a very nice street, newly built, from the town to the sea-shore, which might be a desirable winter residence, and there are several spots where good houses are erecting, not facing the sea, and well sheltered for winter, which your friends and patients might fancy to have been designed and located by yourself, so well they meet your views on these points. But most people prefer the seaward houses, which are constantly occupied.

" The Market-place and street adjoining have been of late years much thrown open and improved; so has the pier, which is now perfect, and the quays on each side large, well paved, and the constant rendezvous of people of all rank and degree, to witness the departure and arrival of steamers. The shops for various articles are numerous, and a few of them really handsome."

My correspondent then proceeds, in a somewhat pert and laconic manner, to the enumeration of the essentials of life, having kept a house in Dover during her residence, as follows : —" Plenty of good water, excellent bread, very bad meat, fish scarce, poultry good, beer indifferent, and (at which I am sorely grieved, as it was not so in former times) warm-baths particularly dirty."

The sea-bathing is reckoned particularly fine, but the steepness of the shore often prevents the bathing, which would be continued in a more sheltered place. There are many good nursery subscription gardens, favourably situated ; and among other objects affording occupation, I must not forget the Museum, an institution of the other day. The formation of an excellent carriage-road over the heights affords a good excuse for taking exercise out of doors, and the stupendous piercing through of Shakspeare Cliff, now completed, leads one to hope that the once almost forlorn project of a railway to Folkstone and London will be realized, so as to bring the capital to Dover in less than four hours.

To visiters who have not secured lodging before hand, the hotels will afford the necessary accommodation for the moment. Some are better than others, but at all of them *on sçait se faire payer*. Though stuffed into a miserable bit of a bed-room at the back of the house, so small that I could touch both the side walls with my hands at the same time, at the York Hotel, whose landlord had evidently not the fear of the forthcoming " Spas of England" before him, to awe him into a more considerate treatment of the author,—I have no reason or inclination to say ought in disparagement of the house. It is generally much liked, and I should always prefer it to any other.

My correspondent once more supplies me with what remains to be said in conclusion, of the present account of Dover :— " During the winter months the society is good, and much amusement is to be had at balls and parties. Dover, in fact, is a most desirable residence, where, besides recovering your health, you may live independent and retired, or you may mix in all its gaiety if you please ; and I feel greatly indebted to you, as others I am sure ought to feel, for having been the first to recommend this now prosperous watering-place to public notice."

CHAPTER XIV.

SOUTHEND.

HOCKLEY SPA.

SOUTHEND under Medical Protection—New Attraction—DISCOVERY of a Mineral Spring near it—HOCKLEY Village—How to find it out—Road and Principal Towns—Favourable View of Essex—RALEIGH—Pretty Approach—HOCKLEY SPA LODGE—History of the Discovery—The First Case of Cure—Practical Reputation—Analysis by PHILLIPS—My Visit—Examination of the Water—Physical and Chemical Characters —Taste and Effect of the Water—COMPLAINTS in which it will be useful—Quantity to be drank—Excellent in Weakness of Bones— STRIKING RECOVERY—Favourable Position of Hockley—IMPROVE- MENTS suggested—How to make it into a Spa—Character of its Cli- mate—Beautiful Scenery Around it—DRIVE to Southend—The KING's ARMS—First View—OLD SOUTHEND—Hope Hotel—The Shore, THE JETTY and the Mount—The CLIFF—Terrace—Hanging Gardens— The ROYAL HOTEL—Sea Bathing—Expenses of Living—Lodging— Preferable Houses.

THE fact that a physician of eminence in London, author of several valuable works, and one of my oldest friends, had, during two summer seasons lodged his numerous family by the sea-side at Southend, after having in previous years tried the effect of the Isle of Wight, Broadstairs, and Ramsgate, none of which he had found useful to them, led me to pay a visit to that home sea-side place. Its loca-

tion in a country having so bad a name with invalids, was
not otherwise likely to have tempted me to such a step:
the less so as I had made up my mind to terminate my tour
of the English Coasts at Dover, leaving the cockneyfied
watering-places of the Isle of Thanet to their own well and
familiarly known merits and recent improvements.

Southend too presented a farther attraction in the circumstance of a new mineral spring having been very recently
discovered within a few miles of that place, at the small village of Hockley, and to which Mr. Richard Phillips, who had
analyzed the water, had called my attention. Thither, therefore, I proceeded in the month of January in the present
year, considering it my duty to include among the Spas that
were to form my second volume, then preparing for press,
one newly come into notice, and under such able chemical
auspices.

Essex is a county with a bad name; and when I heard of
a Spa being about to be established in that part of it which,
like a peninsula, lies between the river Crouch and its
marshes, to the north, and the Thames and its lowlands to
the south, I turned up my nose at the idea. The very name
of the village of Hockley, in which the spring was found, was
quite new to me, nor could I easily detect its topography on
the map. Many of my readers may be in the same predicament, and I shall, therefore, direct them how to find the new
Spa out; for that it will be sought, or looked after so soon as
the accommodations now preparing or meditated on the spot
shall be completed, I have no more doubt than I have of my
having been to see and examine it.

The direct road is the high turnpike and mail road to Ips-
wich, Yarmouth, and Norwich, as far as Shenfield Lodge, a
short distance beyond which it turns to the right, reaching by
good turnpike roads, in various turnings and twistings,
Wickford, and then Raleigh; two miles farther than which,
a little to the left, is Hockley.

The principal places I passed through in my little excursion, escorted by a gentleman well acquainted with the country, were Romford and Brentwood (both of which are now accessible by railway), Billericay, and Raleigh, all nearly of the same size and disposition; though the two last are likely to strike the traveller, even at a distance, from their peculiar situation upon elevated ground, commanding very fine prospects all round. The former of those places was perceived clustered into an almost compact group, upon a rising belt of hills, four or five miles before we reached it; and when once reached, it presented some of the most extensive and striking views, as well as distant peeps of an undulating country, which, in this instance at all events, belied its common reputation of being flat, marshy, and unprofitable. These views are fully enjoyed for the distance of three miles beyond the town, where we took a S.E. direction, and were struck with three or four enchanting *coups d'œil* of extreme beauty, than which few more popular counties can boast of better. To such as are fond of a diversified champaign country, well wooded, and well cultivated, and presenting an infinite variety of undulations, this excursion of a few miles will prove a source of delight.

At Raleigh the singular and almost startling appearance of green mounds, and an escarpment joining two of these, suggests to the traveller who approaches them from London, on his right hand, as he ascends a very steep hill towards Raleigh, the recollection of some Roman entrenchment, or probably some fortification of a more recent date, which must have very effectually commanded the road, and the access to the town. The line of approach to the borders of Hockley parish from Raleigh is very cheering. Just before reaching the turnpike one of the finest and most extensive valleys which lay at our feet on our left, and exhibited to advantage a vast tract of the fairest part of Essex, seemed to be divided in twain by a tongue of lands a portion of the very hill on which we were standing, which projected forward, and whose termination was marked by Hockley Church, well grouped in the landscape. But the beautiful effect of this view vanished on entering the little village of Hockley, which consists merely of a few straggling cottages, and the Bull Inn, at the back of which is the famous Bull Wood, and a superb scenery all the way southward down to the Thames.

Quitting the main road by a bye-lane, not far from the turnpike, we were conducted to the lowest part of the village, where we found three or four cottages, the property of Mr. Fawcett, solicitor; one of which, more showy than the rest, bore the inscription of "Hockley Spa Lodge." In this I took shelter for the night, and there learned from the elderly couple who occupied it, and received us hospitably, the history of the discovery of the well, which was briefly this:—

Mr. and Mrs. Clay, for such was the name of my good-natured and clear-headed host and hostess, had determined upon building for themselves a cottage in this elevated region, after having escaped the relaxing and weakening effects of a long residence in Cheltenham. A well was sunk for water, for the convenience of the cottage, when in throwing out the sod a hard stone was found, about a foot in diameter, which when exposed to the air fell in pieces. It was hollow within, about the size of a two-quart basin, in which was fine clear water. Proceeding further down, a kind of ragstone and gravel appeared, and clear spring-water flowed. Mrs. Clay, who had been asthmatic all her life, and subject to cough, except when she drank Cheltenham water, after drinking of the new well's water for some little time, found that she lost her difficulty of breathing, and her cough became less troublesome. At the end of a twelvemonth, she was so much better in both respects, that she was inclined to attribute her recovery to air and situation only. A visit, however, to some friends in London on one occasion, and somewhere else on another, having taken her away from the well, her constitution became heated, the cough returned, and asthma began to plague her again ; all which symptoms disappeared on returning to Hockley cottage, and beginning the water once more.   This awoke surmises as to the said water possessing medicinal properties.   The notion having once gone abroad, it was immediately seized upon by many in the neighbourhood, who used the water, which was most liberally supplied to them ;   and in the course of three more years such was the healing reputation of Hockley Well, that not only was the water sent for from all parts of Essex, but from greater distances still, and many people of the better classes of society applied on the spot to drink it.   Lastly— by the end of the fourth year from the accidental discovery of the source, a regular Spa was constituted, where I noticed in the book of arrivals that several persons of consequence had employed and derived benefit from the water.

The proprietor, desirous of ascertaining how far the composition of the water might warrant the expectation of patients, and explain its vaunted good effects, at once engaged the valuable services of Mr. Richard Phillips, as before stated ; who, having proceeded to the spot, and made its preliminary analysis at the well, which he afterwards completed by a more extended series of experiments at home, published the result of his inquiries in the form of a pamphlet. His experiments led him to the conclusion that the water contains four distinct ingredients, namely, common salt, bicarbonate of lime, sulphate of magnesia, or Epsom salts, and sulphate of lime.   In my general table will be found his quantitive analysis.

The object for which my services were required was, first, to ascertain to what class of disorders the water might be deemed applicable, and in what quantity it ought to be drank ; and secondly, what disposition and arrangements ought to be made to render the well more available to patients, and the locality more generally suited to the purposes of a Spa.

A pump has been sunk into the well, though the water in it rises to within a few feet of the surface, at a short distance outside, and at the back of the cottage. After pumping for ten minutes I ascertained the temperature to be 47°, that of the room in which the pump was placed being only 39°, and the external air out of doors 33°, with a fine clear sky. The water appeared beautifully limpid, and colourless as crystal: very minute bubbles of air rose in it, and seemed to increase in number for some minutes after it had been drawn. Some of these adhered to the glass. When shaken, these air-bubbles will disappear, and rise again, but at no time does the water become turbid as long as it remains cold.

On drinking it, the first impression on the palate is rather subacid and pleasing, but the general and continuous taste is that of pure spring water. It does not taste or feel harsh to the mouth. I drank a pint tumbler of it without any marked effect, as to any feelings of chilliness or weight at the stomach. When boiled and poured into a glass there is a manifest turbidity, the surface becomes covered almost imperceptibly with a whitish powdery deposit or cream, which, on tilting the glass, will adhere to the surface. After this experiment, the water no longer tastes subacid, and the very minute bubbles of air rise even more abundantly. Placed in contact with metals, it throws down a copious precipitate. It corrodes lead and iron rapidly, and the solder of all metallic vessels. If put into a bottle, it will not deposit any sediment; but if a crack exists in the bottle its edges will presently be furred with the sediment. If a large quantity of the water be boiled, and allowed afterwards to cool, a large proportion of a white magnesia-looking precipitate falls down.

These remarks of mine on the physical character of

2 R 2

Hockley mineral water I purposely made and recorded before I would allow Mr. Phillips to communicate to me his own observations and results, as I did not wish to be biassed by them.

I opened and examined the well, which I found to be about eighteen feet from the surface, with about fifteen feet of water in it. Its diameter is three feet six. During a severe and general drought in all the wells and ponds in the neighbourhood, it still was found to have ten feet of water. It has never frozen, and no landspring seems to affect it.

Judging, _à priori_, from all these data and particulars, I should be inclined to attribute very marked alterative virtues to this mineral water, when taken in small and divided doses. It will act also as an aperient in doses of a pint and a half, drank in the morning at four times, and as an antacid in stomach complaints, as well as in cases of lithic disorders of the kidneys. The water must be drank cold, and immediately after being drawn from the well. I saw and conversed with some of the people who had derived benefit from drinking it, and I have preserved the statement of some of the most interesting cases cured by its means. Into one of these, indeed, that of a nice little child, a nephew of the proprietor of the Spa, who had suffered from rachitic weakness of the bones, and want of ossification, particularly in the breast and bones of the head, I had full opportunities of minutely inquiring, and I felt satisfied that the robustness the child acquired after a residence of some months at the Spa, arose from the use of the water, which I should expect would be found in all similar cases to promote and aid the growth and consolidation of bones. Children or young people of weak frame, inclined to have ricketty and bandy legs, and weak in their ankles, will here find the best means of remedying those constitutional defects.

The air of Hockley is very favourable to such cases, being pure and bracing. The Spa is sheltered from the east, and the rainy winds of the south-west. Hockley itself stands on high ground, and skirts a vast common of the same name. Upon the brow of the highest part, or ridge of this common, where there is now a tolerably good-looking inn, which enjoys the vast prospect of all the fine highly-cultivated country that lies at least two hundred feet below, stretching between the last high ground in the country and the Thames—I would recommend to build a first-rate hotel. Invalids of the superior class, who, upon being made acquainted with the peculiar virtues of this new English mineral spring, and the beauty of the spot, as well as with the purity and invigorating nature of its air and exposure to the south, will not be tardy in availing themselves of such a boon of nature in behalf of their weak or ricketty progeny, should they be afflicted with any such as will require an accommodation of that kind. Many, too, who are liable to acidity and pinky sediment from their kidneys, will flock here, as well as several whose dyspeptic disorders require an alterative pleasant mineral water. The very inn as it now exists, with a more showy front, and some internal amelioration, would do for present purposes; and from it, following the line of the upper crest of the common, detached cottages with a similar aspect of south-east and south, and with the same extensive prospect of river and distant sea, should be erected in the direction towards the well or spa-house which ought to be further enlarged by having a pump-room, and a series of four bath-rooms, on the spot on which Mr. Clay's cottage now stands.

A very sensible and clever lady, residing not many miles from Hockley, and who is a perfectly disinterested party, personally unknown to me, but who has honoured me with her opinion in writing on the subject of this Spa, has greatly confirmed my views as to its capabilities and importance.

" I feel very sanguine," this fair correspondent writes to me, " as to the success of the Spa, provided it be forwarded by men of enterprise and spirit. If interest could be made with Mr. ——, the lord of the manor of Hockley, the common might be built upon at an easy rent (or rather quit-rent) no doubt. A few pretty villas, to begin with immediately, would be desirable. If the pump-room is to be built for the coming summer, it should be set about instanter ; and I know some gentlemen in the neighbourhood who, having a little land thereabout, would be inclined to erect cottages. Hockley is a remarkably healthy village, and the neighbourhood improving very fast."

With this additional recommendation of Hockley Spa, I leave that infant establishment in the hands of those who may feel an interest in its prosperity—not only on mere selfish views, but on the more charitable and philanthropic principle of doing good to their neighbours, by securing to them, in a quarter of England so remote from any well-known and efficient mineral spring, the benefit of one so providentially brought to light.

SOUTHEND.

As was stated in the beginning of this account of Hockley, the vicinity of a sea-bathing place at the mouth of the Thames, with a favourable, and one of the busiest and most enlivening sea-prospects I know of, is a great and a mutual advantage to both places. The Southend people therefore will have reason to rejoice that Hockley Spa has been established so near them; for to Southend, most of the invalids who will have gone through a course of the saline water at Hockley in July, will proceed in August and September to take the benefit of sea-bathing. The drive from the latter place is exceedingly interesting till you get near Prittlewell in the flat country. Between Hockley and Rochford, the ancient church and tower of which, approached by roads flanked with rows of lofty trees, shows well in the landscape, the scenery has always been much admired by strangers; and the cockney who, during the summer, stops short at Gravesend, in his excursion down the Thames, and is in ecstasies at that commonplace sort of retreat, can form no idea of the beauties he would enjoy were he to extend his steaming trip down the river as far as Southend, and stop on the north instead of the south bank.

As the traveller has wound his way through many fantastic girations, along a richly-cultivated plain, after leaving Prittlewell, he little expects to find his carriage halting at a good-looking inn, "THE KING'S ARMS," upon the brow of the cliff overlooking the Thames below it, and enjoying a full view of the sea, which breaks suddenly upon him. From this spot the carriage then descends a pretty steep hill down to the margin of the water, along which is displayed the oldest part of the town, or Old Southend. The first house of entertainment in this part is the Hope Hotel, small but comfortable; the next, and farther east, is the Ship, with an open space before it, and bespeaking by its exterior the excellent accommodation it possesses within. The strand in front here is not quite level with high water, but two or three feet above it, and at low water, the shelving shore is uncovered for nearly a mile out. The wooden jetty at present in existence, and the only convenient place people have to land upon, extends only to about half a mile, and is always left dry at low tides. It is then followed out by a line of shingle, projecting perhaps a quarter of a mile farther, and called the HARD. Then follows a space of clear water, even at low tide, which divides the termination of the Hard and a cluster of piles in the sea called the *Mount*, on which a hut is built of two rooms, inhabited by people deputed to take care of a pharo-light for the safety of vessels at night. To this mount, when it is low water, the Gravesend and Southend steamers land their passengers in the summer, who are then boated over to the Hard, and thence walk to the jetty. At high water, and when the weather is not boisterous, the steamers land their passengers at the jetty itself.

The question of the extension of the latter has engaged the various clashing interests in the place for the last ten years, and there is as little probability as ever that this much-desired continuation will ever be accomplished ; without which accommodation, however, it will be in vain to hope that the company at Southend should increase; for as to the land journey, even with the advantage of rail-convey-ance as far as Brentwood, it is so fatiguing and incon-venient, compared with the facility and rapidity of a down course by steamers on the Thames, that to expect people will prefer that line of communication is absurd.

The aspect of this metropolitan sea-bathing settlement, as I might call it, along the left bank, and at the *embouchure* of the river, taken in its slightly curved sweep, is south inclined to the east in many points, and has Sheerness in front bearing south-south-west. The scene before it is one of bustle and life on the water. The horizon is perpetually filled with every species of vessels and small craft, sailing, rowing, and steaming upon the wide bosom of old father Thames.

The strand is partly sand and partly gravel, but not very clean or inviting at low water. The descent is not imper-ceptible, and at high water, or even half tide, there would be too much water, even at a short distance from the shore, to feel your footing. Bathing-machines, large and commo-dious in every way, stand in front of the Ship Hotel,

The parade and the library are upon this level, and con-stitute the centre of Old Southend. To the north-west of it, the Cliff houses, constituting a part of New Southend, stand nearly sixty feet above the level strand. There are about twenty of them arrayed in a row, along a broad gravel ter-race facing the south-south-west, with all the open sea on the left, and the jetty nearly under them, and the sloping ground from the terrace to the strand, arranged in gardens and zig-zag walks. At the head of this terrace is the crack hotel of the new town, called the Royal Hotel. At this house, the situation of which is certainly the best in the place, and during the summer unquestionably to be preferred, a gentleman may lodge for 2s. 6d. for his bed-room, 3s. 6d. for a sitting-room, and 5s. for his dinner. If you add, for breakfast, tea in the evening, and servants, 5s. more, you have here, as everywhere almost in this blessed country of dear inns, a weekly expenditure of not less than five guineas to live like a gentleman. So no matter whether you be among the fishing-smacks of Southend or the dons of Brighton, there is no getting decent food and lodging for less than your hundred shillings a-week !

Now it is not so at the HOPE, where I stopped, and where one has the advantage of an exceedingly civil and comely landlady, with pretty daughters, all anxious to give satisfaction ; for here you may board, have an excellent bedroom, and a nice sitting-room facing the sea, for just half the money before mentioned. I looked at some of the private lodgings, a few of which are really desirable for such as choose to keep house. At the first house on the left, formerly the Marine Library, immediately at the entrance of Old Southend, and facing the pier or jetty, a very neat and large drawing-room, with a good bedroom at the back, is let for twenty-five shillings a week in June and July, and for thirty in August and September—the two latter being the best months at this watering-place,—which I am inclined, on the whole, to consider as deserving the patronage bestowed upon it by my clever and shrewd friend, the physician alluded to in the beginning of this account of Southend.

CHAPTER XV.

TUNBRIDGE WELLS.

Tunbridge as a Spa—Its slender Claims—Chalybeates of England—
Tunbridge frequented as a Residence—Great Extension of the Place—
Detached Villas—Great Feature of Tunbridge Wells—Its Popu-
larity — The Common—Mount Ephraim — The London Road, Sion
Mount, and Mount Pleasant—The Calverly Estate—Calverly Ter-
race and Parade—The Park and its Villas—The Promenade and
Baths—Architecture of Modern Tunbridge—Splendid Opportunity
for the Display of Taste—The New Churches—Trinity and Christ
Church—Taxation—Window Duty the Bane of Architects—House
Rents — Distances — Assinine Equitation—Walking — The Mineral
Spring—Situation—Reservoir, and Mode of Drinking the Water—
The " Dippers"—Temperature, Appearance, and Taste of the Water
—Not much drank now—Immediate Effect on the Stomach—Sub-
sequent Effect—The *Pro-bono-publico* Basin—Neglected, and not much
cared for—Tunbridge Water wants Carbonic Acid—Might be added,
and Renew the Fame of the Water—The Baths—Their Forlorn Con-
dition—Worse Prospect—What should be done—Chemical Compo-
sition of the Water—Complaints benefited by it— The Author's
Experience—The Sussex Hotel—Advantages and Disadvantages—
The Calverly and the Ephraim Hotels—The Gloucester Family
Boarding House—Provisions—Supply of Water—The Climate—
Fair and Foul Weather—Conclusion.

Tunbridge has risen into importance, and will retain it,
because of its locality, its beautiful environs, the salubrity of
its air, and the judicious manner in which people have availed

themselves of all these advantages to erect houses and accommodation for strangers. Hence Tunbridge Wells will always be a place of great resort for occasional visiters, and may and soon will become one of winter residence also, though the reputation of its mineral waters, which first made the reputation of the place, be nearly gone, and will soon pass away altogether.

No Spa ever had a more slender claim than this insignificant chalybeate to a high-sounding fame. Of such springs there are fifty in the north as well as the south of England. In Yorkshire alone, of chalybeates as good, there is one at every turnpike almost; and in the south we have hardly a town of importance that is not near one of them. But most of the chalybeates of England are cold, heavy, flat, indigestible waters, and lack that which makes medicinal steel water admissible, cheering, easily digested, and exhilarating; they lack, in fine, plenty of carbonic acid; they lack effervescence. Had this very steel stream of Tunbridge Wells possessed an excess of that gaseous ingredient, its effects would have been wonderful and lasting. It is, even now, not too late to impart to it, by easy and effective means, during the hour when invalids and other sojourners in the place usually apply for the water, that all-essential requisite which alone can revive the Spa from its approaching extinction.

It is the unanimous opinion of the best-informed persons residing on the spot, and even of the " dippers " themselves, as the female attendants at the Wells are called,—and I saw the fact vouched by the " dippers' " own registers,—that if Tunbridge Wells be crowded (and I rejoiced to hear it had been so during the preceding summer), it is not with people who come on account of the chalybeate, for few, very few, indeed, had drank of that salutary spring. No: it is the *séjour* that attracted them, and the beauty of *that* cannot be subject to the caprice of fashion. Nay, in proportion, as buildings of a better and superior class rise in eligible situations, on the Nevill property and the Camden property, and other properties lately thrown into the general vortex of speculation for enlarging Tunbridge Wells and its accommodations, so we shall find a greater number of visiters attend the place, and many more invalids inclined to settle there. At no distant period, Tunbridge Wells will have grown as large as Cheltenham.

But the classes of persons who will then frequent the place will be different from those who have hitherto frequented it, both with regard to money and health. With little of either in his possession, let no man attempt Tunbridge Wells. He must get rather into those head-quarters of half-pay, rotten livers, and jaundiced cheeks which stretch upon the blue lias of Gloucestershire. Here he must be endowed with a sound constitution, though temporarily weakened it may be by lapsed diseases, by a fatiguing life, or by any other accidental yet transitory cause. He must have a long purse, too; for, being so very near London, he will have to contend against wealth, and plenty of that aristocratic spirit for spending it during two or three months of each summer, which brings down from the metropolis thousands anxious to enjoy the smiling neighbourhood of Tunbridge Wells, and inhale the bracing and pure breezes from the crests of the holy mounts, be they Ephraim or Sion.

No watering-place except Cheltenham has so many detached villas, mansions, belvederes, bellevues, lodges, and cottages *ornées* as Tunbridge. These, grouped over the most diversified area of plain and hills of undulating ground that can be imagined, or arranged round a common intersected by roads and ways, and fifty winding paths, that have all some important object at their termination; and most of them interspersed with insulated groups of trees, groves, and grotesque masses of rocks peeping above the surface in their grey nakedness;—these buildings, I say, constitute the modern Tunbridge Wells—far different from the " Wells" of old, when quaffing steel-water to patch up old constitutions, like that of Dudley Lord North, and promenading under a narrow wooden arcade, yclept the *Pantiles*, (still in existence), listening to the best musical band Beau Nash could procure, or to his own *fâde* nonsense and priggish civilities, formed the *ne plus* of aristocratic mineral-water drinking in times now almost forgotten.

The great feature of modern Tunbridge Wells is the beautifully irregular amphitheatre it presents, covered nearly, yet not crowded, with houses, all gladdened with lawns, gardens, or plantations, and almost all properly and judiciously located as to compass, and acknowledging in the glory of its own luxuriant hills no superior hill above it to intercept the extensive and magnificent views by which it is surrounded. There are a hundred points from which we can take in a general view of the whole "district;" for to call it a village, or a town even, would be to misapply words. From any one of these points, turn which way you list, you have varied, pleasing, and often striking prospects.

The great popularity of this place of summer resort is not surprising, nor can it be attributed to mere fashion ; for if it be the fashion to repair to Tunbridge Wells, then, so long as taste and good sense shall prevail among the easy classes of society, that fashion will continue. When, after quitting the immediate neighbourhood of the Wells and its pantiles, you step on the common behind the latter, and either by the Castle-road straight across that common, constantly clothed in verdure, or by the more tortuous one called the London-road, you ascend imperceptibly towards the north to reach the highest point, where Grosvenor-road coming from the great centre of Tunbridge joins Ephraim-terrace and Sidney-place at Culverden—you behold equally to the right and to the left a range of detached dwellings more or less imposing, grand, or convenient, but all of them cheering and joyous-looking, bearing single and particular names by which they are known, and under which they are engaged by the visiters lucky enough to get any of them.

On the left, Mount Ephraim spreads its numerous villas, courts, and lodges, with their fronts turned to the south-east, and looking down upon the Old Wells and Mount Sion, with the common and the race-course between; while their back-rooms enjoy a distant view of the Surrey hills. On the right, many more houses are also ranged in an ascending line, which form the north-western border of the newer part of Tunbridge Wells, and like those opposite, stand insulated, and more or less inclosed by gardens and lawns. Their aspect is to the north-west and west, and the common stretches before them.

But if the traveller in search of house-room misses in the two localities just described the object of his wishes, and has no objection to plunge more into the interior of the town, let him, after quitting the Pantiles as a point of departure, follow a north-east direction along Mount Sion, and up to Mount Pleasant, passing the Grove-hill-road, and the Calverly-road on his right, until he has reached Calverly-place, upon the highest confine of the town, and let him then seek in those directions house-room, of which there is no want, and of the best description too, suited to the means and inclination of most classes of persons.

At the termination of his promenade the visiter will find himself in the immediate neighbourhood of by far the most striking portion of modern Tunbridge, being in itself a little town as it were, consisting of a variety of very handsome buildings, erected on the vast and picturesque estate of Calverly. All the roads on this estate are neatly flanked with dwarf-stone walls, handsomely built, and kept in the best order, with well-trimmed quickset hedges surmounting them. Every house here, whether on the Calverly-terrace, or the Calverly-parade, wears the aspect of style and inward ease. Before them there are pleasure-grounds, and the prospect from their upper apartments, both westward and southward, is of the most cheerful description.

Following the Calverly-road in front of the terrace, the stranger arrives at the Calverly Hotel, formerly Calverly House, and the residence once of a most illustrious lady. Just beyond which the Victoria-gate will admit him into Calverly-park, a magnificent embowered and deep dell, whose gently inclined sides, richly clothed with verdure, dotted with groups of trees and shrubberies, and enriched with the dense foliage of a deep and shady wood, offers ample room for first-rate insulated villas, in the style of those which decorate the inclosure of our Regent's-park. The position of Calverly Hotel, with a southern aspect, and its back front peering over the park, is quite unique, and is alone sufficient to tempt people within its ample, highly decorated, showy, and well-furnished apartments.

Another part of this fairy land lies at the threshold of the park, and is itself a curiosity. Within the precincts of an almost imperceptible enclosure, an elliptical sweep of shops, perhaps twenty in number, with convenient private residences over them, and sheltered in front by a spacious colonnade, supporting a running balcony or *terrazza*, presents its front to the south south-east, looking over Calverly-park. At the nearest end of this crescent are the Royal Baths, and its centre house is occupied by a public library. A figured lawn stretches before these buildings, with a fountain marking its centre, and an orchestra-stand facing it, in which I was told a band of musicians performs during the summer. This *bijou* of the Calverly domain is called the " Promenade." The most fastidious, the most difficult to be pleased in matters of house-room, will hardly leave this extensive, elevated, and highly-favoured quarter of the New Town without suiting himself with lodgings for the season.

I have thus presented to my readers, the *carte du pays*, in such a way as will enable them almos' to choose and fix beforehand, and without the trouble of a preliminary journey, upon the dwelling and position they may wish to occupy during a visit to Tunbridge Wells.

The tone and character of the architecture of this place, in which such vast opportunities existed for exhibiting it in perfection, is nevertheless, and in general, rather pleasing than striking. It may be called the " Modern English," which by attempting to follow the severer rules of the Grecian, disdaining the Roman, except to mistake it, and not knowing the Lombard style, or being itself too much akin to the Tudor and Vandalic taste, has fallen into a jumble that can only be designated by the national denomination I have bestowed upon it. This style is like nothing else. It has prevailed for the last twenty years in all places where much building has been going on, whether in the capital or in the chief cities of counties, and at watering-places. You see it triumphant in the Regent's-park, Park-terrace, and Hyde-park-gardens. You meet with it at Brighton, on the extreme East Cliff, and on the King's-road. You cannot mistake it at Cheltenham. It is getting on pretty smartly at Leamington; and we find it here also, [especially on the Calverly estate. A richer, more unique, more magnificent, or extensive locality for the display of sound, yet handsome domestic architecture, than this very domain, no man of taste or judgment could possibly have desired. Yet not one truly striking edifice has been erected upon it; and the hotel, the houses on the terrace and parade, with here and there a detached villa within the park, are the only specimens one can single out as being superior in style to the generality of the " Modern English."

The two new churches stand apart from these general observations. Some say Trinity Church, in Church-road, at the top of Mount Pleasant, and Gothic of course, is good; while others stand by Christ Church, on Mount Sion, a newer edifice, and of the same style, with a Gothic porch of three

arches, which they contend is much better. *Non nostrum
tantas componere lites.*

Captain Marryat has observed somewhere, that the clumsy
and unscientific manner in which the English merchant-
vessels are built in our days, is the result of a desire to evade
channel, port, and river duties.

"We have over-taxed," he says; "our shipping; and our
merchants, in order to carry as much freight as possible, and
at the same time pay as few onerous duties, have given
to their shipping more the form of floating boxes of mer-
chandize than of sailing vessels."

Just so with respect to house-duty, but above all, with
respect to window-tax, in reference to house-building. It has
been remarked of English dwelling-houses in cities, as well as
in the country, that this meting out the light of heaven to
the people by measured and numbered openings or windows,
as gaslight is distributed by meters nowadays, has materially
influenced the nature of architectural designs, and the elevations have suffered in consequence.

On inquiry I found that most of the best houses, and
those which enjoy the best or crack situations, let for high
rents—higher in some cases than in London. Reasonable
prices, however, are demanded for modest and retired private lodgings; but it is of little use to an invalid or a convalescent requiring the bracing iron-air of Tunbridge Wells, to
bury himself in a street-lodging; he must soar and live in
the higher regions, away from the hollow of the Wells, and
upon the sandy soil of the many pretty undulations I have
been describing. Distances here are considered as nothing;
though from the extreme north point of the town, amidst
buildings of high-sounding names, such as Grosvenor House,
and Wilton-place, and Belgrave Villa,—down to Cumberland-
vale and Cumberland-terrace, at the extreme south point;
and again from Calverley Lodge east, to Bishopsdown west,—
two intersecting lines intervene, the one three-quarters of a

mile long, and the other not less than a mile and a quarter. But assinine equitation, first introduced as an appendage to a watering-place at this very Spa by a Lady Seymour nearly forty years ago, and here kept up with spirit and ready facility, shortens these distances, and renders every out-of-door movement perfectly easy. Walking, however, is an exercise much to be encouraged, and these distances offer sufficient excuse for it. Such an exercise at Tunbridge Wells is by no means unpleasant, owing to the nature of the soil, which even after a heavy rain offers a dry footing.

The mineral springs to which the place is indebted for its memorable name, rising first in the small obscure village of Speldhurst, not far off, come down into Tunbridge Wells, and surge again at the lowest point of its narrow valley, over which the original village is built. I descended one morning the few wet steps that lead to the shallow basin, out of the bottom of which, through three round holes, the mineral water ascends, filling its marble receptacle at the rate of one gallon per minute, while its excess runs out of a side-opening into a smaller square reservoir contiguous to the former.

This fountain of health is placed at the east end of the already often mentioned Pantiles, that irregular and multishaped narrow covered shade or wooden arcade, which runs by the side of a paved terrace, raised about three feet from the level of the street on one side, but on the other side even with the common, to which delightful feature of Tunbridge, as previously noticed, there is a free access through one or two openings. Throughout its length, the covered walk is flanked by small shops on the north or last-mentioned side, and by an *allée* or double row of trees on the south side, in the centre of which a permanent wooden stand for an orchestra exists, where a band of music performs three times a-day during the summer, and twice a-day in the winter.

I gave way to a group of young ladies, who were the first I had seen approach the Well that morning, though I had watched from six till nine o'clock, foolishly expecting that early hours here, as at the German Spas, were those at which the Well was most frequented. In the meantime I entered a little unfurnished room, not larger than a cobbler's shed, in which was seated one of the female " dippers," an ancient-looking dame of twenty-nine years' service in the place, watching the simmering process of some of the chalybeate water contained in a ginger-beer bottle, and placed on the hob of a lighted fire-place. The very size of this odd sort of vessel employed for warming the water—which my informant assured me *many* people preferred drinking in that state— shows that the *many* could only have been very *few*,—else a pint or less of water kept warm would soon be disposed of. Be that as it may, I observed that ordinary-sized wine-glasses are used for distributing the chalybeate. The "dipper" dips the said glass into the basin, and hands it full to the strangers.

I found the temperature of the water to be about fifty degrees of Fahrenheit, that of the external air being at the time about forty-five, with clear weather. In no respect could I detect any difference between the taste of this water and that of the pure and transparent water I had drank that morning at the hotel (not far from the Spa), which, by the bye, smelt rather steely. The mineral water, upon being immediately taken from the basin, does not impart at once the notion that steel is present, and many a thirsty soul would quaff it as a pleasant and palatable beverage, without once suspecting that he had drank steel-water, or any other but the purest water from a running brook. Yet the presence of iron is undeniable; for on casting a glance at the little reservoir or stone trough below, the peculiar orange deposit in the shape of powder was fully visible; and so did I see it deposited quite as much in the stone reservoir of the chalybeate spring of Monkswell, near Lincoln.

The Tunbridge Wells Chalybeate feels cold and heavy to the stomach for a few minutes after drinking it, and often fails to produce those warming and stimulating effects which the effervescent chalybeates of Germany produce. A single eructation of air occurs after the ingestion. Drank warm, it is still more insipid. By increasing its temperature its stimulating effect has been augmented in many cases, without injuring the due proportion of oxyde of iron present, which, strange to say, the heating process does not seem to affect, though carried, according to Sir Charles Scudamore, to 140° Fahrenheit.

The Well-women assert that when the wooden cover that protects, with lock and key at night, the basin—which, by the bye, is new, and as I before said, of marble (having before been of a different material)—is removed from over it in the morning, the bottom of the basin is strewed with an ochrey or orange-coloured precipitate, which it is their duty to remove by scouring the basin every morning, before the public is admitted to drink the water.

By the side of this basin is the other before mentioned, which is kept open for the public; but it has, like everything else that belongs to no one in particular, and is for every one's benefit (gratis), been out of repair and unfit for use a long time. The water in it looks like brown tanners' decoction, and runs over in all directions, as it best pleases, no one caring what becomes of this free gift. These two basins are partly sheltered by the friendly steps which lead from the end of the arcade up to the shop of honest silk-mercer Neal, and which form a quarter-arch over the spring,—adjoining to which, by the bye, lies handy a small chemist's shop, ready to supply the mineral-water bibber with any medical aid he may require.

I stated it before, and I may be permitted to repeat it again, that had this water possessed twenty cubic inches or more of carbonic-acid gas in a pint (and it is quite possible to impart this to it), its effects would have surprised the most incredulous as to the efficacy of Tunbridge water. At present that water is not in great vogue; and although from all accounts, about five thousand strangers had sojourned in Tunbridge during the summer, not more than two hundred and forty, from the beginning of June to the 24th of September, had applied for it at the fountain. Their names were recorded in a little book (which I examined), kept by the two female dippers, who are appointed from among the daughters of manor men to the situation, and get the little all produced by such an occupation.

The baths are outside the Pantiles, and at the back of the spring; and their entrance is from the common. The exterior of the building, and no doubt its interior, must have been showy and praiseworthy in former days. At present only a portion of the building is applied for the purpose of the baths, and this is let by the lord of the manor to an upholsterer living on the premises, who uses two rooms on the ground floor for two marble reclining baths, which may be used either warm or cold, and has a cold plunging bath besides; the water of which, five feet deep, is covered on its surface with the reddish ochre peculiar to chalybeates. This bath is only cleared out once during the season, by pumping it out, when it takes ten hours to fill again from the spring.

Hardly fifty names of persons who had used these baths during the preceding season were inserted in the little register: among them was that of an elderly gentleman, a physician from London, who, to recover his lost strength, had dipped into the plunging bath for an instant three successive times every day, for a week, and had gone away satisfied with the good effects the bathing had produced on him. Now, here is steel-water as red as that at Schwalbach, so much extolled by the Old Man of the *brunnen*. Why is it not used then as frequently as we have been told by the old gentleman the Schwalbach baths are used?

The fact is, that the whole concern, whether for drinking or bathing, of the mineral water at Tunbridge Wells, is at a low ebb indeed, compared to the way in which spas in general are conducted nowadays, and is totally unworthy of its former reputation. There is not another place in Great Britain with the pretension of a spa, where the principal features are so neglected: and yet the capabilities of the place, the possibility of rendering the mineral water once more useful to society, and the splendid resources of every sort which Tunbridge Wells possesses as a residence for invalids, convalescents, and people of weak constitutions,—should stir up some of the influential inhabitants to the same exertions which are now being made at Harrogate, and at Bath; thus endeavouring to prevent the reputation of the place as a spa from dwindling into nothing. Both the dippers and the bathwomen spoke but cheerlessly of the prospects of their respective departments; and the Spa, as a spa, is at its eleventh hour, or on its last legs.

It is manifest that a mineral water, a pint of which, according to Sir Charles Scudamore's very minute, and elaborate, and, I doubt not, accurate analysis, contains but seven twenty-fifth parts of a grain of oxyde of iron—a substance of which, let it be borne in mind, as much as eighty grains at a dose have been given when Mr. Hutchinson's steel treatment of tic-doloureux was in vogue—and nineteen hundredth-parts of a grain of muriate of lime, and sixteen hundredth-parts of a grain of common salt, with still more trifling quantities of muriate of magnesia and of glauber-salt, and an unappreciable proportion of manganese,—making altogether hardly one grain of solid ingredients,—I say it is manifest that with such an homœopathic quantity of saline matter in sixteen ounces of the Tunbridge water, we may, with Sir Charles Scudamore, ponder and inquire " whether its powers as a medicine have all the pretensions which it claims; or how far the imagination may have contributed to the credit which the water has acquired."

Sir Charles decides the first part of the proposition in the affirmative, and in the negative the second : and as far as my experience enables me to decide, I am inclined to think with him, that this Tunbridge Wells water has been too highly and undeservedly extolled.

Its salutary effects in many cases, particularly of female complaints, have been undeniable. In weak stomachs, suffering from slow and laborious digestion, accompanied with acidity,—provided the patients or the individuals had not been liable to plethora, or fullness of blood in the head, or congested liver at the same time,—I have found the Tunbridge chalybeate a perfect, safe, and effectual remedy ; but I did so because its administration took place in a climate and atmosphere suited to those particular cases. In any other locality—one less elevated and less bracing, for instance—such a chalybeate would have proved inefficacious.

At my arrival at Tunbridge Wells, I found myself installed (thanks to the instinctive will and pleasure of my post-boy) at the Royal Victoria and Sussex Hotel, an excellent example of a first-rate English establishment of its class. Unfortunately it faces the north, and has, moreover, the ancient lofty trees of the Pantiles-terrace in front; between the trunks of which one beholds that once thronged and lively promenade, now a dull and unfrequented walk, even while the band is performing. This northern aspect renders the front apartments and the coffee-room of the hotel gloomy· It is, besides, situated at the very lowest point of the vale, close to the spring; and the ground around it, north, east, and west, rises immediately, though gently, from near it up to the most distant and highest elevation. The hotel, therefore, will not do for a permanent residence, but admirably so for a temporary *séjour*. Attendance officious, coffee-room appliances unobjectionable, cookery not blameable, civility, cleanliness, and furniture, including beds and bedroom-gear, as good as need be desired, this house offers to a stranger; besides other advantages which the other hotels in Tunbridge have not. With carriages and horses both for town and posting, it is well supplied. A coach-office is at the very next door. The mineral water—the promenade—the band within hearing. The market, and chapel of ease—all are close at hand ; and for such as can be satisfied with the back rooms, a southern sun, and the view of Sussex-gardens adjoining the hotel, will enliven their *séjour*. In fact, the Royal Victoria and Sussex Hotel is what, in the palmy days of Tunbridge Spa, would have been considered as the most desirable spot for a residence, and as the centre of attraction. With all this, however, the establishment will be found eligible only for such of the visiters as intend making a short stay at Tunbridge. Those who, having determined upon a longer residence, prefer an hotel to a private house, will look to the Calverly, which is the Richmond Star and Garter of Tunbridge, but with an infinitely finer and more magnificent prospect before it; or will betake themselves to the more modest, yet also beautifully located Ephraim Hotel, on the mount of that name ; or lastly, to two or three other hotels situated in different parts of the town, and not quite so low down as the Sussex.

For such as prefer family boarding-houses, the Gloucester, opposite the Assembly Rooms, has been generally recommended. It has the advantage of being near to the libraries, of which there are two under the Pantiles, both deserving of patronage and much frequented, and to the Upper Assembly Room, as well as to the mineral springs. The fare at these establishments is said to be unobjectionable, as provisions are excellent at Tunbridge, and the markets of every kind well supplied. Water is a ticklish article at Tunbridge, and there are many people who cannot persuade themselves that any of it is to be got free from iron. This is a mistake : all the pumps and wells in the lower town unquestionably partake of the chalybeate character ; the water is hard, has a somewhat metallic taste, curdles the soap, and leaves the skin quite rough. But this is not the water generally drank; for a supply of a much better sort has of late years been secured, both to the upper town, Mount Ephraim, &c., and to the lower town, including the Sussex Hotel; the first, from what is called the " Jack Boot's Spring," the water of which, of most excellent quality, is pumped from the well into a large reservoir placed on a very elevated ground, and thence distributed; and the second from the Frant reservoir.

The climate of Tunbridge in summer and in dry weather is delightful; the air genial yet invigorating; and no large community of people of fortune, or in easy circumstances, collected together to enjoy life, and the *otium post laborem*, in any one locality in England so near the capital, have, like the community spread luxuriously over these beautiful undulations of Tunbridge, such a nature to admire, and so many advantages from the hand of man to enjoy. The whole scene on a sunny holiday, viewed from any elevated part of the common, is the most inspiriting and gay spectacle that one in love with nature and his fellow-creatures can desire to behold; and such a spectacle greatly enhances the peculiarities of Tunbridge, its air, its situation, and its mineral water, as adjuvants in the recovery of health.

But then it must not rain; for no place in the world loses so much as Tunbridge by the fall of rain, or the withdrawing of the cheering rays of the sun from over its variegated surface. Of this I had a sad example before me on the last day of my visit. All that was lovely, smiling, and delightful yesterday, was now thrown suddenly into mourning. The morning opened with lowering weather. From the south-west there rose presently a strong wind, followed soon after by an incessant fall of rain, which, in a moment, changed the whole aspect of things most woefully. None but those who were compelled to it were abroad. The fine equipages and the gay pedestrians were nowhere to be seen, and the dashing mansions and villas were closely shut up, their inmates being content with peeping through the panes of glass in despair, as they looked up to the heavy clouds. Across the common you might discern a few blue, red, and white lower garments fluttering in the wind, to the great distress of the portly and well-fed cook or housekeeper just returning from market, or of the smart laundress carrying the snow-white linen home to the furnished lodgings on Mount Ephraim. A few umbrellas turned inside out by a sudden and violent gust of the gale, or a bonnet here and there flying off, and just retained by its strangling ribbon, afforded a passing subject for merriment. The flys and the first and second-class carriages plying for fare, were seen crossing and re-crossing the hills upon the Castle and London road; while, on the contrary, the asses seemed to rejoice at the prospect of a holiday from their Spanish and other hard saddles and riders. Lastly, an unfortunate groom, wet to the skin, or some stout coachman, was seen scampering across to Calverley, or Mount Pleasant, or Mount Ephraim, fresh from the Post-office, and carrying to his master, in a smart leathern bag, the letters and papers from the metropolis. Beyond these symptoms of life, none else were visible throughout the Wells in all those places, which, but the day before, when a serene instead of a clouded sky had lighted up the scene, were swarming with life in its most joyous moods.

It would hardly be possible, by theatrical trickery or stage-shift, to produce, as is here produced by foul weather alone, a mutation so sudden, and moreover so complete.

CONCLUSION.

A VERY short journey brought me once more to London, and the conclusion of my task. Long and fatiguing as its execution has been, I shall always consider the gratification I experienced in conducting it as one of its most redeeming features—especially if the manner of communicating its results to the Public, adopted in the present volumes, and the great care taken to impart nothing but useful and original information respecting the manifold subjects treated in them, should meet with the approbation of my readers.

It is a long time since a Medical Tour through England of such an extent, purposely undertaken and written to make known the various resources this country possesses in the class of mineral waters, and embracing, at the same time, all the topics I have introduced to enliven it and render it popular, has issued from the press. Indeed, I am not aware of the existence of any work on English Mineral Waters which can be said to bear a strict analogy or resemblance to the present. In introducing, therefore, for the first time, into the literature of this country a performance of this nature, I must trust to the candour of my readers, that, for the sake of its good intention, they will forgive any defect that may be found in its plan or execution.

That its intention was a good one, I can aver with a pure conscience, for it aimed at inducing English people to read a work of considerable extent concerning their own country, whereby they might renew or augment their own previous knowledge of the many gifts and boons with which Providence has peculiarly blessed them.

INDEX.

WHITING, BEAUFORT HOUSE, STRAND.

EXHIBITING AT ONE VIEW THE CHEMICAL COMPOSITION OF THE WATERS;

N.B. The Springs are arranged in the order in which the Author visited them, for the sake of convenience in referring to the text.

No. of Springs	Degrees of Temp. F.	NAMES OF THE SPRINGS.	AMOUNT, IN GRAINS, AND THOUSANDTH PARTS OF A GRAIN, OF THE MINERALIZING INGREDIENTS HE									ALUM-INE.	SILICA.	OX. OF
			SODA WITH			LIME WITH			MAGNESIA WITH			PURE.	PURE.	PURE.
			M.	S.	C.	M.	S.	C.	M.	S.	C.			
22	83	Buxton.	0.23	0.08		0.07		1.30	0.07					
23	68	Matlock.												
24	54	WOODHALL SPA.	189.6	0.25	Bi-c. 0.75	Dry. 3.33			Dry. 1.41					
25	62	ASHBY-DE-LA-ZOUCH.	133.0 862.5	2.52 —		36.4 106.4	4.24 —		3.72 2.0					
26	48	TENBURY.	62.07			35.22		0.26	0.96	0.10			0.1	
27	50	MALVERN.		0.24		0.23		0.20			Traces			
28	48	LEAMINGTON. {VICTORIA {OLDWELL	35.35 40.77	28.619 40.39		23.51 20.56			8.468 3.26					— Traces
29	50	CHELTENHAM. {PITVILLE {MONTP. (4.) {OLD WELL	27.16 46.40 58.20	17.55 28.64 14.56		— 3.07 6.21		0.20 — —	— 2.02 2.54					
30	49	GLOUCESTER SPA.	50.41	10.35			1.20	0.20						
31	54	VICTORIA SPA.	9.46	60.57		2.05		Bi 3.49		4.06	Bi. 1.84			
32	76	Clifton Wells.		2.02		0.47	0.93	1.68	0.90					
33	116	Bath.	1.89	2.42			10.20	1.35	1.67			0.01	0.41	
34	48	SANDROCK. {ISLE OF WIGHT}	4.00	16.0			10.10			3.60		Sulph. 31.6	0.7	Sulph. 41.40
35	47½	HOCKLEY SPA.	11.96				1.32	Bi c. 9.08		41.26				
36	50	TUNBRIDGE WELLS.	0.30			0.04	0.17	0.03	0.03					
Sea water taken up in the Channel.		N.B. The proportions are calculated as they are present in 1000 grains of water.	27.059				1.406	0.033	3.666	2.295				